THE PRACTICAL OPERATIONS AND MANAGEMENT OF A BANK

•

MARSHALL C. CORNS

•

Second Edition

BANKERS PUBLISHING COMPANY

BOSTON

BANKERS PUBLISHING COMPANY
89 Beach Street
Boston, Massachusetts 02111

First edition 1962
Second edition 1968

Library of Congress catalogue number 68-17247

Printed in the United States of America

To my clients and many other friends in the banking business in sincere appreciation for their valued friendship.

OTHER BOOKS BY Marshall C. Corns

Better Bank Management

How to Audit a Bank

Corns Audit Kit

Practical Cost Accounting for Banks

Organizing Jobs in Banking

PREFACE

As this book is being revised our country continues in one of the most critical periods in its history.

On the international scene our relations with many other countries are strained as our armed forces, maintained in many sections of the free world to insure peace, become involved in undeclared war; and nations continue unchecked to develop nuclear power and atomic weapons for armed conflict.

On the domestic front we are caught in a spiral of wage and price increases with demands for more taxes to provide for a record Federal Budget most of which is appropriated to cover foreign aid, defense projects, rising costs of operating government agencies, additional compensation for those receiving old age benefits, and support of the welfare projects of a paternalistic administration.

While it seems apparent that our problems in connection with maintaining peaceful relations with countries of the Communist world will be with us far into the forseeable future, it is the combination of the factors on the domestic front which at present make up our greatest and most potent enemy.

This enemy is INFLATION, the crippling disease which saps the wealth, ambition, energy and integrity of honest citizens everywhere.

In addition to the problems of inflation, bankers have other important matters to resolve, such as:

A. Need for providing financial assistance and banking facilities to small communities, housing projects, and shopping centers developed as a result of decentralization of industry, or relocation of manufacturing plants close to the source of their labor supply.

B. Branch banking and the expansion of our banking system.

C. The need for some practical way for officers of banks, who have acquired a controlling interest in their bank over the years, to dispose of their holdings without resorting to mergers, liquidation, or the sale to persons whose business is inimical to the best interests of other stockholders, and the community.

D. The encouragement of men of integrity and ability, to seek public office, and the support of them.
E. The encouragement of qualified men, with acceptable social and educational backgrounds, to select banking as a career.

If we carefully review these recognized problems, and analyze each one separately, we find a common factor. We also come to the inescapable conclusion that every one of these problems which has crept up on us over the years because of inertia and failure to take proper steps to aggressively assert ourselves and take action, could have been solved, and can still be solved and the objectives attained, *through aggressive and competent bank leadership.*

Today we appear to be woefully short of this brand of leadership, especially in the smaller banks, not only because of our neglect to provide competent successor management, but because our present executives have such demands on their time that they are unable to contribute to business their most important qualifications — constructive imagination and contemplative thinking to plan for the future.

As of December 31, 1965 there were 14,347 banks and 16,413 branches of banks in the United States. These 30,760 offices employed about 100,000 officers and almost 500,000 full time employees.

It is being forecast that if our economy continues its upward surge, our gross national product will rise to between 700 and 800 billion dollars annually within the next few years.

Considered with these figures are the projections of population which indicate we shall have a population of over 225 million by 1975.

Applying these figures to the banking business indicates vast increases in deposits, and need for more banks and financial institutions to serve the constantly growing population, all of which points out an acute future demand for qualified and well trained men to assume administrative responsibilities in banking.

In every community across the land bankers are called upon to devote a good part of their time to civic undertakings. They are generally acquainted with the effects of our foreign policy on domestic issues, the unbalanced budget on our tax structure, tariff regulations on prices, the causes for high taxes, and probably know more than any other group of citizens about what is going on in the County Seats, State Capitals and Washington. Unfortunately, in too many instances these same bankers refrain from taking an active position in politics or acquainting local citizenry with the situation, either because they are fearful of antagonizing some of their customers, or because they feel inept at leadership.

Many of us too are concerned over the rising power and influence of the labor unions and their philosophy, which contributes to our spiralling inflation.

The power of several million members of labor unions in an election for political office at local, state or municipal levels, and the power of business and professional lobbies in Washington, could be infinitesimal in comparison with the influence the presidents of banks could have through contacts with their depositors.

Each of us – we, the people – are the Government represented by our duly elected senators and congressmen. If we want to maintain our democratic form of Government, reduce Government spending, and operate with a balanced budget which will hold the evils of inflation in check, we need a resurgence of informed leadership to intelligently direct, counsel, and advise our representatives in Congress. Everyone wants freedom and a sound dollar, but too few want to live up to the responsibility of maintaining it.

This leadership could be supplied by local bankers leading a well-informed citizenry, but first we must have better informed personnel and qualified men for successor management, especially in the smaller banks.

It is hoped this book will not only be up to the expectations of those who have encouraged me to undertake the work, but provide a vehicle which will assist chief executive officers of banks to delegate management responsibilities to younger qualified men, thus providing them with time to not only study and work out equitable and satisfactory solutions to banking problems – but most important – assume leadership in political and economic matters, and as elder statesmen, take an active part in directing our country away from the evils of inflation and back to economic sanity.

Marshall C. Corns

November 8, 1967

TABLE OF CONTENTS

LIST OF EXHIBITS

CHAPTER I

INTRODUCTION

THE FUNCTIONS OF COMMERCIAL BANKING and application of the fundamental principles of the depositor-bank relationship have remained essentially the same since about 500 B.C. when Athenian bankers accepted gold and silver coin or bullion for deposit or safekeeping, and transferred credits or receipts for gold and silver coin or bullion from one person to another on presentation of an order; loaned gold and silver coin or bullion at interest; and even paid interest to depositors for use of coin and bullion, while it was in their possession.

Bank operation methods and procedures, on the other hand, have undergone a constant process of evolution because of economic growth, the mounting volume of transactions, and greater use of banking facilities.

As a result of these contributing factors, methods and practices necessary to handle the increased volume of detail work have been developed while shorter and quicker methods have been adopted in order to cope with the increased volume, much of which has been accomplished without unduly increasing the cost of doing business.

This is particularly true in the transit and bookkeeping operations, especially in handling the depositors' accounts where in the past few years we have witnessed the advent and use of magnetic selection, punch card sorting and posting, and computers of all types being installed and used by banks for practically all of their accounting operations.

Our three principal problems today, because of changes in our economy and our industrial growth fostered by inflation, are in connection with services, management and personnel.

During the last twenty years we have experienced a constant transition from the old to the new—from manual to mechanical methods and procedures—from old established practices to current techniques—and to a more scientific approach to the solution of problems brought about by day to day changes in business practices.

"But what now of the future? Will banks accept the competitive challenges that are being thrown at them today from countless sources? Will they come up with new services, new techniques, strong organizations, courageous and visionary personnel, and all of the other requisites that are necessary to build a dynamic forceful banking industry?" Thus wrote Ralph Cox, Managing Editor, *Mid-Continent Banker,* in May 1960.

To cope with changing situations and maintain position, banks must constantly be alert to the opportunities for providing new or improved banking services.

We can no longer close our minds to progress, and the needs of the public we serve, without either becoming swallowed up by the institutions we created by our indifference, or by being absorbed by the nationalization of financial institutions.

Lest we be inclined to lightly dismiss this threat, can we deny that our indifference in the past was responsible for the development of finance companies, savings and loan associations, the production credit associations, and in recent years the growth and development of credit unions?

In connection with personnel and management, let us in the banking business no longer delude ourselves. Banking is a profession which requires a sound foundation in technical operating methods and procedures—knowledge of history, economics and government—intense specialization in the art of communication—but most important, the know-how of getting along with people.

Colleges and universities in past years, while being acutely conscious of the great changes in science and the professions, and often forced into progress and changes by grants and legislative action, have turned out thousands of technicians, engineers, doctors and lawyers who, outside of their specialized talents, do not have the remotest idea of what it means to be a good citizen, lead a good life or shoulder the responsibilities of providing leadership for the country.

Thousands of our college graduates know all the answers if—the questions are asked from the book, but are lost in any field of virgin expression. While we are training men to be specialists, we are also training them to be economic illiterates.

In professional careers many states and the Federal Government have established certain requirements which colleges and universities have adhered to, in order for their graduates to be able to practice within that state.

In comerce and industry on the other hand, the attitude of higher education seems to be one of paternalism. Many colleges and universities are turning out graduates with an education which the educators believe business should have, instead of turning out graduates possessing the knowledge and education which business requires or demands; and have become negligent in providing, or requiring, courses of study which would properly equip graduates with the knowledge required of those who aspire to assume administrative responsibility and executive leadership in banking.

The American Institute of Banking, through its hundreds of chapters and home study courses, has made an excellent contribution to the education of bank personnel, as proven by the number of outstanding bank officers who point with pride to their A.I.B. certificate.

The American Bankers Association through its graduate schools, and the bankers' associations of the various states through their regional schools, provide unequalled facilities for further education of bank officers.

Many of the larger banks today sponsor programs to train their own employees or trainees in the bank's own operations, while in the smaller banks, the practice of learning by association, commonly known as "on the job training" is followed.

These facilities and methods, however, are not sufficient, if our bankers are to be properly trained to cope with the problems of our fast moving economy.

Learning by association, or on the job training can be a practical way to learn, providing techniques which are followed conform to current developments and recognize and incorporate efficient methods and procedures. Often, unfortunately, methods and procedures taught are obsolete and inefficient, and not only reflect the indifference of management, but the incapacity of those in charge of personnel and operations, to properly assume training responsibilities.

Analysis of many factors, and thorough studies undertaken over the years indicate, if we are to properly train bank employees to efficiently perform their work and develop qualified and informed personnel for the future assumption of administrative responsibilities, new approaches must be developed, incorporating all phases of banking into a medium through which employees can learn the theory of banking and its application to daily operation at the some time.

In addition, such mediums should be readily available and used particularly by those considering banking as a career, beginners in banks which have no training program of their own, and those employees of the smaller banks who do not have facilities or opportunities for education available.

It is the hope of the author that until such time as the educational institutions of the country develop and make available practical courses in commercial banking, and fulfill these objectives, that this book will provide a vehicle through which bank executives can develop a well-informed personnel.

Chapters dealing with fundamental principles of economics, as applied to banking and finance, early barter and exchange, coinage, and condensed history of the business we call banking are included; not only to provide background and describe the evolution of banking, but to acquaint the reader with many factors which are prevalent and underlie many of our problems today.

The material in this book is arranged to serve two purposes:

A. As a textbook, for use as a guide by progressive bankers who wish to develop their own vehicle for indoctrinating new employees, further educate present employees, and assist in developing organization and management plans, which will contribute to the future progress of the bank, and
B. For study according to straight line promotion, in order that any employee can become familiar with the application of principles to operating methods and procedures, as he or she advances in banking.

To obtain the best results from this book under the first purpose, no explanation is necessary. To obtain the best results under the second purpose, it is recommended that either:

1. Each employee be instructed to study the contents of the book from beginning to end in order to become thoroughly familiar with all phases of banking, or
2. Be instructed to only study the material which applies to banking in general, such as is contained in Chapters I

through XV *plus* the text material which applies to their particular job, or assumption of assigned duties and responsibilities.

In either event, it is further recommended that after an employee has studied, and become familiar with the material in each chapter or section assigned for study, he be quizzed on the contents by a well informed officer, who can, if necessary, modify the text to conform to certain situations, particular to the individual bank.

CHAPTER II

PRINCIPLES OF ECONOMICS IN BANKING AND COMMERCE

THE SCIENCE OF BANKING as we know it today is often erroneously considered to be a development of the so-called modern age of business. This is a common misconception. The fundamental principles of banking are as old as man himself and came into being when men found it necessary to trade or exchange goods among themselves in order to procure and provide necessities of life.

The word bank, used to designate certain financial institutions which accept deposits and grant loans, is only several centuries old. However, since the beginning of time, landowners, kings, petty chieftains, locksmiths and jewelers have all performed the functions which we today identify with banking. While we perhaps err in referring to all primitive functions dealing with finance as banking, it seems proper to do so, in order to clearly differentiate between periods of time and changes in the application of the fundamental principles, which have come down through the centuries.

Contrary to prevalent beliefs, banks and bankers since the beginning of any records dealing with facts and circumstances which could be classed as being predominantly economic or financial, have undergone changes only in methods of applying principles.

Banks have never pioneered the development of business, or contributed to the ever developing science of business, but rather have been forced to develop and change their methods, practices and procedures to conform to the changing application of the principles of economics and finance instituted by business.

BANKING

Since banking is synonymous with commerce and finance, and since primitive banking was closely allied with coinage and exchange, let us begin by defining banking.

Banking can be defined as the instrumentality or agency through which debits and credits are converted and exchanged between owners. In practice, banking is the middleman of commerce. We then ask, what are debits and credits and how can they be exchanged between owners. Here we become engaged in a controversial matter of economics and a definition of terms. The need for a precise understanding of financial terminology, and a groundwork of practical economics, is obvious if we are to follow the development of banking, and understand the reason why men for centuries have found it necessary to continuously make changes in a system set up to facilitate the exchange and conversion of debits and credits between owners.

LABOR

Let us start off, therefore, by defining labor. We know it to be an indisputable fact that every person, from the time he is born until he dies, is producing something. Every thought, or action, either creates new thoughts in his mind, adds or detracts from ability and knowledge, makes changes in personality, or assists in developing prior thoughts, established knowledge or an acquired ability.

No thought, word, deed or action can take place without subtracting or adding to some part of every human being's makeup. This applies whether the thought, word or action is good or bad, social or unsocial. Every thought, word, deed or action produced by individuals, is a result of an individual's efforts, or labor.

Labor, therefore, we will define, as any action of mind or body which produces results. If such labor creates something immediately useful, then that which is produced has value. On the other hand, if the labor does not produce something immediately useful, or that can be exchanged for something immediately useful, it creates value unto the producer himself. This form of labor contributes to the individual's wealth, but has no value until it is applied to producing something which has use, or which can be exchanged for something else which has use or value.

For example—if by reading this book your mind is stimulated, certain facts will be acquired and portions will be retained in your mind as knowledge. By reading, therefore, you have produced a number of contributions to your wealth. These contributions have added to your wealth, but have no value, until you exchange the result of the stimulation, the facts acquired, or the knowledge retained in your mind, for something that is immediately useful; or you can use the knowledge to procure something that will result in your obtaining something previously created that has value.

RAW MATERIAL

Next let us define raw materials. Now raw materials, in the strict sense of the word, consist of natural resources such as trees in the forests, fish in the water, minerals in the ground, wild animals, wild grain, wild fruit, or anything that has been produced through the influence of nature alone. While raw materials can be considered as having potential value or consist of wealth unto themselves, it is only when such raw materials are combined with labor that they acquire value.

Now by combining labor and raw materials we manufacture a product which has value. It is clearly evident that thus far the object only has value to the producer.

PRIMITIVE WEALTH

If a man, therefore, would fashion a crude blade by rubbing pieces of flint together until they were of a convenient size, then cut a sapling and from it trim down a handle to which he would bind the blade with strips of fibrous grass, he would have a crude axe. Now, this axe didn't grow; all the man had was the raw material in the form of a rock, wood and fiber, but by applying labor to the raw materials he fashioned an axe. Now this axe has value in itself unto the producer (wealth) but no real value unless it can be immediately exchanged for something else which has value. Now this hypothetical man could go on building axes every day and in time he would have accumulated wealth in terms of axes which he could trade for some other article of value that he needed.

In this primitive beginning of civilization, men had all things in common, but as civilization grew and expanded, forming tribes and small nations, it was necessary to trade between one another to obtain the necessities of life. Aristotle said: "It is plain that in the first society there was no such thing as barter, but that it took place when the communities became enlarged where the former had all things in common, the latter must exchange with each other according to their needs, just as many barbarous tribes now subsist by barter and these merely exchange one useful thing for another; for example, giving and receiving wine for grain and other things in like manner."

The history of primitive man, and the accounts of activities of nations in the Bible, refer time and time again to barter and exchange between individuals, tribes and nations. Fertility of the soil, productivity of animals, the skill of workmen, and climatic conditions, were considerations which resulted in certain tribes and nations confining their principal efforts to producing for consumption one or more essential commodities.

These factors later resulted in tribes and nations being recognized principally as producers of grain, fruit, livestock and fish and if not thus engaged, then as producers of transportation facilities, builders of homes, ships or weavers of textiles to be exchanged for commodities required for their needs, or by services whose value could be exchanged for their requirements.

SUPPLY AND DEMAND

Individuals, tribes and nations through the influence of nature and other factors have never been able to become self-sustaining for any length of time, and each yearly period has always disclosed either an over supply or an under supply from the results of their labor or the commodities produced.

The basis for determining supply and demand has to be frequently changed, and the best thing that can be said of any basis, is that it represents at most, an estimate, which if intelligently interpreted shortens the spread between visible supply and anticipated demand. These estimates often contribute to the disruption of our economic life, for if a surplus is on hand, the commodity, in terms of barter and exchange is worth less, while if a shortage occurs, it is worth more. One alternative, when an over supply occurred was to store it until such time as the normal supply was present and a prospective purchaser was found who had other goods wanted by the seller, at which time an exchange was made.

SOME MEDIUMS OF EXCHANGE

It is easy to understand how exchanges were made. For example, two bushels of corn for one chicken, or ten sheep for one cow, or one cow and two pigs for one horse, or one dozen eggs for one pound of butter, all of which exchange values were determined by supply and demand.

In performing acts of labor or services, however, or if a sheep was wanted from a herdsman and you had nothing he wanted or your labor was worth less than one sheep, the trade could not take place unless some other factors entered into the transaction so as to make the exchange balance out.

DEFERRED EXCHANGE

The only two factors available to man to use in balancing up exchanges, which later developed into a second and third basis of conducting business, were (1) use of an intermediate commodity of standard value usually acceptable for immediately consummating the trade or exchange or, (2) a pledge or promise of a future delivery of a certain commodity or the promise to perform certain work at a future date.

Since the beginning of civilization man has been honest and usually his word could be relied on. Through all history we find accounts of trading and exchanging and when we realize how difficult it was at the time, we can reasonably assume that certain transactions could not be consummated unless part of the value exchange was deferred by means of a man's promise to complete the balance due at a future date. This transaction of deferred exchange was comprised of two parts: (1) the seller, later known as the creditor, who gave up wealth or a representation of wealth for a promise and, (2) the promisor who received value on his word to complete the exchange at a later date, known as a debtor.

DEBTOR-CREDITOR

The force of these words creditor and debtor, and their part in banking and finance is more truly brought out by knowledge of the root word from which they were derived. The word creditor is derived from the Latin word "credo" which translated means "I believe." As an example, I believe that you will pay me what you owe me.

The word debtor comes from the Latin "debo" which translated means that which is due from one person to another. The fact that these words have a Latin root presupposes that they were translated into Latin from another language whose origin has been lost in time.

Credit, therefore, always implies wealth represented by something of value that is exchanged for a promise to pay, while debt implies the acceptance and exchange of something of value or the performance of services having equivalent value.

We constantly hear about credit, which term implies wealth, but very little about debt which represents a promise. As a matter of fact, it is debatable which is more important to our economic existence. We cannot have debt without having credit, nor can we have credit without having debt. In studying economic developments it appears that factors of debt have contributed more than factors of credit to business progress.

TRADING AREAS

The extending of credit, or a deferred form of exchange by which one could obtain commodities by the promise either to deliver other commodities or perform certain services at a later date, most probably was used to a great extent in the earliest times. These promises, however, were acceptable only when the seller knew the purchaser, and as travel was only made through need for water or pasture, it is assumed that the credit of individuals was confined to a small area, and that any trading or bartering between families or clans living some distance apart, in the beginning was accomplished solely by an exchange of commodities.

As families and clans grew, however, they found it necessary either to consolidate with other families or clans forming tribes, or to move to larger areas in order to provide from resources and labor their sustenance and wealth to use in trading, or as barter for commodities they needed.

As population increased, each group moved further and further away from other clans or tribes, and as very few were self-sustaining units, raising and growing all feed, fodder, grain, fruit, animals, wool and hides for their own use, they found it necessary to meet periodically with other clans or tribes and exchange the surplus of whatever they produced, for the surplus of whatever the other clan or tribe produced to obtain what they needed.

Undoubtedly the habitat of a tribe was limited, and factors

of safety and convenience restricted the extent of their travel. For example let us presume the center of a circle as shown in the Exhibit 1 to be the tribe headquarters and the circumference of the circle being the maximum distance they could travel safely for food or articles of sustenance.

Exhibit 1

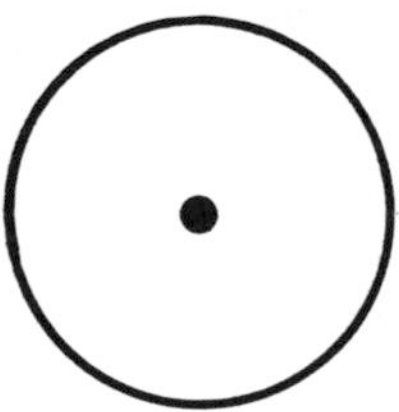

Now if other tribes are located near, we have a series of territories all of which have a common place of trading adjacent to each one's territory so that now we find tribes 1, 2, 3 and 4 all trading among themselves or collectively as shown in Exhibit 2.

Exhibit 2

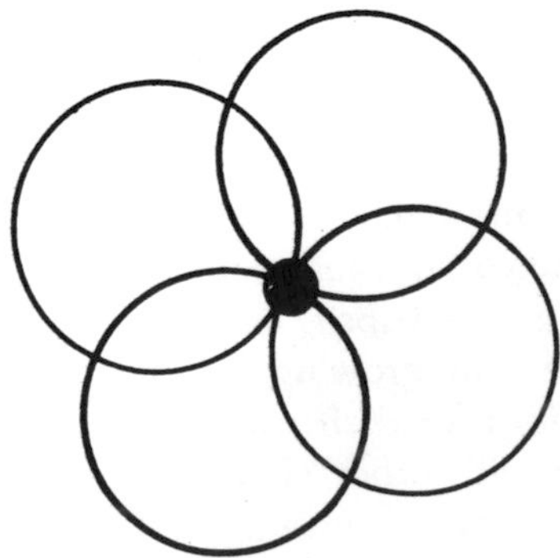

It is conceivable that these tribes did not always trade with each other at the same place, as other tribes were in existence, each having their own territory. As an example, as shown in Exhibit 3, it would only seem practical for tribes 1, 2, 3 and 4; 2, 5, 6 and 7; 5, 10, 11 and 12; 3, 4, 8 and 9; and 6, 11, 13 and 14 to trade with each other, as the distance was too far for tribes 10 and 11 to trade with others at A or for 8 and 9 to trade at E. Several examples are shown in Exhibit 3.

Exhibit 3

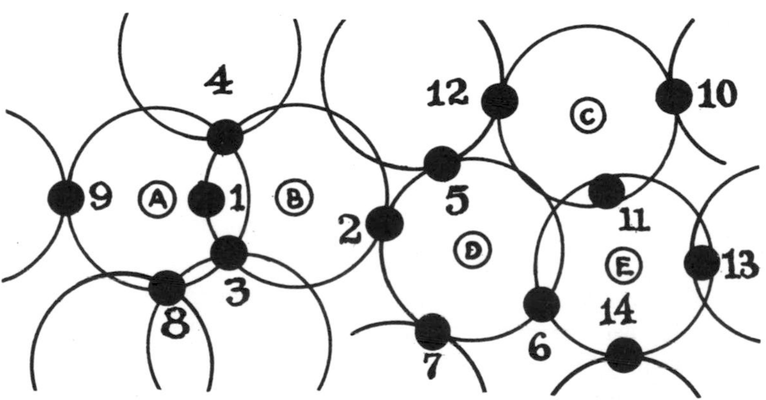

However, through centers of trading and exchanging, commodities of 8 and 9 could often be exchanged for commodities of 4 and 3 and were in turn exchanged with commodities of 1 and 2 at B, and later through interchange at centers, with commodities of 10 and 12. We recognize the fact that there would be no advantage for a man having cattle to sell to exchange his cattle for other cattle, unless for the purpose of breeding, so we conclude that all exchange at these centers consisted of exchanging one or more commodities for one or more other commodities having value. How was the value of new commodities produced determined?

The value of a new commodity or new article produced was determined solely by the already established value of whatever was tendered in trade or exchanged for the new article.

For example: Group 14 lives in the mountains and makes axes out of stone and takes their surplus to center E where Group 11 sells chickens. Now at the trading center one chicken can be exchanged for one and one-half measures of corn, three-fifths measure of oats, one measure of butter, one dozen eggs, and ten chickens can be exchanged for one sheep. This ratio goes on to cover all of the available commodities. The point here to remember is that everything could be obtained by using a chicken or its trading value. But now those in Group 11 see the axe for the first time and want one. After talking back and forth they agree to exchange two chickens for one axe. Now by word of mouth, and depending on the supply and how badly Group 14 needs other commodities, axes should bring at the trading center E the equivalent in trading of two times one chicken.

With a normal supply and demand for axes the trading value would remain consistent, but with an over supply of axes in order to dispose of them, they (Group 14) might exchange axes for less. The fact to establish is that a trading value was determined.

Now if Group 11 had a lot of chickens they might exchange many of them for axes and if they were known in several trading centers, use axes in exchange for other commodities. In certain times in history, axes, spades, iron roasting spits, cattle, grain and even women and children have had trading and exchange value. All of these things were used in exchange for some other commodity because they had a value.

Now if there was a relationship between axes and chickens, axes and goats, axes and cattle, an axe had definite trading value in setting up transactions between buyer and seller and acted as a medium of exchange universally accepted by the group. We define, therefore, a medium of exchange, as any instrument or article of value accepted in trade in lieu of other articles of value.

While it is true that ultimately metals came into use as mediums of exchange, one phase of barter and exchange remains unkown. Throughout recorded history we find that at one time or another, every nation, probably before the advent of so-called civilization, whatever period it was, used baubles of jewelry, beads and precious stones for a time as mediums of exchange and nearly all peaceful conquests of foreign lands were instituted by pioneers using cheap baubles, beads and bright goods in trading, completely hoodwinking the unfortunate natives. What was there about primitive man that he placed such value in appearance? What made him willing to trade on such an unfair basis? History is vague on this point, probably because it was considered of too small value to record, yet it represents a transition period in the history of finance.

Various nations, at some time in their history, have also used salt, beans, silk, fur, tobacco, shells and beads in bartering and as mediums of exchange. Probably the most accurate and authentic record of the use of trinkets and beads is contained in the history of the colonization of America where the first recognized mediums of exchange were beads and tobacco as we shall learn in succeeding chapters.

CHAPTER III

MEDIUMS OF EXCHANGE

WITH THE DISCOVERY of bronze, iron, gold, and silver commodities of sustenance, commodities of use and items of vanity declined as mediums of exchange. History is very definite in recording this transition.

From the earliest records of civilization, believed to be authentic, it has been determined that man discovered bronze, and began to leave written records of his endeavors about 4,000 B.C. The discovery of iron was placed by archeologists to have been about 3,500 B. C. and discovery and use of gold some time between 3,500 and 3,000 B. C.

Gold and other metals were evidently the principal mediums of exchange, either in loose, bar, or piece form, as earliest paintings and sculpture show metals being weighed in scales and Hammurabi, in setting up and codifying laws about 2,100 B.C., provided for the handling and custodianship of gold, silver and other forms of wealth.

Use of scales for determining the weight was only one part in the establishment of the value of gold, silver and other metals as mediums of exchange. The other and most important part, was contributed by those whose knowledge of the metal enabled them to tell the content of actual pure metal in each piece. It was the combination of actual pure metal contained in a certain weight, that determined its value as a medium of exchange. In other words it was the fineness and weight, a combination of the two, which established value as an exchange medium.

The development of commerce in Egypt and Babylon, considered to be the first trading cities, or cities of commerce, created a problem in that certain then known mediums of exchange were not convenient to transport, as their trade value was often in bulk or size.

GOLD AND SILVER AS MEDIUMS OF EXCHANGE

The discovery and use of gold and silver, answered the need for a medium of exchange that had an established definite value in relation to other commodities. It was easier to transport, and was worth in trading, far more than was indicated by its bulk. This establishment of definite concentrated value probably came about through the scarcity of the metal and the difficulty in mining it.

The first use, however, of gold and silver as a convenient medium of exchange was based on fineness and weight. Later history, and the discovery of sculpture and inscriptions however, refer to gold bars and ingots so we can presume that some form of standardization was considered necessary for the convenience of trading.

About the time of the Pharaohs, 3,000 B. C., while gold bars were in use, in order to have a more easily divisible unit of value, gold was formed into rings of a fixed weight. Many of these rings have been found in the tombs of the Pharaohs and when an American, Heinrich Schliemann, discovered the buried treasure of Troy in 1870, thousands of these gold rings were found. Later when he discovered the Mycenaean tombs, more rings and spiral forms of metal all in fixed weights were found.

Discovery of gold molded into shapes of oxen have also been found in ancient tombs, and as we know oxen were used as a base medium of exchange, we can logically suppose that casting the gold in the shape of oxen was to represent the value of the gold in relation to an ox. For example, one piece of gold for one ox. These bars and forms of gold castings were good mediums of exchange and contributed to the expansion of commerce. It was necessary, however, in many countries to still weigh the pieces and determine fineness so as to prevent loss in value through abrasion, clipping and counterfeiting.

COINAGE

Modern names for some fixed forms of gold and silver had their origin in the names of ancient weights and measures. In early Rome payments were made by *tale,* that is by counting, and a talent of silver was a certain fixed count or weight. From the Latin word "Pendo" which means to weigh, is derived the words compensation, expenditure, and stipend, used today in our commercial language. The names shekel, drachma, pound, penny, peso, lire, franc and mark were originally names for ancient weights and measures.

In time, however, probably through expansive trade, certain forms of cast gold and silver made by certain individuals, and stamped with their name or some recognized insignia, became accepted by tradesmen without weighing or investigating as to its contents. The issuer, no doubt a leading merchant, probably guaranteed its quantity and quality, and on account of his reputation, the cast metal bearing his identifying insignia was readily accepted. The great advantage of this form was immediately recognized, and led to universal use, first in cities and then in international commerce among the then known civilized nations.

Aristotle says, relative to the changing from barter and exchange to formed metal, "Not all the necessities of life are easy of carriage, therefore, to effect their exchange men contrived something to give and take amongst themselves which being valuable in itself had the advantage of being easily passed from hand to hand for the needs of life."

Coin, therefore, may be defined as a piece of metal, or combination of metals, bearing a stamp indicative of its weight and fineness, of such shape and character as to be easy of carriage and designed to render counterfeiting difficult and prevent clipping or sweating.

While it is probably true that merchants originally coined metal, the simplicity over other forms of exchange and the possibility of profit later resulted in its issuance being considered a sovereign's right with the result that kings and monarchs took this right unto themselves exclusively.

The first record we find of the use of coin by a sovereign is about 700 B.C. by Gyges, King of Lydia, who stamped the mark of the government on pieces of silver and gold. The Phoenicians are said to have carried this idea over the Mediterranean world.

The prime consideration of acceptibility of coin is in the honesty and accuracy of its manufacture. The first Lydian coins turned out to be short in weight and it remained for Croesus, King of Lydia, (595-546 B.C.) to guarantee both quality and quantity by issuing pure silver and gold coins. Perhaps his honesty and word attracted such attention that others wished to deal with him, and thus established the basis for his fabulous fortune. The expression, "Rich as Croesus" had its origin in his vast fortune.

It is well to remember that metal, passed from hand to hand through all strata of society in all parts of the nation, must be accepted at face value, and with confidence by everybody, if it is to be recognized and utilized as a good medium of exchange. If a false insignia was placed upon a coin, or the metals and the contents were not uniform the acceptor would, when he discovered the fact, either refuse to accept it or, if compelled by law to accept he would either raise prices or resort to reducing the coin to its base value and make the exchange predicated upon the value of the metal in the coin. Unfortunately the very attributes that made coin the most acceptable medium of exchange, that is weight and identifying marks of integrity and character, were the reasons why later abuses developed and devaluations occurred.

RIGHTS OF COINAGE

From the time of the Roman Empire until the Middle Ages, roughly from 400 B.C. to 1300 A.D., with each sovereign issuing his own coin to be used as a medium of exchange, and the fact that all coin was not perfect in weight and fineness, debasement was practiced. To guard against loss it was necessary, in all cities where trade was conducted, before negotiating exchanges, for merchants to employ the services of a specialist to determine the actual value of coin in terms of trade.

As in certain trading areas, certain types, forms or "brands" of coin had greater acceptance; these specialists accumulated this preferred or "prime" coin, and exchanged other coin for this "prime coin." In time, because of this activity, these specialists became known as Money Changers or Exchangers, and were recognized as being important factors in the development of business and commerce.

During the Middle Ages petty princes and free cities were frequently granted the right by their sovereign to coin money. Having this right, they also took it upon themselves to regulate the content of the coin with the result that debasement was frequently practiced and cheaper metals substituted for gold and silver. They also reduced the size of the coin.

This continuation of debasement of coinage, and loss of confidence in the existing forms of metal mediums of exchange, brought back the scales and requirements of personal knowledge of fineness necessary to determine the value of the metal. In order to have a sufficient supply of good coin on hand, exchangers or goldsmiths as they were now sometimes called, found it necessary either to carry large supplies of gold or melt down the debased coin into bullion of fixed content and weight. It was not until commerce and trade developed the necessity for having coin of a uniform size and fixed value, that businessmen and merchants, by protesting, succeeded in having the right of coinage withdrawn from petty princes and instituted again with the government.

BARTER AND EXCHANGE IN THE COLONIES

For further developments of exchange and the principles of banking, in application to the economy of a nation, we will go to the Colonies where, as we shall see, circumstances brought about a return to the earliest form of barter and exchange, and the acceptance of banking principles, as practiced by the Romans, Spanish and English, which later contributed to the banking system as we know it today.

In May 1607, the Colonists sent out by the London Company, a private corporation organized under a grant of the English Crown, reached America and settled in Jamestown, Virginia.

To insure their preservation and welfare all crops for a period of five years, by royal order, were to be gathered into a common storehouse and distributed when needed to the Colonists. While the purpose was undoubtedly to insure sufficient food supply against the uncertainties of climate, it involuntarily encouraged the idle to be supported by the industrious.

Some of the economists of the 17th century were of the opinion that a nation's wealth was measured, not by the amount of goods which it could produce or exchange, but by the quantity of gold and silver it could possess. As a result every nation was trying to buy as little as they could from others, but sell to others as much as possible, so that gold and silver always flowed into the country. The Colonies were considered outlets for goods to be paid for with gold and silver.

This idea of self-sufficiency was responsible for a great deal of the world's economic ills at that time and it was not until the exponents of free trade and commercial expansion convinced businessmen of these fallacies, that nations developed and accumulated real wealth. As a result of this policy however, many of the Colonists spent their time exploring the land for gold, instead of raising crops, and conditions bordering on starvation existed during the wintertime, especially when crops failed or when the supply ships from England failed to get through.

The failure of this country's management to understand the problem, and the unwillingness of the ambitious settlers to continue to support the idle, resulted in the settlers employing their talents in different enterprises to obtain the wherewithal to exchange with the Indians and others for necessities.

The most practical way the Colonists had for exchanging the fruits of their labor for required necessities was by barter and exchange, a reversion to the most primitive type of exchange known to man.

WAMPUM AS A MEDIUM OF EXCHANGE

The close proximity to well regulated Indian tribes made it possible for the Colonists to trade with the Indians, and to effect a trade naturally the medium of exchange had to be that which was acceptable to the Indians.

This medium was known as "Wampumpuage" in some sections and in other sections as "Peage" which consisted of beads made from the inner whorls of certain shells found in sea water which were polished and strung together in belts or sashes. These beads were not only used by the Indians as a medium of exchange but also as articles of adornment. Wampum was of two colors, black and white, of which one black bead had the equivalent exchange value of two white beads.

One of the natural resources greatly in demand through Europe were beaver skins, and the Colonists, finding that the wampum could be exchanged for beaver skins, and that other articles of necessity could be exchanged in relation to the value of the beaver skins, came to use wampum because of its convenience as a medium of exchange.

Being a Colony, the next step was to determine the exchange value in relation to the medium used to express values used by the traders from England, which in this case were pounds and pence. By usage, a unit of wampum, known as the fathom, consisting of 360 white beads worth 60 pence, came into use as a medium of exchange. In 1648 it was so recognized as a legitimate exchange medium that Connecticut legislated on the method used in stringing the beads.

The use of wampum spread throughout the Colonies. In Connecticut, four white beads passed as the equivalent of a penny while in Massachusetts, six passed as the equivalent of a penny. In the Massachusetts settlement, wampum was made legally receivable to the amount of twelve pence for all debts, except taxes, and from 1641 to 1643 was legal tender to the amount of ten pounds. After 1643 it was reduced to 40 shillings.

The Colonial development, which pushed back the Indians, resulted in a decline of the beaver trade, and brought about a repetition of the debasement of established mediums in line with the pattern followed by men throughout history.

Failing to recognize their responsibility, the colonists not only counterfeited wampum beads, that is other beads were made to look like the inner whorls of certain shells, but the practice of dyeing white beads black to arbitrarily increase their value was also resorted to, which brought about a great fluctuation of value and destroyed wampum as a sound medium.

TOBACCO AS A MEDIUM OF EXCHANGE

In Virginia after the reorganization in 1616, the Colonists turned to the raising of tobacco, and later determined values of other commodities by its relationship to tobacco. In fact, in 1619, the General Assembly of Virginia passed a law fixing the price of the best tobacco at 3 shillings, and the second best at 18 pence.

The use of tobacco as a medium of exchange, and also as a basis for determining wealth, resulted in such increased cultivation of tobacco that by 1631 a surplus of tobacco occurred which reduced its price per pound, thus reducing its value as a medium, a practical application of the law of supply and demand. In an effort to stabilize the price of tobacco, the Virginia Assembly in 1642 passed an act forbidding the making of contracts payable in money, virtually making tobacco the sole currency.

In the beginning of the 18th century, however, advantage was taken of nature's fluctuating bounty, and the practice of placing surplus crops in a public warehouse on receipt was followed. Because of the certainty of the quality of tobacco expressed on the receipt, and the integrity of the warehouseman, these receipts became acceptable as mediums of exchange.

In 1727 tobacco receipts issued by reputable warehousemen subject to official inspection by representatives of the Assembly were legalized and declared current and payable for all tobacco debts in the warehouse where they were issued.

BEAVER SKINS AND CORN AS MEDIUMS OF EXCHANGE

The first well known mediums of exchange in Massachusetts were beaver skins which were made legally receivable for debts at 10 shillings per pound. From time to time, however, the General Court in Massachusetts recognized other commodities. In 1631 the Court decreed that corn should pass in payment of all debts at the prevailing price except where in cases coin of the old country or beaver skins were expressly stipulated. In 1635 musket balls were made legal tender to limited extent. In 1640 Indian corn at 4 shillings per pound, wheat at 6 shillings, barley at 5 shillings and peas at 6 shillings per bushel, were made legally receivable for debts and taxes. In other words, any debt payable in shillings or pence, could be paid at the debtor's option in corn at 4 shillings per bushel, beaver skins at 10 shillings per pound, peas at 6 shillings per bushel or in the metallic coin of England. The exporting of gold to England resulted in a shortage of metallic money and in 1654 the General Court decreed that no coin should be exported from the colony except for traveling expenses.

RICE AS A MEDIUM OF EXCHANGE

In South Carolina, rice was made receivable for taxes by the

Assembly in 1719, and the following year a tax levy, by the Assembly to cover expenses was levied in rice. In that year the tax commissioners issued rice orders to public creditors at the rate of 30 shillings per 100 pounds of rice.

Connecticut and eastern Tennessee in the early part of the 19th century recognized coon skins as mediums of exchange and made them receivable for taxes.

COIN AS A MEDIUM OF EXCHANGE

The early Colonists, even with capable administration, were handicapped from the lack of adequate mediums of exchange, an insufficient amount of coin, and almost total absence of capital.

The pushing forward of the frontier and industrial development was severely hampered by the inability to have coin available for trading purposes. Before the adoption of the Constitution, Colonists were entirely dependent upon foreign coin that was in circulation. The Virginia Company endeavored to furnish her Colonists with a medium of exchange and made up coin in shillings and pence stamped with a figure of a hog which was known as "Hogge Money" and in 1652 Massachusetts, in endeavoring to furnish her Colonists with an exchange medium, minted shillings with a figure of a pine tree on its face from which came the name "Pine Tree Shilling"

In spite of the efforts of Colonists, whose attempts at coinage were not well received, the supply was always inadequate and commercial development was handicapped because purchases were made in commodities, which by their bulk and possibility of spoilage, were not easily transported, or practical to accept in any amount.

While there was also some British, French, Spanish and Portuguese minor coin in circulation, their value was reckoned in relation to the Spanish milled dollar. The reason that the Spanish milled dollar was used was due to the fact that the Spanish devised the milled, or corrugated, edge to prevent debasement by clipping or sweating. In briefly covering the development and use of coin, as a medium of exchange, it is interesting to note that the granting of coinage rights by the sovereigns to petty princes, was not restricted to the Middle Ages, for as recently as the 19th century, the right of coinage was granted to any individual here in the United States.

From 1830 to 1864, when the government forbade the private coinage of gold, private manufactories, located in Georgia, North Carolina, California, Oregon, Utah and Colorado did an extensive business. These coins were not counterfeit, and did not imitate the design of the United States Government coin, but bore the name and place of business of the manufacturer and were purported to be worth the number of dollars stamped on them. However, by weight and fineness, the exchange value ranged from $4.36 to $5.00.

Another interesting factor to consider in tracing the history of coinage is the development of the sizes, units, values and methods of reckoning.

Two systems of reckoning presently in use are the English system and the decimal system.

The English system, probably a carry-over from the days of the Romans and employed throughout Europe during the Middle Ages, at the present time is only used in England. Under the English system the unit is a pound sterling, divided into twenty parts called shillings. The word shilling is purported to have come from a word of ancient origin, "Skilling", which meant a cutting from a metal bar. Each shilling is divided into twelve parts called pennies and then again into four parts called farthings.

The decimal system in which the unit is divided into a hundred parts with intermediate parts is now in use practically throughout the world. The decimal system, because of the ease in multiplying by ten, as multiples instead of by twelve and twenty, is vastly superior.

In concluding this chapter on coinage let us say that time has not cured the evils of debasement, or fixed for long the value of gold and silver as a fixed medium of exchange. Throughout the history of coinage we find nation after nation, government after government, practicing the debasement of metals of exchange.

In fact, debasement of metals has been the practice, not the exception. Even in recent years, (1930-1938) the English, French and our own United States government deemed it necessary to arbitrarily set the price of gold and silver, thus increasing in some cases and reducing in others the exchange value of coin. In fact, because of scarcity of metal, the German government in 1937 used aluminum for their 50 pfennig coins to replace nickel.

CHAPTER IV

THE DEVELOPMENT AND USE OF MEDIUMS OF EXCHANGE INTO THE BUSINESS WE CALL BANKING

IN REVIEWING THE HISTORY of exchange and coinage it seems apparent that after principles of exchange were determined somewhere between 4,000 B.C. and 2,000 B.C. that banking developed in cycles. These periods all seemed to have their beginning in the establishing or reestablishing of values by means of scales, the knowledge and integrity of the issuer to determine the weight or fineness of the medium, and the developing of their own practical and convenient form of mediums in connection with trade and commercial development.

With the expansion of trade, as we have seen, the exchangers or specialists accumulated considerable coin and metal which not only represented their own capital but the coin, bullion, and bars of other businessmen placed with them for safekeeping.

The difficulties encountered in transporting bars and coin, not to mention the risk incurred through robbery in transporting gold and silver in quantity from one trading center to another over unprotected travel routes, undoubtedly were responsible for the next development in exchange—use of receipts.

CURRENCY AS A MEDIUM OF EXCHANGE

As specialists in coin at one trading center became known, it logically follows that their reputation and honesty became known also. Therefore in order to prevent possible loss through robbery, merchants contemplating trading at a far away center, deposited their coin or bullion with the local specialist before leaving for their destination, receiving a receipt for gold or silver of certain weight and fineness which upon tendering to another specialist, at another trading center, was converted into coin accepted in that center, as a good medium of exchange. These receipts were returned to the issuer in the same manner later and probably kept in circulation for some time.

These receipts used in the development of commerce and trade, although later modified in form, became known as currency and probably were so termed from the Latin word "curricula" meaning a course or series of moves in circulation. Most probably these receipts were in a form certifying that a certain amount of metal was promised to be tendered in exchange for the receipt, and we can only presume that they were "endorsed" over to the bearer when negotiated in some manner so as to freely circulate.

With the expansion of trade these exchangers or specialists accumulated considerable coin and for protection utilized heavy bound chests, also guards, locks and other safety measures to protect their capital which consisted not only of their own funds, but funds against which they had issued receipts (or currency) for use in business transactions.

From immediate use to safekeeping was only a short step and as individuals had no place to keep coin they placed their surplus with the goldsmiths and exchangers for safety, receiving in exchange a receipt. As more of these receipts came into use, confidence in them increased, so that instead of settling debts by actually turning over coin, the debtor gave his creditor the receipts of the goldsmith, or exchanger which was accepted in payment of the debt. This in time eliminated to a great extent the settlement of debts by actual delivery of metal.

History is uncertain as to the time when written promises or receipts, which we now refer to as currency, began to be used in lieu of gold and silver as a medium of exchange. This is due unquestionably to the fact that probably these early forms of currency, expressed in writing, were impressed on paper, leather or other fragile agents which the elements of time have destroyed. Most of the developments up to the 17th century are conjecture and conclusions arrived at by applications of reason to established facts unearthed by scientists.

Probably the forerunner of currency, where the trading value was implied or based on trust, was the medium used by the Carthaginians about 800 B.C. described by Socrates in his "Dialogue on Wealth" where he relates that the Carthaginians, probably to prevent abrasion, took a piece of metal, wrapped it in leather and sealed it, then used it as a medium of exchange. We do not know how long this was used, but traces of this type of medium, whose value was determined by faith as to what the contents consisted of, have only been found in Carthage.

Evidence unearthed in China, indicates that possibly currency found its beginning in the inventive minds of the Chinese. One curious form of Chinese currency, in use about 100 B.C., consisted of pieces of white deer hide about 12″ square representing a fixed amount of silver. The emperor not only gathered all the white deer together for his own use, but forbade his subjects to own any white deer under penalty of death.

Thomas Francis Carter, in his book "The Invention of Printing in China," states that currency appears to have been used in China about 800 A.D. in the Dynasty of Soung and was known as Pianthsian (flying or convenient) currency, and developed evidently from certificates of debt issued to merchants by the government.

MacLeod found that certificates representing deposits of gold and silver were found in China under the Dynasty of Thang as early as 807 A.D.

History also indicates that these specialists sometimes issued their receipts without having sufficient metal coverage behind them. No one suffered any losses as long as the receipts remained circulating and no demand was made for actual delivery of gold to deplete the metal on hand in the issuer's possesssion. When a deficit became evident, of course, the receipts outstanding became depreciated and bankruptcy resulted.

One of the first situations known where notes or receipts payable in gold or silver were only partially covered by the actual value, the balance presumably by general credit for purposes of raising capital, occurred about 1021 A.D. in China where a group of rich merchants were authorized to issue notes payable in three years. The company met disaster and the emperor forbade the formation of future companies.

Marco Polo, the Venetian, spent from 1260 to 1295 in China observing, and working with, and for, Kublai Khan. From his observations and experience he indicates that currency was in use in China in the form of notes forced in some sections on the population. The value behind these notes was questionable and resulted in inflation and the discontinuance of a paper medium of exchange.

Historians and students of banking history are rather vague as to the first issue of so-called bank notes, that is notes issued by an authorized bank, but evidence seems to attribute the originals to Palmstruch, founder of the Bank of Sweden, about 1658.

Up to the earliest part of the 19th century the issue of notes was considered a common law right executed by individuals and sovereigns. In 1844, however, in Great Britain under the British Bank Act, on the grounds of public policy, issues of currency were limited to bank notes of the Bank of England.

CHARACTERISTICS OF CURRENCY

All forms of currency which are written assurances to redeem the receipts with actual metal, are characteristic in that they do not contain in their own substance, the value being expressed in writing; and only represent the obligation of some person or group of persons to exchange the promise for actual metal. Consequently throughout history the value of currency, by and large, has been based on promises, and the assumption of the acceptors that the paper would be exchanged for its face amount in gold or silver. The theory in back of the use of a paper medium was that by eliminating the debasement of coin it would stabilize it. This, however, has not been the case, as history shows the use of currency has brought with it far more abuses than that of coin. In fact, most of the economic problems of of early America were caused by a breakdown of morals, evidenced in the use of the currency system.

Currency, therefore, while sometimes considered a bill of exchange or bank bill, in that they are both exchangeable into coin of the realm, differ in that a bill of exchange is payable at a future date to certain persons or orders, while a bank bill or currency is payable at sight and payable to bearer. It is a fine point, but nevertheless important as we shall later see.

From the 17th century on the development of currency coinage follows the development of banking as we shall now term the business of money changers, specialists or goldsmiths. It is interesting to note that a study of banking and a study of coinage indicates that most of the economic troubles we have found ourselves in since the beginning of time have had their origin in our coinage system and medium of exchange.

CREDIT AND CREDIT INSTRUMENTS

As mentioned previously the fundamentals of banking have not changed over the years. The principal types of credit and credit instruments used today, namely open accounts, promissory notes, orders to pay, acceptances and bills of exchange are nothing more than an extension and development of forms of deferred credit and exchange whose primary principles were conceived and put in practice several thousand years ago.

The modern forms which we will briefly describe had their beginnings in Central Asia probably about the time in history when commerce between tribes and nations developed.

An "Open Account" is a single, or a series of deferred exchanges, where one party gives up goods or objects of value in return for a verbal or implied promise to pay at a later date. It is this principle that is behind our present charge account system.

A "Promissory Note" is also a deferred exchange except that the promise to pay is in writing.

An "Order to Pay", more commonly known today as a bank check, is an instrument given in exchange for goods or objects having value, or in settlement of deferred exchange, signed by the purchaser, authorizing a third party to immediately pay the seller or payee, on presentation of the order, the amount called for in the instrument.

A "Bill of Exchange" is the same as an "Order to Pay" except that payment is made usually at a fixed future date. An exception is a "Bill Payable at Sight" in which case it is the same as a Bank Draft. Bills of Exchange, payable at sight, are also known as short bills while Bills payable at a fixed future date, are known as long bills, or time bills. In addition, if a bill is drawn on a banker, it is called a Banker's Bill and frequently, depending upon the commodity given in exchange, it is called after the commodity, such as a "Cotton Bill", "Grain Bill", etc.

An "Acceptance" is the same as a long bill except that the drawee indicates his acceptance of the obligation by writing his name across the face of the instrument. When such endorsement is made by a bank it becomes a "Banker's Acceptance" and it is customarily discounted by the acceptor. They are good investments.

A further distinction in bills of exchange is whether they are "Domestic Bills" or "Foreign Bills." If drawn covering a transaction in a certain state or country, depending upon usage, it is known as a "Domestic Bill". If drawn to cover foreign transactions, it is a "Foreign Bill".

LOANING OF DEPOSITS

Because of the increased practice of merchants and others of leaving their excess or surplus coin with the exchangers for safekeeping assured the exchanger of having coin on hand at all times, they first began to loan their own funds at interest, receiving in return, promissory notes secured by commodities in transit, warehouse receipts, assignment of revenue and pledges of property and possessions.

As from experience they were aware that coin and receipts remained on deposit for a considerable length of time, and a balance was accumulated, they next began to loan out the money entrusted to them for safekeeping, at interest. A considerable quantity of the coin was thus loaned by exchangers, specialists and goldsmiths only keeping sufficient on hand to meet their current demand. Later, in order to give greater accommodation, the specialists gradually eliminated the name of the depositor, substituting their own name, and issued the receipts in round amounts. This development is attributed to Greek bankers.

The mechanism of credit while sometimes thought of as a modern invention is practically as old as man himself. Records of transactions involving credit have been discovered in Asia and instruments of credit were used in Assyria at the time that metals passed by weight before the advent of coinage. Traces of credit employing transfer orders are found in Assyria, Phoenicia and Egypt before the system attained full development in Greece and Rome. In the days of Babylon, financial transactions of such were negotiated in conformance with the laws of the land and surrounded with religious rituals.

In the British Museum in London there exist today many clay documents unearthed from Babylon which are recordings of deeds, real estate partitions, and loans of silver at interest. Indications are that these documents were drawn and negotiated in the presence of high priests and copies placed in the temple or other apparently safe place for protection.

Manu, the Sanscript law giver, (1500 B.C.) in his writings refers to judicial proceedings and negotiations governing credit and interest on loans.

Later in history during the reigns of Nebuchadnezzar and Nabopolassar (625 to 604 B.C.) records have been unearthed to indicate it was common practice to make loans of silver at interest.

From what we gather from history, the first bankers of Athens and Rome confined their efforts largely to the exchange of coin. Xenophon, (430 B.C.) in his writings indicates that many large cities in Greece had coinage whose established value existed only at home, with the result that traders, when doing business away from home were forced to resort to the use of commodities as a medium of exchange. The weight and fineness of Athenian gold coin however was so reliable that they were readily accepted everywhere. Undoubtedly the devaluation of coin was practiced in most of the other cities so that coin was only a token of the general credit of the community.

PAYMENT OF INTEREST ON DEPOSITS

Deposits too were regularly received by Athenian bankers, and loans were sufficiently profitable to justify the payment of interest to depositors. Maritime traffic was conducted at such great profit by Greek traders that they were able to borrow at 20 and even 35% interest and make a profit on their ventures. Pledges of valuables were often taken, but disaster sometimes occurred and serious bankruptcies resulted.

Specialists in coinage in Rome were known as "Argenterii" or dealers in silver. According to history, under Roman laws, the Argenterii were required to keep cash books, day books, and deposit books and their operations were subject to official inspection, somewhat similar, no doubt, to the examination of banks made today by banking authorities.

Solon, (635 to 558 B.C.) originated laws governing the transfer of credits on receipt of gold or silver or coin on deposit from one individual to another on presentation of an order to pay.

Probably the first loaning of gold and silver at interest in Rome was done by the Greeks, as history indicates it was not until about 300 B.C. that the Romans became identified with the handling and loaning of coin. In fact, one time in Roman history, it was a disgrace to be an exchanger or money lender. Mark Anthony, (83 to 30 B.C.) made it a subject of derision that Augustus counted an Argentarius among his paternal ancestors, and that on his mother's side an Argentarius was his grandfather.

The development of commerce and the centralization of activity in Rome further developed the business of coinage, the depositing of gold and silver, and the loaning of gold and silver at interest. Regulations in most instances were self imposed, but the need for uniform rules became so great that later a complete jurisprudence developed, most of which was later incorporated in the Code of Justinian, Emperor of the Roman Empire, (483 to 565 A.D.)

The Argenterii, first money changers and receivers of deposits and lenders of gold, later became purchasers of notes and bills of exchange. With the recognition of the Argenterii as members of a profession, the business took on some dignity, and some of the commanders of the Roman armies and proconsuls engaged in this business by loaning their capital at usurious rates. Brutus placed his capital at Kypros at 48%. Verres placed his capital at Sicily at 24% and even Cato watched carefully over his investments and Pompeii loaned hundreds of thousands of sesterces to kings and cities of Greece and Asia.

The early history of banking, unfortunately, must be limited to searching the separate developments of these mechanisms under conditions which account for their use and spread.

In medieval cities about 500 A.D. the role of professional money lender fell to Jews, Lombards and Cahorsins on one hand and the money changers on the other. Judging from history we can attribute this development to three social and economic adjustments which took place around the beginning of that period.

1. The attitude of the Church against interest.

2. The impracticability of transferring metal from one place to the other.
3. The laws of nearly all European countries prohibiting Hebrews from acquiring real property and/or engaging in manufacturing or trade.

From the beginning of Christendom until the 14th century, the Church denied the legitimacy of interest on funds borrowed, with the result that Christians were forced to give up the profitable business of loaning. Naturally, as business had to be carried on, and the loaning of funds on notes, pledging commodities as collateral, was in existence, this part of the business gravitated to the Hebrews who were not bound by Canonical laws.

The merchants with whom they were in constant contact became increasingly accustomed to depositing their monies not immediately needed and were generally charged a fee for safekeeping. The deposit became the basis of a book transfer of local payments.

The deposits were gradually transferred into *depositum irregulare*, often contrary to the original intentions of the depositors. They could be used for extension of credit by the money changers. Moreover, they gave rise to a transfer of interlocal payments established by the money changers through a connection with business colleagues in other cities.

The prohibiting of Jews from carrying on trade and manufacturing and becoming identified with tradesmen skills doesn't seem to be founded on any moral basis, yet the prohibitions were in effect in nearly every country in Europe, and had the effect of forcing them into the goldsmith and exchanger business so as to obtain the necessities of life. This restriction of gainful labor, however, contributed to the growth and development of commerce in that Hebrews, without a country, could conduct business with an Arab, Mohammedan or Christian in behalf of Arab, Mohammedan or Christian without religious, racial, moral or social scruples.

Later when the legitimacy of interest was recognized, merchants and lenders conceived the idea of making bills of exchange payable at a different place from that where it was drawn, and adding to the bill a charge for transportation of the metal to cover payment. This charge, while recognized as being entirely ethical and proper, was merely a subterfuge for interest, as the bills were kept in circulation and never left the country. This, incidentally, has its modern concept in banks charging exchange for cashing or collecting checks, deposited by their customers drawn on banks in other cities and states.

The use of bills of exchange became more recognized after 500 A.D. when permission or licenses were granted by petty rulers to certain individuals to issue coin upon compliance with certain requirements.

Some of these petty princes realizing that their quantity of metal and coin was in the exchanger's possession endeavored by devious ways to obtain this coin for their own use and frequently borrowed it. Unfortunately, in most cases it was never repaid. Therefore, to protect themselves many of the exchangers resorted to keeping their coin in another country, using bills of exchange almost exclusively. Merchants readily accepted these as mediums and in this compact form a fortune could be transferred in a small package.

The development of trade and commerce brought receipts and other forms of credit instruments into wide use. It was these instruments, and the principles followed in the use of these instruments, which resulted in developing the business we today know as banking.

BANKS–BANKERS

As to how the words "bank" and "banker" originated, we have the choice of two explanations, both of which have some basis of fact. MacLeod is of the opinion that the word bank is traceable to public loans made by Italian cities in the Middle Ages. The usual Italian name for a public loan was "Monte" signifying a joint stock fund. The Germans were influential in Venice around 1171 when a forced loan was levied on all citizens, their name for a joint stock fund was "banck", meaning a heap or a mound, which the Italians converted into the word "Banco". Scott, on the other hand, is of the opinion that bank came from the word used to describe the bench "Banken" on which the specialists and money changers placed their chests and strong boxes containing coin.

Between 1100 and 1400 A.D. two situations developed concurrently which had a decided bearing on the later development of commerce and finance—the origin of banks of issue and banks of deposit. It is not that functions of these banks had not been performed before, but, that the universal recognition of such functions makes this period important. Although the developments unfortunately ended in fraud, they did however implant the ideas upon which modern banking is founded. While these so-called banks were not strictly banks of issue yet I term them so primarily because they did issue mediums of exchange using as security not gold or silver but the pledge of wealth, and the taxing power of recognized governments. It was a method of financing public debt.

BANKS OF ISSUE

The first such bank of issue was the Banco O Debito established in Venice in 1171. This bank was organized for the purpose of furnishing the government with money. The fund was accumulated by a 1% levy against property of all citizens of Venice and in return for the gold and silver so paid, receipts passing as curency, were given and passed as mediums of exchange. The second bank of this kind was formed in Florence in 1344 due to the inability of the government to retire its general debt.

Another bank of importance was organized about the same time in Genoa by the issuance of notes secured by the pledge of public revenue to finance punitive wars. Under the plan of finance the lenders were permitted to use their own agents to collect taxes paying the excess of the claim to the city. The multiplicity of these claims was so extensive, however, that in 1407 the Bank of St. George was formed into which were incorporated all of these various claims, and for several decades the new bank was the sole financial agent of the state.

Certain of these banks especially the ones at Florence, made loans to English landowners, using as security the revenue and produce from the land. Edward III, (1312-1377) defaulted to the bank at Florence for 900,000 gold florins, and as a result, the bank was obliged to suspend, ruining many businessmen.

The loans to government by financial houses under these forms resulted in ruin for subscribers. As state bankruptcies occurred the banks failed so that at the end of the 16th century all were out of existence.

BANKS OF DEPOSIT

Banks of deposit on the other hand were the outgrowth of the trade fairs which grew and assisted in the development of commerce. The principal fairs were held at Geneva, Lyons, Genoa, Bruges, Antwerp, the latter two being held all year round. The prominence of bills of exchange, and the maintenance of deposits of gold with money changers over and above needs for the bills of exchange, created large dormant deposit balances.

EARLY LOANING FUNCTIONS OF BANKS

In time, however, as happened in history before, the exchangers and goldsmiths, realizing that these surplus funds remained with them for long periods, began to disregard history and loan out these excess funds. Naturally when income and outgo remained even they functioned, but when the surplus was drawn down and loans couldn't be met, the goldsmiths defaulted causing great loss to the merchants.

Certain small institutions, formed to issue coin of established weight, form and fineness, endeavored to correct the evil but were not of sufficient capital to accomplish this end. Finally, before trade was destroyed, the merchants tired of having coin melted down and debased by goldsmiths and exchangers and having surplus funds loaned out, prevailed upon the municipal authorities, controlled of course by the merchants, to pass laws governing this business.

This pressure brought about the so-called licensing of public transfer banks subject to municipal control and examination. These banks accepted gold or silver of any manufacture or stamp, assayed it, and reduced it to pure metal, giving the depositor a receipt for the value of coin so deposited. These deposit receipts became readily exchangeable at face value for merchandise and were widely used in trade.

The first banks of this kind, historically known, were formed in Barcelona in 1408, Naples in 1539, Venice in 1587, Milan in 1593, Amsterdam in 1609, Hamburg in 1619 and Nuremberg in 1621.

It was in these banks that the basic ethics of modern deposit banking was developed and man's century old cry for a sound and solid foundation for commercial transactions was answered for the first time.

BANK OF AMSTERDAM

The next contribution to the science of modern banking was made by the Bank of Amsterdam which was founded in 1609. In addition to being operated as a municipal bank, giving receipts for coin so deposited, it gave the depositor the right at any time to draw out all or part of his credit in notes or standard money, which sum was deducted from the funds to his credit. Depositors could also make payments of monies owed their creditors, by having the bank transfer by a book entry the amount so owed from their account to the account of their creditor. At first such transfers were made in the banking house itself, but later on as this practice developed, the bank honored such orders as were made in writing which is the forerunner of the present bank check as we know it.

CHAPTER V

FORMATION OF CENTRAL BANKS IN EUROPE

ANY STUDY OF BANKING would be incomplete, without briefly reviewing the next important development in banking—the formation of central banks in European countries in the 17th Century.

In some of the early banks, as we shall now call the business which developed from the functions undertaken by goldsmiths and money changers, not only were the receipts for coin and bullion deposited for safe keeping kept in circulation as currency, but ownership of the metal transferred on the books of the goldsmiths and money changers by endorsement.

In addition, petty princes and sovereigns, when in need of funds, frequently "borrowed" from goldsmiths and money changers, giving in return, a pledge of tax moneys.

Under such a system, as we have seen, fraud was frequently perpetrated, with little chance of detection, until such time as the goldsmith or money changer was unable to redeem the receipts with gold or silver when presented for payment.

Naturally this repudiation of debt disrupted trade, caused bankruptcies, brought about unemployment, and a lowering of living standards in the area.

In order to correct the widespread abuses in the business of money changing, the merchants and wealthy citizens worked toward monetary reform. This combined with the need for standardization of size and value of mediums of exchange, so that commerce could flow smoothly, need for an equitable tax system which would provide sufficient revenue to support the state without resorting to excessive borrowing from the money lenders which usually ended in repudiation of debts and financial ruin, and the need of municipalities and sovereigns for funds to carry on wars and protect trade routes, led to the formation of the so called central banks.

It would appear to those studying a history of banking that central banks were a long time coming into existence although the need was apparently obvious to our forefathers generations ago. This was not the case, however. It is always the tendency of modernism to accept the past without investigating the circumstances which caused the events of the past. This attitude unfortunately colors opinion and often leads to rationalizing.

Any history of banking it seems would be incomplete without some narration to refresh students' minds that it was the political and economic forces of the era which determined, altered or pregnated the germ of central banking which is not only the foundation of modern commerce and finance but the cornerstone of what economic welfare we enjoy today.

The brief resume of the foundation and functions of the central banks of Europe is of additional importance in that it was upon the foundation of these banks that the Bank of England in Great Britain, and the Federal Reserve System in the United States, considered by many to be the finest types of central banking known to man, were founded.

BANK OF ENGLAND

In England until the early part of the 17th century, the functions of the safekeeping of coin and bullion were administered by the goldsmiths who issued their receipts which passed as currency, and were utilized to transfer ownership on their books. Because of the general unrest in European countries the goldsmiths who had large holdings of metal, placed their funds in the Tower of London for safe custody and government protection.

This worked very satisfactorily until 1640 when Charles I, finding himself unable to raise funds by public finance to pay his army, or to get further money from Parliament, seized the coin and bullion in the Tower of London and appropriated it for his own use. As these funds belonged to many of the merchants, the financial situation in London became acute and trade was hampered. Unable to get the money returned, the merchants henceforth avail-ed themselves of either the facilities of the goldsmiths who kept funds in other countries or kept their own funds at home.

When Charles II ascended to the throne in 1660 he too was short of funds, and resorted to borrowing from the goldsmiths in anticipation of taxes voted by Parliament which he pledged as security. Under this plan Parliament would collect taxes and then remit the funds to the goldsmiths for the retirement of the debt. The debt became larger and as income from taxes fell, Charles became so desperate for funds that in 1672 he issued a proclamation stopping all payments by Parliament to the goldsmiths. The freezing of this debt spread ruin and suffering throughout London and paralyzed commerce. This action destroyed confidence in the word of government, and the goldsmiths who were not wiped out and had personal wealth, returned to the business of safekeeping and loaning only to merchants.

In 1694 the increased difficulties of raising money for the government, and the exorbitant rates of interest demanded by goldsmiths, led Parliament, after some difficulty, to approve a plan suggested by William Patterson, an obscure Scotsman, which provided for the organization of a company to be known as the Governor and Company of the Bank of England. The bank was chartered for twelve years, and was allowed to issue notes, receive deposits on which interest was paid, make loans on real estate, deal in bullion and make advances on merchandise.

In the early part of 1697 after the collapse of the land bank which had been formed exclusively to make loans against real estate, the charter of the bank was extended to 1710 and provisions governing the protection of new capital were made. For the next several decades the bank prospered and from 1742 on, had the exclusive right to issue notes.

The war with France brought about a financial crisis and the closing of many country banks, as depositors fearful of French invasion withdrew their coin and hoarded it. This brought about a severe shortage of the circulating medium, the suspension of specie payments and led to the passage of the Bank Restriction Act of 1797. Under this act the bank was forbidden to make any payments in specie, except to the army or navy or by order of the

Privy Council, and gave stability to bank notes by making them valid for the payment of taxes.

When the charter of the bank was renewed in 1826 in order to give more stability to the banking system, the Bank of England was required to establish branches.

After the crisis of 1837-40 a doctrine of finance was developed having its main theme that bank notes were a form of currency distinct from commercial paper and other forms of credit, and that expansion of bank note issues, everywhere redeemable in coin, was the cause of commercial crises and that to prevent crises a fixed limit should be placed on the issue of bank notes. This theory was so generally accepted that in 1844 when the bank charter again came up for renewal, bills were introduced in Parliament whose purposes were to cause a mixed circulation of coin and bank notes to expand and contract, as it would have expanded and contracted under similar circumstances, had it consisted exclusively of coin. These bills which established what we commonly refer to today as a gold standard basis, also prohibited the creation of new banks, and provided for the establishing of British currency to be dependent on the depositing of gold and bullion.

Probably the most important scientific development occurred as a result of the panic of 1857 which consisted of using a discount rate to control the flow of gold and reduced the spread between high and low of commodity prices.

This policy by which the Bank of England established control of economic factors worked as follows:

1. In order to attract gold the rate of discount is raised which induces the general rise of interest rates in banks throughout the country. The high cost of money restricts credit as it makes it advisable to postpone new enterprises and lessens the demand for contractual capital goods. Unemployment usually follows and consumer goods demand is lessened.
2. Merchandise carried with borrowed money is disposed of, depressing the market which causes a decline in the home market. This checks imports and stimulates exports.
3. Capital is attracted by the high rate of interest and not only is gold attracted but home money remains at home.
4. Lowering the rate produces just the opposite effect.

Further developments about this time took place with the organization in 1844 of a bank known as the Check Bank. It was organized to accept deposits and promote the movement of capital.

In brief, funds were deposited to the credit of the depositor for which he received books of checks of fixed denominations making up his balance. It was the privilege of the depositor to fill in these checks for any amount less than the fixed denomination but never for more, thus insuring the honoring of the checks. Such checks were made payable by the Check Bank only through some other bank to escape the prohibition of law against promissory notes payable to bearer. The checks were accepted as cash between individuals and the bank established relationships with over a thousand foreign and domestic banks which agreed to honor these checks. This scheme undoubtedly was the forerunner of the express and bankers' travelers' checks now used and honored throughout the world and the basis for the various and sundry schemes suggested for checking account facilities for small depositors.

The principal functions of the Bank of England are to:

1. Control the credit supply throughout the country.
2. Govern and control interest rates.
3. Have custodianship of the country's gold reserves and control of debt settling functions abroad.
4. Regulate note circulation.
5. Maintain the fiscal agencies for the government.
6. Cooperate with other central banks in other countries for the purpose of currency stabilization.

The Bank of England is governed by a court of 24 directors or governors and deputy governors who serve for one year. Usually the senior director is governor, and the second in seniority is deputy governor.

A portion of the directors, all of whom are drawn from private banks and financial houses are elected every year. These members are usually older men so that the makeup of the board reflects mature judgment.

Stockholders have no voice in the managment although they meet quarterly as provided by the bank charter but this is just a formality.

The bank consists of two departments, the banking or deposit department and the issue department whose functions are distinctly separate.

BANK OF FRANCE

France is one of the few countries which has granted the sole right of note issue to a private bank. This governmental function, vested with a private corporation, seems impractical unless it is realized that the French problem is closely allied with the psychology of the masses who have an intense love for money and financial possession, which encourages speculation, and has been responsible for the money scandals that have rocked the empire throughout generations.

The idea of a royal French bank of state for the purposes of issuing notes is attributed to John Law, a Scotsman, who conceived the idea about 1715. Letters patent were granted, May 2, 1719, and the bank known as Banque General de Law, or Law's Bank began operation.

The functions of the bank were to issue notes, discount commercial paper and act as the physical agency for the treasury. It was an excellent idea, and a sound basis on which to develop a central bank, but Law, the founder, had ideas of a financial empire and set about to unite in a single monopoly, all the various companies organized to develop commerce and trade in America and the colonial empire. Right to establish such a separate company was granted Law, and in August of 1717, the Compagnie D'Occident, representing the consolidaion of companies which controlled the commerce and trade of Louisiana, Canada, and the west coast of Africa, was incorporated. This company made arrangements with the government to farm the taxes, coin money, manage the tobacco monopoly and assume the entire public debt.

In 1718 to further his plans, Law succeeded in having the Banque General de Law transferred into a public institution known as the Banque Royale. As shares of the bank became involved in speculation, it brought on a panic which ended with the closing of the bank in July of 1720. This left France without a principal bank for over 50 years and made the financing of commerce and trade dependent once more on small independent banks.

The next effort to found a bank was in 1776 when the Council of States authorized the establishing of a bank known as the Bank of Commercial Discounts. The bank was forbidden to borrow except by notes payable at sight. The bank was initially successful but the economic crisis beginning in 1788 finally involved the bank so deeply in private and secret loans to the government, including transactions for the Revolutionary government, that the bank was suppressed in 1793 by decree of the National Convention.

During the next three years the Reign of Terror brought circulation of worthless state currency which culminated in a decree of the National Assembly in July of 1795 allowing everyone to transact business in whatever medium of exchange he chose to use.

This law was no sooner promulgated than a group of private bankers organized the Bank of Current Accounts for the purpose of issuing bills and discounting bills of exchange. Not to be outdone by the bankers, a group of businessmen organized the Bank of Commercial Discounts, followed in 1798 by the organization of the Commercial Bank, by retail merchants.

Development of these banks, which were soundly organized into state banks, changed in November of 1797 when Napoleon Bonaparte became First Consul and virtually dictator of France.

One of his first steps was to organize the finances of the state through a national bank and on January of 1800 a decree was passed organizing the Bank of France. The bank weathered the several political upheavals in the ensuing years and until 1830 was regarded principally as a bankers' bank. To meet expanding commercial demand, it contributed its assistance to the organization of many provincial and private banks throughout France.

The overthrow of King Louis Philippe in the Revolution of 1848 brought about a suspension of specie payments, and decrees giving forced legal tender throughout the country to bank notes issued by the Bank of France and legal tender to notes of country banks, only within the boundaries of the area. As this paralyzed the country banks, decrees were passed to provide for the consolidation of the country banks with the Bank of France maintaining them as branches, and limiting the right to issue bills to the Bank of France. From this time on, to the present, the management of debts through times of war and peace has been very ably handled by this bank.

The stock of the Bank of France is owned by the public. The 200 largest stockholders comprise the General Assembly which elects the directors, known as the Board of Regents. These directors, 15 in number, supervise the operation of the bank, examine bills of exchange, fix the rate of discount, define the investment policy of the bank and authorize the issue of bank notes and their withdrawal from circulation.

The administration of the bank is vested in the directors, and a governor and two deputy governors who are appointed by the President of the Republic. The governor is the active head of the bank, directs all of the business, and alone executes contracts and agreements on behalf of the bank. While publicly owned, through the power vested in the governor, it is the treasury and sole fiscal agent of the Republic.

The principal operations of the bank in addition to the issue of notes and currency are to:

1. Discount bills of exchange, warrants maturing in less than three months from date of presentation.
2. Accept deposits for current accounts.
3. Make advances on ingots, bullion and foreign coin, French and colonial securities.

BANK OF ITALY

From the fall of the Roman Empire until the first half of the 19th century Italy was merely a geographical expression. The northern part was held by Austria, the Pope ruled the central part, Sicily, Naples and Sardinia were separate kingdoms and Corsica belonged to France.

Although several banks were organized prior to the 15th century, for the purpose of furnishing funds to the government, the forerunner of the central bank of Italy was the Bank of St. George, formed in the beginning of the 15th century to furnish funds to the government to carry out wars receiving as security the pledge of public taxes.

The bank was formed in 1407 and interposed its advice in every measure of government, even equipping armies at its own expense. The collapse of the French monarchy in 1793, followed by a series of long wars ultimately destroyed all freedom of the Italian cities and put an end to most of the then organized banks.

The next bank of note was formed by the kingdom of Sardinia, which comprised the Island of Sardinia and Piedmont, the northwestern part of Italy. This bank, known as the Bank of Genoa, was organized in Piedmont in March of 1844 and thereafter followed the rise of the Sardinian kingdom, and with the extension of territory opened branches for the serving of commerce. When the Sardinian conquests, under King Victor Emmanuel united all of Italy, the bank continued to grow and opened branches in all territories under its control.

During the last part of 1859, King Victor Emmanuel reorganized the Bank of Genoa as the National Bank of the Kingdom of Italy. The consolidation of the independent protectorate kingdom of Italy, ending in 1870 with King Victor Emmanuel's march into Rome, did not affect, at the time, the operations of the bank in Rome, or the Tuscan Bank of Credit, the National Bank of Tuscany or the Bank of Naples but only resulted in the establishing of new branches of the National Bank of the Kingdom of Italy.

Due to excessive circulation on the part of all of the banks, and disclosure that the politicians had borrowed and connived with the directors for excessive and unwarranted loans and renewals, gave the government an opportunity to unify and consolidate the banking system in 1893 under the name of Bank of Italy, and the continuing of branches and offices operated by the banks which were part of the consolidation.

The functions of the Bank of Italy, as provided for in the statutes are to:

1. Discount commercial paper maturing within four months, endorsed by two or more persons.
2. Discount treasury bills and warehouse receipts, issued by general or bonded warehouses.
3. Advance funds, for periods not exceeding four months, against government stocks, treasury bills, securities payable in gold guaranteed by foreign governments.
4. Sell, or purchase bills payable in gold and drawn on foreign countries, due within three months.
5. Discount bills of the Italian Credit banks.

6. Accept deposits of current accounts, but grant no lines of credit or permit overdrafts.

BANK OF THE NETHERLANDS

The predecessor of the Bank of the Netherlands, the central bank of Holland, was the Bank of Amsterdam, one of the famous banks of the Middle Ages. This bank as we learned was formed by an ordinance of the city of Amsterdam in January 1609, under the administration of the city government, for the purpose of eliminating confusion arising from the mediums of exchange used in financial transactions, and to provide stability for the merchants in handling their commercial transactions.

Under the ordinance as passed

1. All bills of exchange issued by merchants were required to be paid through the bank.
2. Specie was to be sold to anyone on demand.
3. Coin was to be accepted by the bank only at weight and fineness value, and receipts evidencing the deposits were to be issued for the amount brought in, less a charge for handling.
4. The net amount and lawful exchange, as determined by weight and fineness, was credited to the depositor's account.
5. Deposits were subject to a handling or safekeeping charge.
6. The bank was to do no loan or discount business.

The use of receipts as transfers of credit became known as bank money and were a contributing fact to the growth of Amsterdam as a commercial center. So much confidence was placed in these receipts that redemption in coin was practically eliminated, and for the next century it was the accepted conviction that there was at all times, in the vault of the bank, gold and bullion equivalent to the receipts so issued.

In 1789, however, it became known that the bank had allowed overdrafts of accounts and made substantial advances to the Dutch East India Company for development of the colonies. Unable to protect its credit by redeeming these receipts, the bank, in November of 1790, gave notice that silver would be tendered to holders of receipts only to 90% of their claim. As this was an admission of insolvency the bank closed and responsibility for redemption of notes was assumed by the City of Amsterdam.

In 1814 when it was evident that the bank could not be revived the government by granting a royal charter authorized the organization of a bank known as the Bank of the Netherlands, a private institution in the form of a stock company. Under the decree the bank was granted the sole right of issue for the country and limited to function as a bank of issue—that is it could issue currency or bills against coin or bullion, accept deposits and discount bills arising out of commercial transactions—but was forbidden to participate in commercial or industrial enterprises, or make loans against securities or real estate.

The Bank of the Netherlands was unique in that it was permitted by law, to only credit the net value of coin deposited to a customer's account, and make a charge for handling the account. This undoubtedly was the forerunner of present day exchange or collection charges on accounts. The Bank of the Netherlands established further principals of finance, many of which we find today in the administration of the Federal Reserve System.

In other countries of the world other banks were organized but at a much later date than the ones we have covered. As they made little contribution to the science of banking, it is thought sufficient to only briefly cover them.

RUSSIA

Due to the debasement of silver and coin, and in order to consolidate the outstanding note circulation and the floating debt of the empire, the Bank of Russia was organized in 1860. In 1894, it was given permission to make loans on industrial enterprises and to retail merchants. These measures resulted in such confidence that gold began to flow to the bank and reserves were accumulated, so that from 1895 until 1914 the bank bought and sold gold, and paper rubles circulated on an equal term with coin. The war, however, in 1914 brought about a suspension of gold payments and after the Revolution of 1917 all banks were nationalized and put under control of the Central Committee of the U.S.S.R. Shortly thereafter the bank was liquidated, and outstanding issues of currency exchanged for currency representing the debt of the new government.

In November 1920 the State Bank of the United States of Soviet Russia was organized, followed several years later by the organizing of both savings and capital finance banks. In 1925 laws were passed making the State Bank of the United States of Soviet Russia the sole bank of issue.

SWEDEN

The State Bank of Sweden, patterned after the Bank of Amsterdam, was organized as a bank of issue in November of 1656 by Palmstritch. Under his guidance the issue of notes without having a full metal reserve was effected. In 1668 however the bank was unable to cover its redemption requirements and was reorganized as a state bank under government ownership.

For over a hundred years business and private credit was handled by money lenders or by commercial houses who resorted to the open market. In the crises that followed after the Napoleonic Wars nearly all these went out of business and financial transactions were handled by private banks as authorized by law in 1824. Several re-organizations took place, due to the wars in Europe and the problems brought about by changes in economic conditions. In 1897 following a pattern established by many other banks Sweden passed new banking laws giving the State Bank of Sweden the sole right of issue.

GERMANY

Centuries of internal discord made the German nation, until the 19th century, a disjointed group of independent monarchies, the foremost of which was the state of Prussia. The first bank of any importance was organized in 1765 as the Royal Bank of Loans and Current Accounts commonly referred to as the Bank of Prussia. It continued to be a state bank until 1846 when the demand for capital for development of railways and commercial expansion made necessary an increase in capital which was obtained by public subscription. The public were given minor rights, but control remained in the hands of the government. Deposits consisted principally of funds belonging to the government, or governmental agencies, and the discount activities consisted principally of loans on merchandise.

When the North German Federation was formed under leadership of Prussia in March 1870, provision was incorporated into the constitution confining to the Confederation Assembly, the exclusive right of regulating banks of issue and managing circulation which was carried on with the founding of the German Empire in January of 1871.

In May of 1875 following a convention between Prussia and the Empire, plans were made for the organization of a new bank to be known as the Reichsbank, (the Bank of the Empire) which was to be under government management, but private ownership, to take over the rights and privileges of the Bank of Prussia. The new bank came into operation in January of 1876 and succeeded in bringing bank note circulation under control and became the sole bank of issue. This management and direction continued under the government until 1922 when the Republic, by a change in the constitution, placed control of the bank under the bank's Board of Directors thus making it independent of the government except that the bank continued to furnish the needs of the Republic by the issue of bank notes.

NORWAY

When Norway regained her independence from Denmark in 1814 the country was in the throes of an economic and financial panic due to the failure of the crops, the British blockade and a disorganized monetary system caused by the failure of the Danish State Bank in 1813.

Realizing that the progress of the country depended on a sound financial basis, Parliament, in 1816, established a bank for the purpose of providing mediums of exchange, to discount bills, to make loans to agriculture, and to finance real estate. The country was in such poor financial condition that it was impossible to raise capital by subscription, and Parliament was forced to levy taxes on all land owners to obtain capital for the bank.

The bank known as the Bank of Norway opened in January 1817 and moved to Oslo in 1897. Under the charter the bank was permitted to issue currency at the rate of five specie dollars for every two specie dollars of capital, and to make loans on real estate by means of note issues to an amount not exceeding 2/3 of the valuation. The borrower was to make semi-annual payments of interest and principal equivalent to 5% per annum so that the loan was self liquidating in twenty years. This is probably the forerunner of the mortgage plan adopted by the Home Owners Loan Corporation and Federal Housing Authority in the United States in 1933.

While the bank did not redeem its notes in specie except when it was necessary to obtain foreign exchange, it was successful in accumulating sufficient metal to maintain a currency base, so that the price structure was not thrown out of line with the world market. Due to extensive shipping interests and export business Norway enjoyed an uninterrupted era of prosperity until the monetary disturbances caused by the war beginning in 1914.

CHAPTER VI

THE DEVELOPMENT OF BANKING IN THE UNITED STATES

BANKING, AS WE HAVE SEEN through our studies, was originally a common law right. Any citizen could be an exchanger, money lender or goldsmith; and whether or not he functioned as a banker, and accepted deposits, depended on the trust his neighbors, friends and associates had in his honesty and integrity.

The development of banking, from about 1612, beginning with financial transactions in the colonies, until 1913, when the act establishing the Federal Reserve System was passed ushering in the modern era of banking, follows patterns with the accompanying mistakes found in systems tried years before in Europe.

As we read in previous chapters, the attempts of the colonial governments to provide satisfactory mediums of exchange, ended in failure.

Many of the problems faced by the colonists in connection with finance arose from the fact that Colonial governors were unwilling to subscribe to the practice of issuing bills of credit repayable from taxes, and the firm belief of the merchants, that exchange mediums, in the form of currency, were absolutely necessary in the conduct of trade.

Unfortunately, in the beginning, the Colonial assemblies and leaders confused the need for currency with a need for capital, with the result that many public and private banks were formed, whose main purpose was the issuing of bills of credit to be used to circulate as money.

The plan of issuing bills or currency against property and real estate received much support and many experiments were tried, most of which ended in failure. Later banks were formed by provisional governments for the purpose of issuing notes in payment of their debt, with the understanding that notes so issued were to be retired from the collection of taxes.

Both the Colonial governors and the merchants unfortunately failed to realize that a good currency must be properly exchangeable for metal with established value—and that the security behind such currency cannot be subject to depreciation or fluctuation.

As each experiment, however, definitely left its mark on Colonial financial history, and contributed to banking as we know it, a brief review of the principles under which these banks were organized and functioned, is in order. As nearly as is possible they are listed in order of organization. *

THE FUND AT BOSTON NEW ENGLAND

The Fund at Boston New England was formed in September of 1681 in the Colony of Massachusetts for the purpose of providing mediums of exchange or currency for its members. In operation the company received mortgages from each of its members and each member was given a credit on the company's books for the amount so deposited. This credit or parts of this credit could be transferred to any other members of the association in the form of a change bill. The historical knowledge of this bank is very limited and all information available is from the records of a few mortgages in the Suffolk Registry of Deeds and it is presumed the life of the bank was short.

MUNICIPAL NOTES AS MONEY

The first colonial government to issue notes intended to circulate as money was Massachusetts, which in 1690 issued bills in the amount of 40,000 pounds as payments to soldiers who had returned from the unsuccessful expedition against Canada. As they were issued in anticipation of taxes, they should have been readily acceptable at par, but the tradesmen were unwilling to accept them, and in order to negotiate, a considerable discount was extracted.

In 1692 the Assembly made these notes legal tender and receivable for taxes at a premium of 5% over silver. Once it became known that it could be convenient for well regarded colonists to

* The author is indebted to the following for much of the information on colonial banking: White "Money and Banking"; Conant "History of Modern Banks of Issue"; Sumner "Financier and Finances of American Revolution"; Scott "Money and Banking."

pay their obligations with these bills, which in the modern day we could term tax anticipation warrants, other colonial assemblies grasped the opportunity that this scheme presented.

Nearly every state in time resorted to using these bills. Due however to the knowledge the public had as to the basis for issuing the bills, everyone on receiving same would exchange the bill for coin and specie. Quite naturally, if successful in exchanging these bills, the specie was placed out of circulation, which further created a shortage of good mediums of exchange and accentuated the demand for further bills of credit.

Counterfeiting was widely practiced and unscrupulous and greedy individuals often halved and quartered their own bills, uniting them with parts of real bills so that they would pass in trade. Quite naturally, with counterfeiting being practiced, the older such bills became, the less chance there was for full payment, with the result that each year these notes depreciated further in value until ultimately they were fully depreciated.

BANK OF CREDIT IN BOSTON

The Bank of Credit in Boston was formed as a private association in 1714. It had an original capital of 300,000 pounds raised by members making over real estate to the value of the subscription as security for the bills or notes issued by the trustees of the bank.

The rules for the bank provided that each subscriber was pledged to accept the bills on the basis that they were bills of the Colony, and make loans of the bills on iron and other commodities for one-half or two-thirds of the value according to the market. Each subscriber was obliged to keep out at least one-fourth of the amount of his subscription for a period of two years which however could be transferred to any other person on the books of the bank.

This scheme failed due to the fact that the whole system compelled subscribers to receive the notes as the equivalent of silver money in goods, and there was no provision for fixing the price of goods.

In 1720 the House of Commons passed an act known as the Bubble Act which prohibited the transacting of business by joint stock companies in the United Kingdom without the special authority of statute, and imposed severe penalties on those engaged in the business, which temporarily at least put a stop to schemes for organizing so called banks using real estate as security.

NEW LONDON SOCIETY UNITED FOR TRADE AND COMMERCE

In 1729 Solomon Coit, representing a group of individuals, petitioned the Colonial Assembly to organize a company or bank, patterned along the same line and idea as the Bank of Credit in Boston. In addition to capitalizing the bank by a pledge of real estate mortgages, this bank wanted the right and power to issue bills or currency upon their own credit.

The Assembly was unwilling to give power to a private company to issue bills of credit for use as currency. They finally obtained a charter in 1732 which, however, did not grant them the power to issue bills. As soon as the charter was granted, however, the company issued 30,000 pounds in bills and put them in circulation by buying goods from anyone who would take them. When the governor found out what had transpired he called the Colonial Assembly together and dissolved the Society, redeeming the outstanding bills of the company with the new issue of Colonial bills.

RHODE ISLAND BILLS

In 1731 in Rhode Island the Colony organized a bank issuing 100,000 pounds in bills of credit to be made available as loans to individuals. The merchants in Massachusetts and Connecticut, realizing that these bills if readily circulated would depreciate their own currency agreed not to accept these notes in trade. At the same time, a number of prosperous merchants formed a partnership and issued 110,000 pounds of notes for general circulation. These notes were issued as loans at interest, repayable in notes of the same kind or in silver coin of specified weight and fineness. This was a disastrous attempt at stabilization as when the Rhode Island bills came in, they not only caused depreciation in the currency, but a scarcity of good circulating medium as the notes redeemable in silver were hoarded.

THE LAND BANK OF MASSACHUSETTS

The next prominent bank established was the Land Bank, established in Massachusetts in 1739. The bank was patterned after previous banks, but in addition to issuing notes against mortgages, also issued notes against the produce of the Colonies, including hemp, flax, iron, wool, tallow, cord wood and other commodities at a price fixed by the directors.

By provision of the notes which were to circulate as currency, they were to be redeemed in twenty years in manufactured articles of the province and were to be readily acceptable in trade at the rate of value based on silver. This meant nothing in view of the fact that there were no fixed prices for the goods so traded. Since the notes payable at the end of twenty years and the prevailing rate of interest was 5%, the result was that these notes meant a donation of the face value of the notes from the acceptors to the bankers without any return whatsoever. As it was such a great opportunity for profit, over a thousand people subscribed for shares in the bank.

The governor called the Assembly, to fight it, but was unable to prevent its organization and it began to function and issue its own bills in September of 1740.

When the Bubble Act of 1720 was extended to the American Colonies March 17, 1741 it referred specifically to the Land Bank as violating the Act and forced it to suspend. This dealt the Colonies a severe blow in as much as it gave the note holders immediate action against every partner for the full face value, and many of the shareholders were ruined.

These associations were similar to other banks that were in operation throughout the Colonies until the Revolutionary War. It is interesting to note that in the formation of Colonial banks no capital in the form of specie was required, and only land and commodities were used as a basis for issuing bills as mediums of exchange.

CONTINENTAL CONGRESS NOTES

The next development in coinage and exchange came about as a result of the Revolutionary War. Unfortunately, the Continental Congress was not empowered to impose taxes or negotiate loans, consequently the only method available to raise money to pay the army, and finance the expenses of the Congress, was through individual gifts, and the issuance of notes to be redeemed at some indefinite future time. These became known as "due bills" and were given in exchange for merchandise, food stuffs and other supplies required by the army.

The original issue of 2 million dollars, authorized January 22, 1775 was not readily acceptable, and were only taken in at a discount. Funds, however, being necessary at any cost, the Congress authorized an additional issue of 19 million dollars. Unable to retire the notes from tax levies or duties, the depreciation became more pronounced, and as issue was succeeded by issue, the depreciation was so manifest that the expression "Not worth a Continental" came to be attached to this form of money used to finance the Revolutionary War. Issues of such due bills by 1780 reached the staggering sum of 241 million dollars.

ESTABLISHING OF A COINAGE SYSTEM

Because of the need to have a uniform basis for determining mediums of exchange which would be readily acceptable throughout the Colonies, Congress in 1782, upon the recommendations of a committee headed by Robert Morris, adopted the first principles of a coinage system using the spanish mill dollar as a base. These principles called for the use of a decimal system throughout; a coin representing the tenth part of a dollar and a coin of copper for the hundredth part of a dollar, and for supplementary coins, such as a half dollar, double tenth, and a coin representing the twentieth part of a dollar.

Resolutions fixing these fundamental principles of a coinage system were adopted by Congress and made law in July of 1785. This was followed in September 1786 by Congress passing an ordinance establishing the mint, fixing the price of standard gold and of silver. It was not, however, until the new form of government was in operation in March 1789 that these resolutions, brought into being by the Continental Congress, were crystallized when the Treasury Department was provided by law and organized by Alexander Hamilton. It was not until April 2, 1792, that the act establishing the coinage system, in final form, was finally passed.

The history of currency as a medium of exchange, from 1780 until 1863, when the act creating the National Banking System was passed by Congress, follows the pattern, as we shall see in succeeding chapters, of the formation of private banks, or banks originating under the sponsorship of the state; the issuance of bills of exchange and bank notes which were received and accepted out of the immediate territory only at a discount and finally repudiated.

While it was true that most bills and bank notes were payable in gold or silver, the difference in the laws governing the banks of the various states, set up a barrier as to the redemption of these notes at par, and most bank notes in circulation were accepted only on a discount basis, the discount depending on the bank and its distance from financial centers.

It could be of interest to students of banking, that the term exchange, originated during these periods which covered the cost incidental to having a person from a financial center going to the bank which issued the bank note—presenting them for payment or redemption into gold or silver—and transporting the gold and silver back to the bank which had accepted the bank note or bills originally.

THE BANK OF NORTH AMERICA

In 1780, in order to eliminate, if possible, the discouragement and dissention throughout the country caused by a lack of good circulating medium, and depreciation of existing forms of currency; and at the same time to provide funds for carrying on the campaign against England, Alexander Hamilton and Robert Morris, the Superintendent of Finance, conceived the idea of a plan for a bank with a paid up capital of specie which would issue notes for two or three times the amount of its cash on hand.

The Continental Congress granted a charter for such a bank to be known as the Bank of North America in 1781 and of the original capital authorized at $400,000, $250,000 was made in specie in the name of the government.

At the time, however, when the Bank of North America started, there were certain people whose credit was poor, who complained to the Legislature that the bank was guilty of favoritism, and that its attitude was tending to destroy the equality of the citizens which is presumed to exist in a Republic. The Legislature investigated the charges and repealed the charter of the bank in

September, 1785. The bank protested that its charter was irrepealable, but took steps, however, to protect itself by obtaining a charter from Delaware where they intended to operate if they were forced out of business in Pennsylvania.

The State of Pennsylvania, however, then fearing that the bank would transfer its operations to Delaware, again granted the bank a charter, which charter was renewed from time to time. The bank continued in existence until 1929 when it was absorbed by the Pennsylvania Company for Insurance on Lives and Granting Annuities.

MASSACHUSETTS BANK

Up to 1783 the banking needs of Boston were cared for by the prosperous merchants who accepted deposits, made advances and issued drafts on their London correspondents. About 1783, a group of Boston merchants organized the Massachusetts Bank along the lines of the Bank of North America, and received a charter and opened for business in July of 1784. This bank continued in existence and was very profitable. One of the important phases of this bank's charter was that it placed upon the directors personal liability for all debts of the bank incurred with their approval, and prohibited the bank from buying or selling merchandise, or dealing in the shares of any other bank.

When the National Banking Act was passed in 1864, the Massachusetts Bank entered the system. In 1903 it purchased the First National Bank of Boston and assumed the latter's name, although retaining its original charter.

BANK OF NEW YORK

In 1784 merchants in New York, in order to provide circulating medium, prevailed upon Alexander Hamilton and others to organize a bank patterned after the Bank of North America. The Articles of Incorporation were drawn up and the capital subscribed. The State Legislature, however, refused to grant a charter but the organizers, unwilling to allow the lack of approval to stop the bank, which they believed advisable, began business in June of 1784 without a charter. There was no legal penalty for assuming this right except that the stockholder had unlimited liability for all debts of the bank.

The articles and regulations of the bank provided a policy of charging 6% on loans which were only to be extended for a period of 30 days after maturity. In addition they made provision that no note would be discounted to pay a former one, and that payment to the bank would have to be made in its own currency or in specie. In addition it also prohibited overdrafts, and because of the clipping and abrasion in respect to coin, would only receive gold and silver at its weight value.

In spite of numerous petitions the Legislature refused to approve the charter for the bank. Finally in March of 1791 the Legislature granted a charter which among other things provided that

A. The debts of the bank, over and above the monies actually deposited, could not exceed three times the amount of capital actually paid in.
B. It could not hold real estate except as might be required for the accommodation of its own business—or a debt which was acquired by taking titles and land securing debts previously contracted.
C. It could not deal and trade in commodities—or in securities of the United States, except that it might sell such securities as were pledged as security for a loan or purposes of liquidation.

With the passing of the National Banking Act the bank became a member and throughout its history has shown steady progress and greatly participated in the commercial development of New York.

In 1922 the bank changed its name to the Bank of New York and Trust Company and in July 1938 changed its name back to the Bank of New York.

THE FIRST BANK OF THE UNITED STATES

The end of the Revolutionary War found the finances of individuals, and the government very low. The experiences of the Colonists with Continental currency made them reluctant to receive currency or bills as mediums of exchange, so that again the greater part of commerce was conducted with barter and exchange. The Bank of North America, however, performed splendidly and its notes and currency being redeemable in specie, were readily accepted although the supply did not begin to satisfy the demand.

The matter of establishing a strong financial set up for the United States received considerable attention from Congress in 1790 and Alexander Hamilton was delegated to report on a system of coinage and recommend provisions he thought necessary for the establishing of credit. In December he submitted to the House of Representatives a plan for establishing a bank with a constitution similar to the constitution of the Bank of England.

Hamilton would have favored the granting of certain rights to the Bank of North America, on its perpetual charter granted by the Continental Congress, but he and others felt that the position of the bank had been jeopardized by the acceptance of a charter granted by several of the States. Finally, however, opposition to a new bank by certain members of Congress, who believed that the organization of such a bank violated the Constitution, was overcome and on February 25, 1791, President Washington signed the bill approving the establishing of the First Bank of the United States.

This bank operating under a charter limited to twenty years and was capitalized with 25,000 shares of $400 each, of which 8 million dollars was to be subscribed by the public, which could be paid for in 1/4 specie and 3/4 in government obligations bearing 6% interest, with the remainder to be subscribed by the Federal Government.

Among the interesting provisions of this charter was a provision against no more than 3/4 of the directors succeeding themselves; the right of the Secretary of the Treasury to inspect and examine the affairs of the bank; the right of the bank to establish branches wherever the directors might wish; and the limitation of interest on loans to 6%.

The Government continued to be a stockholder of the bank until 1802, when unable to retire debt which it had incurred, sold the balance of the stock to the public.*

PHILADELPHIA NATIONAL BANK

Prior to the removal of the national capital to Washington,

* History continued under Second Bank of the United States.

Philadelphia was one of the principal centers of governmental authority. The city being spread out, with a population of almost 100,000 people, needed additional banking facilities in order to assist in the expansion of trade and commerce.

In August of 1803, almost 200 individuals signed the Articles of Association for a bank to be known as the Philadelphia Bank. Considerable opposition was raised against this bank by the other banks in town, but demands of the merchants were so strong that it was allowed to exist.

The Philadelphia Bank entered the National Banking System in 1865 to become the Philadelphia National Bank. Today this bank is one of the largest in the country and the leading financial institution in Pennsylvania.

TRENTON BANKING COMPANY

One of the oldest banks in the country operating under its original charter is the Trenton Banking Company of Trenton, New Jersey, which was chartered by an act of the New Jersey Legislature in December of 1804. Since opening for business the bank has operated under its original name as a state bank along the lines for which it was originally incorporated.

THE BOSTON EXCHANGE OFFICE

During the first half of the 19th century, because of the absence of uniform banking laws, attempts were made in nearly all of the states to compel shareholders of bank shares to pay for their shares in specie to eliminate speculation which was occuring. Stockholders in many cases were borrowing money from the bank on their own notes to pay for their stock, working on the theory that if the bank survived the dividends would exceed the interest on the notes and the difference would represent a clear profit.

In 1804, several of the charters granted by Massachusetts contained the provision forbidding loans until the capital stock was actually paid for in gold, or silver, coin. While this checked speculation, in more than one case it was proven that banks borrowed the entire amount of their capital in gold and silver from other banks, and after they had exhibited it to the public officers, returned it to the bank they borrowed it from. This considerable speculation in bank shares resulted in the incorporation of the Boston Exchange Office in 1804 for the purpose of dealing in bank shares and bank notes.

SECOND BANK OF THE UNITED STATES

Years of experience of Thomas Jefferson and others did not serve to temper the feeling that the charter for the First Bank of the United States was contrary to the Constitution. Meanwhile, other groups jealous of the prerogative of the Bank, succeeded in establishing other state banks and private banks.

As the charter of the Bank was to expire in 1811, the shareholders began in 1808 to petition for its renewal being opposed, as was to be expected, by supporters of state banks who hoped if the bank expired to share in the business.

In 1809 when it appeared that a war with England was imminent, Secretary of the Treasury, Gallatin, recommended the renewal of the bank's charter and an increase in capital.

The opposition was too great, however, and due to the opposition, and the fact that Congress was unable to pass bills extending the charter, it expired by limitations on February 25, 1811 and was put into liquidation.

Immediately, there was a rush to form new banks. Between January 1, 1811 and January 1, 1815, over a hundred new state banks were established.

The beginning of the second war with England in 1812 destroyed foreign commerce and placed an added debt on the Treasury of the United States. Because of the war, and lack of stability of the state banks, bank notes issued by the banks in existence were accepted only on a discount basis, and in September 1814 nearly all of the banks in the country with the exception of those in New England suspended specie payments.

The bank notes now were accepted only on a discount basis. The principal funds belonging to the Government were on deposit in suspended banks, and the Government found it necessary to default on its public debt bringing about an increase in commodity prices and wild speculation.

The financial condition of the country at that time was so precarious that it led to a great variety of proposals being made in

Congress one of which, by Ex-President Jefferson, that the Treasury issue 20 million dollars in Government promissory notes annually as long as it might be necessary, and at the same time appeal to all State Legislatures to relinquish the right to establish banks.

The situation was so acute, and the need so great for maintaining public credit, that after much deliberation and opposition a bill was introduced and passed by Congress in March 1816, providing for the establishing of a Second Bank of the United States. This bank followed, almost in its entirety, the pattern of the First Bank of the United States.

The section of the bill dealing with the establishment of branches is interesting in that it made it mandatory for the bank to establish a branch bank in the District of Columbia if and when Congress should demand it to provide the Treasurer with an agency to handle the Government's financial transactions. It also provided that a branch should be established in any state upon the application of the Legislature of that state, subject to the condition that at least 2,000 shares of stock were held by residents of the state.

The bank opened for business on January 17, 1817 and by the end of the year had established 17 branches in 14 states, covering the entire eastern seaboard and the Ohio Valley. By 1823, after being plagued with poor management in its early beginning the bank had attained a great measure of success and increased its branches to 26.

The numerous state banks chartered during this period, because the Second Bank of the United States exercised certain privileges not accorded them, made every effort to remove the bank by exercising political influence and attempting through propaganda to influence people against it. Andrew Jackson was President, and in 1829 an avowed opponent of the Bank. As the charter of the bank was to expire in 1836 he called upon Congress to give thought to the practicability of organizing a bank as a branch of the Treasury Department, and followed up with the announcement that after October 1, 1833, Government funds would be withheld entirely from the Second Bank of the United States.

In 1833 the Government deposits were withdrawn from the Second Bank of the United States. Throughout 1834 and the next few years, Congress did everything possible to have the charter extended but was unable to change Jackson's opinion. When the directors of the bank realized the Government was not going to grant them another charter they appealed to the State of Pennsylvania and on February 1, 1836 were granted a charter by the state for 30 years.

Unable to foresee the devastating effects the elimination of the bank would have upon the country, Congress and the President allowed the bank to expire in 1836 by limitation. The capital of the bank, now that it was no longer acting as fiscal agent for the Government, was too large for local needs. In order to be able to pay dividends it made many speculative loans, many of which turned out to be worthless after the crisis of 1837. During this crisis the bank with other banks of the country suspended specie payments and finally in 1841 with its capital impaired, went into liquidation. The depositors were paid in full, but the shareholders lost their entire investment.

NOTABLE PRIVATE BANKS OF THE PERIOD

It is also interesting to note in reviewing this period that not only was banking a common law right but often incidental to other businesses. Often legislatures and government agencies were hostile in granting bank charters, and only by subterfuge could permission be obtained to engage in banking.

Several of the most notable examples of the functions of banking being conducted, incidental to other business, is in connection with the organizations and operations of the Bank of Manhattan Company, Manufacturers Trust Company, Chemical Bank and Trust Company, and the Farmers Loan and Trust Company, now known as the City Bank Farmers Trust Company, which originally was the banking end of the Farmers Fire Insurance Company.

BANK OF THE MANHATTAN COMPANY

The most notable case, of course, is that of the Bank of the Manhattan Company which originally started off in the water business. The City of New York prior to the beginning of the 19th century found itself in need of an adequate water supply system. DeWitt Clinton and Marinus Willett raised the capital and in 1799 formed a company known as the Manhattan Company to furnish pure water to the city, which operation was accomplished by transporting water through bored pine logs laid end to end. The original charter had a provision for the company to employ any surplus capital, not employed in the water supply business, in any business not inconsistent with the existing laws.

The reputation of the founders, and the needs of the community for adequate banking facilities, encouraged the company to accept deposits. The growing city of New York needing more in the way of a water supply system than that furnished by bored logs authorized a so-called Croton system and when it was ready for operation in 1848 the Manhattan Company withdrew from the water business devoting its entire resources to banking, being known as the Bank of the Manhattan Company.

It was a large influential bank, and until it merged with the Chase National on March 31, 1953 the original well and tank on the roof remained as evidence that it was a water company primarily, and a bank secondarily by charter if not by practice.

MANUFACTURERS TRUST COMPANY

In the beginning of the 19th century the New York Manufacturing Company was founded for the purpose of manufacturing cotton looms and supplies. In order to expand sales, it was necessary to make available to customers facilities for payment. The volume of notes and acceptances received in payment of merchandise resulted in 1812 with the Phoenix Bank being formed as a division of the Manufacturing Company.

With the increased development of the deposit and discount business the directors in 1817 divorced the bank from mercantile business and provided separate quarters for them.

The present Manufacturers Trust Company is the result of a combination of two groups of banks, one comprising what is known as the Chatham Phoenix National Bank and Trust Company and the other group known as the Manufacturers National Bank and Trust Company which had its origin in Brooklyn. The Phoenix Bank group which originated from the New York Manufacturing Company and the Manufacturers Trust Company group consolidated in 1932 into what is known as the Manufacturers Trust Company and today remains one of the largest banks in the country.

CHEMICAL BANK AND TRUST COMPANY

The Chemical Bank and Trust Company did not begin business as a banking institution.

In the early part of the 19th century recognizing the growing field of pharmaceuticals, a group of individuals in February of 1823 founded and incorporated the New York Chemical Manufacturing Company.

The company from its inception so strove for quality, that it received from magazines and other periodicals, attestations of quality and in having their products vouched for by the Medical Association of New York which went so far as to recommend to consumers of chemical and drug products that they patronize the products manufactured by this company.

The rapid growth of the country, and inability of merchants to provide adequate exchange, led the company to sell their products on credit or in accepting notes in payment of the merchandise. As with the Manufacturers Trust Company, this volume reached considerable proportions which warranted the directors to apply for a modification of a charter to permit the company to do a discount and deposit business.

On April 1, 1824, the charter was amended, and in August of the same year the company opened an office of discount and deposit. The conservative and conscientious manner in which the company operated, and the quality of their products inspired so much confidence in the management of the bank, that the principal business of the company was transferred from the manufacture of drugs and chemicals to general banking business in 1832. The bank continued to operate under its own name until October 15, 1954 when it merged with the Corn Exchange Bank, which was founded February 1, 1853 and today, as the Chemical Corn Exchange Bank, is one of the largest and best known banks in the country.

NEW ENGLAND BANK

At the end of the War of 1812 with England, the country slowly returned to normalcy. Many of the country banks were in business and had funds on deposit, but had no local demand for loans, with the result that many of them purchased commercial paper in Boston for investment. These notes were acceptable below par because of the cost of converting them into specie, but were used by merchants and manufacturers in the Boston area, who accepted them for use in payment of wages and as change, thus keeping these notes in continuous circulation.

In 1813 the New England Bank was incorporated and began what is known as the "Suffolk System" of banking. This bank was incorporated for the purpose of receiving country bank notes for exchange, charging the depositor only the actual cost involved in making the exchange, or converting the bank notes into coin.

THE SUFFOLK BANK

The return to the old business of barter and exchange as practiced by the exchangers, and the realization that it was bad for business, brought about the chartering of the Suffolk Bank in Boston in 1818.*

It was planned when they incorporated this bank that the bank would redeem the notes of any New England country bank at par, providing the bank of issue would keep a permanent deposit with them of $5,000, plus a deposit sufficient to redeem their notes which would be presented in Boston for payment. It was the bank's thought that the interest on the permanent fund, each bank would maintain, would cover any expense the bank might have either through exchanging the bank's notes between each other by means of debit or credit, or through the handling costs of presenting the notes to the issuing bank and transporting the specie back to the bank. This again was a contribution to the development of exchange charges and clearing of notes between banks. This system gave all the banks who decided to join the system a vehicle for exchanging the notes of other banks on a basis that it would insure parity and redemption of their notes at par.

The plan was not readily acceptable to other banks, but the Suffolk Bank succeeded in having the other banks become members of the system by sending the notes of non-member banks, which were presented for payment, back to the bank of issue for

* So named after the system started by the New England Bank.

redemption in specie which depleted the specie of some of the more distant banks and took notes out of circulation.

About 1838 a branch redemption agency was established through the Merchants Bank of Providence, Rhode Island. Under the operation of this agency, the bank received notes of all the banks in New England and made settlement as far as the Rhode Island banks were concerned. Those notes issued outside of Rhode Island, but presented to them, were sent to Boston to the Suffolk Bank and all Rhode Island notes, received by the Suffolk Bank were sent to the Merchants Bank of Providence for clearing and exchange.

In order to provide more stabilization, the Legislature of Vermont in 1842 levied a tax against bank capital, with a provision that the tax be remitted to any bank which would keep deposits of funds in Boston, so its bills could be redeemed at par. One state after the other gave encouragement of the Suffolk System and by 1857 the Suffolk Bank had a membership, which we today term a correspondent bank relationship, of over 500 banks and was considered a clearing house for all the notes of the banks in New England. Each day these notes were balanced against each other and their respective accounts debited or credited with the net proceeds. This system was undoubtedly the forerunner of the clearing house system which is followed today by banks in cities all over the country.

THE BANK OF MUTUAL REDEMPTION

Profits derived from the loaning of funds kept on deposit by the member banks of the Suffolk Bank were so encouraging, that several efforts were made to set up rival associations and in 1855 a rival institution, the Bank of Mutual Redemption, was established for the purpose of redeeming bank notes at par, without the provision of exchanging notes for specie.

In November of 1858 the Suffolk Bank withdrew from the Suffolk Bank System giving as a reason that "its main feature, the right to send home bills for specie, cannot be given up without destroying its efficacy."

In 1861 as a result of Secretary Chase's issue of Government notes, the redemption plan of the Suffolk System experienced some difficulty, but before the system could recover from the effects of this type of Government financing, the National Bank System was formed which serviced member banks more completely than the Suffolk System.

The Suffolk Bank is notable in that for several decades it maintained New England bank currency at par with gold and established a clearing house system as a principle of banking operation.

THE SAFETY FUND

During the first half of the 19th century, banking in New York was synonymous with politics. In 1828 forty bank charters were in force of which thirty were to expire between 1829 and 1833.

As previous attempts to control the chartering of banks had failed, the Legislature sought to impose new conditions and regulations which would be in the public interest, thus forcing some of the banks which could not comply with some of the regulations out of business, creating monopolies for the remaining banks.

To give wider protection to stockholders and depositors of the banks Joshua Forman of Syracuse prevailed upon Martin Van Buren, then Governor of the State of New York, proposing that a mutual insurance plan for banks be set up under which plan, each bank would contribute a small amount each year to a common fund to be used for the purpose of paying up net losses suffered by depositors in banks that should fail. This was a modification of a plan followed by the Hong merchants in Canton who were made liable for the debts of each other in case of failure by virtue of the rights granted them by the government to trade with foreigners.

This plan which was the forerunner of the Federal Deposit Insurance Corporation, set up by the Banking Act of 1933/35, was passed by the Legislature of the State of New York in April of 1829. The law required that every bank which should be rechartered or when chartered should make a contribution equal to 3% of its capital, in installments, to a fund to be used for the payment of debts of failed banks. A maximum of $500 million was set for the fund and banks were required to make contributions until the fund reached that amount.

Provision was also made that this fund could not be used, however, until the assets of the closed bank were disposed of and the deficiency determined. There was a further provision that if the fund was depleted, when reduced by payment to closed banks, the surviving banks would be called upon for additional contributions.

The Safety Fund was primarily for the purpose of redeeming bank notes at par, preventing loss in case of bank failure. The fact that the law put all creditors at the same level was not clearly understood by the public at the time and resulted in some confusion. In 1842 the law was amended so that after the payment of deposits, the note holders had first claim.

In 1846 due to a number of bank failures the constitution was changed to provide that note holders would be made preferred creditors of all failed banks. This was an excellent law and contributed much to the stabilization of currency, as usually it is not a matter of choice whether the people shall, or shall not, accept the notes of a bank which are offered in payment. The collapse of the Safety Fund occurred principally because it was made to cover all liabilities, instead of simply the liability for note failure.

The Safety Fund is notable however in that it was the forerunner of Deposit Insurance.

THE NATIONAL BANKING SYSTEM

The Civil War brought about similar problems as that experienced by the Continental Congress. In order to provide funds to finance the war, the plan for organizing banking associations, to which the government might furnish circulating notes on the security of United States Bonds deposited in the Treasury developed. This scheme became the foundation for the establishing of the National Banking System in 1864.

In November 1860 when Lincoln was elected President of the United States, the financial condition of the Government was in a very precarious position. Since 1836 the state banks had had the banking field entirely to themselves, and since 1846 the Government, through the independent treasury system, had managed its own finances. The beginning of hostilities between the North and the South completely disorganized the exchange system of the country, as the notes of the state banks made up by far the greater part of the medium of exchange in private transactions, but in payments to the Government only specie was accepted.

The difference in the laws governing the banks of various states also set up a barrier to the redemption of bank notes, and most bank notes issued at the time and which were in circulation were accepted only at a discount, the discount depending on the bank and its distance from the financial center. This happened before in times of crisis and as before, brought back the other elements of exchange. As a result the Federal Treasury found itself in a dilemma. It had no surplus, bank notes were subject to a discount, and current revenues were not sufficient for current expenses. In addition it had no satisfactory plan, either for borrowing or taxation, to provide funds to operate the Government, or for amortizing the constantly increasing deficit.

As soon as war broke out it became evident that in order to quickly raise funds for financing the war, it would be necessary to borrow from the banks that had the transferable capital of the country. In the summer of 1861 the Congress of the United States authorized loans to the Government in several different forms, one of which was the issuing of non-interest bearing-non-legal tender notes, which were to be payable on demand at the office of the Assistant Treasurer in Boston, New York and Philadelphia; and the other consisting of loans secured by three year notes bearing interest of 7-3/10% to retire a public subscription to bonds that were to be made.

The new notes, as they were issued by the Treasury, were reluctantly accepted by the public as currency, and the banks accepted them from the public only as special deposits and protested the use of these notes as a circulating medium.

The public subscription to the bonds fell short and the banks finally had to purchase the bonds, and agree to sell them to the public. (See Jay Cooke in the next chapter.)

The inadequate supply of specie finally forced the Government, like the banks, to refuse to redeem the notes in coin, and placed finances in a further precarious position.

In order to provide some stability to mediums of exchange, and to provide for Government finances, O. B. Potter of New York urged Secretary Chase to adopt a scheme based on the New York Free Banking Law, whereby currency could be issued against securities as obligations of the Government.

After much deliberation, discussion and studies of the laws of the various state banks, a bill to permit banks to issue (currency) bank notes against government bonds was introduced in the House by Representative Hooper of Boston, and in the Senate by Senator Sherman of Ohio, and passed on February 25, 1863.

Hugh McCulloch, the first Comptroller of the Currency under the act, suggested so many amendments, however, that a complete revision was made by Congress the following year, and passed June 3, 1864. It was not until almost ten years later, however, on June 20, 1874, that the official name, National Banking Act, was given this legislation.

The provisions of this law as passed provided that:

1. A banking association could be organized by five or more individuals.
2. Minimum capital requirements were to be based on population.
3. Each association was required to deposit with the Treasury of the United States registered bonds of the United States in an amount equal to at least 1/3 of its capital against which they could issue currency to the extent of 90% of the market value of the bonds.
4. Each bank was required to receive the notes of any other bank belonging to the system at par.
5. Each bank was limited in its operation to the discounting and negotiating of promissory notes, drafts, bills of exchange and other evidences of debt; to receive deposits, buy and sell exchange coin and bullion; and to loan money on personal security, and issue circulating notes.
6. Should a bank default in its redemption of circulating notes, the Comptroller was empowered to declare the security bonds forfeited.
7. Each bank was required to pay to the Treasury of the United States a tax of 1/4 of 1% each half year on the average amount of notes in circulation.
8. No bank could permit any part of its capital to be withdrawn in the form of dividends.
9. The Comptroller of the Currency, with the approval of the Secretary of the Treasury, was given the power to appoint

suitable persons to periodically examine the affairs of every bank and to make a full and detailed report.

10. Any national bank could be designated by the Secretary of the Treasury as a depository of public funds.
11. Sixteen cities of the United States were designated under the Act as reserve cities and were required to maintain 25% of their deposits in lawful money, as a reserve, in lawful coin and in balances maintained in certain banks which were approved by the Comptroller of the Currency. Banks outside of reserve cities were required to keep 15% of their deposits in cash and funds on deposit with the banks approved by the Comptroller of the Currency.
12. Any state bank could enter the National Banking Association by conforming to the provisions of the Act.

The state banks did not willingly embrace membership however, and up to November of 1864 only 168 banks entered the system.

Both President Lincoln and Comptroller McCulloch, convinced that the National Banking System would provide a means to satisfactorily control the finances of government, and exercise restraining power for bank note circulation, attested to that fact in their annual reports.

As a result of Mr. McCulloch's report, the Revenue Act of March 3, 1865 which provided for a 10% tax upon the circulation of state banks paid out by them after July 1, 1866 was passed. This was intended to drive the state banks out of competition with the national banks and to enlarge the market for United States bonds.

Realizing the benefits to be derived from comprehensive banking systems, several of the states passed laws assisting state banks to change over to the national system so that by November 1, 1865, 1,014 banks had become members.

The funding of the National debt, and the great demands placed on financial agencies of the government, as a result of the Civil War, led to banks making large purchases of government securities which in turn were deposited with the Treasury and exchanged for circulating notes.

The next development in the study of banking and mediums of exchange came about in 1873. Between 1850 and 1873 there was such a scarcity of silver in this country, that nearly all mined silver was sold to jewelers and artisans because they paid a higher price than the government. To put a stop to this, Congress in 1873 passed a law which stopped the coinage of silver dollars. About this time, however, silver was discovered in the western states in enormous quantities, with the result that actual silver in the dollar, in terms of purchasing power was worth more than the same weight of silver in coin. For the next 20 years exchange and circulation was closely tied in with prosperity. The tax revenue succeeded in redeeming the government bonds outstanding. As these bonds were redeemed they reduced the national bank notes in circulation, thus reducing the circulating mediums for the country.

SHERMAN SILVER PURCHASE ACT

During this time the discovery and widespread mining of silver, found its way into commercial channels and several acts were passed by Congress to keep up the price of silver. To accomplish this the Sherman Silver Purchase Act was passed in 1890 under which the government committed themselves to purchase 4½ million ounces of silver every month at market prices—and issue legal tender treasury notes to the full amount of the silver purchased.

The progress of the country meanwhile although continuous, suffered from time to time from lack of a sufficiently satisfactory circulating medium, a shortage then an abundance of silver, and attempts to tie in redemption and circulation with gold.

Several of these problems came to the front in the election of 1896 when the Democratic Party objected to the policies of President Cleveland and succeeded in writing into a platform, a plank demanding free and unlimited coinage of silver at the ratio of 16 to 1.

William Jennings Bryan, claiming that he was pleading for and championing the little businessman, swept the delegates off their feet with a stirring oration against the gold standard and for free and unlimited coinage of silver, and on the fifth ballot was nominated as the Democratic candidate for the Presidency.

The Republicans that year nominated Major William McKinley of Ohio, and by the time the campaign got into full swing, Democrats were demanding that the government should take all the silver presented at the mints and coin it into legal currency at the ratio of 16 oz. of silver to 1 oz. of gold. The 16 oz. of silver on the open market were worth only $11.00, against $20.67 for an ounce of gold which meant that the Democratic Party was advocating that the government should maintain in circulation, a legal tender medium worth a dollar in purchasing power that was only actually worth 58 cents.

This was one of the most important elections in history. Bryan by his stand on silver won thousands of converts which split the Democratic Party into two camps while signalizing the ascendency of the Republican Party as the representative party of business.

GOLD STANDARD ACT

McKinley was elected and almost immediately after his inauguration national confidence began to be restored which brought about a revival of business activity. The great need of the time still was for one standard sound circulating medium. It made little difference if it was United States notes, Treasury notes or national banking notes, as long as by virtue of security it stabilized both gold and silver and provided sufficient elasticity so that it would be capable of contracting or expanding with commercial needs.

Demands for radical reform in the banking and monetary system led to the holding of a convention in Indianapolis in January 1897 by bankers, representatives of chambers of commerce, and other commercial bodies, which authorized an executive committee to appoint a monetary commission to deal with the subject, if during the existing session of Congress, a commission was not appointed. While President McKinley did send a recommendation for the appointment of a monetary commission to Congress it was not acted upon.

The Indianapolis Executive Committee then appointed a commission of outstanding businessmen to report on the subject which in brief recommended that

1. Gold be made the standard behind all currency.
2. All obligations of the United States be payable in gold.
3. A reserve of 25% in gold be maintained against all United States Notes.

4. Provision be adopted for retirement of United States Notes, and Treasury notes in ratio to national bank note circulation.

Following the introduction of a bill by Representative McCleary of Minnesota, the bill known as the Gold Standard Act was passed on February 15, 1900, which provided that the dollar consist of 25-8/10 grains of gold nine-tenths fine, to be the standard unit of value, and all forms of money issued as coin by the United States, to be minted at parity with that standard.

While the Gold Standard Act was immediately accepted by the country and was a help to business, there were still certain defects in our financial structure. The principal defect was the fact that each national bank was required under the National Banking Act to keep monies in its vault or on deposit with banks in reserve or central reserve cities, in amounts equal to between 6 and 25% of its deposits as reserve, which was unavailable to use as the basis for currency issues or credit.

The second defect was the failure of the law to provide under the system, either a central bank or an association of some kind sponsored by the Government, where during times of stringency member banks could pledge selected assets and receive in exchange credit or currency to facilitate business transactions.

The result of discovering gold in the Klondike in 1896 and opening of mines in South Africa, greatly added to the gold stocks of the world, and had its effect upon prices and credits. The influx of gold into the banking system stimulated speculation in securities which resulted in 1901 in a general market collapse from the speculative boom, and the failure of many large banks throughout Europe.

America was still expanding. There was increased demand for funds for capital investment. The effect of converting circulating capital into fixed investment brought about a further shortage in circulating capital to meet mercantile demands. As a result from 1900 to 1907 the number of banks almost doubled and the total liabilities of state banking institutions reached more than 500 million dollars while cash reserves expanded only 171 million dollars.

These and other circumstances added up to the Bankers Panic of 1907, the appointing of a National Monetary Commission in 1908 and the passage of the Federal Reserve Act of 1913.

CHAPTER VII

OTHER TYPES OF EARLY BANKS AND FINANCIAL INSTITUTIONS

THE BANKING HISTORY OF THE UNITED STATES would be incomplete if mention were not made of some of the other early banks, both private and state, and other types of financial institutions, whose foresight in providing mediums of exchange and credit and providing financing for industrial development, contributed to the growth of the nation.

The opening of the country by hardy pioneers, the flow of farmers into the Middle West, the discovery of coal in the Central States, development of the cotton fields in the South and the use of cattle ranges in the South West brought forth the necessity for local financing and the organization of local banks. The developing waterway system and the ribboning of the continent with railroad ties bridged the gap between settlements. It was only logical that where lines intersected large cities would grow drawing from their immediate surrounding territory the natural wealth and utilizing the financial institutions in the territory for their own development.

While many public and private banks were organized as the country developed, most of them failed by 1860. Certain of these banks and financial institutions however, stand out because they either made valuable contributions to our present banking system, or accepted certain principles, which were developed, and applied them to their own field.

NOTABLE STATE BANKS

Recognizing the need for some type of Government supervision, over the banking business, if suitable mediums of exchange and credit were to be readily accepted in confidence which would assist in the development of trade and commerce, several states, about this time, either permitted banks to be organized whose principal functions were to act as the instrumentality of the state, or enacted legislation controlling banking functions. The most notable of the banks were the State Banks of Indiana and Ohio, and the most notable legislation enacted in connection with banking was the Louisiana Bank Act.

STATE BANK OF INDIANA

Following the veto of the bill to recharter the Second Bank of the United States, the State Legislature of Indiana in 1834 granted a charter to a bank to be known as the State Bank of Indiana.

Its capital was to be subscribed by both the State and the public. For the initial capital of $1,600,000, all of which was paid in specie (from a loan negotiated in New York) the state advanced the stockholders 62½% of their subscription, taking as security a mortgage on their property and a lien on their shares. The individual shareholders were required to pay the balance of 37½% in actual specie, paid mostly in Spanish and Mexican silver dollars. In addition, the Legislature agreed to permit no other banking corporation to operate in the State during the life of the charter.

The purpose behind the founding of the bank was to provide mediums of exchange (currency) which could be used in commercial transactions, in addition to acting as depositary for the funds of the state, individuals and business. The currency issued by the bank, known as "bank bonds", which each bank could issue to an amount double its capital, were signed by the president of the parent bank and issued to each branch on request, and were interchangeable between branches at par.

In the beginning of its existence, because of the small number of people engaged in industry, the demands on the bank were for funds using land (mortgages) as security. In 1837, however, when the banks of the country experienced difficulty in redeeming currency, or honoring drafts or orders drawn against funds on deposit in specie, because of the difficulty in liquidating mortgage loans, the bank discontinued making such loans, confining its activities in the credit field thereafter to the loaning of funds to farmers and others on personal security, and bills of exchange drawn against shipments of agricultural products.

Originally the bank consisted of the parent bank in Indianapolis, which provided general policy and over-all management, but which did not have any of its own capital; and ten branches, located throughout the state, each of which had capital of $160,000.

This bank is notable in that each branch was managed by local shareholders, subject to the central board in Indianapolis. Another notable provision of the charter was that the earnings of each branch belonged to the shareholders of the branch exclusively but could only be paid out on approval of the parent bank. While each bank was liable for the debts of every other branch, they were independent of each other as far as assets were concerned.

Directors were individually liable for loans resulting from infractions of the law, unless they had voted against such infractions, and each bank was required to redeem its own notes in specie on demand and receive the notes of all the branches at par.

The State Bank of Indiana's charter was not renewed when it expired in 1859 and the bank was liquidated at a profit to all the stockholders.

STATE BANK OF OHIO

To provide similar facilities, the State Bank of Ohio, was chartered under the law of 1845 and followed, to a great extent, the plan of the State Bank of Indiana. The State Bank of Ohio had 36 branches and was highly successful until its charter expired in 1866, when the bank was liquidated.

LOUISIANA BANK ACT OF 1842

In order to improve the financial situation in the South, a number of far-thinking citizens of Louisiana were successful in having an outstanding piece of legislation known as the Louisiana Bank Act passed by the State in 1842. This law was important in that many of the provisions were later used or incorporated by other States in formulating their bank laws.

Some of the notable provisions of this law were:

1. Specie reserves were to be equal to 1/3 of all liabilities with the remainder to be represented by commercial paper having not more than 90 days to run. In other words, for each dollar deposited, the bank was required to keep 33-1/3 cents in the vault in gold or silver coin and could only loan the

balance or 66-2/3 cents, if it was invested in commercial paper which was due and payable within 90 days.

2. All commercial paper was to be paid at maturity; and if not paid, or if an extension were asked, the account of the party was to be closed and his name sent to the other banks as a delinquent.
3. All banks were to be examined by a board of State officers quarterly or oftener.
4. All banks would pay their balances to each other in specie every Saturday, under penalty of being immediately put into liquidation.

This was the first law passed by any state requiring a percentage of specie reserve against deposits.

NOTABLE PRIVATE BANKERS

At the time of the Middle Ages the citizens of European Countries consisted principally of two classes, land owners and serfs. Land owners received their principal income from their land holdings which they leased or rented out to the serfs, receiving payment of rent in either coin, or more often in a portion of the produce of the soil.

Whenever a land owner wished to raise money he would go to a money lender and assign the income from the land for the loan. While advancing of funds at interest against future income was profitable and advantageous to both borrower and lender, it was considered usurious business and received considerable opposition from the Church.

As laws were passed and regulations promulgated covering the charging of interest, it became a not uncommon practice of merchants, who had ships coming in from some foreign port, to assign the merchandise to someone who had a surplus amount of money, and by paying a premium as compensation for the risk involved, plus interest, receive an advance of funds against the merchandise. Sometimes the loan was repaid when the goods were received, other times when the merchant disposed of the goods. The financing of individuals by long term credit developed to such an extent that even countries and municipalities sometimes financed their operations this way. In many cases the financing of business and governments by money lenders laid the foundations for the fortunes of the some of the wealthiest families in Europe.

THE HOUSE OF ROTHSCHILD

One of the most famous of these families was that of the Rothschilds, whose family fortune was founded in Frankfort, Germany, the latter part of the 18th century by Mayer Amschel, more commonly known as Rothschild from his father's signboard called Rothschild or red shield. Rothschild, as he was better known, was educated to become a rabbi—became a money lender—and finally financial adviser to the municipality of Hesse. He had five sons and upon his death in 1822 was succeeded at Frankfort by his oldest son, Solomon.

In order to more conveniently handle trade and commerce, and expand the business, the other sons opened branches in Vienna, London, Naples and Paris. During the war between England and France, becoming convinced that the French would be defeated at Waterloo, Nathan Rothschild used all of the available funds for the purpose of purchasing British securities which, when the result of the battle was known, sky-rocketed in price.

In 1855 Amschel, Son of Solomon, organized the Kreditanstalt in Germany to compete with the Credit Mobilier. In the banking collapse of 1873, following the Franco-Prussian War, the Rothschild Bank, which anticipated the crisis, came through without any difficulty.

The World War split the family, as the powerful London and Paris houses were on the side of the Allies, and the Vienna Bank was with the Central Powers. At the end of World War I the Vienna Bank was in a state of collapse and only help from Paris and London branches kept the bank from failing.

In 1931, however, as a result of the post-war collapse of central Europe the bank failed, bringing with it a serious collapse of other European financial houses.

In 1938 when Hitler marched into Vienna, Baron Louis Rothschild, the last head of the Vienna Bank was arrested and his properties, including the bank, confiscated. The collapse of France in 1940 put an end to this once powerful and unified financial family.

The House of Rothschild was known all over the world as financiers, and negotiated many of the loans made to governments during the 19th century and assisted in developing the railroads of the United States.

Following the lead of older European commercial banking houses, several companies prior to the Civil War undertook the financing of companies on a long term basis. Of these, the following are more prominently known.

JAY COOKE

At the time of the Civil War, with government finances in a most precarious position, Jay Cooke, after a study of the operations of the French investment houses, undertook the sale of United States bonds to banks and to the public, and for the purpose of distribution, hired several thousand salesmen to sell the bonds, paying them a commission for so doing.

Cooke was very successful until the spring and summer of 1873 when the tightening of credit began to be felt. Unable to weather the storm several trust companies in New York and Brooklyn failed in September, which was followed by the collapse of Jay Cooke and Company on September 18, which brought about the panic of 1873.

J. P. MORGAN

After the Civil War, J. P. Morgan, the elder, formed J. P. Morgan and Company; and they, together with Kuhn, Loeb and Company, Brown Brothers and Company, and Harriman Brothers, began to finance the railroads, some of which were in difficulty. Due to the profitable handling of the finances they not only made substantial profits and established themselves as foremost railroad bankers, but contributed to the rapid growth of the vast American railroad system.

N. W. HARRIS

As the public utility business developed through the increased use of power, N. W. Harris in 1882 formed a company in Chicago for the purpose of underwriting and dealing in public utilities and other enterprises. This company became the Harris Trust and

Savings Bank, which today is one of the largest banks in the United States.

Under the Banking Act of 1933, however, all investment houses which also did a deposit business, were required to either retire from the investment end of the business or from the depositing end of the business in one year.

Many of the commercial banks who were engaged also in the securities business disposed of their securities affiliates or liquidated them, while several of the securities or investment houses elected to remain in the commerical banking field, and enjoy the credit and deposit relationship, with top banks, railroad, utility and manufacturing companies.

The outstanding firm of this type was that of J. P. Morgan & Co., Inc., which elected to remain a bank, and did an outstanding commercial banking business, under its own name until April 24, 1959, when it merged with the Guaranty Trust Company of New York and is now known as Morgan Guaranty Trust Company of New York.

INVESTMENT BANKING

With the development and expansion of business, there was great demand for capital with which to build new factories and finance new enterprises. As banks were not supposed to make loans for these purposes, special types of banking houses, known as Investment Banks were organized for the purpose of supplying funds for building plants and buying eqipment for industry through the sale of bonds to the public. Later it became the practice of industry to not only obtain funds for plant and equipment, through the sale of bonds, but also to obtain working capital, through the sale of common and preferred stocks.

In operation, Investment Banking Companies purchase stocks or bonds, issued by those engaged in an enterprise, through a process known as underwriting, and then sell the bonds, or shares of stock to those who have the money to invest, for which they receive an underwriting fee or commission.

Investment Banks are of three principal types—brokerage type, underwriting type—and management type.

The brokerage type is one which acts as agent between the

buyer and seller, and receives a fee or commission for handling the transaction.

The underwriting type is one which finances corporations by the purchase of stocks or bonds, which it sells to the public.

The management type is one which not only finances corporations and supplies their capital requirements through the sale of stocks and bonds to the public, but one which assists in managing the company, for which it receives a fee.

SAVINGS BANKS

Following the French Revolution some of the more intelligent men of Europe, in endeavoring to find the causes and reasons for class upheaval, reached the conclusion that two of the principal contributing factors were:

1. The loophole in the economic system which left no protection for the poor and laboring classes once they were either unable to work or could find no employment.
2. The lack of some means to provide the laboring class with the necessities of life during the periods they were unemployed, or through periods of business inactivity.

From the suggestions for out and out grants to the individuals by the countries to a public dole system, there developed a sound logical plan whereby provisions would be made to educate the public to put away a certain sum of their earnings to be invested so as to provide either income, or something to fall back on when they lost their earning capacity or were temporarily unemployed.

Up to this point the responsibility for the care of the sick, the homeless and the unemployed had fallen on the churches. The idea of making these unfortunate individuals self supporting, or setting up ways and means for them to assist themselves, appealed to the over burdened churches with the result that churches in England, Ireland, Scotland and Germany advocated the formation of savings associations for the benefit of their own members.

The time and place, and the credit for establishing the first savings bank is subject to dispute. We do know, however, an association was established in 1705 in Hamburg, Germany for the purpose of having the workers deposit their surplus money with the association which it would invest at interest.

Under this plan when a worker reached a certain age the association would pay back to them the principal and interest in the form of an annuity. While this association is considered to be one of the first savings associations, as far as the early history of savings banks is concerned, it follows more on the lines of our present insurance companies.

THE PARISH BANK

The first savings bank, strictly speaking, was established at Ruthwell in Dumfriesshire, Scotland in 1810 by Reverend Henry Duncan and was known as the Parish Bank.

In 1814 the Edinburgh Savings Bank was organized in Edinburgh, Scotland.

During the next three years banks were organized in large numbers all over the Continent and their rapid growth, without the guiding force and regulations imposed by higher authorities, often was accompanied by abusive privilege and unethical operation.

In 1817 Parliament passed laws for the regulation of so-called savings banks which laws provided that the administration of these banks was to be under Boards of Trustees. The passage of these regulations established the principals of savings associations on a sound basis and the plan was soon adopted in the United States.

The commercial development of this country, especially the development of manufacturing industries, particularly the textile industry in the East, was a major contributing factor in the establishing of various types of savings banks throughout the United States.

These types of savings banks are:

1. The mutual type
2. The guarantee type
3. The stock type
4. The savings and loan association
5. The type developed through the savings departments of state and national banks
6. Postal Savings

MUTUAL SAVINGS BANKS

The majority of savings banks in the East, particularly in New York, are the mutual savings type. This type has three principal characteristics. It has no capital or stockholders and is managed by a Board of Trustees. Deposits are received and invested for safekeeping. After expenses are paid, the remaining income from investing the deposits are divided among the depositors based on the size of their deposits.

The first mutual savings bank in the United States was the Philadelphia Savings Fund Society which opened for business in November of 1816.

The second mutual savings bank was the Provident Institution for Savings which opened in Boston in December of 1816.

These two banks were followed by the Bank for Savings which opened in Manhattan in 1819 and the Seamen's Bank for Savings which was chartered and opened for business in New York in 1819.

The Greenwich Bank for Savings was chartered and opened for business in 1833 and the Bowery Savings Bank which opened its doors in June of 1834.

Of all these banks, the Bowery has one of the most interesting histories. Bowery comes from the Dutch word "bouwery" which means a farm equipped with buildings and livestock which were offered free to new settlers by the Dutch East India Company. In the early settlement of New York, the Bowery was one of the principal centers of business and the founders of the Bowery Savings Bank included most of the best known and influential brokers, grocers, butchers and others, listed as gentlemen, who today would be known as capitalists.

The success of these savings banks encouraged the formation of similar banks operating under individual charters throughout the Eastern States. Because of the character of the banks and the integrity of the founders, it was not necessary for the states to pass any general laws governing their operations until 1834. In that year Massachusetts adopted the first such general laws with Virginia adopting general laws in 1838, Connecticut in 1843, Rhode Island in 1858 and Maine in 1869. New York State did not pass any laws governing savings banks until 1873.

The early charters granted these banks in the various states made it mandatory that all funds be invested in Government bonds. Permission to depart from these early restrictions were first granted in the charter issued by the State of New York to the Poughkeepsie

Savings Bank in 1831, which permitted loans on real estate having double the value of the sum loaned.

The State of Massachusetts under the General Savings Bank Law, permitted total investment in mortgages to the total of 75% of the amount of the deposits.

GUARANTY SAVINGS BANKS

The second type, or guaranty type of savings bank, exists only in New Hampshire. These banks have no capital, or stockholders. They do have two classes of depositors, special depositors, (who, strictly speaking, are stockholders of the bank) who are responsible to the remaining depositors if the bank fails, and whose return from investment of funds deposited depends on the bank's profit and, the ordinary, or general depositors, who deposit their surplus funds with the bank and in return receive a certain fixed return. After operating expenses of the bank are paid and the interest is paid to the general depositors, the surplus is paid to the special depositors on the basis of their deposits.

STOCK SAVING BANK

The third type of savings bank is the stock savings bank which is a private corporation. It is organized with capital stock, has stockholders, a Board of Directors to manage the affairs of the bank, pays a fixed interest rate on deposits and profits over and above the expenses are paid to the stockholders.

THE COMMERCIAL SAVINGS BANK

The fourth type of savings bank is operated as a department of a state or national commercial bank. They receive deposits and pay a rate of interest fixed by their own regulations or according to law.

The funds, in most instances, are co-mingled with commercial funds resulting in the net profit accruing to the stockholders of the bank.

The establishing of a savings department as a regular operating unit of a commercial bank has only been in existence since around 1900.

SAVINGS AND LOAN ASSOCIATIONS

The first recorded savings and loan corporation in the United States was known as the Oxford Provident Building Association founded in Frankfort, a suburb of Philadelphia, in January 1831.

The original plan of the Oxford associates was to create one issue of stock which was subscribed by the original members of the association. The stock issue had a definite life period and was not supplemental with later stock issues. One result of this plan was the continuance of the association to the life period of the stock issue and the extinguishing of the association when all payments of stock had been completed.

Funds so deposited were loaned out in the form of first mortgage real estate loans which often brought a net return to the depositors in excess of 5%. This association and upwards of fifty similar organizations which were created in Philadelphia between the years 1831 and 1849 were not only voluntary organizations, but were operated without corporate charters from the state. In 1850 the Pennsylvania legislature passed the first law regarding their incorporation.

The savings plan spread rapidly to other sections of the country and in 1847 the State of New Jersey enacted legislation demanding incorporation of such groups.

THE POSTAL SAVINGS BANK

The Postal Savings Bank, under the direction of the Postmaster General and a Board of Trustees, was organized in 1910 with the primary purpose of providing facilities for savings to people in towns where they did not have a bank. One of the features of the postal savings bank was that a depositor could not have on deposit with the postal savings system more than $2,500 at any one time.

INTEREST ON TIME DEPOSITS

The payment of interest on time deposits by a commercial bank is of recent origin, as far as banking history is concerned. One of the first known instances occurred in 1840 when the Farmers Bank of Maryland established the practice. It must be remembered that the monetary problems of the country, up until the middle of the 19th century, were all concerned with the need for a sound currency and acceptable mediums of exchange. Little thought was given to the depositor or the services he required. While it is undoubtedly true the banks used the payment of interest as a device to attract funds, which they could use as a basis for making loans, it was not officially recognized or countenanced by law.

One of the first instances of official recognition of time deposits occurred in May of 1866 when the Appellate Court of Massachusetts ruled that national banking associations could issue Certificates of Deposit and that such certificates were not bank notes within the prohibition of the revised statutes.

Thus receiving legal approval for the instrument, the use of certificates became widespread, and payment of a higher rate of interest was used by a great number of banks to attract deposits thus giving them more funds to loan for the expansion of industry and commerce.

That this practice, when it became widepsread, was not only frowned upon by leading Government banking authorities, but that suggestions were made to banks to prevent such practices is indicated by A. B. Hepburn, Comptroller of the Currency, who in his annual report of 1892 not only condemned this practice, but requested the larger banks to attempt to suppress the practice by refusing to discount Certificates of Deposits, or permit use of Certificates of Deposit as collateral.

The desire of banks to increase deposits by the paying of rates of interest on time and savings deposits, far in excess of what was warranted, was particularly unsound, particularly in the case of national banks as under the National Banking Act no consideration was given the amount of reserves required between time and demand deposits. It was clearly evident, however, to the framers of the Federal Reserve Act, that recognition should be given to time deposits with the result that in the Act as passed, they specifically defined what constituted time deposits.

As a result of the banking crisis in 1932 and 1933, with the passage of the banking act of 1933, as amended in 1935, regulation in respect to the payment of interest on time deposits was vested with the Federal Reserve Board.

INVESTMENT TRUSTS

Another form of investment banking is in the form of associations or companies dealing in investment trusts. In order to protect one's capital it has always been sound practice to diversify investments to the extent that economic changes, which would result in the decrease of the value of certain types of securities, would reflect contrariwise by causing an increase in the price of other securities.

The policy of diversifying investments has been a contributing factor of the development of personal fortunes, as by this means people have been able to weather financial storms without a great impairment of their principal. Unfortunately, the small investor has not usually had sufficient funds to enable him to diversify his holdings, consequently during times of stress the little investor has had his principal depleted and often the savings of a lifetime wiped out

Following the development of savings banks several companies were organized for the purpose of making investments in different types of business and selling participation to the public. Investment in such a company means that an investor would have an interest in a number of companies instead of one, and that competent men, versed in investments and finance, would watch over the operation and management of the company to protect the investment.

Investment trusts generally divide themselves into two classes, the fixed trust, in which type of investment and the amounts so invested are fixed by the incorporators; and the unfixed trust in which the investment and the amount so invested are left to the judgment of the managing officers.

MORTGAGE FINANCE COMPANIES

Mortgage finance companies, another form of investment company, came into prominence about the turn of the century for the purpose of furnishing funds to finance the construction of hotels, apartment houses or office buildings. These companies usually furnish the money for the erection of the buildings, taking back a mortgage on the entire property against which they issue bonds which are sold in various denominations to individual investors.

INDUSTRIAL FINANCE COMPANIES

In order to meet the need for assistance in supplying capital to finance new endeavors, industrial finance companies were formed about 1920 for the purpose of acquiring or advancing capital to start a new enterprise. The capital was first obtained through the sale of securities to the public. Later the companies advanced the capital out of their own funds. In each instance, however, the financing company received remuneration in the form of a block of stock and fees for participating in the management.

MUNICIPAL FINANCING

Other important investment agencies are the municipal investment companies whose functions are concerned with the financing of states, counties, cities, towns, villages, townships and districts.

Because of the very nature of municipal financing, firms having expert knowledge of the municipal financing field, requirements of corporate and individual investors, and laws governing the issue of such municipal obligations, have come to specialize in this type of financing.

Municipal obligations are generally issued in three forms, Direct obligations, Specal obligations, and Revenue obligations.

Direct obligations, on which the payment of principal and interest is dependent on the general tax revenue, or income of the municipality, are generally issued for construction of buildings, to purchase equipment, or provide for the operation of the municipal, fire, and police departments; or for construction and operation of water filtration and garbage disposal plants.

Special obligations, on which the payment of principal and interest is dependent on tax revenue from owners of real estate, for the payment of funds advanced for construction, or paving of streets, alleys; and construction of lighting and sewage disposal facilities.

Revenue obligations, on which payment of principal and interest is dependent on income obtained from the operation of certain projects such as municipal power plants and transportation facilities.

FARM MORTGAGE COMPANIES

To assist farmers in purchasing land, another type of financial institution, known as Farm Mortgage Companies were formed. Such companies engaged in the business of soliciting mortgages from farmers, then selling the bonds or certificates, secured by the mortgages, to the public. The rates of interest were high, and terms of payment stringent, so that in many cases, when the farmer was unable to make his payments, or strictly abide by the terms of the loan, the company foreclosed, taking over the farm, which it often sold later at great profit.

FEDERAL LAND BANKS

In 1908 a Country Life Commission was created by President Roosevelt for the purpose of determining the causes which contributed to the deficiency of country living.

In their report they stated that one of the principal reasons for the poor economic level of the farmer was the absence of an agricultural credit system under which the farmer could secure loans at fair terms. As it was recognized that the commercial banking system of the country was not set up to adequately provide for the farmers' needs, a bill, known as the Federal Farm Loan Act was passed in 1916. This bill as passed, and with amendments adopted in subsequent years, was for the purpose of not only correcting the abuses of private farm mortgage financing, but to provide a convenient and economical means for purchasing farm land and paying off existing debt, and to increase the supply of capital for agricultural development, through the establishing of land banks under federal incorporation.

Funds for financing the operations of the Federal Land Banks were obtained from the sale to the public of Federal Land Bank bonds, guaranteed by the government, and secured by mortgages double the value of the land or five times the value of the permanent improvements.

STOCK EXCHANGES

The history and development of banking in the United States would be incomplete unless some mention was made about the forming of the New York Stock Exchange, which established the pattern for the later establishing of the Chicago Board of Trade, and other exchanges which contributed to the development of the country.

The origin of the Stock Exchange is interesting in that its original purpose was to facilitate the trading and exchanging of United States government securities, particularly the issue of 1789 when the Congress of the United States authorized an 80 million dollar issue to pay for the Revolutionary War, operate the government and provide for peace time activities.

When people wished to trade in these bonds it was necessary to find someone who would trade with them. As price was often a matter of personal opinion there were wide fluctuations in the bid and asked price of these securities. Because of the wide margin of profit, however, men of some means actively went into the business of buying and selling government issues, making a ready market for those who wished to buy or sell. Due to the activity it became difficult for those engaged in trading to get together to consummate the deal and much time was wasted in completing transactions because very often the dealer was acting for other men of means, with whom it was necessary to consult on price before completing the deal.

The first official meeting of these "exchangers" which started the New York Stock Exchange was held on May of 1792 under a buttonwood tree on Wall Street near the East River. After conducting their meetings in the open for about a year they transferred their daily activities to a coffee house.

About this time their value to the community was so established, that they began to handle securities (bills of exchange, notes, and mortgages) of private individuals and independent companies. It was not until 1885, however, that they began active trading in industrial stocks.

In 1816 they rented their own quarters in Wall Street. Finally, because of the increase in business, they moved into the Merchants Exchange Building, where they remained until the end of the Civil War, when they moved into their present quarters at Broad and Wall Street.

With the development of the country, other exchanges, similar to the New York Stock Exchange were formed in the major cities to not only deal in stocks and bonds, but in commodities such as corn, wheat, coffee, cotton, textiles and metals.

CHAPTER VIII

OUR BANKING SYSTEM TODAY

THE BANKING BUSINESS, as we know it today, is composed of three separate and distinct principal functions:

1. The acquiring of funds to invest and loan.
2. The investing of such funds in loans and bonds.
3. The servicing of such funds, such as the providing of checking/savings facilities, and the collection of drafts, notes and checks.

These functions, while differing in detail of operation, follow the same principles established hundreds of years ago by the money lenders and exchangers, when after customary haggling, they accepted coin and bullion, either for exchange into other forms of coin or receipts, the value of which, in terms of purchasing power, was "guaranteed"; or for safekeeping (deposit) for which they gave a receipt, or "promise to pay" which passed for value as currency between merchants and others in negotiating commercial transactions, or in the discharge of debt.

In referring to barter, exchange, and promises to pay, we should be mindful that these terms are reflected and the principles applied, in all forms of financial and banking transactions today. In ancient times persons who wanted to exchange or trade mediums, haggled with the person they wanted to do business with as to the amount, or number of mediums they would accept in exchange, or trade for other mediums or merchandise. Obviously if the merchant or exchanger had a supply of mediums, say salt, sufficient for his needs for some time, for which he paid, or exchanged at the rate of 3 coins for each sack, he didn't particularly need or want more salt. He would, however, buy the salt if he could get it at a price to justify his risk for a profit, and buy the salt for 2 coins a sack. (Remember when the supply exceeds the demand it results in lower prices.) On the other hand if the exchanger or merchant needed the salt he might have to pay or exchange 4 coins for each sack. (When the demand exceeds the supply it results in higher prices.)

In modern times if there is an oversupply of money (commonly referred to when deposits are uninvested and are either kept in cash or invested in short term government securities or commercial paper because there is little demand for loans) banks are willing to loan money at very favorable terms, let us say 3½% per annum for 90 days.

On the other hand if business is prosperous, prices are increasing, and there is a great demand for money, banks might be charging 5% per annum for a loan for 30 days. (The reason for the short period of the loan is that if demand continues, at the end of 30 days they could reloan the funds at a higher rate.)

In connection with promises to pay and exchange, it is also well to remember that when a person deposits money in a bank, he receives in exchange a receipt, or the promise of the bank to pay to that person, or to his order, the sums the person has deposited with the bank for "safekeeping". Further, whenever one person gives a check to another person, he is not only exchanging that check for some other thing of value, but promising that the check represents equal value (funds on deposit to the person's credit in a bank.)

While the principles and general practice of banking today is uniform as between banks, the present status of banking in the United States, has evolved, during the past hundred years, from many types and kinds of banks and financial institutions which we have already briefly reviewed. On the other hand this evolution had brought about many complexities, which can only be resolved by realizing and understanding certain factors which contributed to, and make up, our present system.

TYPES OF BANKS

Today the principal banking and financial facilities available to serve the commercial and financial needs of individuals, and business, are provided, and made available to them through five types of banks.

1. Commercial Banks
2. Trust Companies
3. Savings Banks
4. Savings and Loan Associations
5. Finance Companies.

A current brief re-definition of these types of banks, might be helpful.

COMMERCIAL BANKS

Commercial banks may be defined as "moneyed" corporations, authorized by law to receive deposits and pay such funds to others on order; discount and negotiate promissory notes, drafts, bills of exchange, and other evidences of debt; to lend money on real or personal security; to make collections; and conduct such other moneyed transactions as are not inconsistent with its charter or the laws under which it operates.

TRUST COMPANIES

Trust companies are organized for the purpose of administering estates, acting as trustee, and serving in any fiduciary capacity where there is an advantage to having someone act in capacity of serving one or more people.

Trust companies are chartered and supervised by the state authorities. Many trust companies confine their operation strictly to trust business—some to a single type or a few types of trust service. Others operate banking departments and perform the same kind of banking functions as commercial or savings banks. Some of the largest banks in the United States operate under trust company charters. National banks and state banks have the right to offer trust service, so in the majority of cases there is little difference in the services offered by commercial banks, and trust companies.

SAVINGS BANKS

Savings banks, in general, were formed originally to provide a safe and convenient place for people to put their surplus money, and where they would receive interest for the use of the funds, from the careful investment of their funds.

Many savings banks, when originally started, also conducted a trust business. It is for this reason that we find so many banks today carrying in their name—"Trust and Savings Bank".

Over a period of years there have been many changes in their charters so that today many of these banks provide the same services as commercial banks. Likewise both national and state commercial banks and trust companies, as time went on, began to offer the same facilities as savings banks.

For all practical purposes, therefore, commercial banks, savings banks, and trust companies all render the same type of services.

SAVINGS AND LOAN ASSOCIATIONS

Savings and loan associations, originally known as building and loan associations, are mutual organizations formed for the purpose of assisting members of the association to own their own homes.

Deposits of funds are made to "accounts" which are termed shares. The funds so subscribed in monthly installments are loaned or invested in first mortgages on residential property. Many of these loans are granted under the provisions and guarantee of the Federal Housing Administration, a Government chartered corporation. The earnings from the investment of funds are distributed to the members as dividends.

The principal difference between a savings and loan association and a savings bank, or the savings department of a commercial bank is that in savings banks individuals maintain accounts and receive interest at a prescribed rate, while in a savings and loan association people buy shares and receive earnings in proportion to their investment in the form of dividends.

FINANCE COMPANIES

Finance companies are incorporated under state laws for the purpose of financing the purchase of automobiles, household appliances and for making small loans to individuals for payment of current bills, and for financing the merchandise accounts receivable of business. All sums so borrowed are repayable over a period of months in equal installments.

The method of operation, as well as the interest and terms of the loans granted, are under the regulation and supervision of the state under which they are chartered; or the Small Loans Act of the respective state in order to protect borrowers against usury.

CLASSES OF BANKS

In addition, so called commercial banks, or banks which are

engaged in the business of loaning money, accepting demand deposits or funds, title to which can be transferred by check, almost 15,000 in number, which may be trust companies, or savings banks are of two kinds, either state banks or national banks. That is, they have been given the right to operate and transact their business either by the Federal government under the National Banking Act or under a charter granted by one of the 50 states, the Commonwealth of Puerto Rico, or the Government of the Virgin Islands.

Banks organized under the National Banking Act must have the word National in their name and be a member of the Federal Reserve System. State Banks may, upon application, become a member of the Federal Reserve System.

All national banks are automatically members of the Federal Reserve System and are automatically so-called insured banks, that is the deposits of each individual are insured up to $10,000.00 by the Federal Deposit Insurance Corporation. Because of the fact that we have both state and national banks, that is banks chartered by the government and the various states, our banking system is referred to as the dual system of banking.

In addition to having both national and state banks, some banks under certain state laws which permit it have branches. To clarify this, let it be said that while we have both state and national banks they all must operate in conformance with the laws of the state in which they do business. As a result we have a number of forms under which the corporate structure of banking, and the services of banking operate and function. These classifications are unit banking, branch banking, chain banking, and group banking An explanation of the various types of banking at this point migh be helpful.

A unit bank is one which has one place of business and n bank connection outside of the usual relationship with its corre spondent banks. It is also known as an independent bank, that i it has its own stockholders, its own directors, who manage the af fairs of the bank.

A branch bank is one which maintains a head office and one c more branches controlled from the head office. Such branche may be located in the same city, or may operate throughout the state, depending on the laws and regulations of the state.

A chain bank is one which belongs to a group, that is control and management is exercised through stock ownership in a limited corporation whose officers take an active part in formulating the policies and management of the banks belonging to the chain.

A group bank is one where a substantial portion of the stock is held by a holding company engaged in the business of banking. It differs from a chain or branch bank in that the identity of a local bank remains the same but its policies and operations are determined generally by its own officers and board of directors who, of course, are placed in positions of authority and responsibility by those who control the holding company.

At this point it might be interesting to briefly learn how banks exercise their three principal functions.

In former times acquiring of funds to engage in the business of banking came from two sources. (1) The means or capital which the money changer had acquired from his own operations and which belonged to him and (2) Funds which his customers deposited with him for safekeeping. Today the acquiring of capital is undertaken by organized groups of individuals who apply for a charter from either the federal or state government to engage in the business of banking.

Once stockholders have complied with all provisions of law under which the bank is to be organized, and have their capital paid in and receive their charter, they elect from among their members, a Board of Directors to direct the management of the bank. The Directors in turn appoint the various officers, to whom are delegated actual functions of management. All stockholders share in the profits or losses in proportion to their holdings.

The second source of bank funds are those which are deposited by customers, either for safekeeping (to have a safe and convenient place for their money) or to use the various services offered by banks, which people need to conduct their financial transactions. To obtain these funds, banks, through advertising, and the personal efforts of stockholders, directors, and officers solicit business and encourage people to open checking and savings accounts with them.

Funds deposited in checking accounts are payable on demand, that is the bank agrees to convert the check, or order to pay issued by the depositor, into cash on presentation. Present day checks are nothing more than demand notes, a new form of the old bill of exchange.

Funds deposited in savings accounts generally belong to individuals. With a savings account the bank reserves the right to 30 days notice of withdrawal. This provision of course is to enable the bank, because of the interest which is paid on savings accounts, to invest such funds in bonds and mortgages which yield a greater profit, and provide some protection in case it is necessary to liquidate securities without loss. Funds deposited by people in savings accounts represent funds which are not going to be used for some time or a reserve, and are placed in such an account because the bank is willing to pay them interest for the use of their money, until such time as they need it. All arrangements made by depositors with banks for the handling of funds are in writing. In connection with savings accounts, the depositor signs a signature card or agreement, which provides the authority of the bank to pay out funds upon presentation of a properly signed withdrawal slip accompanied by the pass book.

In connection with a checking account, the customer signs signature cards or an agreement (or both in the case of corporations, and associations, or those engaged in business) which bear the authorized signatures of those authorized to withdraw or transfer funds from the account.

The second function of banks is the investing of capital funds provided by the stockholders, and funds deposited by customers, in loans, and investments. In general loans are made to those engaged in business, including corporations, on their net worth as disclosed by their financial statement, against the pledge of accounts receivable, on inventory, on real estate mortgages and against chattel mortgages on machinery and equipment.

Loans are made to individuals, on their net worth, as disclosed through their financial statement, on marketable collateral and real estate equities, on automobiles and household appliances secured by chattel mortgages, and upon the endorsement of a person of financial standing, or with a co-signer.

The purpose for which loans are made is also of interest. If the loan is made for the purpose of purchasing raw materials which can be converted into finished products, or to discount bills, or to provide funds for a temporary contingency, the loan is generally referred to as a Short Term Loan.

If the loan is made to finance the purchase of machinery or equipment, which can only be repaid out of profits, over a several year period, it is known as a Term Loan or Long Term Loan.

If the loan is made to finance a building, or to make a major installation of equipment, which the borrower expects to finance, when the work is completed, through a long term loan or mortgage using the real estate or machinery or equipment as security, the loan is known as an Intermediate Loan.

If the loan is made for the purpose of purchasing an article of necessity or convenience such as an automobile or washing machine, which will be used while it is being paid for the loan is known as an Installment or Consumer Credit Loan.

Banks also make loans to the Federal, State, and Municipal Governments through the purchase of bonds or other evidences of debt issued by them. All such loans, regardless of purpose, are made with the understanding and promise that they will be repaid out of taxes levied against the income or real property of citizens for their protection, the public welfare, defense or the common good.

In addition to investing funds in bonds, or other evidences of debt, issued by the Federal, State and Municipal Governments, banks also, as permitted by law, invest in bonds of approved rating, issued by Railroads, Utility, and Industrial companies.

The third function of a bank is the servicing of the funds, such as is provided by a number of different departments in the bank such as the paying and receiving tellers who accept checks from other banks for deposit and credit to the presenter's account; the collection from another bank and converting of checks presented by a depositor to cash; a proof department which facilitates the collection of checks drawn on other banks; the bookkeeping department which records deposits made by depositors and checks drawn by the person who maintains the account; and by a number of other departments including secretaries who write letters in connection with bank matters, mail clerks who deliver or process mail, and many others.

MODERN HISTORY CONTINUED

Before we begin to study the technical aspects, detailed functions, and servicing operations of present day banking, it might be well if we continued, once again, with a brief review of the development of banking, from an historical standpoint, since the turn of the century. This period is of particular importance as it was during this era that circumstances developed which brought about the passage of the Federal Reserve Act, creating the Federal Reserve System, and the Banking Act of 1933/5 which, among other matters, provided for the guaranteeing of bank deposits by the Federal Deposit Insurance Corporation.

The development of the country and expansion of commerce, as we have seen, generally brought with it a shortage in the mediums of exchange and the need for revising monetary systems.

In 1905 there was such shortage of circulating medium that on one occasion call money rates in New York (the price people were willing to pay for immediate use of money) was as high a 125%. The fact that money should command such a premium brought to light further deficiencies in our existing system. In order to be able to give considerable study to the entire situation and to make certain recommendations to Congress Jacob H. Schiff the international banker, presented a resolution to the New York Chamber of Commerce in the Fall of 1905 calling for the appointment of a special committee to devise a monetary plan.

Congress paid little attention to this resolution. The fact that there was need for reform was however recognized by President Roosevelt in his annual message in December of 1905 where, in speaking against the evils of inflation stated, that some provision should be made to insure a larger volume of money in the fall and winter months than in the less active seasons of the year. In other words, some type of a currency plan which would expand or contract in accordance with the needs of legitimate business somewhat similar to the operation of the Bank of England. President Roosevelt was confused over the cause of the trouble. He attribute the problem to the rigidity of the volume of money, whereas the problem was in an inadequate supply.

For the next year the committee of the New York Chamber of Commerce reviewed existing systems and consulted with the heads of leading foreign banks. In November of 1906 they rendered their report, approved by the Chamber, which recommended the creation of a central bank of issue under direct control of a Board of Governors appointed, at least in part, by the President of the United States, which bank should perform some of the functions imposed upon the Treasury under existing laws.

In general, this plan recommended a bank molded somewhat after the central banks of France, Germany and the Netherlands and pointed out such a central bank, by issuing all of the currency, could have a currency that would expand or contract depending upon the needs of the country. Further such a bank could control credit expansion or contraction by means of the interest or discount rate similar to what was being brought about by the Bank of England.

While the monetary committee of the Chamber of Commerce was making its extensive studies the American Bankers Association held its annual convention in St. Louis at which time a resolution was adopted authorizing the formation of a committee to consult with the representatives of the Chamber of Commerce to frame a currency measure.

As a result of this meeting, a bill of banking reform was introduced in Congress in 1907 but did not receive consideration. The effect of Roosevelt's idealism to the detriment of the best interests of the American people, was now beginning to be felt.

In the latter part of 1906 and in the early part of 1907 Roosevelt's trust busters succeeded in breaking up several large corporations. As a result, buying power disappeared from the market, wide liquidation of securities took place, and many banks closed as the public, sensing that the banks somehow were suffering losses, presented currency for redemption in specie and brought about the Panic of 1907. The local situation in New York, Chicago and other major cities, was aggravated by the country banks who maintained their reserve deposits in a city bank withdrawing these reserves, and bringing them home so that in the event there was a panic they would have the specie available to pay off their depositors.

To cover these withdrawals the major city banks had no alternative except to liquidate loans the best way they could, often with disastrous results to the community, in order to obtain the gold and silver.

In October, in order to attempt to put a stop to the presenting of currency for gold or silver, the New York Clearing House Committee decided to issue Clearing House Certificates and put a stop to redeeming checks with currency, which in turn was presented to the bank issuing it, for redemption in gold or silver. This policy was followed by Clearing House associations in most of the major cities of the country. The effect of banks paying out Clearing House Certificates in redemption of checks was that currency went to a premium. The general condition was additionally aggravated by a liquidation of securities held in foreign countries, and a conversion of the proceeds into gold.

The hoarding of gold and the restrictions of currency reduced the volume of purchasing power so that existing surpluses were offered at reduced prices. As prices fell it became possible for foreign countries to buy from us with the result that exports increased and imports decreased. As exports exceeded imports, the difference was paid in gold, and as a result of our increased foreign trade, once more gold began to flow back to this country. This withdrawal of gold was immediately felt in European capitals so that in order to stop the outflow of gold, the central banks of England, France and Germany raised the discount rate to make it unattractive to expand credit which consequently restricted the purchasing of goods from the United States.

In order to enable certain banks to remain open, and in an effort to stem the panic, Secretary of the Treasury George B Cortelyou deposited public funds and monies of the government in some banks that were suffering from withdrawals. When it became evident, however, that such switching around of public funds was not going to be sufficient to stem the tide, he determined to demonstrate the ability of the government to fully exercise its power to avert disaster. It was his opinion that the panic could only be stopped if steps were taken to encourage hoarders to either deposit their money again with the banks, or to invest their hoarded funds in securities in which they had confidence, so that the money thus acquired could be redeposited with the banks to enable them to keep open.

In order to accomplish this he announced on Sunday, November 18th, that he would receive subscriptions to an issue of 50 million dollars in 2% bonds for the construction of the Panama Canal which project had been voted by Congress in June of 1902. By the latter part of November the worst part of the panic was over. Currency and gold again flowed into the banks and redemption was gradually resumed.

This panic, sometimes known as the Bankers Panic, again brought to light certain inherent weaknesses in our banking system and in the same year (1907) the Comptroller of the Currency in his annual report, again recommended the formation of a central bank which now had the endorsement of the Bankers Association and the New York Chamber of Commerce. It did not unfortunately have the endorsement of the leaders of the Democratic and Republican parties.

THE ALDRICH VREELAND ACT

This bill, a combination of a bill introduced by Senator Aldrich of Rhode Island in the Senate and a bill introduced earlier in the House by Representative Vreeland of New York, provided for the issuing of notes on the general credit of national banks to the amount of their capital, and the retirement of notes issued under the bond secured system, as provided under the National Banking Act.

This bill provided that:

1. Groups of not less than ten national banks having an aggregate capital surplus of at least 5 million dollars could form what would be known as the National Currency Associations.
2. Such member banks could forward to the Association securities in the form of approved bonds or commercial paper and in exchange receive currency known as Aldrich-Vreeland bank notes. There were only two restrictions on the note issue. First, no member of the association could have an issue of these notes in excess of its capital and surplus, second, the total issue for the Association was not to exceed 500 million dollars.

3. All banks who issued such notes were required to maintain with the Treasury of the United States a redemption fund equal to 5% of the notes so issued.

THE NATIONAL MONETARY COMMISSION

Congress passed the bill known as the Aldrich Vreeland Act on May 30, 1908 and at the same time appointed a committee, to be known as the National Monetary Commission consisting of nine Senators and nine Representatives under the chairmanship of Senator Nelson Aldrich, to make an exhaustive survey of banking, currency issues and credits. It was recognized that the Aldrich Vreeland Act was nothing more than a temporary relief measure to be in effect until such time as a constructive banking legislation could be passed to develop the banking situation along permanent lines.

In January 1912 the committee submitted a report on its findings to Congress. This plan, known as the Aldrich Plan, after Senator Aldrich, proposed to charter an association known as the Reserve Association of America which would be the principal fiscal agent of the government.

The authorized capital would be $300,000,000 and the bank was to be given a charter to run for 50 years. Many of the provisions of the plan, although not passed, were later incorporated into the Federal Reserve Act. The Currency Committee of the American Bankers Association examined the Aldrich Plan and made certain recommendations dealing with modifications for the problem of circulation.

The election in November 1912 put an end to endeavors to have any reform measures adopted, but the discussions between members of the National Monetary Commission the American Bankers Association brought to light facts and opinions which materially contributed to a bill introduced in Congress the following year, which modified the banking system and created the Federal Reserve System.

The agitation created by reports of the New York Chamber of Commerce and the American Bankers Association, and the report of the National Monetary Commission on banking created interest of such widespread magnitude among statesmen, financiers and businessmen, that remedial legislation could no longer be put off.

Presumably guided by public reaction to previous legislation submitted to Congress, and by discussion between members of the National Monetary Commission and the American Banking Association, Representative Carter Glass of Virginia in June 1913 introduced a currency and banking reform bill in the House of Representatives while Senator Owen of Alabama introduced a companion bill in the Senate. These measures had been in preparation for over a year and had had the benefit and counsel of Woodrow Wilson, William G. McAdoo and William Jennings Bryan, who were now President, Secretary of the Treasury, and Secretary of State respectively. The bill, officially known as the Glass-Owens Bill, commonly referred to as the Federal Reserve Act, was passed by Congress and signed by the President December 23, 1913.

That this bill was not intended to be a final cure-all for all of the monetary and currency difficulties, but rather a solid foundation on which to adjust an existing system and create a banking system which would keep abreast of commercial and national development, was indicated by President Wilson in his first annual address following passage of the Act when he said "We shall deal with our economic system as it is and as it may be modified—and step by step we shall make it what it should be."

As membership in the Federal Reserve System under the Act was mandatory, as far as national banks were concerned, they were compelled to either subscribe to Federal Reserve Bank Stock or surrender their charters.

Many national banks immediately reorganized under state charters, but their loss was offset by the influx of state banks to which membership in the system was optional, when they had complied with the reserve and capital requirements of the national banks in their own territory.

FEDERAL RESERVE BANKS

Because of the important position of the Federal Reserve Banks in the national economy, and their influence upon the business of banking, it is well to cover their functions in some detail.

The Federal Reserve Bank system was established as a bankers bank to handle the reserves of the banks that do business directly with the public, render financial services to the Federal government, and to serve as a central bank; that is, as a bank which is operated mainly to stabilize the business and industry of the country.

Every member bank is required by law to keep a percentage of its deposits in the form of reserves, on deposit with the Federal Reserve Bank of the district in which the bank is located. A bank cannot permit its reserve account to fall below its requirements without suffering penalties. On the other hand, a bank ordinarily does not wish to keep its reserve account above its requirements because it receives no income from such excess reserves. As banks acquire excess reserves they tend to lend and invest more readily, and credit becomes easier. As they lose excess reserves they tend to become more selective in their loans and investments, and credit grows tighter.

The United States is divided into twelve Federal Reserve Districts, and each district has one Federal Reserve Bank located in a principal city. While each Federal Reserve Bank is a separate institution, with its own directors and staff of officers, it is not entirely independent in its operations. The Federal Reserve Act provided that major policies were to be determined by the Board of Governors of the Federal Reserve System, which maintains headquarters in Washington, D.C.

This Board consists of seven members, appointed by the President, and confirmed by the Senate. Board members give their full time to the business of the Board of Governors. Appointments are for fourteen years, so arranged that the term of office of one member expires every two years.

It is the function of the Board to:

1. Supervise the operations of the Federal Reserve System.
2. Formulate credit policies of the Federal Reserve System.
3. Establish the reserve requirements of members banks.
4. Review and determine the discount rates of the Reserve Banks.
5. Determine the investment policy of the Federal Reserve System through the Federal Open Market Committee.
6. Set the maximum rates of interest member banks may pay on savings and other time deposits.
7. Determine the requirements for stock market credit.

Federal Open Market Committee. Seven members of the

Board of Governors and five representatives elected by the Reserve banks constitute the Open Market Committee.

This Committee decides on changes to be made in the System's portfolio of Government securities; in other words, when, how much and under what conditions, to buy or sell Government Bonds in the market. Reserve banks are required by law to carry out these decisions. Committee decisions are influenced by national and regional considerations. Purchases and sales of securities for the System open market account are divided among the twelve Reserve banks in accordance with the relative asset size of each.

Federal Advisory Council. This twelve member body consisting of one member selected annually by the Board of Directors of each Reserve Bank, confers with the Board of Governors on business conditions and makes recommendations regarding the affairs of the System.

The Federal Reserve System controls the monetary system of the country through easing or tightening credit by influencing the volume of reserves. It has three general instruments for this purpose:

1. Changes in reserve requirements.
2. Open market operations.
3. Discounting.

These instruments provide the Federal Reserve banks with a considerable amount of flexibility in dealing with credit conditions.

1. *Changes in reserve requirements.* The Board of Governors of the Federal Reserve System is authorized to change, within limits, the minimum percentage of deposits that member banks must keep as reserves.

By reducing reserve requirements, the Board of Governors increases excess reserves of member banks. This increase in excess reserves induces member banks to lend and invest more readily. On the other hand, when reserve requirements are increased, member banks (unless they have excess reserves) must acquire additional reserves to meet the higher requirements, and credit grows tighter.

2. *Open market operations.* The Federal Reserve System can put reserves into the banking system directly by buying Government securities; Federal Reserve can take the reserves out of the

banking system by selling Government securities in the open market.

The System pays for securities with a check drawn on itself. Typically, the seller of the securities deposits the check in his bank. Then the bank in turn deposits the check to its reserve account at the Federal Reserve bank. Since no bank has lost reserves, the operation increases the excess reserves not only of the original receiving bank but also of the banking system as a whole.

When the Federal Reserve buys securities in the market, credit tends to become easier. Conversely, a sale of securities by the System will be paid for by checks, which will reduce both deposits and the reserve balances of the member banks on which the checks are drawn. This action tends to cause both credit and money to become tighter.

3. *Discounting.* A member bank that is short of reserves may restore its position by borrowing from its Federal Reserve bank and depositing proceeds of the loan to its reserve account.

The Reserve banks can influence the volume of reserves created in this way by changing the rate of discount on such borrowing, discouraging borrowers by a higher rate and encouraging borrowers by a lower rate.

Capital. The capital of each Federal Reserve Bank is subscribed to by the member banks of the district in which the Reserve Bank is located.

Each bank is required to subscribe to an amount equal to 6% of its own capital and surplus of which 3% is initially paid in and 3% subject to further call. Annually a cumulative statutory dividend of 6% is paid on the capital stock paid in.

Management. The management of each Federal Reserve Bank is vested in nine Directors whose actions are subject to supervision of the Board of Governors. Three of them are known as Class A directors; three as Class B directors; and three as Class C directors. Class A and B directors are elected by member banks. One of each class (two directors) is elected by small banks; one of each class of banks of medium size; and one of each class of large banks. The three Class A directors may be bankers. The three Class B directors must be actively engaged in the district in business, agriculture or some other commercial pursuit. The Class B directors must not be officers, directors, or employees of any bank.

The three Class C directors are selected by the Board of Governors of the Federal Reserve System. They must not be officers, directors, employees, or stockholders of any bank.

Membership. All national banks chartered by the Comptroller of the Currency are required to be members of the Federal Reserve System. Most of the large state-chartered banks have elected to join the system, thus, although less than half of all banks belong to the System, member banks hold about three-fourths of the total bank deposits.

Services to Banks. The Federal Reserve banks perform for their member banks many of the services that the latter perform for their customers. Among these services are those relating to:

1. Cash.
2. Cash collection.
3. Noncash collection.
4. Wire transfer.
5. Rediscounting.

Each service meets a specific need of the member banks and is performed expeditiously for them by the Federal Reserve banks.

1. *Cash.* When a customer has more cash than he wishes to keep, he deposits the excess in his bank; when he needs more cash, he withdraws it from his bank. The bank, of course, decides how much cash it wishes to keep as a working fund and as vault cash.

When a member bank acquires more cash than it wishes, it sends the excess to its Federal Reserve bank to increase its reserve balance or to a correspondent bank, which sends its excess to the Federal Reserve bank. If a member bank runs short of the desired amount of cash it will draw on its reserve balance. Nonmember banks get their cash from a member bank.

The Federal Reserve banks keep a large stock of all kinds of paper money and coin to meet the demand of member banks for cash. Some of this cash, principally silver certificates, United States notes, and coin, is issued by the Treasury. The Reserve banks pay for such Treasury currency by crediting the Treasury's account, on their books. The largest amount, however, consists of Federal Reserve notes which the Federal Reserve banks are authorized to issue. Thus the Treasury, the twelve Federal Reserve banks, and the thousands of local banks throughout the country distribute currency promptly as needed, and retire it when the need has passed.

2. *Cash collection.* Payments are made by check many times more frequently than they are made with paper money or coins.

The Federal Reserve banks clear and collect checks, and provide commercial banks with a means of settling for the checks that they clear and collect. Included in this system are checks collected by city correspondent banks, or by direct presentation to another bank. The settlement or payment for such checks on member banks is made directly or indirectly through member bank reserve balances with the Federal Reserve banks.

Checks collected and cleared through the Federal Reserve banks must be paid in full by the banks on which they are drawn; in other words, they must be payable at par without deduction of a fee or a charge. Federal Reserve banks will not collect checks drawn on non-par banks.

3. *Noncash collection.* Checks are not the only items that banks convert into usable funds. Notes, acceptances, certificates of deposit, drafts, bills of exchange, bonds, and bond coupons are other items.

4. *Wire transfer.* The Federal Reserve banks operate a leased-wire system that connects every Federal Reserve bank and branch. A member bank may use this service to establish balances or immediately to pay funds in other parts of the country. Such transfers of funds are debited and credited to the reserve accounts of the member banks involved.

5. *Rediscounting.* One of the advantages of membership in the Federal Reserve System is the privilege of borrowing from a Federal Reserve bank. A member mank may rediscount one or more of its customers' notes with a Reserve bank. Also, a member bank may secure an advance from its Federal Reserve bank by giving its own note secured by loans or bonds from its holdings. In either case, the Reserve bank gives the member bank credit in its reserve account. This credit increases the reserve deposit of a member bank at the Reserve bank. For this service a Reserve bank charges interest at a rate known as discount rate.

Service to the Government. The Federal Reserve banks are used by the Government as fiscal agents, custodians, and depositories. They carry the principal checking accounts of the United States Treasury, are responsible for a large part of the work in issuing and redeeming Government obligations, and perform fiscal duties for the Government.

1. *Treasury Deposits.* The Government receives and spends funds in all parts of the country. Receipts come mainly from taxpayers and purchasers of Government securities. Most receipts are deposited initially to the Treasury's account in the commercial banks and are then transferred to the Reserve banks when they are needed by the Treasury. The Government disburses by check, and checks are charged to Treasury accounts at the Reserve banks.

2. *Government Debt.* Reserve banks take applications for the purchase of Government securities, make allotments as instructed by the Treasury, deliver the securities to the purchaser, receive payment, and credit the amounts of the payments to the Treasury account.

Reserve banks redeem Government securities as they mature, make exchanges, and pay interest coupons. They also issue and redeem Savings Bonds.

THE MACFADDEN ACT

The Federal Reserve Act and the National Banking Act underwent very few changes from 1917 to 1927. For several years prior to 1927 however certain agitation was created over the rights and privileges of state banks versus national banks.

The National Banking Act allowed national banks to establish branches if they had a capital and surplus of a million dollars; if permitted by their respective state laws in which the bank was located; and if they had the consent of the Federal Reserve Board. A state bank in a state where branch banks were permitted, on the other hand, could become a member of the National Banking System and continue to operate its branches without having to comply with the other requirements.

Another difference came about due to the fact that under the National Banking Act, national banks were not allowed to engage in the investment business. However some of the larger banks entered the investment banking business through a legal device—that of forming a corporation chartered under the state law to buy and sell securities and having the stockholders of the bank own the stock of the investment company. In this way the national banks did not own the investment company but as the stockholders of the investment company and the stockholders of the bank were one and the same, the profits of the investment company accrued to the bank's stockholders.

Due to some of these differences, and the fact that national banks were not able to maintain branches unless complying with the exceptional provision of the act, a number of banks gave up their national charters and reverted to a state banking status.

In order to overcome this apparent discrimination, the bill known as the MacFadden Act was passed and became law in February, 1927, which briefly provided that:

1. Charters of national banks be extended from 99 years to an indeterminate period.
2. National banks, without forming separte subsidiary corporations, could buy and sell marketable bonds providing their investment in one issue was for an amount not to exceed 25% of their unimpaired capital and surplus.
3. National banks could issue shares having a par value of less than $100.00.
4. National banks could establish branches, within limits of the city or town mentioned in their charter, if the establishment of such branches did not conflict with the state law.

The effect of the passage of this bill was an immediate return by banks to the national banking system.

Even though the passing of the MacFadden Act gave national banks the right to do an investment banking business, it did not give them the right to deal in shares of stock. Certain of the banks therefore that had formed independent investment affiliations kept the affiliate and enlarged their practice so as to incorporate within their scope of business, not only bond transactions, but the purchasing from, and sale to the public, including the underwriting, of stock issues.

The period which witnessed the passage of the Federal Reserve Act also witnessed the passage of two other outstanding pieces of legislation which materially contributed to credit, and brought assistance to the development of agriculture and industry. These pieces of legislation were the United States Warehouse Act and the Federal Bill of Lading Act.

UNITED STATES WAREHOUSE ACT

In previous chapters we covered the practice of people in earlier periods of civilization to deposit coin and merchandise for safekeeping, receiving in return receipts which passed as currency. As commerce developed it became a practice to not only place gold, silver and other valuables in a place of safekeeping, using the receipt as evidence of ownership, but to place agricultural products and manufactured goods such as tobacco, corn, and grain in warehouses on receipt. These receipts would pass for value, and by endorsement transfer of title to such agricultural products and manufactured goods was effected.

Unfortunately there was little law governing the operation of such warehouses, and human nature being what it is, many operators, being aware of the turnover and volume of merchandise entrusted to their care, often "borrowed" the merchandise, probably with every intent to replace it before they would be called upon to deliver it, with results similar to those which arose in conjunction with the loaning out of funds deposited in safekeeping by the goldsmiths and exchangers. In order to prevent fraud and insure value to the holders of receipts, a bill known as the United States Warehouse Act was introduced to Congress and became law in August 1916.

This Act required:

1. The Secretary of Agriculture to license all warehouses storing agricultural products.
2. Made all warehouses so licensed subject to periodical inspection.
3. Required owners to give bond for the faithful discharge of their obligations to the owners of the commodity.
4. Set up certain provisions for the issuing of receipts, so that they would show not only the location of the warehouse and description of the product, but to whom the goods belonged, interest, if any, of the warehousemen, and any advances or liabilities for which the warehouseman claimed a lien.

The passage of this law and supervision has made Warehouse Receipts a valuable and desirable form of collateral.

In recent years, because of the widening development of business and advisability of storing merchandise close to its point of distribution or manufacture, public warehouse companies have provided facilities for the warehousing and storage of such products even on the borrowers premises.

FEDERAL BILL OF LADING ACT

Another important development of the era was the use of Bills of Lading. A Bill of Lading is similar to a Warehouse Receipt, except that where a Warehouse Receipt covers merchandise held in a special, specific or permanent place, a Bill of Lading covers the warehousing of merchandise while being transported from one place to another.

A Bill of Lading performs three functions which facilitate trade and makes it acceptable to banks as collateral for loans.

1. It acts as a receipt for specified goods accepted for shipment by a carrier.
2. It is written evidence of a contract to transport and deliver goods to a designated person, upon specific terms, at a determined place.
3. It is an instrument evidencing title to the goods.

Bills of Lading are of two types, straight bills, which state that the goods are consigned to a specific person; and order bills in which the goods are delivered to the order of a specific person. A straight bill cannot be transferred by endorsement while an order bill, unless it has been rendered non-negotiable, can be transferred by endorsement.

Through the development of the extensive transportation facilities of the country, many frauds were perpetrated against banks and merchants through the use of bills of lading especially in connection with the shipment of cotton and other commodities to Europe. These losses occured because bills of lading in many cases were issued before receipt of the goods and were altered, forged and duplicates issued while the originals were outstanding and uncancelled.

Due to the tremendous losses incurred by merchants and bank

ers, and through petitions to their Congressmen, Congress passed the Federal Bill of Lading Act, in January 1917.

This act provided that all bills of lading must:

1. Show the name of the transportation company.
2. Tell whether or not the bill is negotiable.
3. Show the name of the shipper, and the place, and from whom the goods were received.
4. Contain a contract clause.
5. Contain an itemized list of all goods covered by the bill.
6. Show the name of the consignee and the charges and liens of the carrier.

Since the passage of this bill, bills of lading have attained wide use as collateral for loans in connection with the financing of domestic and foreign trade.

THE DEPRESSION

The far reaching commercial and industrial developments of the country during the latter part of the 19th and early part of the 20th century brought many corresponding changes in the operation of commercial banks.

Under the MacFadden Act, national banks were allowed to maintain branches providing this did note conflict with the laws of the state in which they were located. Taking advantage of the privilege, many banks opened branches, and as of June 1929, 165 national banks were operating approximately 1,000 branches.

Mergers, consolidations, chain banking and group banking become the order of the day. In 1929, according to a report made by the Federal Reserve Board, there were some 257 banking groups in the United States which controlled 2,033 banks. In turn these banks controlled, according to the Economic Policy Committee of the American Bankers Association, in excess of 80% of the banking resources of the United States.

Group and branch banking had many reasons for existence, the principal reasons being:

1. The efficiency and economy of operation.
2. The opportunity for internal housecleaning of personnel and elimination of unprofitable and undesirable business.
3. The ability to render wider banking services.

4. The additional profit due to centralization, control, and overall management.
5. The combining of capital which allowed greater extension of loaning power.

It was the pains of over-extension of credit which gave birth to installment loaning or consumer credit, which enabled a person to enjoy the benefits and use of an article while he was paying for it, which greatly contributed to the depression of the 30's which began with the Stock Market Crash in October 1929.

People who had their savings wiped out in the market found it necessary to restrict their purchases, which resulted in a decreased demand for manufactured goods. With production curtailed, factories suspended operations, throwing millions of people out of work.

The lack of business resulted in a steady withdrawal of deposits by manufacturers and the unemployed, the former to pay up obligations, the latter withdrawing them for living expenses. In order to provide for such unusual demands, banks found it necessary to sell the bonds in their investment portfolio taking, as a result, tremendous losses. The steady decline of bank deposits impregnated the germ of fear and resulted in the American public converting their balances wherever possible to gold and silver and hoarding it away.

The withdrawal of funds was accelerated at a pace more rapid than was possible to convert loans and investments into cash, with the result that in 1930 over 3,600 banks suspended operations. Many of these banks were weak or poorly managed. On the other hand some were financially sound and could have weathered the storm had some means been at their disposal to temporarily borrow currency against assets, which although sound, were not eligible for rediscount with the Federal Reserve banks.

RECONSTRUCTION FINANCE CORPORATION

President Hoover and other leading men of the country, aware of the danger to our financial structure, realized that unless means were provided for advancing funds to the banks against assets not eligible for rediscount that many sound banks would fall.

On October 6, 1931 President Hoover outlined a program in which he called upon the bankers of the country to organize a na tional institution with adequate capital to make advances to banks on sound assets not eligible for rediscount. This bill, known as the Reconstruction Finance Corporation Act of 1932, was passed and became law on January 22, 1932. This Act, in brief, provided for the Reconstruction Finance Corporation to render financial aid directly to agriculture, commerce, industry and financial institutions of the country; also to government agencies or corporations organized to help assist agriculture.

Under the severe conditions of the times (banks being unable to adequately finance industry) many concerns took advantage of the privilege granted under the act and borrowed directly from the Reconstruction Finance Corporation.

Many banks of the country also took advantage of the provision of the Act, and after disposing of their paper, eligible for rediscount with the Federal Reserve banks, pledged other remaining assets with the Reconstruction Finance Corporation, or sold preferred stock to them, to obtain funds to pay off their depositors, and thus kept their banks open.

THE GLASS-STEAGALL BILL

Realizing that the panic, if allowed to go unchecked, would result in the complete breakdown of the economic system, Senator Carter Glass of Virginia, in February of 1932, together with Representative Glynn Steagall of Texas, introduced a bill which would enable the member banks of the Federal Reserve to more adequately cope with the situation. This bill, which was passed and became law, provided that member banks of the Federal Reserve System, after rediscounting with the Federal Reserve Bank, Government bonds and paper eligible for rediscount, could further rediscount with the Federal Reserve Bank, state, municipal, railroad, public utility and industrial bonds; and for the Federal Reserve Bank to issue notes against the security of United States Government securities and 60% of eligible assets.

The reason for the second provision being so important was that in 1932 the volume and quality of commercial paper was so low, that only gold remained in sufficient quantities to act as a reserve on outstanding issues of Federal Reserve notes.

The position of the banks in the various states continued to grow very acute and banks on every hand took advantage of the provisions of the Glass-Steagall Bill and the Reconstruction Finance Corporation to pay off their depositors.

FEDERAL HOME LOAN BANK ACT

The crisis was now affecting home owners. Building and Loan Association officials, and those with real estate interests, claimed that the facilities of the Reconstruction Finance Corporation were not set up to help them. Those who had mortgages coming due were unable to refinance them or pay them off. Many, whose mortgages were not due, found themselves unable to meet taxes and interest payments because surplus funds were tied up in closed banks or they were unemployed.

In order to give relief to distressed home owners a bill introduced in Congress was passed July 22, 1932, known as the Federal Home Loan Bank Act.

The principal provisions of the bill, as originally enacted, set up no less than eight, nor more than twelve, district banks in the United States and possessions, for the purpose of providing a loaning vehicle whereby building and loan associations, savings and loan associations, cooperative banks, homestead associations, insurance companies and savings banks could obtain loans by pledging mortgages as security.

The problems of the Depression also hit the farmer. In order to check the rising tide of foreclosures, Congress, in January, authorized the Secretary of the Treasury to subscribe additional stock in the Federal Land Banks, the funds to be used to make extensions to farmer borrowers, so they could meet back taxes and pay interest. This furnished but temporary relief.

After the election in November 1932, the situation became more acute. Between the 4th and 28th day of February 1933, banking holidays were proclaimed by the Governors of the States of Louisiana, Michigan, Indiana, Maryland, Arkansas and Ohio. The result of these banking holidays left Chicago in the Middle West and Boston, Philadelphia and New York in the East the only financial centers of any importance, and the drain on their financial institutions was tremendous. To try to put a stop to the runs on banks, the Legislature of the State of Iowa passed a law on January

20th, authorizing the Superintendent of Banking to take over and operate any bank for one year without legal formality of a formal receivership, which for practical purposes placed all banks in Iowa on a tentative suspended basis.

On March 1, 1933 banking holidays were declared in Alabama, Kentucky, Tennessee and Nevada and on March 2nd by the Governors of Arizona, California, Louisiana, Mississippi, Oklahoma, Oregon; and on March 3 in Georgia, Idaho, New Mexico, Texas, Utah, Washington and Wisconsin. The steady drain on the banks in states unprotected by banking holidays was so great that had they continued to pay out currency it would have resulted in their being completely put out of business.

Finally on March 4 the Governors of most of the remaining states declared a banking holiday followed two days later by President Roosevelt's Presidential Proclamation which declared a banking holiday throughout the United States and its provinces, up to and including March 9th.

EMERGENCY BANKING ACT

On March 7th the Secretary of the Treasury authorized Clearing House Associations in the principal cities to issue Clearing House Certificates after March 10th against sound assets which were pledged with them.

Congress was called into special session on March 9th by President Roosevelt. At this session he asked that legislation be passed giving him control over the banks and the monetary system of the country. The Emergency Banking Act was accordingly signed which:

1. Gave the President of the United States emergency powers over banking, including the right to control foreign exchange and the movement of gold, silver and currency in banking transactions.
2. Made provision for a conservator to be appointed for national banks when necessary, which made it possible for banks to operate on a restricted basis.
3. Authorized the RFC to purchase the preferred stock of national banks.
4. Authorized the Federal Reserve Banks to issue Federal Reserve notes securing them by direct obligations to the United States.

On the same day after passage of this Act (March 10, 1933) President Roosevelt issued a proclamation extending the banking holiday until further notice, prohibited exportation of gold from the country, and the paying out of gold by any and all banks.

The vast resources of the Government, placed at the disposal of the banks through the RFC and the Federal Reserve System, offered sufficient relief so that on March 11th the President announced banks would open progressively on March 13, 14 and 15. On March 13th all Federal Reserve Banks in the twelve Federal Reserve Cities were to open, followed on March 14th by the banks in 250 other cities.

The opening of banks in this manner was very orderly, and as the banks, during the moratorium, had had an opportunity to take stock of their assets and rediscount with the Federal Reserve banks sufficient paper, they were in a fairly good cash position.

THE BANKING ACT OF 1933 AND 1935

After the moratorium in March, the Government authorities, in collaboration with bankers all over the country, made an exhaustive but rapid study of the existing banking situation. Realizing that reforms, although they might be called drastic, were necessary if the banking structure was to be given stability, a bill was introduced in Congress "to provide for the safe and more effective usage of the assets of the banks, to regulate inner bank control, to prevent the undue diversion of funds into speculative operations; or for other purposes." The bill was only intended as an emergency measure, to be modified when the workability of the plan had been tested.

This bill, known as the Banking Act of 1933, provided for Federal control over credit, regulation of commercial banking and insurance of bank deposits through the creation of the Federal Deposit Corporation and regulation of commercial banking. It was enacted into law and signed by the President on June 16, 1933.*

The Federal Deposit Insurance Corporation maintains principal

---

* As nearly every session of Congress since that time has made amendments to the act, it is suggested that those who wish to make a detailed study procure up to date copies of the act from the office of the Federal Deposit Insurance Corp., Washington, D. C.

headquarters in Washington, D. C., and offices in the principal cities. Principal provisions of the act are:

1. Management is vested in a three man Board of Directors, consisting of the Comptroller of the Currency and two others appointed by the President with the advice and consent of the Senate.
2. All member banks of the Federal Reserve System are required to become members of the F.D.I.C.
3. Nonmember state banks, and mutual savings banks may obtain insurance if they meet F.D.I.C. requirements. (In 1959 about 96% of all banks, holding 97% of the deposits, were insured by F.D.I.C.
4. Insured banks pay to the F.D.I.C. an assessment of one-twelfth of 1% of their yearly deposit liabilities. (In years when F.D.I.C. income exceeds expenses, a percentage of this excess is refunded to the insured banks and the remainder is added to the F.D.I.C. surplus. The F.D.I.C. invests the surplus, and the interest on the investment provides part of the funds for F.D.I.C. operations.)
5. Under the present provisions of the Act each demand and time or savings deposit is insured up to $10,000, (a depositor cannot increase the insurance by placing his deposits in two or more accounts in the same bank. In other words, all deposits maintained in the same bank under the same ownership are insured to $10,000. Accounts maintained under different ownerships or in different banks are each insured up to $10,000.)

SUPERVISION OF BANKS

From a supervisory standpoint, all national banks are supervised by the Comptroller of the Currency who periodically examines the affairs of the bank and at least twice a year issues what is known as a "call," at which time all national banks report their financial condition, a copy of which is published in the local papers.

State banks are examined by, and under the control of either the Superintendent of Banks of the State or some other designated officer of the State who periodically examines the affairs of the bank. As a matter of practice most states follow the practice of the Comptroller, and whenever a Comptroller's call is issued requesting the report on conditions of the national banks, the state banks usually follow suit.

The Federal Deposit Insurance Corporation, while empowered

to make examinations of any insured bank, only examines state banks which are not members of the Federal Reserve System.

The Federal Reserve System may examine any member bank, but as all national banks, which are required to be members of the Federal Reserve System, are examined by the Comptroller's office, the Federal Reserve Examiners confine their activities to state banks which are members of the system.

The state banking authorities on the other hand examine the Trust Departments of all national banks inasmuch as trust powers are granted not by the Federal Government but by the individual states.

In order to exercise control, and avoid duplication, as much as possible, the Comptroller's Office, Federal Deposit Insurance Corporation, and Federal Reserve System provide copies of their report or examination to any other banking agency which is interested.

BANKS, BANKERS AND BANKING

Bankers, like other businessmen, also belong to trade associations, which assist the banks to function as a system and to act together in solving common problems. The clearing of checks, between local banks, makes it necessary for banks to maintain continuous relations with each other. Correspondent bank relations, for collection of out of town items and exchanges of credit information, are among the ways in which banks cooperate with each other.

Bankers also join in associations, conferences, and discussion groups to consider their common problems and to exchange ideas on all phases and aspects of banking.

As banks operate under a variety of circumstances, they have many interests in common. Associations of bankers are organized along geographical lines, such as national, state, city, county, district, and regional associations; and also on the basis of the kind of charter, such as national bank, state bank, trust company, or savings banks.

When there are two or more banks in a city, a Clearing House Association is usually formed for the purpose of simplifying the clearance of local checks between member banks.

Bankers associations are also organized on a functional basis, such as credits, installment loans, investments, mortgages, and public relations. Others are formed to provide specialized help in specific phases of banking, such as Reserve City Bankers Associations, Robert Morris Associates, Financial Public Relations Association and National Association of Bank Auditors and Comptrollers.

There is a State Association in every state and territory, and a nation wide association known as the American Bankers Association of which nearly all banks in the United States, Hawaii, Alaska, Puerto Rico and Virgin Islands are members.

As banking laws are being constantly expanded, revised, amended, and extended, it is one of the duties of the bankers associations to represent bankers' interests at state legislatures, and as a national organization to present the bankers' viewpoint to Congressional committees.

RESEARCH IN BANKING

Study and research are continuous in banking. Every detail of bank operations is the subject of investigation and study, and results are communicated to bankers through conferences, association meetings, in the publication of books, pamphlets, and articles published in banking and financial magazines.

Bankers regularly attend conferences sponsored by their association for discussions of their common problems in connection with agriculture, installment credit, investments or other phases of banking.

THE EDUCATIONAL ACTIVITIES OF BANKING*

The educational activities of organized banking are a unique phenomenon not only in banking but in American education. There is no other industry in the United States which provides an educational program as comprehensive and as well organized.

First and foremost among the educational institutions sponsored by organized banking is the American Institute of Banking. It is the educational section of the American Bankers Association. It was organized in 1900 in response to a petition from bank employees in various cities urging the Association to establish an institute similar to the one in successful operation in England.

*A.I.B. "Principles of Bank Operation" Chapter XXIII.

The Institute carries on its educational program through local chapters, through study groups in localities where the number of bank employees is not sufficient to maintain a chapter, and through individual correspondence courses. Enrollment in classes is open to the personnel of all banks that are members of the American Bankers Association and to the personnel of the bank supervisory agencies.

The objective of the Institute is to:

1. Aid the student in developing his intellectual capacities.
2. Aid the student in acquiring knowledge and understanding of the basic process of banking.
3. Give the student an opportunity for advanced study in the fields of specialized banking, of our monetary system, and of our credit economy.

For the education and development of bank officers the Graduate School of Banking is conducted by the American Bankers Association in cooperation with Rutgers University.

Several state bankers associations also have established schools for advanced study in banking subjects in conjunction with state universities. Some of these schools are Pacific Coast Banking School—University of Washington; School of Banking of the South—Louisiana State University; and School of Banking at the University of Wisconsin. They are conducted along lines similar to that of the Graduate School of Banking with special emphasis being placed on the administrative and management aspects of banking.

Bank personnel, at all levels, are urged to take advantage of these educational opportunities, in the interest of better and progressive banking.

CHAPTER IX

SERVICES OF BANKS

COMMERCE AND TRADE HAVE DEVELOPED through the centuries, as we have seen, first on a cash basis which was followed by a combination of a cash and credit basis.

The cash basis began when mankind conducted commercial transactions through the use of mediums of exchange in the forms of objects produced by the application of labor to raw materials, commodities, shapes of metal, and coins of gold and silver. This was followed by written and printed mediums representing value such as receipts and notes circulating as currency in place of the actual coin or other mediums of exchange which had been deposited with the money changers or bankers for safekeeping.

The cash and credit basis, with which we are more familiar today, and which is the foundation of our present banking system, began when the money changers or bankers started to use the various mediums of exchange such as coin, receipts and other forms of wealth which individuals left with them for safekeeping, for loans to other individuals at interest.

In modern times, these mediums of exchange and the transfers of wealth between one person and another has been accomplished in most parts of the world by means of "orders to pay" commonly known as bank checks.

It is of interest to note that the successful operation of both phases of banking—the deposit and safekeeping function and the withdrawal or transfer function—through which bankers (1) act as depository for funds and mediums of exchange, (2) make loans and investments for, to and in behalf of producers, consumers and governments, and (3) serve the needs of commerce and trade by providing vehicles through which wealth and mediums of exchange are transferred from one person to another—are all based on *promises.*

When a person deposits mediums of exchange or instruments

representing ownership of wealth, which we term money, in a bank, he receives in exchange, a promise of the bank to pay money of equal kind upon surrender of the receipts, or upon his order to pay.

If the money deposited is to be used by the person for immediate payment, the depositor usually places the funds in a checking account, which funds are subject to withdrawal on demand.

If the money deposited is to remain with the bank for a period of time, or will accumulate over a period of time through periodical deposits, the depositor usually places such funds in a savings account where it can be invested by the bank for which the bank receives interest, a portion of which is paid back to the depositor for the use of such funds.

Obviously, under normal economic circumstances, all funds deposited are not used at the same time. Consequently this vast pool of surplus funds is loaned out by the banks to individuals and corporations to finance business.

When a person borrows money from a bank, which money is usually a combination of funds left with the bank for safekeeping, together with funds subscribed by owners of the bank (stockholders) he promises to repay the bank money of equal kind, at a fixed definite date.

Because of the complexity of business, and the need of individuals for financial services today, the basic principles of banking—the deposit and safekeeping function; and the withdrawal and transfer function, have been so developed and modified that they fit each commercial need.

Some of the most important services which banks perform today are in connection with the following, as listed in alphabetical order:

Accounts Receivable Loans. In every business where credit is extended, or where people are able to obtain merchandise on the promise to pay for it at a future time, which could be the first of the month, in case of open or charge accounts; or on terms of 30, 60, 90 days, or over a longer period of time, as in the case of installment loans which are repayable in monthly programs running from

6 to as much as 60 months; such extensions of credit are carried on the books of the business as Accounts Receivable.

When a merchant conducts business in this manner and later requires funds for other purposes or to continue to sell more people on account, he may borrow money from his bank, or a finance company by pledging his so-called Accounts Receivable. Under such a procedure the bank makes the loan against the accounts, and either notifies the people who owe money to the merchant to make payment directly to the bank; or if the merchant is in good standing, will rely on him to make payments on the loan to the bank as he receives payment from his customers.

Agricultural or Farm Loans. These are loans made to farmers, or those engaged in the business of raising livestock, grain and produce, for the purpose of assisting them to: (1) buy land, build a home or other buildings, (2) purchase cattle for feeding or for breeding, (3) purchase feed such as hay, corn and oats for livestock, seed for planting crops, fertilizer and machinery and equipment such as tractors, cultivators, binders, etc.

Such loans can be either short term or seasonal, that is, to be repaid when the purpose for which the loan was made has been fulfilled, such as a seed loan be repaid when the crop is harvested; or over a longer period of time usually through a mortgage loan if the loan is in connection with the purchase of land or construction of a building; or in installments if it is a loan in connection with purchase of equipment and machinery.

Appliance Installment Loans. These are loans generally made to individuals (or to dealers who sell the paper to the bank) for the purpose of purchasing a major appliance for home use such as an ice box, stove, washing machine, dryer, television set, which are repayable in installments over a period of between 6 and 36 months.

Automobile Installment Loans. These are the same as appliance loans except that loans are for the purpose of purchasing an automobile. If a new car is being purchased, the bank will generally loan up to 70% of the sale price. If a used car is being purchased, the bank will generally loan not more than 50% of the appraised value or recognized value.

Banking by Mail Services. To serve modern business efficiently, and provide additional convenience for customers in transacting business, most banks have arranged their deposit and loan repayment operations so that by use of special forms, which the bank provides at no extra charge, customers can conduct banking transactions by mail. By using mail service, a bank is as close as the nearest mailbox.

Business Checking Accounts. These are checking accounts maintained by corporations, partnerships, associations and individuals where the funds deposited to the account arise out of the sale of goods or services, and checks drawn against the account are in payment of merchandise or expenses incurred in connection with providing services or selling goods. Generally in a business account, unless the business is serving a local area, the funds so deposited are in the form of checks drawn on banks not in the immediate area, which must be sent to the bank on which drawn either direct, through their correspondent, or through the Federal Reserve System; while checks issued against the account are payable to other business houses far away, and are presented by their bank to your bank through the other bank's correspondent bank or Federal Reserve System, for payment and credit.

Business Loans on Statement. These are loans made to those engaged in business, for the purchase of (a) raw materials for processing for sale, (b) finished goods and merchandise for resale, (c) new machinery and equipment; (d) financing customer accounts and other business purposes in connection with operating the business.

All these loans are based on the financial position of the company as disclosed by a current balance sheet which is a statement of the assets, liabilities and net worth of the company. The amount of such loan, in addition to the character and the capacity of those operating the business, is generally predicated on the financial position of the corporation, that is its net worth, which is the excess of assets over liabilities—and the relationship between current assets (cash and amounts currently owed to the business) and current liabilities (the amount currently owed by the business for goods or services to others).

Cable Transfers. These are means by which a bank for itself, or on behalf of a customer, transfers funds from this country to an other country, and has such funds available for immediate use. Generally when such a transaction takes place the domestic bank, which has the funds in dollars, advises the foreign bank that funds have been deposited with the domestic bank, or other agency, for the credit and use of the foreign bank here; and for the foreign bank to make such funds available in coin or exchange of that country to a person specified upon proper identification.

Cashiers Checks. These are issued by a bank, signed by the cashier or someone authorized to act on behalf of the cashier. Cashiers checks are direct obligations of the bank authorizing the payment of funds, or the transfer of credit to the individual named as payee in the check upon proper identification, and are used by customers and depositors of the bank in payment of obligations.

Christmas Savings Accounts. These are special purpose accounts opened by individuals, usually around December 1st of each year, for the purpose of making weekly payments to an account which by the end of November in the following year will have an accumulated amount of from $25 to $1,000. When such accounts "mature" the bank mails a check to the customer for the amount paid in which funds can be used for the payment of bills incurred in buying Christmas presents, or for the purchase of Christmas presents.

Collection Service. In order to eliminate the need for customers to go to other banks in town, or to travel to other cities to convert checks they have received in payment of goods or services; or evidences of money owed them such as coupons from bonds, dividends, mortgage payments, notes, etc., into cash funds which they can put in their account and use, banks maintain two collection systems. (1) a check collection system which is an arrangement with other local banks or banks in other towns to transfer funds upon presentation of the check or order to pay from their customers' account, to the account of the bank presenting the item, which in turn will be transferred to the account of the customer and, (2) facilities to collect notes, mortgages, coupons, drafts and other documents for customers, by presenting the items either by messenger, or through the mail, to another bank which collects the obligation in funds which are sent to the presenting bank, which then credits the proceeds, less a charge for collecting, to the account of the person for whom they collected the item.

Credit Information. Banks, through dealings with individuals and business firms, and from knowledge and investigation of their financial tranactions, acquire valuable information which they use in determining the basis for extending credit.

Under proper circumstances, this information is made available to customers and friends of the bank to assist them in extending credit to the company.

Coupon Collections. Customers of the bank, who have invested funds in bonds and mortgages of corporations, periodically collect from the company interest for the use of their funds or on their investment. Evidences of amounts due are in the form of small certificates attached to the bond. In order to collect this interest, owners deposit such coupons in their account, or with the collection teller upon receipt, who sends them directly to a bank in the town in which the corporation is located, or to the bank which acts as the paying agent for the corporation, for collection.

Currency for Payroll Purposes. Many corporations or business houses still follow the practice of paying salaries and compensation to their employees in cash. In order to enable them to do this, with the least amount of effort, banks, if such customers will call in advance, will make up packages containing the proper denominations for assisting the paymaster in making up the payroll.

For other companies when special arrangements are made, the bank will prepare, at intermediate periods, the entire payroll by making up and placing in envelopes the respective amounts of currency or coin called for in the payroll statements which the customer furnishes to the bank.

Currency for Change Purposes. Business houses require quantities of currency and silver in order to make change and conduct their business transactions. Banks provide the service not only at times when representatives of business houses come in for specific amounts of currency or coin, but where proper arrangements are made, will have packages of the proper denominations and specified rolls of silver ready for them when they come to the bank so that there is no delay at the window while the money for change purposes is made up.

Custodianship Service. This service is provided by trust departments of banks. Through such a service, for which the bank charges a fee, it holds stocks and bonds in safekeeping, collecting interest on bonds and collecting other obligations or payments which it remits to the customer or credits to a checking or savings account.

Dental Loan Plans. These are loans made to individuals, upon the endorsement of their dentist, for extensive work in connection with dentures, teeth straightening or orthodontic work. Under this loan plan the patient gives a note to the doctor in payment of the entire bill, which the doctor endorses and presents to the bank for which he receives his funds in cash or by means of a credit to the account. The patient then makes monthly installment payments on the loan. If the patient defaults on payments the loan is charged back to the doctor's account or he is looked to for payment.

Drafts on Domestic Banks. These are bills of exchange, or orders of the issuing banks to another bank, to pay a fixed sum of money at sight or on presentation.

It differs from a Cashiers Check in this regard. A Cashiers Check is an order issued by the bank to pay a certain sum to a payee which is honored by the issuing bank on presentation. A draft, on the other hand, is an order from one bank to another bank which has funds belonging to the first bank on deposit to pay a certain sum to the payee or his order.

Educational Loans. These are loans made to an individual to cover tuition, room and board in connection with obtaining a college education, or degree in science or business. They are made by banks to men and women of good character, with or without the endorsement of another person. Depending on the circumstances, such loans can be made for the entire period, with payments to begin upon completion of the educational program, or be made to cover a current period, with payments being made from employment fees with the unpaid balance being carried over until the end of the period.

Estate Planning. This is a term which applies to the broad services provided by the trust departments of banks to assist individuals in developing investment programs based on their requirements and income needs. This service is of particular help to widows who have problems in connection with raising families, providing for education, upkeep and maintenance of their home.

Escrow Service. This is a function of the trust department of banks. Under such an arrangement, which is covered by a written agreement, stocks, bonds, coin, currency, deeds, mediums of exchange are deposited for safekeeping with the bank, to be delivered to a third party upon the fulfillment of some condition or performance.

Executor. This is a function of the trust department of a bank. In this capacity the bank, so appointed in a will, is designated to act in behalf of a person after his or her death, and carries out the instructions for the disposal of the property as the deceased has provided in the will.

FHA Construction Loans. These are loans made by banks under the Federal Housing Administration Act, a percentage of which is guaranteed by the Federal Government, for the construction of owner-occupied homes. Generally these loans are made for a period not to exceed 20 years and for an amount not exceeding $18,000.

Foreign Drafts. These serve exactly the same purpose in transacting business in foreign countries or transferring funds as a cable transfer, except a draft, which is an order to pay, is usually transported by mail and is a much slower way of effecting the transaction.

Foreign Exchange. This is a medium by which commercial investment, and other transactions are settled between countries and refers to the transferring of credits or debits by individuals through their own banks, by obtaining debits or credits on the books of banks in other countries with which their bank maintains a correspondent bank relationship.

Foreign Exchange Currency Transactions. This is a service some banks render through which a person can obtain the actual mediums of exchange used by a foreign country. This service is only rendered by banks who are actively engaged in handling exchange— that is, exchanging the actual coin or currency issued by a foreign country when presented by one of its nationals or by a citizen who has been travelling in such country for United States currency or coin.

Guardianship. This is a function performed by trust departments of banks under appointment by the court, or under certain conditions of a will, to administer and manage the estate of, or in behalf of, a minor, generally considered to be a person 21 years of age or younger; or a person of any age who because of physical or mental disability is unable or incapable to act or manage his or her own affairs.

Investment Counselling Service. This is a new service made available to customers by some of the larger banks of the country through their trust departments. Because of their facilities for analyzing and investigating investment securities, combined with the fact that they manage estates, they are in a position to counsel and advise customers of the bank, or others, seeking advice in handling their investments and the conversion of unused funds into earning assets.

Inventory Loans. These are loans made by banks to those engaged in business for the purpose of purchasing or stockpiling raw materials which over a period of time are to be processed into finished goods; or finished goods pending sale or delivery. In making such loans the bank generally segregates, or has warehoused, the materials against which the loan has been made. When merchandise is taken out of inventory, a payment representing the value of such merchandise is made on the loan.

Insurance Premium Financing Loans. These are generally made by banks to companies and individuals to enable them to pay the annual premium due and payable on any of the various types of insurance carried by the individual or the company. Such loans are repayable within a year's time.

Life Insurance Loans. These are loans made by banks to individuals and companies, under assignment of the cash surrender value of the policy (that is the amount the insured would receive if he cancelled the policy) as collateral security for the loan.

Life Insurance Savings Accounts. These are of recent origin. They are savings accounts established by banks to provide life insurance for the elderly and a ready fund in addition, in case of death. While there are various types of plans and the interest rates differ they generally provide that the depositor is provided with life insurance or insurance payable upon his death equal to the amount he has on deposit in the account. The coverage generally does not go over $2,000.

Medical Plan Loans. These operate the same as Dental Plan loans except that the loan is made in connection with payment of hospital bills and surgical fees. Such loans are particularly adaptable where health or hospitalization insurance is not sufficient to cover the total expenses.

Mail Services. These are provided by the bank consisting of regular, special delivery and registered and are used in connection with the collection of checks, transferring of securities, collection of drafts, mortgages and notes, handling of mail deposits and the distribution of dividend checks.

Messenger Service. This is provided by most banks particularly for use in personal presentation of collection items, and the collection of checks and other items between banks in the same town.

Machinery Loans. These are made by banks to individuals and companies for the purchase of machinery and equipment.

Such loans, if not made on the general credit of the borrower as warranted by their financial statement are generally made by the bank taking a chattel mortgage on the machinery and equipment as collateral security. Such loans are usually made for 60 to 80% of the cost of such machinery or equipment and are repayable in from 1 to 5 years, depending upon the type and use of such machinery and equipment.

Modernization Loans. These are loans to home owners under FHA guarantee, or under the bank's own plan, for the purpose of remodelling or modernizing kitchens, and bathrooms and for converting basements into family rooms or playrooms. Such loans are made for various periods of time depending on the purpose, and repayable in installments.

Money Orders. These are a form of credit instrument similar to a cashiers check, issued by a bank which shows the name of the payee and also the purchaser. They are widely used by bank customers and others who do not have checking accounts for the payment of bills and the remitting of funds to others.

Money Packets. These are small packages of assorted foreign currency and coin, usually aggregating $10.00 or $25.00 in American money, put up by banks to provide their customers travelling abroad with a supply of change to use on arrival for cab fare, tipping, etc., until they obtain foreign currency and coin for their use, by drawing against their Letter of Credit or cashing Travellers Checks.

Mortgage Servicing. This is a facility developed by banks for the collection of principal, interest, taxes and insurance premiums on real estate mortgages owned by others.

Under such a plan the bank collects in installments the monthly payment of principal, interest, and funds to be set aside for taxes and insurance, records them, and remits the net proceeds to the owner of the mortgage for which the bank receives a fee. Payments for insurance and taxes are remitted direct when due.

Payroll Accounts. These are maintained with banks by companies, or those engaged in businesses employing a number of people, to simplify their accounting methods and procedures.

In operation, the company issues checks in payment of wages and salaries which are drawn on the payroll account, depositing to this account only sufficient funds from their regular account to cover the checks which they have issued. Monthly, or after each pay period, as the case might be, the cancelled checks together with a statement are rendered the customer for reconcilement.

Personal Checking Accounts. These are accounts maintained by individuals, in which they deposit their salary or wage checks, against which they draw checks in payment of household bills.

Personal Loans. These are loans made to individuals, generally with a co-signer or upon the endorsement of a friend with financial reputation, for the purpose of providing funds with which to pay household bills, medical expenses or provide for other contingencies.

These loans are repayable in monthly installments of from 6 to 18 months. Sometimes, in the absence of a co-signer or endorser, a wage assignment is taken which is an order to the company for which the individual works, assigning his salary or wages to the bank in the event of default.

Paying Agent Service. This is a function performed by trust departments of banks under arrangement with the company through which the bank pays dividend checks and coupons when presented by other banks for collection and payment.

Purchase of Bonds and Securities for Customers. This is a special service which banks provide for customers who wish to purchase bonds and securities. To take advantage of this service, a customer signs an order authorizing the bank to purchase so many shares of a certain stock at a certain price, or so many bonds of a certain issue at a certain price, and makes satisfactory arrangements for payment of the securities so purchased, when the order is executed by the broker. When the broker notifies the bank that they have purchased the stock or bonds, the bank remits the funds. Upon receipt of the securities, the bank notifies the customer to pick them up or holds them in safekeeping.

Purchase of United States Savings Bonds. United States Savings Bonds are purchased by banks for customers through the Federal Reserve banks, with the exception of Series E which banks sell directly to customers and others.

Real Estate Mortgage Loans—Conventional. These are made by banks on residential and farm property, using a mortgage or trust deed as collateral to secure the payment of principal and interest.

Conventional mortgages are usually made for 60% of the appraised value and either repayable within 10 years in monthly installments, or set up in such a way that at least 50% of the amount of the loan is paid back within 10 years, with the balance due at the end of the 10 years period.

Real Estate Mortgage Loans—FHA. These are loans made by banks under the guarantee of the Federal Housing Administration Act which guarantees most of the loan as to principal and interest. Such loans are made for a period not to exceed 20 years and for an amount not in excess of $18,000.

Registrar. A registrarship is a service performed by trust departments of banks, through which the bank is appointed by a corporation to certify and register the shares of stock issued by them in the name of the owner.

Remodeling Loans—Residences. These are loans for the purpose of modernizing or remodeling kitchens and bathrooms, or to make additions to the home. They are made by banks, either under an FHA Title II plan through which the loan is partially guaranteed by the Federal Government, or through the bank's own plan. Generally such loans are repayable in monthly installments over a period not to exceed 5 years.

Remodeling Loans—Business. These are loans made by banks either on the financial statement of the company or against a mortgage taken as security. Such loans are usually made to retail establishments for the modernizing of their store fronts, or for equipment, and are repayable in monthly installments over a fixed period of time depending upon the extent and purpose of the remodeling.

Safekeeping Services. These are offered by banks. although the practice is generally discouraged, in view of the fact that banks provide other services which are much more satisfactory from the customers' and banks' standpoint. These are use of a Safe Deposit Box or Custodian service provided by trust departments of banks.

In providing safekeeping service the bank accepts stocks, bonds, mortgages, and other securities or documents of stated value for which it gives its receipt. The bank holds such articles until the customer claims them on presentation of the receipt or receives written orders to dispose of the articles left for safekeeping.

Safe Deposit Boxes. These are strongboxes kept in a vault or safe operated by the bank, where individuals who have their own keys can place their valuables and securities.

Sale of Bonds and Securities for Customers. In performing this service, the customer delivers to the bank securities to be sold, signs an order authorizing the sale and the conditions under which the sale shall be made, and advises the bank the disposition to make of the proceeds.

After the securities have been sold and delivered to the purchaser, the bank either deposits the proceeds to the customer's account or remits the proceeds by check.

Sales of United States Savings Bonds for Customers. This is a service performed by the bank. Banks, through redemption tables, are able to determine the current value of the bonds, and if satisfied as to ownership, can make immediate payment to the customer either by means of a credit to the account or by issuance of a cashiers check.

Savings Accounts. These are funds left on deposit on which the bank agrees to pay interest. As a condition of receiving interest the customer agrees, whenever required, to give the bank at least 30 days' notice of intent to withdraw any or all of the funds.

Interest on savings accounts is generally computed and paid semi-annually, the maximum rate of interest which banks pay is provided for by law, through regulations of the Federal Reserve Board.

Savings Certificates. These are more commonly known as Certificates of Deposit, and represent funds deposited by individuals or corporations for a specific purpose, for which they receive a certificate, or Bill of Exchange, payable to order, which is negotiable, and transferable by endorsement.

If the certificate is payable on demand, it is known as a Demand Certificate, and is not interest bearing. If the certificate is payable at a fixed date or maturity, usually 6 months to 2 years from date of issue, it is known as a Time Certificate and carries a fixed rate of interest.

While title to Time Certificates, like Demand Certificates, passes by endorsement, such certificates are not redeemable, or convertible into cash until the specified maturity. They can, however, be used as collateral security for loans. Generally, because of the length of time such deposits are left on deposit, they bear a higher rate of interest than is paid on regular savings accounts.

Silver for Change Purposes. This is provided by banks to retail stores and other businesses who require quantities of silver in order to make change and conduct their business. As the supply of rolled coin is never sufficient for the demand, banks usually accumulate the loose coin they receive in deposits or order coin from their correspondent bank or the Federal Reserve Bank which comes bagged loose, which they roll in standard packages and have available for their customers to use for change purposes.

Silver for Payroll Purposes. This is provided by banks where businessmen or companies follow the practice of paying out salaries and wages in cash. In such case banks always provide suitable coin, either loose or in rolls, to assist the paymaster in making up the payroll.

Special Checking Accounts. These are maintained by individuals and corporations; in fact by anyone who has reason for maintaining a regular or personal checking account for any specific purpose where they have the privilege of withdrawing the funds on demand or without prior notice.

Among the reasons why "special accounts" are maintained are to record the financial transactions covering a piece of rental property, a farm, the special operation of a business, or to have a record of investment transactions.

Special Savings Accounts. Special savings accounts serve the same purpose as special checking accounts except as there is no need for having the funds on deposit payable on demand they are placed in savings accounts where, in addition to the convenience, they also will draw interest.

Travellers Checks. These are widely used by people traveling abroad or distances from home. They are similar to cashiers checks except that holders are not restricted to cashing them at banks but can negotiate them at any bank and at practically all hotels and travel agencies throughout the world under a guarantee provided by some well known bank or other institution.

Every Travellers Check bears the signature of the person for whose use the check is intended, which is affixed by him at the time of purchase. There is also another space which the purchaser must sign at the time he negotiates the check for cashing as a means of identifying himself as the person who owns the check.

Telegraphic Money Transfers. These are money transfers negotiated through Western Union. This fast form of transferring money is accomplished by the individual or the bank delivering the money to a Western Union office which sends a telegram to the payee in the town designated who upon presentation of proper identification is paid the money so wired. Telegraphic or wire transfers, as they are more commonly known, are in great use between banks in transferring funds from one section of the country to another so banks can make their funds available for the needs of their customers by drawing drafts on these banks.

Travellers Letters of Credit. These are letters issued by domestic banks introducing the bearer to its correspondent in a foreign country, and instructing them to honor drafts up to the amount specified in the letter. Such letters of credit are particularly to the advantage of people purchasing goods in foreign countries, or doing extensive traveling who wish to have maximum funds at their disposal.

Trustee Under Will. This is a service performed by trust departments of banks. As trustee, the bank acts for and in behalf of another person or corporation.

Where the bank acts as Trustee under Will it is empowered to act only in accordance with the provisions of the will. A Trusteeship is usually terminated after a specific period of time when the estate is distributed by the beneficiaries.

Trustee Under Agreement. This is a service provided by banks with trust departments. The functions are similar to acting as Trustee under Will with the exception that generally the individual who created the trust is alive. The bank acts under specific instruction in carrying out the terms of the trust.

Vacation Plan Savings Accounts. These are a form of savings account available in many banks. They are set up specifically to provide funds for a vacation or other travel.

To open such an account the depositor generally determines where he wishes to go, the cost, and how much he can afford to put aside each week or month in order to accumulate the funds by a certain period. When this specified time or period has been reached the bank then mails a check to the customer providing the funds for the vacation or other special purpose.

Transfer Agent. This is a service performed by banks which have trust departments. Stock certificates are personal property, and ownership may pass from one person to another by assignment or endorsement. In case of sale, however, the purchase is not recognized until ownership has been transferred on the books of the company.

To do this it is necessary to present the old certificate. In order to provide accuracy in the transfer of stocks from one owner to the other, after the transfer has been effected, such certificates are then sent to the bank which has been acting as a Registrar who records the certificate, and the name of the owner on the books of the corporation.

Warehouse Loans. These are loans made by banks where the collateral security is raw materials or finished goods stored in a public or bonded warehouse.

Warehouse receipts are generally negotiable, and ownership passes upon surrender of the receipt properly endorsed in payment of the charges to the warehouseman. Warehouse receipts issued by a bonded warehouse under the Warehouse Receipts Act of 1916 also cover commodities and food products of all kinds.

It is also common practice, wherever the merchandise to be warehoused or stored is too far away from the warehouse, to make special arrangements through a bonded warehouse to take custody of the merchandise either on the premises of the customer or in other storage warehouses where they can effect control and protection.

These services which we have briefly enumerated and the manner in which they are performed by the staff of the bank will be covered in greater detail through the later chapters.

OTHER SERVICES OF BANKS

In addition to providing services to their customers and assistance in the development of commerce and trade, banks also have another responsibility—to give service to their communities. This service can only be performed by bankers alert to the needs of the community and interested in developing the commerce and business of the area.

A progressive banker watches the growth and development of his community. He begins to become concerned when the number of vacant stores in the town increases. If a new shopping center has been built, or a new highway has been put through close by the town where a number of merchants have moved their place of business because of the parking facilities, what can be done to bring business back to the town proper?

If this cannot be done and the buildings are run down, should the property be made into parking spaces or parks or other use made which will contribute to the welfare of the town?

An alert banker should also be aware when the streets of his town become a patchwork of ruts and bumps, when holes occasioned by changes in the weather are carelessly filled in with gravel and maybe a dab of asphalt to hold it together. When these situations occur it is time for the alert banker to meet with the city council or the commissioner of streets to find out what the program is for resurfacing.

An alert banker should also be on the lookout for housekeeping in his community particularly in his area. Are the streets littered with papers, leaves? Is seasonal dirt allowed to accumulate and blow hither and yon with every breeze? What is necessary in order to have the community neat and clean?

When merchants complain about business, the alert banker who is interested in his community, will investigate the situation and determine the reasons why business is bad. Many times it is because of poor service. Other times it is because the merchant is not abreast of the times and fails to stock his shelves with merchandise which is in demand by the public.

Many times his furniture and fixtures are antiquated. What he needs is to modernize his store. If modernization is advisable, what better way can a bank serve the community and the individual than by making a loan which will help bring business to the community?

Perhaps the reason for the lack of business, is that parking facilities are inadequate. People hesitate to come into town because they are unable to find parking spaces. They would rather go to the shopping center, or to the adjacent town where the merchants are on their toes and provide places for people to park their cars. Sometimes, too, an alert banker will find a shortage of parking facilities is caused by the employees of the store (and even the owners themselves) parking their own cars in the space which should be provided for customers.

Overcrowded conditions in towns and communities while a good sign because it indicates prosperity, is also a forewarning of danger to the alert and enterprising banker.

To have a progressive community we not only need a balanced population, but recreational facilities for people of all ages, room for expansion for people with families, places for children to play, and facilities and the opportunity for social and cultural activities.

If the town is being crowded because new industries are relocating there and bringing people with them, the alert and progressive banker wants to know if such industries are stable. Are the salaries paid sufficient to enable the workers to own their homes, to become useful citizens of the community, or are they living there because they happen to have a job and will move to another community whenever a better opportunity arises for use of their talents in business?

In such cases the alert banker finds out what the planning commission has in mind. If they are restricting certain property for housing, what is the school board doing about providing educational facilities?

What is the forecast for growth 5 or 10 years from now?

Will new grammar schools and high schools be needed and, if so, where will they be located?

Granted that most bankers are too busy to investigate all of these themselves, as leaders in the community the least they can do is to see that a planning commission is formed to look into the future and make provision for expansion.

A planning commission should be a working organization. Generally they have little money for their activities and operations, and in small communities, serving on such a commission is on a voluntary basis. What better contribution can a banker make to the welfare of his community than by serving on such a committee, and by geting other leading citizens interested in the development of the community, who, like himself are interested in the development of the community, to serve with him?

In view of the limited budget such planning commissions have at their disposal, one of the greatest contributions a progressive bank can make to the community is to start the ball rolling, or to initiate the plan. This can be accomplished by the bank employing the services of experts in community planning, not only to make an appraisal and analysis of the community as it exists, with pictures if possible, but to provide a plan for the future, illustrating by suitable drawings what the community and town would look like if the recommendations made by such experts were placed into effect in the ensuing years by the city council or the municipality, under the urging and guidance of the planning commission.

Planning commissions also have a further function, that is, to work closely with the Chamber of Commerce once a proper appraisal of the facilities of the community has been made, to endeavor to attract new industries to the community. This, of course, is a cooperative effort on the part of the bank and all of the merchants and last, but not least, those owners of strategic real estate where the development of new business in the community would create a demand for houses and real estate developments.

The alert banker will grasp these opportunities for service, knowing full well that with the growth and development of the community, if he provides the banking and financial services, his bank will grow and develop with the community and return substantial profits to his stockholders in the way of dividends, and increased salaries and benefits to himself and other employees of the bank.

In considering community developments an alert banker should also be mindful of the churches as well as the schools. He should keep them advised of the plans for future developments so that they, too, can take adequate steps for enlarging their plants to provide for additional attendance, or for school and recreational facilities for their members.

CHAPTER X

A BANK'S STATEMENT OF CONDITION

MUCH INTERESTING INFORMATION about the progress and financial position of a bank can be learned from studying their various reports of financial condition.

These reports are of two types—"Call Reports", which are published at least twice a year, which reflect the condition of the bank as of a previous, but undeterminable date, and "Statements of Condition" which banks voluntarily issue as of June 30 and December 31.

Both the Call Report, published by order of the supervisory agency which has jurisdiction over the respective type of bank—(Comptroller of the Currency, in the case of all national banks, and the Superintendent or Commissioner of Banking, in the case of state banks in respective states) and the Statement of Condition are public reports of the bank's financial condition and progress. While it is published in condensed form, it nevertheless reflects (as we will see when we study the various "acounts" which make up the control headings) the true financial condition of the bank as of the date of the statement.

A bank's Statement of Condition similar to that shown in Exhibit 4 is composed of two sets of figures of which one represents Assets and the other Liabilities. The totals of both sets of accounts always balance as, under a double entry bookkeeping system, for each debit there must be a credit and for each credit there must be a debit.

Every bank employee should become familiar with the facts pertaining to the condition of his own bank as disclosed by a Statement of Condition, and understand what is represented under the various control headings, in order to be able to intelligently answer any questions which might be asked of him.

Exhibit 4

STATEMENT OF CONDITION

PROGRESSIVE BANK OF PROGRESS

June 30, 1967

ASSETS	
Cash and Due from Banks	$ 639,986.53
U. S. Government Bonds	1,390,044.01
Municipal and Other Bonds	1,304,000.03
Loans and Discounts	1,431,240.87
Overdrafts	2,634.05
Banking House	7,500.00
Furniture and Fixtures	8,607.25
Other Assets	3,450.25
	$4,787,462.99
LIABILITIES	
Demand Deposits	3,459,833.26
Time Deposits	903,460.04
Other Liabilities	1,367.90
Capital	175,000.00
Surplus	100,000.00
Undivided Profits	100,000.00
Reserves	47,801.79
	$4,787,462.99

In order to easily remember the difference between Assets and Liabilities and whether an Asset or a Liability account is affected by a particular financial transaction, it is well to remember, that all Asset Accounts represent what others owe the bank, while all Liability Accounts represents what the bank owes others.

ASSET ACCOUNTS

Cash and Due from Banks. This figure represents:

A. Currency or coin in the possession of the tellers to enable them to cash checks and furnish the cash requirements of depositors.

B. Currency or coin which the bank keeps as a reserve in a special vault or compartment, usually under dual control, known as Reserve Cash.

C. Checks and drafts which have been deposited by depositors for credit to their account, or checks which have been cashed by the tellers for depositors or others, which are in the process of being collected from the issuer on the bank on which drawn.

D. Funds maintained on deposit with the Federal Reserve Bank, or other banks, as a reserve—required by law.

E. Funds maintained on deposit with other banks for the convenience in transferring funds of depositors, and handling other business and financial transactions.

F. Funds in excess of above requirements, available for investment in loans, bonds and mortgages.

United States Government Obligations. This figure represents funds belonging to depositors and capital funds belonging to stockholders, which the bank has invested in:

A. Bonds of the U. S. Government. These are securities, due at a stated future date, which bear a fixed rate of interest, payable semi-annually.

B. Notes of the U. S. Government. These are securities, due at a stated future date, usually within two years from date of issue, on which interest, at a fixed rate, is payable at maturity.

C. Certificates of Indebtedness of the U. S. Government. These are securities which mature 6-12-18 months after date of issue, with interest payable at maturity.

D. U. S. Treasury Bills. These are securities of the U. S. Government, maturing in 30-60-90 days, which are purchased on an interest discount basis.

E. Other Obligations. These are various bonds and notes of governmental instrumentalities, fully or partially guaranteed by the U. S. Government, as to principal and interest.

Municipal Bonds. This figure represents the investment of

funds belonging to the depositors, and capital funds belonging to the stockholders, which the bank has invested in:

A. Bonds, notes, or tax anticipation warrants issued by the state or an instrumentality of the state.

B. Bonds, notes, or tax anticipation warrants issued by a county.

C. Bonds, notes, or tax anticipation warrants issued by a school district.

D. Bonds, notes, or tax anticipation warrants issued by a municipality or city.

Other Bonds. This figure represents the investment of funds belonging to the depositors, and capital funds belonging to the stockholders which the bank has invested in:

A. Bonds, notes and debentures of classified railroads, eligible for bank investment.

B. Bonds, notes and debentures issued by gas, light, power, telephone and other utility companies, eligible for bank investment.

C. Miscellaneous bonds, stocks, and other securities, acquired by the bank, in liquidation of loans, and held temporarily pending disposition.

Loans and Discounts. This figure represents the funds belonging to depositors, and capital funds belonging to stockholders, which the bank has invested in:

A. Time Loans Secured by Marketable Collateral. These are loans, payable at a fixed future date, secured by bonds, debentures, or certificates of stock, issued by corporations, which are listed on one of the recognized Security Exchanges, and are readily marketable.

B. Time Loans Secured by Other Collateral. These are loans payable at a fixed future date, secured by a pledge of bonds, debentures or certificates of stock issued by corporations whose securities are not listed on any recognized Security Exchange, or by other collateral such as notes, mortgages, pledges of accounts receivable, cash surrender value of life insurance policies, warehouse receipts, and similar documents representing value.

C. Time Loans Unsecured. These are loans payable at a future fixed date, based on net worth, as disclosed by a financial statement or on character.

D. Demand Loans Secured. These are loans secured by marketable or other collateral, due and payable on demand or at the pleasure of the bank.

E. Demand Loans Unsecured. These are loans made on financial statements, or on the character of individuals, which are due and payable on demand or at the pleasure of the bank.

F. Discounts. These are drafts, accepted by the drawee, which the bank discounts or advances funds to the payee before maturity.

G. Farm or Agricultural Loans. These are loans made to farmers, or those engaged in agriculture, for the purpose of financing the purchase of cattle for feeding, seed for planting, or other current farm operating purposes.

H. Real Estate Mortgage Loans Conventional. These are first mortgage loans, against equities in residential or business property. They are generally made for 50 to 60% of the appraised valuation and repayable in monthly installments over a maximum period of 10 years.

I. Real Estate Mortgage Loans FHA. These are loans, made by the bank to individuals to acquire, repair, or improve their homes, on which a percentage of the loan and the interest is guaranteed by the Federal Housing Administration. Such loans are made for not more than 80% of appraised value, in maximum amounts of $18,000, and are repayable in monthly installments over a period not to exceed 20 years.

J. Veteran Loans. These are loans made by banks to veterans, under the G.I. Bill of Rights for the purpose of enabling them to purchase or repair their home, or business property, buying a business, or obtaining a working capital for business. Such loans are partially guaranteed by the Veterans Administration.

K. Installment Loans. These are loans made to individuals for the purchase of automobiles and household appliances, or loans made against wage assignments, or on the endorsement of a cosigner, repayable in monthly installments.

L. Other Loans. These are loans against Sight Drafts with securities or documents attached, such as Bills of Lading.

Overdrafts. This represents unsecured loans arising from

debit balances in deposit accounts, caused by payments of checks in excess of the credit balance maintained.

Banking House. This figure represents funds belonging to the stockholders which the bank has invested in:

A. Buildings and real estate properties owned and operated by the bank in conducting its business.

B. Parking Lots.

C. Property on which Drive-In facilities are located.

D. Improved and unimproved property which the bank has acquired in foreclosure proceedings in connection with a loan, and which it holds pending sale; or property it has acquired for future use, either for parking facilities or for construction of a building required for conducting its business.

Furniture, Fixtures, Machinery and Equipment. This figure represents the funds belonging to stockholders which the bank has invested in:

A. Automobiles or vehicles required by the bank in carrying on, and conducting its business.

B. Office furniture such as desks, chairs, counters, cages and carpeting.

C. Machines such as adding machines, typewriters, computers, and bookkeeping machines.

D. Air conditioning units, and electric signs, etc.

Other Assets. This represents miscellaneous items which ultimately will be converted into cash, such as:

A. Interest which has accrued on loans and investments but is unpaid.

B. Commissions or fees earned for which the bank has billed the customer, but has not received payment.

C. Amounts paid out, or amounts disbursed, in payment of current operating expenses of the bank, which have not been charged to the Undivided Profits Account.

D. Letters of Credit issued in behalf of customers to enable them to finance business transactions abroad.

E. Letters of Credit issued to individuals to finance the expenses of travel.

LIABILITIES

Demand Deposits. This figure represents the total funds which depositors of the bank, as classified, have deposited in accounts subject to disbursement on presentation of a properly signed check or order to pay.

A. U. S. Government Deposits. These are funds belonging to various agencies or instrumentalities of the Federal Government held in the name of the Treasurer of the United States.

B. Public Funds. These are funds belonging to states, counties, municipalities or their instrumentalities.

C. Regular Checking Accounts. These are funds maintained by individuals, corporations, partnerships and associations.

D. Special Checking Accounts. These are funds maintained under special arrangement by individuals, corporations, partnerships and associations.

E. Certificates of Deposit. These are funds in the names of individuals, corporations, partnerships and associations evidenced by certificates, transferable by endorsement and payable upon presentation. (The use of demand certificates of deposit in recent years has been largely supplanted by the use of cashier's checks and drafts.)

F. Other Demand Deposits. These are funds deposited by individuals, corporations, partnerships and others with the bank, as surety for loans and other obligations; under special instructions, such as escrow agreements; or representing funds in trust accounts awaiting investment.

G. Due to Banks. These are funds subject to withdrawal by check or draft maintained by other banks.

H. Official Checks. These are funds covering various classes of checks drawn by the bank on itself, either in payment of bank obligations and expenses; or funds which have been provided customers to use in the payment of obligations where their own personal check would not be acceptable such as Certified Checks, Expense Checks, Cashiers Checks and Money Orders.

Time Deposits. This figure represents funds which customers of the bank have deposited in interest bearing accounts, subject to withdrawal upon 30 days notice, upon presentation of a properly signed withdrawal order together with the pass book, classified as follows:

A. U. S. Government Deposits. These are funds belonging to agencies or instrumentalities of the government under control of the Treasurer of the United States.

B. Public Funds. These funds belong to states, counties, municipalities or their instrumentalities.

C. Regular Time Deposits. These are funds deposited by individuals, partnerships, associations subject to withdrawal upon presentation of properly signed withdrawal slips accompanied by the pass book.

D. Time Certificates of Deposit. These are funds in the names of individuals, corporations, partnerships and associations evidenced by certificates, transferable by endorsement, bearing a fixed rate of interest payable as to both principal and interest after a fixed period of time.

E. Special Time Deposits. These are special time deposit accounts, sometimes interest bearing, subject to withdrawal on a definite date or on compliance with other provisions, such as Christmas Club Accounts, Vacation Club Accounts and special purpose accounts.

Other Liabilities. This represents miscellaneous items the bank owes to others in connection with

A. Income Collected but Unearned. This represents interest on loans paid in advance. Under an accrual system the bank onl withdraws daily, weekly or monthly as the procedure might be, the actual interest as earned.

B. Expenses Accrued and Unpaid. This represents earning set aside to pay interest on deposit accounts, taxes and other expenses when payment is due.

C. Income from Operations. This represents the current Cas and Accrued Income account, such as interest on loans and inves ments, service charges, fees, exchange charges, rents received, whic have not been credited into the Undivided Profits account. Whe this is done, either monthly or semi-annually, the Expense Accour which is an Asset account, is then charged against the Undivid Profits account with the difference, representing the net profit f the period.

D. Accounts Payable. This represents funds set aside by the bank which they owe to "creditors", covering the purchase of machinery, equipment, stationery, supplies or other similar property for which they have not been billed.

E. Letters of Credit Outstanding. This figure represents the contingent liabilities of the bank on letters of credit issued in behalf of customers to enable them to finance business transactions abroad or to provide funds for customers of the bank to use while traveling.*

Capital—Common Stock. This represents:

A. The total funds stockholders originally subscribed at the time the bank was formed.

B. Funds subscribed later to provide an increase in capital.

C. Profits from the operation of the bank which were passed on to them in the form of stock dividends.

All earnings, after payment of expenses, dividends on preferred stock, and interest on debentures which are cumulative belong to common shareholders.

Capital—Preferred Stock. This represents the funds stockholders invested in the preferred stock of the bank. Such stock, as the name implies, has preference over the common stock in case of liquidation. The rate of dividends on preferred stock is fixed, that is, it carries a certain fixed rate of return and does not share in the excess earnings of the bank, as does common stock.

Capital—Debentures. This figure represents interest-bearing notes or debentures sold by the bank to obtain additional capital when it is not possible (or conditions are not favorable) to sell common or preferred stock.

Surplus. This figure represents funds belonging to stockholders, originally paid in at the time the bank was formed to provide funds for losses and contingencies; or earnings from operations which have not been distributed as cash dividends or capitalized by the issuance of additional common stock dividends.

Undivided Profits. This figure represents earnings from operations which have not been distributed as cash dividends, or set

* Figures representing Letters of Credit, an asset account, and Letters of Credit Outstanding, a liability account, are generally for the same amount. It is shown in the statement of condition to indicate the bank's liability or guarantee to accept drafts drawn against such letters of credit.

aside in special accounts as reserves for certain purposes, or transferred to the Surplus Account of the bank.

The Undivided Profits Account is a settlement account of the bank, to which, on periodical close-out dates, usually June 30th and December 31st, the balance of all Earning Accounts are tranferred, and against which all Expense Accounts are closed out. After this has been done the net profits for the period are distributed to stockholders by direction of the Board of Directors as dividends or added to Reserve or Surplus Accounts in accordance with the financial requirements and future needs of the bank.

Reserves. This figure represents earnings from operations which have been set aside by the Directors to provide for unforeseen losses on loans and investments, retirement of preferred stock o debentures, new buildings, taxes, etc.

While the records of all banks are similar in their essentials, no all are published in the same form, or show identical items. Thi is due to the fact that while the information called for, by the super visory agencies, whether they be state or federal, is the same, th reporting will vary.

All bank Statements of Condition, however, have one thing i common—that is they can be set up to accurately reflect the finar cial position of a bank as of any given date. The ability to know the exact financial position at the close of business each day, is on of the differences which distinguishes banks from any other busi ness. This is because banks only deal in money and at the en of each day effect a balance of their accounts, complete the financi transactions, and summarize the results, which are posted to r spective control accounts.

Bank Statements of Condition are very informative. By con paring the figures as shown in the current statement with the figur under the same heading as shown in the previous statement it possible to determine both the progress of the bank and the resu of their operations for a given period. For example, let us rememb the principal earning assets of a bank are loans and investments which the dollars of funds entrusted to the bank by depositors, ar the capital belonging to the stockholders have been invested.

Now, if we compare the total loans and investments from o statement with the total loans and investments from the previo statement, and loans show an increase, while investments have r mained constant, we can conclude in general that business has been good and there has been a demand for loans which the bank has supplied.

If, however, investments have declined while loans have increased we can conclude that while business is good because of a demand for loans which carry a greater interest income rate than investments, the bank has sold bonds and placed the proceeds in loans.

If investments have increased while loans have remained stationary, or possibly decreased, we can conclude that while business is good, inventories are being liquidated and because there is little demand for loans, which the bank is willing to make, the bank in order to keep funds employed and obtain income, has invested the uninvested funds in bonds.

Now let us compare the figures on the liability side. If the igures representing demand deposits show an increase, it means business is good and personal income is up. If there is a corresponding increase in savings deposits, it means people are not investing heir surplus funds, but putting them aside in a savings account where they will earn interest until such time as they find something n which to invest their money, or accumulate sufficient funds to buy a home, automobile or any other thing of value they wish.

If deposits decline and loans increase, it indicates that business s buying materials to process, or stocking up on inventory forecasting a period of prosperity; and are buying such merchandise or raw materials in anticipation that prices will increase.

As to determining results of operation, the Capital and Surplus accounts belong to the stockholders. Once funds have been transerred into the Surplus account by the directors, it requires approval f the stockholders to make such funds available for other uses.

Now, if the Capital account, which consists of the Capital, Surplus, Undivided Profits and Reserve accounts, shows a substantial increase, it shows that business has been profitable.

If the increase has been in the Reserve accounts, it indicates e bank is setting aside funds from earnings to provide for antipated losses, taxes or contingencies. If the Surplus account shows n increase, it indicates the Profit and Reserve accounts are sufficient r all contingencies and the directors have earmarked additional nds for the stockholders. These funds have not actually been delivered to them, however. This can only be done through the declaration of a stock dividend.

If the increase has been in the Reserve accounts, it indicates no decision has been reached by the directors, as far as the accumulated earnings are concerned. They may declare a cash dividend, transfer it to surplus and later declare a stock dividend, or perhaps transfer it to a special Reserve account which they will earmark for a special purpose, such as retirement of Preferred Stock or Debentures, the construction of a new building, or for providing new facilities.

Much can be learned about the operation and management of a bank from studying the published condensed Statement of Condition which all banks are required to publish whenever instructed to do so by the supervisory agency which has jurisdiction over their operations and management.

As a well informed staff is an asset of any bank, both officers and employees of banks should study each new Statement of Condition as it is published, to be acquainted with changes which have taken place, and be able to answer intelligently questions about the bank which friends and the public might ask them.

CHAPTER XI

TITLES AND RESPONSIBILITIES OF BANK OFFICERS AND ADMINISTRATIVE PERSONNEL

A BANK'S STATEMENT OF CONDITION, especially hose published to reflect the condition of the bank as of June 30th r December 31st of each year, usually include a list of directors, nd the names and titles of the officers to whom responsibility for ie management of the bank has been delegated by the directors.

It is well to remember that every business becomes successful the degree that talents of properly selected personnel are em- loyed in performing duties and responsibilities which are consid- red to go with or belong to certain titles.

Probably more publicity is given titles of bank officers than titles of officers in other business enterprises. It is of interest everyone, particularly employees, to have a general idea as to st what the functions are of an officer who holds a certain title, what functions an officer holding a certain title performs. It ould be of interest to list both the title and broad duties and re- onsibilities generally believed to be performed by persons hold- g such positions.

Another purpose in listing the titles and functions, generally lieved to be assumed by those holding such titles, is to point t the innumerable opportunities for advancement in a bank and w in the general scheme of promotion a person, once he ob- ins a position of administrative responsibility, can advance if he idies his job and the job ahead, and applies his talents in con- ientiously discharging the duties and responsibilities attached to e particular job to which he is assigned.

This of course is entirely up to the individual—the way he ap- ies himself to the work, the effort he makes to thoroughly learn s job—and, most important, the training of someone else to do s job when he is promoted.

As we shall see later, there are a number of opportunities for a person to advance in banking. It is common practice in banking, to advance and change a person from one position of responsibility to a higher position or responsibility in clerical lines, and to advance a person with an official title to another position carrying greater responsibility and a more important title in administrative lines with a consequential increase in pay, when openings occur.

In order to indicate these opportunities, the following list designates titles and accompanying authority in most banks. The titles of administrative personnel are arranged generally in order of importance or succession, while clerical personnel are listed alphabetically, by job or position, which may or may not have any relation to responsibility.

According to law and generally accepted practice, all person who hold official titles from Chairman of the Board through Executive Vice President, the Secretary and the Cashier, are *electe* by the Board of Directors to hold title and serve for one yea while all other persons holding official titles, are *appointed to serve* either by the Board of Directors or the President.

It is well to point out that in many cases more than one offici title can be held by the same person; that is, a person can hold title designating his administrative capacity, such as Vice Pres dent, and also hold the office of Trust Officer. Similarly, a perso might be a Vice President and also hold the title of Comptrolle The reason for this dual title is generally to give greater recognitio to the office, and to consider it in the "senior" officer class.

The particular responsibilities of each officer from a function standpoint, that is, in the relationship of one department, divisic or section to another department, division or section, is outline in Chapter Twelve.

So that the relationship between functional segments of t banking business is recognized while we briefly describe the duti and responsibilities of administrative personnel, it is well to unde stand that a bank is composed first of departments, usually under senior officer. Departments are divided into divisions under senior or junior officer, while divisions in turn are divided in sections under a manager. Sections in turn are composed of seni and junior tellers, senior and junior clerks and trainees.

The respective positions of authority and responsibility generally assumed to be performed by persons holding such titles are as follows:

Directors are stockholders, elected by other stockholders, to represent them in the management of the bank, as provided by law and under the By-Laws. It is the function of the directors to determine policies and to delegate duties and responsibilities to officers and administrative personnel.

Chairman of the Board is a director elected by the other di- ectors to head up the board of directors and act as liaison be- ween the stockholders and management.

Vice Chairman of the Board is a director elected by other di- ectors to assist the chairman of the board, or to carry out special duties and responsibilities delegated by them.

Chairman of the Executive Committee is a director elected by he board of directors to assume general duties and responsibilities s head of the executive committee which has certain powers del- gated to it by the stockholders, generally in connection with ap- roving loans on behalf of the board of directors.

President is a director, elected by the board of directors, usually s chief executive officer, and held responsible by the board of di- ectors, acting in behalf of the stockholders, for the general admin- tration and management of the bank. The president generally as the responsibility for acting as liaison between the directors nd the other officers.

Executive Vice President is generally a director, elected by the oard of directors, to assume responsibilities, particularly in con- ection with assisting the president, and to assume the responsibil- ies of the president in his absence from the bank or inability to act.

Administrative Vice President is an officer, appointed by the oard of directors, delegated the responsibility for coordinating e operations and functions of the various departments of the bank.

Senior Vice Presidents are appointed officers to whom are dele- ted the responsibility for supervising the activities of a particular epartment, or are assigned general overall duties and respon- bilities not directly identified with the daily operation of the bank.

Vice Presidents are officers to whom are delegated senior administrative responsibility for the operation and management of a department, or a division within such department.

Assistant Vice Presidents are officers to whom are delegated the responsibility of assisting the vice presidents.

Comptroller is an officer to whom is delegated the responsibility for maintaining the accounting system of the bank, the establishing of budgets, and the control of expenses.

Assistant Comptrollers are officers to whom are delegated th responsibility for assisting the comptroller, or assuming respon sibility for the operation of the division or section within the comp troller's department.

Cashier is an officer elected by the board of directors to whor is delegated full responsibility for operating methods and pro cedures used by the bank in conducting its business.

Assistant Cashiers are officers to whom are delegated the re sponsibility of assisting the cashier in discharging his duties an responsibilities.

Trust Officers are officers to whom are delegated the respons bility for supervising one of the divisions within the trust depar ment where the bank is acting in fiduciary capacity such as e ecutor, trustee or administrator.

Assistant Trust Officers are officers to whom are delegated th responsibility of assisting the trust officers, or are in charge of or or more of the sections within a division of the trust department.

District Managers are those to whom are delegated the respons bility for supervising one or more offices or branches of the ban This title is usually given in conjunction with the title of vi president indicating senior status.

Assistant District Managers are those to whom are delegat the responsibility of assisting the district manager and assumi his responsibilities in his absence.

Office Managers are those to whom have been given the respo sibility for the operating, loaning, and public relations activiti in the respective branch office. Generally this title is given in co nection with a title of vice president or assistant vice president dicating senior officer status.

Assistant Office Managers are those to whom are delegated t esponsibility of assisting office managers and acting in their behalf n their absence from the office.

Division Managers are those to whom are delegated the respon- ibility for the overall operation and functions performed by sec- ions within a division.

Assistant Division Managers are those to whom are delegated he responsibility of assisting division managers in performing their uties and responsibilities.

Section Managers are those held responsible by and reporting o the division manager on the operations within a section.

Assistant Section Managers are those who assist the manager in erforming the functions of his office.

Pro-Cashier is a person authorized by the board of directors to gn official checks, letters and other documents on behalf of the ank.

Another group of administrative personnel are those employed the auditing department. This group differs from the other ad- inistrative personnel in that the auditor and his assistants are nployed by, and responsible to, the board of directors to audit nd examine the affairs of the bank on behalf of the board of irectors as provided for under the banking laws; and to execute ch audit program or internal control system in accordance with e routine and procedure established and approved by the board directors. The titles and responsibilities of personnel of the diting department are:

Auditor. A person selected by, and held responsible to, the ard of directors to audit and examine the affairs of the bank; d to periodically report to them on the condition of the financial airs of the bank as disclosed through his procedures.

Assistant Auditors are those selected by the board of directors act as assistant to the auditor, and undertake certain aspects of dit examination and control responsibility as delegated by the ditor.

Audit Clerks are those designated by the auditor or his assistants perform certain routine audit and control functions.

In addition to administrative personnel and those to whom are legated the audit and control responsibilities (which in the small- banks is sometimes assumed by the directors themselves), it is necessary for banks to employ many other people in clerical positions, depending of course on the size of the bank, to provide services for customers and handle the many details of everyday operations.

These various positions, together with a brief description of the functions, duties and responsibilities of each position, are herewith listed in alphabetical order, for reference purposes.

In studying this list we should not be awed by the number of positions, which covers the maximum number of positions, only found in the largest banks. It is well to remember, however, in order to obtain a firm idea of the important functions which banks perform, that the functions which we will describe are performed each day in even the smallest bank in the country, whose personne sometimes consist of only the cashier and one clerk or bookkeeper

Analysis Clerk is one who records the number of checks deposited, checks drawn and other services performed by the bank in behalf of a checking account customer; computes the total cos of services, determines the income from the balance maintained by the customer which the bank has had available to invest, and th net profit or loss of the account.

Addressograph Operator is one who prepares addressograp plates or stencils and operates an addressograph or duplicatin machine on which such plates, which carry the name and addres and other pertinent information on an individual, are transcribe onto envelopes or other bank forms.

Check Filer is one who sorts and files checks alphabetically numerically, whichever is called for under the system being follow ed, or files the checks of checking account customers which hav been paid and posted by the bookkeeping department pendin return to the customer.

Check Sorter is one who sorts out the batches of checks, eith by number or alphabetically, for the convenience of the machin operator in posting the items to the respective accounts.

Clearing Clerk is one who sorts out checks according to th banks on which they are drawn, and prepares them for present tion to the other local banks in town for collection and payme It also refers to the one who actually makes the exchange of chec with other banks in town, or banks which are members of th

Clearing House Association and effects the settlement.

Collateral Clerk is one who writes up, in the collateral register, he description of stocks, bonds, trust deeds, and other negotiable nstruments or securities, pledged with the bank as collateral security for a loan.

Collateral Teller is one who accepts stocks, bonds, and other ecurities pledged as collateral for a loan; examines them to be certain they are in good delivery order and issues the bank's receipt videncing the fact that the securities are in the bank's possession.

The Collateral Teller also delivers securities to the borrower pon proper receipt.

Collection Clerk is one who writes up and indexes in the collection register all drafts, checks, securities, etc., received from ustomers of the bank which the bank is to present to the maker r person on which the collection item is drawn; or on drafts, securities and other items sent by another bank, which are to be presented for payment to a customer or other person residing in the rea.

Collection Teller is one who accepts all items presented by customers for collection through the bank, issuing the bank's receipt fter being certain all items and documents are in proper order; nd who delivers documents or securities upon payment and makes roper remittance to the bank or person for whom the item has een handled.

Collector is one who has the responsibility for contacting, personally or by telephone, borrowers who are delinquent in their an payments.

Commercial Bookkeeper is one who posts all credits, and checks hich have been properly drawn, against the balance to the credit the depositor, who maintains a checking account.

Commercial Loan Bookkeeper is one who posts new loans and yments to the account of a borrower in the commercial loan bility ledger.

Commercial Loan Clerk is one who prepares and sends out tices when a loan matures, and handles the clerical details in nnection with commercial loans.

Commercial Loan Teller is one who handles all details of loan nsactions at the window. After being certain that all documents are in proper order he disperses the proceeds in accordance with instructions of the loaning officer, either by a check or by crediting the proceeds to an account.

Credit Correspondent is one who has the responsibility for prop- erly answering all credit inquiries concerning the credit standing of a customer of the bank.

Credit File Clerk is one who is in charge of filing and indexing all information in the credit files.

Credit Investigator is one who has the responsibility for check ing through business or trade channels on the credit extended; an records of payment for customers of the bank who have applie for a loan. Credit investigators also check on the character, an general reputation of people who have applied for a loan or wh are the subject of a credit investigation.

Credit Analyst is one who analyzes the financial informatio either supplied to the bank by the person who has applied for loan, or which has been prepared by a credit investigator, to dete mine the financial responsibility of the applicant. A credit analys prepares all the financial information for the loaning officer t enable him to reach a decision as to the extension of credit.

Draft or Check Teller is one who exchanges funds presented b a customer or others, either cash or a check, for a draft issued b the bank drawn on one of its correspondents; or for a cashier check, money order or other official check used by the bank.

Draft Clerk is one who handles the recording, and makes u drafts or checks issued by the bank.

File Clerk is one who performs functions in connection wi filing of letters, checks, documents.

Foreign Exchange Clerk is one who maintains records, prepar all documents and performs the clerical work in connection wi the issuance of foreign drafts, letters of credit, and travelers check

Foreign Exchange Teller is one who issues foreign drafts, tra elers checks, letters of credit; and handles all details in connecti with exchanging United States currency or credits, for foreign cu rency or credits.

General Ledger Bookkeeper is one who posts all debits a credits, reflecting business transactions of the bank, to the Gene Ledger and subsidiary ledgers.

Guards are employees of the bank generally with police powers. 't is their principal responsibility to provide protection to cash, :urrency, and negotiable instruments in possession of customers vhile they are in the bank, and protect tellers and others who have ash and securities in their possession, against holdups and robbery. n addition, floor guards have the responsibility of directing traffic, nd answering inquiries.

Vault guards, who also may act as vault attendants, have the esponsibility of providing protection to renters of boxes while they re engaged in depositing or removing things from their safe deosit boxes.

Messenger guards have responsibility of providing protection messengers while they are transporting currency or negotiable istruments from one bank to the other or from one department ithin the bank to another department.

Head Teller is one who has control over the surplus cash of the ank and has the responsibility of seeing that all tellers are proided with adequate amounts of currency and silver to properly ke care of the needs of their customers.

Information Clerk is an employee, usually neat appearing and ssessing a pleasant personality, located in the public space, who swers inquiries on services or the locations of certain individuals departments for customers and others.

Installment Loan Bookkeeper is one who posts new loans and yments to the installment loan liability ledger.

Installment Loan Clerk is the one who prepares all papers in nnection with the installment loan, such as a coupon book, liality card, addressograph plates and the mailing thereto of the upon book to the borrower after the funds have been dispersed.

Installment Loan Interviewer is one who reviews the application r a loan as prepared by a prospective borrower, discusses the ason or purpose for which the loan is to be made, obtains all her necessary information, and turns the file over to a loaning icer who, after review, determines if the loan will be made and e terms for repayment.

Installment Loan Teller is one who reviews the note, determines ether it is correctly signed and in order, and disburses the proeds in accordance with instructions of the loaning officer. In addition, the teller also accepts payments from the borrower which are credited to the customer's account in the liability ledger.

Investment Clerk is one who has the responsibility for maintaining records in connection with the bank's investment account such as the bond ledger, and maturity tickler files. In addition this clerk periodically determines the market value of such securities and prepares or assists in the preparation of the periodical report which goes to the directors for review.

Machine Operators are those specially trained to operate standard type machines such as comptometers, adding machines, proof bookkeeping and accounting machines.

Mail Clerk is one responsible for distributing all incoming mail to the addressees; and seeing to it that all outgoing mail is properly sealed, has the proper amount of postage affixed and is delivered to the Post Office.

Mail Deposit Teller is one to whom are delivered all deposits made by customers to their accounts through the mail. The teller processes the checks and deposits, and returns a receipt, together with another mail envelope to the depositor.

Messenger is one who has a responsibility for delivering checks and documents, between departments of the bank; or between banks in the same town; or of acting in behalf of the bank in directly presenting collection items to customers or others in the area, on whom the items are drawn, for collection and payment.

Microfilm Operator is one who reproduces or photographs checks, documents, and letters. In addition, such a person also generally operates multigraph and duplicating equipment.

Mortgage Loan Bookkeeper is one who posts new loans and payments to the mortgage loan liability ledger.

Mortgage Clerk is one who handles all the details in connection with mortgage loans, such as the preparation of notices of principal and interest which are due, and the checking on payment of tax bills and insurance premiums.

Mortgage Loan Teller is one who determines that mortgage notes are properly signed, are accompanied by proper supporting papers, disburses the proceeds in accordance with instructions of the loaning officer, and accepts payments from the borrower, issuing the bank's receipt therefor.

Pages are usually trainees, or beginners in the bank, whose principal duties are in connection with carrying messages or running errands within the bank for officers, and learning the operation of certain machines or functions of certain positions.

Paying Teller is one who pays out currency and coin on presentation of a check properly signed, drawn against funds on deposit in the bank, payable to persons who are properly known who have endorsed the check; or pays out currency and coin on checks drawn on other banks, presented by customers or others, upon proper identification and approval by an officer.

Personnel Clerk is one who maintains all employee records and assists in preparation of the payroll.

Personnel Interviewer is one who interviews applicants for positions and obtains information as to the person's background, experience and other information for use of the personnel officer, in hiring the applicant as an employee of the bank.

Proof Clerk is one who scrutinizes each deposit before it is processed to determine if the checks so deposited are properly endorsed and who indicates on the deposit slip, for the information of the bookkeeper, information on checks drawn on banks located in other cities so that payment will not be made against such funds until they have been collected.

Proof Operator is one who sorts out checks to respective banks and adds the total of the items listed on the deposit slip, to be certain (prove) the totals of all checks agree with the amount as shown on the deposit slip.

Rack Clerk is one who, after deposits have been proven, sorts the items to respective banks on which drawn; or in connection with items which are drawn on his own bank, sorts the checks to respective bookkeeping sections.

Receiving Teller is one who accepts checks, currency, silver from customers who maintain checking accounts for credit to their account and issues the bank's receipt therefor.

Receptionist is one who greets visitors, presents their name to the officer whom they wish to see, and provides them with books, magazines, or newspapers to make them comfortable while they are waiting to see the officer on whom they have called.

Safe Deposit Attendant is one who assists the renter of a safe deposit box in removing the box from the vault and replacing it when he has finished using it.

Safe Deposit Clerk is one who determines that the person who presents the key is authorized to have access to the box and handles all the clerical details in connection with the renting of new boxes, the sending of notices and collection of rents.

Safekeeping Clerk is one who has responsibility for indexing all items left for safekeeping in the proper bank records and to place them under proper vault control.

Safekeeping Teller is one who accepts stocks, bonds, securities and other documents for safekeeping, being sure they are in proper order, and conform to the regulations of the bank in carrying such items in safekeeping, and issues the bank's receipt for same. The safekeeping teller also releases such securities or documents upon proper identification and return of the receipt properly endorsed.

Savings Bond Teller is one who issues United States Savings Bonds to customers, or accepts orders for such United States Savings Bonds as are only issued by the Federal Reserve banks.

Savings Teller is one who accepts currency and checks for credit to a person who maintains a savings account, issuing the bank's receipt; or who pays out currency or coin to the depositor upon receipt of a properly filled out and signed savings withdrawal slip, and presentation of the pass book.

Secretary is one who in addition to being proficient in the taking of shorthand and typing, performs services of a personal nature for her employer, such as placing telephone calls, arranging his appointment schedule, and assisting him in carrying out the duties and responsibilities of his position.

Signature Payer is one who reviews signatures on all checks presented for payment and determines that the signatures are authentic and provided for by signature cards, resolutions, or other documents pertaining to withdrawing funds from the account.

Statement Clerk is one who prepares statements and cancelled checks for delivery to customers. A statement clerk also refers to a person in the trust department who periodically prepares a statement of the trust accounts showing the stocks, bonds and other securities held in the trust by description, par or market value, and income collected which has been paid or dispersed.

Stenographer is one who is proficient in the taking of shorthand and the operation of a typewriter.

Stop-Payment Clerk is one who accepts stop-payment orders on checks issued by customers which have been lost, stolen or fraudulently obtained. This clerk notifies the bookkeeping department and the paying tellers to be on notice and not cash such checks when presented or pay such checks against the account.

Transit Clerk is one who sends the checks drawn on banks outside of the city in which the bank is located, to either a correspondent bank, Federal Reserve bank or direct to the bank on which the items are drawn for collection and payment.

Transit Operator is one who types up and prepares the collection letter which accompanies the checks drawn on banks located out of the city. Such checks are usually listed by the number of the bank on which drawn, name of the payer, amount and endorser.

Trust Bookkeeper is one who records all transactions affecting trust accounts.

Trust Clerk is one who handles all the details in connection with a trust account such as clipping coupons, sending them out for collection, and seeing to it that dividends and other income is credited to the account.

Typist is one who is proficient in the use of the typewriter and functions in connection with indexing information on forms and registers, or in typing up documents for the bank's use.

This, in brief, describes the duties and responsibilities of employees holding the various positions in a bank.

Generally, in a well organized bank, job descriptions, which we shall cover later, covering the functions performed, and duties and responsibilities of each position, are developed by management to provide guidance for employees in performing the functions of the particular job or position to which they are assigned. Thus the particular functions and duties and responsibilities of each position are clearly defined and operating methods and procedures are more efficiently executed.

CHAPTER XII

BANK ORGANIZATION AND MANAGEMENT

SUCCESSFUL AND PROFITABLE BANKING depends on two principal factors:

A. The manner in which the functions of banking, that is the acquiring of deposits, the investing or converting such deposits into earning assets, and the servicing of such deposits, are performed.

B. The degree to which officers and employees contribute their talents to the progress and welfare of the bank in discharging their duties and responsibilities.

To assist officers and employees to function as a team in discharging such duties and responsibilities, four management tools are available for use by progressive bankers:

1. Organizational Plans and Functional Charts.
2. Job Descriptions.
3. Standard Procedures.
4. Operating Instructions.

Before we study these tools of management and learn how they contribute to profitable banking, it might be well to point out that every bank from an "acquiring of deposits" standpoint is composed of five major operating departments, and from a "converting such funds into earnings assets" and "servicing such deposits" standpoint are reclassified into a number of functional departments and divisions.

The major operating departments of a bank are:

A. The Commercial Department, whose activities are in connection with the servicing of customers who maintain funds on deposit subject to check, and the providing of general banking services and facilities.

B. Savings Department, whose activities are in connection with the servicing of customers who maintain funds on deposit at interest, subject to withdrawal upon notice.

C. The Trust Department, whose activities are in connection with the servicing, investing and managing of funds and property of others where the bank acts in a fiduciary capacity.

D. The Safe Deposit Department, whose activities are in connection with providing a safe and convenient place for people to keep their securities, valuable papers and jewelry.

E. The Capital Department, whose activities are in connection with the providing of capital, acquiring of deposits and general direction and operation of the bank.

The functional departments and divisions of a bank, while varying in number as between banks, are always set up for the purpose of indicating where, or the place where, the operations are performed or methods and procedures undertaken in connection with the:

a. Investment of funds in Commercial Loans.

b. Investment of funds in Consumer Credit Loans.

c. Investment of funds in Mortgage Loans.

d. Investment of funds in obligations of the U. S. Government.

e. Investment of funds in other types of securities.

f. Operations of departments and divisions of the bank.

h. Maintenance of control over expenses of the bank.

i Acquiring of new business for the bank.

j. Conservation of present business of the bank.

k. Maintenance of control over assets of the bank.

While technically these functions apply to *each* of the major departments of the bank, from a practical standpoint they are not only often combined but, depending on the size of the bank, are included in one or more departments.

The tool of management through which lines of authority and responsibility between administrative personnel are shown is the Organization Plan, accompanied by a Functional Chart.

An Organization Plan is a formal program through which duties and responsibilities of stockholders, directors and administrative personnel, as delegated by the stockholders and directors, are outlined and described for the information and guidance of directors, administrative personnel and members of the staff in performing the functions of their respective positions.

Such a program is set up not only to provide all personnel with a thorough knowledge of their functional responsibility and to set up lines of authority from a supervisory standpoint, but also to provide a vehicle through which policies and operating functions can be coordinated.

A Functional Chart, on the other hand, is a vehicle through which functional lines of authority and responsibility, as described in an Organization Plan, are charted and set up for visual reference purposes.

In setting up an Organization Plan it is necessary to first:

1. Analyze the various departments of a bank and break down their functions into respective divisions within the departments.

2. Analyze the functions of the various divisions and break down the divisional functions into respective sections.

3. Analyze the various sections and break down their functions into respective jobs and positions.

4. Describe, for the information and guidance of the staff, the principal functions of each department, division and section.

5. Determine the respective duties and responsibilities of those in charge of their respective departments, divisions and sections; their lines of authority; and to whom they report and are held responsible by for the operations and personnel within their department, division or section.

Let it be said that the most effective and workable Organization Plans are those which are developed only after searching analysis has been made of administrative personnel and selections made to assume administrative responsibilities, based on the qualifications for discharging such duties and responsibilities as determined through personnel evaluation, and as described through job descriptions. This is because such analysis, if properly and conscientiously undertaken, succeeds in utlizing the best qualifications and abilities of each individual in the job for which he is best fitted. In other words, it is the process by which square pegs are taken out of round holes.

In order to illustrate how principles of management can be effectively placed into operation through an Organization Plan and Functional Chart, let us illustrate a typical Organization Plan and Chart, after the analysis and investigation has been completed and it is set up in final form for use and guidance of administrative personnel and members of the staff.

To be most effective an Organization Plan and Functional Chart similar to the following, when distributed to directors, officers, and heads of divisions and sections, for reference purposes should be accompanied by a letter similar to Exhibit 5, which outlines the purpose for which the Plan was set up and objectives to be accomplished.

Because it is the intention that this book be used not only to provide general information on banking but as a textbook for training purposes, special care was used to avoid duplicating of text and material wherever practical.

In this connection to illustrate the working and purpose of the Organization Plan, while general description of the principal functions of departments and divisions are included, the details in connection with the functions and operation of sections within divisions are omitted except by reference. This has been done because details in connection with operating methods and procedures are later included in respective chapters which outline the functions of the various departments, divisions and sections of the bank.

DUTIES AND RESPONSIBILITIES OF STOCKHOLDERS AND BOARD OF DIRECTORS

STOCKHOLDERS

The ownership of (Name of Bank) is vested in the Stockholders, who, at their regular general meeting held on the (Day) in (Month) each year, elect (Number) of their group as Directors, known as the Board of Directors, to represent them in the management of the bank.

The Stockholders, under the By-Laws, delegate to the Directors and administrative personnel certain specific functions and responsibilities, reserving to themselves the exclusive powers of:

1. Amending the By-Laws;
2. Amending the Articles of Incorporation;
3. Increasing or decreasing the Capital Stock of the Bank;

4. Approving the minutes of the previous annual or special meeting of Stockholders;

5. Discussing, considering, approving or disapproving, any other matters which the Chairman of the Board or the President,

Exhibit 5

(Name of Bank)

(Date)

TO: Directors, Officers and
Administrative Personnel:

During the last several months, as you know, a program has been undertaken through which our organization has been reviewed, operations observed, and present duties and responsibilities of administrative and operating personnel analyzed.

This was undertaken because the directors and senior officers were not only conscious of the need to solve certain organizational and operating problems brought about by the rapid growth of the bank, but by the recognized advisability, if the bank is to continue to progress, of having a management plan to follow which would:

1. Permit administrative officers to have time for over-all planning.

2. Provide operating personnel with a thorough knowledge of their functional responsibility.

These objectives have now been formalized in an Organization Plan and Functional Chart, a copy of which is attached for your information, which sets forth the flow of responsibility and outlines the functions and authority of committees and of administrative and operating personnel. So that personnel, under your supervision, may be informed on the program, it is suggested you review all parts of the plan which pertain to your respective department, division or section with them as soon as possible.

While it is understood that it will take several months to effectively place the entire plan into operation, it is the hope of your Directors that when all phases of the Organization Plan are adopted, mutual understanding and cooperation will be increased, greater responsibility be assumed, and the future growth of (Name of Bank) be assured.

Should you have any questions in connection with the operation of the Plan, we shall be pleased to discuss them with you at a mutually convenient time.

Very truly yours,

Chairman President

or the Board of Directors, might consider advisable, in the interest of the Stockholders, to bring to their attention;

6. Examining and approving or disapproving the operations of the bank for the year ending, as disclosed through the annual report, books of account and other records submitted for their attention;

7. Approving the tentative budget for the ensuing year as presented by the President;

8. Electing the Board of Directors;

9. Delegating to the Board of Directors the authority to distribute earnings as dividends as circumstances may dictate.

Stockholders meetings may also be called at any other time of the year on (Number of Days) notice provided: it is so ordered by (Titles of those authorized), a majority of the Board of Directors, or solicited by Stockholders representing one third of the outstanding Capital stock. In calling for such a meeting, notice shall be given to each Stockholder by the Secretary at least (Number) days prior to the date set for the meeting.

Exhibit 6

BANK FUNCTIONAL CHART

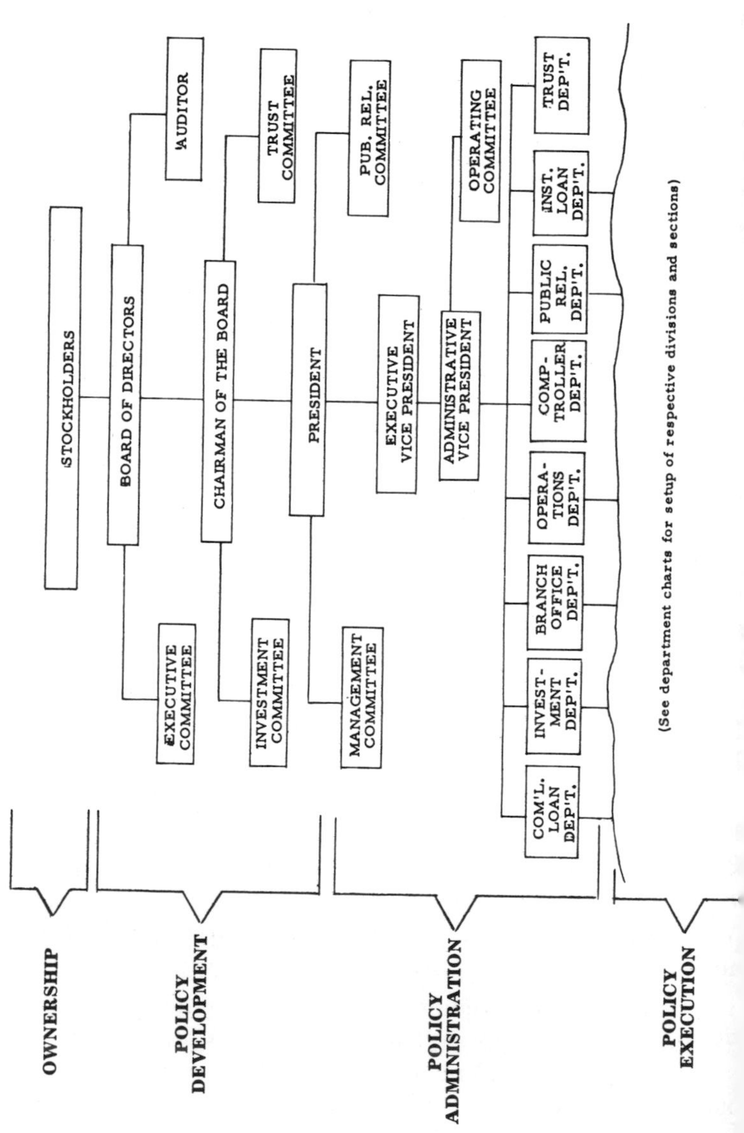

BOARD OF DIRECTORS

The Board of Directors is held responsible by the Stockholders for the management of the bank. Because of the scope of responsibility and detail of management involved, they usually delegate some of the responsibility. Generally, following the Stockholders meeting and their election, the Directors:

1. Elect one of their members as Chairman of the Board and delegate to him the responsibility of presiding at the meetings of the Board of Directors, the annual meeting of Stockholders, and of acting as liaison officer between the Stockholders and the Board of Directors;

2. Elect one of their members as President and Chief Executive officer of the bank;

3. Elect, from among the members of the Board, three or more Directors, including the Chairman of the Board and President, to act as the Executive Committee, and elect one of such members, as Chairman;

4. Elect, upon the recommendation of the Chairman, and President, a Cashier to whom is delegated the responsibility for the overall operations of the bank;

5. Elect a Secretary, to whom is delegated the responsibility for maintaining all corporate records of the bank, the corporate seal, and for recording all action taken by the Board of Directors and Executive Committee;

6. Appoint, by and with the consent of the Chairman and the President, the membership of the various committees which may be set up for the administration of the affairs of the bank;

7. Appoint, upon the recommendation of the Chairman or President, Senior and Junior Officers, to whom are delegated by the President or Board of Directors the responsibility for supervising certain operating and financial functions of the bank;

8. Approve the compensation to be paid to the various officers and employees of the bank;

9. Approve the general assignment of duties and responsibilities of each officer as submitted by the Chairman and President;

10. Determine, approve and set forth, for the guidance of all officers, the loaning limitation of each administrative officer;

11. Approve the amount of surety bonds to be carried on each officer and employee of the bank;

12. Determine the loan and investment policy of the bank, setting forth for the guidance of administrative officers the percentage and amounts of time and demand deposits and capital funds which should be invested in the various types of loans and investments;

13. Approve and decide on all matters involving changes in the capital accounts and the distribution of earnings as dividends, in line with the authority granted by the Stockholders;

14. Approve all loans made to Directors and Officers as to amount and security;

15. Review, and approve or disapprove, the action of the various committees in carrying out their respective functions and responsibilities;

16. Authorize the maintenance of correspondent bank accounts and all borrowing arrangements with other banks;

17. See that suitable books or records of accounts are maintained and approve the form of notes and other documents.

18. Appoint an Auditor; define his duties and responsibilities, the scope of the audit routine, and the manner in which he is to report the results of his work to the Board of Directors.

FUNCTIONS OF COMMITTEES

BOARD OF DIRECTORS

While the Board of Directors has the full and complete authority to decide on all matters pertaining to the bank, it usually delegates certain functional authority and responsibility to the officers and committees such as: the Executive Committee, Investment Committee, Trust Committee, Management Committee, Operations Committee, and the Public Relations Committee.

EXECUTIVE COMMITTEE

Membership: (Number) or more directors, including, the Chairman of the Board, the President, etc., of which one is designated Chairman.

Principal functions: 1. To act as a standing committee of the Board of Directors on all matters when the Board is unable to act as a whole. The Executive Committee is considered to always be in session;

2. To review, and approve or disapprove all loan applications submitted to it, in line with policy established by the Board of Directors;

3. To determine from time to time, in line with general policy as set forth by the Board of Directors, the rates of interest for the various types of loans.

4. To determine from time to time, in line with general policy as set forth by the Board of Directors, the rate of interest to be paid on special Time and Savings Deposits;

5. To approve and authorize, or disapprove, loans and renewals of loans in excess of the loaning limitations of officers;

6. To cause an appraisal to be made at least annually on any real estate owned by the bank;

7. To cause an appraisal to be made at least annually of the bank's other assets.

INVESTMENT COMMITTEE

Membership: The Chairman of the Board as chairman, the President, the officer in charge of the Investment Department, and two non-officer Directors.

Principal functions: 1. To determine the amount and percentages of demand and time deposits and capital funds which should be invested in the various types of loans and investments.

2. To approve the purchase or sale or securities from the banks investment portfolio.

TRUST COMMITTEE

Membership: The Chairman of the Board, the President, the officer in charge of the Trust Department, and two non-officer Directors.

Principal functions: 1. To accept or reject all new accounts in which the bank is to act in fiduciary capacity.

2. To approve or disapprove the investment of all funds in trust accounts.

3. To see that the bank is performing in accordance with terms and conditions of trust indentures.

MANAGEMENT COMMITTEE

Membership: The President as chairman, the Administrative Vice President, the officers in charge of the Departments, the Comptroller, and the Auditor.

Principal functions: 1. To discuss and review any general matters in connection with the administration of the affairs of the bank and to make recommendations in connection with such matters to the Board of Directors;

2. To discuss and review, and recommend for adoption or rejection, major changes in operating routines and procedures as submitted by the Operating Committee.

OPERATING COMMITTEE

Membership: The Administrative Vice President, as chairman, the officer in charge of the Operations Department, the Comptroller, the Cashier, the Auditor, and the officers in charge of the various operating divisions.

Principal functions: 1. To review and analyze from time to time the present operating methods and procedures;

2. To review the reports made by the chairman of sub-committees appointed for the purpose of undertaking detailed studies of departmental, or sectional operations, to bring about economies or greater efficiencies in operating methods or procedures;

3. To consider and approve for reference to the Management Committee recommendations and suggestions for changes and improvements in operating methods and procedures;

4. To establish job classifications and job descriptions for each position within the bank;

5. To determine the practices and policy to be followed in the selection and training of all personnel.

PUBLIC RELATIONS COMMITTEE

Membership: The President as chairman, the officer in charge of the Public Relations Department, two non-officer directors, the Administrative Vice President.

Principal functions: 1. To determine the methods or mediums to be used in carrying out the policies and practices in connection with acquiring new business and conserving present business, as approved by the Board of Directors.

2. To develop and coordinate the advertising and publicity programs of the bank with the new business and conservation activities.

ADMINISTRATIVE RESPONSIBILITIES

Administration and Management. Over-all administration of the bank, from a functional standpoint, is centralized and vested in the Board of Directors, Executive Committee, Chairman of the Board, President, Executive Vice President, Administrative President, and the officers in charge of the:

Commercial Loan Department
Investment Department
Branch Office Department
Comptrollers Department
Public Relations Department
Consumer Loan Department
Trust Department

Policies. Policies of the bank in connection with loans, investments, public relations are recommended by the Management Committee or Executive Committee and approved by the Board of Directors.

Loans. General supervision, and the administration of all policies in connection with commercial and real estate loaning activities, is delegated to the officer in charge of the Commercial Loan Department, with active supervision and management delegated to the officers or managers of the F.H.A. II; Business Loans, and Conventional Mortgage Loans Divisions.

General supervision, and the administration of all policies in connection with automobile and consumer credit loaning activities, is delegated to the officer in charge of the Automobile and Consumer Credit Loan Department with active supervision and management delegated to the officers or managers of the Automobile, F.H.A., and Consumer Credit Loan Divisions.

Investments. All details and functions in connection with the investment of funds in U.S. Government and State and Municipal bonds are under the supervision of the officer in charge of the Investment Department, following policy as established by the Board of Directors covering the investment of funds.

Operations. All supervision pertaining to the general operations of the entire bank is under the officer in charge of the Operations Department. Detail operations in divisions and sections are supervised by officers or managers under the immediate supervision of the officer in charge of the Operations Department or his assistant.

Accounting. All accounting, reporting, and statistical operations are centralized in the Comptroller's Department under an officer who is responsible for accounting procedures to the Administrative Vice President.

Personnel. All personnel matters and personnel direction are under the general supervision of the officer in charge of the Operations Department.

Purchasing. The over-all supervision and handling of purchasing and maintenance of properties used and occupied by the bank is under the supervision of the officer in charge of the Comptroller's Department.

New Business and Conservation. All activities in connection with the obtaining of new business and the conservation of present business and customer relations are under the immediate supervision and direction of the officer in charge of the Public Relations Department.

General. The respective officers who have the responsibility for supervising the functions and administration of policies of the various departments are from an administrative standpoint the managing officers of the bank and are members of the Management Committee under the chairmanship of the President.

The respective officers who have the responsibility for supervising the details of operations in connection with accounting, personnel, departmental routines, and procedures and customer contact are from a functional standpoint the operating officers of the bank and are members of the Operating Committee under the chairmanship of the Administrative Vice President.

All administrative and operating officers and and managers are responsible to the Board of Directors through the President and or Administrative Vice President for supervision of delegated responsibilities, the enforcement of policies delegated to them for enforcement; and the rendering of decisions on all matters which come under the scope of their authority.

DUTIES AND RESPONSIBILITIES OF OFFICERS

Chairman of the Board. The Chairman of the Board is the chief administrative officer of the bank and ex officio member of all committees. It is his duty and responsibility to:

1. Maintain, together with the President, liaison between the Stockholders and the Board of Directors;
2. Maintain, together with the President, liaison between the Board of Directors and the various committees;
3. Preside at all meetings of the Board of Directors;
4. Preside at all meetings of the Executive Committee;
5. Preside at all meetings of the Stockholders;
6. See to it that the Stockholders are kept informed at all imes on affairs of the bank which concern their interest.

President. The President is the chief executive officer of the ank. He is held responsible by the Board of Directors, acting in ehalf of the Stockholders, for the active management of the bank. It is his duty and responsibility to:

1. Preside at all meetings of the Board of Directors and Excutive Committee in the absence of the Chairman;
2. See that action taken by committees and decisions made by fficers and administrative personnel are in conformance with estabshed bank policy;
3. Supervise the business and financial affairs of the bank;
4. Sign jointly with the Cashier, all documents in behalf of e bank;
5. Execute jointly with the Cashier, all notes for the purpose borrowing money for the bank, and pledging of securities as llateral when such action is authorized by the Board of Directors;
6. Delegate to the officers, the details of all duties and responbilities not specifically assigned by the By-Laws or Board of Dictors;
7. Carry out all duties and responsibilities assigned or deleted from time to time by the Board of Directors.

Executive Vice President. The Executive Vice President is the assistant to, and together with the Administrative Vice President acts in behalf of the President in his absence.

Administrative Vice President. The Administrative Vice President is the coordinating officer of the bank and liaison between th President and all the other officers.

Full responsibility for supervising the direct management o the various departments, divisions, sections and branches of th bank is vested in this officer who, in addition, has the responsibilit to see that:

1. The various departments and divisions of the bank ar coordinated in their activities.

2. General policies as set forth by the Board of Directors ar communicated to and followed by administrative personnel.

3. Action taken by administrative personnel is in accordanc with policy as established by the Board of Directors.

Senior Vice Presidents. Senior Vice Presidents are the senio appointed administrative officers. They have the responsibility fo

1. General administration as delegated by the Board of Dire tors, or President.

2. Administering policy and functions as delegated by th board of directors.

Vice Presidents. Vice Presidents are the senior appointed e ecutive officers. They have the responsibility of:

1. Supervising the various divisions of the bank, wherever a signed, from an administrative standpoint in accordance with fun tional authority and responsibility as delegated by the Board Directors, President, or Administrative Vice President.

Cashier. The Cashier is the chief operating officer of the ba and elected, according to law, by the directors. It is his respon bility to:

1. Direct and supervise all the operating and personnel fu tions of the bank, working with the Administrative Vice Preside

Comptroller. The Comptroller is the chief control officer of t bank. It is his responsibility, under direction of the Administrati Vice President, to:

1. Approve the purchasing of all stationery, supplies, furnitu fixtures and equipment.

2. Supervise the real estate, construction, maintenance and r tals of buildings and properties owned by the bank.

3. Direct the preparation of budgets of income and expenses and other statistical information required by the Board of Directors, the President, or the Administrative Vice President.

4. Supervise the general accounting of the bank and the prep-aration of reports for supervisory agencies and others which are equired by management in conducting the affairs of the bank.

Assistant Vice Presidents. Officers designated Assistant Vice Presidents are either assigned as assistants to Vice Presidents or lelegated certain responsibilities in connection with supervising or dministering one of the various divisions, sections, or offices of he bank, wherever assigned, or according to functional authority nd responsibility as delegated by the Board of Directors or the resident.

Assistant Cashiers. Assistant Cashiers are appointed by the oard of Directors to assist the Cashier in carrying out his respon-ibilities. They generally supervise the operations of the various ivisions or sections under the supervision of the Cashier.

Secretary. The Secretary is the chief recording officer of the ank. It is his duty and responsibility to:

1. Maintain all corporate records;

2. Be custodian of the corporate seal which represents the gal authority of the bank;

3. Record all official acts and decisions of the Board of Direc-rs and Executive Committee;

4. Maintain a complete and current list of Stockholders and eir addresses and to notify them of any meetings called.

Auditor. The Auditor is appointed by, and responsible to, the ard of Directors. It is his responsibility to:

1. Periodically undertake an examination or audit of the af-irs of the bank in accordance with the routine approved by the irectors.

2. Report the scope and results of such examinations or audits the Directors in the manner and form prescribed;

3. Establish, with the approval of the Cashier and Administra-e Vice President, a system of internal controls designed to safe-ard the assets of the bank and prevent embezzlements and defal-tions.

4. Examine periodically the correctness of all entries on the

Exhibit 7

COMMERCIAL LOAN DEPARTMENT

FUNCTIONAL CHART

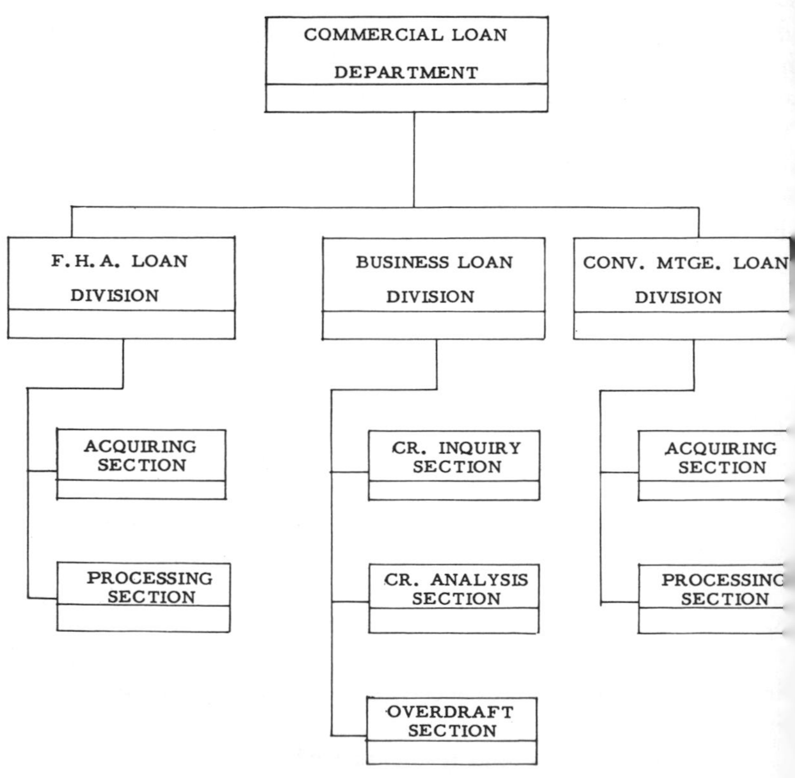

books of the bank, calling to the attention of the Directors, as may be necessary, all matters or transactions which are prejudicial to the interest of the institution, or which, in whatsoever form, may be prejudicial to the bank in its normal functioning, its credit, or its prestige.

COMMERCIAL LOAN DEPARTMENT*

Officer in Charge: ....

Principal functions are to:

1. Invest the funds of the bank in FHA II, Business, and Conventional Real Estate Mortgage Loans in accordance with policy as established by the Board of Directors;

2. Supervise the loaning activities of the respective Divisions of the Department.

In order to provide proper supervision and functional authority over the various types of loans the Department is divided into the following three Divisions, each under the immediate supervision of an officer or manager (who may be in charge of one or more Divisions).

FHA II Loan Division
Business Loan Division
Conventional Mortgage Loan Division

FHA II DIVISION

Officer in Charge: ....

Principal functions are to:

1. Invest funds of the bank in FHA Title II Real Estate Mortgage Loans in accordance with the policy established by the Board of Directors.

---

* The set-up of this department, where both mortgage loans and commercial loans are handled in the same department under the same officer, is an excellent illustration of what is meant when reference is made to an organization plan disclosing functions and lines of authority and responsibility *as they are* to serve the best interests of the bank.

Generally, in most banks, mortgage loan activities would be handled in a separate department similar to automobile installment loans. Here, however, because of factors of control, plus the management and experience of the officer in charge of the department (who is a director-executive vice president and chairman of the executive committee) all types of loans except automobile installment loans are handled in this department.

2. Supervise the activities of the Division in acquiring and processing FHA Title II Loans.

So that the division can function efficiently, it is separated into two sections, each with separate functions under the responsibility of an officer or manager responsible to the manager in charge of the division in all matters in connection with policy; and respon-sible to the officer in charge of the Operations Department or his assistant in all matters in connection with operations. These are:

Acquiring Section
Processing Section

BUSINESS LOANS DIVISION

Officer in Charge: ....

Principal functions are to:

1. Supervise and handle the investment of funds of the ban in loans to business concerns and individuals based on their finan cial position as disclosed through properly prepared financial state ments in accordance with policy as determined by the Board c Directors;

2. Supervise and handle the investment of funds of the ban in loans to business concerns and individuals against acceptabl collateral security, or pledge of assets, in accordance with polic as determined by the Board of Directors.

In order to effectively supervise the functions and respon sibilities of this division it is divided into the three following se tions, each under the supervision of a manager responsible to th officer or manager in charge of the division in all matters in co nection with policy; and responsible to the officer in charge of th Operations Department or his assistant, in all matters in connectio with operations.

Credit Inquiry Section
Credit Analysis Section
Overdraft Section

CONVENTIONAL MORTGAGE LOAN DIVISION

Officer in Charge: ....

Principal functions are to:

1. Invest funds of the bank in conventional real estate mo

Exhibit 8

INVESTMENT DEPARTMENT

FUNCTIONAL CHART

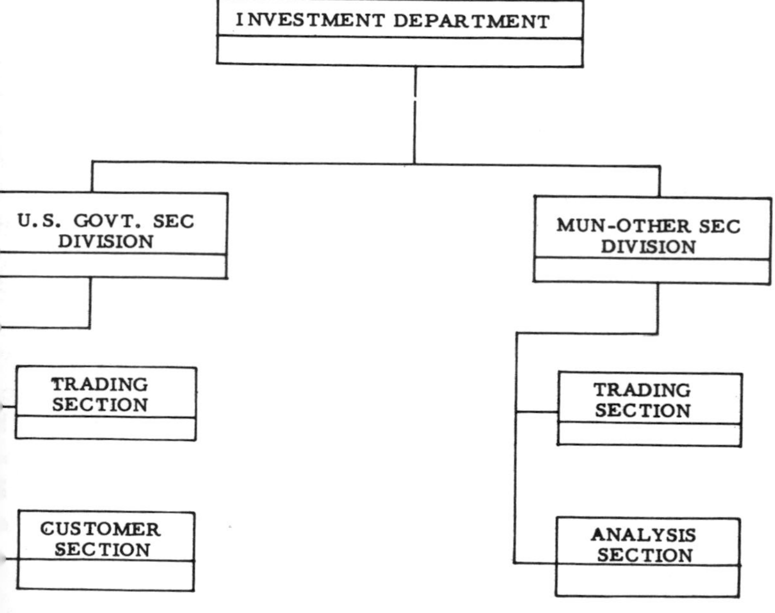

gage loans in accordance with the policy as established by the board of directors;

2. Supervise the activities of the division in acquiring and processing conventional real estate mortgage loans.

In order for the division to function efficiently, it is divided into the two following sections, each with separate functions, under the supervision of a manager responsible to the officer or manager in charge of the division in all matters in connection with policy and responsible to the officer in charge of the Operations Department, or his assistant, in all matters in connection with operations.

Acquiring Section
Processing Section

INVESTMENT DEPARTMENT

Officer in Charge: ....

Principal functions are to:

1. Invest funds of the bank in the various types of bonds and securities in accordance with the policy determined by the Executive Committee or Board of Directors, based on the vulnerability of time and demand deposits and the capital funds structure.

From a functional and policy standpoint all investments are handled in the two following divisions, each under the supervision of an officer responsible to the head of the Department. These are

U. S. Government Division
Municipal or other Securities Division

U. S. GOVERNMENT DIVISION

Officer in Charge: ....

Principal functions are to:

1. Purchase or sell, invest or reinvest, trade or exchange U. S. Government securities for the bank's account in accordance with policy established by the Board of Directors.

So that this division can function effectively, not only in connection with the bank's investment account but in connection with the investment of Trust funds in Government securities, it is separated into two sections.

Trading Section
Customers Section

MUNICIPAL OR OTHER SECURITIES DIVISION

Officer in Charge: ....

Principal functions are to:

1. Analyze the offerings of municipal bond issues, bonds of railroad, industrial and utility companies; and to purchase or sell, nvest or reinvest, trade or exchange such investments in accordance vith policy established by the Board of Directors.

So that this division can properly function, both in connection vith the bank's investment account and trust investments it is eparated into two sections.

Analysis Section
Trading Section

BRANCH OFFICE DEPARTMENT

The Branch Department has the full responsibility for superising the operations, personnel, public relations and business evelopment activities in the branch offices, through the officer in harge of such branch, under the direction of the officer in charge f the Branch Office Department under the supervision of the dministrative Vice President.

Policies, practices and programs in connection with public elations and business development activities are established at e head office by the officer in charge of Public Relations Department, and communicated to the officer in charge of the respective ranch only with the approval of the officer in charge of Branch ffice Department. Public Relations and business development tivities at each branch are under the direction of, and the reonsibility of, the officer in charge of such branch.

All purchasing, the supervision of properties, the origination d development of methods and procedures, and the accounting r the bank are the direct responsibility of the officer in charge Operations Department under the supervision of the Administrave Vice President. The responsibility for operations and execuon of established methods and procedures within each branch, owever, is vested in the head of such branch under the officer in arge of the Branch Office Department.

The hiring, firing, training of all bank personnel is the respon-

Exhibit 9

BRANCH OFFICE DEPARTMENT

FUNCTIONAL CHART

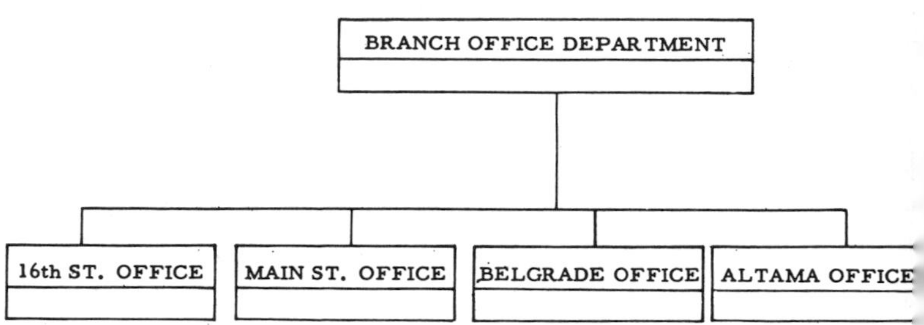

(Each office set up with divisions and sections, according to size and type of services rendered.)

ibility of the officer in charge of the Personnel Section, under he supervision of the Administrative Vice President. Direct su- ervision of personnel within each branch, however, is the respon- ibility of the officer in charge of each respective branch under the fficer in charge of the Branch Office Department.

Officer in Charge: ....

Principal functions are:

1. To approve or disapprove all instructions, programs, or ractices in connection with public relations and new business ctivities originating from the officer in charge of Public Relations epartment, directed to the officer in charge of each branch.

2. To approve or disapprove all operating instructions and irectives covering operating methods and procedures originating rom the officer in charge of the Operations Department, directed the officer in charge of respective branch.

3. To approve or disapprove directives in connection with the iring, firing, transferring of all personnel within districts, offices, nd branches, as directed by the officer in charge of respective ranches.

OPERATIONS DEPARTMENT

Officer in Charge: ....

Principal functions are to:

1. Direct all operating methods and procedures used in the rious departments, divisions, and sections of the bank.

2. Supervise all clerical personnel of the bank and assign their ities and responsibilities.

3. Direct, in conjunction with the officer in charge of the iblic Relations Department, the activities of the officers and per- nnel in their contact with the public and customers of the bank iile on the bank premises.

So that proper functional authority and responsibility can be legated, the department is divided into the following divisions, ch under the supervision of an officer or manager, who is respon- le to the officer in charge of the Operations Department.

Personnel Division

Customer Contact Division

Commercial Division
Savings Division
General Division
Research and Planning Division

PERSONNEL DIVISION

The Personnel Division, under the supervision of an officer wh directly reports to the officer in charge of the Operations Depart ment, has the full responsibility for the employing, training, an dismissal of all staff members below officer level. The employmen supervision, and dismissal of individuals at officer level is generall the responsibility of the Administrative Vice President or th President.

Officer in Charge: ....

Principal functions are to:

1. Interview, and hire all clerical personnel.

2. Develop training programs and supervise the training of a new employees.

3. Develop and maintain job classifications and descriptio covering each position within the bank.

4. Set standards covering each job or position within the ban

5. Develop and maintain an Employees Handbook for t guidance of new employees and the use and information of old employees.

6. Periodically review the performance and record of each e ployee for the purpose of rating, upgrading, salary adjustme transfer or promotion.

7. Prepare the payroll and maintain proper records in conn tion with employees.

8. Dismiss any employee whose services are no longer requ ed, or whose employment, at the discretion of the officer in cha of the Operations Department, is inimical to the best interests the bank.

In order to administer properly the functions of the divisi it is divided into the following sections, under the supervision a

Exhibit 10

OPERATIONS DEPARTMENT

FUNCTIONAL CHART

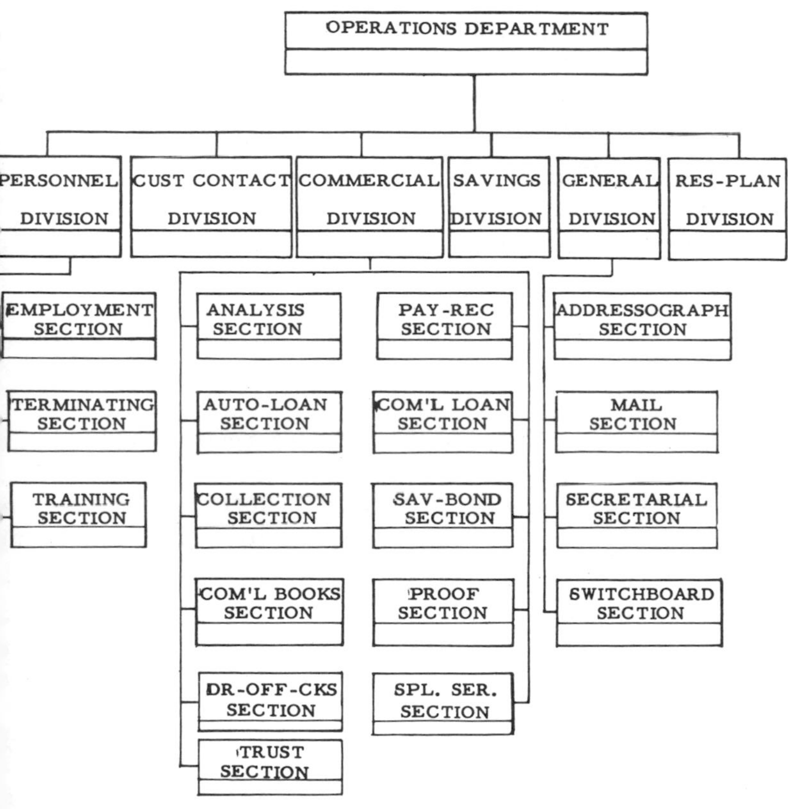

direction of an officer or manager directly responsible to the office in charge of the Personnel Division.

Employing Section
Terminating Section
Training and Supervising Section

CUSTOMER CONTACT DIVISION

The Customer Contact Division has responsibilities generall in connection with providing special services to the customers an handling individuals within the bank who intend to become cus tomers of the bank. (Except in a larger bank, these functions ar usually performed by officers in addition to other duties.)

Officer in Charge: ....

Principal functions are to:

1. Open all new commercial and other types of checking a counts.

2. Open all new savings accounts.

3. Render service to customers and non-customers in conne tion with approving checks for encashment, or exchange for U. Savings Bonds, Cashiers Checks, etc.

4. Answer inquiries and make arrangements for the use of a bank services.

5. Undertake, whenever assigned, public relations activiti in connection with the solicitation of new business or conservati of present business.

COMMERCIAL DIVISION

The Commercial Division of the Operating Department concerned with the operating methods, procedures and supervisi of personnel in sections which directly serve commercial cu tomers. Because of the large volume of items handled, and increa ed use of mechanized equipment, which requires rigid supervisi and direction, these sections are usually segregated from savin and general operations.

Officer in Charge: ....

Principal functions are to:

1. Supervise and coordinate operating methods and pro dures within the respective sections of the division.

2. Maintain liaison between the person in charge of operations n each section of the division and the officer in charge of the Operations Department, on matters of routines, procedures, sys- ems, etc.

3. Analyze existing operating methods and procedures and ake recommendations to the Operating Committee for the adop- on of new methods and procedures to increase efficiency.

In order to supervise all operations and maintain proper dis- ibution of work, the functions of the division are divided into the llowing sections, each under the immediate supervision of a man- ger, responsible to the officer in charge of the division.

Analysis Section
Auto-Consumer Loan Section
Collection Section
Commercial Bookkeeping Section
Commercial Loan Section
Draft-Official Check Section
Paying and Receiving Tellers Section
Proof Section
Savings Bond Section
Special Service Section
Trust Section

SAVINGS DIVISION

The Savings Division is concerned with the operating methods, ocedures, and supervision of personnel in connection with regular vings accounts and Time Certificates of Deposit.

Officer in Charge: ....

Principal functions are to:

1. Supervise and coordinate all operating methods and proce- res within the department, which consists of combination teller- okkeeping functions.

GENERAL DIVISION

The General Division, under the supervision of an officer re- onsible to the officer in charge of the Operations Department, is ncerned with the operating methods and procedures, and supervision of personnel of the various sections which serve other section or which serve the bank as a whole.

Officer in Charge: ....

Principal functions are to:

1. See that all sections of the bank are properly serviced.

In order to supervise all operations and maintain proper dis tribution of work, the functions of this division are divided into th following sections, each under the immediate supervision of a ma ager who is responsible to the officer in charge of the division.

- Addressograph Section
- Mail Section
- Secretarial Section
- Switchboard Section
- Police and Guard Section
- Parking Lot Section
- Safe Deposit Company Section (unless it is a wholly-owned subsidiary)

RESEARCH AND PLANNING DIVISION

Officer in Charge: ....

Principal responsibilities are to:

1. Undertake, under the supervision and direction of the offic in charge of the Operations Department, investigations, analysis a studies of present operating methods, systems, and procedures f the purpose of recommending changes which will result in incre ed efficiency or reduction of expense.

2. Undertake, under the supervision and direction of the offic in charge of the Operations Department, investigation of new c erating methods and procedures developed and used by other bar for the purpose of determining if the adoption of such new metho and procedures will contribute to increased efficiency or reducti of expense.

COMPTROLLERS DEPARTMENT

Officer in Charge: ....

Principal functions are to:

1. Direct and approve the purchasing of stationery suppli

Exhibit 11

COMPTROLLERS DEPARTMENT
FUNCTIONAL CHART

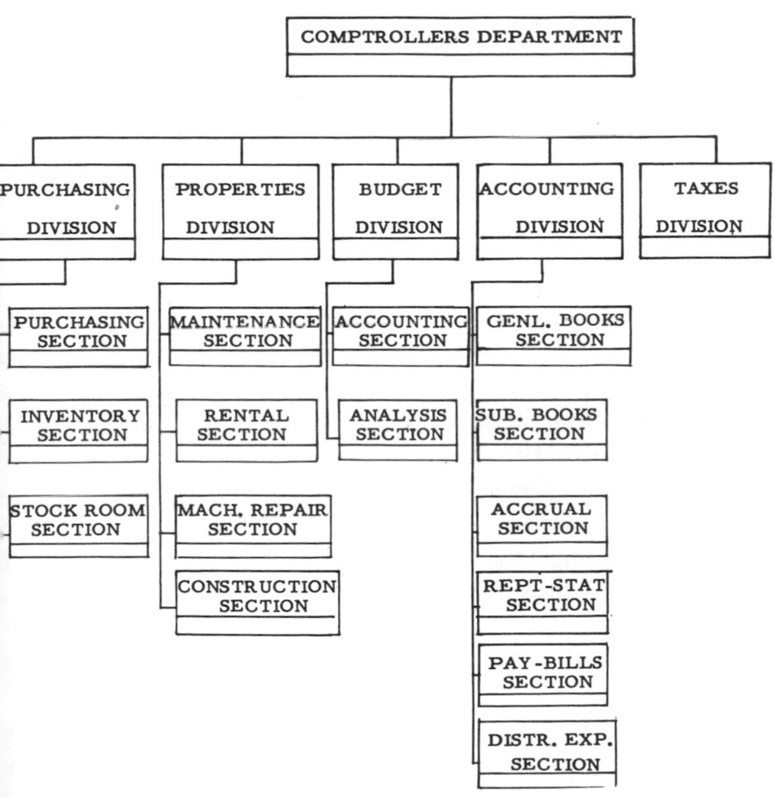

machinery, and equipment for the departments, divisions, sections and branches of the bank.

2. Supervise the maintenance of properties owned, leased, or used by the bank in its operations.

3. Supervise all accounting functions of departments, divisions, sections and branches through the officer in such department, division, section or branch charged with accounting responsibility.

4. Supervise the development and application of the cost system and to develop departmental, district, office and branch costs of operation and functional or unit costs, within such groups, for the information and guidance of the Administrative Vice President.

5. Prepare all reports required by the federal or municipal governments or instrumentalities.

6. Prepare all budgets and internal reports in connection with departmental, divisional and branch cost distribution, profit or loss and activity; and review and analyze such reports with the Administrative Vice President.

In order to maintain proper supervision and direction, the department is divided into the following divisions, each under the immediate supervision of an officer responsible to the officer in charge of the Comptrollers Department.

Purchasing Division
Properties Division
Budget Division
Accounting Division
Tax and Insurance Division

PURCHASING DIVISION

Officer in Charge: ....

Principal functions are:

1. To place purchase orders for all stationery, forms, office supplies, machinery and equipment.

2. To maintain perpetual inventory control of all stationery, supplies, and forms.

3. To supervise the delivery of stationery, forms, and supplies to the various offices and departments, divisions and sections upon receipt of requisitions.

In order to supervise properly all functions, the division is divi-ed into the following sections, each under a manager responsible to the officer in charge of the division.

Purchasing Section
Inventory Control Section
Stock Room Section

PROPERTIES DIVISION

Officer in Charge: ....

Principal functions are to:

1. See that all real estate, buildings, and properties owned, operated or leased by the bank are properly maintained as to cleaning, repairs, janitor service, etc.

2. Handle all matters in connection with the rental of properties, owned by the bank, to others.

3. See that all machinery, equipment, furniture and fixtures owned or leased by the bank, are kept in repair and efficient working order.

4. Supervise all matters in connection with remodeling or new construction of properties owned by the bank.

In order to fix responsibility and properly supervise all functions, the division is divided into the following sections each under a manager responsible to the officer in charge of the division.

Maintenance (janitors) Section
Rental Section
Machinery-Repair Section
Construction Section

BUDGET DIVISION

Officer in Charge: ....

Principal functions are to:

1. Prepare the annual budget of income and expense for submission to the officer in charge of Comptrollers Department and Administrative Vice President.

2. Check and compare actual expenditures and income received with the budget figures and to report to the officer in charge of the Comptrollers Department and Administrative Vice President, on current status.

In order to fix responsibility and properly supervise all functions, this division is divided into the following sections, each under the direct supervision of a manager responsible to the officer in charge of the division.

Accounting and Distributing Section
Analysis Section

ACCOUNTING DIVISION

Officer in Charge: ....

Principal functions are to:

1. Maintain the general books and other records of the bank.
2. Maintain the records of income and expenses of the departments, divisions and branches of the bank.
3. Supervise and maintain the accrual system operated by departments, divisions and branches of the bank.
4. Prepare the daily Statements of Condition.
5. Prepare the periodical consolidated reports, as required for the directors or management of the bank.
6. Complete and furnish all reports required by the supervising authorities.
7. Pay all bills for expenses incurred in the operation of the bank.

In order to properly supervise all functions, and effect economies in operation, the division is separated into the following sec tions each under the supervision of a manager responsible to the officer in charge of the division.

General Books Section
Subsidiary Books Section
Accrual Section
Reports and Statistics Section
Payment of Bills Section
Distribution of Expense Section

TAX AND INSURANCE DIVISION

Officer in charge: ....

Principle functions are to:

1. See that all buildings, properties, furniture, fixtures, ma chinery and equipment owned, leased or used by the bank are prop erly covered by respective types of insurance.

Exhibit 12

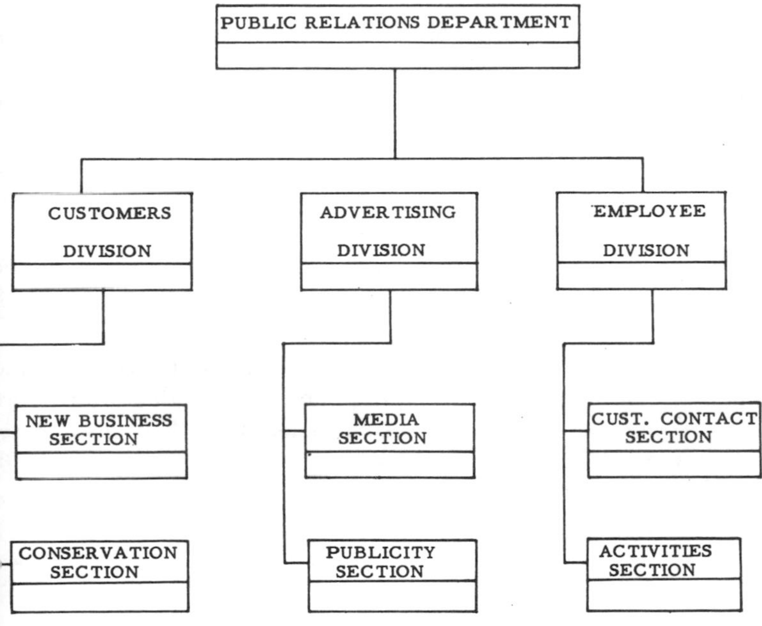
PUBLIC RELATIONS DEPARTMENT
FUNCTIONAL CHART
PUBLIC RELATIONS DEPARTMENT
CUSTOMERS DIVISION
ADVERTISING DIVISION
EMPLOYEE DIVISION
NEW BUSINESS SECTION
MEDIA SECTION
CUST. CONTACT SECTION
CONSERVATION SECTION
PUBLICITY SECTION
ACTIVITIES SECTION

2. See that the bank is protected by having all types of insurance in connection with public liability, fire, theft and exposure.

3. Maintain whatever records are required and prepare the various tax returns required by Federal or State governments.

PUBLIC RELATIONS DEPARTMENT

Officer in charge: ....

Principle functions are to:

1. Direct the activities of officers and employees in soliciting new business.

2. Direct the activities of officers and employees in conserving present business.

3. Execute, in accordance with policy as established by the Public Relations Committee, all programs in connection with advertising the services of the bank.

4. See that all publicity in connection with activities of the bank, its officers or employees is presented in a manner whicl favorably reflects the bank.

In order to obtain the best results from these activities anc exercise proper supervision, the functions of this department ar separated into the following divisions, each with their distinct re sponsibilities under the administration of an officer responsible t the officer in charge of the Public Relations Department:

Customer Division
Employee Division
Advertising Division

CUSTOMER DIVISION

Officer in charge: ....

Principle functions are to:

1. Develop and maintain a list of customers, who have need o or who should be prevailed upon to use, additional services of th bank.

2. Develop and maintain a list of the larger and more importa customers of the bank who should be cultivated through occasion calls or contacts.

3. Develop and maintain a list of the more important peop

or businesses in the service area of the bank, who should be contacted or solicited to do business with the bank.

4. Maintain a Central File, which discloses each service used, or the relationship maintained, by each and every customer of the bank.

As certain functions of this department are distinct and require certain or special administrations, the department is separated into the following sections, each under the direction of a manager to whom is assigned specific responsibilities:

New Business Section
Conservation Section

EMPLOYEE DIVISION

Officer in charge: ....

Principle functions are to:

1. Direct and supervise the attitudes, appearances, and the communicating practices of all personnel in their contact with the public and customers within the premises of the bank.

2. See that suggestions made by personnel through the Suggestion Box are directed to the proper parties, and that satisfactory acknowledgement and recognition is given to all personnel submitting suggestions.

So that proper supervision can be exercised over the functions of this division, it is separated into the following sections, each under the direction of a manager responsible to the officer in charge of the division:

Activities Section
Customer Contact Section

ADVERTISING DIVISION

Officer in charge: ....

Principle functions are to:

1. Direct, so as to reflect a favorable image of the bank, all publicity in connection with the activities of the bank, and happenings about, or to, directors, officers and employees.

2. Develop and prepare for submission and approval by the Public Relations Committee, or President, the overall advertising program, covering the use of all types of media such as newspapers,

radio, statement insertion pieces, direct mail, billboards, "give aways" and other types of advertising used by the bank.

To properly supervise and coordinate the respective activities and avoid conflict with the agency through which advertising is placed, the division is separated into two sections, each under the direction of an officer responsible to the officer in charge of the division:

Advertising Media Section

Publicity Section

AUTOMOBILE AND CONSUMER CREDIT LOAN DEPARTMENT

Officer in charge: ....

Principle functions are to:

1. Invest the funds of the bank in FHA I and Home Improvement, Automobile, and Consumer Credit Loans, repayable in monthly installments, in accordance with policy as established by the Board of Directors.

2. Supervise the loaning activities of the respective divisions of the departments.

In order to establish functional authority, and provide proper supervision over the various types of loans the department is divided into the following divisions, each under the immediate supervision of an officer or manager (who may be in charge of more than one department):

Automobile Loan Division

FHA I and Home Improvement Loan Division

Consumer Credit Loan Division

AUTOMOBILE DIVISION

Officer in charge: ....

Principle functions are to:

1. Invest funds of the bank, either on a recourse or non recourse basis, in loans on new and used automobiles.

2. Invest funds of the bank in direct loans to individuals on new and used automobiles.

Exhibit 13

AUTO - CONSUMER CREDIT DEPARTMENT
FUNCTIONAL CHART

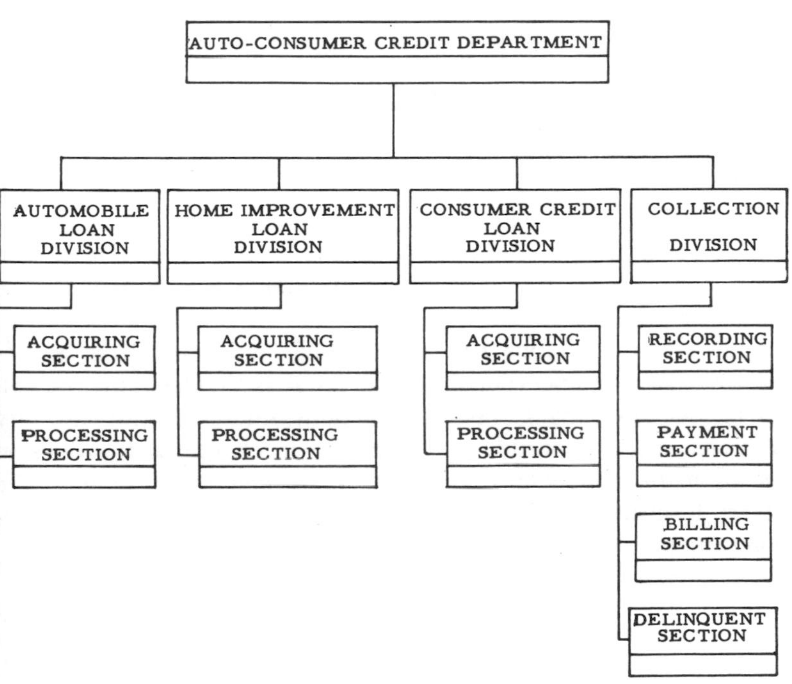

So that the division can function efficiently both from an administrative and operational standpoint it is divided into the following sections having separate functions, under the responsibility of a manager responsible to the officer in charge of the division in all matters in connection with policy, and responsible to the officer in charge of the Operations Department on all matters in connection with operations:

Acquiring Section
Processing Section

FHA TITLE I AND HOME IMPROVEMENT LOAN DIVISION

Officer in charge: ....

Principle functions are to:

1. Invest funds of the bank in FHA Title I and Home Improvement Loans in accordance with policy established by the Board of Directors.

So that the division can function efficiently both from an administrative and operational standpoint it is divided into the following sections having separate functions, under the responsibility of a manager responsible to the officer in charge of the division on all matters in connection with policy and responsible to the officer in charge of the Operations Department on all matters in connection with operations:

Acquiring Section
Processing Section

CONSUMER CREDIT LOAN DIVISION

Officer in charge: ....

Principle functions are to:

1. Supervise and handle the investment of funds of the bank in unsecured loans repayable in monthly installments to individuals, based on their financial statements or salary assignment, or with co-signer, in accordance with policy as determined by the Board of Directors.

2. Supervise and handle the investment of funds of the bank in loans repayable in monthly installments to individuals against

acceptable collateral, chattel mortgage, or conditional sales contracts on automobiles or household appliances, in accordance with policy as established by the Board of Directors.

In order to effectively supervise the functions and responsibilities of this division, it is divided into the following sections, each under the responsibility of a manager, responsible to the officer in charge of the division in all matters in connection with policy, and responsible to the officer in charge of the Operations Department on all matters in connection with operations:

Acquiring-Interviewing Section
Processing Section

COLLECTION DIVISION

Officer in charge: ....

Principle functions are to:

1. Handle the mechanical and operating details in connection with the investing and collecting of funds placed in FHA I, Automobile, and Consumer Credit Loans.

2. Maintain custody, and control over all chattel mortgages or other papers supporting the loan.

3. Collect and process loans and loan payments.

In order to exercise proper supervision, the division is divided into the following sections, each under the supervision of a manager, who is responsible to the officer in charge of the division in matters of policy and to the officer in charge of the Operations Department in connection with operations:

Recording Section
Payment Section
Billing Section
Delinquent Section

TRUST DEPARTMENT

The Trust Department of bank is set up to function where the bank acts in fiduciary capacity, in accordance with the powers and authority granted to it under state law.

Officer in charge: ....

Principle functions are to:

Exhibit 14

TRUST DEPARTMENT

FUNCTIONAL CHART

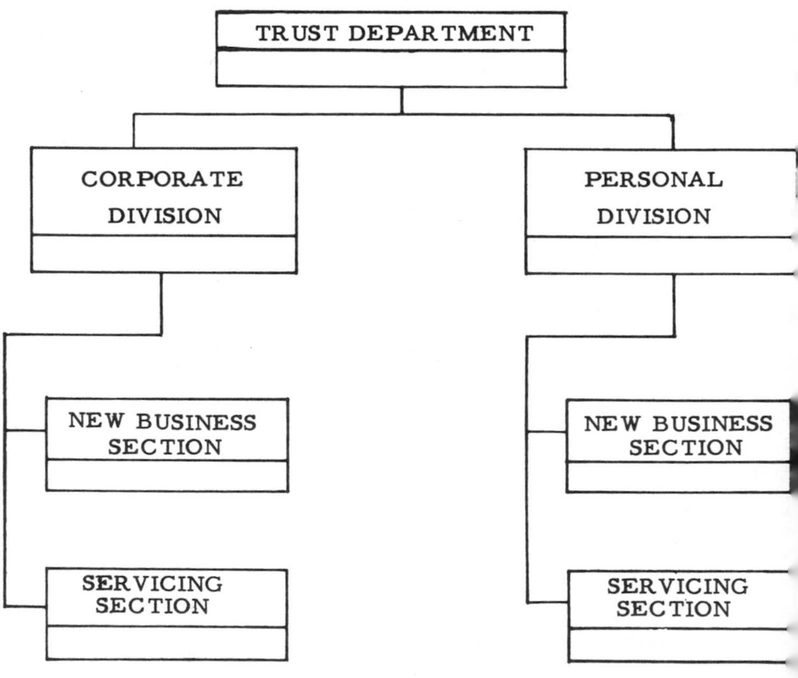

1. Solicit and acquire all types of new trust business in accordance with policy as established by the Board of Directors.

2. Perform all functions and services required in connection with the management of trust accounts.

3. Sell, invest and reinvest trust funds in accordance with the provisions of the trust agreement and bank policy.

4. Distribute income and principal of trust accounts in accordance with the terms and provisions of the trust agreement.

From an operating standpoint, the functions of the department are divided into the following divisions, each under the supervision of an officer responsible to the officer in charge of the Trust Department who in turn is responsible to the Administrative Vice President:

Corporate Trust Division
Personal Trust Division

CORPORATE TRUST DIVISION

Officer in charge: ....

Principle functions are to act as:

1. Trustee under Trust Deed.
2. Trustee under Agreement.
3. Registrar for securities issued by corporations.
4. Transfer Agent for securities issued by corporations.
5. Paying Agent for interest on bonds issued by corporations and municipalities.
6. Dividend Disbursing Agent for dividends declared on stocks issued by corporations.
7. Escrow Agent.

In order to establish functional authority and provide supervision, the division is separated into the following sections, each under the direction of a manager who is responsible to the officer in charge of the division:

New Business Section
Servicing Section

PERSONAL TRUST DIVISION

Officer in charge: ....

Principal functions are to act as:

1. Administrator of Estates,

2. Trustee of Estates under Will.

3. Trustee under Agreement.

4. Executor of Estates under Will.

5. Guardian, under appointment of a court, of estates of minors or incompetents.

6. Agent for individuals in the safekeeping, investing and managing of their securities and property.

So that the division can function efficiently both from an administrative and operational standpoint, it is divided into the following sections under the responsibility of a manager who is responsible to the officer in charge of the division:

New Business Section

Servicing Section

In connection with the operations of a Trust Department it is common practice, depending upon the size of the bank, to have certain functions in connection with solicitation of trust business either undertaken by the officers in charge of the respective divisions, or by officers of the bank who have contacts with commercial customers and thus are in a position to know their need and can encourage them to make use of the trust facilities available through the bank.

In like manner, and again depending upon the size of the bank, sometimes the commercial departments handle the mechanical operations in connection with the accounting, investing, selling, or reinvesting of funds for trust accounts.

Regardless, however, of whether the bank is of sufficient size to have a Trust Department (which is a self-contained unit) or whether it functions for a relatively few accounts, or the management of trust activities is under a commercial or other officer of the bank, the proper investing of trust funds and administration of trust accounts is the responsibility of the Directors.

Before proceeding with the other important phases of operation and management, it is well to rememeber that Organization Plans and Charts represent lines of authority and responsibility from a functional standpoint only. It is quite possible, in setting up a well prepared Organization Chart, to find that the officer in charge of the Commercial Loaning Department will be a Senior

Vice President while the officer in charge of the Investment Department will be an Assistant Vice President. This only indicates that the Commercial Loan Department and the Investment Department are on the same management level from a *functional standpoint* and that the officers in charge of such departments report to, and are under the direct supervision and authority, again from a functional standpoint, of the Administrative Vice President.

Another situation which occurs very frequently can be in connection with a Public Relations Department. Here it is headed by a Vice President. From a functional standpoint, the head of the Customer Relations Division is an Assistant Cashier, while the head of the Employees Relation Division is the Cashier. In this case, particularly in large banks, where they have a number of countermen, the head of the Customers Contact Section and the Employees Relation Division could be even a Vice President.

No two banks are set up the same. Obviously, the larger the bank the more need there is for specialization and fine delegation of duties and responsibilities between individuals. In this connection it is also well to remember that all of the functions we have described, as performed by departments, divisions and sections in the Organization Plan used as an example, are performed by officers in even the smallest banks in their day-by-day operations, although it is not generally recognized.

This can be well illustrated in the following Functional Chart for a small bank, where the committee functions we previously described are undertaken by the Board of Directors who meet weekly, and where the operating and management functions of banking are performed by:

A. A President who also handles all loans and investments.

B. A Cashier who is in charge of all operations.

C. An Assistant Cashier, also a Teller, who after hours solicits new business.

D. Two clerks who act as tellers and three other clerks who perform functions in connection with Proof, Bookkeeping, General Books, and all other functions in connection with operations of a bank.

Most of the confusion which arises from use of an Organization Plan occurs because the one who develops the plan endeavors to

Exhibit 15

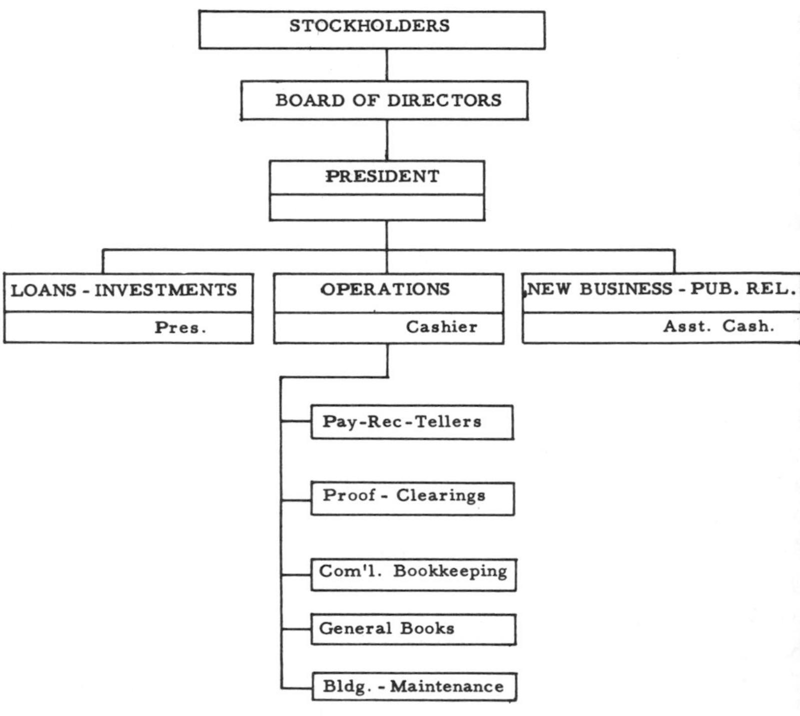
SMALL BANK
FUNCTIONAL CHART
STOCKHOLDERS
BOARD OF DIRECTORS
PRESIDENT
LOANS - INVESTMENTS
Pres.
OPERATIONS
Cashier
NEW BUSINESS - PUB. REL.
Asst. Cash.
Pay-Rec-Tellers
Proof - Clearings
Com'l. Bookkeeping
General Books
Bldg. - Maintenance

assign duties and responsibilities according to titles. This pitfall can be avoided if in developing the Plan and Functional Chart the objectives are approached from the standpoint of functions.

Once departments, divisions, and sections have been set up, and respective functions determined, then and only then should qualified persons to whom the duties and responsibilities of re-pective positions within departments, divisions and sections are to be assigned be selected by management.

Frequently under this procedure it is found that "senior" of-icers from a functional standpoint are responsible to "junior" officers. This disclosure should be welcome as it provides an op-portunity to correct previous "mistakes" of management brought bout by promotions based on seniority.

Another factor to be mindful of in studying bank organization nd management is that titles do not necessarily reflect rank or ositions of authority and responsibility. For example, a bank has a Chairman of the Board, Vice Chairman of the Board, Chair-man of the Executive Committee, President, Executive Vice Presi-dent, and several Senior Vice Presidents. Depending on the Directors, who have the responsibility for delegating duties and esponsibilities, one is always named "and Chief Executive Officer" n addition to his other title. It is well to remember in our dealings ith banks that regardless of title, the one referred to as "Chief xecutive Officer" is the "top man" and the officer to whom all the other officers and Directors look to in all matters affecting the man-agement of the bank.

CHAPTER XIII

OTHER TOOLS OF BANK ORGANIZATION AND MANAGEMENT

NO BANK CAN BE EXPECTED TO OPERATE efficiently unless all employees within a department, division c section know:

A. *From whom* they are to receive the work they are to dc or the items they are to process.

B. *What* they are supposed to do with the work or the ite after they receive it.

C. *How* they are supposed to handle the operation or proce the item.

D. *When* they are supposed to do the work, perform the oper tion or handle the item.

E. *To whom* they give the item, or what they are to do wit the work after they have performed the operation or function an have finished with it.

The answers to these questions, together with a description the way in which internal work or functions are performed an items processed or handled, are found in a department manual operations, sometimes known as a manual of procedure.

A manual of procedure is just what the name implies. It is book which details, for the information and guidance of personne the various operations or functions performed within the divisic and by sections of the division.

In a well managed bank, a manual of operations or manual procedure is written for every division shown on its organizatic chart and should cover the following:

Floor Plan Lay-Out

Organizational Chart

Job Descriptions

Standard Procedures

Operating Instructions

If best results are to be obtained from the use of a manual of ·perations or manual of procedure, the above subjects should not ·e formalized until analysis has been undertaken of each position vithin the division or section and flow studies made of the operaions.

These studies are required because it is only through such nalysis that we are able to trace the processes through which an em is handled or function performed. A study of job analysis ·ill determine if greater efficiency can be obtained by changing ıethods and procedures; or economies in operation can be brought bout through elimination of unnecessary work, avoidance of duication, or simplification in the procedure which is being used.

The purpose of a manual of operations is not only to provide medium for training personnel by having them become familiar ith the operating methods and procedures as used within a department or division, together with duties and responsibilities of l personnel, but also to provide the officer in charge of the sysms and planning division of the operating department with comete records which he continuously studies in order to devise new improve present operating methods and procedures to increase ficiency of operations. Some definitions are in order:

FLOOR PLAN LAYOUT

A floor plan layout is a drawing to scale of the locations of all the desks, cabinets, machinery and equipment used within the vision or section.

The way the department, division or section is laid out at the ne of the study, becomes the basis for time, motion, and flow ıdies. After the flow of items has been traced and study disɔses the routine which provides for greater efficiency, the floor plan yout can then be placed into final form.

ORGANIZATION CHART

The organization chart shows the working of the department ·m a functional standpoint and the lines of authority and responsibility, as have been set up and approved by the directors, or th chief executive officer.

JOB DESCRIPTIONS

Job descriptions, which should be developed for each job o position within the division and section, cover the functions of particular job; the duties and responsibilities connected with th particular job or position; and the qualifications or training th person should possess in order to efficiently perform the function of the job or position and properly discharge its duties and respon sibilities.

STANDARD PROCEDURES

A standard procedure is the description of the approved an accepted manner in which an item is handled, or function pe formed.

OPERATING INSTRUCTIONS

Operating instructions are rules of procedure written by, approved by, the officer in charge of the operations departme covering the handling of certain operations and transactions; modifying or changing certain procedures not incorporated in standard procedures or covering operations of a fluctuating or ten porary nature. The function of operating instructions is to s forth the approved way of undertaking an operation or function.

In many banks operating instructions cover not only operati matters, which are subject to periodical change, but also very oft include standard procedures.

In order to illustrate the principles of management we ha been discussing and point out how the use of manuals of operati can contribute to more efficient methods and procedures, let build a manual of operations for the bookkeeping section in t commercial division of the operations department.

First of all, let us refer to the functional chart for the boo keeping section. This is shown in Exhibit 16, set up according the instructions of the board of directors, and shows the operatio of the department from a functional standpoint.

Next let us refer to the organization plan to determine t

Exhibit 16

ORGANIZATION CHART

BOOKKEEPING SECTION
OF
COMMERCIAL DIVISION
IN
OPERATIONS DEPARTMENT

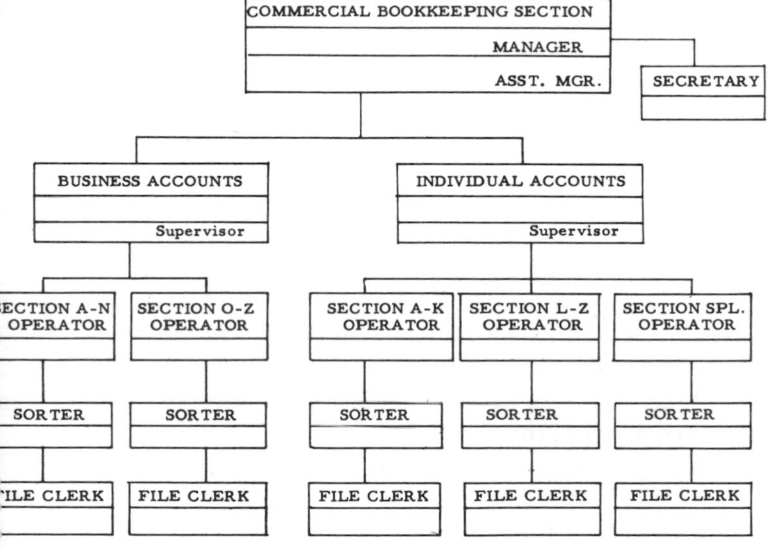

positions within the bookkeeping section and the principal functions, duties and responsibilities of each position within the section

According to the organization plan there are seven position within this section, with titles and responsibilities as follows:

MANAGER

Principal responsibilities are to:

1. Supervise and direct all methods, procedures, functions an operations within the department.

2. Approve all overdrafts in accordance with instructions o the loaning officers.

3. Approve the payment of checks against uncollected fund

4. Review and approve all signature cards and resolutions, i connection with new accounts.

5. Approve all transfers of funds in accordance with schedule and instructions.

6. Verify and approve credits to and checks drawn again inactive accounts jointly with the cashier.

7. Receive all garnishments and attachments, and provide th attorneys with all necessary information.

8. Approve all stop payment orders.

9. See that all reports of the section are correctly prepared an forwarded to the proper officers.

ASSISTANT MANAGERS

Principal responsibilities are to:

1. Supervise the mechanical operations of the departme through the supervisors of respective groups.

2. See that all settlements are properly made between oth divisions and sections.

3. Train and assign duties and responsibilities to personn within the department.

4. Maintain running records on uncollected funds on specifi accounts.

5. Take the place of the supervisors when they are ill or vacation.

6. Maintain activity records and other statistical informatic pertaining to the section.

7. Handle the work of the manager in his absence or while he s on vacation.

SUPERVISORS

Principal responsibilities are to:

1. "Pay" the signatures and endorsements on all checks.
2. "Pay" dates on all checks.
3. See that all items are properly posted and that the sections re in balance.
4. Perform the work of the bookkeepers in their absence or hile on vacations if no trainee is available.
5. Assist the bookkeepers in performing the functions of their bs.
6. Answer inquiries from customers or others in respect to alances, and the payment of items.
7. See that all service charges are properly computed and ut through.
8. See that all charges are made for returning items for insufficient funds and for overdrafts.
9. See that all mis-sorts, items that are going to be returned presenter for insufficient funds, date or other reason are properly arged back to the proof section.
10. Prepare specal statements, required by customers, on the proval of the manager or assistant manager.

BOOKKEEPERS

Principal responsibilities are to:

1. Post all deposits to respective accounts.
2. Post all checks to respective accounts.
3. Watch for stop-payment orders on all checks.
4. Post lists of checks to statements.
5. Post individual checks on each list to the ledger sheets.
6. List each account which is overdrawn after checks present- have been posted to the ledger sheets, and give such list to the pervisor.
7. List the accounts which, after posting, show checks drawn ainst uncollected funds and give such list to the supervisor.

SORTERS

Principal responsibilities are to:

1. Receive all checks from the proof section and sort them first alphabetically, then fine-sort them to individuals within an alphabetical section.

2. Combine and run on an adding machine, 8 or more check drawn by the same customer.

3. Fine-sort and intersort all deposits and credits.

4. Interleaf deposits and checks in front of the ledger sheet of the account on which the items are drawn or items credited a the close of business each day, for the bookkeepers to start postin the next morning.

FILE CLERKS

Principal responsibilities are to:

1. Cancel and file all paid checks.

2. File all ledger sheets when filled, in the vault.

3. Collect from each bookkeeper ledger sheets on closed accounts for filing in the vault.

4. Remove from the signature file and resolutions file signatu cards and resolutions on closed out accounts and file in the vault.

5. Remove checks from file drawers and deliver to authoriz clerks on receipt for makeup of monthly statements.

SECRETARY

Principal responsibilities are to:

1. Take all dictation in connection with reports, written i quiries, correspondence of the manager and assistant manager.

2. Follow up and see that current resolutions are on file.

3. See that proper signature cards covering each account a received.

4. Take over the work of the stenographer in case of absen or vacation.

TYPIST

Principal responsibilities are to:

1. Type up the overdraft list and list the checks returned

Exhibit 17

FUNCTIONAL QUESTIONNAIRE

ection ______________________ No. ____________

repared by ______________________ Date ____________

Describe briefly the functions of this section. (What work is performed)

What are the sources of work for this section?
(from what other divisions does the work come from)

To which section does the work of this division go when completed or processed?

List the individual positions in this section.

Exhibit 18

POSITION ANALYSIS - Questionnaire

(One of these must be made up for each job listed under Question 4 of functional questionnaire)

Position ______________________ Section __________ Division ______

Prepared by __________________________ Date __________________

Please read all questions carefully before making entries. When answering questions be as brief as possible.

1. Briefly describe the general duties of this position (daily routine).

2. Indicate the time spent on each duty that takes more than 10% of the tin

3. Which of the above duties are performed on a weekly, monthly basis?

4. What machinery or equipment is used in performing the duties of this position?

5. In performing duties of this position what percentage of time is spent:

   Standing - %, Sitting - %, Moving about - %

6. What is the most difficult or troublesome feature of the position?

7. Why is it difficult or troublesome?

8. What feature of the work is disagreeable?

9. Why is it disagreeable?

Exhibit 19

FLOOR PLAN LAYOUT OF BOOKKEEPING SECTION

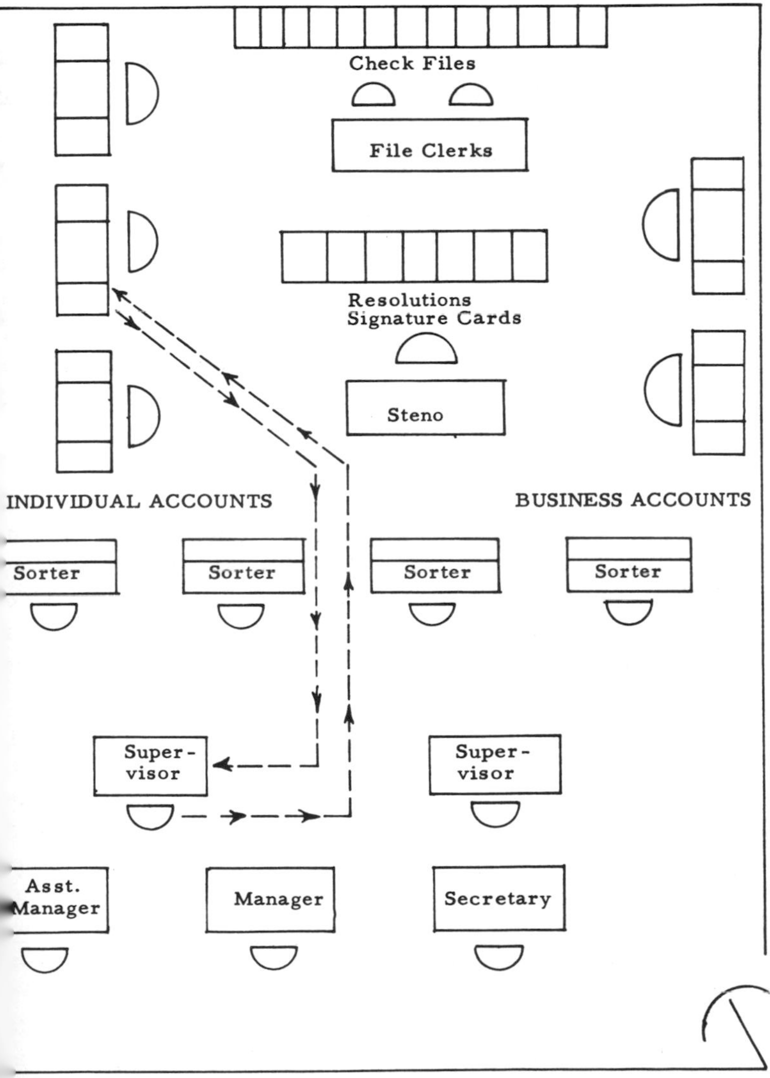

insufficient funds on a stencil and deliver same to addressograp section for processing.

2. Type up the charges and notices of all items returned fo insufficient funds or other reason.

3. Prepare and mail the overdraft notices.

4. Head up ledger and statement sheets on all new account

5. Type up new envelopes for accounts where there has bee a change of address.

6. Prepare and send to addressograph section address slip on new accounts.

Information from which functions of the sections within th divisions were determined as shown, and duties and responsibiliti of each employee within the section delegated, as described, w provided by the officer in charge of the commercial division of th operating department from review of completed functional que tionnaires similar to that shown in Exhibit 17, and position analys questionnaires similar to that shown in Exhibit 18.

FLOOR PLAN LAYOUT

The next step is to prepare a flow chart for the bookkeepi section. This is done by making first a floor plan layout similar that shown in Exhibit 19 showing the respective positions or loc tions of all personnel within that section. This type of layout cha is used in tracing the course of every operation or function p formed within the section.

When charts covering all of the respective operations ha been prepared, they are studied and analyzed together with t position analysis questionnaire in order to determine the most dire line of progress or straight line procedure and the most efficie way in which the operation is to be performed. In setting up flow chart and developing a floor plan layout, it is helpful if u is made of templates, which are cutouts representing the amount space generally occupied or needed by the operation of a m chine or occupancy of a desk or file. These can be moved arou for experimental purposes and are of great help until the final l out has been decided upon when they can be glued into positi Samples of these are shown in Exhibit 20.

Exhibit 20

TEMPLATES FOR FLOOR PLAN LAYOUT

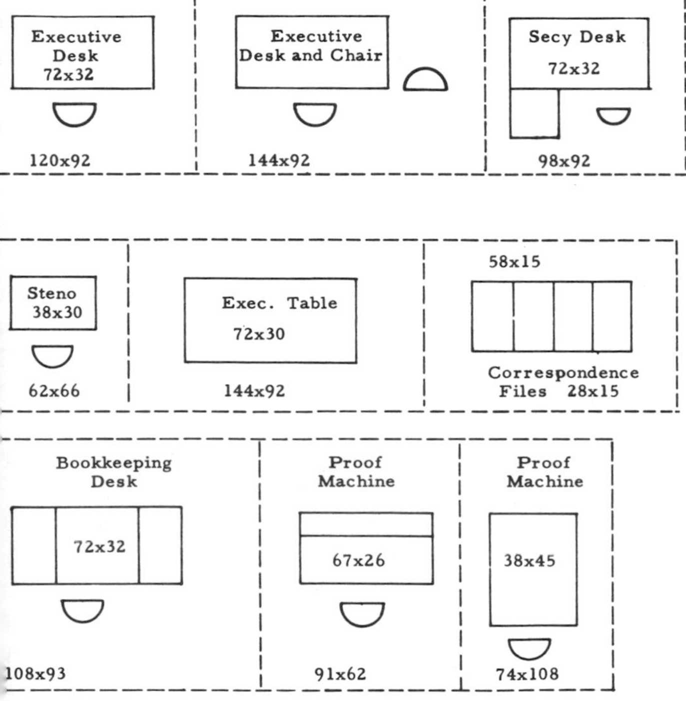

Scale - 1/4 = 1'

---- Functioning Space required as indicated is NOT to Scale. Reduce space required if desks or machines are "backed up" against other machines or desks or to a wall.

In order to follow through on the use of a flow chart let u take the one operation—the handling of balance requests. Th handling of balance requests in the bookkeeping department aris from two sources.

1. Tellers and others who wish to check on the balance of customer's account in order to determine that the balance is suffi cient to cover the checks presented for encashment or to acce before releasing documents.

2. Customers who wish to check up on the amount of mon they have on deposit.

At the time this analysis was undertaken, all such requests we directed first to the supervisor of either the business accounts gro or the individual account group.

In order to get the information it was necessary for the supe visor to either call out to the bookkeeper, in whose group the a count was carried, or to leave his desk and walk down to the i dividual bookkeeper to get the information and then walk back his desk (as shown by the dotted lines) to answer the inquiry.

Analysis made it apparent that when a supervisor called o for information it not only disturbed others in the section and i terrupted personnel from concentrating on what they were doi but contributed to opportunities for errors. It was also obvio that when the supervisor left his desk to go to the bookkeepe desk to obtain information, he not only wasted his time but t time of the bookkeeper, who had to stop what he was doing a refer to the account on which the information was wanted. A alysis and review of the flow chart, together with a study of Exhi 18, position analysis questionnaire of the bookkeeper, showed t the ledgers were actively used by the bookkeepers about two ho a day.

As a result of this study, a considerable saving of time and ficiency of operations was brought about by rearranging the partment so that the supervisor's desk was set directly behind machine operators, as shown in Exhibit 21. In addition, after ledgers were posted, they were rolled to the side of the supervis desk available for ready access and reference to each accou This change not only saved considerable time in handling bala requests, but eliminated, to a great extent, the annoyance and

Exhibit 21

REVISED FLOOR PLAN LAYOUT

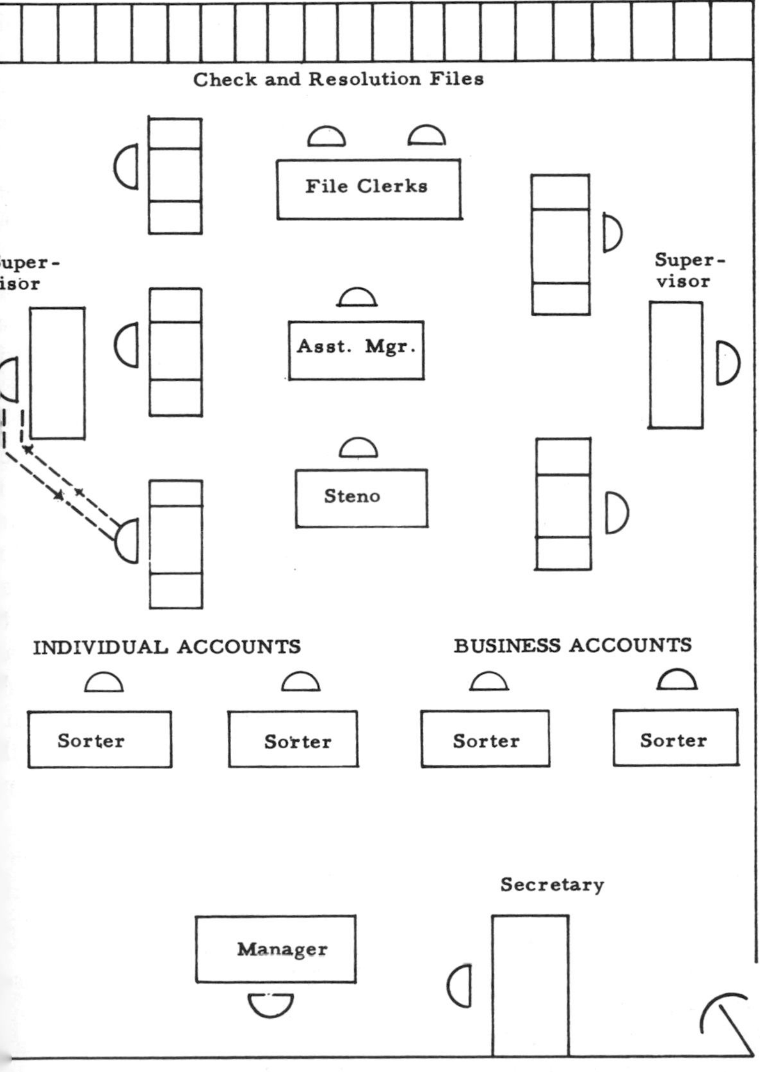

terruption of work resulting from loud talking or questioning t obtain a balance.

JOB DESCRIPTIONS

The next step in building a manual of operations is to develo job descriptions covering the various positions within the section.

As we have seen, job descriptions in a well managed bank ar necessary not only to acquaint personnel with the duties and re sponsibilities of the respective positions they hold, the functio they are to perform, and the routines they are to follow in pe forming the functions and discharging the duties and responsibil ties of their position, but to acquaint them with the duties, respo sibilities, functions and routines of other positions within th section.

By referring to the answer to question 4 of the function questionnaire Exhibit 17, we find there are eight positions in th bookkeeping section. (The principal responsibilities of which we covered in the organization plan)

Manager

Assistant Manager

Supervisors

Bookkeepers (Machine Operators)

Sorters

File Clerks

Secretary

Typist

The position questionnaire (Exhibit 18) for each of the po tions was reviewed and analyzed, together with studies of the ti and motions undertaken in performing the functions or operatio of each job or position within the section. From this study, j descriptions were written and standard procedures developed.

As an example, to show the results of these studies and analys let us review the completed job description for the file clerk in t bookkeeping section, as shown in Exhibit 22.

Exhibit 22

JOB DESCRIPTION

DATE__________ POSITION File Clerk

DEPARTMENT Operating

DIVISION Commercial

SECTION Bookkeeping

WORK SCHEDULE	START	MORNING RELIEF	LUNCH PERIOD	AFTERNOON RELIEF	TERMINATION
	8:30 AM	9:45/10:00	11:30/12:30	2:45/3:00	5:00 PM

DUTIES AND RESPONSIBILITIES

1. Cancel all checks posted and paid by bookkeepers.

2. File all paid checks in the paid file in the vault under the ıame of the account.

3. Collect all filled ledger sheets from bookkeepers.

4. File all filled ledger sheets in vault under name of account.

5. Remove signature cards on closed accounts from signature le under control of the supervisor, and file in vault in signature file-losed accounts.

6. Remove resolutions, or other authorizations, on closed ac-ɔunts from file maintained by manager, and file in vault in resolu-ɔn file-closed accounts.

7. Collect ledger sheets on closed accounts from bookkeepers ıd file in vault under name of account.

8. Remove check drawers from files in vault and deliver to ıthorized clerks at end of month for make up of monthly state-ents.

9. Relieve or assist sorters as directed by the supervisor.

ROUTINE PROCEDURE

1. After arriving at the bank, place wearing apparel you will t be using in locker, and proceed to time station to which you ve been assigned.

2. Remove time card from rack, record "time in," refile, and ɔceed to your desk.

3. Change dates on daters to the correct date.

4. Fill sponge cup with water.

5. Pick up filled ledger sheets from bookkeeper and take to vault for filing.

6. Remove signature cards on closed accounts from the supervisor's file.

7. Remove resolutions on all accounts closed, from the manager's file.

8. Take filled ledger sheets, signature cards on closed accounts, resolutions on closed accounts to vault and file in respective files.

9. Remove checks paid by the bookkeeper the previous da from overnight file, put through cancelling machine and file ir vault under proper name in file drawers.

10. Remove cancelled checks from file together with statemen on all accounts which were closed the previous day and refer to th assistant manager for disposition or mailing.

11. Prepare new envelopes for all accounts which appear o the change of address slips, file in alphabetical order in envelop file.

12. When the bookkeepers have finished posting items to th ledger sheets, and have made up their overdrafts and uncollecte fund list, check names against deposits which have not been postec

If a deposit is found, index the total amount of the deposit o a pink substitute slip, initial, and leave in place of the original de posit slip.

13. Refer overdraft list, together with any deposit slips, to ma ager for approval as to payment of the overdraft, or against unco lected funds, or for reference to the officer to whom the account assigned.

14. When work is complete, report to supervisor for assignme as to assisting with sorting of checks; or if the bookkeepers hav completed their posting, to practice using the machine.

STANDARD PROCEDURE

Another important step to take in building a manual of oper tions, is to develop standard procedures. The term standard pr cedures can be, and is, applied to two distinct phases of manag ment:

A. The approved routine and procedure a division, section

individual should follow in carrying out the general duties and responsibilities of the division, section or position.

B. The approved or suggested routine a person should follow in performing a particular function, or operation in connection with the duties and responsibilities of his position.

As the first phase is generally incorporated into job descriptions, such as recording "time in" *before* proceeding with the filing of checks, or changing the dates on the daters, let us devote our attention to the second phase: the suggested routine a person should follow in performing a particular function.

While there are a number of functions performed by the file clerk, as we know from referring to the job descriptions, only a few of these functions, such as the following, require additional or supplemental instructions, because of the importance of the work, to operate in an efficient manner.

Cancelling and filing of checks

Filing of deposits

Filing of ledger sheets

Preparation of checks for statement makeup

As an example of a standard procedure, let us review the one covering the "filing of checks," in completed form as shown in Exhibit 23.

Exhibit 23

STANDARD PROCEDURE

FOR Cancelling and Filing of Checks DATE 7-7-60

DEPARTMENT Operating POSITION File Clerk

DIVISION Commercial

SECTION Bookkeeping

FUNCTION

Cancelling and filing of paid checks

STANDARD PROCEDURE

1. Remove paid checks from overnight safe and take to perforator machine for cancelling.

2. Select checks from the batch, for cancelling, by using thumb and forefinger of *left hand.* Pick up bunches of checks, if possible, according to alphabetical breakdown of check file drawer.

3. Insert checks selected in perforator using thumb and forefinger of *left hand.*

4. Press *right foot* on pedal, to operate machine.

5. Remove perforated checks with thumb and forefinger of *right hand* and turn face down on pile. Criss cross alphabetical batches.

6. After all checks have been cancelled and sorted according to alphabetical breakdown of drawers, place checks on sorter shelves which can be attached to each drawer.

7. Select and remove checks for filing according to account using the thumb and forefinger of the *left hand.*

8. Select the pocket in which the checks are to be filed, using the thumb and forefinger of the *right hand.*

9. Pull other checks in the pocket forward so as to leave space in the rear for checks which are to be filed.

10. Insert checks to be filed in space thus provided, using the thumb and forefinger of the *left hand.*

OPERATING INSTRUCTIONS

The final step in building a manual of operations is in develop ing operating instructions through which changes in operatin methods, procedures or routines are communicated to the depart ments, divisions and sections, by the officer in charge of the opera tions department as approved by the administrative vice presiden

To provide proper authority and approval, *only* the officer i charge of the operations department should issue and sign opera ing instructions, although they may originate within any depar ment, division, or section. As a matter of good practice, operatin instructions, when issued, are sent to *all* administrative personn (officers including managers of sections) not because the instru tions particularly apply to their functions, but to keep them cu rently informed on all phases of operations.

Exhibit 24

OPERATING INSTRUCTIONS

NO: 14 - A

DATE ______________

TO: All Officers and Managers

RE: Handling of deposit slips on commercial accounts which have been posted and filed.

At the present time, after commercial deposit slips have been posted to ledger and statement sheets of respective accounts, they are filed in the bookkeeping vault for a period of 12 months after which they are transferred to the storage vault, where they are maintained for a period of seven years and then destroyed by the auditor.

Effective as of this date, in order to conserve space and more efficientl handle posted deposit slips, such items, after a period of 12 months, are to be transferred to the auditing department. After being photographed they are to be destroyed and the film permanently filed in the old records vault.

By:

Vice President and Cashier

Approved:

Administrative Vice President

(1) This supersedes Operating Instruction 14, dated August 30, 1957 which should be removed from the binder and destroyed.

ALL OPERATING INSTRUCTIONS SHOULD BE FILED IN BINDER FOR READY REFERENCE.

When operating instructions are received, each administrative officer, if the instructions apply to some operation or function of divisions or sections under his supervision, has the responsibility to communicate the instructions to members of such divisions or sections, and to obtain an additional copy for insertion in the manual of operations.

Generally, operating instructions, when received by administrative personnel, are filed in a binder provided for the purpose, in numerical order for ready reference purposes. Periodically, detailed indexes are provided to enable administrative personnel to readily refer to instructions covering a particular operation or function.

To illustrate the use of operating instructions, let us take one which has been issued covering the handling of deposit slips on commercial accounts, as shown in Exhibit 24.

QUALIFICATIONS AND SPECIFICATIONS

In connection with this chapter on organization and manage ment, it might be well to conclude by briefly covering one of the most important and yet seemingly neglected phases of manage ment—the selection of qualified personnel at all levels to properly discharge the duties and responsibilities of positions.

Personnel placement agencies over the years have been almos unanimous in stating that the most difficult phase in obtaining ser vices of an individual to fill a certain position in a bank arises no because qualified people are unavailable but because those in ad ministrative positions, in many cases, not only lack knowledge a to the duties and responsibilities of the position they seek to fil but also knowledge of the qualifications, background, and exper ence a person should possess to be able to properly discharge th duties and responsibilities of the position.

It has been facetiously said—but never doubt the seriousne or sincerity of the remark—that when many executives seek a ma for a top administrative position, they look for a man 30 to 3 years of age, with at least 20 years of "greying" experience, wh is presently getting an annual salary of $18,000, but by any stan ards should be getting $25,000, and whom they hope to hire f $10,000.

Unfortunately this attitude is so prevalent that it is not only difficult to attract the right type of men to the banking business, but to keep men interested in staying in banking.

In order to overcome and correct this situation, it is the practice of management counselors and administrative heads of many of the larger banks, working very closely with a well qualified man in charge of personnel, to have heads of departments, divisions and sections, fill out and complete a qualifications questionnaire similar to Exhibit 25 on which they list their own opinion as to duties and responsibilities, qualifications, experience and other requirements for every position under their supervision. Once it is completed it is returned to the personnel officer or to a person experienced in job analysis and placement, who competently analyzes the questionnaire and determines just what the actual requirements are for each respective position.

After the proper analysis and appraisal of qualifications and requirements for each position has been completed, the information is indexed on a position specification schedule similar to Exhibit 26. Once these schedules have been prepared for every position within the bank, they serve as a guide for the personnel officer in hiring, transferring employees from one position to another, and in determining what additional education is required to fill higher positions once it has been indicated that background, personality and experience otherwise qualify them for such position.

Incidentally, while speaking of well qualified men for personnel work we should be mindful of the fact that personnel relations are just as important in the profitable operation of a bank as is new business and the investing of funds in loans and securities. To do a top job in personnel work requires that a person not only have a proper educational background, including preferably a master's degree in psychology, but a very fine working knowledge of labor relations.

Exhibit 25

QUALIFICATION QUESTIONNAIRE

POSITION ______________________________

DEPARTMENT ______________ PREPARED BY ______________

DIVISION ______________ TITLE ______________

SECTION ______________ DATE ______________

1. DUTIES AND RESPONSIBILITIES OF POSITION

2. In order to satisfactorily perform the duties and responsibilities of this position, as described, what are the educational requirements?

   Grammar School ______________
   High School ______________ Number of years ______
   College ______________ Number of years ______
   Special studies or knowledge ______ Number of years ______

3. What experience is necessary to have in order to satisfactorily learn this position? (What previous experience is necessary?)

4. If an employee possessed the education and experience required for this position, how many months would it take for the employee to become:

   Satisfactory ________ Good ________ Proficient ________

5. What is the most difficult feature of this position to learn? Why?

6. What are the physical requirements for the position?

   Excellent ________ Good ________ Fair ________

7. What degree of responsibility is required for this position?

   Superior ________ High ________ Medium ________ Low ________

Exhibit 26

POSITION SPECIFICATION

POSITION ______________________ DATE ______________

DEPARTMENT ______________________ SALARY RANGE $ ________

DIVISION ______________________ AGE ________

SECTION ______________________ PERSONALITY __________

SPECIFICATIONS (If important)

HEIGHT __________ WEIGHT __________ APPEARANCE __________

MACHINE KNOWLEDGE REQUIRED ______________________

WORDS OR ITEMS PER MINUTE ______________________

PERVIOUS BANK EXPERIENCE ______________________

EDUCATIONAL REQUIREMENTS ______________________

BRIEF OUTLINE OF DUTIES AND RESPONSIBILITIES OF POSITION:

CHAPTER XIV

BANKING AS A CAREER

UP TO NOW WE HAVE BEEN LEARNING how barter and exchange developed into the business we call banking. We have traced the functions of the money changers and goldsmiths into modern banks where all the facilities required by individuals and business concerns in conducting their financial affairs are provided.

We have also learned of the way modern banks function in providing their many services, and how duties and responsibilities are delegated within the bank organization to provide management.

It is important that every person should know about banks and the services they render, because without using the facilities banks provide, business would be as handicapped as though there were no highways or railroads to transport goods to market. It can be said that banks are equally as important as highways and railroads in the conduct of commerce and trade. Highways and railroads are the ways by which products are brought from the producer to the consumer. Banks, on the other hand, are the means through which the payments for products are brought from the consumer to the producer.

Now let us consider banking as a career. As of December 3 1965, according to Rand McNally's International Bankers Director there were 14,347 unit banks in the United States, and 16,41 branches or offices, making a total of 30,760 areas in the Unite States where banking facilities were provided.

Study indicates that every community of any size has its ow locally owned bank. In addition, nearly every village, town, an city, if it does not have its own home owned bank, is either provid ed with banking facilities through a branch of a bank located another city, or through facilities available in a nearby town.

Because many of the buildings which house banks are built

stone, brick, marble and concrete, we come to think of banks as being cold and their personnel lacking in feeling. This is not true. A bank is more than a well built edifice with steel vaults and grilled windows. It is an organization of human beings, like ourselves, who desire to contribute their talents to the development and progress of business and who assist other individuals in providing the means to obtain the necessities and conveniences of life. At the present time, approximately 600,000 people are engaged in the business of banking, of which approximately 98,000, or one out of every five, are officers engaged in administrative functions.

Because functions, services, and operations are practically the same in every bank and only differ in volume, there are multiple advantages to those selecting banking as a career.

If a person enjoys a warm and sunny climate where he can play golf, tennis, swim, fish and sail the year round, there are opportunities for employment with banks in California, Florida, Hawaii and Puerto Rico, to mention a few such locations.

If a person likes the changes in weather and finds seasonal enjoyment in hunting, fishing and sports activities attractive, there are banks located in the eastern and midwestern states ready to employ their talents.

If a person likes to travel and see the world, there are opportunities to enjoy this type of living by being employed by some of the larger banks in the country which maintain foreign branches.

If a person enjoys the excitement of big city life with its theaters, places of amusement and diversified activities, many banks in major cities or their suburban areas are eager to employ their services.

If a person is attracted to the soil and is interested in farming, mining, cattle raising, or fruit growing, there are jobs awaiting him with many banks located in the central, midwest, and southwest states.

In addition to location, many people choose banking as a career because:

1. Banks offer continuous employment and security.
2. The work is interesting.
3. The hours are pleasant.

4. Employee benefits, such as paid vacations, insurance and pension are better than those offered by any other type of business.

5. Conditions under which a person works are generally pleasant. (Good lighting, air conditioning, etc.)

6. People engaged in banking are above the average in intelligence and character and are therefore likely to prove congenial to fellow workers.

7. Banking provides an opportunity to serve others.

8. There is opportunity for advancement for a person who applies himself well and is willing to assume responsibilities.

9. It provides an opportunity to become acquainted with those engaged in other lines of business and it opens a wide field for personal progress.

Work in a bank is interesting and covers a multitude of jobs and positions. As we have learned in previous chapters, the basic functions of banking are performed in every bank whether it has resources of half a million dollars and employs two or three people or whether it has resources of several billion dollars and employs thousands of people. The great difference, of course, is that in a large bank we have specialists, that is, individuals who spend most of their lives in the same department, doing perhaps the same thing; while in a small bank, because of the volume, we may find one person performing functions which in a larger bank might be performed by ten or twenty different individuals. In a large bank, however, because of specialization, there is greater efficiency, because it is possible for a well qualified individual to perform a certain function and devote all of his time to performing that function, whereas in a smaller bank it is necessary for a person to perform many functions at which he is not always adept.

This also brings up the question as to whether working in small bank or working in a larger bank provides the greater opportunity.

In a small bank, let it be said, a person must know or at lea have a general idea about all the operations and functions of bank, and during a normal day will shift from one position to the other.

In a larger bank, on the other hand, the volume and routine may be such that a person is engaged in performing only one op eration or function and a period of years will be required to obtain a working knowledge of all of the functions of banking. This reason itself is sufficient for studying this book, which provides those in a small bank with information as to policies, organizational planning, systems, and routines not generally found in a smaller bank; and brings to the employee of a larger bank the information on all functions of banking which, because of specialization, is generally not available to him except over a long period of time as he progresses from one position to another.

If a person elects to begin his banking career in a small bank he generally will be employed as a clerk where his job will be to learn to run an adding machine, assist in the sorting and filing of checks, run errands and perform many of the menial jobs which someone has to do.

Later, as he progresses and develops, he will become assistant bookkeeper, then bookkeeper and progress possibly to teller, handling savings and commercial deposits and withdrawals, collections, and loan and discount transactions. About this time he will receive official recognition and be made a junior officer. In a smaller bank even when an official title is given to an employee very often he continues to perform his former duties such as teller, head bookkeeper, etc., but with this title obtains additional responsibility and additional authority. As time moves on and he progresses, he earns to undertake credit investigations and analysis, to make oans, and enter into the top echelon of banking, which can take him to the presidency.

In a large bank on the other hand, the new employee is usually tarted out as a page or messenger. Pages, as we have seen, act s messengers between individuals within the bank while messengers are used outside the bank for delivering securities, presenting ollections, and carrying checks to other banks of the clearing ouse. In addition, messengers also handle the mail, delivering it and from the Post Office. They also open, sort, and deliver incoming mail to the department or the addressee.

Following a term of service as page or messenger, the normal ne of progression in large banks would be then to the proof or earing house section where they learn to sort checks, make listgs on the adding machine, learn to operate a proof machine.

The work of sorting checks and listing gives the clerk experience in using bank machinery, mainly the adding machine. It also enables him to learn about such bank instruments as checks, drafts, and notes. If a person has imagination and initiative, he will also acquire a good general idea of bank operations. He will, therefore, be prepared when new opportunities occur.

The next opportunity may arise in any of the departments, divisions, or sections of the bank, some of which will be discussed later; but is likely to occur in the commercial bookkeeping section. It is here that speed and accuracy in sorting, and in the use of the adding machine are essential.

The commercial bookkeeping section has charge of the ledgers in which the accounts of depositors are kept. These accounts must be balanced daily, deposits being credited and paid checks charged. The bookkeeper must keep in touch constantly with changes in balance resulting from deposits or checks being paid, for at any moment a check may be presented for payment and the paying teller may need to know the balance in a certain account.

In some banks the bookkeeper first serves an apprenticeship as a statement clerk. The statement is really a duplicate of the ledger and is sent to the depositor periodically. The statement clerk compares balances with the bookkeeper daily, thus verifying the work of both. Under the direction of the bookkeeper, the statement clerk becomes familiar with the signatures and the characteristics of the various customers. As he develops skill he may be promoted to the position of bookkeeper.

Bookkeeping methods vary greatly according to the size of the bank and the activity, (number of deposits and checks paid) of the depositors. In banks where large corporations deposit and draw thousands of checks daily, the systems may be entirely mechanized all operations being performed on machines of remarkable variety

The next promotions to paying or receiving teller are usually based on ability and the proficiency with which they handle work in the proof and bookkeeping sections. While it is true that they do come in contact with the officers, it is not until they are promoted to clerks in a "contact" section or become tellers, or are selected for training in the credit section, that they come into daily contact with the officers where their appearance and personality receive attention, and serious consideration is given to selecting them for training which will develop them into future officers of the bank.

The receiving teller deals directly with customers and must therefore be a person of pleasing personality, as well as one of good judgment and technical experience. He receives the deposits of cash, checks, and coupons made by the customers, verifies their accuracy, and gives receipts, usually in a special book issued to the customer, called a pass book.

He must be familiar with the law of negotiable instruments (checks, drafts, etc.), understand endorsements, be able to detect counterfeit money at sight and have the ability to work with speed and accuracy under pressure without losing his cordiality and good humor.

From the position of receiving teller to that of paying teller is usually the next step. Paying tellers have the responsibility of cashing checks presented for payment. Practically every transaction is a cash one, involving checking or verifying the signature on the check, the sufficiency of the balance of the account to cover it, and the genuineness and identification of the endorser.

In the savings section, where deposits and withdrawals are usually made personally and require a passbook, one teller generally handles both deposits and withdrawals. It is not uncommon also, even in large banks, for one individual to act as both paying teller and receiving teller for checking account customers. This, of course, calls for the skill and experience required by both kinds of tellers.

Some of the other sections to which a person may be advanced next are the collection section, which collects payments on notes, drafts with documents attached, and other items which cannot be credited to a customer until payment is actually received; also the loan and discount section, which keeps the records of loans, has the custody of notes and collateral, and eventually collects the loans made by the bank.

To complete the picture of the many jobs available in large metropolitan banks, mention must be made of a number of independent departments and divisions, all of them important and some calling for special talents and training. For all practical purposes, they may be considered as banks within the banks, with their own records and staffs.

In this class is the trust department, which generally handles the financial affairs of others in fiduciary capacity; the safe deposit department, which provides a means for keeping one's valuables safely in their own compartment at small expense; the foreign department, which provides the facilities for handling foreign transactions; and last but not least, the commercial, installment, and mortgage loan departments and investment departments, which invest the funds belonging to stockholders and depositors in the various types of loans and investments.

All of these departments and services offer jobs to many people and a chance for those with talent and technical training to rise in the banking world.

Assignment to any of these departments, divisions or sections in a junior capacity may come directly from the page or messenger section, or from minor positions anywhere. Transfer to a senior position may come after bookkeeping or teller experience. This may be pure chance as far as the individual can see, but is more likely to be based on the considered judgment of the personnel director or manager.

From this brief description it is apparent that bank work provides a great variety of experience and gives scope for the exercise of many aptitudes and abilities.

Whenever an individual enters the employ of a bank, regardless of its size, he has the opportunity to progress through the organization to a senior position, ultimately becoming president. Advancement in every case depends on knowledge of banking principles and their application, familiarity with operating methods and procedures, the ability to get along with other people, and competence in performing each duty and responsibility required by the job or position assigned.

There are fairly well defined lines of progression in banking for those who apply themselves. Such progression is shown in Exhibit 27.

In studying this chart of progress, it is well to be mindful hat the vertical lines only indicate the path or progression for an ndividual who remains doing a certain type of work. In most oanks it is a practice, wherever a person is qualified or shows ability n other lines, to promote horizontally as well as vertically. In other vords, just because a person has attained the position of trust teller loesn't mean that he must always remain in the trust department. Providing he has other qualifications, and the opportunity presents tself, he can be transferred to a position as teller in another department or division of the bank, or even promoted or advanced o a "new business solicitor," "junior investment officer" or "junior ommercial loan officer."

The stage of one's experience is taken into account by sometimes classifying bank personnel as "junior" and "senior." The erms indicate the amount of responsibility involved and the experince and judgment required, rather than the age of the person ssigned to the task.

The terms, however, are always relative. A person may work p from a "junior" to a "senior" position in a certain department, ivision or section, and then be promoted to a "junior" position in nother department, division or section where the responsibility is reater. There are, in fact, such positions as "junior vice president" n large banks. Practically everyone in a bank has before him a till higher position as a goal. First assignments in a bank are, so ar as an individual is concerned, largely a matter of chance; that , they depend upon the jobs that are open in various departnents. However, an employee should always make every effort to nderstand the purpose of his work, and to prepare himself for ther assignments. As time goes on, promotion will be less and ss a matter of blind chance and more a matter of proved ability.

In discussing banking as a career and in choosing the various elds of banking, it might be of interest to know that banks in eneral serve three distinct areas: country banking, city banking, nd intermediate banking.

The primary services of a country bank are in connection with rming and mining. The country banker is concerned about the ondition of the crops. He must follow the markets and be able give sound advice on planting so as to extend credit for grain and for seed. He must know livestock, the markets, so as to be abl to intelligently loan money to farmers for the buying and feedin of cattle. He must know farm management, including the use o farm machinery and equipment, and be able to judge a man as t whether or not he is a good farmer worthy of the bank to risk it money in financing his operations.

The services of a city bank, on the other hand, is in connectio with manufacturing instead of farming. The city banker mus know the markets for raw materials, something of the marketing o finished products, understand the economy, and whether or not th products which are being manufactured can be sold to repay th loan.

The intermediate banks, which by far are in the greatest num ber, are just what the term implies. They are neither city bank in a strict sense of the word, nor country banks. They do no have the large demand for loans to industry and business nor d they have any large demand for extending credit to farmers. Ger erally, the intermediate banker is concerned with supplying th credit needs and services to those in retail trade and householder in a community.

In addition to *location* and *type* of bank, a person selectin banking as a career has a wide choice as to the *size* of the ban in which he wants to work. As of December 31, 1965 there wer 14,347 banks in the United States with total resources classified a follows:

572	under	$ 1,000,000.		
5890	between	1,000,000.	and	$ 5,000,000.
4699	between	5,000,000.	and	15,000,000.
1265	between	15,000,000.	and	25,000,000.
900	between	25,000,000.	and	50,000,000.
1021	over	50,000,000.		

Working in an intermediate or country bank has many a vantages. A person engaged in banking in such cities often liv the community, participates in its cultural activities and enjoys any other advantages not available to those employed by banks larger cities.

From the standpoint of compensation, it is generally agreed at banks located in the larger cities pay the higher salaries. It ust be remembered on the other hand, however, that rentals and e cost of living are higher in the cities than in the smaller towns. ery often, too, additional expenses are incurred through the fact at employees of city banks live in suburban or country areas nd must commute each day to their jobs.

All things considered, there are many compensations in working r a bank besides the pay check. While it is true that those skilled a trade or profession sometimes earn a higher hourly or daily age, often they are not continuously employed; that is they may ork for two months and then be laid off for several weeks or may ork only a few days each week. On the other hand, bank work steady, salary is on an annual basis and grades upward with age nd seniority.

Banks, in addition, generally make every effort to keep their nployees happy and satisfied by providing many fringe benefits, ich as a two weeks annual vacation with pay; health, hospitaliza-on and accident insurance, which protects the savings of an em-loyee in case of prolonged illness or medical expenses; and life surance, under a group plan, which provides for certain sums to e paid to beneficiaries in the event of death.

Many banks also have pension and retirement plans to which ich employee is eligible to belong after being with the bank for fixed period of time and which provide income after they reach tirement age.

In addition, many progressive banks have profit sharing plans order to permit bank officers and employees to participate in the ntributions they make to the earnings or profits of the bank.

One of the greatest satisfactions which comes to a person is e sense of being respected, of belonging to somebody, or being part of a group or organization. This satisfaction can be attained banking where each employee is a member of the team, and nsidered as being a part of the bank in or out of the bank arters.

Another source of satisfaction in life comes from serving This satisfaction can be found through banking which provide facilities through which individuals and business concerns conduc their financial affairs.

Nearly everyone aspires to leadership, recognition for hi accomplishments, and wants to be appreciated, either in busines or at home. At home we all want to be appreciated as either dutiful daughter, respectful son, as a husband who is a good pro vider and father, or as a wife who is a good housekeeper and moth er. In business we want to be recognized not only as a loyal an conscientious employee, but as one who has some qualities c leadership.

Bank officers, beginning with their first official appointment are recognized as leaders. They are constantly sought out to b officers and take active part in activities of civic organizations suc as Rotary, Lions, and Optimist clubs, and as members of th school, library, or hospital boards. Very seldom is there a com munity development or project which does not have a banke playing one of the leading roles.

There is no business like the banking business. Banks, small c large, in big cities or small towns, are located everywhere: Nort South, East, and West; where it is cold, where it is hot, where the have steady seasons, where they have changing seasons, where is mountainous, where there are lakes, where there are plain In fact, once a person has selected banking as a career, he ca enjoy practicing his profession any place which suits his health pleasure; and can obtain great satisfaction from life by contributin his talents and abilities to both the attainment of personal recogn tion and in service to the community.

CHAPTER XV

THE INDIVIDUAL AS A BANK EMPLOYEE

FROM THE STUDY THUS FAR MADE of the func-
'ons of banking, we cannot arrive at any conclusion other than
ıat the most important product of banking is service. Only peo-
le can supply service; therefore, successful banking is nothing
ıore than the results of the efforts of people, what they do, how
ıey do it, and for whom they do it. Because banking is principally
science of dealing with people, and we have looked at the func-
ons of banking from the standpoint of the general public, let us
ow look at banking from the standpoint of those who provide the
ervices—the bank employee and the bank employer.

Unfortunately, over the years the personnel policies and prac-
ces of banks too often have developed without any plan or well
ormulated program. In the smaller institutions the chief executive
fficer of the bank is in very close touch with all staff members and
epends upon his judgment as to the selection of employees for
dvancement and those who merit increases in salary.

In the absence of any soundly formulated program dealing
ith human relations, the chief executive's policy in assigning
ork, granting salary increases and recognizing ability by promo-
on, is generally well known to everyone on the staff. To those who
re recipients of his favors, he is looked upon as a person of good
ıdgment, capable, a fine man to work for; while to those who are
assed by when it comes to salary increases or promotions, he is a
erson lacking in judgment, prejudiced, playing favorites and hold-
ıg grudges. Fortunately, this situation has the habit of correcting
self. It soon becomes evident that the chief executive is unfair,
oes not recognize ability, and only grants increases in salary
nd promotion to his favorites. As a result good men will seek
nployment elsewhere, which ultimately works against the growth
nd progress of the bank. Also, no one is compelled to work for an

unfair boss. The banking field is constantly seeking men wit initiative and ability.

In larger banks, however, and even in the smallest bank, wher the chief executive officer is considered to be a progressive thinke much of the guess work has been taken out of personnel relation in recent years. While human relationships cannot be measure entirely in dollars and cents, nevertheless, it is possible to measur abilities and character in relationship to a job or position, selec the right man for the right job and develop a coordinated tear through which the individual members are well compensated fo the services they perform, and the stockholders receive a fair re turn for the investment they have in the employee.

A well managed and efficient operating business, like a ban is similar to a baseball team. In baseball, for example, a team i composed of 9 players. To be able to put 9 men on the field, pro vide for illness and injury, a well managed team always has othe men on the squad in reserve who can fill in for any of the so-calle "regular" players when they are incapacitated or unable to pla This, however, merely makes a baseball team.

This team, on the other hand, can be of championship qualit only if there are capable men for each position and they functio together at all times as a unit.

It is possible to have the best defensive infield in baseba yet, if the outfielders are unable to field ground balls and fr quently lose fly balls in the sun, the defense has little value. like manner, it would be possible to have the best defensive an offensive team in baseball with the three outfielders leading th league in hitting, yet without capable pitching it would be ju another team. To correct this situation, top management of baseball team is constantly on the alert to acquire players not on for their individual skill and ability, but because they compleme the other members of the team and assist in developing a coord nated unit.

This is also very true in banking. We need individuals wh possess varied abilities, qualifications and distinctive personaliti to build a good bank "team." It is for the purpose of proper selecting men and women whose abilities and qualifications w contribute to team work, and in furthering the "Plan of Progres r the bank and providing service—which is the tool through which e progress of a bank is measured—that proper personnel policies re formulated, and responsibility for the handling of personnel elegated to a qualified member of the staff.

From our study of the organization plan, it has been determined that the principal functions and responsibilities of the personnel division are to:

1. Interview, evaluate and hire all clerical personnel.

2. Develop and supervise proper indoctrination or training rograms for all new employees.

3. Develop job descriptions for each position for employees use as a guide in becoming familiar with the duties, responsibilies and functions of their jobs.

4. Set standards covering each job or position within the bank.

5. Develop and maintain an Employees Handbook or Manual r the guidance of new employees and for information of older nployees.

6. Periodically review the performance of each employee for ading and salary adjustments.

A great responsibility rests upon the person in charge of pernnel. He can only be expected to do a good job if he occupies a sition of recognized authority, has the respect of associates in s judgment and is considered by the employees to possess the alifications of friendliness, fairness, understanding and justice.

Because we are dealing with personalities and human relans, the selection and training of personnel can bring progress, ace or dissension to any bank. It is because personnel relations e so important that banks today, wherever possible, establish ed policies in respect to the hiring, training and firing of personl; set up standards for the evaluation of personnel; and make use job descriptions and other tools of personnel management in der to build a cooperative team which will contribute to the ogress of the bank.

Analysis and review of all factors indicates that the following ms up the purpose and objectives of personnel relations:

A. Attracting qualified personnel.

B. The hiring and orientation of new personnel.

C. Having satisfied and happy employees who will contribut their abilities and talents to the progress of the bank.

D. Providing the proper facilities for carrying out the ob jectives.

The first objective, attracting qualified personnel, takes o additional importance in this era, in view of the intense recruitmer programs instituted by business to attract the graduates of ou colleges and universities. In view of our population growth an expansion of banking facilities, it daily becomes more importa for banks to attract men and women of the highest caliber, t assume administrative positions.

Whether or not banks will continue to be successful in attrac ing the right type of personnel will depend on their ability t develop sound methods of recruitment, incentives, and use of pro erly devised programs for orienting and training.

Two of the most effective methods used in the recruitme of personnel are recruitment through contacts and recruitme through advertising. Both of these efforts, however, will produ little in the way of qualified applicants unless *what is said* abo the aggressiveness, administration, accomplishments, attractivenes attitudes and atmosphere of the bank *is based on factual evidenc* In other words, we *live* public relations and service, we don't ju *talk* about them.

Probably the best vehicle for attracting new personnel through our present employees who have found working conditio and salary schedules so satisfactory and pleasing, and are so prou to be working at the bank, that they recommend the bank to the friends as a place to work.

Another source of personnel is through customers. If we tre our customers properly, many mothers and fathers who are i pressed with the courteous service rendered by people in the ba will suggest to their sons and daughters, when it comes time f them to go to work, that they apply at the bank. Customers als when they are impressed with the bank or its personnel and t services they render, often can recommend to sons and daughte of their friends who are seeking advice as to their vocations, th they apply to the bank or see Mr.————, that very nice ma about a job.

High schools and colleges are most cooperative in finding mployment for their graduates. By acquainting the deans of ɑen and women, or placement directors in colleges and universi-es; the professors in charge of the business administrating or ac-ɔunting sections; and teachers of commercial courses in high ·hools, with the specific positions the bank has available, and the ualifications applicants should have, it it possible to develop a orking relationship both of benefit to the bank and the school.

Employment agencies also are a source of supplying personnel ıd can be most helpful if they are discreetly and honestly used. lany people avail themselves of the facilities of recognized and ·ensed employment agencies to better themselves position-wise ıd salary-wise, and to relocate. Unfortunately, both individuals ıd bank personnel directors use employment agencies as a sound-g board and as a means to interview applicants seeking senior ɔsitions which they hope to hire for junior positions. Knowing ıis to be the case, many employment agencies either refuse to nd applicants to certain banks or, if they do, build up the appli-ınt to the position they believe the personnel director is endeavor-g to fill. Employment agencies can be relied upon to supply the ·eds of banks if banks will be honest as to their requirements by nscientiously describing the qualifications and requirements of e position they wish to fill, which can be obtained from position ecifications, and the salary they are willing to pay.

The other source of attracting personnel is through newspaper d advertising media. Probably the most satisfactory medium is e local newspaper, not only because it is read by people residing the area, some of whom might be employed by banks located other towns and be interested in working in a bank closer to me, but because the ad indicates to the townspeople that the nk is growing and requires additional personnel to provide serv-·.

Such newspaper ads are consistently effective in attracting ə services of secretaries, stenographers, trainees, bookkeepers, ıchine operators and clerks.

In addition, so called "blind ads", or ads which describe the sition and the qualifications required of the applicant without ·closing the name of the employer, are sometimes effective especially if properly used in connection with the hiring of supe visory and administrative personnel. Careful consideration, how ever, should be given as to the manner in which such ads ar placed. Replies can be directed either to the bank or directed to post office box or to a box number, which newspapers and ma azines provide for their advertisers. Should a bank elect to hav replies come to the bank, it is well, depending upon the position course, to acquaint the personnel of the bank with the ad and th particular qualifications of the position, so that they are in a pos tion to intelligently answer any inquiries which might be made them through friends or acquaintances who have seen the ad.

The attaining of the second objective of personnel relation proper hiring and orientation of new employees, begins at th moment a person enters the personnel office. If the objective friendly personnel relations is to be attained, the applicant shou be greeted in a friendly and warm manner, then with courtesy an a helpful attitude, given the application blank to fill out.

Frequently an applicant is given the wrong impression of th bank because the application form is given to him without any wo of friendly assistance or explanation. In addition, the form, many cases, without a satisfactory explanation, appears to be t inquisitive and curious about matters which have little to do wi the position being applied for. As the purpose of an applicati form is to initially provide information which will enable the pe sonnel manager to determine if the applicant is qualified for t position for which he has applied, or for other positions with t bank, the form should be informative yet simple, similar to th shown in Exhibit 28.

As a further means to establishing initial friendly relationsh with an applicant, help should be given in filling out the bla

After the application blank has been filled out, the next st in the establishing of friendly relations is to be interviewed in friendly manner by a person capable of tactfully weeding out th not qualified for the position, or those who do not have the init qualifications or minimum requirements for other positions in bank.

One of the greatest opportunities to build friends for a ba is in the turning down or declining of an application for a positi

Exhibit 28

APPLICATION FOR EMPLOYMENT

FRONT SIDE

RP-1

Photograph here

APPLICATION FOR EMPLOYMENT

WITH

___________________________19____

Dear Sirs:

I hereby apply to the for a position as ______________

It is my understanding that the filing of an application is a preliminary step to employment and does not imply that I will eventually be engaged.

I have completed the questionnaire on the reverse hereof and affirm that I have answered all questions to the best of my ability.

Should I receive an appointment to a position with the bank I agree to abide by all of the rules and regulations of the bank and to dedicate my time to the service of the bank.

I understand that such an appointment is subject to satisfactory work, and that such appointment may be terminated at any time at the discretion of the management. Should such appointment be terminated within the first six months, which shall be a trial period, it is understood that the only compensation due me will be that which has been earned to the date of termination.

If, upon completion of the six month trial period, I desire to leave the employment of the bank, I agree to give at least two weeks advance notice of my resignation in writing.

Exhibit 28A

APPLICATION FOR EMPLOYMENT

REVERSE SIDE

(Please Print)

Name Address Tel.

Soc. Sec. No. Nationality Religion

Date of Birth Marital Status No. of Dependents

FAMILY MEMBERS or DEPENDENTS

NAME	RELATIONSHIP	OCCUPATION	ADDRESS

Names of relatives or friends employed in this company

Date of last Physical Examination Physician Address

Nature of last illness

Who recommended you to this company

Of what fraternities, clubs or lodges are you a member

What are your hobies

EDUCATION

Grade or school	NAME	FROM	TO	GRADUATE OR SUBJECTS
Grammar school				
High School				
College				
Business Coll.				

Specialized Subjects

REFERENCES

Please list the names and addressess of three persons not related to you as character references.

NAME	ADDRESS	OCCUPATION AND YEARS KNOWN

EXPERIENCE

By whom have you been employed during the past ten years? Place name of present employer first.

FROM	TO	NAME OF COMPANY	ADDRESS	BUSINESS	POSITION	SALAR

If presently employed why do you desire to make a change?

If not employed why did you leave your last employer?

With what business machines operation are you familiar?

DO NOT FILL IN.

DATE INTERVIEWED BY

DATE HIRED BY SALARY

REMARKS

Many times the personnel officer, by making helpful suggestions to ne applicant as to where his talents might be used profitably, can nake a friend for the bank who will, in return, recommend the ank to friends who might be seeking employment, or using the cilities of the bank when in need of financial assistance or services.

Many progressive banks, even though it is necessary to turn own an applicant, often tell him they will keep the application n file and notify him in case a position opens up for which his lents qualify him. In these cases, sometimes the personnel officer ves the applicant a little booklet, which tells him something about ne bank and its services which can make the person a good friend the bank.

Very often, following the screening interview and before a erson is hired or given further consideration as to employment, pplicants are given certain mechanical, learning ability, manual exterity, comprehension, and aptitude tests. Should it be the olicy of the bank to give these tests, it is well to remember that ne friendliness and personality of the person who administers ese tests not only can influence the outcome of the tests but also ovide the initial impressions which the applicant carries with m in his future relationship with the bank.

The hiring and selection of personnel, we might add, is simified under modern employment practices especially in seeking ersonnel to fill certain clerical positions, due to the fact that the ersonnel officer has position specifications for each position. By mparing information in the application with the specifications can readily determine if the person has the qualifications to disarge the duties and responsibilities of the respective position.

Once an applicant has passed the initial interview, satisfacrily completed the tests and thus becomes eligible for employent, the most important phase of his initial relationship with the nk begins—the interview with the Personnel Officer.

As the seed for good employee morale is planted during this al interview, it is important that the personnel officer thoroughly ver the relationship between the bank and the new employee. must be remembered that a bank cannot expect to benefit from e proper use of the abilities of an employee, neither can an emoyee contribute his best work and talents to the bank, unless the employee knows what he is expected to do, and what rewards h can expect to receive from the intelligent and conscientious us of his talents and abilities in the bank's interest.

First of all, in the interview, the personnel officer should infor the new employee about salary and that the base salary of eac position is being constantly reviewed, through job analysis, wi adjustments being made, based on the requirements for the positio

At this point it might be interesting to cover some of th principles of job analysis or job evaluation frequently used to e tablish the salary range for a particular position and its wag relationship to another position of similar responsibility.

Job analysis or job evaluation, starting with definitions, is th minimum qualifications, abilities, and other requirements a pers must, or should possess, to satisfactorily perform the functions a particular job or position.

As the application of the principles of job analysis or evalu tion is a study in itself, let it suffice here to outline the princip under which job evaluation operates.

First of all the basic factors in connection with any job, be for messenger or president, are minimum requirements in rega to:

Education
Experience
Skill (Machine or mechanized operations)
Physical Condition
Appearance
Personality
Responsibility
Working Conditions (Clerical positions)

By establishing "weights" for degrees of proficiency or complishment in each of the above factors, as applied to a position, we can establish minimum "weight" requirements for t functions of each position within the bank.

Then if we assign dollar values to each of the "weights" a multiply the respective weights in each position by the dol value, we arrive at the base pay for each position so evaluat based on the factors.

To this we add additional weights for each year of servi

lus a weight for the volume of work the individual is capable of roducing or handling in a given time.

Base pay, plus weights for length of service, plus weights for olume of work performed, establishes the minimum and maximum alary ranges for each position.

The personnel officer should also inform the new employee bout the permanent record the bank maintains on each employee, milar to Exhibit 29, and how periodically, usually on the employee's anniversary date, each division manager or supervisor, is equired to prepare a formalized report similar to Exhibit 30 for e purpose of rating, upgrading, and adjusting of the salary of e employee.

Further, the personnel officer should explain that once a person proficient in a particular position, the bank provides every opportunity for that employee to advance both in position of responsiility and compensation.

The explanation of such policies and practices gives assurance the applicants or employees, who have the qualities for success, at promotion and advancement is not a matter of luck or guessork but is based on recognition of ability and performance. In e final analysis all a conscientious and ambitious employee seeks opportunity and assurance that he will be trained to perform e functions of the position to which he is assigned in the most ficient manner possible, in order to obtain maximum rewards in osition and compensation.

It is desirable, also, that the personnel officer during this interew, inform the new employee about the bank, its policies, the rvices it provides for use of customers and the public, and the osition of the bank in community affairs. Because it is expected at each new employee will become a valuable member of the ganization, it is important that the personnel officer thoroughly quaint the new employee with the rules and customs of the ank he is expected to follow, especially the hours of work, payays, absenteeism, the various employee benefits which the bank ovides in the way of health, life, and hospitalization insurance, d profit sharing and retirement benefits.

Finally, in order to thoroughly remind the employee of the atters discussed during the interview, and to provide him with

Exhibit 29

EMPLOYEE RECORD

FRONT SIDE

ADG M/C	Type	Steno	C.H. Proof	Bkpg. M/C	Calc. Comp.	B X	Rec. Tel.	Pay Tel.	Cy. Silver Tel.	Sav. Tel.	Coll. Tel.	Disc. Tel.	Tran.	Anal.	File	New A/C	R.E.L.	PL AL	Bond
JOB OR POSITION EXPERIENCE																			

JAN.	FEB.	MAR.	APR.	MAY	JUN.	JUL.	AUG.	SEP.	OCT.	NOV.	DEC.
ANNIVERSARY DATE											

Name__________ Address__________ Tel. No.__________ Social Sec. No.__________

Nationality__________ Date of Birth__________ Religion__________ Marital Status__________ No. Dependents__________

EDUCATION

GRADE OF SCHOOL	NAME OF SCHOOL	FROM	TO	GRADUATE
GRAMMAR SCHOOL				
HIGH SCHOOL				
COLLEGE				
BUS. COLLEGE				

DEPENDENTS

NAME	REL.	DATE OF BIRTH

Other Schools or Specialized Banking Subjects

BUSINESS EXPERIENCE (Last Three Positions)

FROM	TO	NAME OF COMPANY	ADDRESS	BUSINESS	POSITION HELD	SALARY

BANK EXPERIENCE

DATE	DEPARTMENT	POSITION	SALARY	COMMENTS	DATE	DEPARTMENT	POSITION	SALARY	COMMENTS

PAYROLL DEDUCTION DATA

DATE	SALARY	F.O.A.B.	WITH. TAX	WAR BONDS	HOSPITAL PLAN	GROUP INS.	PERSONAL INS.	COM. FUND	ADV.—MISCL.	NET PAY	

Exhibit 29A

EMPLOYEE RECORD

REVERSE SIDE

COMMENTS	
DATE	

PERIODIC REVIEW OR APPRAISAL	
QUANTITY OF PRODUCTION	
QUALITY OF PRODUCTION	
INDUSTRY	
INITIATIVE	
ADAPTABILITY	
TACT	
GENERAL ATTITUDE	
SUPERVISION REQUIRED	
SUITABILITY	
SOCIAL ATTITUDE	
NEATNESS	
HEALTH	
ABSENCE	
BY	
DATE	

Exhibit 30

SALARY REVIEW REPORT

FRONT SIDE

SALARY REVIEW REPORT

☐ ANNIVERSARY DATE__________ ☐ SEMI ANNUAL ANNIVERSARY DATE__________ ☐ SPECIAL__________

To____________________ Department____________________

From: PERSONNEL DEPARTMENT

Please review the salary and qualifications of the following employee, fill in the information on this report, and return to this department with your recommendations.

Name____________________ Position____________________

Present Salary $__________. Last increase was for $__________ on____________________

Person has been in the employ of the bank since____________________

MANAGER'S RECOMMENDATIONS	COMMITTEE ACTION
☐ Increase Salary $__________ per annum.	__________
☐ Promote in position from__________ to__________	__________
☐ Recommend Employee be transferred to__________	__________
☐ Recommend services be terminated on__________	__________
☐ Defer consideration at this time.	

REASONS FOR THIS RECOMMENDATION

____

____

____

____

____
Department Manager

COMMITTEE COMMENTS

____

____

____

COMMITTEE ACTION APPROVED. DATE____________________ BY____________________

Exhibit 30A

SALARY REVIEW REPORT

REVERSE SIDE

Underscore below and mark symbol in right hand column, the characteristics applicable to the individual being considered. Additional comments should be added in the space provided.

		DO NOT USE	
QUANTITY OF PRODUCTION	A. Above average. B. Average. C. Below average. Comment:		
QUALITY OF PRODUCTION	A. Accurate. B. Occasional errors. C. Frequent errors. Comment:		
INDUSTRY	A. Industrious. B. Average worker. C. Spasmodic. Comment:		
INITIATIVE	A. Acts without being told. B. Must be told what to do. C. Requires detailed instructions. Comment:		
ADAPTABILITY	A. Retains instructions well. B. Must be retold occasionally. C. Must be retold frequently. Comment:		
TACT	A. Diplomatic. B. Usually tactful. C. Lacking in tact. D. Antagonistic. Comment:		
GENERAL ATTITUDE	A. Enthusiastic or energetic. B. Satisfied but ambitious. C. Discontented. D. Trouble maker. Comment:		
UPERVISION EQUIRED	A. No supervision. B. Occasional supervision. C. Frequent supervision D. Not dependable even with supervision. Comment:		
UITABILITY	A. Prospects for future development. B. Might be better in some other position. C. Has reached limit. Comment:		
OCIAL TTITUDE	A. Pleasant. B. Temperamental. C. Sullen. Comment:		
EATNESS	A. Very neat and orderly. B. Average in neatness and order. C. Untidy. Comment:		
EALTH	A. Healthy. B. Occasionally ill. C. Unhealthy. Comment:		
BSENCE	A. Never absent. B. Occasionally absent. C. Frequently absent. Comment:		

NOTATION FROM PERSONNEL RECORDS

Absent__________Days During Last__________Months

UTSTANDING HARACTERISTICS______________________________

OTHER REMARKS

____

____

____

information for reference purposes, he should be given a copy of the Employees Handbook, which tells about the bank and details some of the other subjects touched upon during the interview.

Such Employees Handbook, if it is to assist in properly indoctrinating new employees and guide older employees, should include sections covering some, or all, of the following subjects:

Welcoming the new employee.
Summarized history of banking.
Background and history of the subject bank.
The community or area served by the bank.
Services the bank has to offer customers and the public.
Employee benefits.
Rules of conduct.
Text for guidance and inspiration.

In order to illustrate the coverage of an Employees Handbook and at the same time spell out certain sections which should be included in order to obtain the greatest benefits, let us outline the text which a bank can use as a guide in developing a Handbook for its own particular use and need.

First of all there should be a warm and sincere word of wel come to the new employee. This can either be personally ad dressed to the individual or set up in blank. Likewise the name of the president can either be printed or signed. It should, how ever, have a personal touch and be so designed as to make th new employee feel at home and as belonging to the organizatior similar to the following.

(Letter of Welcome to the New Employee)

WELCOME to the staff of the (name of bank).

We know you will enjoy working here. As you become ac quainted, you will find we are a friendly group of people, happ to cooperate with you in working together to serve our value customers.

In our bank we believe we all have the responsibility to eac other for a high quality of personal conduct inside and outside th bank, and trust that your conduct, character, dress, talk, an manners, at all times, will reflect this responsibility.

This little booklet has been prepared to acquaint you with our bank, and the business you have chosen as a career. In addition it contains rules of conduct to guide you in your work as a member of the staff, and helpful suggestions to assist you in pursuing a successful career in banking. Should you have any questions, or wish further information on any of the subjects contained in the booklet, any of the officers will be glad to discuss them with you.

It is the hope of the Directors and other officers, as well as myself, that you will be happy in your work as a member of our staff.

Sincerely yours,

President

The first section covering the "Summarized history of banking" could be titled:

SECTION I

OUR BUSINESS OF BANKING

This section should contain an outline, as lengthy or as brief, as management believes necessary, (but not to exceed 2,000 words) taken from the text in Chapters I to VIII, covering:

A. Definition of word "Bank."

B. Early functions of money changers as "Bankers."

C. Present types and classes of banks.

D. The purpose and function of the Federal Reserve System.

E. The purpose and function of the Federal Deposit Insurance Corporation.

F. Membership in and purposes of belonging to Banking Associations.

The next section, "Background and history of the subject bank" could be titled:

SECTION II

YOUR BANK

This section should be written so as to inform the new employee about the history of the bank, its progress over the years, and present management. The text should cover:

A. When the bank was founded.

B. By whom the bank was founded.

C. Changes in name or status of bank, if any.

D. Growth over the years.

E. The bank Statement of Condition. The meaning of the account headings (Chapter X). A space should be provided for attaching a copy of the current published statement.

F. Present management. (Names and affiliations of the Directors. Names and titles of present officers if not listed on current statement).

The next section "The community or area served by the bank" could be titled:

SECTION III
YOUR COMMUNITY or THE COMMUNITY WE SERVE

This section should inform the new employee about the community in which the bank is located, so they can understand the part the bank plays in the development of the community. To provide this information the text should cover:

A. The geographical area served by the bank.

B. The population in the area served by the bank.

C. Principal industries in area.

D. Economy of area. (Farming, manufacturing, residential, etc.)

E. Purchasing power of the area.

F. Outstanding community undertakings. (Fairs, commemorations, etc.)

G. Any thing for which the community is noted. (Location of colleges, parks, etc.)

The next section, covering the "Services the bank has to offer customers and the public" can be titled:

SECTION IV
OUR SERVICES TO THE COMMUNITY

This section should outline the principal services the bank ha available for the use of customers and the public. Those provided can be listed from Chapter IX.

After this listing, the following could be added to remind the employee of the operations in connection with providing these services, and acquaint him with the purpose of the Organization Plan.

"In order to efficiently handle these transactions, it is necessary to centralize certain activities and services in special departments, divisions and sections. It is also necessary to have the bank organized from a functional standpoint.

"So that each employee will have knowledge and understanding as to how the bank functions in its day by day operations, the bank has available, through its officers and department managers, an Organization Plan which it follows. This plan sets forth the authority and responsibility of each committee, officer, department, division and section and the continuity of operation and administration from a functional standpoint.

"Copies of the Plan, kept currently revised, are maintained for reference purposes by each divisional officer and section manager. In order that you will become familiar with lines of responsibility and know the proper person to contact or refer matters to in case your immediate superior is unavailable, it is suggested you ask the manager of your division or section to review the plan, especially the sections pertaining to your responsibility, with you."

The next section "Employee benefits" which is generally of the utmost interest to each employee can be properly titled:

SECTION V
YOU AS A BANK EMPLOYEE

This section should describe the compensation and benefits the bank offers each employee in exchange for his loyalty and service, and should cover such matters as hours of work, pay days, absenteeism, and fringe benefits, similar, if applicable, to the following:

1. *Hours of Work*

Because the volume of work in the bank varies, depending upon the commercial activity, a fixed number of hours in each day or week can not be determined. It is the policy of the bank, however, to have the employees work only 40 hours per week, unless longer hours are necessary.

The hours during which the bank is open for business are:

Monday	——— A.M	to	———	P.M.
Tuesday	——— A.M	to	———	P.M.
Wednesday	——— A.M	to	———	P.M.
Thursday	——— A.M	to	———	P.M.
Friday	——— A.M	to	———	P.M.
and	——— P.M.	to	———	P.M.
Saturday	——— A.M	to	———	P.M.

Unless otherwise instructed, all employees should be at their desks or cages, ready to work, no later than ——— A.M., and should remain until their work is finished.

While the time set for the beginning of work in the morning is set by management, all employees are permitted to leave the bank as soon after the close of business as their work has been completed, or there are no additional assignments.

2. *Over-Time*

Banks, like industrial companies, are covered by the Fair Labor Standards Act, which provides that any employee working in excess of 40 hours a week shall be entitled to receive over-time pay at the rate of time and one-half of their regular hourly pay. In the case of bank employees whose wages are computed on an annual basis, the hourly rate for computing over-time is determined by dividing the annual salary by 52 weeks and then by 40 hours, which establishes the hourly rate used in computing the hourly rate of overtime.

3. *Lunch Room and Relief Periods*

The bank, for the convenience of the personnel, maintains a lunch room where lunch is served and coffee and rolls and soft drink can be enjoyed throughout the day. Lunch and relief periods are periodically assigned by the division manager or officer in charge of personnel so as not to disrupt the continuity of work.

4. *Pay Days*

Bank employees are employed to perform certain duties and

assume certain responsibilities for which they receive compensation on an annual basis. This annual compensation is payable as salary, semi-monthly, the fifteenth and last day of each month, or the day preceding if such day falls on a holiday, Saturday or Sunday.

5. *Holidays*

The six major holidays, namely, New Year's Day, Memorial Day, Fourth of July, Labor Day, Thanksgiving Day and Christmas Day plus the following: Lincoln's Birthday, Washington's Birthday, Good Friday, Columbus Day, Presidential Election Day, Veterans' Day are observed.

6. *Vacations*

Each person employed by the bank for 12 months prior to June first of the current year is entitled to a two week vacation with pay. However, persons employed less than twelve months, but over six months are entitled to one week vacation with pay. Time of vacations to be taken is up to the discretion of the division manager, with the approval of the officer in charge of personnel.

7. *Leave of Absence*

Leave of absence may be granted for cause at the employee's own expense, at the discretion of the officer in charge of the Operations Department.

8. *Absenteeism*

No salary deductions will be made for absence caused by illness unless the period exceeds that equal to one day for each month of employment, with a maximum of two weeks. Compensation for periods in excess of the above requirement may be made at the discretion of the bank.

9. *Promotions*

All new employees at the time of their employment and present employees when promoted or changed from one job to another, should immediately familiarize themselves with the operating instructions related to the specific functions of the job in which they are assigned.

10. *Profit Sharing*

All officers and employees, after being in the employ of the bank for one year, annually thereafter, share in a certain percentage of the net operating profits of the bank, as determined by the directors.

Participation is based on the cumulative total of one point for each year of service up to 25 years, PLUS one-half point for each $500, or fraction of annual salary, up to $——— for each eligible officer and employee, in relation to the total years of service and annual salaries of all eligible personnel.

Further details in connection with the Profit Sharing Plan can be obtained from the officer in charge of personnel.

11. *Hospitalization Insurance*

All officers, employees and their families, after 30 days employment, are protected against hospitalization and accident expense through a comprehensive policy issued by (Name of Company), carried by the bank for their benefit.

Details of this coverage, as it applies to you and your family, can be obtained from the officer in charge of personnel.

12. *Life Insurance*

All officers and employees after being employed by the bank for 90 days are covered by life insurance on their lives, which amount is payable to their designated beneficiary at death.

Details of this coverage as it applies to you and your family can be obtained from the officer in charge of personnel.

13. *Retirement*

All officers and employees, after being employed by the bank for three years, are eligible to participate in the retirement or pension plan of the bank. This plan, which is non-contributory, provides for a percentage of the annual salary earned during the last five years prior to retirement age, which is 65 with optional retirement at age 60, to be paid to them annually in monthly installments as long as they shall live after retiring from the bank, after at least 20 years of continuous service.

Details of the coverage as it applies to you, can be obtained from the officer in charge of personnel.

14. *Banking Facilities*

The privilege of having a checking account and use of a safe deposit box without charge is extended to all employees upon application to, and approval of, the officer in charge of the Operations Department. Imprinted checks will also be furnished without charge. It is understood, however, that all employees who avail themselves of these privileges will conduct their financial affairs according to generally accepted banking principles.

15. *Employee Activities*

In order to promote good fellowship, cooperation and general welfare, the bank, under the direction of the ———— CLUB, an organization directed by officers elected by the employees, to which all employees are cordially encouraged to belong, sponsors social, recreational and educational activities, such as the House organ, Christmas party, annual outing, bowling, baseball and basketball teams, and other activities and benefits in which the members are interested.

Monthly membership dues, as determined by the club, will be a payroll deduction each month.

16. *Suggestion Box*

A "Suggestion Box" in the employees' lunch room is available for employees to present suggestions which will contribute to more efficient operation, better service, or improved public relations. All suggestions will receive courteous consideration by the Officer's Committee, and suitable rewards will be made for suggestions adopted.

17. *Education*

The bank recommends the American Institute of Banking for its many fine courses.

Tuition fee will be refunded to each employee who receives a passing grade at the end of each completed course.

The next section covering "Rules of conduct" could well be titled:

SECTION VI
THE BANK AND YOU

This section likewise should be of interest to each employee because it outlines certain rules and regulations governing conduct, which management expects employees to follow as they progress upward through the various divisions and sections of the bank, as they advance to administrative positions.

The section should cover such matters as the regulations in

connection with reporting accidents, illness, smoking, etc., similar, if applicable, to the following:

A. *Care of Apparel*

Suitable space is provided for each employee to keep his surplus wearing apparel. Coats, hats, sweaters, galoshes, etc., when not worn, should be kept in the space provided or assigned in the lounge.

B. *Time Cards*

All employees are required to report daily on time cards the actual time they enter the bank for work and when they leave, as well as the time they depart for lunch, and upon their return to resume their duties. The cards are to be totaled and signed at the end of each week.

C. *Reporting of Illness*

Any employee who is ill and unable to report for work should notify the officer in charge of personnel no later than 9:00 A.M. of the same day. If the employee is personally unable to do so, he should see to it that some member of the immediate family advises the bank accordingly.

D. *Accidents*

Accidents occurring in the bank to an employee or to a customer (however slight or trivial) should be reported to the officer in charge of personnel immediately. Upon making such report, employees will receive all necessary medical and surgical attention, as provided by the Workmen's Compensation Act, from our physicians, free of cost, but if any physician other than the one selected by our insurance company is consulted, the bank is not responsible for the charges.

The physicians who have been selected to render medical and surgical attention under the Act are posted on the employees' bulletin board for your reference.

E. *Changes in Address and Residences*

Any employee who moves or changes his address and telephone number, should notify the officer in charge of personnel immediately.

F. *Errands*

Employees will not leave the bank during business hours for

personal business without permission of their section manager or approval of the officer in charge of personnel.

G. *Rest Rooms*

Suitable rest rooms are provided for both men and women personnel. It is respectfully suggested that all employees will be considerate of others and be neat in their habits.

H. *Operating Instructions*

Rules and procedures governing the operations of departments, divisions or sections of the bank, or the method of procedure to be followed in handling certain operations, or performing functions, are issued from time to time to the staff. These memorandums are known as Operating Instructions and should be read carefully and studied by each person who receives them so that no error will occur in handling specific transactions.

I. *Neatness and Order*

Cages and desks should be neat at all times. After the completion of the day's work, machines should be covered and desks and working equipment placed in order. Calendars, pictures, etc., should not be placed in the cages where they can be observed through the glass partitions.

J. *Waste Receptacles*

Suitable receptacles are furnished for waste paper and should be used for that purpose.

K. *Records*

Accurate records are very essential, and tickets and other memorandum entries should be complete in detail and neat in form.

L. *Telephone*

Employees should not use the telephone for private purposes during business hours except on matters of great importance.

M. *Visiting*

Employees should not encourage their friends to visit them at the bank and, if they do come in, not to engage in irrelevant conversation or loud talk and laughter.

N. *Smoking*

Smoking in the bank quarters by employees during banking hours shall only be enjoyed in the lunch room and rest rooms.

Common courtesy demands that smoking by officers will not be enjoyed wherever it interferes with work or where there is a possibility that it might be offensive to the customers. The term 'banking hours' covers all departments under our posted banking hours with the exception of the Real Estate and Installment Loan Departments, which is ——— P.M. daily except Saturday.

O. *Late Hours and Intoxicants*

Late hours and the habitual use of intoxicating liquors and the frequenting of places of questionable repute are deemed sufficient cause for dismissal and should be avoided.

P. *Gambling*

Gambling and betting and speculation in any form will not be tolerated or condoned.

Q. *Business with other Employees*

Employees are not permitted to traffic among themselves, or in the interests of persons outside the bank. Employees are cautioned not to enter into outside business enterprises.

R. *Getting into Debt*

Avoid getting into debt. Borrowing from another employee is not permitted. If an employee deems it advisable or necessary to borrow from another bank or loaning agency, he should first consult the officer in charge of personnel before making any commitment.

S. *Confidential Business*

Employees must keep in strict confidence whatever knowledge they may acquire in affairs of the bank and its customers, and all questions of a confidential nature should be referred to the proper official for reply.

T. *Conduct and Courtesy*

Orderly conduct and courtesy towards the public should be observed by employees at all times.

U. *Personal Assistance*

The officer in charge of personnel will be glad to extend a considerate hearing at any time to any employee who might desire to confer with him upon any matter either of an official or personal nature.

The purpose of the final section covering "Text for guidance and inspiration" is to provide some advice for a person who aspires to succeed in banking. While undoubtedly many such texts have been written, the following, which is a combination of advice and words of wisdom, to which no one person can claim authorship, appears to serve the purpose. It could be titled:

SECTION VII
ATTRIBUTES OF A BANKER

A banker is a unique and special type of person. To be successful as a banker, a person must not only understand the principles of banking and finance, possess a good accounting and analytical mind, like people and understand human nature; but possess the attributes and qualities of enthusiasm, courtesy, cooperation, accuracy, initiative, loyalty, judgment, inspire confidence on the part of fellow employees and customers of the bank, and constantly be seeking additional knowledge which will help him to be a better banker.

A man may possess a number of these qualifications, but unless he possesses all of them, he is no banker, as indicated by a study of the following definitions as applied to the business of banking.

ENTHUSIASM

Enthusiasm is the manifestation of interest in what a person is doing and the satisfaction that comes from doing a good job.

Enthusiasm is contagious. When a person is enthusiastic not only do people around him become encouraged to do better work, but the individual himself acts as a potential leader.

COURTESY

Courtesy is the ability to make other people like us and treat others in the same manner as we wish them to treat us. Courtesy in banking is very important because after all our business is dependent on people and on people liking us.

The use of the words "please," "thank you," "I will be happy to do this for you," "I am sorry," or any other little phrases that express courtesy should be remembered.

Also saying "may I suggest" instead of "you have to do this," "I will appreciate it if" instead of "do this" and other similar phrases all express courtesy.

There is also a courteous way to say "no." In fact we should take more time to say "no" than to say "yes." We should figure out how to turn down an individual and at the same time keep his personal regard for us. If we want to be successful in banking we should all try to be courteous. If we look around we find that the people at the top, the people advancing upward and the people we admire, generally are very courteous and kind in their relationship with others.

COOPERATION

We all have a particular job to do or duties to perform in life. Everything worthwhile in this world is accomplished, not only by people doing their own job, but by individuals working together.

Cooperation can be expressed in many ways, but particularly in the banking business where the flow of work generally varies, resulting in one person being through with his particular job before others have completed theirs. It is then that we have an opportunity to be cooperative by inquiring if we can help other people with their jobs, or assist them in some way. This is a common form of cooperation.

The most important form of cooperation in a bank, however, comes from the realization that most work flows through the bank, and that work from one division or section is dependent on work first handled in another division or section. For example: the proof section cannot operate until they receive the deposits and checks from the tellers. Likewise the bookkeeping section cannot operate until they have the work from the proof section. To cooperate, work should be performed as promptly as possible so as to avoid delaying some other section in performing its work.

A cooperative person is a happy person, not only because he is helping others, but because of the benefits he receives from cooperation. As an aid to cooperation, the bank follows an Organization Plan which you will learn about from the manager of the division or section to which you will be assigned. By following the lines of authority and responsibility we can contribute to this cooperative spirit.

In the operation of every department the most efficient method and procedures have been determined. These have been set forth for the guidance of every employee through Manuals of Operation nd Operating Instructions you will study when you are located in he division or section to which you are assigned.

ACCURACY

Our customers believe our records are absolutely correct. Be-ause of this no one is willing to excuse a bank for making the lightest mistake. Carelessness in putting down figures can lead to rrors which not only create confusion within the bank but also re-uire the expenditure of many hours seeking the cause of the mis-ake. When a cusomer's account is affected, he blames not only the mployee who made the mistake, but the entire bank as well. We hould always remember the first principle of double entry ac-ounting, that wherever there is a debit, there must be a credit. aying attention to our work, concentrating on the particular work e are performing, and not letting our mind wander to other ubjects will assist us in being more accurate.

INITIATIVE

Ambition is the driving power to success. It is a desire to chieve something but our objective can only be attained if we work or it. While everyone has ambitions to a greater or lesser degree e all have one main ambition. One person may want to be resident of a bank, another one might want to own his own home, nother person might want to advance in the banking business, to ave money, to travel.

The attainment of objectives requires planning. One of the ost important aspects of ambition is what we call initiative which eans that a person is a self-starter. He does not always have to be ld to do something, to be watched over, or to have his work ecked after he has completed it.

One of the qualities looked for in people to be trained to assume lministrative responsibilities in banking is the degree of initiative ey possess. Ideas, while considered to be a mark of a person ving initiative, are only worthwhile when the suggestions made, ograms developed, and plans proposed for adoption, are based reliable information. These ideas, if adopted, will either result a saving of time, reduction in labor cost, increase in income, or velopment of additional or new business.

Banking offers a wide field for those who possess initiative and ambition. Every idea, every thought and every plan you as an em ployee have for improving operating methods and procedures, de veloping new business, improving relationships with the public an customers, will at all times be given courteous attention by your im mediate superior or you can describe your plan or idea in a lette and place it in the "SUGGESTION BOX" where it will be carefull reviewed by the Operating Committee and make you eligible for reward, if it is adopted.

LOYALTY

Every bank, for all practical purposes, can be considered public institution. It is the public, having confidence in the ban and its management, who deposit its funds which the bank loan to produce income. The security and well being of many peopl depend on the manner in which affairs of the bank are conducte Because of the credit facilities the bank extends to businessmen an individuals to finance their business transactions, the communit is dependent on the bank for its economic development.

In addition to confidence, the quality of loyalty is present i every successful bank. Loyalty not only means respect and co fidence, but a profound belief in the policies under which the ban is operated.

Customers are loyal when they give us their business; as a employee we are loyal when we perform our work accuratel refrain from making unkind remarks about our associates or t officers and stoutly defend the bank's actions.

Loyalty is earned. Unless we can be loyal to our friends, loy to our associates, loyal to the bank, that is believe in them and b willing to defend them against outsiders, we should change o position and seek employment with a firm to which we can expre loyalty.

JUDGMENT

One of the principal characteristics of a leader or a person w aspires to hold a top executive position in the bank is the quality judgment.

Judgment comes from experience, the ability to assimilate a evaluate facts and be able to render a decision which most of t time is correct. Every action we perform in life is the result of t legree of judgment we have acquired in respective fields. We ither do something, or do not do it; we either say something, or do ot say it; we either do something this way or that way. The extent o which our decisions are the right ones depends on the degree of ıdgment and experience we have acquired.

It is important that whenever a person in a bank possesses uthority he has knowledge or has had experience. Without this ackground a person is not prepared to have good judgment or roperly evaluate all factors from which to render a decision in ıe best interest of the bank.

Remember the greater our information and experience the etter equipped we are to judge and render correct decisions.

We should not be afraid to make decisions within our scope f authority and responsibility as set forth in the Organization Plan.

CONFIDENTIAL

There is no business which has such a degree of secrecy surounding the transactions as those which take place in a bank. eople do business with the bank because they have confidence in ıe bank, believe the management is capable, and that each member the staff of the bank will handle customer's business in absolute onfidence.

Divulging the amount of money a person has in a checking or vings account; the name of persons to whom checks are payable who they receive money from; the type of collateral they have edged as security for a loan, etc., is prohibited. Customers enred into these transactions originally because they were certain eir trust would not be betrayed and that the transaction would be eated with the utmost confidence. Breaches of confidence can deroy an individual, make his position precarious and expose the ınk to possible loss.

Every employee of a bank should realize the trust placed in m by the customer, the bank officers, and his fellow employees ıd should do whatever is within his power to keep the relationship hich exists between the customer and the bank confidential.

KNOWLEDGE

The opportunities for advancement in banking are many, but e cannot advance unless we show we have the ability to assume greater responsibilities, or are capable of performing more difficul work. Naturally when we assume additional responsibilities o perform more difficult work, we are rewarded by increases in salar and promotions.

Ambition is a wonderful quality for anyone to have, but want ing a thing does not make it so. A thing will only happen if w are willing to work and contribute our time to make it happen.

The first step in getting ahead is to learn thoroughly everythin there is to learn about the particular job we are to do. The ne step is to learn everything there is to know about the job ahead, ho it is handled, its responsibilities, any policies in connection with th job, and about the person who supervises the job. Most importan however, is that we train or acquaint someone in our section, or se to it that someone in our section knows everything about our jo and can take over this responsibility when the opportunity com for us to advance.

Building a successful career is similar to building a house. I order to build a good house which will stand strong and last throug the years, it is necessary to have a solid and firm foundation. W can likewise only be successful in banking if we have a solid fou dation.

There are many ways to acquire knowledge:

1. Through reading books on banking.

2. Inquiring of our superiors and fellow workers about t job, learning all you can.

3. Outside studies. Attend the courses offered by the Ame can Institute of Banking.

Knowledge is power, and when a person knows how, why, a when to perform certain operations or undertake certain functio he is preparing himself for advancement in his chosen career.

No better way exists to accomplish this than to become th oughly familiar with the Manual of Operations of each division section in which you work, become thoroughly conversant with t Operating Instructions which apply to the particular functions, a learn in detail the work performed by each employee in the divisi or section in which you work.

Banks which adopt sound personnel policies and friendly hiri and indoctrination procedures realize many benefits, principally b cause such policies not only result in having salary increases a romotions based on merit instead of seniority, which contributes to ttracting the finest calibre of men to the banking profession; but ecause friendly hiring and indoctrination practices and procedures ake friends for the bank and install an esprit de corps which conibutes to the progress and development of the bank.

Progressive and constructive employee relations, however, do ot end with friendly indoctrination customs, use of Handbooks and lanuals of Operation, or sound salary review practices. This is nly a beginning. The entire bank must be friendly and possess spirit of cooperation.

Constructive personnel relations, contrary to what is sometimes elieved, do not start at the bottom and grow upward, but to be fective must either rub off, or like rain, come from above and seep ownward, where it can softly fall on young sprouts, and assist em to grow in stature and strength, to where they become strong ough to assume the mantle of management responsibility.

In conclusion, it is well to remember that a courteous and iendly bank is generally nothing more than the reflection of its ief executive officer.

CHAPTER XVI

DEVELOPMENT, USE AND TYPES OF NEGOTIABLE INSTRUMENTS

THE DEVELOPMENT OF COMMERCE and trad while predicated on expansion of territories and economic factor was restricted, as we have seen, by two factors—lack of a satisfactor medium of exchange easy to transport and whose value was n based on weight or fineness, and frequent borrowing (confiscatio of the wealth of merchants and money changers by sovereign ruler

To overcome these deterrents to commercial progress, me chants realized that some form of credit instrument was necessa as a medium of exchange and turned more and more to use of "O ders to Pay" or "Bills of Exchange" to complete business and trad transactions.

Originally merchants, following the practice of the mone changers, maintained credit balances with other merchants locate in the principal cities where they did business. These credit ba ances originated from the sale of goods, the proceeds of which th did not "bring home." Thereafter a merchant completed tradi with other merchants in the town where he maintained a cred balance by "ordering" the merchant with whom he had funds deposit, by letter, to use all or part of these funds to complete t transaction.

These "Orders to Pay", commonly known as Bills of Exchang increased in use as commerce developed and, in conducting co mercial and financial transactions, took a number of forms to ser special purposes.

Many of these forms of Bills of Exchange are today commor referred to as:

- Acceptances
- Bank Checks
- Bank Drafts
- Bank Money Orders
- Bank Registered Checks

Bills of Exchange (Foreign and Domestic)
Cashier's Checks
Certified Checks
Drafts (Time and Sight)
Promissory Notes
Treasurer's Checks

The characteristics which made these forms of Bills of Exiange important in conducting trade and commerce was the fact iat they were "negotiable" that is title could be transferred by enorsement or merely "receipting for" or "signing over" the value or terest which the document represented.

Before describing the various types or forms of Bills of Exiange which are a vital part of modern commerce, let us first efine or describe what constitutes a Bill of Exchange, and the contions, requirements and characteristics which make such instruents "negotiable."

A Bill of Exchange may be defined as an unconditional order in riting, addressed by one person (the creditor or payee) to another erson (the debtor or drawee) instructing that payment of a certain m of money be made to a third person, or his order (payee), on emand, or at a fixed or determinable future time.

As over the years, and in the course of numerous business transtions, use of these instruments were subject to dispute and diffilties, often the disputes were taken to court where decision was ndered based on common law. As a result, vast sections of the d Roman, Spanish and English law were concerned with cases and ecisions involving use of such instruments.

The first statement of principles of common law in connection ith negotiable instruments was the British Bill of Exchange Act ssed in 1882. This was followed by the drafting of the Negotiable struments Law for the United States which was initially adopted the states of Florida, Connecticut, New York and Virginia in 97. Prior to enactment of the law, which was later adopted in me form by all the states, (and even at the present time, 1960, is bject to further amendments and changes to make it uniform) ses growing out of litigation covering checks and notes were verned by common law, which is still resorted to where the egotiable Instruments Law does not cover the case.

While there are slight differences in the Negotiable Instruments

Laws of the various states, they are all uniform in the requiremer that every document, in order to qualify as a negotiable instrumen must have the following characteristics:

1. It must be an unconditional promise, or order to pay, a sur certain in money.

2. It must be in writing and must be signed by the maker c drawer.

3. It must be payable on demand, or at a fixed or determinab future date.

4. It must be payable to a certain person, to order, or to beare

5. It must not contain any conditions except those necessary fix the time and place for payment of the money.

6. It must be possible for the instrument to pass readily fro one holder to another in such a manner that the holder receiving can obtain the full and complete benefits, as set forth in the instr ment.

Negotiable instruments are divided into two classes

A. *Promises to Pay,* such as Notes, Acceptances and Bills Exchange, and

B. *Orders to Pay,* such as Checks and Drafts.

"Promises to Pay" differ from "Orders to Pay" in several r spects. A "Promise to Pay" which is an unconditional promise one person to pay a certain sum of money to another person, i volves two persons, the drawer and the payee.

An "Order to Pay" which is an unconditional order from o person to another person ordering them to pay a certain sum money to a third person, involves three persons, the drawer w issues and signs the order; the drawee, to whom the order is addre ed; and the payee, to whom the payment is to be made.

While a negotiable instrument is created by the drawer or t maker, it is not effective or of value until it has been formally livered to the payee.

Proper delivery is one of the important conditions of nego ability. To have such proper delivery the person who has possessi of the instrument must tender the instrument to another person w the intention of transferring good legal title. Instruments which not intentionally delivered, such as those which are lost or stol are not considered legally to have been properly negotiated.

Once, however, the payee has the instrument in his possessi

the instrument is payable to his order, he can transfer his legal tle to another person for value, simply by endorsement or by riting his name on the reverse side as it appears on the face of the strument, and physically delivering the instrument to the person whom he intends to transfer his rights. If the instrument is payble to "bearer," the holder may transfer title merely by making hysical delivery of the instrument.

ENDORSEMENTS

In order that the condition of negotiability, the transfer of title d rights in the instrument from one person to another, be underood, knowledge of endorsements is necessary.

Endorsements refer to either the handwritten signature or the amped or typed name of the payee, or a subsequent holder of an strument and are usually placed on the reverse side for the rpose of transferring the holder's rights in the instrument to meone else. They are of six types:

1. Blank
2. Special
3. Restrictive
4. Qualified
5. Conditional
6. Combination

Blank Endorsement

A Blank Endorsement consists simply of the endorser's signare on the reverse side of the instrument. If the signature is the dorsement of the payee, it must agree with the name of the payee pearing on the face of the instrument. The effect of a blank or a neral endorsement is to make the instrument payable to the arer, and is transferable simply by delivery.

Special Endorsement

A Special endorsement names the person to whom the title the instrument is being tranferred. For instance, a check made yable to George Brown might bear a special endorsement reading follows:

Pay to the order of
William Smith
(signed) George Brown

The endorsement of the designated endorser (William Smith) necessary for further negotiations of the instrument.

Restrictive Endorsement

A restrictive endorsement is one that imposes limitations the transferee such as naming the specific purpose of the transfe There are several forms of restrictive endorsements. The mc common is the one used when the holder deposits a check in h bank for collection and for credit to his account in the bank. Su restrictive endorsement might read as follows:

For deposit only in the
First National Bank
(signed) Willis Allen

Qualified Endorsement

A qualified endorsement is one in which the words "witho recourse" or a similar expression appear above the endorser's si nature. It has the effect of relieving the endorser of certain liabi ties that usually accompany an endorsement. A qualified endors ment implies that while the party transferring the instrument h the right to do so, he does not guarantee payment.

Such a qualified endorsement might read as follows:

Without recourse
(signed) George S. Olson

Conditional Endorsement

A conditional endorsement imposes upon subsequent endors the responsibility of determining whether the conditions includ in the endorsement have been fulfilled. Such an endorsement mig read:

Pay to the order of
William Smith
When my car is repaired
(signed) George S. Allen

It should be fairly obvious that no one should accept an inst ment bearing a qualified or a conditional endorsement unless he fully aware of the circumstances surrounding the transfer of instrument in this manner and have full knowledge of the le consequences of such an endorsement.

Combination Endorsement

It may be noted that various combinations of the five principal rms of endorsements are possible. The following is a combination f a special endorsement and a restrictive endorsement:

Pay to the order of the
First National Bank
for deposit only
(signed) Thomas H. Smith

Endorsers of negotiable instruments not only incur a serious ability but assume grave responsibility when they sign their name the reverse side of a negotiable instrument.

When a person endorses a negotiable instrument he not only uarantees all prior endorsements," which means that if any preous endorsement proves to be forged or unauthorized he will reburse the holder, but warrants that:

1. The instrument is genuine.
2. He has good title to it and the right to transfer the title.
3. He has no knowledge of any defect in the instrument.
4. If the instrument is not paid upon presentation he will pay providing he has been properly notified as to non-payment.

These provisions of the law are both insuring and logical for if e holder of a dishonored check did not have the privilege of revering the money from the person from whom he received the strument, and this person in turn could not recover from the preding endorser, no one would be willing to accept endorsed checks ce in most instances there is no assurance that the check is good, will be paid on presentation.

Because the liabilities of an endorser have been firmly esblished by law, it has brought about the universal and widespread e of negotiable instruments as prime mediums of exchange.

It is also important to note that regardless of dispute or question volving the original transaction and the possible effect on the hts of the original payee, the rights of a subsequent holder are t affected as long as he accepted the instrument "for value," and d no knowledge either of a defect in the instrument itself or in the ht of the person to negotiate it. Such a person is known as a older in due course" and looks to the previous endorsers for pannt.

Banks are particularly interested in the liability of endorse because of the huge volume of checks they handle daily. When bank accepts checks and other cash items for deposit, it gives th depositor immediate credit. and the bank has the right to charg or debit the depositor's account with any item which is dishonore upon presentment.

When checks are cashed by a bank's teller for customers, th situation is slightly different. Courts in some states have held tha a cashed check which is subsequently dishonored may be charge to the depositor's account. Courts in other states have held tha such items are not chargeable to the depositor's account. In th latter instance, however, there is no question about the custome liability to the bank because of his endorsement on the check. *

With the widespread use of negotiable instruments, there we many lawsuits involving the liability of endorsers. Because of th absence of substantiating information, resulting in contradicto evidence, it was quite difficult to determine the facts. Holde would claim they had made proper presentation, but the endors would deny it. Then if the holder claimed he had given prop notice of dishonor, the endorser claimed he had never received Finally, in order to provide proper protection to endorsers wi irrefutable evidence, the practice of "Protest" came into wide use.

Under such practice, when a negotiable instrument is dishono ed, it is delivered by the holder to a notary public or other qualifi public official who formally presents the instrument. If payment refused, he notifies the maker and all endorsers, and attaches to th instrument an official statement bearing his official seal relating a the facts concerning the non-payment of the instrument and th action taken.

Under this practice, when a dishonored instrument is offer as evidence in court, the protest documents establish the fact th presentation was properly made, at the proper place, at the prop time, and that all endorsers, as well as the principals, were du notified.

PRINCIPAL TYPES OF NEGOTIABLE INSTRUMENTS

Acceptances

An acceptance is a bill of exchange payable at a future da

* A. I. B. "Principles of Bank Operations"

·hich has been "accepted" (honored) by the drawee, signifying his ıtention to pay the bill at maturity. Acceptance consists of writing ıe word "ACCEPTED" across the face of the instrument, together ·ith the date, name of the bank where payable, and followed by ıe signature of payee.

Acceptances are of two general classes, bank acceptances, and ·ade acceptances.

A Bank Acceptance (Exhibit 31) is a bill of exchange used to ıance foreign and domestic transactions and arises out of drafts rawn under Letters of Credit issued by the accepting bank. By ccepting the draft, the bank substitutes its credit for that of its ıstomer and guarantees the draft will be paid at maturity.

Exhibit 31

BANK ACCEPTANCE

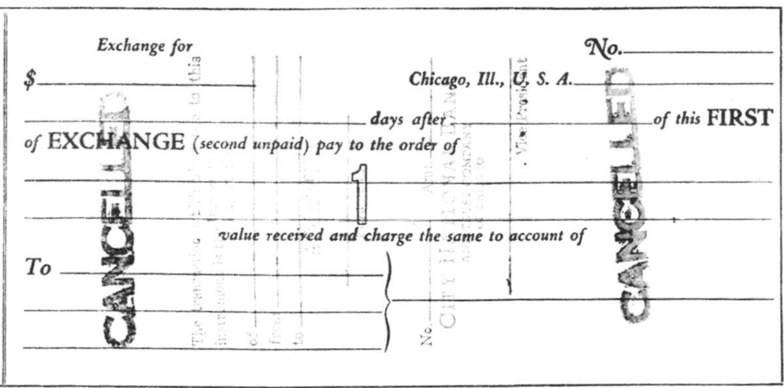
Exchange for No.
$ *Chicago, Ill., U. S. A.*
days after *of this* FIRST
of EXCHANGE *(second unpaid) pay to the order of*
1
value received and charge the same to account of
To
CANCELLED
CANCELLED

A Trade Acceptance (Exhibit 32) used to finance domestic trade a bill of exchange drawn by the seller on the purchaser of goods hich has been "accepted" or acknowledged by the purchaser. nce accepted, with name of the bank where payable affixed, the ocument is equivalent to an order on the bank to charge the in-ument to the purchaser's account, when presented for payment ı maturity date.

Exhibit 32

TRADE ACCEPTANCE

TRADE ACCEPTANCE

No. ______ ______ 19____
(CITY OF DRAWER) (DATE)

TO ______ ______
(NAME OF DRAWEE) (ADDRESS OF DRAWEE)

ON ______ PAY TO THE ORDER OF ______
(DATE OF MATURITY) (NAME OF PAYEE)

______ DOLLARS, ($______)

THE TRANSACTION WHICH GIVES RISE TO THIS INSTRUMENT IS THE PURCHASE OF GOODS BY THE ACCEPTOR FROM THE DRAWER. THE DRAWEE MAY ACCEPT THIS BILL PAYABLE AT ANY BANK, BANKER OR TRUST COMPANY IN THE UNITED STATES WHICH SUCH DRAWEE MAY DESIGNATE.

ACCEPTED AT ______ ON ______ 19____
(CITY) (DATE)

PAYABLE AT ______
(NAME OF BANK)

LOCATION ______

______
(SIGNATURE OF DRAWER)

BY ______

No. L1-29 (SIGNATURE OF ACCEPTOR)

Bank Check

A Bank Check (Exhibit 33) is an order to pay given in exchang for goods or objects having value, or in settlement of deferred ex change signed by the purchaser authorizing a third party (bank to immediately pay the seller or payee on presentation of the orde the amount called for in the instrument.

Exhibit 33

BANK CHECK

THE FIRST COMMERCIAL BANK

2-43
710

CHICAGO, ILL. ______ 195___ NO.

PAY TO THE ORDER OF ______ $______

______ DOLLAR

Bank Draft

A Bank Draft (Exhibit 34) is a written order (check) drawn by ne bank ordering another bank, with whom the first bank mainains a credit balance (account), to pay a certain sum of money to a hird party.

Exhibit 34

BANK DRAFT

CIVIC CENTER BANK AND TRUST CO.
LA SALLE AT RANDOLPH
CHICAGO, ILLINOIS 60601
2-129
710

102

DATE June 29, 1966

1-2
210

PAY TO THE ORDER OF American Red Cross

EXACTLY $1 AND 00 CTS

THE CHASE MANHATTAN BANK
National Association
1 Chase Manhattan Plaza, New York, N. Y.

Pres.

⑈0210⑈0002⑆ 920⑈1⑈0510761⑈

Bank Money Orders

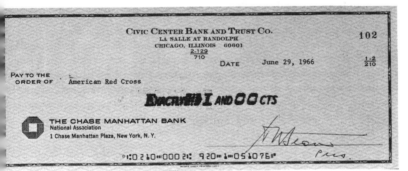

Bank Money Orders (Exhibit 35) are similar to Cashier's Checks ıd Treasurer's Checks, except that the bank money orders are not rawn for official business purposes but are sold to depositors and thers usually for the payment of bills.

Exhibit 35

BANK MONEY ORDER

BANK MONEY ORDER No. 291549
FIRST NATIONAL BANK AND TRUST COMPANY
OF EVANSTON
EVANSTON, ILL.
70-114
710
M.C.Corns
REMITTER
SEP 26 1960
Pay to the order of American Red Cross $ 1.00
1ST NAT'L BK.& TR. CO. EVANSTON $$1 00 CTS
NOT VALID IF DRAWN IN EXCESS OF $500
PAYABLE THROUGH CHICAGO CLEARING HOUSE OR IF DESIRED THROUGH THE
Morgan Guaranty Trust Company of New York
CASHIER

Bank Registered Checks

Registered Checks (Exhibit 36) are used for much the sam purpose as Bank Money Orders, but they are handled by the ban in a slightly different manner. When a Registered Check is pu chased, the bank merely cuts the desired amount in a prepare check with a check writer, dates the instrument, and delivers it t the purchaser, who fills in the name of the payee and signs his ow name as maker.

Registered Checks are not technically "Bank" checks but check the purchaser has drawn against the total balance of a account opened for a single special purpose.

Bills of Exchange

A Bill of Exchange, as we have noted previously, is any un conditional order in writing addressed by one person to anoth person, instructing that payment of a certain sum of money b paid to a third person on demand, or at a fixed or determinable fu ture time.

When such instruments are payable on presentation or deman they are the same as an "Order to Pay" such as bank checks

Exhibit 36

BANK REGISTERED CHECK or PERSONAL MONEY ORDER

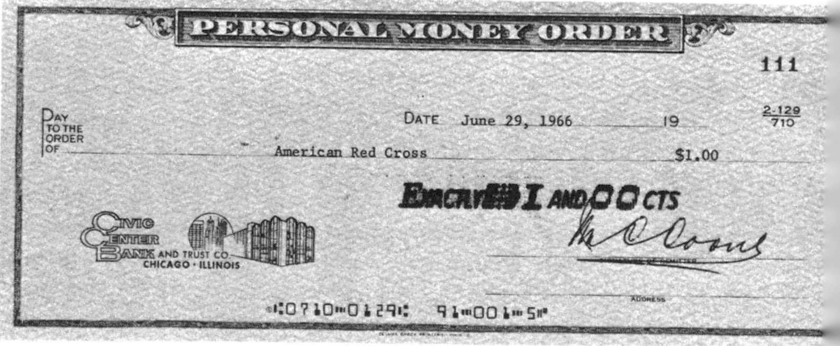

PERSONAL MONEY ORDER

111

DATE June 29, 1966 19

2-129
710

PAY TO THE ORDER OF American Red Cross $1.00

EXACTLY 1 AND 00 CTS

CIVIC CENTER BANK AND TRUST CO.
CHICAGO · ILLINOIS

ADDRESS

⑆0710⑈0129⑆ 91⑈001⑈5⑈

drafts. When such instruments are payable at a determinable future time, they may become Acceptances or take the form of one of the various types of drafts.

There are certain additional distinctions covering all types of Bills of Exchange. If drawn covering a transaction in a certain state or country, depending upon usage, they are known as a "Domestic Bill." If drawn to cover transactions in foreign countries, they are known as "Foreign Bills." Frequently, too, depending upon the commodity given in exchange, they are called after the commodity such as "cotton bill," "grain bill," etc.

Cashier's Check

A Cashier's Check (Exhibit 37) is a draft drawn by a bank on itself. In legal effect, cashier's checks are considered to have the qualifications of acceptances or promises to pay. Since the drawer and drawee are identical, acceptances or acknowledgment of the instrument by the drawee is implied.

Certified Check

A Certified Check (Exhibit 38) is a Bill of Exchange (check) payable on presentation or demand, drawn by a depositor on a bank,

Exhibit 37

CASHIER'S CHECK

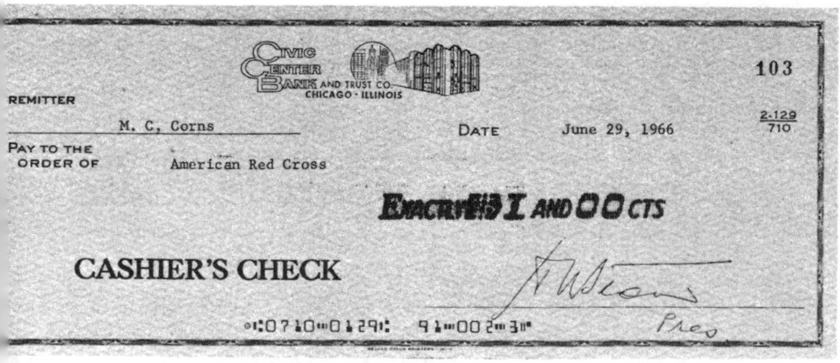

Civic Center Bank and Trust Co. Chicago · Illinois

103

REMITTER M. C. Corns

DATE June 29, 1966

2-129
710

PAY TO THE ORDER OF American Red Cross

CASHIER'S CHECK

Pres

Exhibit 38

CERTIFIED CHECK

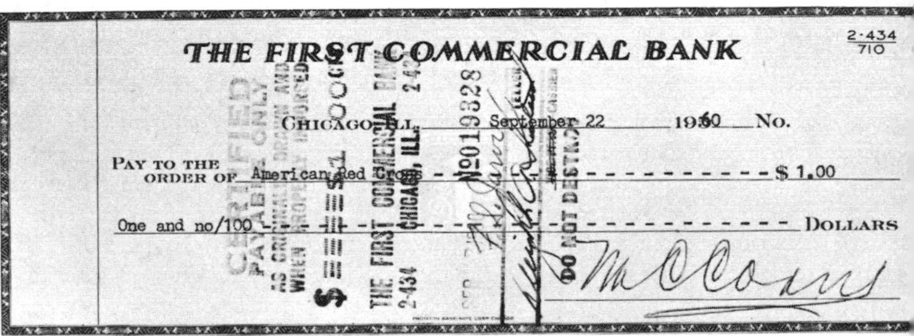
THE FIRST COMMERCIAL BANK 2-434/710

CHICAGO, ILL. September 22 1960 No.

PAY TO THE ORDER OF American Red Cross $ 1.00

One and no/100 DOLLARS

CERTIFIED PAYABLE ONLY AS ORIGINALLY DRAWN AND WHEN PROPERLY ENDORSED

THE FIRST COMMERCIAL BANK CHICAGO, ILL. 2-434

No019328

DO NOT DESTROY

which the bank legally "accepts" by writing the word "CERTIFIED" across the face of the check.

Certified Checks differ from Acceptances in that while both ar drawn by a depositor, when a check is "certified" the amount o the check is immediately charged against the credit balance of th customer; but under an "acceptance" arrangement, the instrumen is drawn under a loan or credit agreement which becomes the ob ligation of the depositor payable at maturity, or future date.

Drafts

A draft is the same as a Bill of Exchange except that in thi country the term "Draft" is used in domestic transactions whil both of the terms "Draft" and "Bill of Exchange" are used in foreig transactions.

A draft differs from a check in that it is an instrument drawn o an individual, firm, corporation, or bank where the initiative fo payment is instituted by the seller and not the buyer. Anothe difference is that in case of a draft, the debtor or merchant has th custody of the money, while in the case of a bank check, the ban has custodianship.

Drafts are of several principal types:

1. Commercial Drafts
2. Security or Collection Drafts
3. Dunning Drafts

Commercial Drafts (Exhibit 39) usually arise out of commercial or trade transactions where the buyer and seller are located in different sections of the country, and where arrangements have been made between buyer and seller for the seller to draw drafts on the buyer in settlement of the transactions. In such cases the seller sends the draft, with shipping documents attached, to the buyer's bank, usually through their correspondent bank. Upon presentation and payment, the shipping documents are released to the buyer either upon payment of the draft or "ACCEPTANCE." (See ACCEPTANCE)

Security or Collection Drafts (Exhibit 40) do not arise out of commercial transactions, but are used to secure payment of funds against delivery of securities, deeds, or other instruments.

Dunning Drafts (Exhibit 41), which have no documents attached, are merely "demands for payment" of past due bills and

Exhibit 39

COMMERCIAL DRAFT

DRAFT

Chicago, Illinois________________

____________________ Pay to the order of

______________________________ Dollars-$____________

o

Exhibit 40

SECURITY or COLLECTION DRAFT

THE FIRST COMMERCIAL BANK

$______ CHICAGO, ILL.__________19___ NO.______

________________ PAY TO THE ORDER OF THE FIRST COMMERCIAL BANK

____________________________ DOLLARS

WITH EXCHANGE

VALUE RECEIVED AND CHARGE SAME TO ACCOUNT OF

TO________________

FORM 58 - 2M-10-56-R.P.P.

Exhibit 41

DUNNING DRAFT

$______ __________19___

Pay to the order of ________________

________________ WITH EXCHANGE Dollars

Value received and charge the same to account of

To ________________

No. ________________

NO. L1-4420

generally are only presented by a bank to the payer upon prior payment of a collection or presentation fee.

The time when various drafts are due and payable is generally used in describing the types of drafts.

A. Sight Drafts

B. Arrival Drafts

C. Time Drafts

Sight Drafts are payable on presentation or demand.

Arrival Drafts are payable upon arrival of the goods at the destination of the drawee, or place of delivery designated by him.

Time Drafts are payable on a fixed date, or on a date a certain number of days after presentation. A time draft payment "30 days after sight" must be presented for acceptance, and presented at maturity for payment.

Promissory Notes

A Promissory Note is an unconditional promise in writing, signed by the maker, to pay on demand or at a fixed or determinable future time, a certain sum of dollars, at a certain place, to order or to bearer, given in consideration for value of services or goods previously received.

Promissory Notes are of two kinds, time or demand. In addition, each kind may be of two types, secured or unsecured (Exhibits 42-43).

A Time Promissory Note is a promise to pay the amount of money so stated in the instrument on the date of payment, or after the number of days specified in the instrument at the place specified in the instrument.

A Demand Promissory Note is a promise to pay the amount of money so stated in the instrument whenever the holder of the note demands payment of the maker. Such demand usually must be accompanied by notice and presentation of the instrument at the place of payment specified in the instrument.

Promissory Notes generally bear interest from date of the instrument until date of maturity or demand for payment, at a rate not exceeding the maximum rate of interest allowable by the state in which the note was made.

Where time or demand promissory notes are "secured," it means that securities or other documents of value acceptable to the

Exhibit 42

PROMISSORY NOTE UNSECURED
(Front side)

$__________ *Wilmette, Illinois*__________19___

________________*days after date, for value received, the undersigned, and each of them, promise to pay to the order of* **THE WILMETTE STATE BANK** *at its banking house in Wilmette, the sum of*____________________*Dollars*

with interest at the rate of_____per cent per annum after {date / maturity} until paid and said bank or its assigns is hereby authorized to apply upon this note or upon any other indebtedness of the undersigned or either of them to said bank at its option, at any time before or after the maturity thereof, any money or other property in the possession of said bank or its assigns belonging to the undersigned or either or any of them. And to further secure the payment of this note the undersigned hereby irrevocably authorizes any attorney of any court of record to appear for the undersigned, or either or any of them, in such court, in term time or in vacation, or at any time hereafter, and confess judgment, without process in favor of the holder of this note for such amount as may appear to be unpaid thereon, including interest, whether due or not, together with costs and reasonable attorney's fees, and to waive and release all errors which may intervene in any such proceedings and consent to immediate execution upon such judgment and to waive all benefit under the exemption laws of the State of Illinois, hereby ratifying and confirming all said attorney may do by virtue hereof.

No._______*Due*_____________ ________________

Address____________________ ________________

(Reverse side)

FOR value received the undersigned hereby guarantees the prompt payment of this note at maturity and at all times thereafter, hereby expressly waiving demand, protest, notice of protest or non-payment, or other notice of any kind.

Exhibit 43

Wilmette, Illinois,..19......

$.................... ....days after date for value received.....................promise to pay to the order of

THE WILMETTE STATE BANK

....Dollars

at its offices in Wilmette, Illinois, with interest at the rate of...............per cent per annum after {date / maturity} until paid.

The undersigned ha____deposited with, and pledged to said THE WILMETTE STATE BANK as collateral security for the payment of the above and foregoing note, and also of all other liabilities of any kind of all or any one or more of the undersigned to said Bank due or to become due, heretofore or hereafter contracted, or which may hereafter arise, the following property owned by the undersigned namely:

----

the market value of which is now $____________________.

In case said THE WILMETTE STATE BANK shall at any time be of the opinion that said property is or may be of less value than above stated or that the whole or any part of said property has declined or may decline in value, or in case said Bank shall feel insecure, or in case any bank may, in its discretion, call for additional security, satisfactory to it, and if the same is not furnished on demand, may, at its option, declare this note, and also any and all other liabilities of all or any one or more of the undersigned to said Bank immediately due and payable, without notice or demand. And said Bank is hereby given further authority and power, from time to time, to sell or cause to be sold, all or any part of said pledged property and any property substituted therefor, and any additions which shall be made or accrue thereto, either on the maturity of any such liability or at any time thereafter, or before, if the property or substitutes or additions shall depreciate in value, or if said Bank shall feel insecure, at the discretion of said Bank, at public or private sale, without advertising the same or giving notice of such sale to any person or corporation, and without demand of payment, with the right of said Bank to buy the same or any part thereof at any public sale made hereunder, and upon such purchase thereafter to hold the same absolutely discharged from any claim or interest of the undersigned therein, and with the right also to said Bank at its discretion and in lieu of such sale to collect or cause to be collected or otherwise converted into money all or any part of said pledged, substituted or additional property and securities; hereby also giving the said Bank authority, after first deducting from the proceeds of any such sale, collection or conversion, all costs, attorney's fees and expenses made, or incurred in respect thereto, to apply such proceeds then remaining to the payment of all, either or any part of the said liabilities to said Bank, due or not due, in such order and manner as said Bank shall at its discretion choose, returning the overplus, if any, to or holding the same for the undersigned; and in case such proceeds shall not satisfy the whole of all said liabilities, costs and expenses, the undersigned agree____to pay the deficiency forthwith to said Bank.

In case of any exchange of, or substitution for, or addition to said property so pledged, or any part thereof, all of the provisions of this agreement shall extend to such new, exchanged, substitute or additional property. And the undersigned hereby authorize____said Bank, at any time, at its discretion, to apply any money or moneys which said Bank may have or hold on deposit or otherwise, or in transit to it, for the undersigned, or either of them, toward the payment of said note and other liabilities, whether due or not. The undersigned hereby gives to said Bank the option from time to time by written notice to the undersigned to change the rate of interest thereafter to accrue on the foregoing note, and hereby agree____to pay the said rate as changed, unless the undersigned shall at once elect to and forthwith pay said note, with the interest then due thereon, which notice of change of rate shall be sufficient if mailed to the address of the undersigned. All the provisions and powers hereof shall inure to the benefit of the assigns of said Bank. And to further secure the payment of this note the undersigned hereby irrevocably authorizes any attorney of any court of record to appear for the undersigned, or either or any of them, in such court, in term time or in vacation, or at any time hereafter, and confess judgment, without process in favor of the holder of this note for such amount as may appear to be unpaid thereon, including interest, whether due or not, together with costs and reasonable attorney's fees, and to waive and release all errors which may intervene in any such proceedings and consent to immediate execution upon such judgment and to waive all benefit under the exemption laws of the State of Illinois, hereby ratifying and confirming all said attorney may do by virtue hereof.

No............................ Due.................................... ....

Address ....

ender have been pledged as collateral to secure the payment of the note.

Treasurer's Checks

A Treasurer's Check is the same as a Cashier's Check. Cashier's Checks are the official instruments of a state or national bank where the official, who is responsible for operations, is usually known as the Cashier. The same official in many Trust Companies or other state chartered institutions, who has the same or similar responsibilities, is known as the Treasurer, and instruments drawn by such institution on itself are known as Treasurer's Checks.

CHAPTER XVII

THE RELATIONSHIP OF A BANK WITH ITS CUSTOMERS [1]

EVERY PERSON WHO DOES BUSINESS with a bank generally does so because of an agency, fiduciary, debtor or creditor relationship founded on a contract.

Sometimes the contract covering this relationship is expressed by a written agreement and other times it is unwritten. Where the contract or arrangement for the relationship is unwritten, banking laws and customs supply the framework of rules and regulations based on common law under which transactions are handled.

In order to better understand the relationship between banks and their customers, a brief explanation of the types of relationships is in order. Here let it be said that the more relationships an individual, firm, corporation, partnership, or association has with a bank, the more valuable they become; and it is the objective of an aggressive bank to encourage customers with whom it only has one relationship, to maintain other relationships.

An agency relationship exists between a bank and a customer when the bank performs or provides certain single services for or in behalf of a person, individual, firm, corporation, partnership, or association, such as the purchase and sale of securities for their account; collecting interest on bonds, notes and mortgages, providing safekeeping and safe deposit services; selling cashier's checks and drafts and money orders, all of which assist them in conducting their business transactions. These and many other services are detailed in Chapter IX under Services of Banks.

A fiduciary relationship exists between a bank and a customer when the bank acts as a trustee, executor, administrator or agent

[1] Acknowledgment for much of the information used in this chapter is made to the authors of "Principles of Bank Operation" American Institute of Banking, Chapter VII "Legal Relationship with Depositors."

for an estate on matters in which the customer has an interest either as principal or beneficiary. The various types of fiduciary relationships are listed in Chapter IX under Services of Banks and explained in greater detail in the chapter dealing with the Trust Department.

A *debtor relationship* exists between a bank and a customer whenever an individual, firm, corporation, partnership or association borrows money from a bank. The various instruments through which a person can borrow money from a bank, the many purposes for which money can be borrowed, and the many terms under which such money can be repaid are listed in Chapter IX under Services of Banks and covered in the chapters dealing with Credit and Loaning Operations.

A *creditor relationship* exists between a bank and a customer whenever an individual, firm, corporation, partnership or association deposits certain sums of money or instruments representing sums of money for collection with the bank, under conditions, provisions, arrangements or agreement covering the withdrawal and use of such funds.

According to law a contract is enforceable only if the parties to the contract have the legal power to enter into a contract or make an agreement. In the relationship of a bank with its customers, most of the obligations under whatever agreement or contract is entered into, rest upon the bank.

The bank's authority to enter into contracts is established and limited by provisions of its charter which, in the case of a state bank, is granted by the state in which it is incorporated, or by the Comptroller of the Currency in the case of a national bank. In the latter case, however, such authority never conflicts with the laws of the state in which the bank is located.

A bank's authority to enter into contracts may also be limited by the By-Laws of the bank and the acts of the Board of Directors. In every case, however, employees of the bank empowered to enter into contracts on behalf of the bank, are granted this authority and are appointed either by the Board of Directors or Executive Officer acting in behalf of the stockholders.

An individual, member of a partnership, officer of a corporation or association, likewise, has certain authority to enter into contracts. This is either granted by law, by provision of the articles of association, or under the corporation charter under which the business is conducted.

The reason that contracts are entered into covering such relationships is clearly evident. When a party who intends to establish a relationship with a bank comes to the bank and deals with a representative of the bank, generally seated in official quarters, they can rightfully assume that the person representing the bank has the authority to bind the bank in ordinary contracts having to do with the business of banking.

The bank officer, on the other hand, finds himself in quite a different position. Many of the people who approach his desk are complete strangers. A person may represent himself to be a certain individual, a partner, a corporation officer, a trustee, a member of an association, or an individual doing business under a trade name. Before entering into such a contract with a customer, it is necessary that bank officers thoroughly satisfy themselves concerning the identity of the individual. If the individual is not acting for himself, the bank officers must satisfy themselves that the person has authority to act in the capacity he represents.

As in a bank we first must have deposits before we can invest them to provide interest income, and must have accounts before we can obtain income from providing services, let us first study the creditor relationship between the bank and its customers.

The creditor relationship divides itself into two principal types, the relationship of the bank with the demand, or checking account depositors, and the relationship of the bank with a time, or savings account depositor. In both of these relationships particular attention is paid by the bank to the identification of the individual, firm, corporation, partnership or association which deposits the funds. This is important because the bank, in accepting deposits, must be certain that the individual, firm, corporation, partnership or association has the legal right and title to the funds deposited. Also the bank, in honoring checks or withdrawals, must be certain it is paying out such funds on the authorization of the proper individual or the person certified by the firm, corporation, partnership or association as authorized to make disbursement of funds.

THE DEMAND ACCOUNT RELATIONSHIP

As demand deposit accounts of individuals, etc., constitute the largest volume of any form of funds on deposit with banks, let us review the relationship of the bank with the demand depositor.

Under the demand deposit relationship the customer deposits funds with the bank for collection and credit to his account, for the purpose of safekeeping and for the privilege of drawing checks up to the full amount of the balance to his credit, at any time and without prior notice to the bank.

The bank, as part of its contract, agrees to have available at all times liquid funds with which to redeem in cash any checks which have been presented by a person authorized to receive the funds, provided the order to pay is properly authorized and there are sufficient funds on deposit to cover the check.

As it is important that the bank have definite knowledge of such relationships, in order to avoid fraud being committed for which the bank might be held liable, let us describe the various classes of accounts included in this relationship.

ACCOUNT CLASSIFIED ACCORDING TO AUTHORITY

On the basis of authority, accounts may be classified as:

- Individual Accounts
- Joint Accounts, involving two or more persons
- Partnership Accounts
- Trade Name or Proprietorship Accounts
- Corporation Accounts
- Fiduciary Accounts
- Club, Church, or Association Accounts
- Public Funds

Individual Accounts

The proper opening of an individual account is not very involved for only the identification of the person presenting the deposit is required. The question of identification itself is by no means a simple matter. There is no absolutely positive means of identification or set procedure for a bank to follow. Bank officers establish identification satisfactorily by a combination of experience and judgment. The circumstances surrounding each particular case reveal how far a bank can go in its efforts to establish the desired identification. Naturally, the signature of the person presenting such evidence should be compared with the signature appearing on identifying papers.

Once the identity of a prospective individual depositor has been established, only that person has the authority to withdraw the funds deposited. By signing his name to a signature card, similar to that shown in Exhibit 44, the depositor accepts all rules and regulations printed on the card and authorizes the bank to honor orders for the withdrawal of funds, either in the form of checks or in some other form, provided that the checks or orders bear his genuine signature and that there are sufficient funds in the account.

Since an individual depositor has complete control of an account opened in his own name, he may confer full or limited powers on some other person or persons with respect to the account. Anyone so authorized is known as an Attorney in Fact. The depositor must give the bank written confirmation and explanation of the authority vested in the attorney. This document, Exhibit 45, which the bank keeps permanently in its file, is known as Power of Attorney.

An Attorney in Fact acts in the name of his principal, the depositor, and signs checks in the name of the depositor by himself as attorney. The authority granted to him is effective only during the lifetime of his principal. The depositor's death automatically invalidates any and all powers of attorney. Therefore, when a bank receives notice of the death of a depositor, who had previously filed with it a document of this kind, it can no longer regard the signature of the attorney as effective in connection with the deceased depositor's account.

In the case of joint accounts, the power of attorney should be signed by each of the joint depositors.

Joint Accounts Involving Two or More Persons

There are two general types of joint accounts.

1. Joint accounts which carry the right of survivorship.
2. Joint accounts without the right of survivorship, or which require all co-depositors to sign.

In an account carrying the right of survivorship, each of the

Exhibit 44

SIGNATURE CARD FOR INDIVIDUAL ACCOUNT

TO CITY NATIONAL BANK AND TRUST COMPANY OF CHICAGO

The Bank is hereby authorized to reeognize and act upon the signatures recorded hereon in the transaction of all business relating to this account, including but not limited to withdrawals therefrom, deposits therein and the indorsement, negotiation and collection of items deposited.

The agreement now or hereafter printed on the Bank's commercial deposit tickets and any authorization or certification pertaining to this account are hereby accepted and approved.

DATE NUMBER OF SIGNATURES REQUIRED

E-19

(PLEASE SIGN ON OTHER SIDE)

Business

Address

Telephone

Sole Ownership Letter 19

Partnership Letter 19

Certificate of Authority 19

Power of Attorney 19

ACCEPTED: By *for Cashier's Division on*

ACCEPTED: By *for Resolutions Division on*

E-19

Exhibit 45

POWER OF ATTORNEY - INDIVIDUAL ACCOUNT

Limited Power of Attorney

TO: CITY NATIONAL BANK AND TRUST COMPANY OF CHICAGO

I, the undersigned, do hereby appoint____
(Name of attorney in fact)

____

as attorney in fact for me and in my name and behalf, to make, sign, and indorse checks, to draw, sign, and indorse drafts, to waive demand, presentment, protest and notices of protest, non-payment, and dishonor in connection with any checks or drafts so indorsed or drawn, and generally to execute such other papers and to exercise such other powers as may be necessary or convenient in transacting business pertaining to the making of and checking against deposits with you in my name and the negotiation with you of any and all checks and drafts payable or indorsed to me or to my order or to bearer, to as full an extent as the undersigned could do if personally present, hereby ratifying and confirming all that such attorney in fact may do in the premises.

By virtue of such appointment you are hereby authorized and empowered to honor, pay, and charge to the account of the undersigned all checks and other orders of every kind whatsoever for the payment of money drawn on you and signed by said attorney in fact, including, without limitation, any and all checks and other orders payable to or to the individual order of said attorney in fact or tendered for deposit to his individual account; and to accept and treat as the indorsement of the undersigned the indorsement made by said attorney in fact on any and all checks and other orders for the payment of money either for the purpose of giving cash or credit to said attorney in fact individually or for any other purpose.

The undersigned certifies that the signature of said attorney in fact appearing below in this document is genuine.

It is understood and agreed that the authority hereby given shall continue in effect until written revocation thereof is actually received by one of your executive officers, and in the event of the death of the undersigned before such revocation that such authority shall continue after such death and be binding upon the legal representatives of the undersigned until actual written notice of the fact of such death shall be received by one of your executive officers.

"The undersigned" as used herein shall refer to the one or more persons who sign and seal this instrument, regardless of the use of verbs and pronouns importing the singular member. Execution hereof by two or more of the undersigned shall bind them jointly and severally. "Attorney in fact" as used herein shall refer to the person or persons so appointed hereby, and in case two or more persons are so appointed, their power and authority shall be both joint and several and may be exercised by any one or more of them. Notwithstanding the death or incapacity of any of the undersigned or any of the attorneys in fact, this instrument shall remain in full force and effect with respect to the surviving or other persons.

Dated at Chicago, Illinois, this____________day of____________________, 19___

______________________________[SEAL]

______________________________[SEAL]

SIGNATURE OF ATTORNEY IN FACT: ______________________________

____

Signed, sealed and delivered in the presence of:

____

E-5

Exhibit 46

JOINT ACCOUNT WITH RIGHT OF SURVIVORSHIP

(Front side)

JOINT SURVIVORSHIP

TO CITY NATIONAL BANK AND TRUST COMPANY OF CHICAGO

The undersigned hereby agree that all deposits to this account, or any part thereof, or any interest or dividend thereon, may be paid to or upon the order of any one or more of the undersigned, whether the other or others be living or not, on the check, draft or other order, receipt or acquittance of any one or more of the undersigned; it being the intention of the undersigned to create a joint tenancy in this account with the right of survivorship.

The Bank is hereby authorized to recognize and act upon any of the signatures recorded hereon in the transaction of all business relating to this account of the undersigned, including (without limitation on the generality of the foregoing) withdrawals therefrom, deposits therein, and the indorsement, negotiation and collection of items deposited. The undersigned further agree that any of the undersigned may deposit to this account moneys, checks, drafts and other items belonging to any other or others of the undersigned, whether such checks, drafts or other items are unindorsed or are indorsed in any manner by any person whomsoever. Each of the undersigned hereby guarantees to the Bank all prior indorsements on all items deposited to this account or cashed for any of the undersigned.

IT IS HEREBY AGREED that the Bank shall have the right to charge against this account and any other account of any of the undersigned, whether or not such account is now in existence, any liabilities at any time existing of any one or more of the undersigned to the Bank. All the terms and provisions printed in the deposit book shall form a part hereof as though printed herein. Unless and until another and different address is furnished in writing by any of the undersigned to the bank, all communications relating to this account or said business may be addressed to any of the undersigned and mailed or otherwise sent to the address given on the reverse side of this card and shall constitute notice to each of the undersigned.

DATE SIGNATURES REQUIRED

E20

(Reverse side)

(PLEASE SIGN ON OTHER SIDE)

Business

Address

Telephone

Introduced by

ACCEPTED: By *for Cashier's Division on*

ACCEPTED: By *for Resolutions Division on*

joint co-depositors generally signs an agreement with the bank authorizing the bank to deal with each depositor during the lives of the signatories and with the survivor or survivors as the owner or owners of all funds on deposit, similar to Exhibit 46. Thus, each depositor agrees that upon his death all his rights, title and interest in the funds on deposit shall immediately pass to the surviving depositor, or depositors, and that neither his estate, nor his heirs, nor assigns, shall acquire any interest in the funds. Although the joint account would seem to be an excellent means of transferring funds to others in anticipation of death and to avoid the payment of inheritance taxes, the laws of many states require that the bank notify the State Department of Revenue in the event of the death of any party to a joint account.

With respect to accounts in which there is no right of survivorship, generally such accounts are opened for business reasons between persons not related, and where the principals do not wish, or where it is not practical or expedient, to enter into a partnership arrangement. Under such an arrangement, should one of the co-signers die, the share of the deceased does not pass automatically to the survivors, and the bank is obliged to deal with the executor or administrator of the decedent's estate before disposing of the decedent's share. Obviously this also requires considerable work on the part of the estate of the deceased in order to determine whatever rights, title and interest exist.

In order to avoid problems, many banks refuse to accept such accounts unless they are in the form of an individual account, with power of attorney, or are covered by a special agreement providing for withdrawal of funds in event of death of one of the parties similar to that shown in Exhibit 47.

Not only should every joint account arrangement be based on a written agreement, similar to those shown in Exhibits 46 and 47 but the agreement should clearly specify whether orders for the withdrwal of funds are to be signed by any one of the depositors or by all depositors signing jointly.

Although banks ordinarily accept the instructions of customers calling for either one or for all of the signatures, a good many banks take more than casual interest in these instructions because of past experience.

Exhibit 47

JOINT ACCOUNT AGREEMENT WITHOUT RIGHT OF SURVIVORSHIP

Date______________________

ontinental Illinois National Bank
nd Trust Company of Chicago
hicago, Illinois

entlemen:

he undersigned,________________ and __________________, desire to establish a joint checking account without the right of survivorship in he name of "__________________ and __________________".

hecks, drafts, notes, bills of exchange and orders for the payment of oney payable to or belonging to either of us, may be endorsed by either f us and deposited with you for the credit of the said account and ndorsements for deposit may be made in writing or by stamp and without esignation of the person so endorsing. Checks or orders for the withrawal of funds from this account must be signed jointly by____________ ____________and______________________.

n the event of the death of either of the undersigned, you are authorized disburse any funds in this account on the joint order of the survivor d the legal representative of the deceased.

Yours very truly

____

____

Normally, a bank would prefer to be instructed to hono withdrawals on the signature of any one of the depositors. Difficult situations sometimes arise in connection with joint account which do not permit withdrawals except on the signature of al depositors.

Sometimes one of the joint depositors becomes critically il or suffers a stroke which leaves him alive but incapable of acting or, as has happened, one of the joint depositors may simply disappear and never be heard from again. Without the signature o the ailing or missing depositor, the deposited funds are complete and effectively frozen. There is no immediate possibility of anyon qualifying to sign for such a depositor in the absence of proof o incompetency or satisfactory proof of death. To attempt to unfreeze the account through legal process would be tedious an time-consuming. These situations do arise from time to time much to the discomfort and inconvenience of the remaining join depositors and oftentimes to the extreme embarrassment of th bank, which is without authority to accept any instructions fro the remaining depositors.

Partnership Accounts

A partnership account is a business account carried in th names of two or more partners. A partnership is based on a mutua agreement, usually in writing, between the various partners. Fo the purpose of setting up a bank account in a partnership name many banks require the partners to sign a form similar to Exhibit 48 and 49 which covers the authority relating to banking tran actions, such as the signing of checks and the making of loan Signature cards similar to that shown in Exhibit 44, for individu accounts are used.

Many states have adopted the Uniform Partnership Act, whic is a special body of law dealing with partnership affairs. Bank in these states must be familiar with the general principles partnership law so that they may properly handle the situatio that may arise. Among other things, partnership law provides th each partner is responsible for the business contracts of the othe partners, and that one partner can bind all the other partners b his contracts. To be enforceable, the contracts entered into by single partner must be within the scope of this partnership busines

Exhibit 48

PARTNERSHIP AGREEMENT (Front side)

PARTNERSHIP

:ITY NATIONAL BANK AND TRUST COMPANY OF CHICAGO

·ENTLEMEN:

We hereby certify that the undersigned, ______________________________

____

____

____

-re engaged in business or profession as partners under the name and style of ______________

____

: the following address ______________________________

____

ıd that the undersigned represent and constitute all the members of said partnership.

This will further evidence the agreement and authorization of the undersigned that:

1. City National Bank and Trust Company of Chicago (hereinafter called "the Bank") be, and it hereby is ·signated as a depositary of the funds of said partnership and that any one of the undersigned partners, their agents employees be, and each of them hereby is, authorized to deposit funds of said partnership with the Bank to the ·edit of the partnership account and for that purpose to endorse in the name of said partnership checks, drafts, ·tes and other like obligations payable or endorsed to or to the order of said partnership, which endorsements may written or stamped without designation of the individual partner, agent or employee making such endorsement; ·d the undersigned partners hereby guarantee to the Bank all prior endorsements on every such check, draft, note other like obligation.

2. Any ______________ of the following ______________
(Number of Signatures on Each Check)

____

____

____

______ hereby specifically authorized for and on behalf of the undersigned partners and in the partnership name,
s or are)
issue to the Bank instructions for the payment of money, and to make, execute and deliver checks, drafts and ·ers drawn upon the Bank, including but not limited to checks, drafts and orders drawn to the individual order, tendered for deposit to the individual account of any of the said partners, agents or employees signing or counter- ·ning the same, and the Bank hereby is authorized to pay out funds on deposit from time to time to the credit of ·d partnership upon checks, drafts and orders drawn upon or instructions issued to the Bank and signed in the ·ne of said partnership in conformity with the foregoing authorization.

, 4-59

Exhibit 49

PARTNERSHIP AGREEMENT (Reverse side)

3. Any ____________ (One or Two, etc.) of the following persons ____________

____

____

____________ (is or are) hereby authorized, in addition to and not in limitation of the rights inherent in a partner, for and i behalf of said partnership and in the partnership name; from time to time to borrow money from the Bank in suc amounts, for such lengths of time, at such rates of interest and upon such terms and conditions as to such persc or persons may seem expedient; to secure payment of money so borrowed and to evidence the indebtedness therel created, to execute and deliver promissory notes, judgment promissory notes and other like obligations of sa partnership, in such form and containing such terms and provisions as may to such person or persons seem necessa and advisable; and to pledge or hypothecate as security for the payment of said notes and other obligations a receivables, securities, or property of any character whatsoever now or hereafter belonging to said partnership; discount with the Bank any receivables now or hereafter owing to said partnership; to withdraw, receipt fc execute, and deliver trust receipts for securities, or other property of any kind whatsoever purchased from, left wit or held by the Bank for safekeeping, or as collateral security, or for delivery or collection or otherwise held for t account of said partnership; and the Bank is specifically authorized to deliver to the person or persons so designat any such securities, or other property of any kind whatsoever, upon receipts or trust receipts executed by su person or persons in his or their individual name and without requiring the execution of such receipts in the nar of the partnership.

4. The Bank shall not be in any way responsible for or required to see to the application of any of the fun deposited with it or borrowed from it as hereinabove provided.

5. As between the Bank and each partner it is agreed that in the event of the death of any partner h personal representatives shall look exclusively and in all events to the surviving partner or partners for an accounti for any funds which may be due the estate of such deceased partner and that the surviving partner or partners sh have full power and authority to continue to maintain and operate all bank accounts of said partnership with t Bank and make deposits thereto and withdrawals therefrom in the same manner in all respects as if such deceas partner had never been a member of said partnership.

6. All transactions above authorized shall be conclusive and binding upon the undersigned and each of t undersigned until written notice of the revocvation of the authority hereby granted, or until a new authorizati superseding the foregoing, executed by all of the partners then comprising the partnership, shall have been deliver to the Bank at its office in Chicago, Illinois.

7. This instrument shall be binding upon the heirs, executors and administrators of each of the undersign partners.

IN WITNESS WHEREOF, we have hereunto subscribed our respective hands and seals this ________

day of ____________, A.D. 19______.

____________(SEA

____________(SEA

____________(SEA

____________(SEA

____________(SEA

Exhibit 50

SOLE OWNERSHIP AGREEMENT

SOLE OWNERSHIP

(One copy to be filed with Bank)

o City National Bank and Trust Company of Chicago,
Chicago, Illinois:

o induce you to open or continue a bank account in the trade name of ....

....

....,

ıd in consideration of your so doing, I, ...

r myself and my heirs, executors, administrators and assigns, do hereby (1) represent and warrant to you that I n the sole owner of the trade name and of the business enterprise conducted in that name, and (2) agree to protect, efend and indemnify you and your successors and assigns from and against any and all claims, demands, liabilities, dgments, decrees, costs and expenses, including but not limited to the fees of your attorneys, which you may suffer incur or which may be entered or recovered against you as a direct or indirect result of your opening or continuing id bank account, or your receiving for deposit to said bank account checks, drafts, orders, notes and other like instruents payable or indorsed to or to the order of the trade name, or your acting in accordance with this instrument.

You are hereby authorized and directed to pay and charge to said bank account, any and all checks, drafts, ders, or instructions drawn upon or issued to you, when signed in the trade name by the undersigned or by any .... of the following:
(one, two, etc.)

....

....

....

ithout inquiry as to the circumstances of the issuance or the disposition of the proceeds of such checks, drafts, ders or instructions, including but not limited to checks, drafts, and orders payable or indorsed to or to the order any one or more of the persons signing the same on behalf of the drawer, or tendered for deposit to the individual count of any such person.

You are further hereby authorized and directed to accept for deposit to said bank account, cash, instruments yable or indorsed to bearer and any and all checks, drafts, orders, notes and other like instruments payable or dorsed to me or my order or to or to the order of the trade name, when indorsed by any person in my name or in e trade name, and such indorsements may be written or stamped without designation of the person or persons aking such indorsements. Each such indorsement, irrespective of its form or kind, shall make me an unqualified dorser to you of the instruments so indorsed and a guarantor to you of all prior indorsements.

I do further hereby authorize any .... of the following:
(one, two, etc.)

....

....

....,

ereinafter for convenience called "the attorney",) for me, in the trade name, to borrow money from you at any ne and from time to time; to make, execute and deliver, as evidences of the sums so borrowed, acceptances, notes, dgment notes and other instruments for the payment of money, whether negotiable or not, in such amounts, upon ch terms, with such maturities and at such rates of interest or discount as to the attorney shall seem proper; to dge, indorse, guarantee, assign, transfer and deliver bills and accounts receivable, bills of lading, warehouse eipts, stocks, bonds, notes, bills of exchange and other property of mine, whether or not standing in the trade me, as security for any moneys borrowed and as security for any liability incurred or to be incurred in the trade me, all upon such terms and with such provisions and conditions as to the attorney shall seem proper; and to hdraw, receive and receipt for and to withdraw upon trust receipt, all on my responsibility and at my risk, and to n any and all orders for the withdrawal, substitution or exchange of, any and all collateral securities or other operty pledged, assigned, transferred or otherwise held for my account. You shall have no duty or obligation to to the application or disposition of moneys borrowed pursuant hereto or of other property withdrawn or received the attorney.

This instrument shall remain in full force and effect until revoked by notice in writing, signed by me and vered to you, but no revocation of this instrument, by notice or by operation of law, shall affect or impair your nt to indemnity hereunder with respect to any transaction that occurred before such revocation.

IN WITNESS WHEREOF, I have subscribed my hand and seal at Chicago, Illinois, this .... day of

...., 19........

....(Seal)

While the death of a partner ordinarily terminates the part nership, the law gives the surviving partners the right to carry o the business during liquidation and this right carries with it th power to handle all assets, including funds on deposit in bank Thus, the estate of the deceased partner ordinarily is without powe to step in and claim or seize control of bank deposits which are i the partnership name. The surviving partner(s), however, ar required to render an accounting to the estate and to disclos fully the financial data incident to the liquidation.

Trade Name or Proprietorship Accounts

In business people frequently find it advisable to use a trad or an assumed name (sometimes known as fictitious name). Thoug a common business practice, the use of a trade name is a privileg which could be abused. Many states have laws designed to regu late the use of trade names to legitimate purposes and to requi that the name be registered in order to identify the person or pe sons who wish to do business under a trade name and fix respons bility with respect to contracts or liabilities incurred in the nam of the business.

Where such registration is necessary, banks generally requi the person opening the account to furnish them with a certifie copy of the certificate, showing that the trade name has bee registered. In addition they require such customers to execu a Sole Ownership Agreement, similar to Exhibit 50, which warran the person to be the sole owner of the business and agrees protect and indemnify the bank against any liability incurred handling the account and signature cards similar to the one show in Exhibit 51.

Where an account is opened in a trade name by more th one person, the bank should carefully scrutinize the arrangeme for more than likely they are not dealing with a proprietorshi but with a partnership which requires a different type of agre ment to protect the bank in its relationship with the depositors.

Corporation Accounts

A corporation is a legal entity created by law, under whi a number of people, generally more than three, can conduct bu ness, enter into contracts, bring suit against others, and be sue where their personal liability for acts committed by their age

Exhibit 51

PROPRIETORSHIP ACCOUNT SIGNATURE CARDS

TO CITY NATIONAL BANK AND TRUST COMPANY OF CHICAGO

The Bank is hereby authorized to recognize and act upon the signatures recorded hereon in the transaction of all business relating to this account, including but not limited to withdrawals therefrom, deposits therein and the indorsement, negotiation and collection of items deposited.

The agreement now or hereafter printed on the Bank's commercial deposit tickets and any authorization or certification pertaining to this account are hereby accepted and approved.

DATE NUMBER OF SIGNATURES REQUIRED

E-19

(PLEASE SIGN ON OTHER SIDE)

usiness

ddress

elephone

ole Ownership Letter 19

artnership Letter 19

ertificate of Authority 19

ower of Attorney 19

CCEPTED: By for Cashier's Division on

CCEPTED: By for Resolutions Division on

E-19

or representatives, in conducting the activities for which the com pany was charted, is limited to their financial investment.

Authorization for such a group to engage in business is ev denced by a document, known as a Corporate Charter, issued b the state which has granted the group the right to engage in bus ness. Such charters set forth the purpose for which the corporatio was formed and prescribe the kind of business they may engage i or the functions they may undertake. Sometimes the charter als will contain a prohibitory clause; that is while granting certai powers, rights, and privileges, it will also prohibit the corporatio undertaking certain allied activities.

Corporation charters can be revoked or rescinded, or the co poration can be dissolved, either voluntarily or through bankruptc

Ownership of a corporation is ordinarily evidenced by share of stock, and the owners of these shares are called stockholder The stockholders may adopt by-laws which describe the activitie of the corporation, and elect a Board of Directors whose duty to manage and direct corporation affairs, appoint the active e ecutive officers, and to approve contracts.

The question confronting a bank, as well as anyone else doin business with a corporation, is the proper level of authority th must be sought in order to enter into contracts with the corporatio safely. The stockholders are the real owners, but obviously would be impossible to conduct business with what may be a larg and scattered group.

It is well established by law and custom that the Board Directors is the active governing body of a corporation, and a thority given by the Board of Directors is normally sufficient ev dence of the validity of any business negotiations carried on the corporate name.

When a bank opens an account in the name of a corporatio the basis for all future dealings is a Certified Copy of a Corpor tion Resolution, similar to that shown in Exhibits 52 and 5 adopted by the Board of Directors, authorizing the opening of account with the bank, and empowering certain corporation office and representatives to act in behalf of the corporation in t handling of ordinary banking transactions.

The wording of this document contains an appropriate resol

Exhibit 52

CORPORATE RESOLUTION (Front side)

Corporation Resolution

the undersigned, do hereby certify that I am the..Secretary of..........................

....,

orporation duly organized and existing under the laws of the State of...................................and the keeper of the rporate records and the corporate seal of said corporation; that the following is a true and complete copy of cer-n resolutions unanimously adopted at a meeting of the Board of Directors of said corporation duly and regularly lled and held in accordance with law and the by-laws of said corporation on the..day of

........................, 19....... at which meeting a majority and quorum were personally present; that said resolutions ve not been rescinded, repealed, or in any way amended, and are still in full force and effect:

IT RESOLVED:

1. That the City National Bank and Trust Company of Chicago be and it hereby is designated as a depositary in which funds of this corporation may be deposited by its officers, agents, or employees, and that any of said officers, agents, or employees of this corporation be, and each of them hereby is, authorized for the purpose of deposit with said depositary, to the account or accounts of this corporation, to endorse in the name of this corporation any and all checks, drafts, and orders for the payment of money either belonging to or coming into the possession of this corporation, and that such endorsements may be written or stamped in the name of this corporation without designation of the individual officer, agent, or employee making such endorsement; it being understood and agreed that on all such items deposited, all prior endorsements are guaranteed by this corporation whether or not an express guaranty is incorporated in such endorsements.

2. That the City National Bank and Trust Company of Chicago be and it hereby is authorized to pay out funds on deposit with it from time to time to the credit of this corporation, upon any and all checks, drafts, and orders drawn upon or instructions issued to said depositary and signed in the name of this corporation by

any .... of the following:
(One, two, etc.)

President, any Vice President, the Treasurer, any Assistant Treasurer, the Secretary, any Assistant Secretary,
(Rule out any of above titles, if such officials are not authorized under this section.)

....

....
(Use blank space for additional titles or to authorize countersignatures—and rule out space not used.)

including any and all checks, drafts and orders drawn to the individual order of any officer or other person signing or countersigning the same or tendered for deposit to the individual account of any such officer or person.

3. That any .... of the following:
(One, two, etc.)

President, any Vice President, the Treasurer, any Assistant Treasurer, the Secretary, any Assistant Secretary,
(Rule out any of above titles, if such officials are not authorized under this section.)

....

....
(Use blank space for additional titles or to authorize countersignatures—and rule out space not used.)

of this corporation be authorized upon such terms and conditions as to him/them shall seem proper:

To borrow money and incur liabilities for and on behalf and in the name of this corporation, to make agreements for the payment, purchase or repurchase of bills and notes which are the obligations of any other corporation or corporations, to sell or discount its bills and accounts receivable and to enter into, make, sign and deliver acceptances and promissory notes, judgment promissory notes and other obligations of this corporation in and for such amounts, for such time, at such rate of interest or discount and upon such conditions as to him/them shall seem proper, and

To sign, execute and deliver applications and contracts for letters of credit and travellers' checks and guaranties thereof containing such provisions as to him/them seem proper and as may be required, and

To endorse for negotiation, negotiate, assign and transfer and receive the proceeds of any and all negotiable instruments and non-negotiable instruments and other orders for the payment of money payable to or belonging to this corporation, and

To pledge, endorse, guarantee, assign, transfer and deliver bills and accounts receivable, bills of lading, warehouse receipts, stocks and bonds and other property of this corporation as security for any moneys borrowed and as security for any liability incurred or to be incurred by this corporation in connection with any and all acceptances, notes, letters of credit, guaranties, trust receipts or otherwise as may be required, all upon such terms, provisions and conditions as may be deemed proper by him/them, and

To sell, transfer and endorse for sale or for transfer any and all securities, bonds, stock certificates, interim, participation and other certificates and to identify and guarantee signatures and endorsements thereon, and on bond or stock powers of attorney executed in connection therewith, or otherwise, and

To withdraw, receive and receipt for and to withdraw upon trust receipt, or otherwise, all on the responsibility of, and at the risk of this corporation and to sign any and all orders for the withdrawal, substitution

Exhibit 53

CORPORATE RESOLUTION (Reverse side)

or exchange of any and all collateral, securities or other property pledged, assigned, transferred, held in safekeeping, or otherwise held for its account. Such withdrawals, substitutions and exchanges may also be made by the bearer of any order, receipt or request signed by any person or persons authorized and empowered by these resolutions to sign on behalf of this corporation as aforesaid.

4. That each of the aforementioned officers or other persons, authorized to act for this corporation in any case aforesaid, shall be and hereby is further authorized, without the concurrence of any other officer or persons:

To identify, approve and guarantee the endorsements of any payee or endorser of any and all checks and drafts drawn by this corporation, and

To waive presentment, demand, protest and notice of dishonor or protest and to give instructions in regard to the handling or delivery of any negotiable or non-negotiable papers or documents involved in any of said transactions, and

To act for this corporation in the transaction of all other business (whether or not it is of the kind, nature or character specified in these resolutions) for its account with the City National Bank and Trust Company of Chicago.

5. That the City National Bank and Trust Company of Chicago, as such depositary, shall be entitled to rely upon the terms of these resolutions as vesting in the designated officers of the corporation and other persons complete authority to act on its behalf in the manner and to the extent herein set forth, and shall be under no obligation to make further inquiry with respect thereto and shall assume no responsibility or liability for the application of any of the funds deposited with it or borrowed from it pursuant to the provisions of these resolutions.

6. That the Secretary or Assistant Secretary of this corporation is directed to file with the City National Bank and Trust Company of Chicago a copy of these resolutions duly certified under the seal of this corporation, and to certify (with or without the seal of this corporation) from time to time a list of the names and signatures of the persons who are the duly elected and qualified officers of the corporation hereby empowered to act hereunder, and that the City National Bank and Trust Company of Chicago shall be entitled as against this corporation to assume conclusively that the authority of the persons so certified as such officers and of the other person or persons named hereinabove, to act on behalf of this corporation, continues until expressly notified in writing to the contrary.

7. That the City National Bank and Trust Company of Chicago shall be entitled to assume conclusively that each of the foregoing resolutions continues in full force and effect until express written notice of its rescission or modification, accompanied by a copy of the proper resolution effecting such modification or rescission duly certified by the Secretary, or Assistant Secretary of the corporation over its seal, shall have been delivered to it at its office in the City of Chicago, Illinois, and shall be indemnified and saved harmless from any loss suffered or liability incurred by it in reliance on the authority delegated by the terms of said resolutions prior to receipt of such notice of rescission or modification.

8. That these resolutions shall supersede any and all previous resolutions of similar import.

IN WITNESS WHEREOF, I have affixed my name as ....Secretary and have caused the corporate seal of said corporation to be hereunto affixed this..................................day of.......................................,
19............

Affix corporate seal below

....
Secretary

I,.., a Director of said corporation, do hereby certify that the foregoing is a correct copy of certain resolutions passed as therein set forth.

....
Director.

Exhibit 54

CORPORATION ACCOUNTS SIGNATURE CARDS

CORPORATION

TO: CITY NATIONAL BANK AND TRUST COMPANY OF CHICAGO

The corporation named above hereby agrees to all the terms and provisions printed in the deposit book.

TYPE OR PRINT NAMES	SIGNATURES	
MR.	SIGNS	President
MR.	SIGNS	Vice-President
MR.	SIGNS	Treasurer
MR.	SIGNS	Secretary
MR.	SIGNS	Asst. Treasurer
MR.	SIGNS	Asst. Secretary

-14 NUMBER OF SIGNATURES REQUIRED ________

PLEASE SIGN THIS CERTIFICATION

certify that the above are the genuine signatures of the persons authorized in accordance with documents on file with you.

Date________________ ________________ Secretary (or other officer)

(PLEASE SIGN ON OTHER SIDE)

Business

Address

Telephone

RESOLUTION 19

ACCEPTED: By *for Cashier's Division on*

ACCEPTED: By *for Resolutions Division on*

-14

Exhibit 55

CORPORATION CERTIFICATE

Corporation Certificate

TO: CITY NATIONAL BANK AND TRUST COMPANY OF CHICAGO:

I, the undersigned, do hereby certify that I am the duly elected, qualified, and acting .... Secretary of ....

a corporation organized and existing under the laws of ...., and the keeper of the corpora records and the custodian of the seal of said corporation, and that the following named persons have be appointed or elected, have duly qualified, and are now acting as officers or employees of said corporation the capacities indicated under their respective names:

.... President	.... Treasurer
.... Vice-President	.... Secretary
.... Vice-President	.... Vice-President
.... *	.... *
.... *	.... *
.... *	.... *

I do further hereby certify that the resolutions of the board of directors of said corporation, pursuance of which this certificate is given, are in full force and effect, without alteration, amendment modification, and do not in anv respect contravene or conflict with the by-laws of said corporation.

IN WITNESS WHEREOF, I have hereunto subscribed my name as said .... Secret and have affixed the corporate seal of said corporation, this .... day of ...., 19...

(Affix Corporate Seal below)

....
Secret

Approved ....
Presid
Vice-Presid

*** Indicate here the title of the person named or his relation to the corporation.**

E-1

on which was adopted by the corporation's Board of Directors t a regular or special meeting. In addition to the Corporate esolution and signature cards, similar to those shown in Exhibit 4, which are usually signed in duplicate or triplicate, the bank equires a Corporation Certificate, similar to that shown in Exhibit 5, signed by the Secretary, which states that the Resolution was uly adopted by proper action of the Board of Directors and bears e corporate seal.

In some cases, the corporate by-laws confer on certain officers e power to handle bank accounts. When officers have this power, e bank obtains a certified copy of the section of the by-laws ntaining this specific authorization instead of obtaining a resolu-on of the Board of Directors.

It is important for a bank to examine each corporate resolution refully to make certain that it is in proper form and that it con-ins the necessary authority to cover completely the action of the rporate officers or designated representatives in depositing and ithdrawing funds and in performing other acts necessary to con-ct business pertaining to the corporation's account.

Fiduciary Accounts

Generally speaking, a fiduciary is a person or a corporation thorized to handle property for the benefit of others. Circum-nces often make it desirable or convenient for individuals or rporations to be given possession of the property of others and act on their behalf in various ways.

Sometimes property is given by a court to a guardian, with in-uctions to administer the property for the benefit of a minor, an ompetent, or someone who does not enjoy the legal capacity to t for himself.

When a person dies, an executor (who is named in the will) an administrator (when the will mentions no name, when there no will, or when the executor does not serve) becomes the de-dent's legal representative. He administers the estate for the nefit of heirs and creditors. The term fiduciary is a broad one ich includes all persons, such as trustees, guardians, administra-s, and executors who administer property for the benefit of ers.

Banks are frequently requested to open accounts in the

names of individuals or corporations acting in fiduciary capacity. In each case it is important for the bank to determine the validit of the appointment and to obtain for its file proper evidence o authority to act. Most accounts of this kind are formal in natur

A fiduciary may be appointed by a trust agreement which ha been filed as a matter of public record; he may be appointed unde a will which has been probated and made a part of the publi record; he may receive his authority by court appointment, whic is a matter of public record; or his authority may come from som other type of formal document which has been properly recorde in public archives. In each case, the bank should request an receive a copy of the document or certificate of appointment s that it may examine the authority vested in the fiduciary and ma determine whether there are any important limitations whic would affect the fiduciary's relationship with the bank.

Sometimes trusts are more or less informal in nature; eith they are not evidenced by a formal document or, if a writte agreement does exist, the document has never been recorded. Th most frequently encountered informal trust of this kind is th account opened by a parent, an aunt, an uncle, an older sister brother, or some other relative in trust for a minor child.

In handling such accounts, once authorization has been e tablished, banks generally have the person acting in fiducia capacity sign signature cards used in opening an account for a individual, similar to that shown in Exhibit 44.

Club, Church, or Association Accounts

Unincorporated associations formed for social or charitab purposes and not for profit, usually have informal organization a few regulations. In such cases, a bank should exercise reasonab care to ascertain that persons dealing with it in the name of such group or association have proper authority. However, for a ba to require unincorporated associations the same letter-perfect a thority and technical adherence to legal details that it requir of the modern business corporation obviously would impose u reasonable inconveniences upon the officers of the informal gro The procedure adopted by a bank may vary according to the c cumstances confronting it. A large social or charitable organizati with a substantial treasury probably would be expected to confo easonably to the type of authorization furnished by a corporation. small club or neighborhood group, with a modest treasury and ith an entirely new slate of officers elected each year, may receive ss exacting treatment. Usually signature cards together with a tter or resolution, warranted under the circumstances, are re- uired by the bank.

Public Fund Accounts

Public fund accounts are maintained with banks for con- enience in handling financial transactions by incorporated areas, llages, towns, cities, counties, states and the Federal Government well as the instrumentalities of respective governments set up connection with parks, recreation, transportation, utilities and her. services of government.

Generally, conditions and provisions under which funds are eposited in so-called public fund accounts, and authorization for ithdrawal and disbursement of funds, are provided for by law.

The initial establishment of such a relationship is generally ubject to scrutiny and review of the law governing the particular stumentality, or legal opinion from counsel of the bank confirm- g that certain powers granted by law are vested in the operation the account and the persons authorized to withdraw funds. ecause of the complexities, varieties and provisions of law govern- g the deposit or withdrawal of funds under the control of the ublic trust, it is general practice to accept, maintain and handle ch accounts only after the rights of all parties concerned have een established by legal counsel.

Demand Certificates of Deposit Accounts

Under special circumstances, customers might wish to place sum of money on deposit with a bank, retain official evidence of e deposit, and have it in such form that title can be transferred endorsement and delivery of the instrument. Such an instru- ent is known as a Certificate of Deposit which is defined as an strument evidencing the deposit with the bank of a certain sum ecified on the face of the certificate, payable to the depositor, other payee, or his order, upon presentation of the certificate at e bank on which drawn.

A Certificate of Deposit performs the same function that a shier's Check does and the same negotiability applies. Even

Exhibit 56

NEW ACCOUNT MEMORANDUM

NEW ACCOUNT MEMORANDUM

DATE OPENED ....

ACCOUNT TITLE	MR. / MRS. (GIVEN NAME) / MISS .... RELATIONS
MAILING ADDRESS	FIRM NAME—C/O—ATT'N OF—ETC. / NUMBER—STREET · CITY · POSTAL UNIT NO. · STATE · TELEPHONE
ALTERNATE ADDRESS ☐ RESIDENCE ☐ OFFICE	FIRM NAME—C/O—ATT'N OF—ETC. / NUMBER—STREET · CITY · POSTAL UNIT NO. · STATE · TELEPHONE
BUSINESS OCCUPATION OR PROFESSION	OCCUPATION—PROFESSION—TITLE OR POSITION · BUSINESS ☐ MFG. ☐ WH'SALE ☐ RETAIL ☐ · PRODUCT (S) · ☐ NEW VENT · ☐ ESTAB. FI
TYPE OF ACCOUNT	☐ PERSONAL ☐ S/O ☐ PART. ☐ ASS'N. ☐ CORP. ☐ ....
GENERAL INFORMATION	NON-RESIDENT ALIEN? · SUBJECT TO EXEC. ORDER 8389? · IF REPLY IS "YES" EXPLA IN DETAIL ON OTHER SID HOW IDENTIFIED OPENED BY · ACCOUNT OBTAINED BY · INITIAL DEPOSIT $ · NEW BUSINESS $ REASONS FOR SELECTION OF THIS BANK, CHANGE OF CONNECTION, TRANSFER, REOPENING AND OTHER REMARKS ACCOUNT FORMERLY AT OTHER ACCOUNTS AT ACQUAINTANCES IN THIS BANK
AFFILIATED ACCOUNTS IN THIS BANK	SAVINGS ACCT. HERE NO. · IN NAME OF · DATE OPENED · AV. BAL. LAST 6 MO. · PRESENT BAL. OR DATE CLOSED · IDENT. SATISFACTO
REFERENCES	NAME · ADDRESS
HANDLING INSTRUCTIONS	ASSIGN THIS ACCOUNT TO MR. INSTRUCTIONS FOR DELIVERY OF STATEMENT ☐ MAIL ☐ HOLD ☐ .... CHECKING ACCOUNT FEE ☐ MEASURED ☐ COST PLUS ☐ ANALYZE AND REFER TO .... IN .... DAYS ☐ NO FEE — REASON: SIGNATURE CARDS— ☐ TEMPORARY CARDS RECEIVED ☐ PERMANENT CARDS RECEIVED ☐ TO FOLLOW AUTHORITY DOCUMENTS ☐ RECEIVED ☐ TO FOLLOW SPECIAL INSTRUCTIONS—NOTATIONS USE REVERSE SIDE FOR ADDITIONAL NOTATIONS

E-12

Exhibit 57

COMMERCIAL ACCOUNT DEPOSIT SLIP

Front side

COMMERCIAL DEPOSIT TICKET

DEPOSITED WITH

CITY NATIONAL BANK

AND TRUST COMPANY *of Chicago*

Subject to conditions of agreement printed on back hereof.

CHECKS ON CHICAGO	CHECKS ON OTHER CITIES (EXCEPT NEW YORK CITY)	CHECKS ON NEW YORK CITY
		CHECKS ON THIS BANK
	CURRENCY	
	COIN	
	CHICAGO	
	OTHER CITIES	
	NEW YORK CITY	
	CHECKS ON THIS BANK	
	TOTAL	

FOR ACCOUNT OF

(Please write full title of account.)

DATE ____________

Reverse side

AGREEMENT

(Amended August, 1945)

In receiving and handling items for deposit or collection (including items received in payment of collections), this Bank acts only as the depositor's collecting agent and assumes no responsibility beyond the exercise of due care. This Bank will not be liable for default or negligence of its duly selected correspondents or for losses in transit. This Bank or its correspondents, as depositor's agents, may send items directly or indirectly to any bank or to any maker, drawee, acceptor, or payor of any such items, and may accept the draft, check, or credit of such bank or of the maker, drawee, acceptor, or payor, or of the agent of any of them, as conditional payment in lieu of cash. This Bank or its correspondents may, but shall not be required to, request certification in any case.

All items are credited or cashed subject to final payment in cash or solvent credits, and this Bank may decline to honor or pay checks drawn against conditional credits. This Bank may charge back to the depositor any items, whether returned or not, including items drawn on it, at any time before final payment. It is expressly understood that irrespective of the form of endorsement thereon, by deposit of items with this Bank either for credit or collection, the depositor guarantees all prior endorsements.

This Bank endeavors to credit promptly all items deposited, but neither undertakes, represents, nor warrants that deposits made on any certain day, whether such deposit comprised currency, items drawn on this Bank, or other items, will be credited in time to support payment of items drawn against the depositor's account on the same (or current) day.

Items may be transmitted for collection to any Federal Reserve Bank. All such items shall be subject to the rules and regulations of such Federal Reserve Bank and of the Federal Reserve Board in force from time to time. Items payable in the City of Chicago, or in any suburb thereof, may be collected through the Chicago Clearing House Association (in which event they may be carried over for presentation through the Clearing House on the following business day) and will be subject to its rules and regulations in force from time to time, or they may be collected in any other manner. This Bank will make reasonable effort to transmit every item by its usual and customary methods of transmission, so that it will be presented for payment at maturity, but the Bank does not warrant that such presentation will be made.

This Bank shall have a lien on all items handled by it and on the proceeds thereof for its charges, expenses (including court costs and attorneys' fees), and any advances made by it in connection therewith.

Delivery to the Bank of items for collection or credit shall constitute acceptance by the depositor of all the provisions of this agreement in the absence of written notice to the contrary.

Deposits received and not verified in detail at the time of acceptance are subject to later detail verification, and correcting entries may be made if any error is discovered.

When the depositor makes use of the bank's Day and Night Depository, the bailor-bailee relationship (for the sole benefit of the depositor-bailor) shall arise when this bank shall have removed from such depository any deposit placed therein by the depositor, and until such removal all risks of loss of the deposit shall be borne exclusively by the depositor. This bank's removal and subsequent handling of the deposit shall be governed in all respects by the rules and conditions in this bank's then current form of Day and Night Depository Agreement—a copy of which will be furnished to the depositor at any time on request.

Failure at any time or times on the part of the Bank to enforce compliance with any of the provisions of this agreement shall not constitute or be deemed a waiver thereof.

though it is a deposit account, the bank in issuing a Demand Certificate of Deposit, is only concerned with the goodness of the funds tendered in payment of the certificate and the right title and interest of the individual who presents the funds for conversion into a certificate. In accepting a Certificate of Deposit for conversion into cash or other type of credit, the bank's only responsibility is in the identification and the right title and interest of the payee or endorser. A Certificate of Deposit differs from a checking account, too, in that there are no signature cards, resolutions or other authorization involved as there would be if the funds were deposited in any other type of account.

In order to provide some vehicle of identification, where the purchaser of a Certificate of Deposit is a non-customer and therefore has not otherwise established a relationship with the bank for identification purposes, it is suggested that the "requisition form" be signed by the purchaser at the time the certificate is issued.

OPENING THE NEW ACCOUNT

Once the type of account covering the relationship has been determined, the next step is filling out the New Account Memorandum sheet, similar to that shown in Exhibit 56, for the purpose of recording pertinent information about the depositor such as name, address, business, affiliations and connections.

The New Account Memorandum sheet is usually made up in triplicate. The original goes to the credit section for filing in the file of the customer; the duplicate to the resolution section for review and follow up, if necessary, of resolutions and other documents which might be required and distribution of signature cards for use of tellers and bookkeepers in paying signatures on checks drawn against the funds on deposit in the account; and the triplicate to the addressograph section for make up of the addressograph plate from which the new ledger and statement sheets and envelope will be prepared and delivered to the bookkeeping section.

The next step is to head up a deposit slip, similar to that shown in Exhibit 57, with the name and address of the depositor. The name on the deposit slip should be exactly the same as that shown on the New Account Memorandum Sheet and have the words "New Account" written across the top, unless it is the practice of the bank to use special deposit slips in connection with the opening of a new account.

After the deposit slip has been headed up, the checks with which the account is to be opened are scrutinized to be certain they are payable to those in whose name the account will be carried, and properly endorsed over to the bank for collection and credit.

The next step is to enter the amount of the deposit in the Deposit Book. This book contains the general rules and regulations governing the relationship of the depositor with the bank and collection and crediting of checks. These regulations also appear on the reverse side of the deposit slip, as shown. The person opening an account may take the deposit slip, together with the checks, to the Receiving Teller's window for acceptance and the issuance of a receipt by the tellers machine.

The final step in establishing the relationship is either to provide the depositor with a supply of checks, or take an order for special checks upon which the name and address will be printed.

THE TIME ACCOUNT RELATIONSHIP

The second type of a creditor relationship with a bank is in connection with maintaining time deposit accounts.

Time deposit accounts are generally described as funds deposited with the bank on which it pays interest in consideration of the depositor giving prior notice of withdrawal.

Time deposit accounts are of four types:

1. Regular Savings
2. Special Savings
3. Time Certificates of Deposit
4. Special Time Accounts

Regular Savings Accounts

Regular savings accounts represent funds deposited with banks evidenced by a pass book receipt on which, in consideration of requiring at least 30 days prior notice of withdrawal, the bank agrees to pay interest at periodical intervals.

This relationship generally is maintained only with individuals acting in their own behalf; jointly with others; as agents in fiduciary capacity; or as members of a club, church or association. Signature cards, resolutions, and authorizations similar to those used in the demand deposit relationship are required.

Special Savings Accounts

Special savings accounts are funds deposited by individuals for a special purpose such as a Christmas Savings Club account, a Vacation Club account, or other special purpose account where receipts for funds are evidenced by coupons or stamps, or similar mediums. As such funds, after a specified period of time, are payable to the depositor or his order only, a simple signature card for identification purposes is required.

Time Certificates of Deposit Accounts

Time Certificates of Deposit accounts are the same as Demand Certificates of Deposit except that they have a definite maturity date, which is at least 30 days after date of issue, and bear a fixed rate of interest during the period for which they are issued.

Special Time Accounts

Special time accounts are interest bearing accounts maintained principally by corporations who find themselves in possession of temporary funds which they would like to invest. Special time accounts are deposit accounts, that is book accounts, subject to withdrawal on presentation of a properly signed check. The feature of special time accounts is that they are covered by a written agreement which provides that the funds will either be available 30-60-90-180 or more days *after* date; or subject to 30-60-90-180 or more prior days notice of withdrawal, in consideration of which the bank pays a fixed rate of interest depending on the terms of the agreement.

In connection with the establishing of a Special Time Account relationship, signature cards, resolutions, and authorizations similar to those used in the demand deposit relationship are required.

In connection with time deposit accounts it is well to remember that the maximum rate of interest banks are permitted to pay on any of the various types of time deposit accounts, is fixed by regulation of the Federal Reserve Board and in some instances by the laws of the state in which the bank is located or does business.

Exhibit 58

SAVINGS ACCOUNT SIGNATURE CARD

I hereby agree to be bound by all of the present and future rules and conditions governing accounts in the Savings Department of

CITY NATIONAL BANK

AND TRUST COMPANY *of Chicago*

Sign Here ______________________________

Address ______________________________

Occupation ______________________________

Place of Birth ______________ Date of Birth ______________

Introduced by ______________________________

NN-19

Exhibit 59

SAVINGS ACCOUNT DEPOSIT SLIP

Front side

SAVINGS DEPOSIT TICKET

BANK BOOK NUMBER ____________________

DEPOSITED WITH

CITY NATIONAL BANK
AND TRUST COMPANY *of Chicago*

FOR SAVINGS ACCOUNT OF

Name ____________________

____

Address ____________________

____

Subject to conditions of agreement printed on back hereof

Chicago, ______________ 19____

	DOLLARS	CENTS
CASH.		
CHECKS, COUPONS OR OTHER ITEMS . . . . (List each item separately)		
TOTAL		
LESS AMOUNT RETURNED. . . . . . . Receipt Thereof Acknowledged		
Signature NET DEPOSIT		

PLEASE NOTIFY THE BANK PROMPTLY OF ANY CHANGE OF ADDRESS

NN-4

Reverse side

EXCERPT FROM RULES AND CONDITIONS FOR SAVINGS DEPOSITS.

(As amended March 17, 1953)

3. DEPOSITS. In receiving and handling items for deposit or collection (including items received in payment of collections), this Ban
acts only as the depositor's collecting agent and assumes no responsibilit
beyond the exercise of due care. This Bank will not be liable for defaul
or negligence of its duly selected correspondents or for losses in transit
This Bank or its correspondents, as depositor's agents, may send item
directly or indirectly to any bank or to any maker, drawee, acceptor, o
payor of any such items, and may accept the draft, check, or credit of suc
bank or of the maker, drawee, acceptor, or payer, or of the agent of any
them, as conditional payment in lieu of cash. This Bank or its correspon
dents may, but shall not be required to, request certification in any cas
All items are credited or cashed subject to final payment in cash o
solvent credits, and this Bank may decline to honor or pay again
conditional credits. This Bank may charge back to the depositor an
items, whether returned or not, including items drawn on it, at any tim
before final payment.

It is expressly understood that irrespective of the form of endorsemen
thereon, by deposit of items with this Bank either for credit or collectio
the depositor guarantees all prior endorsements.

Items may be transmitted for collection to any Federal Reserve Bank
All such items shall be subject to the rules and regulations of such Fed
eral Reserve Bank and of the Federal Reserve Board in force from tim
to time.

Items payable in the City of Chicago, or in any suburb thereof, may b
collected through the Chicago Clearing House Association (in which eve
they may be carried over for presentation through the Clearing House o
the following business day) and will be subject to its rules and regula
tions in force from time to time, or they may be collected in any othe
manner.

This Bank will make reasonable effort to transmit every item by i
usual and customary methods of transmission, so that it will be present
for payment at maturity, but the Bank does not warrant that such prese
tation will be made. If the depositor of items for collection hereund
shall at any time have a right of recovery for any reason against a
property, credits or balances belonging to any other person, firm, or co
poration in the possession of the Bank, all such rights shall be subord
nate to the rights of the Bank against such property, credits or balance

The Bank may decline to receive savings deposits from any person
limit the amount thereof whenever any officer in his discretion may
elect, and may at any time return to any depositor all or part of t
amount standing to the depositor's credit provided that notice to that eff
shall be served personally upon the depositor or deposited in the Unit
States Mail, postage prepaid and registered, addressed to the deposit
at the address as shown on the records of the Bank, and such deposit
portion of deposit shall cease to bear interest from and after the date up
which said notice shall be personally served or mailed, except that
interest shall accrue upon any deposit declared by law or regulation to
ineligible for classification as a savings deposit.

When the depositor makes use of the Bank's Day and Night D
pository, the bailor-bailee relationship (for the sole benefit of t
depositor-bailor) shall arise when this Bank shall have removed from su
depository any deposit placed therein by the depositor, and until su
removal all risks of loss of the deposit shall be borne exclusively by t
depositor. This Bank's removal and subsequent handling of the depo
shall be governed in all respects by the rules and conditions in th
Bank's then current form of Day and Night Depository Agreement—
copy of which will be furnished to the depositor at any time on reque

OPENING A TIME DEPOSIT ACCOUNT

In opening a time deposit account the bank takes the same precautionary measures as to identification, and scrutiny of checks tendered in opening the account, as it does in the case of the demand deposit account.

Although a New Account Memorandum sheet is not generally used in connection with a time deposit account, information for identification purposes, such as in connection with date and place of birth, is usually indexed on the signature card similar to that shown in Exhibit 58.

Rules and regulations covering the relationship of the bank with the time depositor are set forth in the pass book, a copy of which, in connection with depositing and collection of checks, usually appears on the reverse side of the deposit slip as shown in Exhibit 59.

All in all, the relationship between the bank and the demand or time depositor is the same except as to "notice or time of withdrawal" and "payment of interest."

CHAPTER XVIII

ACCOUNTING AS APPLIED TO BANKING

ACCOUNTING, THE SCIENCE, IS THE system through which financial transactions are recorded. The purpose of accounting is to:

1. Record all transactions which result in an increase or decrease in values or worth.

2. Determine, at any given time, the financial position of an individual or a business enterprise.

3. Establish the net worth of an individual or business enterprise which is the difference between assets and liabilities, or what we own and are owed by others, and what we owe others.

4. Determine, at the end of a certain number of days, months or years, the net profit or loss from financial activities covering that period.

The need for accurate accounting in banking transactions is quite apparent when we consider the volume of activity which takes place daily in every bank and the relationship of the bank with its stockholders, depositors, and the public.

Accounting, from the standpoint of the bank's relationship with the stockholders, is contained in the various records management is required by law to maintain in conducting the affairs of the bank.

Accounting, from the standpoint of the depositor and the public, is contained in the accounting reports which every bank, whether it is operating under a state or national charter, is required by law to make several times a year to the supervisory authorities. A condensed copy of these reports is required to be published in a paper serving the community in which the bank is located.

The principles of accounting, whether applied to financial or mercantile transactions, are the same except that a mercantile establishment deals in merchandise or goods and a bank deals with money and the various mediums of exchange. Further, the transactions entered into by both types of business enterprises are based upon agreements and promises. For example: A retail merchant buys shoes from the manufacturer for which he agrees (promises) to remit payment on or before a certain date. A bank receives deposits which it agrees (promises) to return to the depositor on demand or at a fixed time.

The retail merchant, in selling shoes, permits the purchaser to take the shoes and wear them, on his promise (agreement) to remit payment on or before a certain time or number of days. The bank, on the other hand, "sells" money to a customer on his promise (agreement) to repay the amount on demand or after a certain number of days.

Bank accounting is of two principal classes:

A. Corporate accounting

B. Financial accounting

CORPORATE ACCOUNTING

Corporate accounting consists of the recording of information in connection with ownership of the bank and recording of information which affects the interests of the stockholders in the enterprise.

This information is generally found in the following records or ledgers which are kept by the secretary, or officer of the bank, to whom the Board of Directors has delegated responsibility for the maintenance of the official records of the bank and the custodianship of the corporate seal:

1. Stock Ledger Book
2. Stock Certificate Ledger
3. Stock Transfer Ledger
4. Minute Books of Committees
5. Minute Book of the Board of Directors

The Stock Ledger Book is maintained to record the ownership of the stock of the bank. This ledger contains a sheet for each stockholder showing in alphabetical order the name, address, and details in connection with the purchase or sale of the bank stock such as date acquired or sold, number of shares acquired or sold, price paid or received and the present number of shares owned.

The Stock Certificate Ledger is similar to a check book. It has a stub on which is indexed the name of the stockholder, the date, number of the certificate, number of shares, from whom the stock was transferred, and a receipt. This corresponds to the information on the stock certificate which is delivered to the stockholder as evidence of ownership of shares in the bank. Whenever a stock certificate is transferred or cancelled, the old certificate is attached to the stub as evidence of cancellation.

The Stock Transfer Ledger is a chronological record of changes in stock ownership. It shows by date the number of the old stock certificate, number of the new certificate, from whom it was received and to whom the new certificate was issued. A Stock Transfer Ledger is generally used only where the stock is traded actively, and for the purpose of recording the day by day transactions as a guide or check in completing stock transfer records.

Minute Books of committees are maintained for the purpose of recording the proceedings and actions taken by committees of the bank engaged in official business. Every minute book, in the final analysis, is nothing more than the recording of the history and progress of the bank as it is being made.

In a well managed bank, minutes are kept by the secretary of each committee. Such minutes, because the committees are organized and set up for a specific purpose, generally consist of:

A. The roll call or reading and recording of names of members present.

B. The reading of the minutes of the previous meeting, or reading of the proceedings or action taken at the previous meeting.

C. The formal approval of such minutes as read, as evidence of approval of action taken on all matters submitted to the members of the committee who were present at the previous meeting.

D. The disposal of unfinished business or matters before the committee at the previous meeting on which no decision was reached before adjournment.

E. The taking up of new matters on which the committee should take action.

F. Adjournment.

AGENDA OF MEETINGS OF THE BOARD OF DIRECTORS

The minutes of the Board of Directors meetings, however, because they are the official records of the bank, are written in more detail.

First of all the minute book, for reference purposes, generally starts off with the Articles of Incorporation and By-Laws. It then records the action taken at periodic meetings, whether held at regular times as provided by the By-Laws, or when called at special times by the stockholders or directors.

The proceedings of each meeting, as recorded in the minute book, should show the date and time the meeting was held, the place where it was held, and the name and title of the person who presided as chairman.

In addition to following the routine which is described and recording the action taken at all annual or special meetings of the stockholders or regular or special meetings of the Board of Directors, the minutes should record:

1. The election or resignation of directors.

2. The election, appointment, dismissal or resignation of officers.

3. The compensation to be paid officers and employees, or the approval of the Board authorizing the President or other officer to act in behalf of the Board in connection with salary matters.

4. The appointment of directors and officers as members of committees.

5. The approval of assignments of duties and responsibilities to administrative personnel, or the authorization of the president or other officer to act in behalf of the Board in assigning duties and responsibilities.

6. Amendments or changes to the By-Laws.

7. Action taken by the directors in any and all matters, the authority and responsibility for which is vested in them by either the By-Laws or Organization Plan, as approved.

In studying the minute book and action of the Board of Directors, it is well to remember that all actions or decisions recorded in the minute book either begin with the reading of a report followed by a motion for adoption or rejection of a recommendation, or with the offering of a resolution which the chairman submits to the members of the Board for approval or rejection.

Every regular Directors' meeting generally is conducted in accordance with the following agenda and the action or procedure followed, with respect to the items on the agenda, recorded by the secretary in the minute book.

A. Roll call of members present.

B. Reading of minutes of previous meeting.

C. Approval or rejection of the minutes of the previous meeting which is the approval or rejection of the action taken or decisions made at the previous meeting.

D. Review of the current Statement of Condition. This is generally done on a comparative basis which shows the position of the bank for the current month, previous month and same month in the prior year.

E. Review and analysis of income and expense for the current period. This is generally on a comparative basis showing income and expense for current month, for the previous month, or the same month in the prior year or "year to date" in comparison with "previous year to date." After expenses have been reviewed, they are approved or disapproved and the decisions recorded in the minute book.

F. Review of all new loans made and loans renewed during the current period, or since the date of the previous meeting. The action in connection with the loans is entered in the minute book.

In some banks, depending upon the state laws and the By-Laws of the bank, loans under a specified amount are generally approved by number. Where it is the practice to have loans over a certain amount approved individually, the vote of the individual Director as to approval or rejection of such loans, should be recorded.

G. Review and discussion of applications for new loans. These applications generally cover loans in excess of the authorization or authority granted the officers or Executive Committee.

H. Analysis and review of the investment portfolio of the bank for the current period, together with approval or rejection of securities purchased or sold for the bank's account.

I. Review of all new accounts opened during the current period. This generally only covers the larger and more important accounts, depending upon the policy of the bank.

J. Review of closed accounts. Such accounts are usually listed by name, the balance at the time of closing, average balance maintained in recent months, and reason for closing if known. It is essential that the reason for closing be determined because, outside of those given for "moving away," "transferred," or "deceased," other causes or reasons could be a reflection on the policy of the bank, discourtesy on the part of employees, or other factors inimicable to the best interests of the bank, which should be corrected.

K. Review of overdrafts by name, amount and the name of the officer who approved.

L. Completion of unfinished business or decision on matters under discussion at the time of adjournment of the previous meeting.

M. Introduction of new matters for review and decision of Directors. This covers any matter which requires the attention and decision of the Board of Directors in connection with policies, major personnel problems, advertising, etc.

N. Adjournment.

FINANCIAL ACCOUNTING

The financial records of a bank are generally considered to be of two types, temporary records and permanent records.

Temporary records, such as adding machine lists, copies of proof or transit letters, records in connection with the return of checks for insufficient funds, various forms of collection or check registers, are rendered obsolete either when the transaction has been completed or after a reasonable length of time when it is certain that the transaction was properly handled.

Permanent records are those which, according to law, must be maintained forever. These records consist primarily of commercial, savings, stockholders, general, and subsidiary ledgers; loans and collateral ledgers; and collection and official check registers. While these records are supposed to be maintained permanently, common practice and the Statute of Limitations have worked so that in many cases they can be destroyed after a fixed number of years. In addition, it is now legally permissible, in many states, for banks to microfilm and then destroy financial records which, because of their bulk and size, take up a large amount of storage space.

The financial records of a bank will vary according to the size of the bank and need for keeping detailed records of transactions. Every bank, however, regardless of size will have the following financial records maintained under generally acceptable accounting procedures.

A. A form of Journal which is a record or summary of the daily transactions which take place.

B. A General Ledger in which the summarizations of the day's transactions, as shown on the Daily Journal, are entered as a permanent record to principal assets and liability accounts.

C. Subledgers or records in which detailed accounting is made of transactions which are summarized in the General Ledger.

D. A Daily Statement of Condition which lists the balances of the principal asset and liability control accounts in the General Ledger as of the close of business the previous day.

Accounting procedures are the ways and means used to record the financial transactions in the various accounting records. The procedure or manner in which results of financial transactions are recorded and the results they portray, provide the basis for internal control systems. Likewise, the figures which are shown in the accounting records provide the basis for review, analysis and confirmation under an audit program.

In reviewing accounting procedures, it is necessary to be certain that the details of all transactions are correctly indexed in the accounting records to correctly reflect the result of financial transactions in the Statements of Condition and Profit and Loss Statements. It is also important to set up subsidiary accounts to properly reflect all movements and changes.

A proper accounting system also should provide adequatel for the proper segregation of the different types and values o classes of accounts based on income, tax and most important, th reporting requirements of the various federal, state and super visory authorities.

Last, but not least, the accounting system should be set up t properly reflect the operations of the bank from a profit and los standpoint.

Accounting records, if properly set up therefore, should revea the details in connection with the assets of the bank which represen what people owe the bank and all details in connection with th liabilities of the bank which represents the amounts the bank ow others.

Every bank, regardless of location or whether it be large small, essentially performs the same type of work. The differenc as we have pointed out, is not so much in the way it is done but b whom it is done. The smaller the bank the greater number functions are performed by the same individual; the larger th bank, the more operations are departmentalized, and a person's activities are entirely in connection with performing one function, or the operation of one section, or in connection with providing one service.

In order to describe properly an accounting set up for a bank, we must use for reference purposes either a small country bank or a large city bank. Regardless of which type of bank we take, the principles and fundamentals of bookkeeping must be observed and followed, in order to keep the records in proper order and correctly reflect the operation of the bank.

Inasmuch as nearly every bank, regardless of size, performs the same functions and provides the same services, it might be more informative, as long as we realize that the need for subsidiary accounts and breakdowns of control accounts to their component parts is predicated entirely upon the size and activity of the bank, to take the accounting setup of a large bank which carries nearly every type of an account necessary to reflect the scope of its business transactions.

CHART OF ACCOUNTS

The various classes and types of accounts a bank should carry, in order to properly reflect the scope and activity of its business, can only be determined after studying its activity, policies, management and objectives. Once these factors are known, the setup and nomenclature of respective accounts, known as a Chart of Accounts can be decided upon.

Generally an individual ledger sheet is carried for each account maintained by the bank, with a CONTROL ACCOUNT (upper case type) reflecting the totals of respective accounts under the major classifications. In many banks it is the policy to only show on the Daily Statement of Condition the detail of the Control Account "CASH AND DUE FROM BANKS" and the total of the other accounts as reflected in the CONTROL ACCOUNT.

Such a Chart of Accounts showing both control and subsidiary accounts for Asset and Liability Accounts as used by a large bank, is shown in Exhibits 60 and 61. In reviewing this Chart of Accounts attention is called to the use of numbers and the use of upper case letters in designating the control accounts.

Use of numbers not only facilitates the heading up of General

Exhibit 60

CHART OF ACCOUNTS

ASSET ACCOUNTS

Classification	Number
Cash	1
Exchange for Clearings	3
Clearings between Main Office and Dist. Offices	7
Cash Items in Transit to Correspondent Banks	9
Cash Items in Transit to Other Banks	11
Cash Items in Process of Collection	13
Due from Federal Reserve Bank	17
Due from Domestic Banks	19
Due from Foreign Banks	21
TOTAL CASH AND DUE FROM BANKS	25
Time Loans Secured - Marketable Collateral	27
Time Loans Secured - Other Collateral	27-1
Time Loans Unsecured	27-2
Demand Loans Secured - Marketable Collateral	29
Demand Loans Secured - Other Collateral	29-1
Demand Loans Unsecured	29-2
Discounts	31
Farm Loans	33
Discounted Sight Drafts in Process of Collection	37
Commercial Paper	39
Construction Loans - Conventional	41
Construction Loans Under F.H.A. Commit.	41-1
F.H.A. Title II Loans 4-1/2%	43
F.H.A. Title II Loans 4-1/4%	43-1
F.H.A. TITLE VI Loans	43-2
F.H.A. Loans Offered for Sale	43-3
Veterans Loans	43-4
F.H.A. Title I Loans	43-5

Exhibit 60

Conventional R. E. Mortgage Loans	47
Loans to Auto Dealers	49
Discounts to Auto Dealers	51
Installment Loans - Personal	53
Installment Loans - Automobile	53-1
Installment Loans - Appliance	53-2
Overdrafts	57
Bills of Exchange	59
Payment Made under Letters of Credit	61
Acceptances	63
TOTAL LOANS AND DISCOUNTS	65
U.S. Govt. Bonds - Unpledged	67
U.S. Govt. Bonds - Pledged	67-1
U.S. Govt. Notes - Unpledged	69
U.S. Govt. Notes - Pledged	69-1
U.S. Govt. Cert. of Ind. - Unpledged	71
U.S. Govt. Cert. of Ind. - Pledged	71-1
U.S. Treasury Bills	73
Other U.S. Govt. Obligations	77
State Obligations - Unpledged	79
State Obligations - Pledged	79-1
County Obligations - Unpledged	81
County Obligations - Pledged	81-1
Municipal Obligations - Unpledged	83
Municipal Obligations - Pledged	83-1
Railroad Bonds; Debentures	87
Utility Bonds; Debentures	89
Federal Reserve Bank Stock	91
Other Bonds, Notes, Debentures	93
TOTAL BONDS AND INVESTMENTS	95
Bank Premises	97
Bank Premises, Equipment	99
Bank Premises under Construction	101
Other Real Estate	109

Exhibit 60

Buses, Cars, Motorcycles, etc.	111
Office Furniture and Fixtures	113
Office Machines and Equipment	117
Fix., Equip., Leasehold Imp. Bldg. Under Con.	119
Fixtures - Equipment Leasehold Improve.	121
TOTAL PROPERTIES	125
Accrued Interest Receivable	127
Interest Earned but Not Collected	129
Other Income Earned or Accrued but Not Collected	131
TOTAL INCOME EARNED BUT NOT COLLECTED	135
Interest and Discount on Borrowed Money	137
Interest Paid on Deposits	139
Taxes Paid	141
Depreciation	143
Fees Paid to Directors and Committees	147
Salaries and Overtime Paid	149
Other Operating Expenses	151
TOTAL CURRENT EXPENSES FROM OPERAT.	155
Losses on Loans	157
Sundry Losses	159
Losses on the Sale of Securities	161
Losses on the Sale of Other Property	163
TOTAL CHARGES OR LOSSES	165
Accounts Receivable	167
Teller's Difference	169
Hold Over Debits	171
Customer's Liability under Letters of Credit	173
Prepaid Expenses	177
Sundry Resources	181
TOTAL OTHER RESOURCES	185
TOTAL RESOURCES	

Exhibit 61

CHART OF ACCOUNTS

LIABILITY ACCOUNTS

Classification	Number
State Deposits Sec. by Collateral (Demand)	2
County Deposits Sec. by Collateral (Demand)	6
City Deposits Sec. by Collateral (Demand)	8
Other Pub. Fd. Deposits Sec. by Coll. (Demand)	12
TOTAL PUBLIC FUND DEMAND DEPOSITS SECURED BY COLLATERAL	20
U.S. Treas. Gen. Acct. Sec. by Coll. (Demand)	22
Army, Navy, and Air Force Funds Secured by Collateral (Demand)	24
U.S. Treasury Tax and Loan Account Secured by Collateral (Demand)	26
Postal Savings Funds - Sec. by Coll. (Demand)	28
TOTAL U.S. GOVT. DEPOSITS SECURED BY COLLATERAL	30
Regular Checking Deposits	32
Special Checking Deposits	34
Inactive Checking Deposits	36
Certificates of Deposit	38
TOTAL REGULAR AND SPECIAL DEMAND DEPOSITS	40
Marginal Deposits	42
Undisbursed Loans and Related Deposits (F. H. A.)	44
Customers Guarantee on Estab. Comm'l. Credits	46
Installment payments to Auto Dealers	48
TOTAL DEPOSITS SECURING LIABILITIES	50
Deposits under Special Instructions	52
Trust Funds or Escrows	54
Escrow Funds for Taxes/Ins. F. H. A. and Vet. Loans	56
Escrow Funds for Prin./Int. F. H. A. and Vet. Loans	58
TOTAL ESCROW AND FIDUCIARY DEPOSITS	60
TOTAL DUE TO BANKS	70

Exhibit 61

Certified Checks	72
Expense Checks	74
Administrative Checks; Cashier Checks	76
Dividend Checks	78
Christmas Club Checks	82
Money Orders	84
Due to Local Banks for Returned Clear. Items	88
TOTAL OFFICIAL CHECKS, ETC.	90
State Deposits Sec. by Collateral (Time)	92
County Deposits Sec. by Collateral (Time)	96
City Deposits Sec. by Collateral (Time)	98
Other Pub. Fund Sec. by Coll. (Time)	102
TOTAL PUB. FUND TIME DEP. SEC. BY COLL.	110
U.S. Treas. Gen. Acct. Secured by Coll. (Time)	112
Army, Navy, and Air Forces Funds Secured by Collateral (Time)	114
Postal Sav. Funds - Sec. by Coll. (Time)	118
TOTAL U.S. GOVT. TIME DEPOSITS SECURED BY COLLATERAL	120
Savings Deposits	122
Christmas Club Deposits	124
Savings Deposits (Personal Loans)	126
Time Deposits Open Accounts	128
Inactive Savings Deposits	132
Unclaimed Balances	134
Certificates of Deposit	136
TOTAL REGULAR AND SPECIAL TIME DEP.	140
Capital Stock Common	142
Capital Stock Preferred Class A	142-1
Capital Stock Preferred Class B	142-2
Capital Notes or Debentures	144
Surplus	146
Undivided Profits	148
TOTAL CAPITAL ACCOUNTS	150

Exhibit 61

eserves for Depreciation	152
eserve for Dividends	154
eserve for Income Tax	156
eserve for Interest	158
eserve for Insurance	162
eserve for Municipal Taxes	164
eserve for Real Estate Taxes	166
ther Special Reserves	168
OTAL RESERVES	170
nearned Discount	172
nearned F.H.A. Service Fee Income	176
OTAL INCOME COLLECTED BUT UNEARNED	180
ccrued Interest Payable	182
ccrued Expenses Payable	184
ccrued Taxes Payable	186
OTAL EXPENSES ACCRUED BUT UNPAID	190
nterest Earned; Loans and Discounts	192
nterest Earned; Investments	194
ervice Charges and Fees on Loans	196
ervice Charges on Checking Accounts	198
ther Charges and Fees	202
ommissions	204
xchange Charges	206
ents Received	208
afe Deposit Box Rent	212
rust Department Fees	214
OTAL CURRENT INCOME FROM OPERATIONS	220
ecoveries on Loans	222
undry Recoveries	224
rofits from the Sale of Securities	226
rofits from the Sale of Other Property	228
OTAL RECOVERIES AND PROFITS	230
ccounts Payable	232
eller's Difference	234
old Over Credits	236
etters of Credit Outstanding	238
ividends Declared but not Payable	242
ediscounts	244
cceptances	246
dvances Secured by Pledges of Securities	248
ndry Liabilities	252
OTAL OTHER LIABILITIES	260
OTAL LIABILITIES	

Ledger tickets, but simplifies intersorting and classifying of th tickets which affect both control and subsidiary accounts.

Generally in using numbers, the odd numbered digits such a 1, 3, 7, 9, etc. are used for Asset Accounts, while the even digi numbers such as 2, 4, 6, 8, etc. are used for Liability Accounts.

In using numbers, it is also the accepted practice in allocatin numbers, to spread numbers and leave some numbers unassigned i the various classifications, so as to provide for expansion, and th inclusion of additional accounts.

To more properly systematize the numerical setup, number ending with the numeral 5 such as 5, 15, 25, etc. can be assigned t the Asset Control Accounts while numbers ending in zero such a 10, 20, 30 etc. can be assigned to Liability Control Accounts.

Under such a numerical system, if additional accounts or mor detail is required, the use of suffix numbers following Control Ac counts such as 27-1 and 27-2, etc. will provide further expansion, a will the use of alphabetical letters A, B, C, etc. in connection wit classifying certain subsidiary accounts.

While studying the various accounts which make up a Cha of Accounts in every bank, it is well to remember that *each* an *every* time a bank performs a function or provides a service involv ing money or credit, a General Ledger ticket has to be prepared fc recording the transaction, each of which affects the balance of tw or more accounts. This may be in the form of a General Ledg ticket in connection with a single transaction, as in the case c recording the commission from the sale of Travellers Checks t *one* customer; or it may be in the form of a General Ledger tick representing *many* transactions, such as the total deposits made t Regular Savings Accounts, the details of which individual tran actions are recorded in the Savings Ledgers.

In order to increase efficiency and eliminate unnecessary wor especially in cases where a bank is departmentalized, considerab time can be saved by having the General Ledger tickets used by tl respective divisions or sections pre-headed with the name an Chart of Account number of respective accounts.

Entries affecting the principal accounting records of a bar originate in the various departments, divisions and sections whic handle financial transactions. Once prepared, General Ledg ickets covering individual transactions are either sent by the re-pective divisions and sections throughout the day to the Proof ection as part of the transaction, where they are charged to the ;eneral Bookkeeping Section; or the respective divisions and sec-ions prepare such General Ledger tickets at the end of the day) reflect the summarization of totals of a number of individual ransactions.

If such tickets go directly to the General Bookkeeper, and this done in cases where the Central Proof Section does not effect ie balancing of the bank, it is customary for such divisions or sec-ions to include their journal or blotter sheet. This is a record f the transactions between divisions, sections and tellers, and rovides the General Bookkeeper with information with respect to ash on hand at the beginning of business, transfers of cash be-veen divisions and sections, and cash on hand at the close of usiness.

If such General Ledger Tickets come from the Proof Section ey are usually accompanied by a tape which shows the total of e debit tickets and the total of the credit tickets to balance.

THE DAILY JOURNAL

Once these tickets have been received by the General Book-eeper and have been balanced as to batches as received, they are rted to respective accounts and entered on the Daily Journal.

The purpose of listing all daily transactions in summary in the urnal and balancing, is to prove that the current transactions of e bank balance, and that for every debit there has been a cor-sponding credit, before the totals covering the various types of ansactions are posted to the General Ledger.

After all General Ledger tickets affecting respective General edger or Subsidiary accounts have been posted to the Journal, e summarized Journal entries are either posted to the respective ccounts in the General Ledger or the original tickets are used as emos to post the accounts.

It should be noted that in many banks which have adopted achine or mechanized posting of the General Ledger, the Gen-ral Ledger is posted directly from the General Ledger tickets, liminating the make-up and use of the Journal.

THE GENERAL LEDGER

After all tickets have been posted to the respective account in the Journal, the entries are posted directly from the Journal t the corresponding account in the General Ledger. In the case o banks which, under machine or mechanized posting have eliminat ed the Journal as such using as a "journal" the carbon copy of th posting record which is a by-product of the machine posting t "prove" posting totals, the tickets themselves are used to record th details of transactions to the respective General Ledger accounts.

In recording the daily individual debit and credit transaction which affect the respective balance totals of each class and type c control or subcontrol account, the figures are either first posted t the subcontrol accounts from the Journal (or from the individu tickets) and then to the control account; or the summarized or tot of each type or class of account is first posted to the principal co trol account under which procedure the detail to the individu subcontrol accounts is posted *after* all the General Ledger Contr accounts have been posted and balanced and the Daily Stateme of Condition taken off.

The General Ledger setup, under the accounting princip that such a ledger is nothing but a summarization of other recor which contain essential details, carries an account for each class property, each class and type of loan and investment, and eac class and type of deposit account.

All accounts in the General Ledger are known either as Co trol Accounts or Subcontrol Accounts. Control and Subcontr accounts are those which reflect the changes and remaining ba ances of the principal classes and types of asset and liability a counts, similar to those we studied in Chapter X "The Bank Statement of Condition," and which are designated by capit letters in the Chart of Accounts.

Such control or subcontrol accounts may or may not, depen ing on the volume of transactions, be supported by subsidia ledgers, which are maintained whenever, in the judgment of ma agement, additional records are required to provide detail or oth information. For example: When the X Bank began business it ha so few loans that it carried individual accounts under the name each borrower in the General Ledger. As business increase owever, this practice not only entailed too much work for the eneral Bookkeeper, but failed to provide sufficient information r management. Therefore, the control account "LOANS and ISCOUNTS" was divided into two subcontrol accounts "TIME OANS" and "DEMAND LOANS" reflecting only totals while the etail in connection with such loans was recorded in subsidiary dgers.

Later, when the volume of loans further increased, manage-ent decided it required additional information. It, therefore, set p other subcontrol accounts and ledgers separating "TIME OANS" into "TIME LOANS SECURED" and "TIME LOANS NSECURED."

Depending on the wishes of management, control, subcontrol, id sub-subcontrols can be established to cover practically every cet. An idea of the possibilities of setting up such accounts in nnection with "LOANS and DISCOUNTS" is shown in Exhibit .

While the number of control, subcontrol, and sub-subcontrol counts and the number of subsidiary ledgers is predicated on the ze of the bank, activity of respective accounts and the policy of anagement to require detailed information on which to base cisions, the general practice of most banks, regardless of size, to maintain only subsidiary ledgers in connection with the follow-g control or subcontrol accounts, which may have more than one issification.

1. Accounts Payable
2. Accounts Receivable
3. Bank Building and Premises
4. Cash
5. Commercial Loans
6. Demand Deposits
7. Due from Banks
8. Due to Banks
9. Expenses
10. Furniture and Fixtures
11. Income Received
12. Installment Loans
13. Letters of Credit

Exhibit 62

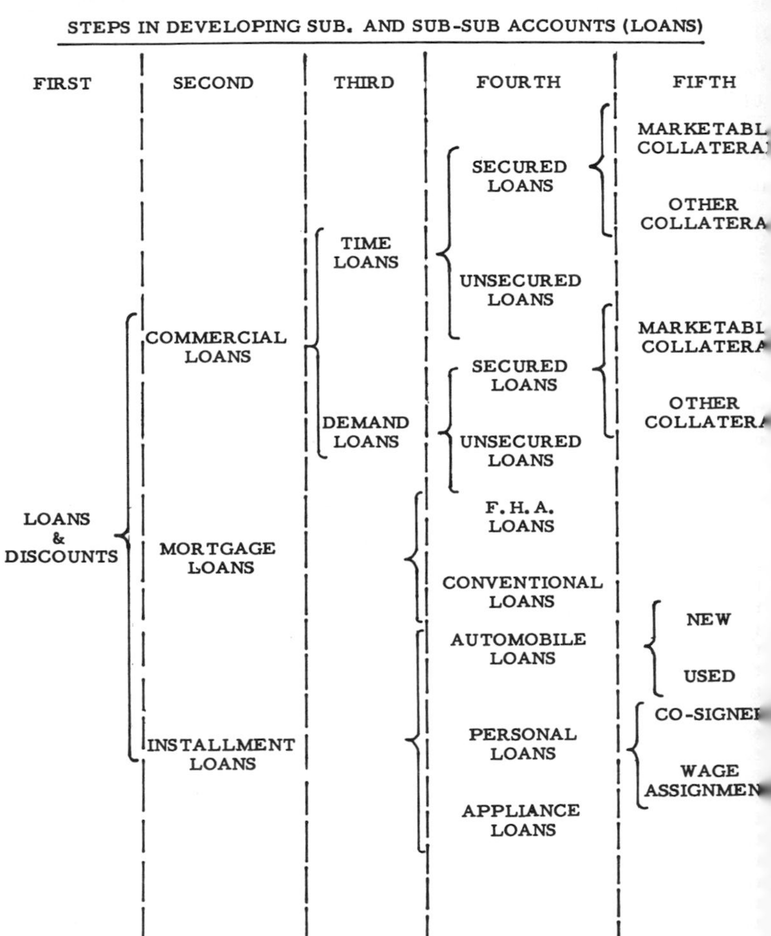

STEPS IN DEVELOPING SUB. AND SUB-SUB ACCOUNTS (LOANS)
FIRST
SECOND
THIRD
FOURTH
FIFTH
LOANS & DISCOUNTS
COMMERCIAL LOANS
MORTGAGE LOANS
INSTALLMENT LOANS
TIME LOANS
DEMAND LOANS
SECURED LOANS
UNSECURED LOANS
SECURED LOANS
UNSECURED LOANS
F.H.A. LOANS
CONVENTIONAL LOANS
AUTOMOBILE LOANS
PERSONAL LOANS
APPLIANCE LOANS
NEW
USED

Exhibit 63

INCOME

URRENT INCOME FROM OPERATIONS ACCOUNTS	220
ıterest Earned; Loans and Discounts	192
ıterest Earned; Investments	194
ervice Charges and Fees on Loans	196
ervice Charges on Checking Accounts	198
ther Charges and Fees	202
ommissions	204
xchange Charges	206
ents Received	208
ıfe Deposit Box Rents	212
rust Department Fees	214

INDIVIDUAL ACCOUNTS

Description	Account No.
t. Earned; Time Loans	192-1
t. Earned; Demand Loans	192-2
t. Earned; Discounts	192-3
t. Earned; Farm Loans	192-4
t. Earned; Disc. Sight Drafts in Col.	192-5
t. Earned; Const. Loans - Conventional	192-6
t. Earned; Const. Loans - F.H.A. Commit.	192-7
t. Earned; F.H.A. Title II	192-8
t. Earned; F.H.A. Title VI	192-9
t. Earned; Veterans Loans	192-10
t. Earned; F.H.A. Title I	192-11
t. Earned; Conventional R. E. Mtg. Loans	192-12
t. Earned; Loans to Auto Dealers	192-13
t. Earned; Disc. to Auto Dealers	192-14
t. Earned; Install. Loans--Personal	192-15
t. Earned; Install. Loans--Automobile	192-16
t. Earned; Install. Loans--Appliance	192-17
t. Earned; Overdrafts	192-18
t. Earned; Letters of Credit	192-19
)TAL INTEREST EARNED ON LOANS AND DISCOUNTS	192

Exhibit 63

Int. Earned; U.S. Govt. Bonds--Taxable	194-1
Int. Earned; U.S. Govt. Bonds--Non Tax.	194-2
Int. Earned; U.S. Govt. Notes	194-3
Int. Earned; U.S. Govt. Ctf. of Ind.	194-4
Disc. Int. Earned; U.S. Treas. Bills	194-5
Int. Earned; Other U.S. Govt. Oblig.	194-6
Int. Earned; State Obligations	194-7
Int. Earned; County Obligations	194-8
Int. Earned; Municipal Obligations	194-9
Int. Earned; Railroad Bonds--Debentures	194-10
Int. Earned; Utility Bonds--Debentures	194-11
Int. Earned; Other Bonds or Debentures	194-12
TOTAL INTEREST ON INVESTMENTS	194
Delayed Pay. Cha; Installment Loans	196-1
Delayed Pay. Chg; F.H.A. Title II and VI	196-2
Delayed Pay. Chg; F.H.A. Title I	196-3
Fees--New F.H.A. Loans	196-4
Fees--Commercial Loans and Discounts	196-5
Fees--Auto Dealers	196-6
TOTAL CHARGES AND FEES ON LOANS	196
Service Charges--Reg. Checking Accounts	198-1
Service Charges--Personal Checking Accounts	198-2
TOTAL SERVICE CHARGES ON CHECKING ACCOUNTS	198
Stop Payment and Return Check Fees	202-1
Charges on Savings Accounts	202-2
Miscellaneous Charges	202-3
F.H.A. Servicing Fees	202-4
Redemption Fees; Defense Savings Bonds	202-5
TOTAL OTHER CHARGES AND FEES	202
Commissions; Commercial Letters of Credit	204-1
Commissions; Documentary Drafts in Transit	204-2
Commissions; Collections	204-3
Commissions; Miscellaneous	204-4
Commissions; Travellers Letters of Credit	204-5
Commissions; Travellers Checks Sold	204-6
TOTAL COMMISSIONS	204

Exhibit 63

xchange Charges; Checks Dep. /Cashed	206-1
xchange Charges; Sale of Foreign Drafts	206-2
xchange Charges; Purchase of Foreign Dr.	206-3
OTAL EXCHANGE CHARGES RECEIVED	206
ents Received; Main Office Building	208-1
ents Received; District Offices	208-2
ents Received; Other Buildings--Property	208-3
OTAL RENTS RECEIVED	208
AFE DEPOSIT BOX RENTALS	212
RUST DEPARTMENT FEES	214
OTAL CURRENT INCOME FROM OPERATIONS	220

14. Machinery and Equipment
15. Mortgage Loans
16. Municipal Bonds
17. Official Checks (Drafts—Cashier's Checks—Expense Checks etc.)
18. Other Bonds
19. Time Deposits, Regular
20. Time Deposits, Special
21. U. S. Government Bonds

Because of the necessity for having complete information fc budgeting, cost control, cost analysis and tax purposes, the accoun of INCOME and EXPENSE (which are major control accounts) a maintained in detail, with control, sub, and sub-subcontrol accoun carried for individual items of income and expense, similar to th shown in Exhibits 63 and 64.

USING THE CASH OR ACCRUAL BASIS FOR RECORDING INCOME AND EXPENSE

In recording items of income and expense banks may u either one of two methods.

1. The cash basis
2. The accrual basis

Under the cash basis, used by many of the smaller bank income is entered as earnings on the bank's books when receive and expenses are deducted on the bank's books from earnings whe paid. Obviously, this method results in a distortion of net profi for any period under review, as large fees, commissions or intere paid in advance, are immediately reflected in earnings, where such income is earned only over the period for which the servi is rendered or over the period for which the money is loaned.

Likewise, when a bank makes a loan, the terms of which pr vide for the interest to be paid when the principal amount is pa at maturity; or invests funds in bonds where the interest is pa semi-annually; current earnings do not reflect the interest incor due the bank during the time the money is loaned out or investe

By the same token, if a bank pays in advance for goods services which will be used over a long period of time, it resu

Exhibit 64

EXPENSES

OTAL CURRENT EXPENSES FROM OPERATIONS	155
t. and Disc. on Borrowed Money	137
terest Paid on Deposits	139
axes Paid	141
epreciation	143
ees Paid to Directors and Committees	147
laries and Overtime Paid	149
her Operating Expenses	151

INDIVIDUAL ACCOUNTS

Description	Account No.
t. on Overdrafts	137-1
t. on Advances for Other Purposes	137-2
iscount on Acceptances	137-3
TAL INT. AND DISC. ON BORROWED MONEY	137
t. Paid on Public Demand Funds	139-1
t. Paid on Public Time Funds	139-2
t. Paid on Savings Deposits	139-3
t. Paid on Time Dep. Open Accounts	139-4
t. Paid on Sav. Dep. (Personal Loans)	129-5
TAL INTEREST PAID ON DEPOSITS	139
operty Taxes (R.E.; Pers. Prop.)	141-1
unicipal License Tax	141-2
cial Security Tax	141-3
cise Tax & Internal Revenue Stamps	141-4
to; Bus; Motorcycle; Bus License Tax	141-5
come Tax	141-6
TAL TAXES PAID	141
preciation; Office Furniture/Fixtures	143-1
preciation; Machines and Equipment	143-2
preciation; Bank Bldg. Equipment	143-3

Exhibit 64

Depreciation; Bank Building	143-4
Depreciation; Buses, Cars, etc.	143-5
TOTAL DEPRECIATION	143
FEES PAID TO DIRECTORS AND COMMITTEES	147
Salaries; Bank Employees	149-1
Salaries; Bank Officers	149-2
Overtime; Bank Employees	149-3
Salaries; Building Employees	149-4
Overtime; Building Employees	149-5
TOTAL SALARIES AND OVERTIME PAID	149
Advertising---Calendars	151-1
Direct Mail	151-1-A
Magazines	151-1-B
Newspapers	151-1-C
Publicity	151-1-D
Attorney Fees	151-2
Automobile Allowances	151-3
Building Improvement Amortization	151-4
Cables--Bank Account	151-5
Customers Accounts	151-51A
Contributions-- Bank	151-6
Employees Welfare	151-6-A
Donations------Charitable	151-7
Civic	151-7-A
Other	151-7-B
Dues----------Association	151-8
Club	151-8-A
Society	151-8-B
Entertainment--Customers	151-9
Convention	151-9-A
New Business	151-9-B
Examination--- State Banking Dept. or Office	151-10
Fed. Banking Dept. or Office	151-10-A
Express	151-11
Flowers	151-12
Freight	151-13
Gasoline--Oil	151-14
Gifts---Honorariums	151-15
Hotels	151-16
Ins.--Fire, etc. Machines, Equip., Fur. Fixt.	151-17
Blanket Bond	151-17-A
Accident	151-17-B
Cash or Sec. Transferred	151-17-C
Public Liability	151-17-D
Safe Deposit Liability	151-17-E

Exhibit 64

	State Ins. (Workman Comp.)	151-17-F
	F.D.I.C.	151-17-G
	Fire-Earthquake on Bldgs.	151-17-H
Light--Power		151-18
Luncheons-----	Customers	151-19
	Employees	151-19-A
	New Business	151-19-B
Maintenance---	Buildings	151-20
	Building Equipment	151-20-A
	Furniture & Fixtures	151-20-B
	Machinery & Equipment	151-20-C
	Mobile Units	151-20-D
	Mobile Units Equipment	151-20-E
	Other Real Estate	151-20-F
Medical Examination & Expenses		151-21
Pension Plan --	Regular	151-22
	Special	151-22-A
Photographs		151-23
Postage		151-24
Professional Services		151-25
Rent----------	Automobiles	151-26
	Bank Premises	151-26-A
	Garages & Others	151-26-B
	Machinery & Equipment	151-26-C
Repairs-------	Building	151-27
	Building Equipment	151-27-A
	Furniture & Fixtures	151-27-B
	Machinery & Equipment	151-27-C
	Mobile Units	151-27-D
	Mobile Units Equipment	151-27-E
	Other Real Estate	151-27-F
Stationery---Printing---Office Supplies		151-28
Subscriptions---	Magazines	151-29
	Newspapers	151-29-A
	Other	151-29-B
Supplies-------	Building	151-30
	Others	151-30-A
Taxi		151-31
Telegraph		151-32
Telephone-----	Local	151-33
	Long Distance	151-33-A
	Overseas	151-33-B
Transportation-	Bank Business--Air	151-34
	Boat	151-34-A
	Railroad	151-34-B
Transportation-	Other---Air	151-34-C
	Boat	151-34-D
	Railroad	151-34-E
Uniforms------	Building	151-35
	Band	151-35-A

Exhibit 64

Water ---------	Buildings	151-36
	Drinking	151-36-A
Unallocated		151-37
TOTAL OTHER OPERATING EXPENSES		151
TOTAL CURRENT EXPENSES FROM OPERATIONS		155

in understating its net profits for the period in which the goods or services are paid for, and in overstating its net profits during the remaining periods when the goods are used or services are performed. For example: a bank can save a considerable amount of money if it contracts for certain types of insurance on a three year basis. Obviously if the entire cost of the three year premium is charged to Expense in the first year, the net profits for that year are reduced, while the profits for the second and third year are greater than they would have been if the proportionate amount of the insurance premium had been charged to Expense in the year in which it was actually spent.

To avoid all this distortion in net profits, banks, particularly the larger banks, use what is known as an accrual system of accounting. Under this system, interest paid in advance is entered on the bank's books when it is received as a deferred item, and credited to an account "Interest Paid but Unearned," and only taken into the bank's income account periodically as it is actually earned.

Likewise, interest on loans due to be paid at maturity or interest on investments to be paid at a future time, is taken into income as earned. This is done by charging such amounts to a deferred income account "Interest Earned but Unpaid" which is credited with the amount of interest earned when paid by the borrower, thus cancelling the amount advanced during the time the funds were earning interest income.

In like manner expenses incurred for services which are to be rendered over a long period of time; stationery and supplies which are to be used over a long period of time; machinery and equipment which is to be used for a number of years; or repairs or additions to buildings and property which will be used over the life of the lease of building are capitalized by setting them up as Asset Accounts and paying for them during the time they are being used by having a proportionate amount of the cost periodically charged to expense and such amounts credited to respective accounts. A good example of this is in connection with funds spent for new accounting machines. Obviously, if the total cost of $6,000 were immediately charged to expense it would affect the profits of the bank for the period. If, on the other hand, it is determined that the useful life of the machine is 5 years, it could be set up in a deferred account with only $1,200 to be charged against expense for each year, thus increasing the net profits in the first year by $4,800.

Another and more current example of accrued expenses is in connection with "Interest Paid on Time Deposits." Most banks credit the interest earned on regular savings accounts to individual accounts as of June 30 and December 31. Obviously, if the entire amount of interest for the previous six months is charged to expense in the months of June and December, the net profits from operations for those months would be distorted. Therefore, in order to more correctly reflect operating results, progressive bank management charges to expense each month 1/6 of the estimated interest due to be paid at the end of the period, crediting such amounts to a "Reserve for Interest" account from which it is transferred to respective accounts at the end of the period.

The items or classes of income generally set up under an accrual system are in connection with:

1. Interest on Investments
2. Interest on Loans
3. Service Fees and Commissions

The items or classes of expense usually set up under an accrual system, through which a proportionate amount or percentage of the original expense is periodically charged to expense and the like amount either credited to a Reserve Account for future payment or distribution or immediately applied against amounts originally capitalized (as Asset Accounts), are generally in connection with:

1. Depreciation (Building—Building Improvements, Furniture Fixtures, Machinery and Equipment)
2. Dividends
3. Employee Benefits (Bonus—Pension Plans—Profit Sharing)
4. Federal Income Tax
5. Federal Deposit Ins. Corp. Assessment
6. Interest on Time Deposits
7. Local Real Estate, and other Taxes
8. Prepaid Expenses (Insurance, Supplies, Advertising, Commissions and Fees)
9. Retirement of Preferred Stock or Debentures.

THE BANK'S DAILY STATEMENT OF CONDITION

The last, but probably the most important record of bank financial accounting is the Daily Statement of Condition, similar to that shown in Exhibit 65, which is prepared by the general bookkeeper from the Control Accounts in the General Ledger after all debit and credit tickets affecting such accounts have been posted, and balances of Asset and Liability Accounts run and proven to be in balance.

The Daily Statement of Condition, which shows the financial position of the bank as of the close of business each day, is either prepared late in the afternoon after the posting has been completed or the first thing the following morning.

The purpose of the Daily Statement of Condition is not only to show that the bank is in balance and that all assets and liabilities have been accounted for, but most important, to provide the administrative and executive officers of the bank with information to assist them in making management decisions.

The composition of the Daily Statement of Condition may and often does vary between banks. It will, however, always reflect the totals of the control accounts which appear in capital letters on the Chart of Accounts plus whatever subsidiary accounts management finds it necessary to include in order to efficiently operate and manage the affairs of the bank.

Through study of the current Statement of Condition and comparison with the figures as shown therein with the Daily Statement of Condition for the previous day, or possibly several prior days, management is able to determine quickly the increase or decrease in loans and deposits and the bank's cash position. This, together with information supplied by the bookkeeping section in connection with large withdrawals or transfers from checking and savings accounts together with information supplied by the proof section in connection with large deposits made to checking and savings accounts, enables management to take the necessary action in connection with the conversion of assets,

If the deposits are declining and loans are steady or increasing (which reduces cash and the balances of funds which the bank maintains on deposit with other banks) management must either liquidate loans or investments, or borrow, by pledging securities as collateral for a loan, to provide funds for honoring withdrawals.

If, on the other hand, deposits are increasing and loans are steady or declining (which increases cash and balances with other banks) management will, based on information as to the length of time such increased deposits will remain on deposit with the bank, invest such funds in securities in order to earn income for the bank during the time funds remain with the bank on deposit.

Exhibit 65

DAILY STATEMENT OF CONDITION

DATE ____________

ASSETS		LIABILITIES	
CASH ON HAND	$	PUBLIC FUND DEMAND DEP.	$
EXCHANGE FOR CH		U.S. GOVT. DEMAND DEP.	
ITEMS IN TRANSIT			
		REG. CHECKING DEM. DEP.	
DUE FROM			
DUE FROM		SPL. CHECKING DEM. DEP.	
DUE FROM			
DUE FROM		FIDUCIARY DEM. DEPOSITS	
TIME LOANS SEC		DUE TO BANKS	
TIME LOANS UNSEC.			
		OFFICIAL CHECKS	
DEMAND LOANS SEC.			
DEMAND LOANS UNSEC.		PUBLIC FUND TIME DEPOSITS	
INSTAL LOANS PERS.		U.S. GOVT. TIME DEPOSITS	
INSTAL LOANS AUTO			
		REGULAR TIME DEPOSITS	
MORTGAGE LOANS			
		SPECIAL TIME DEPOSITS	
U.S. GOVT. SEC.			
		TIME C.D's	
MUNICIPAL SEC.			
		CAPITAL	
OTHER SEC.			
		SURPLUS	
BANK PREMISES			
FURN-FIXTURES		UNDIVIDED PROFITS	
INC. EARNED NOT COL.			
CHG. OFF-LOSSES		RESERVES	
CURRENT EXP. OPR.		CURRENT INCOME OPR.	
OTHER ASSETS		OTHER LIABILITIES	
TOTAL ASSETS		TOTAL LIABILITIES	

CHAPTER XIX

PUBLIC RELATIONS AND NEW BUSINESS

OF THE THREE PRINCIPAL PHASES of the business of banking there is no doubt that the acquiring of funds is the most important phase, for if we did not have funds we could not loan them out, and if we did not have customers and accounts we could not serve them.

Because of this, it is logical to state that the most important single factor of any successful business is people; for without people who manufacture things to sell, without people who have things to sell, and without people to buy things we have to sell we wouldn't have any business.

Success, it can be said, depends upon the manner in which we influence people to buy what we have to offer, whether it is goods, services or ourselves. Therefore, our greatest and most important job in life, and the principal factor which more than anything else contributes to success, is our relationships with others or the ability and degree to which we get along with other people.

This getting along with people, be it our husbands, wives, members of our family, business associates, neighbors, people we buy from or the people we sell to is nothing more than following the Golden Rule, of doing unto others as we expect them to do unto us. When this factor of getting along with people becomes a group action, or the action of those who make up the personnel of a company, it is then referred to as public relations or the way the company gets along with the customers and the public. The laws underlying human relations and public relations are the same. Mostly this relationship deals with the instinctive need of all people to be recognized, the need to feel they are important and the need to know that they belong.

Good relations with the public are the result not only of the way we think or the way we feel, but the way we treat other people.

Relationship is a human process. When we say we like a company, what we mean is we like the people who work for the company, and our attitude toward the company is nothing more than the reflection of the people working for that company.

If we study the reason for success, we find that a person who is successful is generally well liked. Why is he liked? Generally, we find that the reason he is liked and successful is because he has mastered the art of getting along with others, and people like him because he treats them the way they want to be treated.

Some of the ways in which we can treat a person the way he wants to be treated is by:

1. *Calling him by name.* Calling a person by name makes him important. The very fact that we call a customer by name indicates to the customer that he is part of the bank and belongs to the bank.

2. *Greeting him with a smile.* Probably the most effective creator of good will at our disposal is a smile. Most people like to do business with a friendly person and a smile is an evidence of friendliness and by action says, "I like you." Unfortunately, in too many banks, too many people greet newcomers and people who come up to their window or the desk, with the attitude that they are interrupting their work.

People who take this attitude should remember, if there were not customers to interrupt them, they would not have a job.

3. *Saying "Thank you."* These two little words express, as no other words can, gratitude and appreciation for what a person has done.

In a bank relationship, a bank employee says "Thank you" to indicate to the customer that he appreciates the business he has been privileged to transact. The customer says "Thank you" to the bank employee to indicate that he appreciates the service he has received.

4. *Being sympathetic and understanding.* Many of the little irritations in life are caused because we do not understand either the cause or the motives behind them.

When we understand a person's attitude and are sympathetic with his viewpoint, even though we do not agree, we show him respect and a willingness to understand his point of view.

5. *Being a good listener.* Generally when a customer comes in the bank, whether to sit at our desk, or stand in front of our window to make a deposit, he feels important. In gratifying this feeling of importance he likes to talk—everyone does—and nothing so inflates a person's ego and makes him feel important as to have someone listen to what he has to say.

If a person comes into the bank grouchy, irritable, and complaining, the more he talks, or rather the more you let him talk, the less angry he becomes. If he talks long enough and you listen, he'll run out of complaints. Then, with a few kind words, you can pave the way to rebuild the friendship.

6. *Never discuss matters to the point where an argument occurs.* Nearly every transaction in a bank is governed by law and if we are unable to satisfactorily express an opinion, it is better to refer the matter to someone in higher authority who can tactfully disagree with the opinion of the customer and assure him of the correctness of the bank's position.

7. *Being humble.* Never act superior to people or high-hat them. In a bank no customer is so unimportant that he can be neglected, or a service too small to render. Many of our best customers are not versed or familiar with banking practices, and when they make inquiry of us, even though we believe the matter unimportant, we should, as tactfully as possible, answer their inquiry with the greatest consideration, kindness and understanding, and make it appear that the question they ask is a normal and common one.

Public relations, therefore, is the attitude we show, the courtesy we extend, the ways and means in which we provide friendliness in selling or providing services.

While these functions as performed in every bank to a greater or lesser degree by every officer and employee, certain phases in large banks require the full time responsibility of an officer, generally holding a senior position, to whom is delegated full responsibility for the relationship with others which we term Public Relations and New Business.

Public Relations and New Business are synonymous. We cannot have one without the other. In order to efficiently carry out the public relation functions of a bank, the activities of well organized departments are all in connection with:

1. New Business.
2. Conservation of present business.
3. Customer contact.
4. Activities in connection with publicity.
5. Advertising the bank and its services.

NEW BUSINESS

New business activities are those in connection with:

A. The acquiring of new business from those who heretofore have had no relationship with the bank.

B. Interesting customers of the bank or those who already have established a relationship with the bank in one or more departments, to use services provided by other departments of the bank.

While both activities are in connection with acquiring new business, the sources of new business and the techniques of acquiring such business are separate and distinct.

The acquiring of new business is an activity which should be engaged in by everyone connected with the bank — stockholders, directors, officers, employees even customers.

The best sources of new business are our friends or those we associate with socially or through church, lodge, club, or neighborhood activities. Such people are good prospects for new business because we are known to them and can make inquiry as to where they transact their banking business on a personal basis. Once we know where they bank it is a simple matter to mention the many services which our bank has available and point out how well our bank is equipped to provide for their particular requirements.

New families moving to town are another source of new business for the bank and potential friends of the bank. Contacting such families, however, should be the responsibility of the officers of the bank, or someone who has the authority to make decisions in connection with loans or credit applications.

In order to be in the position to make contacts with families moving into the community, it is helpful if the officers of the bank cultivate the friendship of those engaged in the real estate business. They can supply the banker with the name, present address, number of members of the family and other information about the new family which is renting a house or has just bought a home in the community.

Fortified with these facts, the alert banker can then either write or telephone the person who expects to make his home in town and not only offer the regular services of the bank but the special services such as those in connection with transferring accounts and securities, introducing him to the local merchants, helping him to establish his credit (if warranted) and acquainting him with the medical, dental, church, school and recreational facilities of the community. In other words, making him feel welcome.

Newly organized businesses which intend to establish their plant or office in the community and established businesses from other sections of the country which are relocating in the area served by the bank are also excellent sources of new business. Here, too, close association with the Chamber of Commerce and real estate agents is important. Once it becomes known that a new company is going to locate in the area served by the bank, the officers of the bank, who undoubtedly are acquainted with the bank in the town where the company is presently located, can contact them about the company, arrange for an introduction to the principals and enlist the assistance of the company's present bank in recommending their bank when the company moves.

Another source of new business and a very profitable one is in connection with industrial development where the banker serves on the Planning Board or works closely with the Chamber of Commerce to bring new industries to the town. Through such contacts as may be developed, the banker is in an excellent position not only to make banking facilities available to the company but to the officers, employees and their families who will be relocating with the company and are seeking places to live. It is well to remember that many opportunities for new business can be obtained by a bank through its interest in assisting others to become established in their community.

In contacting people for the purpose of soliciting business

it is well to remember that people, in general, do not think of a business organization or a bank in abstract terms but in terms of those they know who are employed by such organizations. Consequently, in the eyes and opinion of the person whose business is being solicited, the person who makes the initial contact in behalf of the bank is THE BANK.

Therefore, it follows that if the person soliciting business is courteous, considerate and makes the prospect feel important, the latter will have a high regard for the individual representing the bank and consequently an initial high regard towards the bank. Whether or not this opinion he forms of the bank is maintained, depends upon the way the prospect is treated by everyone in the bank from the janitor up to the Chairman of the Board after he becomes a customer.

In soliciting new business it is important to know what we are doing in order to successfuly acquire new business and avoid making mistakes, or duplicating effort. Very often an officer, director or employee knows of a new person or family moving to town; a new business being located; a new store being rented; and, because of his interest and initiative, will without investigation contact the person for his account or other business. In many cases such a prospect might already have been approached by another officer or director who discussed with him certain terms of a relationship.

CENTRAL FILE OF INFORMATION

Many banks, in order to have information immediately available on their customers maintain what is known as a Central File of Information. This file with a card for each customer, similar to Exhibit 66, set up in alphabetical order, shows the name, address and business connection of the customer. It shows also the various departments with which the customer maintains a relationship, the date the relationship was established with the respective department, the date the respective relationship was terminated, and a list of the officers of the bank to whom the customer is known. It is obvious that reference to such a card will disclose immediately the extent of the relationship of the customer with the bank.

So that the Central File of Information may be used effectively

Exhibit 66

CENTRAL FILE CARD (Front)

1	2	3	4	5	6	7	8

BUSINESS

BUSINESS ADDRESS

TEL. TEL. No.

ASSIGNED TO INTRODUCED BY OR KNOWN TO

OFFICERS OR PARTNERS	AFFILIATED ACCOUNTS	BANK RELATIONSHIP			
			RELATIONSHIP	DATE OPENED	DATE CLOSED
		1	STOCK HOLDER		
		2	CHECKING		
		3	SAVINGS		
		4	LOAN-DISCOUNT		
		5			
		6			
		7	MTGE. LOAN		
		8	SAFE DEPOSIT		

SPECIAL INSTRUCTIONS

BALANCE RECORD

MIN. - MAX. BALANCES MAX. LOANS (IN THOUSANDS AND HUNDREDS)

YEAR																								
MONTH	MIN.	MAX.	S.C.	LOAN	MIN.	MAX.	S.C.	LOAN	MIN.	MAX.	S.C.	LOAN	MIN.	MAX.	S.C.	LOAN	MIN.	MAX.	S.C.	LOAN	MIN.	MAX.	S.C.	LOAN
JAN.																								
FEB.																								
MAR.																								
APR.																								
MAY																								
JUNE																								
JULY																								
AUG.																								
SEPT.																								
OCT.																								
NOV.																								
DEC.																								
AVE.																								

CHECKS RETURNED | OVERDRAFTS

RECORD OF CALLS OR CONTACTS

(SEE REVERSE SIDE FOR PERTINENT INFORMATION)

NO.	DATE	BY	NO.	DATE	BY	NO.	DATE	BY
1			6			11		
2			7			12		
3			8			13		
4			9			14		
5			10			15		

Exhibit 66

CENTRAL FILE CARD (Reverse Side)

1	2	3	4	5
6	7	8	9	10
11	12	13	14	15

FORM 111 - 6M—7-56—R.P.P.

in new business activities, each director, officer or employee, whenever they come across an individual or company they believe would be a prospect for new business, should first check the name with the Central File. Should they find the name of the prospect already in the file or already having been suggested by another officer, they should contact the officer telling him of their interest and exchange information, some of which might be of help in interesting the prospect to do business with the bank.

If, however, the name does not appear in the file, then the director, officer or employee should immediately prepare a prospect form similar to Exhibit 67, which should show all information in connection with the prospect from which a Central File card marked "Prospect" will be prepared.

In connection with public relations and new business activities, it is also helpful in obtaining new business, to have the officer in charge of public relations and new business undertake a survey of the area served by the bank so as to develop and maintain a

Exhibit 67

PROSPECT FORM

PROSPECT REPORT

NAME ______________________________ DATE ______________

ADDRESS ______________________________ BY ______________

IF A BUSINESS ACCOUNT, LIST PRINCIPAL OFFICER AND NAME OF PERSON CONTACTED ON REVERSE SIDE, TOGETHER WITH BRIEF DESCRIPTION OF BUSINESS ACTIVITY.

REASON FOR SOLICITATION-OR SOURCE OF LEAD ______________

____

PROSPECT FOR		RESULTS OF CALL
REGULAR CHECKING ACCOUNT	___	______________
SPECIAL CHECKING ACCOUNT	___	______________
PAYROLL ACCOUNT	___	______________
SAFE DEPOSIT BOX	___	______________
TRUST SERVICE	___	______________
______________	___	______________
SPECIAL SERVICE		______________
______________	___	TO BE REFERRED FOR FOLLOW UP
		______________

current list of prospects who should be cultivated and solicited to become customers of the bank.

After such names have been listed and checked against the Central File, cards should be made up for each account which does not have a card already in the file, after which they should be reviewed by the directors and officers to determine if the prospect is known to any of the directors and officers, and for proper assignment to directors and officers for cultivation.

In order that the bank may be kept currently informed on the status of the account, the director or officer to whom the name is assigned for cultivation should periodically report to the officer in charge of public relations and new business on the progress being made in making the prospect a customer, which information should be indexed on the Central File Prospect Card.

Central File cards are currently maintained by having each department or division which provides services which the bank wishes to record, report daily to the section which maintains the Central File all new and closed relationships, which information is indexed on the card in the proper space. The only exception to this is in connection with the relationship of a customer with the Consumer Credit or Installment Loan Department where experience indicates once a customer, frequently a customer. It becomes practical, therefore, to save time and also because it is necessary to contact each department with whom the customer maintains a relationship in order to obtain the current status of of the account, merely to indicate the opening date of a relationship with the Consumer Credit or Installment Loan Department.

Another and most practical use of a central file card is in connection with recording leads or indications of additional business from present customers. In using the cards for this purpose, the officer to whom the account is assigned for handling or who knows the customer, reviews the relationship after which he advises the Central File section of the services provided by other departments which, in his opinion, the customer could use.

Upon receiving this information the officer in charge of the Central File affixes tabs of different colors on the top of the card indicating the particular service for which the customer might be a prospect for direct mail contact. In addition memos are made on the officers' assignment card to the effect that when contacting the customer, the contacting officer should discuss the matter o a trust relationship or insurance premium financing, or whatever service the person is a prospect for.

CONSERVATION OF PRESENT BUSINESS

While obtaining new business is most important if the bank i to grow, have funds to invest, and have customers to serve, one o the most important aspects of public relations is to maintain friendl relationships with the important customers of the bank, especiall those who maintain substantial accounts.

This can be accomplished either through visits when th customer comes into the bank to make a loan or transact othe business, a friendly greeting when an officer sees an importan customer on the floor making a deposit, or by indicating the interes of the bank in the customer by calling on him periodically at hi place of business.

While the Central File card provides information as to th various relationships a customer maintains with the bank, such a being a stockholder; maintaining a checking account; being renter of a safe deposit box; it generally does not, unless specia provision is made, indicate the scope or trend of the balance whic the customer maintains in his checking account.

In order to provide this information for the use and guidanc of the officers, many banks maintain what is known as an Averag Balance Record. This record, similar to that shown in Exhibit 6 records the monthly deposit balance (also at times the number o checks drawn and service charge) and loan balance of all customer of the bank who maintain a checking account.

The recording of deposit balance information generally is mad under one of three forms (a) the average balance basis which i obtained by adding the balance as shown on the ledger at the clos of business each day and dividing by 30 or 31 to obtain the dail average balance; (b) the minimum balance basis which is th lowest balance maintained by the customer during the mont and (c) the "high" and "low" balance basis which is the recordin of the high balance of the month as well as the low balance. I recording loan balances it is most generally the practice to sho the "high" and the "low" borrowings for the month.

In addition, in order to currently determine the balance trend

Exhibit 68

AVERAGE BALANCE RECORD (Front)

NAME

BUSINESS

OPENED

ASSIGNED TO

SOURCE

SPECIAL INSTRUCTIONS:

ENDORSERS OR GUARANTORS (PENCIL)

OFFICERS OR PARTNERS:

AFFILIATED COMMERCIAL ACCOUNTS (CALL CENTRAL FILE FOR OTHER CONNECTIONS):

LINES OF CREDIT (IN THOUSANDS OF DOLLARS)

DATE
BASIS
AMOUNT

FINANCIAL STATEMENTS (IN THOUSANDS OF DOLLARS)

DATE
CASH & RECEIVABLES
CURRENT ASSETS
CURRENT LIABILITIES
WORKING CAPITAL
TOTAL LIABILITIES
NET WORTH
SALES
PROFITS
CHECKS RETURNED

0-1f

Exhibit 68

AVERAGE BALANCE RECORD (Reverse Side)

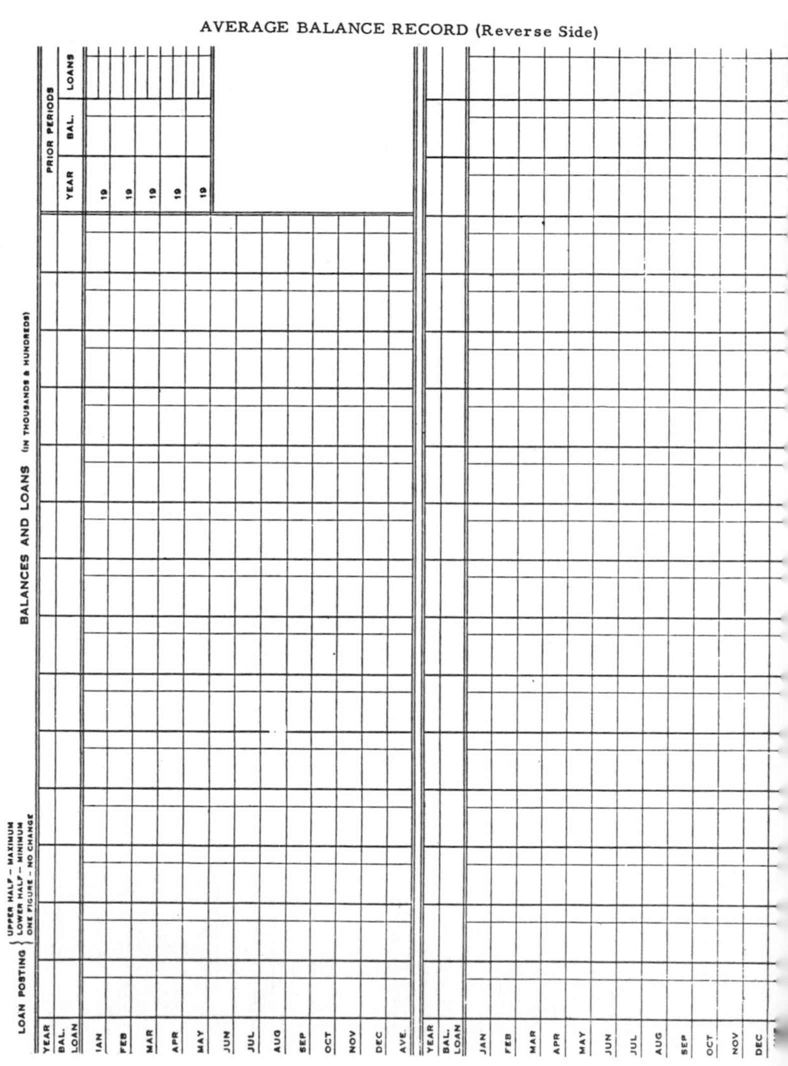

BALANCES AND LOANS (IN THOUSANDS & HUNDREDS)

LOAN POSTING { UPPER HALF – MAXIMUM
LOWER HALF – MINIMUM
ONE FIGURE – NO CHANGE

PRIOR PERIODS
YEAR | BAL. | LOANS
19
19
19
19
19

YEAR
BAL. LOAN
JAN FEB MAR APR MAY JUN JUL AUG SEP OCT NOV DEC AVE.

YEAR
BAL. LOAN
JAN FEB MAR APR MAY JUN JUL AUG SEP OCT NOV DEC

Exhibit 69

WEEKLY BALANCE RECORD

REPORT OF BALANCES $5,000.00 AND OVER	Assigned to
Account of NOTE: Address shown hereon is not kept current.	

1959													
	Jan. 6	Jan. 13	Jan. 20	Jan. 27	Feb. 3	Feb. 10	Feb. 17	Feb. 24	Mar. 3	Mar. 10	Mar. 17	Mar. 24	Mar. 31
	Apr. 7	Apr. 14	Apr. 21	Apr. 28	May 5	May 12	May 19	May 26	June 2	June 9	June 16	June 23	June 30
	July 7	July 14	July 21	July 28	Aug. 4	Aug. 11	Aug. 18	Aug. 25	Sept. 1	Sept. 8	Sept. 15	Sept. 22	Sept. 29
	Oct. 6	Oct. 13	Oct. 20	Oct. 27	Nov. 3	Nov. 10	Nov. 17	Nov. 24	Dec. 1	Dec. 8	Dec. 15	Dec. 22	Dec. 29

1960													
	Jan. 5	Jan. 12	Jan. 19	Jan. 26	Feb. 2	Feb. 9	Feb. 16	Feb. 23	Mar. 1	Mar. 8	Mar. 15	Mar. 22	Mar. 29
	Apr. 5	Apr. 12	Apr. 19	Apr. 26	May 3	May 10	May 17	May 24	May 31	June 7	June 14	June 21	June 28
	July 5	July 12	July 19	July 26	Aug. 2	Aug. 9	Aug. 16	Aug. 23	Aug. 30	Sept. 6	Sept. 13	Sept. 20	Sept. 27
	Oct. 4	Oct. 11	Oct. 18	Oct. 25	Nov. 1	Nov. 8	Nov. 15	Nov. 22	Nov. 29	Dec. 6	Dec. 13	Dec. 20	Dec. 27

Use symbols only to indicate: Balances below $1,000__"__" Overdraft__"O.D." Account closed__"C"

Report balances in even thousands. PLEASE POST CAREFULLY

of the most important customers, many progressive banks, in addi tion, maintain what is known as a Weekly Balance Record. Thi is a loose leaf ledger which contains a sheet, similar to Exhibit 69 for each account which maintains a balance in excess of a certai amount.

WEEKLY BALANCE RECORD

The record is maintained by having the bookkeepers, on th same day each week (after the close of business) index the amour of the balance on the sheet. If an account at the time of postin has a balance for the first time in excess of the certain amoun a sheet is prepared, the balance posted, and the sheet placed in th binder. All posting is by decimals, that is, if the ledger balanc is $6,221.43, the bookkeeper, in indexing the amount in the Weekl Balance Record, would post the amount as 6.2.

After the sheets have been posted, the binder is then forwarde either to the officer in charge of Public Relations Department one of his assistants or to some other designated person, to revie the accounts and advise the officer to whom the account is assigne of any substantial changes which have taken place. Obviously th record is of little value until it has been established for some peric of time so as to indicate the normal trend. Once this has bee established, however, any increases or decreases in the balan should be called to the attention of the officer to whom the accou is assigned so that, in case he does not know the reason for th change, he may contact the depositor.

It goes without saying that a marked decline in the balan indicates the customer is either doing business elsewhere or is a low cash position. Perhaps his accounts receivable are slow which case he might possibly be over extending himself, or might be stock-piling inventory. In either of these cases, howeve an opportunity exists for the alert banker to offer the facilities the bank to help the depositor or the customer conduct his busine affairs.

It is likewise important to note balances when they increa This can be the result of increased sales, which means better bu ness, or it can mean a liquidation of inventory. In any event, increase in balance provides the officer to whom the account assigned with a splendid opportunity to contact the customer a xpress appreciation for being favored with the increased balance.

It is a very simple matter to maintain these records as accounts enerally maintain balances within a fixed range. Through the veekly review, of course, accounts whose balances have reached he minimum balance for recording purposes will be added. Likewise certain accounts whose balances are below the fixed minimum vill not be posted. In order to keep the ledgers current, it is dvisable to have someone in authority periodically go through he ledgers and remove from the balance records those accounts which are consistently below the established figure.

DAILY CHANGES IN BALANCES

One of the most important phases in connection with the onservation of business is for officers to have knowledge of the aily changes which substantially effect a depositor's account or ossibly the relationship of the depositor with the bank. We refer ere to two things, substantial deposits and substantial withdrawals. n the case of substantial deposits the bookkeepers should immediately report to the head bookkeeper any substantial deposits nd if, in the opinion of the head bookkeeper, this represents an nusual transaction—say a customer who normally makes deposits etween $5,000 and $10,000 and suddenly makes a deposit of 30,000—it should be reported to the officer who handles the account, r to whom the account is assigned, in order that the officer can ndertake whatever investigation is necessary to determine the ource of funds and the reason for the increase.

Should investigation disclose that the funds will probably emain with the bank for some time, the officer in charge of investments should be notified so as to take proper steps to invest such unds for the period of time the funds will remain, in order that he bank may receive the income.

The most important change to notice in an account is in connection with checks of large amounts drawn by a customer against is balance. The reason the investigation of such checks is important is that it could indicate an adverse change in the relationship etween the customer and the bank, for example:

A. A check drawn by our customer payable to himself and eposited with another bank might disclose he is maintaining or has opened an account with another bank, certainly a matter whic should be investigated.

B. A check drawn by our customer and payable to anothe business concern could indicate a financial interest; or if the part is not a customer of our bank, that our customer does sufficien business with such a firm as to be able to influence them to main tain an account with our bank.

C. A check drawn by our customer payable to another ban could indicate our customer is borrowing from another bank an the check in question is either in payment of the loan or a paymen on account, certainly a situation which should be investigated b an alert bank officer.

D. A check drawn by our customer payable to another ban could also be in payment of collection items which, if properl handled, could result in having the item sent to our bank for co lection so we could receive the collection fee.

In connection with business conservation it is most importan that accounts be assigned to officers who are charged with th responsibility of maintaining the contact and relationship with th customer. This presents no problem in banks where new accour sheets are used or records are maintained which show the name of the officers of the bank who are acquainted with the custome

ASSIGNMENT OF ACCOUNTS

If present account records do not already show the names the officers who know the customer, it is recommended that all the commercial accounts, especially those over a certain amoun be listed and circularized among the officers so they may indica their knowledge of the account. This information should then b indexed on a signature card, a central file card, an analysis car or a credit file card for reference purposes.

Should an important account not be well known to any one the officers, then such an account is arbitrarily assigned to an offic who then has the responsibility of becoming acquainted with th depositor and maintaining the relationship.

It is also very important, when a depositor is only known to or officer, that arrangements be made to have him become acquainte with other officers so that in the event a change takes place in th bank, the relationship may be cordially maintained.

CUSTOMER CONTACT

Another important phase of public relations is in connection ·ith customer contact which covers the attitudes, appearances and onduct of all personnel in their communicating activities with the ublic and customers *within* the bank.

As mentioned previously, every officer and employee of the ank within the bank or outside the bank is THE BANK.

Outside the bank our conduct, as we mentioned in the study f the employee's handbook, reflects the bank. Here, however, e refer to the officer and employee while they are in the bank.

First of all we should remember that bank personnel occupy very confidential and responsible position.

It is confidential because information in connection with the ecords of a bank and the transactions of customers could effect their ves, welfare and the financial well being if disclosed to others.

It is responsible because in dealing with the bank, customers xpect that all transactions will be accurately handled in a cometent manner.

This being the case, the art of courtesy and ability to render tisfactory service are two of the most important assets a person ould have who wishes to be successful in banking.

Banking, in addition to being a business which sells money, lso through its officers and employees sells service. As such you, a bank officer or employee, should always remember the most portant part of any bank is its customers and whenever you rform work or render a service for a customer, meet or wait a customer face to face, write a letter to a customer or prospect, talk to a customer or prospect on the telephone–in his eyes– OU – ARE – THE – BANK.

WHEN YOU PERFORM WORK OR RENDER A SERVICE OR A CUSTOMER–YOU ARE THE BANK–because–customers pect accuracy and neatness in records. By being accurate and at you show him you are interested in serving him. By being ompt you show him you are interested in rendering the type of rvice which says "Thanks! Come back again."

WHEN YOU MEET OR WAIT ON A CUSTOMER FACE O FACE–YOU ARE THE BANK–because–when you wait on a customer face to face, the customer is not thinking of the ban as a building made out of marble, brick, stone and steel—or as machine—but what you, as an individual, are doing to provid courteous service for him. This being the case, when a custome comes up to your window or desk:

A. Don't keep him standing or waiting for an interview. what you are doing must be finished before you can take care him, at least stop long enough to greet him and apologize for keepin him waiting. If you are sitting at a desk, by all means invite hi to be seated and proceed as quickly as possible to take care of hir

B. Always greet your customer pleasantly and always by nam if you know it. If you are serving customers at your desk, it is th courteous mark of a gentleman to arise and greet him. Never giv the impression that he is interrupting your work. While a perso is sitting at your desk, remember it is your present job to take ca of him.

C. Courteously listen to what he wishes to talk to you abo before interrupting him. Should there be a number of facts yo might later wish to refer to, it is always permissible to pick up pencil and jot down figures on a piece of paper and explain to hi the reason you are doing it is to have points for reference purpos after he has completed telling his story. If, after listening to wh he has to say, you find it necessary to refer him to someone els either have the courtesy to accompany him to the other officer direct him to the other officer. If, however, you are a teller in cage and it is impossible for you to leave, then call the guard or flo man and have him take the customer to the proper official for t answer.

D. Remember it is a mark of courtesy to apologize and endeav to make amends if a customer has been poorly treated and handl in a discourteous manner by someone else, or handled in such manner as to reflect on the service or safety of the bank or reputation. Banks should never, however, apologize or ma excuses for the service charge, fee or interest rate it is policy charge a customer for services rendered or for money borrowe

E. Cautiously observe your attitude in your relationship wi others. Are you a person who is easily upset and, if so, are y given to carrying over a grudge? Be careful that you do not ca over, into a current interview or visit, the effects or ill hum ngendered during a previous conversation or visit. If a previous onversation has left you somewhat disturbed and unnerved, find n excuse to get away for a few minutes lest you offend the innocent ustomer presently sitting at your desk.

Whenever you face a customer you have a wonderful opporınity to build better friendships for the bank through cordial and ncere attitudes, and build business for the bank because the best rospects for new business are well served present customers.

In order to take advantage of opportunities to build better iendships for the bank when you wait on a customer face to face:

1. Be well groomed.
2. Be pleasant. It costs nothing.
3. Be interested. This is a matter of attitude toward work.
4. Be sincere. Honest sincerity is just about the best good ill builder there is.
5. Be patient. What seems simple to you due to daily contact, ay be complex to others.
6. Be efficient. Most people liked to be served swiftly and ccurately.
7. Be well informed about the bank and its services.

WHENEVER YOU SEND A LETTER TO A CUSTOMER R PROSPECT INQUIRING INTO SOME PHASE OF BANKING ROCEDURE OR SERVICE—YOU ARE THE BANK—because— ery letter which goes out from the bank is an intimate form of ntact with a customer or a prospect and is a very important phase a bank's program of creating good will.

Whether you dictate the letter, whether you type it, or whether is your job to mail it, the customer is going to judge the bank in rms of the helpfulness, service, neatness and accuracy of the tter. In the case of a letter, the dictator, the secretary who anscribes the letter and the clerk who mails the letter IS THE ANK.

Form letters should be avoided wherever possible and, if cessary, they should be individually typed with the name and dress spelled out correctly. You can be sure that your letters ill build good will for the bank if you:

A. Use correct grammatical English.

Avoid stock expressions such as "yours of the 16th received," e beg to advise," etc.

The art of good letter writing is to write as you speak. I your signature is illegible, it should appear somewhere on th letterhead in print or be typed in.

It is often said the way to create good will through a letter i to enhance the person's sense of importance. This can be accomp lished by using the word Y-O-U wherever practical and possibl

B. Avoid compliments and false flattery. Be liberal wit praise and compliments but here, as in other matters, use good tast and don't overdo it.

C. If the matter is such that it cannot be handled tactfully c diplomatically by letter or telephone, a personal visit is in orde

D. In writing letters avoid giving the opinion that a decisio has already been reached.

E. If it is necessary to tell a customer the bank must tak action which you are certain the customer will not like, state th facts simply and logically.

F. It is good business technique, in replying to a letter a cu tomer has written in anger or complaint about some act of the ban to restate in simple terms the customer's complaint. This indicat to the customer that you thoroughly understand his position ar reason for writing, which then can be followed up by a statement the bank's position. This is especially helpful if the bank has be in error and made a mistake. If it is necessary to apologize, l simple and avoid excuses or alibis.

In order to build good will for the bank when you wri letters, be:

1. *Accurate.* The name should be spelled exactly right ar correctly addressed.

2. *Prompt.* Letters should be answered the same day if all possible.

3. *Direct.* People are busy. Come to the point. Expre thoughts clearly.

4. *Friendly.* It requires practice to acquire just the rig balance between dignity and informality. The result, however, a "friendly tone" that characterizes an effective bank letter.

WHEN YOU TALK TO A CUSTOMER OR PROSPECT C THE TELEPHONE—YOU ARE THE BANK—because—it is hum nature to build a picture of the person we are talking to, his si his age, his appearance, by the sound of his voice. This image c e favorable and complimentary, both to you and to the bank if ou take the necessary steps to take advantage of these opportunities o build good will and create a favorable impression.

While the telephone is one of the most important instruments of ommunication for maintaining relationships with customers, prosects and the public, unfortunately calls are often marred by disourtesy both by the caller and the recipient of the call.

In order to have what is known as a good telephone technique, ou should:

A. Never give the impression that the telephone call is an nterruption of your work, rather a welcome opportunity to be of ervice.

B. Answer the telephone promptly when it rings. After quietly emoving the receiver you should state the name of the department nd your name. When answering any phone other than your own, ou should first state the name of the person whose phone you are nswering and then take the message or transfer the call to the roper party. Under no circumstances, when an inquiry is made egarding a person who is not presently at the desk, should you eply "I don't know," "he didn't tell me," or similar answers. In uch cases, you should say, "I am sorry he is not at his desk right ow," or "he has stepped away from his desk," and find out who calling and inquire if the person for whom the call was intended an return the call.

In order to avoid confusion when making inter office calls, if ne extension is not answered by the third ring, it is evident that he person is busy or away from his desk. You should hang up and lace the call at a later time.

C. Always arrange to be on the phone when the person you re calling comes on. It is your business to wait for him since ou instigated the call, it is not up to him to wait for you. This is ne of the greatest faults committed by executives who have ecretaries or others place their calls and invariably antagonizes ne person who is called.

D. Cultivate a friendly tone of voice when saying good-by hen the purpose for which the call was made has been accompshed. Then hang up the receiver softly so as to not bang the eceiver in the other person's ear.

E. Always make certain, when you leave your desk, that some one will answer your phone should it ring while you are away.

It is well to remember the opportunities to make the telephon a vehicle for creating good will are increased by:

1. Cultivating a friendly voice. A natural, friendly manne produces a good reaction. An irritated or cross tone produce irritation in others.

2. Cultivating a clear speaking voice. People can not under stand unless they hear clearly. It is best to talk slowly and directl into the mouthpiece.

3. Giving the caller prompt, accurate and complete answer to his questions. If you don't know the answer, connect him wit someone who has the information.

4. Giving extra service such as getting additional data an calling back, mailing literature and helping in other ways.

5. Being sincere. The telephone can hide a face but not person's true attitude.

PUBLICITY

Another important phase of public relations is in connectio with the publicity attending the activities of directors, officers an employees, such as social activities, business promotions, awardin of civic and fraternal honors, public recognition for some outstandin achievement, appointments to boards of charitable, education and religious institutions, in other words any happening in whic the director, officer, employee is involved and has news value.

Good public relations in connection with activities means th all the publicity and news is so presented in the newspaper th it reflects favorably toward the bank. For example, let us take th situation where Mr. J. J. Scott, Vice President of the First Nation Bank is going to Boston to attend a class reunion.

The news item probably would be reported in the local pap thus:

> Mr. J. J. Scott of 420 Center Street left yesterday for Boston where he will attend the 25th reunion of the Class of 1935 at Union College.

If however, the bank was publicity conscious and proper reported the news to the local newspaper, the item could appe thus:

> Mr. Joseph J. (Whitey) Scott, Vice President in charge of Loans of the First National Bank of Meridian, left on Tuesday with his wife, Mary, for Boston where he will attend the 25th reunion of the class of 1935 at Union College. Old time residents of Meridian will remember Whitey as the All-State Quarterback in 1930 when he played for Central High School and at Union when he won letters in his sophomore, junior and senior year in football, basketball, baseball, and was mentioned on several All-American Football teams.

When, as it unfortunately happens, the activities or doings of ome director, officer or employee is such that publicity reflects gainst the bank, then it is good public relations to play down the ame of the bank or the connection of the director, officer or nployee with the bank.

In order to obtain favorable publicity, banks should cultivate litors and publishers of local newspapers. Cultivation is not eant as doing anything which might be construed as begging voritism. It is the job of a newspaper to print news. It is the b of the editor of a newspaper to select and present the news such a manner that people see and read the advertising which, ter all, produces the income which supports the newspaper.

The best way to be assured of the fairness of a newspaper is be fair with them—to confide in them and present them with the cts. Any company or bank which plays fair with a newspaper can e assured that information told in confidence will remain in confi-ence. They can always be assured of a fair public trial.

In connection with activities, it should also be the function of e public relations department to maintain liaison between em-loyees and administrative personnel in connection with suggestions ade through a Suggestion Box, or if this is the function of the ersonnel or Operation Department, to see that the utmost in ourtesy is extended the employees who make recommendations nd suggestions for improving service, for making operations more ficient, for providing services which will help the growth and evelopment of the bank. It is also most important that suitable cognition be given to such employees for their recommendations d suggestions. Remember, we all like to be important, we all like be recognized, we all like to be made to feel we belong.

ADVERTISING THE BANK AND ITS SERVICES

The final, but undoubtedly one of the most important phase of public relations activities is in connection with advertising th bank and its services.

Advertising, according to its universal purpose and in the fina analysis, is nothing more than the vehicle through which we:

1. Tell people about the product we have to sell, or of th services we can provide.

2. Develop their interest in owning the product we have t sell or in using our services.

3. Have them exchange their wealth in order to own th product we have to sell, or use the service we can provide.

4. Keep customers satisfied with the product or service the have purchased.

5. Have them continue to purchase our product or use ou service.

In order to be productive, advertising should be based on tw kinds of facts—facts about the product or service, and facts abo the people who do, or should, buy our product or use our servic

These facts are used in developing our advertising, not onl to find new users of our product or service, but to encourage peop to make more frequent use of our product or service.

In addition, good advertising should not only provide th answer to the question "Who buys our product or service?" BU to other questions "Why do they buy our product or service?" an "Who should buy our product or service?"

It is also important to know why people who do not purcha our product or use our service, do not use them. Proper analys of the answers to these questions often results in the developme of new products or services, or changes in present services whic produce additional income for the bank and widen the scope service activities available for its customers and the public.

In connection with developing informative answers to th questions "Who purchases our product or service?" and "Why d they purchase our product or service?", the following inquirie made in connection with each service the bank has to offer, shou provide the basis for sound productive advertising text.

A. WHO uses the product or service?

B. WHEN is the product or service used?
C. WHERE is the product or service used?
D. HOW do people purchase the product or service?
E. WHY do people use the product or service?
F. DO others produce the product or provide the service?

In order to obtain the answer to the first question, "Who uses he product or service?" the logical questions to ask would be: "Is he service used by men?—by women?—by children?—by all three?" urther, one question begets another such as "Should the person vho uses this service be young or old?—should the service be used y a person with a certain income?—is the service used by people vho live on a farm?—in the city?—is it a service which can be used y an individual, or a person engaged in business?"

To illustrate the effect the answers to these questions have on dvertising a service, let us take a checking account. Obviously, rom what we have learned about checking accounts, everyone vho needs to keep a record of his financial transactions, the onvenience of disbursing funds in payment of bills and obligations y check, or a medium for the collection of checks and funds lue—has need for a checking account.

As to the answer to the second question "When is the service ised?", it is obviously not a service of a seasonal nature, therefore he answer is "Whenever it is necessary to deposit funds, collect a heck or pay a bill by check."

In connection with the third question "Where is the service ised?", the correct answer is "Wherever we wish to transact finan- ial affairs—at home—at the office.

The answer to the question "How do people purchase the ervice?" brings up a very interesting point, partially answered by eferring to the answers to the first question, as to who uses the ervice. It could be a corporation using special checks, or an in- lividual where the charge for a service rendered is not only based n the balance maintained, number of checks issued, but other ervices rendered.

The answer to the fifth question "Why do people use the serv- ce?", in this case seems obvious. They use the service (checking ccount) to have a convenient medium through which to handle heir financial transactions.

We all know the answer to the last question "Do others provide the same service?"—"Every bank", which brings us back to the most important reason for people doing business with a particular bank—the type of friendly and courteous service.

ADVERTISING MEDIUMS

Banks advertise their services through eight principal mediums:

1. Direct mail
2. Statement insertion pieces
3. Billboards
4. Newspapers
5. Hand outs
6. Service pieces
7. Radio
8. Television

Direct mail advertising refers to letters individually addressec to a prospect, outlining the particular services available, and signec by the person soliciting the account. Direct mail is used in solicit ing all types of business and services, but particularly with individ uals in connection with financing automobiles, homes, trust account and trust services. It is used with corporations in connection wit financing, or warehousing.

Statement insertion pieces are advertising mediums includec with cancelled checks being returned to individuals and consist o pluggers, or letters in connection with personal loans, financing o automobiles and household appliances, use of travellers' checks safe deposit boxes, Christmas club accounts and other services of personal nature.

Billboard advertising generally carries text which is institu tional in nature, commonly on the type of bank; that is—the oldest - the strongest—the most friendly—or the bank which gives the greate service. Sometimes billboards are used as direct mediums, that is to advertise a particular service such as a checking account, variou types of loans, or use of a checking account, advantages of a saving account, rates of interest and similar services.

Newspaper advertising is of two classes, institutional and thos in connection with services.

Institutional advertising is that which is commonly placed i newspapers on the occasion of national holidays, or in connectio with seasonal greetings, and are merely a friendly manner in which to extend the wishes of the bank to the public on the occasion.

Newspaper advertising in connection with services, on the other hand, are generally directed to the attention of those to whom the service should appeal and cover such matters as the advantages of maintaining a checking account, the advantages of a safety deposit box, the advantages of a savings account, the value of trust services, the assistance the bank renders to those buying an automobile, remodeling their homes or buying a home. The secret, however, in taking full advantage of newspaper advertising, is to coordinate the newspaper advertising with hand outs and the simultaneous personal solicitation of directors, officers and employees of those who might be interested in the particular service being advertised.

Hand Outs are similar to statement insertion pieces except that they have greater universal use within a bank and are usually given to the customers of one department urging or encouraging them to use the facilities of another department. For example:

A. Hand outs in connection with use of a safe deposit box would be handed out at the commercial and savings paying and receiving teller's windows and the collateral window.

B. Hand outs in connection with trust services, and the use of safe deposit boxes would be handed out by the collateral teller.

C. Hand outs in connection with personal loans and automobile loans would be handed out by the paying-receiving tellers, collection tellers, personal trust tellers and by the draft tellers.

In other words, the practical use of hand outs is to have them given out by personnel of departments where it is obvious the customer can use the service of another department.

Service pieces are merely informative vehicles and consist of such things as clocks on the building, weather bells, or similar devices which either by sound or by appearance, call people's attention to the bank.

Radio is an excellent means of advertising provided the program used is properly keyed to the bank and its activities. The most effective use of radio is in connection with spot broadcasts of the weather, or the news or; if the budget provides, in sponsoring special programs, such as concerts, local football, baseball or basketball games or other activities which have general public interest.

One of the most effective bank advertising mediums, especially in a small or medium-sized town, or in an agricultural area, where the newspaper is either issued daily in the morning or evening, or weekly, is the bank's news broadcast between 5 and 7 PM where mention is made of those in the community who died in the last 24 hours, together with information as to where the wake will be held, and funeral arrangements if known. This is a great service, particularly in an agricultural area where the evening news broadcast is the most prompt and immediate means of notifying friends of the death of a loved one.

Television programs can also be a very good source of good will and advertising to the bank. It is generally recognized, however, that great care must be used in televising activities in order to obtain maximum benefits. Here, as in radio, the most effective television programs are those in connection with televising events of general public interest such as basketball, football games, concerts or programs in connection with some phase of the economy, such as educational films dealing with farming, manufacturing, mining.

Another opportunity for the bank to benefit from the use of advertising is for astute bank management to keep the stockholders informed on the activities of the bank in connection with promotion of new business and services. In order to accomplish this it should be the policy of the Chairman of the Board or President, whenever new types of direct mail, or statement insertion pieces are to be used, or where a new radio or television program has been approved, or even new billboard advertising is to be put up, to write a short note to the respective stockholders informing them of the development and enclosing a sample of the piece to be used.

In order to encourage employees to think about the bank and its services, they can be asked to submit their ideas on advertising by drafting the text they would use in advertising certain services of the bank. This can even take the form of a contest, where all employees working for a suitable prize or for personal recognition are invited to submit advertising copy in connection with a certain service incorporating the various points of advertising media as discussed in this chapter.

Such a program has many advantages. In addition to providing the bank with good ideas, it will assist the employee in studying each service. They will want to learn the benefits which accrue to a customer who uses the different services and in doing so will also learn the importance of their job. This could be a long range project providing personnel with innumerable opportunities to study the many services banks provide for use of the public and their customers.

One of the most important phases in developing an advertising program for a bank is for the officer in charge of the public relations department to prepare a program showing by month, well in advance, the various services which are to be advertised and the respective media to be used. In addition to developing the program, the officer in charge of public relations should also work out a budget showing in detail the respective cost for each type of advertising. Only when this has been completed should the entire advertising program be submitted, through the President, to the Board of Directors, or the Public Relations Committee for final approval and execution.

It should be evident to every progressive employee or student of banking that a bank must have customers to serve, and deposits to invest if:

A. Stockholders are to receive a return from the investment of their funds commensurate with risk.

B. Officers and employees are to be rewarded for faithfully discharging the duties and responsibilities of their position.

C. Customers and people who reside in the area served by the bank can be provided with all types of banking services required in conducting their financial affairs.

In order to fully attain these objectives it is necessary that stockholders, directors, officers, employees and customers of the bank fully contribute their best efforts to helping the bank grow and progress. The following outlines some of the ways stockholders, directors, officers, employees and customers can help the bank.

THE STOCKHOLDER CAN HELP HIS BANK BY:

1. Using the services the bank has to offer.
2. Recommending the bank services to his friends.
3. Seeing that the business firm with which he is connected does business with his bank.

4. Recommending services of his bank to clubs, churches, lodges and organizations of which he is a member.

5. Endeavoring to have civic organizations, or municipal organizations of which he is a member or officer, conduct their financial transactions with his bank.

6. Bringing to the attention of the officers of the bank the names of individuals or businesses who are moving into the community.

7. Introducing his friends, who are not customers of the bank or presently using any of its services, to officers of the bank.

8. Cooperating with the officers and directors in civic and community undertakings.

9. By naming the bank as executor of his estate or trustee under his will.

A DIRECTOR CAN HELP HIS BANK BY:

1. Carrying out all the recommendations made above, due to the fact that to be a director he must be a stockholder.

2. Being careful to conduct his affairs as a borrower or depositor in strict conformity with the laws, by-laws and policies established by the Board of Directors in the interest of the stockholders.

3. Encouraging friends and associates to discuss their financial problems with him, or introducing them to the proper officer in the bank who can assist the prospect or customer in solving his financial affairs.

4. A willingness to serve municipal organizations, such as the library board, the hospital board, planning commission where contacts with others could result not only in serving the community but in additional business for the bank.

5. Closely cooperating with other directors or officers of the bank; and being available to contact and call on prospects on behalf of the interests of the bank in the acquiring of new business.

6. Actively, willingly and cooperatively serving on the committees of the bank when appointed.

7. Making his experience, knowledge and wisdom available at all times to the officers and other directors in furthering the best interests of the bank.

OFFICERS AND EMPLOYEES CAN HELP THE BANK BY:

1. Remembering they are the bank in their contacts with customers.

2. Remembering they are the bank when they write a letter, answer the telephone; being friendly and considerate, and so conduct themselves that people respect them and have confidence in them.

3. Being alert to the needs and services required by a customer or prospect in conducting their financial affairs.

4. Studying ways and means to make operations more efficient, more systematic, less costly.

5. Conscientiously taking steps to reduce expenses, avoid waste of machinery, equipment, light, heat, power and supplies.

6. Being alert and encouraging prospects or customers to avail themselves of the services of the bank, thus increasing the income in which they will ultimately participate through salary increases.

7. Helping to promote the interests of bank customers and prospects.

8. Becoming familar with the various services the bank has available for its customers and the public.

9. Keeping abreast of financial matters so as to be able to answer intelligently the questions about the bank or its services asked by customers or prospects.

CUSTOMERS CAN HELP THE BANK BY:

1. Making practical use of all the services the bank has to offer.

2. Calling the attention of management to omissions in service, discourtesy, or services which are needed by business, which the bank presently is not supplying, such as financial assistance in the discounting of paper, warehousing of raw material, which are services a bank would be happy to supply or provide if they knew they would help their customers in transacting their financial affairs.

3. Complimenting employees on good service and letting management know when officers and employees have gone out of their way to give exceptional service. It is only through being appreciated and knowing they are part of an organization, or belong to a group that personnel get the encouragment to make further efforts to please others and thus obtain the rewards which result from courtesy and service.

CHAPTER XX

CONVERSION OF FUNDS INTO EARNING ASSETS

THE SECOND MOST IMPORTANT PHASE in banking, especially as it applies to bank management, is in connection with the conversion of capital funds provided by the stockholders and funds deposited with the bank in checking and savings accounts by customers into earning assets. It is important because the interest income produced from the sound investment of such funds in loans and securities enables the bank to:

A. Pay for the cost of investing such funds.

B. Provide services for customers and others.

C. Pay "rent," in the form of interest, to time depositors for the use of their funds.

D. Reward the stockholders through payment of dividends for the risk involved in investing their funds.

The actual work in connection with converting such funds into the various types of loans and investments is an operating function, performed by and through the Loan Department and the Investment Department whose methods and procedures of operation we shall cover separately. The program, however, which the loan and investment departments follow in converting such funds into the various types of loans and investments is determined by the policy established by the Directors or the Executive Committee, which is formalized into what is known as a Conversion of Funds Program.

Such Conversion of Funds Program, in turn, is only established by the Board of Directors or the Executive Committee after a careful analysis has been made of the make up or content of all the funds available for investment. In other words, any formalizing of the Conversion of Funds Program is based on the exposure and vulnerability of such funds available for investment and the cash requirements of the bank.

Before we develop a Conversion of Funds Program and review the important functions of the loan and investment departments in connection with converting funds available for investment into earning assets, it might be of interest to explain what is meant by such terms as:

Gross funds available for conversion.
Cash requirements.
Reserve requirements.
Excess reserves.
Secondary reserve requirements.
Net funds available for investment.
Exposure of funds available for investment.
Vulnerability of funds available for investment.

Gross funds available for conversion represent the total of funds deposited in checking accounts, savings accounts, and certificates of deposit by depositors plus the funds belonging to the stockholders. These are represented by funds in the capital, surplus, undivided profits and reserve for losses accounts, less the outstanding balances, as shown on the statement, which have been expended for land, building, furniture, fixtures, machinery and equipment. Reserves for taxes, insurance, expenses, and other like reserves are not included inasmuch as they represent an accumulation of funds currently set aside from earnings in payment of services rendered or amounts already owed which will be payable at a future date.

Cash requirements represent respective amounts of currency and coin which the bank, after study and analysis, has prudently determined (A) should be maintained on the bank premises in order to cash checks which have been presented to them; (B) provide the current needs for currency and coin required by their customers and (C) should be maintained on deposit with other banks for payment of their drafts and checks of their customers presented for payment through them.

Reserve requirements represent the percentage of time and demand deposits (or funds customers of the bank keep in checking and savings accounts) which member banks of the Federal Reserve System must keep on deposit with the Federal Reserve Bank in whose district they are located; or respective percentages of funds deposited by customers in checking and savings accounts which, according to the law of the state in which the bank is located, the bank must maintain in cash or on deposit with properly designated banks.

Excess reserves represent the amount of cash or funds on deposit with the Federal Reserve Bank, over and above the amount which the bank is required by the law to maintain on deposit, and represents funds which the bank has available to invest in the various types of loans and securities.

Secondary reserve requirements represent a percentage of the funds which customers have deposited in checking accounts, savings accounts and certificates of deposit, which prudent bank management believes should be invested in loans and securities which readily can be converted into cash. Formerly it was the principle of bank management that secondary reserves should be invested in commercial paper, Treasury Bills and Certificates of Indebtedness maturing within 90 days. In recent years, however, because of a change in the provisions of the Federal Reserve Act in connection with the discounting of loans and borrowing privileges, the necessity for investing large amounts of funds in low income securities to provide such reserve, has lessened. It is also becoming more evident that loans themselves, under a properly devised conversion of funds program, provide necessary liquidity to take care of contingencies which might arise.

Net funds available for investment represent the total funds deposited by customers in checking accounts, savings accounts and certificates of deposit plus the net funds belonging to the stockholders less fixed assets and amounts set aside for cash and legal reserve requirements.

Exposure of funds available for investment is the extent to which percentages of funds of individual depositors, in respective classes of accounts, bear in relationship to the total of such class of funds, or in other words, the percentages of the total funds deposited by customers in checking accounts, savings accounts or any other type of account who maintain balances under, over, or between certain amounts.

It is axiomatic in formulating an investment program that the greater the percentages of deposits represented by the fewer number of accounts, the greater the need for liquidity and investment of such funds in short term loans or investments.

Vulnerability of Funds Available for Investment represents (A) funds temporarily on deposit with the bank; (B) the balance of accounts maintained as a compliment to a Director or Officer of the bank; (C) uninvested trust funds; (D) special time deposits; (E) or the excess funds of depositors placed with the bank pending investment or other use. In other words, vulnerable deposits are those which it is not prudent for the bank to invest except in loans and investments which, by their very nature can be immediately converted into cash.

For practical and analytical purposes in this study, however, deposits both from the standpoint of exposure and from the standpoint of vulnerability are considered as one.

A Conversion of Funds Program, therefore, is a program based on a study of the vulnerability and exposure of the deposit structure which provides for the investment of such funds in amounts and in various classes and types of loans and investments, which will provide maximum income based on minimum exposure, and provide at all times for the orderly liquidation and conversion of loans and investments into cash without loss.

It is axiomatic, from a public relations standpoint of a progressive bank, that a bank's second duty to depositors and the community is to provide for the credit needs of the businesses serving the community and the people residing in the community. The first obligation, of course, is the safety of the funds which customers have entrusted to the bank by depositing such funds in checking and savings accounts. To accomplish this objective it is essential that bank management study the local needs and requirements of their depositors and the community in order to have funds available at all times to supply their credit requirements.

For example: in a farming community the bank must have funds available in the spring to loan to the farmers to buy seed. In order to accomplish this, a certain percentage of funds, as determined by study, must be available at that time. In such a bank, their loans would be repaid as soon as the grain is harvested, thus reducing loans and increasing balances which would place the bank in the position of having excess reserves and funds available for investment. It is obvious, if such funds are to be required by the customers of the bank again the next spring, that the bank's only opportunity to obtain income is to invest such funds in securities and loans which will mature or which can be liquidated in the spring.

In so-called community banks where the customers are retail merchants and home owners, banks generally have demands made on them for funds at tax periods. If a bank is located in a manufacturing community and business is seasonal, an investment program must provide funds when people need them for living expenses.

It can be seen that a Conversion of Funds policy for each bank is an individual project, based, of course, on the economic conditions of the area served by the bank and seasonal demands.

It can be said, however, that every Conversion of Funds program is fundamentally developed to:

A. Provide for the credit needs of businesses located in the area served by the bank or for the people residing in the community served by the bank.

B. Provide for percentages of funds to be invested in the various classes of loans and investments which will provide sufficient flexibility to meet all changes in economic conditions.

C. Avoid excesses of credit expansion and contraction by basing the investment program on such expansion or contraction.

D. Invest funds only in loans and securities which provide reasonable liquidity based on the make up of the deposit structure.

E. Obtain maximum income from funds available for investment by proper correlating of loan practices with investment practices.

It is pertinent to the establishment of a Conversion of Funds Program to state that such a program should make ample provision for supplying the normal credit needs of businesses and people in the area served by the bank, even though the general overall economy should be on a downward trend. To bring this about, prudent bank management avoids having too large a percentage of funds invested in term loans, or loans secured by marketable collateral, and endeavors to have the loan portfolio represent extensions of credit arising from normal business and commercial transactions.

However, where circumstances and conditions in the local economy are such that it is necessary for a bank, in order to properly serve the community, to invest a large percentage of funds in particular types of loans, liquidity must be provided for in the investment program. Under such circumstances prudent bank management carries a larger percentage of funds available for investment in short term Government Bonds and other types of securities which mature within a reasonable period of time or which can speedily be converted into cash without loss.

All of the objectives to be attained through the development of a Conversion of Funds Program, namely, provision for taking care of the credit requirements of businesses and people located in the area served by the bank, and liquidity, provided by study and analysis of exposure and vulnerability of the deposit structure as shown by the following.

In order to develop a Conversion of Funds Program applicable to the individual bank, it is necessary first to classify checking accounts and savings accounts by balance and number, and then determine the percentages of funds, in respective classes, which should be invested in the various types of loans and securities to attain the over all objective.

The first step in accomplishing this objective is by counting the number of accounts in respective classifications and determining the respective balances as represented by the total number of accounts in each class. This information can be obtained from the work sheet on which the latest proof was made in balancing up the checking and savings account ledgers. Results of such a study are shown in Exhibit 70.

In studying this Exhibit, which reflects statistics and figures typically found in a bank of approximate deposit size located in a medium size town which has diversified interests, particular attention is called to the large number of checking accounts maintaining balances under $500 which account for such a small percentage (9.9) of the total funds available for investment. Obviously the investment of such funds does not begin to provide sufficient income to cover the cost of providing the services required or used by this large number of customers. Yet, on the other hand, the bank is reluctant to compensate for these low balances by the assessing of proper service charges based on cost plus a profit.

It is interesting, likewise, to notice the large percentage of funds represented by the few accounts in number which maintain balances in excess of $5,000. It is this large percentage of demand deposits (58.6) represented by a small number of accounts (50) which makes necessary the formulation of a sound Conversion of Funds Program based on whatever exposure such figures disclose.

It is also of interest to note, in reviewing this exhibit, the situation of which many bankers are aware—the large number of savings accounts which maintain relatively small balances. Many of these savings accounts we know from experience, if we have made a detailed analysis of the activity, serve both the purpose of "safe keeping" and "convenience" as exemplified by the frequent number of withdrawals from the small accounts. Here too, it is obvious that the investment of such funds does not begin to compensate for the expense incurred in servicing such accounts.

Bankers, it appears, have lost sight of the fact that bona fide savings deposits, while providing the base, according to law, for investments in mortgage loans, consist primarily of funds set aside by individuals for a special purpose or as a reserve for emergencies. If this is the purpose, do we have a right to employ such funds in long maturing assets? From a theoretical yet sound viewpoint individuals or families, depending on individual circumstances should strive to have a reserve fund equal to 1/6 of their annual income to provide for unexepected illness, temporary loss of job of the breadwinner or other contingency. This being the case, the balances of bona fide savings accounts should run between $500 and $5,000. Others who come into funds through the exchange or sale of personal property believe it advisable to segregate such funds so they won't be used for another purpose and, therefore, place these funds in a special or savings account while awaiting investment. In both instances the interest allowance is of secondary consideration. The prime consideration is that they will be able to have use of their funds when they want or need them. By intent they are funds considered to become payable on demand which raises other important questions. Do we have the right to employ such funds in long maturing assets to be able to pay a larger rate of interest? Do we have the right to risk the stockholders' equity to satisfy our desire for size?

For years we have had the mistaken idea that we could encourage thrift by encouraging people to "Save for a Rainy Day" with little thought as to what kind of weather to provide for. Maybe the rain would be a drizzle, or perhaps it would be a cloudburst

Exhibit 70

CLASSIFICATION OF ACCOUNTS				
CLASSIFICATION	NUMBER OF ACCOUNTS	% OF ACCOUNTS	REPRESENTED IN DOLLARS	% OF TOTAL DEPOSITS
CHECKING ACCOUNTS				
UNDER $ 200.	417	30.3	$ 38,000.	1.5
$ 200. - 499.	540	38.3	213,000.	8.4
500. - 999.	179	12.	157,000.	6.2
1000. - 2499.	147	10.4	310,000.	12.2
2500. - 4999.	77	5.5	334,000.	13.1
5000. - 9999.	28	2.	232,000.	9.1
10000. - OVER	22	1.5	1,258,000.	49.5
	1410	100.%	2,542,000.	100.%
SAVINGS ACCOUNTS				
UNDER $ 100.	846	41.	21,000.	1.1
$ 100. - 499.	474	23	108,000.	6.
500. - 999.	198	9.6	120,000.	6.5
1000. - 2499.	267	12.9	372,000.	20.3
2500. - 4999.	156	7.5	438,000.	24.
5000. - OVER	123	6.	771,000.	42.1
	2064	100.%	1,830,000.	100.%
CERTIFICATES OF DEPOSIT	62		268,000.	
CAPITAL			150,000.	
SURPLUS			100,000.	
UNDIVIDED PROFITS (NET)			62,000.	
			312,000.	
TOTAL FUNDS FOR INVESTMENT			4,952,000.	

Both kinds of weather require a different type of protection. We have also made the mistake of erroneously believing we could encourage thrift by suggesting people open a savings account with $1.00.

Proof that bankers have lost sight of the real need of bona fide savings accounts is borne out in every bank by analyzing the balances maintained in the savings ledgers. Analysis will disclose that approximately

46% of the savings accounts maintain balances of less than $100, average about $18 each, and represent less than 7/10 of 1% of the total savings funds.

20% of such accounts maintain balances beteween $100 and $500, average $240 each, and represent about 4% of the total savings funds.

29% of such accounts maintain balances between $500 and $5,000, average about $1,800 each, and represent about 45% of the total savings funds.

Less than 5% of the number of accounts maintain balances of $5,000 and over, average about $11,000 each, and represent better than 50% of the total savings funds.

The accounts which maintain balances under $500 represent about 66% of the number of accounts, and less than 5% of the total savings funds, yet are the most active and account conservatively for more than 50% of the operating expense. Should banks encourage these accounts, and if the answer is "yes," shouldn't banks make some effort to either build them up for bona fide purposes, or make some arrangement for them to bear their proportionate share of expense?

If we follow through on the economic need for bona fide savings accounts, what real justification is there for less than 5% of the total number of accounts to represent more than 50% of the total savings funds? As they exceed the normal requirement for bona fide savings accounts, we can only arrive at the inescapable conclusion that these are "investment" funds and should be so considered.

If we adjust accounts maintaining balances over $5,000 to a maximum of $5,000, we find that 34% of the number of accounts comprising 93% of the total funds would be strictly bona fide savings, be responsible for a very small percentage of the operating cost, incur no real investment problem, and would represent a sound class of accounts whose primary interest was safety and availability of funds when needed, rather than the interest the funds earned.

Should not, therefore, prudent bankers, approach the whole matter of interest rates on savings deposits to the effect it would have on bona fide savings accounts or those accounts maintaining balances between $500 and $5,000, and not be too concerned with the smaller account which in too many instances are costly, and a circumvention of a checking account—or the larger account which for practical purposes, is in the investment class.

If we can accept this philosophy, then banks could set up a special type of account (a common investment trust fund) with restrictions as to withdrawals which would permit them to invest such segregated funds without fear of withdrawals or demand, which would entail possible losses through conversion of such assets to cash.

The next step, once the make up of the deposit structure and funds available for investment has been determined, is to analyze respective classes of accounts and determine their exposure and vulnerability. In other words, under adverse economic conditions, what would be the anticipated fall off or decline in balances in each class of account, and what class of loans and investments should these funds be invested in to provide for conversion into cash without loss, should liquidation be necessary.

By sampling and analyzing a representative number of accounts. taking into consideration the factors of:

A. Population of area by status and age (retired couples 65 or over, producing couples 25/65 years of age, young people and young married couples 18/25 years of age, school children 6/18 years of age).

B. Balances and borrowings maintained with the bank by business concerns located in the area served by the bank and number of people employed.

C. Balances and borrowings maintained with the bank by retail establishments located in the area served by the bank and number of people employed.

D. Balances and borrowings maintained with the bank by employees of such business concerns, retail establishments and householders (people who reside and trade in the community but whose income is earned in another community).

E. Balances of accounts maintained in excess of FDIC coverage.

F. Balances maintained as a compliment to a director or officer. The percentage of such funds which should be invested in respective classes of loans and investments can be estimated, as shown in Exhibit 71.

Note:

Because the purpose of a Conversion of Funds Program is to act as a guide, it is not essential that such percentages represent actual figures or that figures reflect the results of actual mathematical computations. In other words, if it has been determined that 18.5% of the funds in checking accounts which maintain balances between $2,500 and $4,999 should be invested in Installment Loans, use the closest percentage unit of 5 or 20%. Further, in applying such percentage to the aggregate balances, use the closest even thousand dollar amount adjusting respective dollar amounts to cash and reserve requirements EXCEPT in connection with checking accounts maintaining balances over $10,000 and savings accounts maintaining balances of $5,000, where the excess over such amounts is maintained in cash or invested in short term Government securities, with the balance of such accounts under $10,000 and $5,000 respectively being subject to conversion as shown.

The next step is to reflect these respective percentages of class of accounts to respective dollar amounts of the various types of loans and investments as shown in Exhibit 72; compare with present policy; and determine the bank's present position both from a liquidity/conversion of funds position and earning standpoint.

In order to disclose the difference and possible benefits to be obtained from following a Conversion of Funds Program, as against an Investment Policy unbased on the deposit structure, let us make a comparison between the Program and Policy followed by Bank "A," which is similar in size to the one we have been using for illustrative purposes. It should be thoroughly understood, however, that where there is not sufficient demand for the type of loans permissible under the Conversion of Funds Program, that such unin-

Exhibit 71

PERCENTAGES OF FUNDS IN RESPECTIVE CLASSES OF ACCOUNTS TO BE INVESTED IN RESPECTIVE TYPES OF LOANS AND INVESTMENTS								
CLASSIFICATION	BALANCES 000. OMITTED	CASH	U. S. GOV'T BONDS			LOANS		
CHECKING ACCOUNTS			UNDER 1 yr	1 to 5 years	6 to 10 years	COM'L	INSTAL	MTGE
UNDER $ 200.	$ 38.	10	10	10	10	20	20	20
$ 200. - 499.	213.	10	10	10	10	20	20	20
500. - 999.	157.	10	10	10	10	20	20	20
1000. - 2499.	310.	10	10	10	10	30	30	
2500. - 4999.	334	10	20	20		30	20	
5000. - 9999.	232.	10	20	20		40	10	
10000. - OVER	1258.	(See footnote)				50	50	
TOTAL	2542.							
SAVINGS ACCOUNTS								
UNDER $ 100.	21.						50	50
$ 100. - 499.	108.						50	50
500. - 999.	120.						50	50
1000. - 2499.	372.	5				20	35	40
2500. - 4999.	438.	5	15			20	20	40
5000. - OVER	771.	(See footnote)				40	30	30
TOTAL								
CERT. OF DEPOSIT	268.		50			25	25	
CAPITAL	150.					25	50	25
SURPLUS	100.					25	50	25
UP & RESERVES	62.		50	50				
TOTAL	312.							
TOTAL FUNDS FOR INVESTMENT	4952.							

Exhibit 72

INVESTMENT OF FUNDS IN RESPECTIVE TYPES OF LOANS AND INVESTMENTS (000.00 omitted)								
CLASSIFICATIONS			U. S. GOV'T BONDS			LOANS		
CHECKING ACCOUNTS	BALANCES	CASH	UNDER 1 yr	1 to 5 years	6 to 10 years	COM'L	INSTAL	MTGE
UNDER $ 200.	$ 38.	2.	4.	4.	4.	8.	8.	8.
$ 200. - 499.	213.	24.	21.	21.	21.	42.	42.	42.
500. - 999.	157.	13.	16.	16.	16.	32.	32.	32.
1000. - 2499.	310.	31.	31.	31.	31.	93.	93.	
2500. - 4999.	334.	37.	66.	66.		99.	66.	
5000. - 9999.	232.	25.	46.	46.		92.	23.	
10000. - OVER	1258.	250.	788.			110.	110.	
TOTAL	2542.	382.	972.	184.	72.	476.	374.	82.
SAVINGS ACCOUNTS								
UNDER $ 100.	$ 21.	1.					10.	10.
$ 100. - 499.	108.						54.	54.
500. - 999.	120.						60.	60.
1000. - 2499.	372.	20.				74.	130.	148.
2500. - 4999.	438.	26.	64.			87.	87.	174
5000. - OVER	771.	80.	81.			244.	183.	183.
TOTAL	1830.	127.	145.			405.	524.	629.
CERTIFICATES OF DEPOSIT	268.		134.			67.	67.	
CAPITAL	150.					38.	75.	37.
SURPLUS	100.					25.	50.	25.
UNDIVIDED PROFITS RESERVES-NET	62.	31.	31.					
TOTAL	312.							
TOTAL FUNDS FOR INVESTMENT	4952.	509.	1282.	215.	72.	1011.	1090.	773.

vested funds are to be invested in U. S. Government securities of similar maturity.

The Directors of our subject bank undertook a study of the economic situation in the area served by the bank. Because the demand for loans from local retail business was seasonal, balances maintained by manufacturing enterprises were subject to wide fluctuations, and most of the depositors of the bank were employed by the major companies or in related fields, policy was established which provided that of the gross funds available for conversion into earning assets, 20% should be maintained in cash or in accounts with other banks, 40% should be invested in United States and municipal bonds, 20% invested in commercial or installment loans, with the balance of 20% in real estate mortgages up to 50% of the total savings deposits. This, of course, was a good policy and served to guide the administrative officers of the bank in making loans and investments. It did not, however, take into consideration the exposure and vulnerability of the deposit structure, closeness of the relationship of the depositors with the bank, or other factors.

The extent to which liquidity and conversion of funds received *improper* consideration under *both* arrangements is illustrated by reviewing the following comparisons:

USE OF FUNDS AVAILABLE FOR INVESTMENT	COMPOSITION UNDER POLICY	COMPOSITION UNDER CONVERSION OF FUNDS PROGRAM	DIFFERENCE BETWEEN POLICY AND PROGRAM
	000.00	omitted	
CASH	$ 992.	$ 509.	$ + 483.
U.S. GOVT. SEC.	1980.	1569.	+ 411.
COMMERCIAL LOANS	495.	1011.	- 516.
INSTALLMENT LOANS	495.	1090.	- 595.
MORTGAGE LOANS	990.	773.	+ 117.
TOTAL FUNDS FOR INVESTMENT	4952.	4952.	-0-

The effect a sound investment program based on a Conversion of Funds Program can have on earnings is illustrated by applying the interest income return of Bank "A" to respective types of loans and investments as shown in the previous chart, which in this instance, would increase interest income in excess of 33%.

USE OF FUNDS AVAILABLE FOR INVESTMENT	RATE	COMPARISON OF GROSS INCOME			
		UNDER BANK POLICY		UNDER CONVERSION PROGRAM	
		FUNDS INVESTED	INCOME	FUNDS INVESTED	INCOME
CASH		$ 992.	$ -0-	$ 509.	$ -0-
U. S. GOVT. SEC.	2.7	1980.	53,500.	1569.	42,400.
COMMERCIAL LOANS	6.0	495.	29,700	1011.	60,700.
INSTAL LOANS NET	8.6	495.	42,600.	1090.	93,700.
MORTGAGE LOANS	5.4	990.	53,500	773.	41,800
TOTAL FUNDS FOR INVESTMENT		4952.	179,300.	4952.	238,600

While it is readily admitted that the basis for such a formul is subject to questioning, it nevertheless provides a basis for analysi and discussion—and for the formulation of a policy or program fo the guidance of management, and makes directors more aware o their responsibilities.

On the other hand, it is well to point out such a program als sets up a "sales quota" for the officers in charge of the respectiv types of loans and investments and provides, at least in theory, goal, which if attained and worked towards, will result in a ban receiving maximum income from the investment of funds based o liquidity.

CHAPTER XXI

THE INVESTMENT DEPARTMENT

ONCE THE CONVERSION OF FUNDS PROGRAM has been established by the Board of Directors, the administration or execution of such program becomes the function and responsibility of the investment department and the loan department in accordance with duties and responsibilities assigned to them by the Board of Directors, as outlined in the organization plan.

The Investment Department from a functional and operating standpoint has relatively few transactions in comparison with the number of transactions handled in the various divisions of the Loan Department. Because of this, even though the volume of investments in many banks will approximate or exceed the volume of loans, we will study the Investment Department first.

The principal functions of the Investment Department in a well managed bank, are in connection with investing the available funds of the bank in the various types and classes of bonds. The amounts, in accordance with policy and the Conversion of Funds, are determined by the Board of Directors based on the vulnerability and exposure of the deposits and capital funds structure.

To carry out the Conversion of Funds Program the Investment Department is generally divided from a functional standpoint into two divisions: the U. S. Government Division and the Municipal and Other Securities Division.

The U. S. Government Division is charged with the responsibility of handling the purchase, exchange, and sale of U. S. Government securities for customers and the bank's own investment portfolio.

The Municipal and Other Securities Division is charged with the responsibility of analyzing, trading, purchasing, and selling municipal and other securities for the bank's own investment portfolio.

In a large bank it is generally also the responsibility of the

Investment Department to handle all security transactions for the Trust Department.

In order to function properly and again depending on the size of the bank but usually in the larger banks, certain officers and clerks will have as their principal responsibility, either the analysis trading, and clerical work in connection with delivery and payment of securities, or the custody of securities. In the smaller bank, the officer in charge of investment, who might even be the president will not only undertake analysis and place the order, but prepare the confirmation, letters of transmittal with instructions for delivering the securities for payment, and arrange for the payment and handling of proceeds.

Generally the officer in charge of the Investment Department will not only undertake full management of the bank's investment portfolio, but the maintaining and control of the bank's reserve position. These dual functions are undertaken by the officer in charge of the Investment Department or his assistant in order that the bank obtain income from maximum investment of funds for investment even though they are of a temporary nature.

In reviewing the functions of the Investment Department it is well to point out that here we are only considering the functions of the Investment Department from the standpoint of a bank converting its funds available for investment into bonds in order to obtain income in the form of interest earned. We mention this in order to differentiate between *investment* of funds and the practice of certain banks to *trade* in the securities held in their investment account in order to realize a profit when the securities increase in price; or when others are willing to pay the bank more for the bonds than they paid for them; or when the bank sees an opportunity to take a loss by selling certain securities in the investment accounts to offset capital, or other gains, which losses will benefit them from a tax standpoint.

In managing the investment portfolio of a bank, the officer who has the responsibility for the conversion of funds available for investment into bonds and maintenance of the bank's cash and reserve position has the use of six important tools:

1. Conversion of Funds Program.
2. Investment Ledger.

3. Maturity Schedule.

4. Daily Statement of Condition for previous day.

5. Report of total amounts of checks drawn on the bank, re-ceived from other banks in the current day's clearings, or received in the cash letter from the Federal Reserve Bank or correspondent banks, payment for which will reduce "Due From Bank Accounts."

6. Report of large deposits made to, or large checks drawn and paid against, commercial accounts on the previous day.

The Conversion of Funds Program determines the policy and practice as to investing funds in securities; and sets the maximum amount which should be invested in the various classes of bonds.

The Investment Ledger provides the officer in charge of invest-ments with a detailed record of all bonds held in the bank's port-folio by name or class, date of issue, par value, interest rate, ma-turity, optional call date if any, cost, and where located (deposited to secure deposits—safe keeping with another bank—in vault).

The Maturity Schedule shows the holding of the various classes of bonds projected to maturity, together with remaining balances.

In order to avoid taking losses, if forced to liquidate invest-ments and to provide for orderly maturity, it is generally the policy of banks to arrange their investments so that a certain percentage of their portfolio will mature quarterly and that, based on exposure, up to 80% of securities of respective classification or issue will turn over in equal installments within five years. This provides a re-volving fund which is reinvested, depending on economic condi-tions.

It is from this projection and knowledge of the trend of deposits and loans during respective periods of the year which enables the officer in charge of investments to determine the disposition of pro-ceeds of maturing obligations. Under normal conditions, and pro-viding there has not been any unforeseen change in the deposit and loan structure (abnormal increases or decreases) such funds will be:

A. Maintained in cash, to provide either for seasonal decline in deposits—or conversion into seasonal loans,

B. Reinvested in securities of similar class and maturity to maintain policy, or

C. Reinvested in other types of bonds or loans in accordance with approved modifications in the Conversion of Funds Program.

The Daily Statement of Condition reflects the financial positio of the bank as of the beginning of business on the current day (close of business for previous day).

The officer in charge of investments and the bank's cash an reserve position pays particular attention to the figure showin amounts due from the Federal Reserve Bank and respective co respondent banks, for it is against balances maintained with thes banks that drafts are drawn to pay for checks "on us" presente for payment by other banks.

Reports of Checks Drawn and Deposits Made. After receivin the report from the Clearings Department as to the net amount funds required to pay for checks "on us" presented by other bank or the amount of net funds which will be credited to such accoun after settlement with other banks, (which occurs when the tota of the checks which are drawn on and presented to the other ban exceed the totals of checks "on us" which they present for paymen the officer makes the adjustment of balances on the memo settl ment sheet.

If the balances in respective bank accounts are not sufficie to cover a draft drawn in payment of the checks presented throug that bank for payment, it is then necessary for the officer to transf funds from another bank to cover. This is done either by tel phone, wire transfer, or the depositing of a draft drawn on anoth bank in which surplus funds are maintained.

Once settlements with other banks have been made, the offic makes his computations and determines that reserves based time and demand deposits are sufficient to comply with legal reser requirements. If the bank is a member of the Federal Reser System and the balances maintained with the Federal Reserve Ba is below legal reserve requirements, the officer either increases t balance with the Federal Reserve Bank by transferring funds fro other banks; sells U. S. Government short term securities; borro from the Federal Reserve Bank by pledging U. S. Government s curities; rediscounts eligible paper with the Federal Reserve Ba sells mortgage loans, or sells loans secured by marketable coll eral to its correspondent bank.

If, on the other hand, after making settlement with oth banks, the balance maintained with the Federal Reserve Ba exceeds the reserve requirements, and funds maintained on depo vith correspondent banks exceed amounts required for normal ›usiness transactions, the bank has "funds available for investment." t is then up to the officer in charge of investments and the bank's eserve requirements to analyze the increase in deposits or funds .vailable for investment and by review and analysis of reports of arge deposits made, determine, if possible, if such increases rep-esent funds which will remain permanently or temporarily on eposit—and if the latter is the case—how long such funds will re-nain on deposit before being used. Once this has been deter-nined the officer takes steps to convert such funds into earning ssets.

Should the demand for loans exceed the supply of funds, and ıch demand is in conformance with the Conversion of Funds Pro-ram, the funds will be immediately used. If there is normal de-and for loans (which has been provided for under the Conversion Funds Program) the increase is invested in bonds in accordance ith the program. If, on the other hand, the increase in funds ailable for investment is temporary—or experience and analysis dicates such increase will shortly be absorbed through a seasonal emand for loans—such funds will be invested in short term U. S. overnment bonds, bills, or certificates.

Regardless of the decision—whether to convert bonds into sh, or cash (deposits) into earning assets through the purchase of nds, the transaction must be handled through a broker or an ency licensed to buy and sell securities.

U. S. Government Securities. Since the time of Jay Cooke, ring the Civil War, there have have been a number of reputable ms whose principal business has been in connection with the ying, selling and trading in securities of the United States Gov-nment. In recent years the activities of such firms have been gmented by the services performed by a number of the larger nks in the country which are authorized to buy, sell, and trade United States Government securities. In order to have this vilege they are registered with the Securities and Exchange mmission and are known as Registered Dealers. It is these nks and investment houses authorized to deal in Government urities, working closely with the Treasury Department and Fed-l Reserve Banks, which maintain markets at all times through which United States Government securities can be bought, sold and traded.

U. S. Government securities of the various classes which banks insurance companies, individuals and corporations hold in their in vestment portfolios, represent the funded debt of the federal gov ernment. These securities are generally in the form of bonds havin various maturities from 5 to 20 years or longer bearing a fixed rat of interest, Certificates of Indebtedness or Treasury Certificates is sued for shorter periods and which either bear a fixed rate o interest, or are sold on a discount basis.

If the federal government is seeking new money, banks an others are invited to subscribe to the issue or are invited to enter subscription for the amount they wish to invest. Such subscriptio blanks always show the full amount of the issue, the various ma turities and the rate. Due to the widespread demand for suc investments in recent years, particularly because of the increase i bank deposits, the demand for such bonds has exceeded the suppl When such situations occur, then the subscriptions entered by th various banks are filled on pro rata basis, that is the banks ar awarded bonds in direct percentage of the total subscriptions re ceived to the amount of bonds available.

In cases where the federal government is refinancing maturin bonds (generally at a lower or higher rate than the original bond due to changing economic conditions) present holders of the bond are extended the privilege of obtaining new bonds in like amoun for the bonds which they presently hold and which generally matur as of the day of the exchange. Should a bank elect to exchang maturing bonds for new bonds having a longer maturity, it ente the exchange order which is honored by the Treasury Departme through the Federal Reserve Bank. If, however, the bank does n elect to exchange the bonds, it sends the maturing bonds to th Federal Reserve Bank for collection and credit to the bank's reser account.

When exchange privileges are not exercised to the full exte by banks or others holding such securities, the bonds not taken are generally purchased through the open market committee the Federal Reserve System, respective Federal Reserve Banks, by commercial banks and investment houses who are authoriz registered dealers.

When the officer in charge of the Investment Department decides bonds are to be purchased or sold, he either places the order directly or, depending on the size of the bank, instructs the trading section to contact the dealer or correspondent bank and execute the order.

Where the bank is purchasing bonds it is the customary procedure to place the order by telephone, and then formally confirm he transaction by letter. Such letter, in order to protect both the bank and the dealer should:

A. Include authorization to the bank or dealer to purchase bonds as described at the price as set forth.

B. Contain instructions as to delivery of the bonds.

C. Advise the bank or dealer as to how payment for the bonds is to be made.

Generally the delivery instructions will inform the bank or the investment dealer either to deliver the bonds direct to the bank which has purchased them—or deliver them to a correspondent bank or the Federal Reserve Bank where they are placed in safe eeping for the bank which made the purchase.

As to payment—generally the bank making the purchase either remits direct to the bank or broker for the amount of the purchase including principal and interest, upon receipt of the advice that the bonds have been purchased; instructs its correspondent bank r the Federal Reserve Bank to pay for the bonds upon delivery; r, if the transaction is handled through its own correspondent bank, to charge its account upon presentation and good delivery of the bonds.

When a bank sells bonds, the same general procedure is followed except that in addition to the letter of confirmation containing uthorization as to the sale of bonds as described, and at a price set forth, letters or instructions are given to the correspondent bank r Federal Reserve Bank, where the bonds are kept in safe keeping, s to:

A. Delivery of the bonds upon payment of proceeds,

B. Disposition of proceeds.

Generally the bank selling the securities will instruct the bank holding the bonds in safe keeping to present the bonds to the bank r dealer who negotiated the sale, for delivery upon payment of roceeds. Payment should always be made either by bank draft or certified check. Proceeds are usually deposited by the bank making the delivery in the account of the bank which sold the bonds.

When the confirmation of the purchase or sale of bonds fo the bank's account is received by the bank, and it is determine how payment is to be made if bonds were purchased, or what is t be done with the proceeds if the bonds were sold, the officer i charge of the Investment Department or trading section prepare the necessary general ledger debit or credit tickets effecting th transaction, and the corresponding credit or debit to the correspon dent bank account which sets the transaction up on the books of th bank.

In connection with safe keeping arrangements, once the secur ties are received by the correspondent bank for the account of th purchasing bank they issue a safe keeping receipt which they sen to the bank which purchased the bonds as evidence of ownership.

Municipal Securities. While the operating procedures i connection with the purchase or sale of municipal bonds, or func tions performed by the trading section of the Municipal or Othe Bond Division of the Investment Department are the same as thos performed by the U. S. Government Division, the work preliminar to the execution of such orders is entirely different.

Municipal securities, issued by villages, towns, cities and state or municipalities, depending upon their purpose and use, are eithe tax exempt or taxable. That is, the income or interest from th bonds is subject to the normal federal and/or state income tax.

Municipal bonds, not only because of the security and stabilit but because of the interest rate, are looked upon as prime inves ments. There is considerable competition for such bonds, howeve not only because the total issue for any particular purpose, such street paving or lighting, may run as low as $10,000, but becau such bonds mature serially. This means that they are payab from taxes or revenue over a period of time and therefore have or 10 per cent of the total issue maturing each year, which mak maturities under five years highly desirable for bank investment.

Many banks, of course, are familar with the type of financi undertaken within their own community or county, but in order have sufficient volume of municipal bonds, it is necessary for the to make investments in other sections of their state, or even into other states where lack of financial assistance from ban nakes it extremely difficult for the municipalities to finance their perations.

Banks generally restrict the amount they will invest in any one ssue to a minimum of $5,000 or a maximum of $25,000.

It is the general practice of most banks engaged in the investing f funds in municipal obligations to be close to the municipal bond narket. This is a field of its own, served by a number of investment ouses which specialize in the handling of municipal securities. One of the reasons for banks dealing directly with such investment ouses which handle municipal bonds, is to receive assurance of the egality of such bonds. In other words, to protect their investment n the securities of municipalities, both the investment house and he bank must be certain that the municipality or the instrumentality f the municipality has the legal right—and is empowered—to issue uch securities. Therefore, most issues of municipal securities are lways accompanied by a legal opinion as to the right of the muni-ipality to issue such bonds, which opinion is prepared by lawyers who specialize in municipal law.

Banks, when investing in municipal securities also as a matter f policy and practice, diversify their investments as much as they an. In other words, they like to spread their investments be-ween various sections of the county, state or country so that in the vent of economic slump or catastrophe, their entire investment vould not be jeopardized or perhaps the payment of interest and rincipal deferred.

It is likewise the policy of many banks to diversify their invest-nent in municipal bonds as to class and purpose. That is, it is a ound policy not to invest *all* their municipal bond investments olely in school bonds, bonds for transportation systems, highway onstruction or for utilities.

The bank which is engaged in the purchasing of a municipal ond for investment generally either personally investigates nearby tuations; is kept informed on current developments by the invest-nent banking house from which the securities are purchased; or aintains an individual investigation and research in connection ith certain sections of the country in which they have invested inds in municipal securities. Very often, once a bank has begun invest funds in a certain town or a certain area, it can develop market for such type of securities, which it sells to its customers or perhaps other banks for whom it acts as agent. Through such an arrangement over a period of time the municipality, instead of generally advertising for bids or that it has bonds to sell for a specific purpose, negotiates directly with the bank which handles its financial requirements.

Because of the limited market in municipal securities and the difficulty in trading or selling municipal bonds, in case it becomes necessary to convert to some other investment, municipal bonds are not looked upon generally as possessing the qualifications of a primary or secondary reserve and are purchased for the purpose of being held until maturity. It is therefore obvious, if investments are made in connection with Conversion of Funds Program based on exposure and vulnerability, that only the most stable type of deposits should be invested in municipal bonds. Generally the investment of funds in municipal bonds is looked upon the same as an investment of funds in long term Government bonds and mortgages. Investments available for quick conversion into cash or for conversion into loans, therefore, should be restricted to U. S. Government bonds maturing within six months.

CHAPTER XXII

THE LOAN DEPARTMENT

IN THE PREVIOUS CHAPTER WE COVERED the functions of the Investment Department and the mechanics of operation in connection with converting funds available for investment into bonds. Let us now cover the conversion of funds available for investment into the various types of loans.

The Loan Department, while it shares the responsibility for the conversion of funds belonging to the depositors and stockholders into earning assets with the Investment Department, is without question the most important department in the bank. This is true not only because of the income the Loan Department produces, but because of the invaluable service this department renders customers of the bank and others in providing funds for their financial needs, and the assistance rendered the economy in the area served by the bank through the supplying of credit information.

The nature and functions of credit are many and varied. Credit had its beginning many thousands of years ago when the money changers made loans of coin at interest to enable merchants to conduct their business on their promise to repay the amount so borrowed at a future date.

It was the extension of credit and the belief that promises to pay would be kept which built the railroads which spanned the country, made possible the development of water power providing electricity which runs our factories, developed our air line transportation system which criss-crosses the country, and provided the means to construct our vast housing developments.

Credit and credit functions are the life blood of business and develop factors which are responsible for our standard of living. Without credit we would be dependent upon barter and exchange in conducting commercial and business transactions. Credit is the lubricant which keeps the wheels of commerce turning. In discussing credit it is well to remember:

Credit is the power to borrow money and the ability to com-

mand capital. Where the credit system is highly developed, active and profitable demand for capital exists. Where credit is lacking or undeveloped, we find business in a crude state, wages small and finances generally in an unsatisfactory condition. Once money is borrowed, it becomes capital for the borrower to use in conducting his business affairs. The industries of the world are carried on through borrowed capital, assembled in private hands and in banks through which it is loaned to those who can best employ the funds.

Credit is the present right to a future payment. When a bill of goods is sold, the legal title passes to the buyer, and the seller simply holds the right to collect the equivalent at the time and place appointed. He can sell the right and the holder in due course will have good title to this right of enforcement.

Credit is a commodity. When a merchant sells goods to a purchaser on the promise to pay, he trusts the individual to make payment at the appointed time. The merchant, because he owns this promise to pay or credit, can sell the account and vest in the buyer all the rights which he possesses to enable him to collect his credit. Anything a person owns he can sell. Credit, therefore, is bought and sold like any other commodity because of its standing in law. It is an intangible asset on the balance sheet, yet it is an asset which is used in conducting business.

Credit is respect. It is the reputation an individual, firm or corporation has for being honest, for being fair in their dealings with others, and the measure of their ability and willingness to meet their obligations.

All credit is based upon a transfer of property for without such transfer of property, credit cannot exist. A lender gives or exchanges property or something of value, or transfers title to property or something of value, only upon the promise, based on trust of the individual, to return such property or something of equal value at a future time.

In the final analysis, the basis of all credit is confidence. In fact, the whole modern financial system is built upon the confidence that we have in others that they will conform or comply with the terms of an agreement.

Where a merchant sells goods for cash, the confidence is on the part of the purchaser that the merchandise possesses the qualities it is advertised or reputed to have. Where, however, the merchant parts with goods on the promise that the purchaser will pay for the goods at a future time, it is only done because the merchant has confidence that the purchaser will pay. Therefore, this promise to pay at a later date is nothing more than a credit that is based on the belief of the seller that the buyer has the ability to pay, and is willing to take care of his obligations in the manner provided, or the way promised.

Expressed in the simplest language, credit is the belief that men will keep their promises; and it is the mark of a competent loaning officer or credit man to properly judge and evaluate the promises and know that they will be fulfiilled.

A loan or extension of credit is an advance of cash, or a credit to an account which can be withdrawn in cash or used for the payment of bills, or liquidation of promises to pay against the belief of the lender that the funds so borrowed or so advanced, will be repaid at a future date. The form the loan takes will depend to a great extent upon the maker's desire, the purpose for which the loan is requested, and the basis on which the bank is willing to grant the extension of credit.

In general, bank loans are made for a stated period of time or payable on demand. In addition, they are either secured or unsecured. Further, loans are either "made" or "discounted." Generally in bank nomenclature, a loan is "made" when the interest is paid at maturity. It is referred to as a "discount" when the interest is paid in advance, or deducted from the amount of the principal at the time the loan is put through. In banking, the term also refers to notes, including commercial paper, which banks have bought or made advances against, on behalf of their customers.

A test of sound banking is to have funds constantly employed and to have a steady stream of money always available, by way of maturing loans, so that the credit demands of customers can be met. The practice behind such operations is shown in the Conversion of Funds program which provides for liquidation of loans or investments, and availability of funds at all times for the normal and seasonal demands of customers.

Of course the ultimate test of the soundness of any loan is the ability to liquidate itself at maturity. It is for this reason that those regarded as experts in the field of credit rate mercantile loans higher than loans secured by stock exchange or other classes of collateral security which can be liquidated only through the sale of the property, such as loans secured by real estate.

The reason for this goes back to the times of crises, times of economic upheavals, or when the economy of a country is disjointed because of war or depression when it was found that loans secured by marketable collateral or real estate could only be liquidated by private sale, often with loss to the borrower as well as to the bank. However, loans based on commodities such as wheat, corn, etc. would, by the law of consumption, turn themselves into money by the very fact of people consuming or using the merchandise purchased with the proceeds of the loan.

Policies covering the investment of the various classes of funds into the various types of loans, as we have noted, are determined by the Board of Directors, and formalized into a loan and investment policy. In addition, in a well managed bank, the Board of Directors establishes loaning limitations for each of the officers who are granted the authority to make loans.

These loaning limitations, which are set up for the individua officer based on his experience and judgment, set forth the maxi mum amounts of credit under the various forms, that he can loan one individual or company. Such limitations, as shown for illus trative purposes in Exhibit 73, usually permit or provide for officer to join together in approving loans. The maximum amount which they can loan one individual or company is the total of their re spective limitations for the particular class or form of loan. In addition, such loaning limitations usually provide that application for loans over or above certain amounts be referred to the Executiv Committee, or Board of Directors for approval.

Officers who are granted the loan authority and responsibilit by the Board of Directors have three particular functions (an sometimes four). First, they are the interpreters of bank policy as i applies to the investing of funds in loans. Second, they are th ones who evaluate the information which is collected and assemble regarding the prospective borrower. Third, on the basis of the information and judgment, they either make or decline the loan As the functions, duties and responsibilities of officers will vary a between banks, their fourth function might not only be to evalu ate information assembled regarding the prospective borrower, bu also to obtain the information on which they are to base their decision.

Exhibit 73

LOANING LIMITATIONS

TYPE OF LOAN	MR. A Asst. V. President	MR. B Vice President	MR. C President	EXECUTIVE COMMITTEE*
Line of Credit	--	10,000.	20,000.	20,000. / 50,000.
Loan on Statement	2,500.	10,000.	20,000.	20,000. / 50,000.
Secured U.S. Bonds	25,000.	100,000.	100,000.	100,000. /over
Secured Marketable Collateral	10,000.	25,000.	50,000.	75,000. /200,000. (1)
Secured Other Collateral	10,000.	25,000.	25,000.	50,000. /100,000. (1)
Secured-Chattel Mtge on Equipment-Appliances	500.	2,500.	5,000.	5,000. /over
Secured Chattel Mtge on New Car		80% of cost		
Secured Chattel Mtge on Used Car		60% of book value		
Secured Accounts Receivable	10,000.	25,000.	25,000.	25,000. /100,000.
Secured by Inventory	--	25,000.	25,000.	50,000. /100,000. (1)
Secured by F.H.A. Mtge.	--	15,000.	15,000.	15,000. / 22,500.
Secured, Conventional Mtge.	10,000.	15,000.	15,000.	15,000. / 25,000.
Secured Dealer Floor Plan	--	20,000.	30,000.	50,000. /100,000. (1)

* All loans over maximum, up to and including the legal limit, to be referred to the Board of Directors.

(1) Both the President and Vice President are required to approve loans up to the minimum limit of Executive Committee.

Once the loan is made, it is the loaning officer's responsibility to see that the loan is paid at maturity or according to the terms of the loan agreement. Officers in a loaning department or in one of the divisions within the department, are generally divided into senior and junior officers. Unless the bank is departmentalized according to industry, borrowing customers generally do business with the officer to whom they are known.

Because the fundamental principles of credit involved and the methods of handling respective types and classes of loans differ, most banks with any volume of loans segregate loaning responsibilities into three divisions. The Mortgage Loan Division has the responsibility for all loans secured by real estate equities. The Consumer Credit Loan or Installment Loan Division handles loans repayable in monthly installments, secured by chattel mortgages on automobiles and home appliances and personal loans with or without co-signers or secured by wage assignments. The Commercial Loan Division has the responsibility for handling loans to individuals on statement or secured by collateral; or to business concerns on their statement or through pledge of accounts receivable or inventory. As the functions of all divisions except the

Commercial Loan Division are similar in that the primary basis for making loans is the collateral security in the form of real property or chattel mortgages on automobiles or household appliances, we will cover such loans first from the functional standpoint of investigating, approving and processing the loan.

THE MORTGAGE LOAN DIVISION

Mortgage loans, or loans where real property on real estate owned by the borrower is pledged as security for the loan, are of a number of types and classes. The most common type of loan using real estate as collateral, in which a mortgage is given to secure payment of both the principal and interest, is a first mortgage loan made by commercial and savings banks, under provisions of the law of the state in which the bank is located, by mortgage investment companies, savings and loan associations and farm mortgage companies.

First mortgage loans made by banks and savings and loan associations are of two types, FHA and conventional.

FHA loans are loans guaranteed by the Federal Government through the Federal Housing Administration and made by banks and other associations licensed by the administration to make loans. Such loans can be made on residential real estate, that is homes, up to 80% of the appraised valuation, but not to exceed $22,500. They are repayable in monthly installments covering payment of principal, interest, taxes and insurance over a thirty year period.

In making an FHA loan, the bank or other agency submits the formal application to the office of the Federal Housing Administration which makes an independent investigation and approves or disapproves the loan application. In connection with construction loans, however, where approval is made for a loan to enable a home owner to construct a house, payments can only be made by the bank or agency to the contractor or builder for work performed after the FHA office has examined the work and approved it as in conformance to their standards.

Conventional real estate mortgage loans, on the other hand, are made without an outside guarantee, based on the appraisal of the directors or officers of the bank or an outside agency.

Generally conventional real estate mortgage loans, whether

on existing houses or homes to be built, known as construction loans, are made for 50-60% of the appraised evaluation and repayable in equal monthly installments over a 10-20 year period. Because of the large equity which acts as security for the loan, it is common practice, particularly with loans of larger amounts, to arrange to have 50-60% of the loan repayable over a 10 year period, with the balance of 30-40% to be paid at maturity.

In connection with real estate mortgage loans, the Mortgage Loan Division, from a functional standpoint is divided into three sections– the Acquiring Section; the Processing Section; and the Servicing Section. In a small bank all respective functions might be performed by the same person, while in a larger bank such functions might be performed by separate individuals.

The Acquiring Section is the new business section of the Mortgage Loan Division. This division is charged with the responsibility of obtaining new loans. This takes on great importance, particularly with some of the larger banks which have sufficient facilities for processing and servicing such loans, and are located in an area that is undergoing extensive urban development. Because of the security which real estate mortgage loans offer, they are considered a prime investment by savings banks and insurance companies. Because of their rapid growth and need for investment of funds, insurance companies and savings banks are often unable to obtain sufficient mortgage loans to meet their requirements, It is a common practice for commercial banks, where such loans are available, to acquire and process the loans and then sell them to the savings banks or insurance companies. Under such a procedure, while title to the loans passes to the purchaser, arrangements are made with the seller to continue the servicing of the loans. Through this arrangement, the borrower continues to make payments of principal and interest, and funds set aside as reserves for taxes and insurance to the bank which made the loan. The mortgagor bank, on the other hand, remits the proceeds of principal and interest to the owner, retaining the proportionate amount to cover payment of taxes and insurance which it takes care of when due. For this service, the mortgagor or bank receives a percentage of interest income as a service or handling fee.

As commercial banks have markets for such loans, the acquiring of such loans is of such great importance that the banks actively seek prospective borrowers. This is accomplished by general advertising which stresses the services of the bank in assisting people to own their own homes or to finance the purchase of a home.

The officers or personnel of the acquiring section of the bank also maintain close contact with real estate agents and others so as to be favorably recommended to a prospective borrower.

Such representatives also maintain close liaison with building contractors, architects and the smaller banks in the area which perhaps do not have excess funds, yet wish to be able to accommodate residents of the community or their customers who have need for this type of financing.

Banks active in this field make use of direct mail advertising with their customers to acquaint them with their mortgage loan policies. They not only invite them to make use of the bank's facilities but acquaint them with all the services of the bank so that they are in a position to recommend the bank to their friends who are in need of this type of financing and other services.

The first step in making a first mortgage real estate loan is to have the prospective borrower fill out an application for a loan. While these forms will vary between banks, they are set up to provide the bank with the essential information and generally disclose:

A. The amount of money required.

B. The location of the property.

C. The dimensions of the lot on which the house is located or to be located.

D. The dimensions of the house or building to be erected, if it is a construction loan. Specifications as to materials to be used and contractors bids are also generally submitted.

E. The appraised value of the ground.

F. The type, style and value of the construction, if the house is already built. The number of rooms, baths, etc.

G. The position or business connection of the individual applying for the loan.

H. The number of dependents in the family and their ages.

I. The applicant's annual income or salary.

While some of these questions would appear on the surface

to be personal, it is not the case. The purpose of having information as to the number of dependents, their ages and the applicant's position and annual income, is to assist the loan committee to demine if the applicant's income, after making provisions for obligations in connection with family life, education, etc., is sufficient to cover payments of principal, interest, taxes and insurance, and maintain the property in good repair.

Once the application blank has been filled out and signed, the general practice is for the application to go to the appraisal committee or those delegated the responsibility of appraising the property.

The appraisal committee visits the property, and after making whichever investigations it believes necessary under the circumstances, estimates the value of the land and buildings, and submits it to the loan committee.

If the property is located in an approved area, if there is a proper margin of security, and if the applicant is acceptable from a character and capacity standpoint, the loan application is approved. The applicant is notified as to the approval and the loan application is turned over to the processing section for handling.

The first step, after the application has been approved, is to have the prospective borrower bring either the Abstract of Title or Title Guaranty Policy to the bank from which the legal description of the property and other information will be obtained.

An Abstract of Title is a document which legally describes a piece of land, recites how the land was originally acquired, and gives the various changes in ownership. It also lists in chronological order any restrictions as to the use of the land and any encumbrances or liens against the property.

A Title Guaranty Policy is the same as an Abstract except that it is issued by a corporation chartered to examine and insure titles to real property. Such corporations, for a fee, will insure the owner of the land against any flaw in the title and against other claimants.

It might be said that both Abstracts of Title and Title Guaranty Policies are nothing more than a legal copy of the records of deeds, conveyances, judgments and liens which have been filed in a municipal office of the county in which the property is located as a public record against the property or affecting the owners of the property.

Once the Abstract of Title or Title Guaranty Policy has been received, the personnel of the processing section draw or prepare the necessary papers in connection with a mortgage loan. These usually consist of a trust deed, which is a conveyance of title to the mortgagor for the amount of the loan. It contains a legal description of the property, the amount of indebtedness, terms of repayment, interest charges, warranty that the borrower has the right to pledge such property as collateral security, a promissory note which is evidence of the amount borrowed, payment or receipt books, ledger sheets and other records which the bank must maintain in connection with the loan.

After the deed and note have been signed by the borrower, they are then recorded in the municipal office or office in the county where such documents are registered. Then the Abstract, or the Letter of Opinion rendered by a Title Guaranty Company showing any liens of record, including the current mortgage, is brought down to date.

When the property is already encumbered by a mortgage which has been picked up by the present lenders, such mortgage is then released, after the Letter of Opinion or attorneys' opinion in connection with the bringing down to date of the Abstract, shows it to be of record. Once this is released, the current mortgage then becomes a first mortgage and stands in the record as being the first real estate mortgage lien against the property.

After the title has been brought down, the municipal records are then usually checked to be sure that all taxes levied against the property have been paid, and that no judgments or other liens have been filed of record against the owners of the property. Meanwhile, the processing section has checked to be certain the property is adequately covered by fire, hail, tornado, or other types of insurance, which, in the judgment of the mortgagor, should be provided to insure payment of the loan should such contingencies arise. Following this, the officer in charge of the processing section or in charge of the mortgage loan division then undertakes the process known as "closing."

In the process of closing a loan both the lender and the borrower, or their representatives, are present. The lender usually prepares a settlement statement which shows the gross amount of the loan and any deductions which have been made, such as payment to obtain the deed to the property or picking up of the previous mortgage; amount expended for attorneys for review of the Abstract or to the title company for their Letter of Opinion and Guaranty Policy; the amounts paid out for insurance; the commission or fee charged by the lender for making the loan; and the net proceeds from the loan. The net proceeds are usually paid out by check which requires endorsement and is evidence of receipt of the funds. The borrower also receives a payment book or schedule in which the bank will receipt monthly the amounts which the borrower will pay on principal, interest, and as a reserve for taxes and insurance.

The methods and procedures followed by the bank in handling such payments is an operating function performed by the servicing section which is covered under Operations.

CONSUMER CREDIT OR INSTALLMENT LOAN DIVISION

In connection with the study of the Loan Department of the bank, let us next review the functions and operations of the Consumer Credit or Installment Loan Division.

Loans handled by this division are made in amounts between $100 and $5,000 and are repayable in monthly installments which, depending on the type of loan, generally do not exceed 60 months.

The types and classes of loans handled in the division consist of the following:

A. Loans on new and used automobiles.
B. Loans on household appliances.
C. Loans to individuals (personal loans).
D. Loans in payment of dental and medical expenses.
E. Loans to finance a college education or post graduate work.
F. Loans for home improvements.

In reviewing the Consumer Credit Loan Division, and the functions undertaken by the personnel of the various sections, it is well to remember that the functions, as outlined, are performed in every bank, regardless of size. In a large bank such functions might well be performed by several people, each handling and being resposible for some particular function, while in a smaller bank the same officer will handle all functions including the interviewing of the applicant, processing of the application, undertaking the credit investigation, paying out of the proceeds, handling delinquent accounts and maintaining contacts with the automobile and appliance dealers.

Regardless of the fact that all loans payable in monthly installments are generally handled in the Consumer Credit Loan Division, which is also in some banks called the Installment Loan Division, all such loans by their terms are made in accordance with bank policy, and the maximum amount outstanding is governed by the amount set forth in the Conversion of Funds Program.

The fixing of the maximum amount outstanding under a Conversion Fund Program has several advantages, foremost of which is that in the judgment and opinion of the directors, it sets the maximum exposure of the bank for the particular types of loans. It also has other advantages which are sometimes overlooked by bank management. First of all, the maximum amount acts as a sales quota and encourages the officer in charge of the division to constantly seek new loans in order to maintain the maximum outstanding amount approved under the Conversion of Funds Program. Second, should the division be headed by an officer who is very aggressive, it acts as a check on his activity, with the result that he is more selective in the class of loan he approves.

Let us now review the various types of loans and their terms.

Loans on New and Used Automobiles. Generally loans on new automobiles are made for 80% of their retail cost, the loan to be repaid within 36 months. Loans on used cars are generally made for 60% of the appraised or Blue Book value, for periods of repayment not to exceed 18 months, depending on the make, year, and model of the car. Automobile loans are secured by a chattel mortgage for the amount of the loan.

Loans on Household Appliances. Loans for the purchase of household appliances such as washing machines, radios, stoves, refrigerators, television sets, etc., are generally made in amounts not to exceed 90% of the retail price and are repayable in from 6 to 18 months. Such loans, depending on the article and amount, are secured by a chattel mortgage.

Loans to Individuals (Personal Loans). Loans to individuals for the payment of household bills are made generally for periods of from 6 to 18 months, for amounts not more than 3 times the monthly salary of the individual. Such loans are either secured by a wage assignment, guaranty of an endorser, or by a co-signer.

Loans in Payment of Medical and Dental Expenses. Loans in payment of medical and dental expense are generally made for a period not to exceed 36 months and are made for 100% of the bill. The full amount of these loans is granted, due to the fact that they are endorsed or guaranteed by the doctor or the dentist who performed the work, and technically are loans discounted by the bank for the doctor or the dentist.

Loans to Finance a College Education or Post Graduate Work. Loans for educational purposes will vary as to time, terms, and security, depending on the purpose of the loan. In some instances one loan can be made to finance a period of schooling, while in other instances the loan can be set up as a revolving credit. Under such arrangements periodical advances are made, with the outstanding balance reduced through payment made by the borrower from wages earned through part-time or vacation employment. Generally arrangements for payment of the final outstanding balance become effective upon completion of the program, and are predicated on the earnings and position of the borrower.

Loans for Home Improvements. Loans for home improvements are just what the name implies. They are loans made for the improvement of homes such as remodeling of a kitchen or bathroom, adding on a room, putting on a new roof, or revamping the heating or electrical system. Such loans are either made under the bank's own home improvement loan plan, which is similar to the conventional mortgage loan plan, or the FHA remodeling plan which is guaranteed by the Federal Housing Administration.

While home improvement loans may be either a first lien on a property or a second lien on the property, in other words a second mortgage, they are repayable in equal monthly installments, over a period of time generally not to exceed 60 months or 5 years. Generally, with such loans, a trust deed with note, signed by the owners of the property, is taken by the lender and recorded as collateral security.

In home improvement loans the application is generally accompanied by an estimate of the cost of the work performed. Likewise, the property on which the work is to be performed or the improvement made is appraised to be certain there is sufficient equity to act as collateral security for the new loan.

The first step in making any type of installment loan begins by having the prospective borrower complete and sign a loan application form, either before or during the conference with the loan interviewer. Such application, in addition to stating the amount and purpose of the loan, the name, address, information as to employment, names and ages of husband or wife and dependents, ownership of property if any, also contains information as to outstanding indebtedness and terms of repayment.

Should review of the application indicate favorable action will be taken, it is turned over to the credit investigator for checking and verification of the information given on the application.

In checking out a loan application, the first thing the investigator determines is that the name and address is correct. He next confirms the fact that the person signing the application is employed by the company whose name was placed on the form. In the case of an application for an automobile loan, the investigator checks with an automobile credit agency, or similar service bureau, which maintain records of all chattel mortgages filed on automobiles owned by people who reside in the area, to be certain the automobile is free from all liens or encumbrances. Should no lien appear of record, the automobile is checked over to be certain it fits the description placed on the application.

After the investigation has been completed the application, together with the report of investigation, is reviewed by the officer in charge of the division for approval or disapproval.

Should the loan application be approved, the applicant is notified, terms of repayment and any conditions agreed upon, and the applicant asked to come in the bank to sign the note (if the note was not signed at the time the application was made) and receive the check for the proceeds.

Following notification and confirmation of terms, the processing section is notified to prepare the note and chattel mortgage for signature, obtain insurance if required, and prepare the coupon book and other required or necessary papers.

The chattel mortgage contains all the information and description of the property, together with any registry numbers or other information which will assist in identifying the article or automobile. In the case of an automobile, home improvement, and sometimes in connection with personal loans, banks require the loan be covered with applicable insurance. Therefore, if the prospective borrower does not already have insurance, the bank request the borrower to procure such insurance with a loss payable clause in favor of the bank. A loss payable clause, which is attached to the insurance policy, is notification to any parties of interest that the bank has a lien on the property insured and that in event of a loss or claim against the policy, the proceeds will first be applied to the outstanding balance of the loan.

When the prospective borrower comes to the bank, he signs the note (and chattel mortgage, if required) and receives a check for proceeds of the loan together with pass book in which the amounts of the monthly payments will be recorded, or a coupon book, one of which is to accompany each monthly payment when made. Following disbursement of the funds, the chattel mortgage is recorded and the ledger sheet set up in the liability ledger in the name of the borrower.

If the loan application is disapproved, the applicant is contacted and advised of the decision. In declining an application it is well to remember that turning down a request for a loan CAN be a means of creating good will—if properly handled. Loan officers, alert to aspects of good public relations, never say "No" in so many words to a loan request. They say "Yes" we will be happy to make the loan BUT (we will have to have a co-signer—more information before we can decide—collateral—etc.); or PROVIDING (certain conditions which will make the loan acceptable are conformed to or complied with).

Automobile, home improvement and appliance loans generally come to the bank either on a direct basis in which the borrower makes application for the loan directly to the bank or on an indirect or discount basis where the loans are made by the seller of the merchandise and the notes (sometimes on the bank's own form) are purchased by the bank.

Such notes which are purchased by the bank are generally

bought by the bank either on a recourse or non-recourse basis. Notes purchased by the bank on a non-recourse basis become the bank's liability in the event of default. Loans that are purchased under a recourse basis become the obligation of the seller of the merchandise in the event of default.

Where loans are purchased on a recourse basis, it is the generally accepted practice and custom for banks to withhold a portion of the face value or face amount of the loan which is set up in a reserve account to which are charged any losses which might occur. Obviously, where loans are purchased with recourse, the loans can be for a greater percentage of the amount and generally the bank takes all of the paper which is offered. Contrariwise, where the loans are purchased by the bank only on a non-recourse basis, each credit is analyzed and only accepted when it measures up to certain standards.

Once installment or consumer credit loans are placed on the books, the handling of the loan is the responsibility of the service section, which processes payments, maintains records of insurance, etc.; and the collection section which has the responsibility of following up and collecting delinquent accounts. As functions of both of these sections are in connection with methods and procedures, they will more properly be covered under Operations.

CHAPTER XXIII

COMMERCIAL LOANS

NEGOTIABLE INSTRUMENTS, AS WE LEARNED in Chapter XVI, are divided into two main classes: Orders to Pay, which consist of checks and drafts and Promises to Pay, which consist of trade acceptances, bank acceptances, and promissory notes.

A trade acceptance, we know, is a draft drawn by the seller of the merchandise on the buyer, which is acknowledged by the buyer by writing the word "ACCEPTED" across the face of the draft, and designating the place of payment and date of acceptance. After a draft is "accepted" it can be discounted by a bank and the proceeds advanced to the seller, who is obligated to pay the draft in case the buyer fails to do so at maturity.

A bank acceptance, on the other hand, is a draft drawn by the seller of the merchandise on the buyer, which a *bank* acknowledges by writing the word "ACCEPTED" across the face of the draft, and designating the place of payment and date of acceptance. A bank acceptance is the same as a trade acceptance *except* that the bank, by "accepting" the draft, exchanges its credit for that of the person or party on which drawn. Once a draft is accepted by a bank, it becomes the obligation of the bank and can be discounted or sold by the seller of the merchandise by endorsement or order, without further liability or recourse to him.

Promissory notes, however, which are unrestricted promises to pay an amount certain in money to bearer or order, at a certain place, on or before a certain fixed future time, are the most widely used instruments in commercial and financial transactions.

The most common form of promissory note is that used in connection with commercial loans, which by their terms are either payable on demand, on or before a future date, or in installments over a fixed period of time. In addition, such loans are either made against a pledge or something of value as collateral security; based on the financial standing of the borrower as disclosed through the rendering of a financial statement; or by a combination of both.

The majority of loans made by a bank are dependent on th general financial standing of the borrower where the only evidenc of debt is an unsecured promissory note similar to that shown i Exhibit 42. It is the use of unsecured credit, as evidenced b promissory notes and open accounts, which has provided th means to develop and expand American industry. For example under an open account method of extending credit, the manufac turer delivers the goods purchased to the retailer on the implie promise that the retailer will pay for the merchandise within 1C 30, 60, or 90 days, whichever the terms might be.

The retailer in turn sells and delivers the merchandise to th consumer for cash, or on the implied promise that he will pay fo the goods within 30 days, at which time the retailer will pay th manufacturer.

Meanwhile, should the manufacturer require funds with whic to pay operating expenses or purchase raw materials for proces ing, he can obtain such funds from the bank either by borrowin unsecured on his statement, by a pledge of accounts receivabl warehouse receipts, other acceptable collateral, or by discountin trade acceptances and bills of lading.

The retailer, likewise, should he be in need of funds wit which to pay expenses and remit to the manufacturer for the good previously purchased, because his customers are slow in payin their bills, can obtain funds from the bank by borrowing uns cured on his statement, by pledging accounts receivable, warehous receipts, or other suitable articles representing wealth as collater security.

The consumer (customer), on the other hand, if in need funds to pay the retailer, can obtain such funds from the bank (pr viding he qualifies for credit) by borrowing unsecured on h statement, by pledging stocks, bonds, mortgages or notes which h owns as collateral security, on cash surrender value of life i surance, or on the endorsement or guaranty of a responsible pe son of financial means.

For the purposes of our study, applicants for commerci loans fall into one of the following categories:

1. Individuals, corporations and partnerships who are custon

ers of the bank and want to borrow by pledging securities, assets or articles representing wealth as collateral for the loan.

2. Individuals, corporations and partnerships who are not customers of the bank at the time of applying for a loan and wish o borrow by pledging securities, assets, or articles representing vealth as collateral for the loan.

3. Individuals, corporations and partnerships who are customrs of the bank and wish to borrow unsecured on their statement or the first time.

4. Individuals, corporations and partnerships who are customrs of the bank and have occasionally borrowed unsecured on heir statement.

5. Individuals, corporations and partnerships who are customrs of the bank and frequently borrow on their statement.

6. Individuals, corporations and partnerships who are not ustomers of the bank at the time of applying for a loan and wish borrow unsecured on their statement.

Because many of the conditions and provisions of loans secured re similar to conditions and provisions of mortgage loans secured y real estate, and installment or consumer credit loans secured by attel mortgages and endorsements, let us first cover commercial ans secured, before getting into the life blood of commercial anking—the unsecured commercial loan—where the credit exnded is not only predicated on a "promise to pay," but on the ssurance that the "wealth" as disclosed on the various forms of ancial statements submitted, truly and honorably represents e financial position of the borrower.

To be classified as good collateral, the evidence of wealth not ly must have stability under adverse business conditions, but be such form that in event of default or non-payment of the loan, e title or ownership to such collateral can be readily transferred others for cash, or the collateral sold and converted into cash hich can be applied against the outstanding balance of the loan.

Evidence of a commercial secured loan is by means of a llateral form note similar to that shown in Exhibit 43. In addin to containing the general provisions of a promissory note, it thorizes the lender to sell or convert such collateral into cash d apply the proceeds to the outstanding balance of the loan if the borrower defaults on payment, fails to make payment, or does not comply with other conditions.

While commercial loans secured can be made against the pledge of various types and classes of securities or articles representing wealth, the principal types and classes generally used as collateral in connection with commercial transactions are:

1. Bonds and stocks of industrial and utility corporations
2. United States Government Bonds and Notes
3. Savings Accounts
4. Chattel Mortgages
5. Real Estate Mortgages
6. Cash Surrender Value of Life Insurance
7. Accounts Receivable
8. Bills of Lading
9. Warehouse Receipts

BONDS AND STOCKS OF INDUSTRIAL AND UTILITY CORPORATIONS

Bonds, as we have seen, are interest-bearing promissory notes i writing in which the borrower agrees to pay an amount certain i money to the bearer or order, at a certain place on a certain futur date. The interest on bonds, which is evidenced by coupons whic are attached, is payable generally every six months. Bonds ar secured by the pledge of real estate, machinery, equipment, lease hold improvements and other property which act as collater security.

Stock, on the other hand, is ownership in the net assets of company, which is evidenced by a certificate signed by officers the company, and registered on the books of the company certif ing that the person whose name appears on the face of the cert ficate is the owner of a stated number of shares of stock.

Stock is of two classes: preferred stock and common stoc Preferred stock, of which there are several types, is just what t name signifies, preferred as to payment. In cases of liquidatio however, and depending on the solvency of the company, t preferred stockholders receive as a maximum the amount of p value specified on the certificate, while the common stockholde share in the remainder.

In the payment of dividends, the preferred stockholders are ntitled to the dividends, when authorized by the Board of Direc- ors, according to the rate so specified on their certificates. They ave a first lien as far as the earnings are concerned while common tockholders, on the other hand, are entitled to whatever dividends he Directors deem prudent to pay after taking into consideration roper provisions for taxes, possible losses and other obligations.

Bonds and stocks as to ready convertibility are of two classes— sted and unlisted. Listed securities are those which can be bought, old or traded through a recognized and registered exchange, hich, as we have seen, is an organization of individuals engaged the business of buying and selling securities, under rules and egulations established and enforced by the exchange.

Unlisted securities, on the other hand, are those which are ealt in privately by dealers who maintain a market for the pur- hase, sale or trade of such securities in which they might have an terest or maintain a position. One of the principal differences etween listed and unlisted securities is that in the latter case, in mes of economic upheaval, there is no ready market for them. s a result, the price at which such securities can be sold, traded exchanged is entirely up to the whim or judgment of the in- erested parties.

Normal adjustments, which periodically occur in our dynamic onomic system, at times bring about temporary curtailment of oduction, liquidation of inventories and unemployment. Such anges reduce not only the earnings of individuals and busi- esses, but the demand for ownership of securities and other evi- ences of wealth, thus reducing the price which investors, or those ith funds to invest, are willing to pay for them.

Because of these factors, bank regulatory authorities and pru- ent bank management see to it that loans against which market- le and other collateral has been pledged, are adequately secured. other words, there must be at all times a sufficient margin or fference between the balance of the loan and the price at which ch collateral can be sold so that, in event it becomes necessary liquidate or sell the collateral in a declining market, the pro- eds will be sufficient to pay the balance due on the loan plus interest and any other charges or expenses in connection with liq uidating the collateral.

UNITED STATES GOVERNMENT BONDS AND NOTES

Bearer bonds, Certificates of Indebtedness and Treasury Cer tificates issued by the United States Government are considere prime collateral. They are frequently pledged by individuals an corporations as security for a loan with which to pay taxes or fo other business purposes. Many individuals and corporations fr quently have need for short term loans and maintain a percentag of their quick assets in United States Government securities fo this purpose.

Unted States Savings Bonds, however, are not eligible f collateral as they do not conform to the law of negotiabiilty that title cannot be transferred by endorsement to holders in du course.

SAVINGS ACCOUNTS

The rules of most savings departments provide that funds ca only be withdrawn from a bona fide savings account upon prese tation of the pass book and a savings withdrawal properly signe Interest on savings accounts is generally paid semi-annually as June 30th and December 31st.

People who maintain sizable savings accounts often do so f a special purpose. It also happens occasionally that such peop have need for cash funds between interest periods and do not ha any other type of wealth which they can use as security for temporary loan. It has become a practice of banks, therefore, make loans to such depositors using the pass book and a withdra al slip properly signed as collateral to secure the loan. By use such a vehicle, the funds remain in the bank for the purpose f which they were intended and the customer does not suffer t loss of interest by withdrawing the funds from the account.

CHATTEL MORTGAGES

A chattel mortgage loan is one which is secured by a pled of the equity the borrower has in the personal property or artic uch as as automobile, refrigerator, stove, television set, air con-itioner, farm machinery or equipment and office machinery or quipment. Practically any article which comes under the heading f appliance, machinery or equipment can be pledged as security or a loan.

Under the terms of a chattel mortgage loan, if the borrower oes not make payments in accordance with the agreement, the ender has the right to take possession of the property, sell it and ay off the loan from the proceeds.

Another form of time payment contract which acts similarly to chattel mortgage is an installment contract. The main difference that under the installment contract the seller usually retains title the property until all installments are paid, whereas under a hattel mortgage the title to the property is in the name of the urchaser or owner, subject, of course, to the lien or the loan gainst such property.

Both chattel mortgage loans and installment contracts are xtensively used to finance the sale of a variety of all types of ersonal property, both on a direct basis and an indirect basis.

REAL ESTATE MORTGAGES

When real estate is used as collateral security for a commercial an, the general practice is to prepare and record a trust deed and ote, and follow the procedure for completion as previously out-ied in making a real estate mortgage loan (appraisal-abstract—uaranty policy—insurance, etc.).

The amount and terms of payment of such mortgages, how-ver, may differ in that instead of the amount of the mortgage loan eing for 60% of the regularly appraised value, with the terms of payment to be in monthly installments over a five to ten year eriod, the loan may be for a period of one to five years for an nount payable at maturity only sufficient to provide a margin of curity between the amount of the mortgage and loan. Where real estate mortgage is pledged as collateral security for a com-ercial loan, the terms of the real estate mortgage are not ap-icable (as to payment) until such time as it is necessary to take ssession and sell the mortgage and apply the proceeds to the an.

CASH SURRENDER VALUE OF LIFE INSURANCE

Under the usual terms and conditions covering life insuranc policies, the insured at stated times pays a certain sum of mone known as a premium, to the company for which they promise t pay a certain sum of money to the estate, or to the beneficiarie of the insured, upon his death; or at the termination of the contrac By virtue of the terms and conditions covering payments made b the insured, a cash value to the policy is provided which the in sured may withdraw at any time during the life of the policy. A this cash value may be pledged, loans secured by the assignme of the cash surrender value of life insurance are looked upon a being prime loans and generally command a prime rate.

It is necessary, however, in connection with loans on the cas surrender value of life insurance which is assigned, for the lende to periodically check with the insurance company, or have th borrower present the receipts for the payments of premiums du to be certain that the margin has not been depleted or reduce because of the failure of the insured to pay the premiums whe due, and by arrangement, having such cash surrender value ap plied against premiums.

ACCOUNTS RECEIVABLE

When a seller of merchandise allows the purchaser of th goods to take immediate delivery of the merchandise, upon th promse to pay for the merchandise at a future time—or permits customer to "charge it" to an account which will be paid aft receipt of a periodical bill, such transactions are referred to, on th financial records of the seller as "accounts receivable" (accoun which are due). Accounts receivable, if current, next to cash an government bonds, represent the most liquid assets of any busine

Where a merchant or manufacturer is not in sufficient go standing to warrant the extension of credit on an unsecured ba and sells to others on open accounts, these accounts may be pled ed to the bank as collateral security for a loan. In addition banks there are finance companies and commercial paper hous who make a business of loaning against accounts receivable, rather "buying" these accounts.

In making accounts receivable loans, it is generally the accept-d and legal practice for the lender to make a notation on the ·dger sheet of each account pledged as collateral security to the ffect that the lender has a lien on the account; and to notify the ebtor that payments should be made to the lender instead of the ıerchant or manufacturer from whom the merchandise was pur-hased.

It is also acceptable practice, where a company in good ıancial standing which sells its products to customers on open ccounts, for banks to make loans on accounts receivable without otification to the customers. In such cases the customers (pur-hasers) continue to make payments to the seller who in turn, laily or weekly), remits the funds paid or collected to the bank ·hich applies the funds to the balance of the loan.

Where loans are made on accounts receivable, the borrower's ooks should be checked periodically to be sure the ledgers are roperly marked to show that accounts are pledged, and to con-rm that collections are being remitted as received.

While loans on accounts receivable are not considered a prime ·pe of loan for a commercial bank, they are often made in order · provide a merchant or manufacturer, whose business is rapidly xpanding, with temporary working capital to enable him to dis-ount his bills for raw materials and extend credit to acceptable urchasers.

In making accounts receivable loans, the laws of the respective ates should be carefully checked to be certain that the formalities ı assigning the accounts, as provided by law, are complied with. rudent bankers will refer such matters to legal counsel and base ıeir practice in connection with making such loans on their opin-n.

BILLS OF LADING

A bill of lading is an instrument issued by a common carrier ailroad, steamship line, public transportation system) acknowl-lging receipt of specified goods for transportation to a certain ərson at a certain place. They are two types, a straight bill or ı order bill.

A straight bill of lading, which is generally non-negotiable, provides for delivery of goods only to the person named on th bill and does not require the bill of lading to be surrendered, al though the carrier must be certain of the identification of th person and that the person so named is entitled to receive th goods.

An order bill of lading, on the other hand, is negotiable be cause it provides for delivery of the goods only to the person t whom the goods are assigned, or his order, and only on prope endorsement and surrender of the bill of lading to the carrie Because of negotiability and the fact that the goods and title pa upon endorsement, order bills of lading are good collateral fo loans under the usual conditions of margin and the ready conve sion of such goods into cash. Once such goods are delivered b the carrier, they can either be placed in a warehouse and covere by a warehouse receipt, in which case the goods become collater to a warehouse loan; or they can be stored on the premises o property of the borrower, in which case the goods can be pledge as collateral to an inventory loan.

WAREHOUSE RECEIPTS

Not all those engaged in manufacturing or retailing busine have sufficient space of their own to store raw materials awaitin processing or finished goods awaiting sale and delivery. To pr vide storage facilities, warehouse companies, which are bonded an licensed by the Federal Government, provide space in which me chandise can be stored, for which it receives a fee. When the good are placed with the warehouse company, the warehouse compan issues a receipt evidencing the fact that the goods so named in th receipt are in storage under the control and responsibility of th warehouse company.

Warehouse receipts are of two types, non-negotiable an negotiable. Non-negotiable receipts are sometimes called straig receipts and provide for the delivery of the goods only to th person named in the receipt, upon payment of the storage charg of the warehouse. This, of course, is similar to the provisions a bill of lading.

On the other hand, a negotiable or order receipt, which is a ceptable collateral security for a loan, provides for delivery of th oods to the person named, or to his order, on proper endorsement nd surrender of the warehouse receipt together with payment of harges.

It can be said that a warehouse receipt is a bill of lading cov- ring goods stored in a permanent place, and that a bill of lading a warehouse receipt covering storage and custody of goods in ansit.

Loans secured by warehouse receipts are also frequently made se of by those engaged in handling commodities where large mounts of credit, in proportion to net worth, are needed to finance e purchase, storage and processing of raw materials such as orn, wheat, butter, cheese, eggs, oil, poultry, etc.

The credit and loan machinery of a bank begins to function e minute a request is made for a loan.

If the request is in connection with a loan on an automobile, ousehold appliance, guaranty of an endorser, or co-signer, repay- ble in installments, or in connection with real estate, the machin- y begins to turn with the filing of an application for the respec- ve type of loan, as previously described.

If the application, however, is for a loan secured by the pledge something of wealth or value as collateral security, or is to be ased on the financial position of the applicant, the machinery egins to turn at the time of the interview with the loaning officer.

If the applicant for a loan on a secured basis is a customer of e bank, the loaning officer will generally refer to the credit file r information as to the account and data on the applicant. He ill satisfy himself as to the ownership of the collateral, that the urpose for which the loan is requested is legitimate and that it n be made in accordance with the rules and regulations of the upervisory authorities and policy of the bank. He also satisfies mself that the securities tendered as collateral are marketable, ve sufficient margin to protect the loan, and are in good delivery der that is either endorsed or accompanied by a power of at- rney.

If the applicant for a loan on a secured basis is not a customer the bank at the time the request for a loan is made, the loaning ficer, after satisfying himself as to the identity of the applicant d acceptability of the collateral, will probably have the credit section make certain investigations of the individual, before ap proving or disapproving the loan.

COMMERCIAL LOANS UNSECURED

Up to now we have been covering the converting of func available for investment into the various classes and types of loar and investments, where the amounts so advanced have either bee guaranteed or secured by the pledge of acceptable collateral. W now enter the most interesting field of finance, which supplies th life blood to commercial banking and economic development loans based on the credit and worth of the applicant, as disclose through a financial statement—known as unsecured loans. Th introductory step in the granting of an unsecured loan general begins with an interview with a loaning officer.

If the applicant for unsecured credit is a customer of th bank but has never applied for a loan, the loaning officer will fir obtain from the applicant information as to the purpose of the loa and require certain financial information in the generally accepte form. Unless the prospective borrower has a current balan sheet and profit and loss statement prepared by a public or Ce tified Public Accountant available, the loaning officer will provi the applicant with statement forms similar to those shown Exhibits 74-77 which were prepared and approved by the Robe Morris Associates. Such statements are to be completed eith by the individual borrower, the firm's own accountant or financi officer, or outside accountant, and returned to the bank for analy and review.

If the applicant is a customer of the bank, the credit secti should have in their files information as to when the account w opened, how the account has been conducted, the range of t balances maintained, the type of business engaged in, the nam of the officers, a record of garnishments or law suits to which t bank was made a party, and possibly some correspondence connection with credit inquiries. Should this be the situation, t credit investigating section will proceed to augment this inform tion with outside information as warranted under the circu stances.

If the applicant is a customer of the bank and has occasiona

Exhibit 74

PERSONAL FINANCIAL STATEMENT (FRONT SIDE)

Please do not leave any questions unanswered.

PERSONAL STATEMENT

CONFIDENTIAL

To

Name____________________ Address____________________

For the purpose of procuring and maintaining credit from time to time in any form whatsoever with the above named Bank, for claims and demands against the undersigned, the undersigned submits the following as being a true and accurate statement of his financial condition on the following date, and agree that if any change occurs that materially reduces the means or ability of the undersigned to pay all claims or demands against him, the undersigned will immediately and without delay notify the said Bank, and unless the Bank is so notified it may continue to rely upon the statement herein given as a true and accurate statement of the financial condition of the undersigned as of the close of business.

(Month)____________________ (Day)____________ 19____

ASSETS				LIABILITIES			
Cash on hand and in Banks				Notes payable to Banks — Secured			
U. S. Gov. Securities — see schedule				Notes payable to Banks — Unsecured			
Listed Securities — see schedule				Notes payable to relatives			
Unlisted Securities — see schedule				Notes payable to others			
Accounts and Notes Receivable Due from relatives and friends				Accounts and bills due			
				Unpaid Income Tax			
Accounts and Notes Receivable Due from others — good				Other unpaid taxes and interest			
				Real Estate Mortgages payable — see schedule			
Accounts and Notes Receivable Doubtful				Chattel Mortgages and other Liens payable			
Real Estate owned — see schedule				Other debts — itemize			
Real Estate Mortgages Receivable							
Automobiles and other Personal Property							
Cash Value — Life Insurance							
Other assets — itemize							
				TOTAL LIABILITIES			
				NET WORTH			
TOTAL ASSETS				TOTAL LIAB. & NET WORTH			

SOURCES OF INCOME		PERSONAL INFORMATION	
Salary	$	Business or occupation	Age
Bonus and Commissions	$		
Dividends	$	Partner or officer in any other venture	
Real Estate Income	$		
Other income — itemize	$	Married	Children
		Single	Dependents
TOTAL	$		

CONTINGENT LIABILITIES		GENERAL INFORMATION
As endorser, comaker or guarantor	$	Are any assets pledged? — see schedule
On leases or contracts	$	Are you defendant in any suits or legal actions?
Legal claims	$	
Provision for Federal Income Taxes	$	Personal Bank Accounts carried at
Other special debt	$	Have you ever taken bankruptcy? Explain:

(COMPLETE SCHEDULES ON REVERSE SIDE)

Carried in Stock by Cadwallader & Johnson, Inc., Chicago.

Exhibit 74A

PERSONAL FINANCIAL STATEMENT (REVERSE SIDE)

SCHEDULE OF U. S. GOVERNMENTS, STOCKS AND BONDS OWNED			
No. of shares or Face value (Bonds)	Description	In name of	Market value

SCHEDULE OF REAL ESTATE MORTGAGES RECEIVABLE				
Description of Property covered	Date of Acquisition	In name of	Amount	Maturity

SCHEDULE OF REAL ESTATE OWNED						
Description of property and Improvements	Date Acquired	Title in Name of	Cost	Market Value	Mortgage	
					Amount	Maturity

SCHEDULE OF LIFE INSURANCE CARRIED, INCL. N.S.L.I. AND GROUP INSURANCE				
Amount	Name of Company	Beneficiary	Cash Surrender Value	Loans

SCHEDULE OF ASSETS PLEDGED		
Description	Value	To Whom Pledged

GIVE NAMES OF BANKS OR FINANCE COMPANIES WHERE CREDIT HAS BEEN OBTAINED			
Name	Date	High credit	Basis

THE UNDERSIGNED CERTIFIES THAT BOTH SIDES HEREOF AND THE INFORMATION INSERTED THEREIN HAS BEEN CAREFULLY READ AND IS TRUE AND CORRECT.

____________________19____________________________

Date signed — Signature

Exhibit 75

CORPORATION FINANCIAL STATEMENT (FRONT SIDE)

Please do not leave any questions unanswered.

FINANCIAL STATEMENT AND SUPPORTING INFORMATION

Confidential

To:

Name__________ Address__________

Business__________ ☐ Proprietorship ☐ Partnership ☐ Corporation

For the purpose of procuring and maintaining credit from time to time in any form whatsoever with the above named Bank, for claims and demands against the undersigned, the undersigned submits the following as being a true and accurate statement of its financial condition on the following date, and agree that if any change occurs that materially reduces the means or ability of the undersigned to pay all claims or demands against it, the undersigned will immediately and without delay notify the said Bank, and unless the Bank is so notified it may continue to rely upon the statement herein given as a true and accurate statement of the financial condition of the undersigned as of the close of business.

BALANCE SHEET			
DATED			
ASSETS			
Cash	$		
Marketable Securities (C)			
Receivables (Net)—Customers (A)			
Merchandise (Net)—(B)			
TOTAL CURRENT ASSETS	$		
Deferred Receivables			
Due from Officers and Employees			
Investment in Affiliations—Subsidiaries (D)			
Due from Affiliations—Subsidiaries (D)			
Investments—Other (C)			
Deferred Charges and Prepaid Expenses			
Fixed Assets (Net)—(E & F)			
TOTAL	$		
LIABILITIES			
Notes Payable—Banks			
Notes Payable—Trade			
Accounts Payable—Trade			
Due to Officers and Employees			
Due to Affiliations—Subsidiaries (D)			
Taxes			
TOTAL CURRENT LIABILITIES	$		
TOTAL LIABILITIES	$		
Capital Stock—Preferred*			
Capital Stock—Common*			
Earned Surplus *			
Capital Surplus *			
NET WORTH	$		
TOTAL	$		
AMT. OF CONTINGENT LIABILITIES			
AMOUNT OF ASSETS PLEDGED			
AMOUNT OF LIABILITIES SECURED			

PROFIT AND LOSS STATEMENT			
FROM TO			
NET SALES	$		
Less—Cost of Goods Sold:			
Beginning Inventory			
Add—Purchases			
If Manufacturer Add { Labor			
Manufacturing Expense			
Total			
Less—Closing Inventory			
Total Cost of Goods Sold	$		
GROSS PROFIT	$		
Less—Selling Expense			
General and Administrative			
Provision for Bad Debts			
Reserve for Taxes (Excl. Fed. Taxes)			
Total Operating Expenses	$		
NET OPERATING PROFIT			
Add—Other Income			
Total Other Income	$		
Less—Other Expenses			
Total Other Expenses	$		
Less—Provision for Federal Taxes			
NET PROFIT	$		
Included Above—Depreciation Charges			
Executive Remuneration			

Is above profit and loss statement on cash ☐ or accrual basis ☐

Are Federal taxes paid on cash ☐ or accrual basis ☐

SURPLUS RECONCILIATION			
Beginning Surplus	$		
Add—Profit			
Less—Dividends or Withdrawals			
Adjustments			
Closing Surplus	$		

*Not to be filled in by proprietorship or partnership

Schedules on reverse side

Exhibit 75A

CORPORATION FINANCIAL STATEMENT (REVERSE SIDE)

(OMIT PENNIES)

(A) TRADE RECEIVABLES—Selling Terms..........days		(B) INVENTORY—Purchase Terms..........days	
Accounts—Not Due		Finished Goods	
Past due....to....days		Work in Process	
Past due....to....days		Raw Materials	
Past due....to....days		Supplies	
Past due....to....days		Out on Consignment	
Unclassified		Miscellaneous	
Total Trade Accounts		GROSS INVENTORY	
Notes—Current		*Less*—Reserve	
Deferred		NET INVENTORY	
GROSS TRADE RECEIVABLES		Purchase Commitments	
Less—Reserve for Bad Debts		% of Discounts Earned on Purchases	
NET TRADE RECEIVABLES		% of Returns & Allow. on Gross Sales	
Charge-offs in Period		Basis of inventory pricing?	
Recoveries in Period		Was physical count taken?	

(C) INVESTMENTS	Units	Mkt. Val.	Total	(D) AFFL.—SUBSID.	% Owned	Invest.	Due From	Due To
Total				Totals				

(E) FIXED ASSETS	Title in Whose Name	Appraisal Val.	Res. for Dep.	Net Value	Mortgage	Yr. Due
Totals						

(F) FIXED ASSET CHANGES IN PERIOD:

DESCRIPTION	PURCHASES	SOLD OR TRADED	RETIREMENTS	DEP'R'N THEREON
Totals				

(G) LIFE INSURANCE (M indicates thousands of dollars):

INSURED	COMPANY	FACE VALUE	CASH VALUE	LOAN	BENEFICIARY	TYPE	MDSE.	PLANT
		M	M	M		Fire	M	M
		M	M	M		Wind	M	M
		M	M	M		Burglary	M	M
		M	M	M		War Risk	M	M
		M	M	M			M	M
		M	M	M			M	M

(H) MONTH END BALANCES (12 Mos. to Date)

	SALES	MDSE. PAY.	BANK LOANS
1			
2			
3			
4			
5			
6			
7			
8			
9			
10			
11			
12			

Date Signed..........

(I) OWNERSHIP OF BUSINESS:

NAME	Title	Per Cent Interest	Remuneration

*Incorporated in.......... Date..........

*Shares Authorized..........Outstanding..........Par Value $..........

Last independent audit by..........as of..........

Income Tax Payments approved thru..........19....

Outstanding Sales Commitments $..........

Unsatisfied Judgments $.......... Any suits pending?..........

*Not to be answered by proprietorship or partnership.

The undersigned certifies that both sides hereof and the information inserted therein has been carefully read and is true and correct.

Company Name..........

By..........Title..........

Exhibit 76

FINANCIAL STATEMENT AND SUPPORTING INFORMATION (FRONT SIDE)

Please do not leave any questions unanswered.

FINANCIAL STATEMENT AND SUPPORTING INFORMATION

Confidential

To:

Name ______________________ Address ______________________

Business ______________________ ☐ Proprietorship ☐ Partnership ☐ Corporation

For the purpose of procuring and maintaining credit from time to time in any form whatsoever with the above named Bank, for claims and demands against the undersigned, the undersigned submits the following as being a true and accurate statement of its financial condition on the following date, and agree that if any change occurs that materially reduces the means or ability of the undersigned to pay all claims or demands against it, the undersigned will immediately and without delay notify the said Bank, and unless the Bank is so notified it may continue to rely upon the statement herein given as a true and accurate statement of the financial condition of the undersigned as of the close of business.

BALANCE SHEET			
DATED			
ASSETS			
Cash	$		
Marketable Securities (C)			
Receivables (Net)—Customers (A)			
Merchandise (Net)—(B)			
TOTAL CURRENT ASSETS	$		
Deferred Receivables			
Due from Officers and Employees			
Investment in Affiliations—Subsidiaries (D)			
Due from Affiliations—Subsidiaries (D)			
Investments—Other (C)			
Deferred Charges and Prepaid Expenses			
Fixed Assets (Net)—(E & F)			
TOTAL	$		
LIABILITIES			
Notes Payable—Banks			
Notes Payable—Trade			
Accounts Payable—Trade			
Due to Officers and Employees			
Due to Affiliations—Subsidiaries (D)			
Taxes			
TOTAL CURRENT LIABILITIES	$		
TOTAL LIABILITIES	$		
Capital Stock—Preferred*			
Capital Stock—Common*			
Earned Surplus *			
Capital Surplus *			
NET WORTH	$		
TOTAL	$		
AMT. OF CONTINGENT LIABILITIES			
AMOUNT OF ASSETS PLEDGED			
AMOUNT OF LIABILITIES SECURED			

PROFIT AND LOSS STATEMENT			
FROM TO			
NET SALES	$		
Less—Cost of Goods Sold:			
Beginning Inventory			
Add—Purchases			
If Manufacturer Add { Labor			
If Manufacturer Add { Manufacturing Expense			
Total			
Less—Closing Inventory			
Total Cost of Goods Sold	$		
GROSS PROFIT	$		
Less—Selling Expense			
General and Administrative			
Provision for Bad Debts			
Reserve for Taxes (Excl. Fed. Taxes)			
Total Operating Expenses	$		
NET OPERATING PROFIT			
Add—Other Income			
Total Other Income	$		
Less—Other Expenses			
Total Other Expenses	$		
Less—Provision for Federal Taxes			
NET PROFIT	$		
Included Above—Depreciation Charges			
Executive Remuneration			

Is above profit and loss statement on cash ☐ or accrual basis ☐

Are Federal taxes paid on cash ☐ or accrual basis ☐

SURPLUS RECONCILIATION			
Beginning Surplus	$		
Add—Profit			
Less—Dividends or Withdrawals			
Adjustments			
Closing Surplus	$		

*Not to be filled in by proprietorship or partnership

Schedules on reverse side

Exhibit 76A

FINANCIAL STATEMENT AND SUPPORTING INFORMATION (REVERSE SIDE)

(OMIT PENNIES)

(A) TRADE RECEIVABLES—Selling Terms............days		(B) INVENTORY—Purchase Terms............days	
Accounts—Not Due		Finished Goods	
Past due......to......days		Work in Process	
Past due......to......days		Raw Materials	
Past due......to......days		Supplies	
Past due......to......days		Out on Consignment	
Unclassified		Miscellaneous	
Total Trade Accounts		GROSS INVENTORY	
Notes—Current		*Less*—Reserve	
Deferred		NET INVENTORY	
GROSS TRADE RECEIVABLES		Purchase Commitments	
Less—Reserve for Bad Debts		% of Discounts Earned on Purchases	
NET TRADE RECEIVABLES		% of Returns & Allow. on Gross Sales	
Charge-offs in Period		Basis of inventory pricing?	
Recoveries in Period		Was physical count taken?	

(C) INVESTMENTS	Units	Mkt. Val.	Total	(D) AFFL.—SUBSID.	% Owned	Invest.	Due From	Due To
Total				Totals				

(E) FIXED ASSETS	Title in Whose Name	Appraisal Val.	Res. for Dep.	Net Value	Mortgage	Yr. Due
Totals						

(F) FIXED ASSET CHANGES IN PERIOD:

DESCRIPTION	PURCHASES	SOLD OR TRADED	RETIREMENTS	DEP'R'N THEREON
Totals				

(G) LIFE INSURANCE (M indicates thousands of dollars):

INSURED	COMPANY	FACE VALUE	CASH VALUE	LOAN	BENEFICIARY	TYPE	MDSE.	PLANT
		M	M	M		Fire	M	M
		M	M	M		Wind	M	M
		M	M	M		Burglary	M	M
		M	M	M		War Risk	M	M
		M	M	M			M	M
							M	M

(H) MONTH END BALANCES (12 Mos. to Date)		
SALES	MDSE. PAY.	BANK LOANS
1		
2		
3		
4		
5		
6		
7		
8		
9		
10		
11		
12		

(I) OWNERSHIP OF BUSINESS:

NAME	Title	Per Cent Interest	Remuneration

*Incorporated in............ Date............

*Shares Authorized............Outstanding............Par Value $............

Last independent audit by............as of............

Income Tax Payments approved thru............19......

Outstanding Sales Commitments $............

Unsatisfied Judgments $............ Any suits pending?............

*Not to be answered by proprietorship or partnership.

The undersigned certifies that both sides hereof and he information inserted therein has been carefully read and is true and correct.

Date Signed............

Company Name............

By............Title............

Exhibit 77

FINANCIAL STATEMENT--AGRICULTURAL (FRONT SIDE)

FINANCIAL STATEMENT — AGRICULTURAL

From____________________ Address____________________

To

For the purpose of obtaining credit from the above bank, the undersigned makes the following statements of all my (our) assets and liabilities on the______day of____________, 19____

(Fill All Blanks, Writing "No" or "None" Where Necessary To Complete Information)

ASSETS	(Omit Cents)		LIABILITIES	(Omit Cents)	
Cash on Hand and in Bank			Owing this Bank (Schedule 7)		
Cash Value of Life Ins. (Sched. 1)			Owing Other Banks (Schedule 7)		
Securities at Market Value (Schedule 2)			Notes Payable to Merchants: (Schedule 7)		
Accounts Receivable			Owing to Relatives and Friends (Sched. 7)		
Grain & Feed on Hand—Exclusive of Growing Crops (Schedule 3)			Accounts Payable		
Livestock (Schedule 4)			Loans on Life Insurance Policies (Sched. 7)		
Other Current Assets (Describe)			Federal & State Income Taxes		
			Cash Rent Owed and Interest Due		
			Real Estate Taxes Due but Unpaid		
	$		Other Liabilities Due Within One Year (Describe)		
TOTAL CURRENT ASSETS					
Notes or Mortgages Due Me (Us)					
Farm Lands & Improvements (Sched. 5)			*TOTAL CURRENT LIABILITIES	$	
City and Town Property (Schedule 5)			Mortgages on Farm Lands & Other Real Estate (Schedule 7)		
Farm Machinery, Autos, Trucks, Tractors & Other Equip. (Schedule 6)			All Other Debts (Describe)		
Other Assets (Describe)					
			TOTAL LIABILITIES	$	
			NET WORTH	$	
TOTAL ASSETS	$		TOTAL LIABILITIES & NET WORTH		

*INCLUDE UNDER CURRENT LIABILITIES DEBTS DUE WITHIN 12 MONTHS

SCHEDULE 1 — LIFE INSURANCE

Company	Face of Policy	Cash Surrender Value	Loan	Beneficiary
	$	$	$	
TOTAL	$	$	$	

SCHEDULE 2 — SECURITIES OWNED (Including U. S. Govt. Bonds)

Description	Cost Price	Market Value	Amount Pledged To Secure Loans
	$	$	$
TOTAL	$	$	$

SCHEDULE 3 — GRAIN AND FARM PRODUCTS

On Hand				Growing Crops (do not include in assets)	Other Crops (Describe):
____ Bu. Corn	@	$____	$____	____ Acres Corn	____ Acres ____
____ Bu. Wheat	@	____	____	____ Acres Wheat	____ Acres ____
____ Bu. Soy Beans	@	____	____	____ Acres Soy Beans	____ Acres ____
____ Bu. Oats	@	____	____	____ Acres Oats	____ Acres ____
____ Bu. Barley	@	____	____	____ Acres Barley	____ Acres ____
____ Tons Hay	@	____	____	____ Acres Hay	____ Acres ____
____ Bales Cotton	@	____	____	____ Acres Cotton	____
____	@	____	____		
		Total	$____		

Exhibit 77A

FINANCIAL STATEMENT--AGRICULTURAL (REVERSE SIDE)

SCHEDULE 4 — LIVESTOCK

Number		Weight				Number		Weight			
____	Horses	@	$____	per head	$____	____	Hogs, Pigs	@	$____	per head	$____
____	Colts	@	____	per head	____	____	Hogs, Sows	@	____	per head	____
____	Mules	@	____	per head	____	____	Hogs, Feeders	@	____	per head	____
____	Pure Br. Cows	@	____	per head	____	____	Sheeps, Ewes	@	____	per head	____
____	Grade Cows	@	____	per head	____	____	Sheep, Lambs	@	____	per head	____
____	Calves	@	____	per head	____	____	Sheep, Bucks	@	____	per head	____
____	Steers, 1's	@	____	per head	____	____	Poultry	@	____	per head	____
____	Steers, 2's	@	____	per head	____	____	____	@	____	per head	____
____	Heifers	@	____	per head	____	____	____	@	____	per head	____
____	Bulls	@	____	per head	____					Total	$____

SCHEDULE 5 — REAL ESTATE

Description & Location of Property	Title in Name of	Unimproved Improved or	Acres or Lots	Present Value	Amount of Mortgage	How Payable

SCHEDULE 6 — FARM MACHINERY, AUTOS, TRUCKS, TRACTORS & OTHER EQUIPMENT

Units	Type of Equipment	Make	Age	Condition	Market Value	Encumbrances (if any)
				TOTAL	$	$

SCHEDULE 7 — NOTES, MORTGAGES AND LOANS PAYABLE

Amount	To Whom Payable	Dated	When Due	Security Pledged
$				

I rent________acres from________________at a rental of $________cash per acre, ____% corn, ____% grain, per year.

Liability as Endorser, etc. .... $________ Fire Insurance on Buildings .... $________

Cattle and Hogs Insured for .... $________ Other Insurance, Itemize .... $________

Fire Insurance on Grain .... $________

Have you ever made a compromise settlement with creditors or been adjudged bankrupt? ________

Are any suits, judgments or litigation pending either for or against you? ________

The undersigned hereby represents and guarantees that the foregoing statement is in all respects true and correct. In the event of any material change in the financial condition, as set forth herein, the undersigned agrees to notify said bank immediately in writing.

________, 19____ ________________

Date Signed Signature

STATE OF ________ }
COUNTY OF ________ } ss.

________being first duly sworn on oath, deposes and says that he is the person who signed the above and foregoing instrument; that he has read the contents thereof, both written and printed matter, and that same are true and correct.

Subscribed and sworn to before me this______day of________________19____

Notary Public________________

(Seal) My commission expires________________19____

or frequently borrowed and such borrowing has been in recent months, the credit file should contain sufficient essential information to enable the loaning officer to arrive at an immediate decision. Of course, circumstances may warrant additional information which the credit investigator will obtain on a current basis, or from a current balance sheet and profit and loss statement for the interim period which the borrower will provide.

The rendering of an immediate decision is possible because it is a general practice in most banks, especially the larger banks, to review annually the credit file of former borrowers and revise them to reflect current conditions.

If the applicant is not a customer of the bank, the loaning officer will obtain information as to the reason for selecting the bank, the applicant's business, the purpose of the loan, terms of repayment if the loan is granted. If the bank is interested in making the loan based on preliminary information, (unless the applicant presents a balance sheet and profit and loss statement for current and past periods) the loaning officer will provide the applicant with statement and other forms required under the circumstances, which are to be completed by the firm's accountant. During the course of the initial interview, the loaning officer usually obtains from such applicant, information as to the banks with which the applicant does business, business firms with which the company is dealing and the nature and extent of the relationship, together with purpose of the loan.

Should such a non-customer applicant be located in the area served by the bank, it is reasonable to assume that most of the information on the company is already in the credit file, as it is the general policy and practice with aggressive banks to maintain reasonable current information on companies in the area which might be prospects for a sometime relationship.

Following the interview, a memorandum covering the preliminary information is usually prepared by the officer and forwarded for processing to the credit section or officer charged with the responsibility of undertaking credit investigation. It is up to the credit section to investigate the borrower, gather the facts and information covering the condition of the business, the reputation and character of the principals, obtain all financial information such as is contained on balance sheets, and make a comprehensive report to the loan officer to enable him to analyze the situation and arrive at an intelligent conclusion and decision.

The ability to analyze and evaluate financial information which it is necessary for a loan officer to possess in order to safely convert funds available for investment into unsecured loans, in contrast to the process of investing funds in securities or in making loans secured by a pledge of acceptable collateral, is a science predicated on judgment acquired through years of experience in the various phases of credit investigation and credit analysis. Experience provides the judgment which differentiates a good sound loan officer, who has few losses, from a loan officer whose judgment results in losses for the bank, or work outs of slow loans, both of which are costly and time consuming.

Generally it can be said that 40% of the attributes of a good loan officer are acquired by study of the fundamentals of credit and 60% by experience. Nowhere in the banking field is it so important to acquire knowledge by doing, in order to gain the experience and know-how, than in the matter of loaning money unsecured.

Experience cannot be learned from books. The principles of credit investigation and analysis can be learned. However it is only through constant application, under the supervision and guidance of men of vast experiences, that one becomes a competent loan officer.

Another attribute of a good loan officer is that he must have knowledge of economic factors. He must understand business conditions. He must be astute and have a good working knowledge of the businesses to which he loans the funds entrusted to the bank by the depositors and the stockholders.

The experience through which a person develops into a competent loan officer is generally acquired by serving both an apprenticeship and mastership as a

Credit Correspondent
Credit Investigator
Credit Analyst

Because of the importance of these positions in the loaning of funds for investment on an unsecured basis, we will cover their respective functions separately.

CHAPTER XXIV

FUNCTIONS OF A CREDIT CORRESPONDENT AND CREDIT INVESTIGATOR

ONE OF THE MOST IMPORTANT FUNCTIONS of the Credit Department is the answering of credit inquiries pertaining to customers of the bank; and the answering of credit inquiries on those who are not customers of the bank, but who reside in the area serviced by the bank. It is the function of the credit correspondent, in line with general policy established by the directors, to see that such inquiries are handled in a manner to engender good will to the bank, cooperate with the sources of the request, and provide leads for new business.

Prior to assuming the responsibilities of this position, however, the employee has generally had some experience in the other departments of the bank, knows the flow of work, and possesses some knowledge of negotiable instruments. After being assigned to the credit department he generally has performed functions in connection with filing information in the credit file, and checking balances on accounts on which the bank has received a credit inquiry. He has also been taught to check out the relationship of a customer with the bank, either through the central file, or by going from department to department to obtain the necessary information. In addition he has been trained to check death notices, scan newspapers and check to see if the news about bankruptcies, mergers, fires, which are of sufficient importance to find their way into the newspapers, apply to the customers of the bank. If so, it is a customary practice to clip the article to an information sheet in the file, showing the source and the date.

When inquiries for credit information are received from other banks, customers of the bank, department stores, local merchants and others who have a right to credit information, they are referred to the credit correspondent. Generally the first thing the credit correspondent does is to requisition the credit file on the person who is the subject of the inquiry. When a file is removed from the file drawer, it is good practice for the file clerk (or person making the request) to insert an "OUT" card in place of the file, which shows the name of the account and person to whom the file has been delivered. This will serve as notice to others, who might be checking on the same name that there *is* a file and that "something is up" in connection with the account.

If there is a credit file and it contains current information, the the correspondent is in a position to answer the credit inquiry in the manner generally provided for without much delay. If, however, there is no current material in the file, then the correspondent will, depending on the source of the inquiry and importance of the subject of the inquiry, either request the credit investigator to undertake a general investigation, as warranted under the circumstances; or obtain the current balance and other information, available through records of the bank, and reply.

Should the subject of the inquiry, however, be neither a customer of the bank, nor of sufficient local importance to have a credit file, then again, depending on the source of the inquiry and importance of the subject of the inquiry, the correspondent will either request the credit investigator to undertake an investigation, after which the correspondent will reply to the inquiry—or the correspondent will advise the party asking the inquiry that no information is available and possibly suggest another source.

In the answering and replying to credit inquiries, the reply will depend to a great extent upon the right of the inquirer to have interest in the subject. In most instances the person making the inquiry or requesting credit information, if it is a legitimate credit request, will state the reason for the request; or it can be surmised that it is a legitimate request based on the knowledge of the type of business in which the inquirer is engaged. Before a bank answers a credit inquiry it determines if the inquirer is trustworthy, has a legitimate reason for his interest, and is entitled to the service provided by the bank because of business connections, or because he has been referred to the bank by one of its bank correspondents.

Under ordinary circumstances and general conditions, banks,

in replying to a credit inquiry, generally cover the following points:

1. A short history of the individual, corporation or partnership.

2. Approximate length of time such individual, corporation or partnership has maintained a relationship with the bank.

3. A general description of any loaning or credit extended.

4. How the relationship has been conducted.

5. Expression as to the integrity and ability of the individual, partners, or management in the case of a business.

6. An estimate of the net worth based on analysis of financial statements, if available, and provided they are not confidential.

In answering credit inquiries banks generally have printed on the inquiry sheet a disclaimer clause holding that while the bank is furnishing the information which has been obtained from sources they believe are reliable, they do not guarantee the information.

While most inquiries received by a bank concern their own depositors, a number of inquiries will be received concerning companies which are not customers of the bank and, therefore, require investigation.

In order to provide the utmost in service, many progressive banks not only maintain an up-to-date credit file on their customers periodically suggesting they provide them with current balance sheet and profit and loss information, but have current information from independent inquiries on the important customers or important businesses located in the service area of the bank.

The providing of credit information can also produce new business for the bank because an alert credit department, from the inquiries received, often can determine the need of the company, which is the subject of the inquiry, for additional service or credit. This information, when passed on to the loaning officer or one of the officers in the New Business Department, sometimes can be invaluable in developing a bank relationship.

Credit Investigator. When a request is made for an unsecured loan, or loan based on the financial position or wealth of the applicant, as evidenced by financial statements, it is the function of the credit investigator to seek out and obtain reliable and complete information in connection with the business experience or record of the applicant, and to undertake the painstaking investigation of the affairs of the applicant through banking, trade and competitive sources. It is this information, together with the analysis of comparative balance sheets and profit and loss statements made by the credit analyst, which assists the loaning officer to arrive at an intelligent conclusion and decision.

"Mistakes in making loans," Guy C. Kiddoo, former vice president of the First National Bank of Chicago, once said, "are due more largely to failure to get complete information than to errors of judgment. The first essential for making sound loans is exhaustive investigation and careful consideration of every pertinent fact as to financial condition, earnings, and prospects.

"Making loans to prime credit risks is not difficult, where complete and detailed audited balance sheets and earning figures are available and the borrower is well established with a long, successful record. One note of caution is to make sure that companies once in the prime classification, stay there. Managements sometimes go to seed and become complacent with years of success."

The credit investigation generally begins on receipt of a memorandum from the loan officer, which outlines pertinent information in connection with the proposed loan gathered during the visit with the applicant, and the scope of additional information required. Such memorandum is either attached to the credit file, if one is made up, or serves as a basis for undertaking the investigation.

If the memorandum concerns a customer who is currently borrowing, or who borrows occasionally, it can be reasonably assumed that information in the credit file is current. Most progressive banks, in order to maintain current information particularly in the case of borrowing accounts, follow the practice of maintaining a tickler or reminder file, so that at least once a year, at the close of the fiscal year, the customer is asked to provide current figures so that the file can be revised and brought up to date.

Generally, after such revision, the file is reviewed by the credit analyst. Should the new information indicate changes in the financial position or operation of the company which could possibly affect the relationship, such changes are discussed with the officer to whom the account is assigned.

Credit files, if properly prepared and kept current, provide the loaning officers with the essential information, outside perhaps of an interim statement, which enables them to promptly reach a decision on loan applications received from frequent borrowers.

If, however, there is no credit file, or if there is a file and the information is stale, the credit investigator undertakes a new and complete investigation as warranted.

In undertaking a credit investigation, there are a number of sources of information to which the credit investigator refers, of which the following are the most important:

1. The applicant, from information obtained by the loaning officer during the interview which is outlined in the memorandum.
2. Financial statements.
3. The bank's own records.
4. Credit agency reports.
5. Other banks with whom the applicant maintains accounts.
6. Business concerns who sell the applicant raw materials for processing or finished goods for resale.
7. A visit to the plant or office of the applicant.

The Applicant. Generally the loaning officer, when interviewing the applicant, determines what use is to be made of the funds; the method or schedule of repayment, if collateral security is to be required under circumstances; how it is to be delivered or pledged to the bank; inquiries as to other banks with which the applicant does business; firms from whom the applicant makes puchases; customers to whom the applicant sells products and names of accountants who prepare their financial reports and income tax returns. He also discusses the present operation of the business, and asks pertinent questions regarding sales and management.

Following the initial interview, the loaning officer makes a notation in the file, or prepares a memorandum covering the request for the loan. All pertinent information obtained through conversation with the applicant, together with the financial statements, is then sent to the credit investigator.

Financial Statements. The statements, to be of value, must be complete, accurate, and sufficiently detailed to show the book value of the assets and liabilities. They should be supplemented and supported by such additional schedules and explanatory data as may be needed for a complete understanding of the borrower's affairs.

Assets should be neither understated or overstated.

Fixed Assets in particular should, by applying disclosed reserves, reasonably reflect current values.

Accounts Receivable should disclose the accounts which are current, and those which are delinquent or should be charged off, according to general understanding in the trade.

Inventories, both raw materials and finished products should reflect, unless proper reserves have been set up, values at which respective inventory items could be currently and reasonably liquidated.

Liabilities should be fully disclosed, including actual figures together with an estimate of any liabilities which might be contingent upon future performance, pending lawsuits or tax liability.

The loan application should also be accompanied by a profit and loss statement for the current period or the most recent period which is ended, showing the volume of business, the various profit percentages and a reconcilement of surplus or net worth with the previous period.

It is also of help to the credit analyst and loan officer in evaluating the loan application, to be provided with a cash budget forecast. Such projection, covering the term of the loan, should include an estimate of net sales, cost of sales, other disbursements and net receipts; or to make it simpler, a statement of estimated income, expense and profits.

Should the statements tendered by the applicant fail to disclose accurately the true condition of his affairs it is prudent for the loan officer to suggest (and request) that a member of the credit department of the bank make a direct examination of the applicant's books. This may show, among other things, the amount and the age of receivables, the current position of inventory, the amounts owing to the company by principals, which may necessarily have to be subrogated in connection with any loan which is granted.

If the opportunity presents itself for the credit investigator to visit the plant or office of the applicant or to discuss certain aspects of operation with the financial officer or public accountant who handles the preparation of financial reports for the applicant, the answers to many management and operating questions, which may arise in the course of the investigation, can be obtained by using as a guide and where applicable, the following questionnaire check list.

1. Is perpetual inventory control maintained over raw materials, goods in process and finished goods? How often reconciled?

2. Are the accounting procedures used by the company modern and mechanized?

3. Are personnel of the subject firm who handle or have access to money properly bonded?

4. Does the company maintain adequate insurance on its land, buildings, machinery and equipment? Is it protected against public liability and occupational hazards?

5. Are personnel who handle customers' ledgers and collection of charge accounts separated from sales and shipping departments?

6. Are accounts receivable maintained in good order? How often are they audited? How often are they confirmed directly with the creditor?

7. Are the accounts receivable periodically aged? Are the agings properly reflected in the balance sheet submitted to the bank?

8. Are bank accounts reconciled by someone other than the person who authorized the disbursement of funds?

9. Are controls set up over expense accounts to prevent cash from being extracted for unauthorized purposes?

10. Are proceeds from the sale of waste and by-products properly accounted for?

11. Are deductions from remittances of commissions properly verified?

12. Is the payroll of the subject company disbursed by cash or check, and if by cash, are the persons making the disbursements properly bonded and protected from holdup?

13. Are the credit policies of the subject company adequate in line with current economic conditions?

14. Is sufficient credit checking undertaken in connection with new customers in order to avoid bad or slow accounts?

15. Is there effective cooperation between the sales department and the credit department?

16. Does the company have definite and effective policies and practices in connection with handling delinquent accounts?

17. What procedure is followed in curtailing or restricting

deliveries or shipments when an account becomes slow; and how often, or under what circumstances, are reports of delinquent accounts made to the treasurer or chief executive officer?

18. Does the company follow a complete working budget for all operations?

19. Does the company have a good system of production control?

20. Are requirements for materials and goods to be processed forecast sufficiently in advance to provide a normal flow of manufacturing without upsetting or forcing a change in the sales price?

21. Are there any income tax liabilities for prior years? How recently have returns been audited and approved?

Customers or prospects interested in developing a satisfactory credit relationship with a bank should be willing to completely answer such questions or cooperate so that answers are obtained. Should they hesitate, or hedge their replies, an alert credit investigator or loan officer should discover, if possible, the reason for reluctance in cooperating.

The Bank's Own Records. It is the practice in some banks to maintain a file or record which they refer to as a central file of information. Sometimes this consists of a form on which is noted the various relationships a person maintains with the bank. Other banks maintain one or several files in which a new account memorandum if used, copies of letters, correspondence in connection with a credit reference or inquiry, and newpspaper reports of legal action or important information affecting the subject are filed. Such files are as extensive or simple as is desired by management.

Regardless, however, of the practice followed, an alert credit investigator will always check for information on the subject of investigation within the bank, for the reason that on occasion a fact of apparent insignificance turns out to be the key of great importance in credit decisions.

An alert credit investigator, who is also astute, will, after making a check of the sources of information within the bank, summarize his findings and file it in the credit file for future use and reference.

Credit Agencies. As this is the first time we have referred to credit agencies as such, it might be well to tell something about their founding and commercial function.

In studying mediums of exchange, it was pointed out that mediums such as receipts, or objects used in place of gold, had value because of the warranty of the issuer of the medium, and that such medium represented, and could be exchanged for, gold or articles of fixed value.

The reputation of the person issuing such mediums was not only based on the fact that it was *believed* there was actual gold available in exchange for such medium, but that the person issuing such medium properly conducted his business affairs; that other persons vouched for his character and honesty; and that he would redeem such medium in gold upon presentation.

In like manner, merchants who entrusted their wealth for safekeeping to the goldsmith could refer those with whom they wished to do business to the goldsmith, who would assure the prospective purchaser of the honesty and integrity of the seller. In other words the goldsmith rendered a "credit report" on the seller.

With the expansion and development of business, it became quite common practice, when a person was moving or relocating in another part of the country, to take with him a letter of introduction or reference signed by a banker, or someone with an excellent reputation who was widely known, which when presented to a local banker or merchant, succeeded in establishing his credit and reputation.

Once credit was established with one merchant, the party referred others to this merchant for reference as to his financial position and manner of conducting his business affairs.

In time, as cities grew, commerce developed and trade was expanded using open accounts. Merchants pooled their information and experience on the credit standing and payment habits of their customers, thus forming credit bureaus. Men of reputation, who because of their position were frequently called upon to vouch for a person or give reference, began to provide information on the financial standing, method of operation, and personal reputation of individuals and businesses for a fee. Thus were born the credit agencies whose functions and services today provide information for the impartial evaluation and financial position of individuals, partnerships and corporations.

The principal services rendered by such agencies are in connection with reporting on the:

1. History of the enteprise—date organized or founded.
2. Corporate setup—class of stock—debt.
3. Type of operation—manufacturing—wholesale—retail.
4. Management—titles—ages—background—directors—officers.
5. Financial position—balance sheet—profit and loss figures.
6. Real estate holdings.
7. Liabilities—claims or judgments.
8. Purchasing terms—method of paying bills—discounting.
9. Selling terms—discounts—30 days—cash.

Many of these agencies, such as Dun and Bradstreet, Hills Reports, and National Credit Office, to mention a few, function on a nationwide basis, and have offices in the principal cities. Others providing similar services function in a particular area.

In addition, many local associations such as the Chamber of Commerce, Association of Commerce, and Better Business Bureau, provide certain types of financial and other information on business located in the town or adjacent area, and are often contacted by credit investigators for particular information.

Whenever a loaning officer is evaluating an application for credit of a sizeable amount, and wishes to corroborate information and data independently gathered by the credit investigator, or wishes to obtain special information, he will in his memorandum, unless it is accepted procedure, request the investigator to obtain a credit or agency report. It is up to the credit investigator to select the agency to make the report which in his opinion and judgment is set up to provide the particular information required under the circumstances. Such a report, together with other information gathered by the credit investigator in undertaking the investigation, is invaluable to the credit analyst in making his evaluation of the credit, and in making his report to the loan officer which will assist him in making his decision.

Other Banks with Which the Applicant Maintains Accounts. This type of investigation is undertaken in connection with three situations: (a) where a business firm or company maintains accounts with more than one bank, (b) where a company or business firm is changing banking relationships, (c) where an investigation of a company or business is being undertaken with a bank in connection with a credit inquiry received from the bank's customer or another bank.

Generally when a company or business maintains accounts and a borrowing relationship with more than one bank, there is a free exchange of information at all times, and comparison of information when the file is revised following receipt of annual or periodical financial reports.

In checking a company or business name with another bank in connection with a change in relationship, or in behalf of a customer or another bank, answers to questions on the following check list should be obtained, to the extent required or warranted under the circumstances.

1. When (date) was the company or business established?

2. If incorporated, under what laws, and the amount of authorized and paid capital?

3. What is the background of the officers of the business if it was recently incorporated?

4. How long have the officers been associated with the company?

5. Are they connected with any other business?

6. Is the company controlled by another?

7. Have the principals ever failed in business? If so, obtain full particulars.

8. Is the management capable, conservative and morally responsible?

9. Has there been any change in the organization recently? If so, what effect will it have on the business?

10. Do the financial statements show progress or loss over a period of years? Explain changes.

11. What is the date of the last financial statement filed with the bank?

12. How does the bank regard the firm's position as reflected by its statements?

13. Does the bank recommend the concern as worthy of confidence and credit?

14. What other banks have the account?

15. How high and to what extent does the bank grant accommodation and in what form?

16. If notes are endorsed or guaranteed, who are the endorsers or guarantors?

17. Is borrowing continuous?

18. Have accommodations ever been refused? Why?
19. Have accommodations ever been secured?
20. What class of assets were pledged as collateral security?
21. Have borrowings been seasonal?
22. What range of balances is maintained in the account?
23. Are overdrafts permitted? Under what circumstances?
24. Have checks been returned for insufficient funds?
25. Have checks been returned drawn against uncollected funds?
26. When did the bank last investigate the name?
27. Was the information secured favorable or unfavorable?

If the subject of the bank investigation is an individual, the following questions should be asked—where applicable.

1. How old is the individual?
2. With what company or enterprise is he connected?
3. What is his present position?
4. How long has he been employed in his present position, or engaged in professional work?
5. What is his annual salary or income?
6. Does he have any other source of income?
7. Does he own his own home?
8. What was his previous connection or business?
9. How many years so engaged before entering present business?
10. Is he considered to be a solid citizen?
11. How is he regarded by his associates?
12. Are there any judgments against him?
13. What is the condition of his health?
14. Is he prompt in meeting his obligations?
15. Would you consider him responsible for the amount of the accommodation requested?

Business Concerns Who Sell the Applicant. In checking with suppliers who sell raw materials to the company for processing, or finished goods for re-sale or distribution, answers to the questions on the following check list, where applicable, will assist in establishing the position of the company in the trade.

1. How long have they been selling the subject?
2. What amount of credit is extended?
3. Are regular, special or cash terms granted?

4. If special or cash terms are granted, what is the reason?
5. How are bills paid?
6. If not paid according to terms, what is the reason?
7. If sold in the past, would credit relations be resumed at the present time?
8. What is the general condition in the trade?
9. Do you have a personal acquaintance with the management?
10. How do you regard management?
11. Is management conservative or speculatively inclined?
12. What other concerns are selling the subject?

A Visit to the Plant or Office of the Applicant. One of the most important sources of information in connection with a credit investigation is an observation visit to the office, or tour of the plant of the applicant. This is in addition to obtaining financial information, as previously recommended, if the occasion warrants. The investigator may not be an expert in the processes going on, but he can sense the atmosphere of the place, whether the employees are cheerful and busy, whether the housekeeping is clean and whether the management is concentrated in the hands of one man, or whether there is a competent staff of assistants to whom authority and responsibility is soundly delegated.

Upon completion of the investigation, and to the extent warranted under the circumstances, the credit investigator summarizes his findings in a report to which is attached copies of letters written in connection with the investigation, the replies, and supporting data which after possible use and review by the credit analyst or loaning officer, is filed in the proper section in the credit file.

In order to present the results and findings of the credit investigation in an orderly and efficient manner, credit investigators in many banks, especially those which have a large volume of loans, report the results of their findings in orderly sequence under the following or similar headings.

1. *History.* The history of the business—date of its inception—dates of consolidation or mergers, if any—general background and experience of those charged with management responsibility—information pertaining to operations which the credit investigator might have discovered through a visit to the office or plant of the company—fire losses—litigation which might affect the reputation, progress or standing of the firm, or its earnings.

2. *Method of Operations.* Whether the company operates as manufacturer, retailer, importer or wholesaler—terms of purchas-ng—general methods of distribution—selling or credit terms—gen-ral type or class of customers—the markup and profit on goods old.

3. *Subsidiary or Affiliated Businesses.* Connections or affilia-ions with other companies—subsidiary operations—the extent of the elationship particularly in connection with financial and manage-nent assistance. (Should the interest in subsidiaries be substantial, r there is a close relationship between the company being investi-ated and other companies, it might be necessary to request the pplicant to provide a consolidated balance sheet and profit and oss statement so that the entire operating picture can be available evaluating the credit.)

4. *Other Bank Connections.* Names of banks with which the pplicant maintains a relationship—date account was opened—range f balance maintained.

5. *Credit Extensions and Borrowings.* Names of banks or nancial institutions with which the applicant maintains a borrow-ng relationship—type and form of the borrowing—endorsements—uarantees—pledge of accounts receivable, inventory or other assets f the company—line of credit—individual term borrowings.

6. *The Current Balance Sheet.* Explanation of any extraordinary tems on the balance sheet which is attached, with particular at-ention being paid to the suporting comments.

7. *Profit and Loss Statements.* Statements which are attached hould show on a comparative basis, the profit or loss for prior ears to enable the credit analyst and loaning officer to determine he progress of the company based on annual sales. (It is the credit nvestigator's responsibility to see that the financial statements and chedules, required under the circumstances, are in the file or at-ached to the report so they are available for use of the credit nalyst.)

8. *Management Details.* Pertinent information regarding the pplicant disclosed through contacts made with the officers, di-ectors or administrative personnel of the company or based on bservations made by the investigator during contacts with the ersonnel of the company.

9. *Credit Agency Reports and Trade Comments.* Credit report provided by recognized mercantile agencies—condensed reports o the company obtained by the investigator through checking wit those in the trade—those engaged in similar lines of business, o suppliers of materials to the company.

10. *Concluding Remarks.* Observations of the credit investi gator not otherwise stated—investigator's opinion as to the manage ment, operations and financial condition of the company in lin with the request for credit. (Where a place in the report is pro vided for the "opinion" of the investigator, it is usually done s for the purpose of training, that is, to enable the credit analyst an loaning officer to become familiar with the thinking of the cred investigator so they can point out to him certain objectives and b giving him the benefit of their experience, thus contribute to h training and development as a future credit analyst and loanin officer.)

This report, together with balance sheets and profit and los statements, is then referred to the credit analyst for spreading an analysis of financial figures. The credit analyst also reviews the in formation supplied by the investigator to determine if figures, a submitted, are substantiated or confirmed by the information pre sented by the credit investigator through his checkings and in quiries.

Upon completion of the review, together with pertinent com ments of the credit analyst, the file is either referred to the loa officer, or the contents discussed with the loan officer, to assi him in reaching a decision in connection with the loan applicatio

It is common practice in many banks in connection with a ne account, to have the credit investigator make a check to ascertai whether or not the new depositor is morally responsible, and if th business will measure up to the standards set up by the manageme of the bank.

In order to protect the reputation of the bank and avoid an reflections against those who are customers and depositors of th bank, most banks are very selective as to the character of those wh seek to do business with them. Whenever a credit investigatio of a new customer discloses a reputation which reflects against th honesty or integrity of the person, it is a general practice for bank to request the subject party to close the account and termina he relationship. This is to avoid the bank becoming involved in nswering credit inquiries and being requested to produce their ecords in case of tax or other litigation.

This preliminary investigation also provides information which s sometimes helpful in answering future credit inquiries. Bankers n making such investigation should not hesitate to check with ompeting banks, as failure to do so may result in having an un- esirable or troublesome account unloaded on them which may be he source of future embarrassment.

CHAPTER XXV

THE FUNCTIONS OF A CREDIT ANALYST

THE CREDIT ANALYST HAS A NUMBER OF func tions to perform in discharging the responsibilities of the positior of which the most important are to:

1. Analyze and evaluate financial and operating informatio obtained by the credit investigator, or supplied by the applican The information supplied by the applicant generally includes balance sheet showing the current assets and liabilities, togethe with a profit or loss statement covering the results of operation fc the current annual or semi-annual period.

2. Condense such financial information from the balance shee and spread to the bank's own form.

3. Review and analyze the operating results of the busine as reflected in the profit and loss statement.

4. Undertake the necessary computations and determine th respective operating ratios to be used in anlyzing the progress the business.

6. Analyze and evaluate the historical and financial informatio gathered and developed by the credit investigator and from trad and agency reports, and condense for information and guidance the loan officer.

THE BALANCE SHEET

Information required by a loaning officer in reaching a decisio as to approving or declining a loan application will vary, dependin on the nature of the business, the amount of loan requested, an terms and conditions of payment. To be assured of obtaining a curate and reliable information, loan officers, in an ever increasin number, are requiring prospective borrowers to submit figures i the form of an audit prepared by a public or certified accountan In undertaking an audit which meets all the requirements and full discloses the financial condition of the company being audite e accountant must be permitted not only to make such tests and hecks as he considers necessary in order to give an unqualified rofessional opinion, but disclose the extent to which receivables nd inventory were confirmed and verified, and make full disclosure s to any possible contingent liabilities.

Audit reports are classified into two groups, the short form hich contains only the financial statement and an opinion; and e long form which in addition to the financial statements and pinion contains explanatory and analytical schedules together with escriptive supplementary comments on the quality and nature of e assets and liabilities.

The long form is generally considered to be the most acceptable banks, but most of all to the businessman because it provides him ith information which assists him in more profitable operation, nd in conducting negotiations with the bank for forms of credit.

In order to assist the credit analyst in properly evaluating and nalyzing the information provided through financial statements, se of the following descriptive outline of disclosure and question- aire, which follows the order of listing of assets and liabilities gen- rally found in balance sheets, will be found helpful.

Cash. Cash should be segregated as to the amount on hand in ossession of the treasurer or cashier; funds deposited with banks; nd any funds restricted, pledged or earmarked for some special urpose, or which are not immediately available.

1. Are there any memorandums covering withdrawals or ad- ances made to officers or employees of the company, or for ex- enses, included in cash? If so, they should be indicated.

2. Is any cash represented by funds held by subsidiary com- anies? If so, such amounts should be deducted and only included a consolidated statement is being analyzed.

3. Are funds deposited with foreign banks, whose withdrawal nd use is restricted, included in cash? If so, this should be clearly ated in order that proper accounting can be made in determining e quick assets.

4. Are any funds represented by cash held by companies in the rocess of liquidation, or where the funds are not readily available r use by the company? If so, this should be stated so that the re- ective amounts can be properly classified.

Notes Receivable. Notes Receivable should be classified as to amounts (a) due from officers or principals (b) owed by affiliates c subsidiaries (c) arising out of bona fide sale of goods or service which constitutes the regular business of the company.

Notes given in trade should be aged by date of origin an analyzed to show those not due, those past due, which are secure and which unsecured. If the notes are secured, the nature of th securities should be disclosed. Notes other than those taken i trade should be itemized by date of origin, the maker, the maturit the security and the purpose for which taken.

1. Is it the usual practice of the business to accept customer notes in payment of invoices?

2. Are such notes held by the company or are they pledge with a bank or finance company?

3. If so, do the figures represent the total amount of the not or are they the net entries deducting hypothecated and pledge notes which should be carried in notes or accounts payable. (notes payable are deducted, the statement does not correctly refle the condition of the business. All liabilities and assets should b correctly stated, and no deductions made which can be misleadin in evaluating the financial condition of the company. Such note if discounted, should be carried in the accounts or notes payabl on the liability side.)

4. Are the notes given to cover actual purchases? If not, b certain that the notes are not given in lieu of payment by concer which in the trade are considered to be slow or of dubious characte

5. Are notes of affiliated or subsidiary companies carried i notes receivable? If so, they should be properly evaluated b reference to a consolidated statement.

6. Are notes of officers and employees, covering withdrawa or loans carried in accounts receivable? If so, they should b clearly stated and deducted from quick assets. Generally, unle they are amply secured by non-affiliated collateral, they are nor collectable in case of failure or financial difficulty of the company.

7. Do notes given in settlement of trade cover current transa tions? Are they renewal notes or notes given in payment of pa due or delinquent accounts? Notes covering not recent transactior should be carefully checked as they may indicate a weakness i credit, laxity in sales policy and neglect in collecting accounts du

8. Are the notes payable within a six-month period or do they xtend over a long period of time? If notes are given and repayable ver a relatively long period of time, particular attention should e given as to setting up proper reserves or eliminating them as uick assets.

9. Are notes which are uncollected and considered worthless eing carried under notes receivable? If so, such notes should e immediately charged off, or deducted from the assets in evaluatg the net worth of the company.

Accounts Receivable. Accounts Receivable should be classified to amounts (a) due from officers or principals, (b) owed by afiates or from subsidiaries, (c) arising out of bona fide sale of goods services which constitute the regular business of the company.

Accounts Receivable from trade customers, in like manner, ould be aged to show accounts (I) current and not yet due, (II) ose due and payable, and (III) those 30-60-90 days past due from rms of sale.

Should this information not be readily available from reports rnished, then a report similar to that shown in Exhibit 78 should prepared for the information of the bank, either by the comny's auditor, outside accountant, or a member of the bank's edit investigation staff.

1. What percentage of the outstanding accounts receivable are accordance with the general policy of the company regarding les on open account? The answer to this question determines the gree of liquidity of accounts receivable.

2. Are any accounts due from subsidiary or affiliated companies account of advances made to them? Unless this is a consolidated port, particular attention should be paid to any such items and ey should be properly analyzed and segregated from other quick sets.

3. Do any of the accounts receivable represent amounts due om officers, directors, employees for advances against salary, exnses or other purposes? Particular attention should be paid to ch items, as such items or obligations reflect against management.

4. Have any of the accounts receivable been sold or assigned? sclosure should be made of any accounts pledged or assigned secure indebtedness, and on any accounts sold without recourse.

Exhibit 78

AUDITORS ACCOUNT RECEIVABLE REPORT

AUDITORS ACCOUNT RECEIVABLE REPORT

ACCOUNT_____ DATE_____ AUDITOR_____

_____ BUSINESS_____ LAST AUDIT_____

CORPORATION ☐ PARTNERSHIP ☐ SOLE OWNER ☐ Officer Handling Account_____

From last statement dated_____ Source_____ Period_____

Current Assets .... $_____ Sales .... $_____

Current Liabilities .... _____ Returns .... _____

Fixed Assets .... _____

Net Worth .... _____ Net Profits Before/After Taxes .... _____

Withdrawals .... _____

Amount of Loan $_____ Collateral per our records $_____

Loan Basis_____

Rate_____

CONDITION OF RECORDS: Excellent ☐ Good ☐ Fair ☐ Poor ☐

General Ledger posted to:_____ Do records indicate assignment:_____

Subsidiary records posted to:_____ Cash Book posted to:_____

Are inventory records adequate?_____

Give details of other loans, mortgages or financing:_____

Usual selling terms:_____

	Portion Checked	Current	Past Due: 1-30	30-60	60-90	Over 90
Receivables	_____	$	$	$	$	$
Payables		$	$	$	$	$

Comment:_____

COLLATERAL IRREGULARITIES:

Unreported Collections .... $_____ Disputed Accounts .... $_____

Unreported Returns .... _____ Consignments .... _____

Past Due Accounts .... _____ Miscellaneous .... _____

Contra Accounts .... _____ Total.................. _____

Percentage of loan to clean collateral_____

Disposition of irregularities_____

1. Were verifications made:_____ No. sent_____ No. reported_____
2. Were bank statements reconciled?_____ for month of_____
3. Other bank accounts_____
4. Were cancelled checks inspected and in order?_____
5. Were cash receipts test checked and in order?_____
6. Were disbursements test checked and in order?_____
7. Were repurchases checked through cash book and bank account?_____
8. Percentage of receivables assigned to us is_____
9. Average amount of invoices assigned to us is_____
10. Does the company make a practice of not pledging certain active accounts?_____
11. Were evidences of shipment checked?_____
12. What is income tax status?_____ Withholding Taxes_____ Social Security_____
13. Is insurance adequate?_____
14. What was bad debt experience?_____ Recoveries?_____

Note—Auditor will set forth on the reverse side other items of importance, explanation of any irregularities noticed, and explanatio adverse information contained herein, together with his general reaction to the account.

Signed_____

Carried in Stock by Cadwallader & Johnson, Chicago. Form No. C-114. Robert Morris Associates.

Should such accounts have been sold or pledged, they should be correctly reflected in accounts payable.

5. Are accounts, where goods have been assigned on consignment, included in accounts receivable? Where goods are under consignment, they should be carried in inventory and disclose that they are under consignment. In no case should they be included in accounts receivable which indicates that the merchandise has been sold or that a contract exists for the payment.

6. Are any uncollectable, old or worthless accounts included in the accounts receivable? Accounts receivable to truly reflect current assets should be current. Accounts carried over and beyond the normal time should be charged off, and proper notations made for claims against the reserve account.

7. Based on the aging of the receivables, are reserves for bad debts sufficient to provide for slow and deliquent accounts? In case proper reserves have not been set up, an estimate, based on normal reserve requirements for that type of business, should be set up by deducting from undivided profits or surplus an amount sufficient for the purpose intended.

Inventory. Whenever practical, inventory should be broken down by stages of manufacture, that is (a) raw materials, (b) goods in process, (c) finished goods. In addition, the various forms of inventory should be classified by location, departments or products. In this connection, any finished goods shipped out on consignment should be so marked and so indicated on the statement.

As a further indication of sound business practice, a footnote should fully explain the basis for valuing merchandise and inventory whether it is on a (1) first-in, first-out; (2) last-in, first-out; (3) cost or market; or whatever method is used for valuation purposes. In addition, where such inventory system of valuation has been used, it is a help to the banker to indicate if the method followed by the company has been approved by the Internal Revenue Department.

Raw Materials. This figure should show the raw materials unprocessed, and if they are carried on the books at cost or market, in order that proper valuation can be made.

1. Does the raw material, or goods awaiting processing, consist of merchandise of such a character that it could be sold without

loss, or does it consist of special parts or special classes of merchan dise adaptable for only one purpose for which there would be littl market in the event of a liquidation? Should such material no have a ready market, it is obvious that adjustment should be mad in the reserve account to provide for such material to be costed a market.

2. Does the raw material figure include all materials purchase and delivered for which payment has not been made? If so, ac counts payable should disclose the amount owed for such ra material.

Goods in Process. This figure should disclose the amount o goods taken out of raw material inventory, which is in the proces of being converted, at the price at which it was carried in the ra material inventory.

1. Does test checking indicate material removed from "Ra Material Inventory" and placed into "Work in Process Inventory" truly reflect the actual cost of such material? If not, adjustmen should be made to correctly reflect this transaction.

Inventory—Finished or Processed. Such inventory should con sist of manufactured or processed goods immediately available fo sale or shipment, and represent the cost of the raw material plus th addition of conversion costs and administrative expense applicabl to conversion.

1. Does the finished merchandise consist of staple articles fo which there is a constant demand or ready sale?

2. Does the merchandise carried in finished or processed good consist of up-to-date and marketable merchandise; or are there old obsolete, out of date types of merchandise for which there is littl market included in this figure? Should this be the case, the ol or obsolete stock should be deducted from the finished merchandis with a corresponding adjustment made in the surplus or net wort accounts.

3. Does the company make a practice of periodically evaluat ing its finished goods inventory and liquidating it; or carry it i current inventory by making a proper adjustment to reserves Proper analysis of this factor should be undertaken in order t determine that finished merchandise or goods which are warehouse have an established current value.

Investments. Investments which consist of marketable stock onds, and other securities, should be itemized and carry a detailed escription of the security; when it was purchased; price at which was purchased; the rate of interest or dividends; and, in the case f a bond, when it matures.

1. Are any securities in the investment portfolio those of ffiliated, or subsidiary companies?

2. If securities in the investment portfolio are stocks or bonds f affiliated companies, are there any contingent liabilities or con-actual obligations incurred through ownership? It is important fully understand this situation, as any contingent liability should e noted and proper reserves set aside, or adjustments made in the apital account to provide for it.

3. Are securities carried in the investment portfolio thoroughly arketable? If not, reasons for carrying such securities should be efinitely understood. Unless there are good and legitimate rea-ons for carrying such securities and they are readily marketable, ey should not be considered as fixed assets.

4. Are any securities carried in the investment account of a eculative nature, or have funds of the company been invested ith the thought that the company could profit from an apprecia-on in the value? If securities are being carried for speculative urposes, it reflects on the management of the company who might so be speculating in raw material inventory, and over-extensions f credit to the trade in order to increase sales.

Cash Surrender Value of Life Insurance. Often as a protection the stockholders a company will insure the lives of the prin-pals so that in the event of death, the sum will be paid to the ompany to partially compensate them for the loss incurred through bsence of management. Should this be the case, the records ould clearly show the name of the insured, the insurer, the bene-ciaries, the cash surrender value, and the description of any in-ebtedness secured by the assignment of any of the policies listed.

1. Is it the policy of the company to carry life insurance on the ves of the principals? If so, are the assignments in order, and is e company named as the beneficiary?

Land, Buildings, Other Real Estate. The total investment of e company in real estate, land, and buildings, should be clearly own, plus the amount set aside for depreciation.

1. Does the amount as shown on the balance sheet for rea estate and plant represent the gross or net value after deductin the mortgage, if any? If the property is subject to an encum brance, it should be clearly shown. Also, if the property is in th name of any person other than the company, it should be shown.

2. If the property is subject to a mortgage, does it cover onl the land and buildings, or also the machinery and equipment other additions and chattels to the property? If at all possible mortgages should cover specific property.

3. Is the property suited or adaptable for the business con ducted, and is it maintained in good condition? Failure of a com pany to take proper care of their land and buildings only result in extraordinary expenses at a later period. Current provisio should be made to properly maintain buildings.

4. Are buildings properly protected by insurance of all type necessary under the circumstances to provide ample protection i the event of fire, wind storm, and public liability? Unless this i done, recommendation should be made to provide proper coverag to protect the bank against any contingent liability in the event o fire, wind storm or other damage.

5. Are there any general, special assessments or other ta liens unpaid against the property? This should be checked an if there are liens, proper reserves should be set up by deductin such amount from net worth.

Machinery and Fixtures. Machinery and fixtures should be rep resented on the balance sheet at cost, less normal depreciation or with ample reserves in case machinery and equipment has bee used beyond its life expectancy.

1. Is machinery and equipment modern so as to provide effi ciency in operation? If not, have ample reserve provisions bee made to replace such machinery and equipment?

2. Does machinery and equipment carried as assets of th company have current market value in case of liquidation of th company; or trade in value in the event of exchanging such ma chinery and equipment for new machinery and equipment? Ma chinery and equipment should be appraised so as to prove th reserve for depreciation plus asset value, as disclosed in the bal ance sheet of the company, is sufficient for replacement.

3. Is machinery and equipment covered by a chattel mortgage, or are amounts owed others for such machinery and equipment? If chattel mortgages have been given on the machinery and equipment, either in payment or to raise money, it should be so disclosed in the financial statement by a corresponding entry in accounts or notes payable.

Other Assets. Other charges or expenses which are deferred or prepaid should be itemized in efficient detail so they can be readily identified. This includes tax refund claims, which should be described in detail; and the value and basis of value of such intangible assets as copyrights, patents, franchises, advertising, good will. The latter items which have no particular value from a credit standpoint, only have value to the company in the event of sale, consolidation or merger. If carried for any other than nominal amounts they should be properly adjusted by a reserve, or deduction from net worth accounts.

Notes Payable. Notes payable should be classified as to amounts (a) owed banks, (b) owed the trade, (c) owed principals of the company and others.

Notes payable should be set up on a separate schedule showing the name of the payee, date, terms, maturity, security if any, and scrutinized for any subordination agreements or restrictions covering the payment of the notes.

If such notes are guaranteed or endorsed, the name of the guarantor or endorser should be given; likewise, if such notes are secured, a complete description of the collateral should be stated in the schedule.

1. Are notes payable issued in settlement of trade accounts?

2. Is this a customary practice in this type of business or are notes given for overdue accounts? If given for overdue accounts, is it an indication that the company is getting careless in their collection practices, maintaining too loose control over credit, or failing to properly budget and control expenses?

3. In connection with notes for borrowed money given to their own bank, is borrowing seasonal or steady?

4. Are any of these borrowings from banks in the form of commercial paper, that is notes which have been sold by note brokers? The type and duration of borrowing from a bank will

indicate whether the concern is maintaining adequate credit channels to take care of an emergency.

5. Are any notes secured by collateral? This is a point to watch because if any outstanding indebtedness is guaranteed or secured, and the company endeavors to obtain credit from a bank, the bank should share in the collateral.

6. Do any notes represent loans or advances from officers, directors, members of the family, or persons closely associated with the company? This is a good point to watch as while it might indicate that those closely identified with the company are willing to risk additional funds, there is also a possibility that because of their closeness, in the event of impending trouble, they might endeavor to get out from under to the detriment of other creditors; or obtain security or agreements giving them a prior claim.

7. Does the amount of notes payable include all outstanding notes, or have some been deducted from accounts and notes receivable? Deductions of such type or offsets are never permissable as they clearly understate the liability.

8. In tracing the application of funds, has money borrowed been used for taking discounts, settling open accounts, or making additional purchases?

9. Has the money borrowed been used to purchase machinery and equipment, property, or to fund additions to the plant? This should be carefully checked as it is generally not good policy for a company to borrow funds repayable over a short period of time to purchase fixed or slow assets, which should be properly funded over a long period of time.

10. Were the proceeds of such notes used for paying dividends? This is a poor policy and should be discouraged by the bank because all obligations should be provided for before distributing profits to shareholders.

Accounts Payable. Accounts payable to other than trade creditors should be segregated, itemized and described. Trade accounts should be summarized by date of origin and customary purchase terms. Items accrued, such as interest and taxes, should be set forth as to class of item.

1. Are there any amounts due to affiliated or subsidiary companies?

2. Are there any amounts due to stockholders, directors, officers or employees, or to those closely identified with the business? If so, the reason for such indebtedness should be explained.

3. What percentage of the accounts are past due?

4. Are satisfactory efforts being made to retire these obligations? Explain.

5. Have any of the accounts been secured in any manner as by the pledging of security, or a guarantee which makes them a preferred creditor? Such items should be carefully investigated and securities, if pledged, deducted from quick assets in evaluating the statement.

6. Have all the liabilities of each and every kind, and all bills owed by the company in payment of merchandise, been properly reflected in accounts payable? As this is absolutely necessary to maintain good credit, this item should be carefully checked.

Bonded Debt. A full description should be made of any mortgages and non-current indebtedness so as to indicate the payee, security, interest rate, maturity, any sinking fund requirements, and major covenants which must be observed.

1. Does the bond issue or mortgage represent a lien on only the real estate and the buildings?

2. Does the bond issue or mortgage cover general assets in addition to the real estate and buildings? This should be determined, because if the mortgage or bond issue covers general assets, the bond holder has a first lien on all such assets.

3. Are there sinking fund provisions, and if so, are they being complied with? It is important that sinking fund provisions be currently maintained in order for the company to continue in good credit standing.

Other Liabilities. Any accruals such as for interest, taxes, acceptances, or the existence of any contingent liabilities such as guarantees, endorsements, discounted receivables, commitments for the purchase of machinery, contracts covering construction, and the amount of outstanding purchase commitments should be stated.

1. Does review and examination disclose that accrued items in connection with taxes, interest, wages, rents and other items have not been taken into consideration in making up the state-

ment? These items should be frankly and honestly stated to correctly reflect the financial position of the company.

Should there be a question as to the tax liability or insurance coverage, the company should be requested to complete an Insurance and Tax Questionnaire, similar to that shown in Exhibit 79.

Reserves. Reserve accounts are of three types; (a) those which are deducted from an asset, (b) funds reserved for a definite liability, (c) or a portion of earned surplus which is earmarked for a specific purpose. All reserve accounts should be clearly identified as to nature and purpose and an explanation provided covering all changes in the reserve accounts during the accounting period, or since the last accounting period. In a soundly operated business enterprise proper reserves should always be maintained.

1. Are reserves adequate to provide for maturing obligations?

2. Are reserves set up to provide for depreciation of buildings, machinery, equipment or their replacement, adequate and sufficient under current valuations. This is particularly important during a period of increased costs where perhaps a replacement for a piece of machinery or equipment being depreciated is now two or three times the original cost. Obviously depreciation cannot be changed, but differences should be compensated for by the setting up of adequate reserves. (See "Machinery and Equipment")

3. Are reserves for bad accounts sufficient, based on losses and items charged off during the past several years?

Capital Accounts. The various classes of stock representing ownership in the business should be clearly stated as to type, par value, dividend rights, number of shares authorized, number of shares issued and outstanding, and number of shares held in the treasury. Preferred stock should be described as to whether it is convertible, cumulative, or callable; provisions, if any, for retirement; and what provisions cover the preferred stock in the event of dividend suspension.

1. Are all classes of stock showing amount authorized, amount issued, and amount retained in the treasury correctly reflected on the statement?

2. Are there notes and accounts payable which, because of

Exhibit 79

INSURANCE AND TAX QUESTIONNAIRE

Confidential

INSURANCE AND TAX QUESTIONNAIRE

To Be Submitted With Your Robert Morris Associates Form No. C-110H Financial Statement or Audit Report.

TO:______________________________

BY: Name______________________________

Address______________________________

STATEMENT DATED____________________ Do not leave any questions unanswered.

INSURANCE COVERAGE

It is suggested that your Insurance Broker may be helpful in the preparation of this section.

PLEASE LIST AMOUNTS IN EVEN THOUSANDS	AMOUNT	% OF CO-INS.
Contents — Fire & Extended Coverage		
Contents — Sprinkler		
Building — Fire & Extended Coverage		
Use and Occupancy (Business Interruption)		
Machinery and Equipment		
Premises — Public Liability		
Fidelity Bond on Employees		
Vehicles: Public Liability		
Vehicles: Property Damage		

Please list any other types of insurance on reverse side.

TAXES

1) Have you filed federal income tax returns for all years to date?____________________
2) Furnish name of accountant, attorney, or other person who supervises the preparation of your federal income tax returns____________________
3) For what year was your return last examined and approved?____________________
   Have you waived any rights?____________________
4) Are there any claims for prior years federal income taxes against you?____________________
   If yes, Year(s)____________________ Amount(s)____________________
   Contested____________________ Not Contested____________________
5) Does the attached statement include liability for (a) deficiencies?____________________
   (b) adequate current provisions?__________ (c) claims?____________________
6) Were any sales made to U. S. Governmental Agencies which are subject to renegotiation?__________
   Are amounts owing for price redetermination?____________________
   Have they been adjusted?__________ If answer is yes on any of (6) questions, please explain on reverse side.
7) Are any amounts owing for:
   (a) Excise taxes?__________ Amount(s)__________ Period(s)__________
   (b) Unemployment compensation taxes?__________ Amount(s)__________ Period(s)__________
   (c) Withholding taxes?__________ Amount(s)__________ Period(s)__________
   (d) State sales taxes?__________ Amount(s)__________ Period(s)__________
   (e) State income taxes?__________ Amount(s)__________ Period(s)__________
   (f) Other taxes? Please explain on reverse side.

   Are all tax liabilities reflected on the balance sheet?____________________

The foregoing information, supplementing our financial statement of____________________ is submitted for the purpose of obtaining credit, and the information contained herein is true and correct to the best of my knowledge and belief.

COMPANY NAME____________________

DATED:____________________ BY____________________ TITLE____________________ their origination, should be more properly converted into common and preferred stock?

3. Are there any arrearages in connection with dividends on preferred stock?

4. What is the rate of dividend on the common stock?

5. What is the past record of the company in regard to dividend payments on common and preferred stock?

6. Have dividend payments been justified by earnings after adequate provisions for proper write down of fixed assets and reserve accounts?

Earned Surplus. All retained income in surplus accounts should be segregated as to origin and reflect changes during the current accounting period.

1. Does the statement, or supporting schedule, clearly and adequately disclose dispersal reconcilement of net profits to the various respective surplus, reserve, and dividend accounts?

THE SPREAD SHEET

After the balance sheet is analyzed, the credit analyst condenses and spreads the information on spread sheets similar to those shown in Exhibits 80 and 81. This is done to enable the credit analyst and loaning officer to compare the sales and financial progress of the company between periods and, quite naturally provokes many questions on which the loan officer must be completely informed if he is to properly appraise and evaluate the risk, and determine the basis and form on which credit will be extended.

With this in mind all asset accounts shown on the balance sheet are classified in accordance with certain accepted theories that is classified into one group designated as "current assets" or those which can readily be converted into cash after a period of time, or when certain conditions have been complied with.

The same classification applies to liabilities—those which are "current" or those which must be immediately paid or are currently owed, such as for merchandise, or salaries and wages, and "other liabilities" which are those on which payment may be deferred until current liabilities have been taken care of, such as loans funded debt, and return of capital.

Finally, for the information and guidance of the loaning officer, the net worth, or that portion of the net assets of the company which belongs to the stockholders, is broken down as to the different classes of capital.

In making this allocation, a full explanation should be made of the specific and particular items which do not arise from normal business transactions. Items such as sums "due from officers, directors," and amounts "due from subsidiaries or affiliated companies" should be questioned and carefully scrutinized.

Foot and explanatory notes on the balance sheet should also be investigated to be certain that full disclosure is made, and that such items do not disguise contingent liabilities which would affect the credit standing of the company and the collectability of a loan.

To properly reflect the financial position of the company, any and all contingent liabilities should be set up, as such, on the liability side and the amount deducted from the surplus account.

Likewise reserves set aside for bad debts should be deducted from accounts receivable, thus reducing the total assets.

The reserves set aside against the value of buildings, furniture, fixtures, machinery and equipment, should be shown as a deduction from the cost so that the asset items, furniture, fixtures, machinery, equipment, and land, represent current or net value, that is cost less depreciation.

It is also well to observe that in evaluating current assets, securities, unless readily marketable and convertible into cash, should not be included with the "current assets" but in "other assets."

THE PROFIT OR LOSS STATEMENT

The balance sheet with its various classifications of assets and liabilities, discloses the financial position of a company or enterprise.

The profit or loss statement, on the other hand, discloses the results from the employment of capital in the business; and reflects the degree, or extent, to which those entrusted with management or operational duties have discharged their responsibilities.

Exhibit 80

SPREAD SHEET

NAME BUSINESS

No.	ASSETS (Spread in Hundreds / Thousands)		%		%		%		%		%
1	Cash										
2	Marketable Securities										
3	Receivables (Net) and Ave. Day's Turn. of Trade A/Cs.										
4	Inventory (Net) and Ave. Day's Supply										
5											
6											
7	TOTAL CURRENT ASSETS										
8	Fixed Assets (Net)										
9	Deferred Receivables										
10											
11											
12	Deferred Charges and Prepaid Expenses										
13											
14											
15	TOTAL ASSETS										
	LIABILITIES										
16	Notes Payable—Banks										
17	Notes Payable—Trade } Ave. Day's Purchases										
18	Account Payable—Trade } Ave. Day's Purchases										
19											
20	Miscellaneous Accruals										
21	Taxes (Due and or Accrued)										
22											
23											
24	TOTAL CURRENT LIABILITIES										
25											
26											
27	TOTAL LIABILITIES										
28											
29	Capital Stock—Preferred (% to Line 33)										
30	Capital Stock—Common										
31	Earned Surplus										
32	Capital Surplus										
33	NET WORTH (Excl. Intang. & Treas. Stock)										
34	TOTAL NET WORTH & LIABILITIES										
35	WORKING CAPITAL (and Ratio)										
36	Equity Working Capital (Lines 7 Minus 27)										
37	NET SALES (and Working Capital Turnover)										
38	Materials Used (% to Cost of Sales)										
39	Labor (% to Cost of Sales)										
40	Manufacturing Expenses (% to Cost of Sales)										
41	COST OF GOODS SOLD (% to Sales)										
42	GROSS PROFIT (% to Sales)										
43	Selling Expense (% to Sales)										
44	General & Admn. Expense (% to Sales)										
45	OPERATING PROFIT (% to Sales)										
46	Other Income (% to Sales)										
47	Other Expense (% to Sales)										
48	NET PROFIT (Before Fed. Taxes and Special Items)										
49	Special Items										
50	Federal Taxes (% to Sales)										
51	NET PROFIT (% to Sales)										
52	Dividends or Withdrawals										
53	Surplus Adjustments—Debit (Red)										
54	Credit (Black)										
55	Addition to Surplus (% to Beginning Net Worth)										
56	MEMO—Depreciation Incl. in Above Exp.										
57	Executive Remuneration (Excl. Div.)										
58	Contingent Liabilities										

5 Column Spread Sheet for use with Financial Statement Forms C-110H or C110T
Robert Morris Associates—Stock Form No. C-108A—Order from Cadwallader & Johnson, Inc., Chicago 10, Illinois

Exhibit 81

PROJECTION OF FINANCIAL STATEMENTS FORM
SCHEDULE SIDE

PROJECTION OF FINANCIAL STATEMENTS

SUBMITTED BY______________________________________

			ACTUAL	PROJECTIONS				
		SPREAD IN HUNDREDS ☐ DATE						
		SPREAD IN THOUSANDS ☐ PERIOD						
	1	NET SALES						1
P	2	Less: Materials Used						2
R	3	Direct Labor						3
O	4	Other Manufacturing Expense						4
F	5							5
I	6	COST OF GOODS SOLD .						6
T	7	GROSS PROFIT						7
	8	Less: Sales Expense						8
and	9	General and Administrative Expense						9
	10							10
L	11	OPERATING PROFIT						11
O	12	Less: Other Expense or *Income* (Net)						12
S	13	Income Tax Provision						13
S	14							14
	15	NET PROFIT						15
	16	CASH BALANCE (Opening)						16
C	17	Plus RECEIPTS: Receivable Collections						17
A	18							18
S	19							19
H	20	Bank Loan Proceeds						20
	21	Total						21
P	22	Less: DISBURSEMENTS: Trade Payables						22
R	23	Direct Labor						23
O	24	Other M'fg Expense						24
J	25	Sales, Gen'l and Adm. Exp.						25
E	26	Fixed Asset Additions						26
C	27	Income Taxes						27
T	28							28
I	29	Dividends or Withdrawals						29
O	30							30
N	31	Bank Loan Repayment						31
	32	Total						32
	33	CASH BALANCE (Closing)						33
	34	ASSETS: Cash						34
	35	Marketable Securities						35
	36	Receivables (Net)						36
	37	Inventory (Net)						37
	38							38
	39	CURRENT ASSETS						39
B	40	Fixed Assets (Net)						40
A	41							41
L	42							42
A	43							43
N	44	Deferred Charges						44
C	45	TOTAL ASSETS						45
E	46	LIABILITIES: Notes Payable—Banks						46
	47	Trade Payables						47
S	48	Income Tax						48
H	49							49
E	50							50
E	51	Accruals						51
T	52	CURRENT LIABILITIES						52
	53							53
	54							54
	55							55
	56	CAPITAL STOCK } Net Worth for						56
	57	SURPLUS } Partnership or Individual						57
	58	TOTAL LIABILITIES AND NET WORTH						58
	59	WORKING CAPITAL						59

Robert Morris Associates. Form C117
Carried in Stock by Cadwallader & Johnson, Inc., 225 W. Huron St., Chicago 10, Ill.

Exhibit 81A

PROJECTION OF FINANCIAL STATEMENT FORM
REVERSE SIDE

SALES FORECAST

Consider (1) Previous years business; (2) estimates of (a) Sales Department (b) Purchasing Department (c) Production Department; and (3) Allowances for (a) Economic Outlook (b) Government regulations (c) Market (d) Styles (e) Peak periods. Space for comments at right. ☛

INDICATE FACTORS USED IN PREPARING PROJECTION

1. Average receivable collection period in days __________
2. Inventory Turnover in Days __________
3. Trade Payable Turnover in Days __________
4. % Federal Tax to Profits before Tax %__________
5. Depreciation per Year $__________
6. Total Officers' or Partners' Compensation per month $__________

SUGGESTIONS FOR PREPARATION OF PROJECTION

Other Estimates needed for each period of the Projection are underlined below.

Blank lines in Projection are to accommodate unusual items of significance.

References to the Divisions of the Projection are abbreviated as follows:

Profit and Loss Statement	is PL
Cash Projection Receipts	is CR
Cash Projection Disbursements	is CD
Balance Sheet Assets	is BA
Balance Sheet Liabilities	is BL

In the first column, record the actual PROFIT AND LOSS STATEMENT and BALANCE SHEET of date immediately prior to projection period.

In each subsequent column covering a projection period (month, quarter, etc.):

1. Enter on date line, projection period covered and ending date thereof.

2. Complete PL, recording NET SALES, less all discounts and allowances; showing costs and expenses as indicated. *Compute NET PROFIT OR LOSS.

3. Record in CD on lines indicated, PL entries for DIRECT LABOR. OTHER MF'G EXPENSE, SALES, GENERAL and ADMINISTRATIVE EXPENSE and OTHER EXPENSE, less depreciation expense included therein. Record in CR, OTHER INCOME (PL).

4. Combine FIXED ASSETS (per prior column BA) and fixed asset additions, subtract depreciation expense and enter result in FIXED ASSETS (BA). Record cost of fixed asset additions in CD.

5. Combine INCOME TAX PROVISION (PL) with INCOME TAXES (per prior column BL), subtract payment of income tax and record result as INCOME TAXES (BL). Record income tax payment in CD.

6. Combine NET PROFIT or LOSS (PL) with SURPLUS or NET WORTH (per prior column BL), subtract DIVIDENDS OR WITHDRAWALS, record result as SURPLUS or NET WORTH (BL). Record DIVIDENDS or WITHDRAWALS in CD.

7. Record CASH (per prior column BA) as CASH BALANCE (opening) (CR).

8. Combine RECEIVABLES (per prior column BA) with NET SALES (PL), allocate resulting total between RECEIVABLE COLLECTIONS (CR) and RECEIVABLES (BA) per average collection period (Factor 1 above).

9. Combine TRADE PAYABLES (per prior column BL), with cost of material purchased (less discounts), allocate resulting total between TRADE PAYABLES (CD) and TRADE PAYABLES (BL) per turnover of payables (Factor 3 above).

10. Combine INVENTORY (per prior column BA), cost of materials purchased (less discounts) and DIRECT LABOR and OTHER M'FG EXPENSE (PL), subtract COST OF GOODS SOLD (PL), record result in INVENTORY (BA).

11. Review all items in prior column Balance Sheet (except CASH and NOTES PAYABLE—BANKS) for which no entries have been made in present period BALANCE SHEET. If there is no change in these items, transfer to present period BALANCE SHEET. If items are changed, reflect changes through CR or CD. Carry deferred charges (BA) and accruals (BL) without change.

12. Foot CASH PROJECTION: If cash deficiency indicated, enter amount to adjust in BANK LOAN PROCEEDS (CR); Combine this adjustment with NOTES PAYABLE—BANKS (per prior column BL) and enter as NOTES PAYABLE—BANKS (BL); if excessive cash is indicated, and NOTES PAYABLE—BANKS (per prior column BL) appears, provide BANK LOAN REPAYMENT (CD); reduce NOTES PAYABLE—BANKS (per prior column BL) by this provision, entering result as NOTES PAYABLE—BANKS (BL). Refoot CASH PROJECTION and enter resulting CASH BALANCE (closing) as CASH (BA).

13. Foot and balance BALANCE SHEET.

COMMENTS

****For Manufacturer projecting substantial increases or decreases in inventor[y] during projection period.***
Enter as title on Line No. 5(PL).
"INCREASE OR DECREASE IN WORK IN PROCESS AN[D] FINISHED INVENTORIES" — record increase in red, decrease i[n] black.

A profit or loss statement, to correctly reflect the results of operation, should report the following information:

Net Sales—which figure represents the total sales of merchandise or goods produced, less goods returned.

Materials Used—which is the difference between the inventory at the beginning of the period, plus materials purchased during the period, less material on hand at the end of the period.

Labor Expense—which represents the salaries, wages directly incurred in processing or converting materials into finished products.

Manufacturing Expense—representing amounts expended for rent, light, heat, maintenance, depreciation, etc., in converting materials into finished goods.

Cost of Goods Sold—representing the total funds expended for materials, labor and manufacturing as disclosed under headings, Materials Used, Labor Expense, and Manufacturing Expense.

Gross Profit or Loss—which is the difference between net sales and cost of goods sold.

Selling Expense—which represents the amounts expended for advertising, compensation and expenses of salesmen, discounts and allowances to trade, and cost of delivery distribution.

Administrative Expense—representing amounts expended for executive and general office salaries, travel, maintenance, etc.

Operating Profit or Loss—which is the difference between gross profit or loss, less selling, plus administrative expenses.

Net Profit or Loss—representing operating profit or loss plus income from dividends, subsidiaries, affiliates, etc., less expenses for federal income tax, payments on funded debt, etc.

Application of Funds—disclosing the distribution of net profits in dividends, extra executive remuneration or profit sharing plans; expenditures for equipment or additions to the plant not capitalized; and additions to earned surplus and reserve accounts.

The application of funds statement together with reconcilement to capital accounts is of great importance in that it often points out the company's past policy and may indicate future trends.

Minor variations may not be of material consequence. Major or wide variations, on the other hand could indicate the exercise of caution. For example: continuous sums expended for plant and equipment could indicate obsolescence with ultimate replacement being required to maintain efficiency and competitive position, which raises the question as to how this project is to be financed, and what possible effect it might have on the company-bank credit relationship.

In like manner a comparison of dividends paid against earnings may indicate an unwise policy in that dividends are being paid at the same rate regardless of earnings with the result that working capital is being depleted; insufficient provision is being made for expansion, research and development; and inadequate reserves are being set up for replacement of machinery and equipment.

In order to properly analyze a profit and loss statement, sources of income and expense should be presented clearly and stated in detail. Wherever it is possible and practical, the statements of income, sales, and production cost figures should be accompanied, or supplemented, by figures showing the breakdown by departments, divisions, and branches; or by class of goods and products.

It is of importance to a loan officer in evaluating a loan application particularly in connection with term loans, for the treasurer or financial officer of the company to submit copies of the annual budget so that the loaning officer can determine if sufficient provision has been made for the retirement of debt and any contingencies which might arise.

It is also of help to a loan officer, in evaluating the progress of a company, particularly in the case of a revolving credit of some duration, to be provided monthly, quarterly, or semi-annually, as warranted under the circumstances, with supplementary schedules or reports showing the period and balances of:

1. Cash
2. Trade accounts
3. Notes receivable
4. Raw materials inventory
5. Goods in process inventory
6. Finished goods inventory
7. Notes payable
8. Accounts payable

9. Gross sales and returns

In addition to disclosures resulting from analyzing figures set forth in the profit and loss statement, answers to the following questions might also be of assistance to the credit analyst in evaluating the progress and management of the company.

1. Are sales returns and allowances clearly stated and considered normal for the business?

2. Are freight in and freight out charges in line with the type of business and volume of sales?

3. Are charges for depreciation, amortization and depletion adequate?

4. Is the compensation paid to the officers or principals commensurate with duties and responsibilities?

5. Are provisions for charging off bad debts or adjustments to the reserve account adequate?

6. Are amounts set aside for traveling and entertainment normal for a business of the type engaged in?

7. Is the auditing and legal expense in line with the operations of the company, and considered normal for the particular type of business engaged in? (Legal expenses if excessive could indicate the payment of fees or retainers out of line with services performed; or that the company is engaged in certain practices or procedures which require correction and attention.)

If the auditing expense is small or nominal, in the absence of adequate internal accounting officers, it indicates the company is not getting the full benefit of proper accounting counsel from the standpoint of management and taxes.

8. Is the profit and loss statement sufficiently comprehensive and detailed to disclose all operating factors in connection with costs, manufacturing, or cost of sales, to enable management to function properly?

9. Are the net profits of the business commensurate with the volume of sales and capital employed?

RATIOS AND PERCENTAGES

While the value of properly prepared financial statements continues important in the extension of bank credit, because of the widespread specialization, larger risk involved, and tax burden, increased importance is being placed by credit officers on ratios and operating percentages as tools for analyzing the financial health of business.

Although it is recognized that ratios and percentages will vary between industries and types of business conducted, they are invaluable to credit analysts and loaning officers because they provide a yardstick whereby the strength or weakness of businesses similar in type of operation, can be measured and evaluated.

The principal ratios and percentages generally used by loaning officers in considering loan applications and the method of preparation by the credit analyst, are as follows:

CURRENT ASSETS TO CURRENT LIABILITIES

(Divide Current Assets by Current Liabilities)

This is a most important ratio and traditionally analysts have used a ratio of two to one as a general guide. At statement date the latter should coincide with the end of the seasonal year. Lower ratios may be satisfactory at seasonal peaks and in certain industries.

Where selling terms require payment of 90 days or less and inventory shows a rapid turnover, this ratio may not exceed 1½ to 1.

NET PROFITS ON NET SALES

(Divide Net Profits by Net Sales)

This represents the percentage of net profits earned, after taxes, and generally is the controlling figure on the amount of dividends paid by corporations or withdrawals made by partners in a partnership.

Net profits will vary widely from industry to industry.

NET PROFITS ON NET WORTH

(Divide Net Profits by Net Worth)

This represents the return on the investment of the owners of the business and will show a wide variation from one industry to another. Sound, aggressive management will show a greater return than one that lacks these qualities. Capital is invested in anticipation of a fair return, generally conceded to be around 6%.

The higher the profit after taxes to net worth, the greater is the probability of making appreciable addition to owners' equity, and the more attractive the appeal to long term investors seeking a place to invest their funds.

NET SALES TO NET WORTH

(Divide Net Sales by Net Worth)

This ratio reflects the activity of owners' capital during the year. When the relation increases from year to year, it indicates that owners' capital is being used more frequently during the year. A high ratio may indicate an excessive volume of business on a thin margin of invested capital with a consequent over-use of credit. This is over-trading and under-capitalization. It is apt to bring on loss to creditors if the business is closed.

The converse is under-trading based on over-capitalization, and while good for creditors, is usually not profitable to owners, and shows poor management for stockholders' interests.

QUICK ASSETS TO CURRENT LIABILITIES

(Divide total of Cash, Government Bonds and Net Current Receivables by Current Liabilities)

If quick assets amount to one dollar for each dollar of current liabilities, then the company is truly in a liquid position, particularly if the current liabilities represent total liabilities. If this ratio is less than 1 to 1 then look to see how much of the debt liquidation must come through the sale and/or reduction of inventory.

TOTAL DEBT TO NET WORTH

(Divide Net Worth by the total of Accounts Payable, Notes Payable, and Mortgages or Liens on Real Estate, Buildings, and Equipment)

When comparing the total debt to the tangible net worth, one must not lose sight of the fact that the distinction between current liabilities and a long term debt may be overemphasized. In the event of trouble, the latter quickly ranks with the other liabilities. Restrictive covenants in a term agreement may contain an acceleration clause and usually provide for a minimum current ratio and a working capital stop. In the event of default the term debt becomes due, thereby ranking with the other liabilities. Therefore this ratio comparison becomes of vital interest.

Although the analysts have set a standard of not over one dollar of debt to each dollar of net worth, based upon the assumption that the owners of the business shall have an investment equal to outside creditors, variations from this rule are not necessarily a sign of danger especially with growth companies, or new enterprises which are temporarily short of working capital.

AVERAGE TIME OF COLLECTIONS (DAYS)

(First divide the net annual credit sales by 365, second divide total of notes and accounts receivable by result, which gives number of days sales represented by receivables are outstanding)

A comparison of this figure with the terms of sale for the industry will show the extent of control over credit and collections. The greater number of days outstanding, the greater is the possibility of delinquencies in accounts receivable.

Average collection period should be no more than one-third greater than the net selling terms. For example, if selling terms are 2% net 30, outstanding receivables should not represent more than 40 to 45 days' sales.

NET SALES TO INVENTORY

(Divide the average Net Monthly Sales by the average monthly inventory)

The purpose of such computation is to determine the number of times during the year merchandise, or goods on hand is sold and stock replenished. Generally, and depending on the type of business, the greater the turnover the more maintenance of goods readily saleable is indicated.

THE CREDIT OR AGENCY REPORTS

In studying and analyzing the financial information pertaining to the loan applicant, the credit analyst and loaning officer also makes use of the reports and data on the applicant which the credit investigator has obtained from credit and mercantile agencies.

The foremost firm in this field is generally considered to be Dun & Bradstreet, Inc. In addition to investigating and reporting financial information in connection with individuals and corporations for subscribers to its service, it also edits and publishes the DUN & BRADSTREET REFERENCE BOOK which is widely used by mercantile concerns and banks. This book is made available by banks to their customers for checking the financial strength and credit standing of those who wish credit terms. It is with the permission of Dun & Bradstreet, gratefully acknowledged, that excerpts from their publications and reports are interposed and reproduced in this section.

In developing a report similar to that shown in Exhibit 82, investigators carefully investigate the subject of the inquiry from every standpoint and, similarly to a bank, report their findings in the following order and as defined and described.

Identification of subject
Financial rating of subject
Summary of credit standing
History of business
Method of operation
Financial position
Record of handling financial obligations

Identification of Subject. The identification section discloses the name, address, county, and state location of the corporation, partnership or individual, which is the subject of the investigation. In addition, if the subject is a partnership or an individual doing business under a trade name or trade style, the report discloses the name under which the business is conducted.

Financial Rating of Interest. A rating is a device by which the financial strength and composite credit appraisal of a business are reflected by a symbol. It is a meaningful way of classifying concerns by size and credit standing, and makes possible the listing of over 3 million names in the REFERENCE BOOK for the convenience of suppliers. RATINGS form the basis for the daily approval of millions of dollars in small orders.

Exhibit 82

SAMPLE OF DUN & BRADSTREET AGENCY REPORT

Dun & Bradstreet, Inc. Report — RATING UNCHANGED

5411
FOOD CENTER
GOLDSON, HAROLD J., OWNER

CD 69 JAN 5 19--
GROCERIES & MEATS

BUTLER GA
TAYLOR COUNTY
600 TURNBULL ST

RATING: F 2½

STARTED: 1954
NET WORTH: $12,540

PAYMENTS: Discount and Prompt
SALES: $7,500 monthly

SUMMARY

GOLDSON HAS DEVELOPED A STEADY TRADE IN HIS NEIGHBORHOOD AND MAINTAINED HIS AFFAIRS IN GOOD SHAPE.

HISTORY

Style registered by the owner January 2, 1954.

Goldson is 36, married, a native of Butler. He went into the Navy from school in 1942 and served until 1946. He was employed by Butler Paper Box Company from 1946 to 1951. From 1951 to December 15, 1953 he was employed by Kane's Chain Grocery Stores, Inc. as branch store manager and left voluntarily. He started business January 2, 1954 with $5,000 savings.

OPERATION-LOCATION

Retails groceries (85%) including a wide variety of canned, dry, and frozen foods; fresh and frozen meats (10%) and fresh fruits and vegetables (5%). All sales for cash. This residential neighborhood store occupies 1,400 square feet of floor space in a one-story frame building. Owner assisted by two full-time employees and his wife helps out on Saturdays. Store open 8 A.M. to 7 P.M. Premises well-maintained.

FINANCIAL INFORMATION

Estimated financial condition at Jan. 4, 19--:

ASSETS		LIABILITIES	
Cash on hand	$ 200	Accts Pay not due	$ 1,150
Cash in bank	2,221	Owing on Fixt & Equip	931
Mdse	6,500		
Total Current	8,921	Total Current	2,081
Fixt & Equip	5,200		
1953 Truck	500	NET WORTH	12,540
Total Assets	14,621	Total	14,621

Net Sales monthly $7,500; monthly rent $125; lease expires in three years; fire insurance on merchandise and fixtures $10,000.
Signed Jan 4, 19-- FOOD CENTER By Harold J. Goldson, owner.

------0------

Goldson has built up a nice little business for himself. During 19--, sales totaled $90,000, out of which he was able to net $3,000 after monthly drawings of $350. One of the things that has helped is that he opens up earlier and stays open later than the supermarkets in the nearby shopping center. In addition, Goldson and his wife are well liked by his customers, most of whom live in the immediate vicinity and give him steady trade.

Cash was confirmed and Goldson has not had to borrow from bank. The $931 owing on fixtures and equipment represents the last nine monthly installments on a new refrigerator cabinet. He and his wife own their home, valued at $15,000, free and clear.

PAYMENTS

HC	OWE	P DUE	TERMS	Dec 30 19--	
1000	400		2-10-30	Disc	Sold over 3 yrs
200			2%-10 days	Disc	Sold 2 yrs
1000	200		Net 30	Prompt	Sold 3 yrs
300			7 days	Prompt	Sold 2 yrs
(5)			C.O.D.		Cash to all

1-5-6- (744 12)

A RATING is composed of a letter-numeral symbol, indicating a concern's financial stability, character, and payment record.

The absence of a RATING, expressed by the dash (–) is not to be construed as unfavorable but signifies circumstances difficult to classify within condensed RATING symbols and should suggest to the subscriber the advisability of obtaining additional information.

However, no RATING is permanent. A RATING is assigned as of a given date, and is subject to review at subsequent intervals. RATINGS are changed as circumstances may warrant. Supplementary reports, including rating changes, are sent to subscribers periodically under "Continuous Service." RATINGS, in conjunction with the Standard Industrial Code number, are often studied by sales departments in planning sales programs, and many concerns include them both on ledger sheets and sales records. They aid salesmen to select and classify their prospective customers. Frequently, manufacturers seeking agencies and dealers for their products screen likely prospects by use of RATINGS and SIC members.

Summary of Credit Standing. The SUMMARY section consists of two parts. The first covers STARTING DATE, NET WORTH, PAYMENTS AND SALES. The second part is a narrative section describing the outstanding features of the case. In the simpler cases, the SUMMARY provides a condensation of the information needed by the sales or credit manager to reach a decision regarding the desirability of a customer or prospect. In more complicated cases, where a careful study of the entire report is necessary, the SUMMARY serves as an introduction to the detailed information in the sections of the report described on this page.

History of Business. The HISTORY section reveals the names and ages of the principals or owners of a concern and gives their past business experience. Basic features covered in the HISTORY are the length of time the individuals have been in the line of business in which they are currently engaged, length of time in other lines, outside business affiliations, and a record of any financial difficulties that may have been experienced in the past.

There are many important uses for the antecedent information found in the HISTORY—verifying orders, identifying owners, partners, and officers, and revealing any outside business interests of the principals. The information in the HISTORY forms the basis for many credit decisions. By knowing the ages of the principals, it is often possible to draw certain conclusions regarding their general business experience. The HISTORY, by shedding light on the principals, gives a picture of the enterprise and its proprietors and makes it easier to establish confident business relations.

Method of Operation. This section describes what a concern does and the nature of the neighborhood. Described also are the lines of merchandise sold or services rendered, price range, class of customers, selling terms, percentage of cash and credit sales, size of floor space, location, seasonal aspects, and type of equipment.

By describing the machinery of production and distribution, the section prepares the reader for a better understanding of the balance sheet and profit and loss figures which follow in the report. Unless the analyst knows the principal operating features, he is unable to judge whether capital is adequate or debt is excessive. Information contained in this section is used by sales departments to determine whether the subject of the report would make a profitable outlet for merchandise. Purchasing departments find this information of special value in determining the capacity of a manufacturer to deliver an order, maintain schedules, and support guarantees. In certain lines, operation details indicate the most efficient method of making shipment.

Financial Position. The balance sheet gives the essential facts for determining the financial health of a business. The purpose of this financial statement is to show the amount of capital in use, how it is applied, and how much of it is borrowed. Most reports contain a financial statement. Where principals of some concerns decline to furnish detailed figures, financial information is given based on bank interviews, calls on the "trade," investigation of public records, and other sources of business information available to DUN & BRADSTREET.

Balance sheet figures are generally supplemented by profit and loss details, plus information regarding leases, insurance coverage, and other pertinent data. The comment following the statement is devoted to further explanation of the figures and a description of sales and profit trends.

The ability of a concern to meet its liabilities as they fall due is usually indicated by an analysis of the financial information. The

RATING assigned is based to a marked extent upon the degree of financial stability and indicated trend as reflected in this section.

Record of Handling Financial Obligations. The purpose of this section is to record the manner in which the credit seeker pays his bills. It gives him the benefit of his trading record, and often indicates to the source of supply his relative importance as a customer. Each line in this section represents the experience of a specific supplier. Indicated are the approximations of the highest credit granted during the past year (HC), amount owing, and the amount past due, if any. Other columns indicate terms of sale, manner of payment, and any explanatory remarks about the account. Trade information is obtained directly from the ledgers of a representative number of suppliers covering all markets and lines.

The PAYMENTS section serves several important functions. If a supplier intends to open a new account, he can tell you from the paying experiences of others what to expect in his dealings with the prospective customer. If he has been selling the account, he is able to guide his own selling activity and credit policy by checking the relation of his sales with those of other suppliers. Besides being able to determine the amount of credit being granted by others, he can also see the terms which they have granted. Occasionally, a study of the PAYMENTS section reveals that one creditor is receiving prompt payments at the expense of slow payments to others.

A change in paying habits usually means there is some internal change in the financial condition of the business. This prompts the reporter to investigate more closely to determine the reason for the change. It also indicates to a supplier the danger of relying on his own ledger experience as the sole guide to credit judgment.

DUN & BRADSTREET REFERENCE BOOK

The Dun & Bradstreet Reference Book includes the names of more than 3 million business concerns in the United States and Canada. These are manufacturers, wholesalers, retailers and other businesses buying on credit terms. Not included are some service and professional establishments.

Each reference book listing is condensed from information in the credit report on the concern.

Credit ratings, as shown in Exhibit 83, which disclose the estimated financial strength and credit appraisal of the subject are assigned by credit analysts of the agency based on interviews with principals in the concern, the concern's financial statement, payment experiences of suppliers, comments from the local banker, as well as courthouse information on suits, liens, and mortgages.

The reference book is revised and issued every two months in January, March, May, July, September, and November. These revisions are necessary to keep pace with the more than 5,000 changes which occur among business concerns every business day.

During the course of a year approximately two out of three listings in the reference book are affected by a change of major or minor significance.

FAILURES IN PERSPECTIVE

As our economy strides along, the business population shifts and changes with unceasing vigor. In recent years over 400,000 concerns have been started annually, between 350,000 and 400,000 have been discontinued, and a slightly larger number have transferred ownership or control. On every business day more than 5,000 listings in the Dun & Bradstreet Reference Book are changed—new names are added, discontinued businesses are deleted, ratings are revised both upward and downward, and name styles are altered.

Of this vast turnover, business failures represent the fractional portion involving court proceedings or voluntary action likely to end in loss to creditors. Not all concerns going out of business are failures by this definition. Most withdrawals are transfers of ownership or voluntary liquidations in which there is no loss to creditors. These discontinuances outnumber failures by a wide margin, estimated at twenty-five to one in recent years. However, the discontinuances in which the owner manages to pay his creditors but loses his own capital and courage actually are failures of a less "formal" variety and are of serious concern to all of us. Discontinuances and failures tend to follow similar trends. Failures, reflecting the most drastic effects of the wear and tear on our economy, provide a measure of the vulnerability of businesses in different industries and trades, in different locales, and in different age and size groups. Naturally, this vulnerability varies from year to year as our economy pushes upward or sinks downward.

In studying the history and financial development of a business

Exhibit 83

DUN & BRADSTREET CREDIT RATING

KEY TO RATINGS

ESTIMATED FINANCIAL STRENGTH				COMPOSITE CREDIT APPRAISAL			
				HIGH	GOOD	FAIR	LIMITED
AA	Over		$1,000,000	A1	1	1½	2
A+	Over		750,000	A1	1	1½	2
A	$500,000	to	750,000	A1	1	1½	2
B+	300,000	to	500,000	1	1½	2	2½
B	200,000	to	300,000	1	1½	2	2½
C+	125,000	to	200,000	1	1½	2	2½
C	75,000	to	125,000	1½	2	2½	3
D+	50,000	to	75,000	1½	2	2½	3
D	35,000	to	50,000	1½	2	2½	3
E	20,000	to	35,000	2	2½	3	3½
F	10,000	to	20,000	2½	3	3½	4
G	5,000	to	10,000	3	3½	4	4½
H	3,000	to	5,000	3	3½	4	4½
J	2,000	to	3,000	3	3½	4	4½
K	1,000	to	2,000	3	3½	4	4½
L		Up to	1,000	3½	4	4½	5

CLASSIFICATION AS TO BOTH ESTIMATED FINANCIAL STRENGTH AND CREDIT APPRAISAL

FINANCIAL STRENGTH BRACKET			
1	$125,000	to	$1,000,000 and Over
2	20,000	to	125,000
3	2,000	to	20,000
4	Up	to	2,000

EXPLANATION

When only the numeral (1, 2, 3, or 4) appears, it is an indication that the estimated financial strength, while not definitely classified, is presumed to be within the range of the ($) figures in the corresponding bracket and that a condition is believed to exist which warrants credit in keeping with that assumption.

NOT CLASSIFIED OR ABSENCE OF RATING

The absence of a rating, expressed by the dash (—), is not to be construed as unfavorable but signifies circumstances difficult to classify within condensed rating symbols and should suggest to the subscriber the advisability of obtaining additional information.

INVESTIGATING

"Inv" in place of the rating is an abbreviation of "investigating." It signifies nothing more than that a pending investigation was incomplete when the book in which it appears went to press.

The letters "N. Q." on any written report mean not listed in the Reference Book.

Dun & Bradstreet, Inc.

it is helpful, and generally of importance to the credit analyst and loan officer, to be familiar with, and have information regarding the mortality and causes of failure of respective types or classes of business. So that students of banking become familiar with the availability of such information, in studying the functions of the credit analyst, results of the 1965 studies undertaken by Dun & Bradstreet and made available by them for reproducing are shown in Exhibits 84, 85, and 86.

It is interesting to note that 13,514 businesses with an average liability of $97,800. failed in 1965, in contrast with 1932, the peak period in the 1920/65 period when a record 31,822 firms failed with an average liability of $29,172. and in 1945, the lowest year in the 1920/65 period when only 809 firms failed with an average liability of $37,361.

Analysis of failures in 1965, in all business categories, indicates approximately 29% of all failures could be attributed to lack of previous experience, or familiarity with the business engaged in; 22% to lack of administrative or managerial ability to direct operations; 41% to general incompetence resulting in heavy operating expenses, inadequacy of sales and/or injudicious extensions of credit; 4% to neglect because of family difficulties or health problems, and the remainder to fraud on the part of the principals, fire not covered by insurance, and various other reasons.

It is the duty and responsibility of the credit analyst to evaluate the quality and strength or weakness of the assets and liabilities as disclosed by the balance sheet and, from experience, to be aware of the limitations surrounding the accuracy of financial reports. An astute analyst develops sound opinions by studying and evaluating past operating results, and comparing with present financial position, budget estimates, and the projection of future sales.

An astute credit analyst also learns to study, analyze, and evaluate the human factors involved in any business enterprise.

Final assistance in summarizing the results of his analysis and findings can often be obtained through use of the following questionnaire, or check list, against the credit report, mortality tables and information in the credit folder as developed by the credit investigator.

1. Is there a record of changes in the firm name? This should be particularly checked in order to determine that there has been no

Exhibit 84

FAILURE TRENDS 1920-1965

FAILURE TRENDS 1920-1965

Year	Number of Failures	Total Failure Liabilities	Failure Rate Per 10,000 Listed Concerns	Average Liability Per Failure
1920	8,881	$ 295,121,000	48	$33,230
1921	19,652	627,401,000	102	31,926
1922	23,676	623,895,000	120	26,351
1923	18,718	539,387,000	93	28,817
1924	20,615	543,226,000	100	26,351
1925	21,214	443,744,000	100	20,918
1926	21,773	409,233,000	101	18,795
1927	23,146	520,105,000	106	22,471
1928	23,842	489,559,000	109	20,534
1929	22,909	483,252,000	104	21,094
1930	26,355	668,282,000	122	25,357
1931	28,285	736,310,000	133	26,032
1932	31,822	928,313,000	154	29,172
1933	19,859	457,520,000	100	23,038
1934	12,091	333,959,000	61	27,621
1935	12,244	310,580,000	62	25,366
1936	9,607	203,173,000	48	21,148
1937	9,490	183,253,000	46	19,310
1938	12,836	246,505,000	61	19,204
1939	14,768	182,520,000	70	12,359
1940	13,619	166,684,000	63	12,239
1941	11,848	136,104,000	55	11,488
1942	9,405	100,763,000	45	10,713
1943	3,221	45,339,000	16	14,076
1944	1,222	31,660,000	7	25,908
1945	809	30,225,000	4	37,361
1946	1,129	67,349,000	5	59,654
1947	3,474	204,612,000	14	58,898
1948	5,250	234,620,000	20	44,690
1949	9,246	308,109,000	34	33,323
1950	9,162	248,283,000	34	27,099
1951	8,058	259,547,000	31	32,210
1952	7,611	283,314,000	29	37,224
1953	8,862	394,153,000	33	44,477
1954	11,086	462,628,000	42	41,731
1955	10,969	449,380,000	42	40,968
1956	12,686	562,697,000	48	44,356
1957	13,739	615,293,000	52	44,784
1958	14,964	728,258,000	56	48,667
1959	14,053	692,808,000	52	49,300
1960	15,445	938,630,000	57	60,772
1961	17,075	1,090,123,000	64	63,843
1962	15,782	1,213,601,000	61	76,898
1963	14,374	1,352,593,000	56	94,100
1964	13,501	1,329,223,000	53	98,454
1965	13,514	1,321,666,000	53	97,800

Exhibit 85

FAILURE TRENDS IN SPECIFIC MANUFACTURING AND RETAIL LINES 1965

FAILURE RATES IN SPECIFIC MANUFACTURING AND RETAIL LINES, 1965

MANUFACTURING INDUSTRIES RANKED BY RATE
Year 1965

Line of Industry	Failure Rate Per 10,000 Operating Concerns
Furniture	196
Transportation Equipment	161
Electric Machinery	146
Leather & Shoes	102
Apparel	94
Metals, Primary & Fabricated	67
Chemicals & Drugs	64
Textile	57
Machinery	55
Printing & Publishing	51
Paper	47
Lumber	37
Food	37
Stone, Clay & Glass	27

RETAIL FAILURES RANKED BY FAILURE RATES
Year 1965

Line of Business	Failure Rate Per 10,000 Operating Concerns
Infants' and Children's Wear	105
Toys and Hobby Crafts	102
Appliances, Radios & Television	80
Furniture and Furnishings	79
Gifts	74
Women's Ready-to-Wear	71
Men's Wear	69
Bakeries	67
Books and Stationery	67
Sporting Goods	59
Cameras and Photographic Supplies	55
Lumber and Building Materials	50
Shoes	43
Eating and Drinking Places	42
Dry Goods and General Merchandise	41
Jewelry	38
Auto Parts and Accessories	38
Automobiles	35
Women's Accessories	34
Drugs	34
Hardware	31
Groceries	22
Farm Implements	20

Exhibit 86

AGE OF BUSINESS FAILURES BY FUNCTIONS IN 1965

AGE OF BUSINESS FAILURES BY FUNCTIONS IN 1965

Age in Years	Manu-facturing	Wholesale	Retail	Construction	Service	All Concerns
One Year or Less	2.3%	1.7%	3.6%	1.2%	2.4%	2.7%
Two	14.0	10.9	20.4	10.3	16.2	16.1
Three	14.9	16.2	18.9	15.8	15.1	17.0
Total Three Years or Less	31.2	28.8	42.9	27.3	33.7	35.8
Four	10.8	10.7	12.5	12.3	13.6	12.1
Five	8.8	8.9	8.5	10.6	8.6	9.0
Total Five Years or Less	50.8	48.4	63.9	50.2	55.9	56.9
Six	6.8	5.3	6.1	7.8	7.8	6.6
Seven	4.8	5.4	4.6	6.9	7.0	5.4
Eight	3.5	4.2	3.3	4.7	3.6	3.7
Nine	3.3	3.8	2.5	3.5	2.5	2.9
Ten	3.0	3.1	2.3	3.5	3.4	2.8
Total Six-Ten Years	21.4	21.8	18.8	26.4	24.3	21.4
Over Ten Years	27.8	29.8	17.3	23.4	19.8	21.7
Total	100.0%	100.0%	100.0%	100.0%	100.0%	100.0%
Number of Failures	2,097	1,355	6,250	2,513	1,299	13,514

manipulation of assets to the detriment of the creditors, or that prior business practices have not made it necessary for them to change their name.

2. Is this particular business normally considered to be a hazardous risk, or is it a business subject to excessive competition and price cutting?

3. Does this type of business generally attract an irresponsible or "fast" type of proprietor?

4. Is this business generally considered to be speculative, or pertinent to a particular undertaking or economic condition? If so, are the terms of the loan sufficient to provide for liquidation over the period for which the business is organized?

5. Is the industry of which this business is a part subject to periodic instability or handicapped by excessive periodical production?

6. Is this business sensitive to local economic conditions, such as crop failures and strikes?

7. Would strikes or shut-downs in other businesses in the area affect the production of this business?

8. What is the relationship of this company with respective unions to which its employees belong?

9. Is the location of the business such that it can operate economically and advantageously with respect to sources of raw materials and markets for finished goods?

10. Is the company a major supplier of several companies, the termination of which would seriously affect the production and sales of the company? Explain.

11. If the company deals extensively with foreign countries, what effect would currency problems, economic disturbances, and/ or tariffs have on its business? Explain.

12. Is the real property, building, machinery and equipment properly covered by insurance of the required type to cover possible losses, including use and occupancy, or interruption of business?

13. Do figures representing inventory of raw material or finished goods reflect or represent goods or merchandise which can be used in current production, or for which there is a current demand?

14. Is the request for credit in line with seasonal requirements of the business, or for the particular purpose for which they request the loan?

15. Would a general depression or recession affect the repayment of the loan?

16. Does the financial information furnished by public accountants or certified public accountants, in your opinion, accurately reflect the financial position and condition of the company? Explain.

17. Is the company family-owned? If so, is active management vested in men qualified to manage affairs of the company or is nepotism practiced? Explain.

18. Do the directors contribute to or assist in the management, or are they merely figureheads?

19. Are all of the officers active in the management of the company? Explain.

20. Are the officers and administrative personnel experienced and qualified to discharge the responsibilities of the respective positions?

21. Are the principal officers and administrative personnel of the company backed up with qualified understudies?

22. Would the company, in its operations, be seriously affected by the death, resignation or withdrawal from activity of any of the principal officers or administrative personnel? Give details and explain.

23. Have there been any recent changes in management or ownership which indicate instability, or any management weaknesses? Explain.

24. Does the company make use of an organization plan through which duties and responsibilities are charted and defined for the information and guidance of the staff?

25. To what extent is active management delegated to administrative personnel 55 or more years of age? List key personnel by title or position, name and age.

26. Is there need for new blood at the top administrative or management level? If so, how is it being provided for? Explain.

27. Does the company have a definite program for retirement? Explain.

28. Is retirement of personnel covered by a suitable pension plan? Explain type of coverage.

After the credit analyst has finally reviewed and analyzed the information in the file, or new information gathered by the credit investigator, and is satisfied as to the sufficiency of the financial and historical information, he writes up his report, which together with the file is delivered to the loaning officer for review, further analysis and decision.

CHAPTER XXVI

THE LOAN OFFICER

A PERSON QUALIFIED AS A LOAN OFFICER has the ombined knowledge and experience of a credit investigator and redit analyst and the judgment acquired from association with nior loan officers.

It is not so much what he is but what he has been, which idenfies and marks a good loan officer. In the final anlysis he is only good or capable as his judgment—and his judgment is only as ood as his training and experience as a credit investigator, his nalytical ability developed as a credit analyst, and experience has roven him to be.

Upon receipt of the credit file, together with information gathred by the credit investigator, and the summary report prepared y the credit analyst, it becomes the responsibility of the loan officer analyze and evaluate the information in light of the credit appliation, and arrive at the proper decision—to decline the loan or pprove the loan in line with authority and limitations granted by e board of directors.

In arriving at a decision, the following five fundamental conderations for credit are generally taken into consideration by a aning officer in addition to, and in connection with, the information and reports in the credit file.

1. *Character.* The moral risk, the reliability of the individual, r of management; their reputation, their honesty.

2. *Capacity.* Knowledge and knowhow which the principals ngaged in the business can contribute to profitable and successful anagement and operation.

3. *Capital.* The property risk, resources of the individuals or ompany; the ability to provide sufficient funds to profitably operte.

4. *Collateral.* Securities, or fixed assets, which if required can e pledged to secure a loan. The net worth of individuals connect-

ed with the enterprise which can be used as additional collateral or security by having them endorse the paper.

5. *Conditions.* The economic characteristics of the business which may contribute to its success or failure.

Sound credit cannot be based on the integrity, honesty or ability of the individual or principals of the business enterprise alone. In addition, the business must have capable management and have sufficient assets and unburdening liabilities to warrant credit consideration.

Today, as never before, competent credit and loan officers place importance on such often intangible assets as:

1. Informed and capable leadership and management.
2. Sufficiency of capable and qualified men as understudies to the principals.
3. Use of modern and efficient machinery and equipment.
4. Modern design and marketability of the products.
5. Progressive research facilities for development of new products.

While the scope of information in the credit file is generally developed by the credit investigator and credit analyst in accordance with the request submitted by the loan officer, following the initial interview with the prospective borrower, or later directly provided by the applicant; the loan officer most probably will seek the answers to these additional questions in connection with the loan application.

1. Are there any inactive assets which should or could be converted into cash?
2. Will any excess of cash over current requirements be available to liquidate bank loans?
3. Are the balance sheet ratios in line with the standards for the industry?
4. Does the budget provide for the company to be out of debt within the 12-month period?
5. If the budget provides for a loss, is adequate provision made for ample working capital?
6. Are production schedules in line with sales estimates?
7. Are supplies and sources of materials properly gauged?
8. Is the size of the inventory justified by present production and projected sales?

9. Does the present system of production control guard against tying up too much working capital in inventories?

10. Is full use being made of commercial credit instruments such as customers' notes, drafts secured by bills of lading, warehouse receipts, for additional working capital?

11. Does the budget disclose how much working capital is needed for all operations at all times?

12. Is the working capital large enough to provide for increased sales volume on present credit terms?

13. Would it be advisable to shorten credit terms so that less working capital would be required?

14. Is the working capital sufficient to permit the lengthening of credit terms?

15. Is the compensation paid salesmen sufficient to attract the right type of salesmen?

16. Under the sales policy and practices of the company, do salesmen sell the product or are they merely order takers?

17. Are the general sales policies of the company designed to keep distribution in the strong hands of highly rated and regarded wholesalers and distributors?

18. Does the company adequately protect dealers against price ompetition?

19. Does the profit margin provide distributors with an attractive profit?

20. Does company policy provide for teaching or assisting dealers and distributors to do a better sales job?

21. Is the company's budget provision for promotion and new usiness out of line in comparison to provisions to keep present customers satisfied and develop present customers into bigger uyers?

22. Is the advertising provision in the budget sufficient to produce necessary sales results?

23. Is the research department acting independently to constently improve the product?

24. Are the products attractively packaged and modernized to onform to current trends?

After analyzing the information provided by the applicant; esults of investigation by the credit investigator; studies of financial ffairs made by the credit analyst; plus application of his own factors of experience and judgment; the loan officer makes known the favorable or unfavorable decision of the bank in connection with the loan application.

If the application is approved, once the terms of repayment rate of interest, provisions and other conditions of the loan are agreed upon and the note signed, the note, together with necessary supporting papers or securities pledged as collateral, is delivered to the loan and discount cage through which the proceeds are made available to the borrower, either through credit to an account, or by issuance of a cashier's check.

Should the loaning officer reach the conclusion that approval of the loan is not warranted, it is then that the tact and diplomacy of a successful and seasoned credit officer comes into action.

From a public relations and business development standpoint an astute loan officer never flatly or finally declines a loan application. Being mindful of maintaining the good will of the applicant and further developing the prestige of the bank, a successful loan officer always declines a loan application with a conditional rejection. That is, the application can be approved *providing* certain terms and conditions are fulfilled, or it will be favorably reconsidered, if, when, and providing, changes in management, policy or operations, which the loan officer has recommended or suggested are adopted or placed into operation.

By following such a policy in declining loans, not only does the loan officer safeguard the interest of the bank and build good will for the bank, but often assists the applicant in strengthening his company, possibly increasing sales, and in producing greater profits.

The ordinary procedure in connection with the processing of loans, distribution of proceeds and the collection and payment of loans is an operating function covered in the operating section.

The handling of past due, defaulted, or delinquent commercial loans, however, is another phase which takes on real importance in times of economic stress or times of business recession.

Generally the matter of handling a loan delinquent as to payment becomes the responsibility of the loan officer who approved the loan. He works with the company or individual in developing a program which will enable the borrower to ultimately repay the loan without detriment to the welfare of the company or loss to the bank. In some of the larger banks, however, the collection of loans which are delinquent, or where certain terms or conditions must be made in order to have the loan ultimately repaid, is handled by a separate department, the personnel of which actively participate in the affairs and management of the company until such time as the loan is repaid or certain conditions have been complied with to restore the loan to prime status.

Bad loans are made in so-called good times as well as in bad times. Both good loans and bad loans are also made in times of economic prosperity, not due to economic factors, but to the human elements of management, inability of the borrower either through negligence or lack of experience to cope with ever changing business conditions, or through the perverted judgment of the loan officer.

A loaning officer may be influenced in approving a loan application by friendship, business or family connections. He may also hesitate to decline the loan because of the connections which the prospective borrower has with the bank, or the influence which the applicant exercises in the community. In addition a banker may be ambitious to build up the bank and be willing to exchange credit for additional deposits in the hope that the loans made will be collectable at maturity.

It is axiomatic that generally all loans are good when made—and, if the loan is paid at maturity—it was a good loan. Whether or not a loan is good or bad, in the final analysis, depends on the ability of the loan officer to correctly appraise and evaluate facts.

Mistakes made in making loans generally are more attributable to the neglect of the loan officer to get complete information than to errors in judgment.

The first rule for a loan officer to follow in making a sound loan is to be certain that he is in possession of all of the facts, which can only be obtained after an exhaustive investigation, and proper consideration of every pertinent fact as to financial condition.

The second rule is for the loan officer to be certain of the productivity and efficiency of operations; the soundness of sales and distribution policies; and to be reasonably sure that future sales will be sufficient to turn over inventory at a profit, and provide funds for the repayment of the loan.

Generally when the loan officer is provided with the facts and has had extensive experience, it is not difficult to make a loan to a prime credit risk. All in all, regardless of the angle from which we approach the extension of credit, we ultimately return to the focal point of having complete and audited balance sheets, detailed profit or loss statements, and historical and financial information, which has been provided by the credit investigators and credit analysts.

Ways and means are constantly being sought to improve the scope of activity of the credit departments of banks. It is their increased objective to have credit investigators, or those charged with the responsibility, develop more reliable and complete sources of information and simplify the painstaking work in connection with the investigation of the applicant in bank and trade quarters which together with the financial information as shown in the balance sheet and profit and loss statement, which is analyzed by the credit analyst to enable the loan officer to arrive at an intelligent conclusion, and make the correct decision, without undue risk to either the funds belonging to the stockholders, or entrusted to the bank for safekeeping by the depositors.

From the study of the functions of a loan officer, it should readily be understood how the judgment necessary to make decisions regarding the loaning of stockholders' and depositors' funds, in the various types of loans, is developed only through years of experience both as a credit investigator and as a credit analyst.

The position of loan officer is one which can provide great personal satisfaction to a conscientious person, not only because the conversion of funds into loans provides interest income for the bank but because the granting of loans provides jobs in industry, constructs homes, enables people to purchase homes, automobiles, and household appliances, which not only contribute to the growth and economic development of the community, but assist people to lead happier and more satisfying lives.

CHAPTER XXVII

THE MAIL AND MESSENGER SECTION

IN CHAPTER VIII WE LEARNED THAT THE business of banking is composed of three principal functions: (a) the acquiring of funds to invest and loan, (b) the converting of such funds into bonds and loans, and (c) the servicing of such funds, or the providing of services to accounts which provided the funds.

We also learned that such functions were generally performed within departments, divisions and sections, which from a management and supervisory standpoint were classified as: (a) Operating groups, or those whose functions were performed in connection with providing services to, or in behalf of customers and the public, handling or processing items, or performing certain services; (b) Non-Operating groups whose functions were in connection with the conversion of funds; (c) Capital groups whose functions were in connection with directly serving, acting for, or in behalf of the stockholders; (d) Administrative groups whose responsibilities were directly in connection with management and supervisory functions; and (e) Service groups whose responsibilities and functions were in connection with either directly serving the public or customers—or in assisting other departments, divisions and sections in discharging their responsibilities or in carrying out their functions.

The departments, divisions and sections whose functions are in connection with the acquiring and conversion of funds have been covered in previous chapters. We will now cover the functions of the various operating and service sections of the commercial department whose responsibilities are either in connection with performing an operation, processing an item, or providing a service, for or in behalf of a customer, the public, or some other department, division or section of the bank.

Before taking up the functions and responsibilities of the operating and service sections, it is again well to point out that each and every function or responsibility, as described in connection with performing an operation, processing an item, or providing a service, is performed in every bank regardless of size. In a smal bank the respective functions might be undertaken or be performe by the same person; while in another bank, depending on size an volume of activity, the functions would be departmentalized.

In a large bank, which we will use for our study because o the opportunity it provides to detail the scope of most activities such operating functions would be handled within or by the fol lowing sections, which are listed in order of general succession, o lines of progression through the operating departments and divi sions of the bank.

Mail and Messenger Section
Proof-Clearings and Transit Section
Bookkeeping Section
Savings Section
Commercial Receiving Section
Commercial Paying Section
Drafts and Official Checks Section
Collection Section
Loan Tellers Section

In studying these various sections we will first take up th Mail and Messenger Section.

The responsibility for handling mail depends to a great exten on the size of the bank. In a small bank generally the cashier o even the president looks over the incoming mail and directs it t the proper person for handling. The reason an officer handles th incoming mail, in some of the smaller banks, is in order to be thor oughly informed and acquainted at all times with what is going o in the bank. In other banks, the handling of the incoming mai might be the responsibility of a junior officer or a clerk.

The handling of outgoing mail, on the other hand, in a smal or medium sized bank is usually handled by one of the clerks as a part-time job. It is his responsibility to see that the proper postag is affixed, that the envelopes have been sealed and to take the mai to the post office after the close of business.

In a large bank, however, the handling of mail is generally th function of the mail section, which has the principal responsibilitie in connection with:

1. Picking up from the post office, sorting, analyzing and distributing incoming mail.

2. Picking up and delivering internal mail from and to inter bank stations.

3. Processing outgoing mail, and delivering it to the post office.

4. Performing messenger services in connection with outside presentation of collections and checks on other banks.

Incoming Mail. The first pickup of incoming mail is generally made by the bank messenger from the bank's own post office box at the post office as soon as the post office opens, which is usually around 7:00 AM. As soon as the mail is received at the bank it is sorted to addressees for the first internal delivery, so that it can be processed immediately by them as soon as they arrive at their desks.

Other pickups are made from the post office throughout the day, usually at 8:30 AM, 11:00 AM and 1:00 PM, depending on the time that incoming mail is received by the post office and sorted by them to the box holders.

Generally, all mail which comes to the bank comes in under one of three forms: (A) that which is addressed to the bank without further identification, (B) that which is addressed to a department of the bank and (C) that which is addresser to an officer of the bank.

Mail addressed to the bank usually consists of the following, and can be classified as follows:

1. Registered mail, which consists mostly of stock certificates, bonds, notes and drafts for collection; or coupons, and checks for deposit.

2. Envelopes addressed to the bank, which the bank has provided, or addressed to the bank by the mailer, containing checks which customers wish to have deposited to their own account; items from other banks sent for collection; and remittances from collections previously sent out by the bank.

3. Letters of acknowledgement in connection with items sent to another bank for collection.

4. Replies to credit inquiries or replies to matters in connection with credit investigations.

5. Miscellaneous mail such as circulars, magazines, and bond offerings.

6. Cash letters from correspondent banks containing checks or remittances.

As soon as the mail is received from the post office, the first step is to sort out the mail to delivery or distribution points.

Large envelopes from correspondent banks usually contain checks for presentation and payment and are delivered to the proof department.

The bank's own envelopes used in connection with mail deposits are sorted and delivered to the mail teller for processing.

Envelopes addressed to a particular department of the bank are sorted to that particular department, while envelopes addressed to a particular officer are sorted for personal delivery to him.

The remainder of the mail addressed to the bank, which cannot be readily identified, is then opened by the mail clerk, contents noted, and properly directed to the person or department which will handle the item.

In connection with handling of the mail addressed to an officer of the bank or individual, confusion often exists as to the proper handling of such mail. Mail addressed to an officer of the bank will generally come in one of the three following forms.

Mr. John Banker, Vice President
First National Bank
Town and State

First National Bank
Town and State
Attention:
Mr. John Banker
Vice President

or

Mr. John Banker
c/o First National Bank
Town and State

The generally accepted procedure in handling such mail, from a standpoint of management efficiency and courtesy, is that mail so addressed should be delivered to the officer whose name appears on the envelope.

However, mail addressed to an individual as Vice President or to the bank for the attention of an individual or an officer, should the officer not be there, should be immediately opened by his secretary or some other officer who has responsibility for handling his affairs when he is absent from the bank. Letters addressed to an individual in care of the bank are considered personal and should only be opened by the addressee.

Incoming registered mail, unless specifically directed to a particular department or an officer, is generally opened by the mail clerk. When the mail clerk has determined the contents of the envelope, it is then entered on a register sheet by date, number of the registered envelope, from whom received, description of the contents, and name of the department to which the envelope will be delivered for handling. When it is received by the department to which delivered, a proper receipt should be made on the register sheet as proof of delivery.

Inter-office Mail. The efficient handling of inter-office mail or delivery of documents, mail, etc., between departments, divisions, sections and individuals of the bank, is another function of the mail and messenger section.

Generally, in order to avoid waste of time in delivering letters, documents, memorandums, etc. for proper attention, and to simplify the delivery of incoming regular mail and process outgoing regular mail, progressive banks either set up a series of stations—usually one in each section—or use double baskets on officers' desks, to which a messenger deposits all incoming mail directed to the attention of the individual or personnel within the section, and picks up mail for the post office or for delivery to other sections or individuals within the bank.

These stations are set up in proper sequence, and regular schedules maintained so that pickups and deliveries are made to and from each section at least once every hour.

In delivering inter-bank mail and memorandums from one section to another, it is the customary practice to provide interested personnel with a supply of INTER-BANK ENVELOPES similar to that shown in Exhibit 87.

Such envelopes are usually made up in colored stock, to distinguish them from regular mailing envelopes, with non-seal flaps, in size 5 x 10½. In addition they have peep holes to distinguish any contents and are printed up with horizontal lines for affixing of name and addressee. Upon receipt of such an envelope, after removing contents, the addressee crosses off his name and the envelope is ready for further use.

In case the system of section stations is used, in order to eliminate the use of "incoming" and "outgoing" trays on officers' desks, it is the responsibility of someone within the section to make inter section delivery of incoming mail. Individuals having mail to be delivered to another person or to the post office, however, deposit the items in the "outgoing" tray themselves.

Outgoing Mail. The handling of outgoing mail is another important function of the mail and messenger section. Here again, depending on the size of the bank, one of several procedures is followed.

In a small bank, as previously mentioned, the sealing of outgoing mail, affixing of proper postage, and delivery to the post office might be the responsibility of one of the clerks, while in a large bank, the handling of outgoing mail is the responsibility of the mail section.

Where a bank has a mail section, one of several procedures is

Exhibit 87

FOR INTER BANK USE ONLY			
To:	Section	To:	Section

followed in handling outgoing mail (a) outgoing mail originating from a section is periodically deposited in the "outgoing" tray in that section for pickup and processing at convenient intervals by the mail clerk, or (b) delivered at the end of the day by clerks or secretaries to the mail section for processing.

Items which are to be sent by registered mail, when received in the mail section, are entered in the register by number, name and address of addressee, and description. The register is taken to the post office, together with the items, where it is stamped officially for receipt and insurance purposes.

In situations where a bank has a quantity of individual pieces of mail from various sources within the bank going to the same addressee, it usually is sent to the mail section, either without an envelope, or with an envelope addressed to the person to whom the item is directed for attention, where it is segregated. At the end of the day all such items of mail are placed in one large envelope and mailed resulting in a considerable saving in postage expense. When such envelopes are received by the addressee bank, they are opened and the mail distributed.

In connection with mail schedules, an efficiently operated mail section will keep currently informed as to the times during the day the post office delivers out regular, air, and foreign mail to various points; and arrange, wherever possible, to make such deliveries of mail from the bank to the post office so they are included in the sending. This is necessary and desirable not only to effect the rapid presentation and collection of documents which are interest bearing for the protection of the bank, but to provide service to the customers of the bank as well.

Where a bank handles a large volume of incoming mail, practical use is often made of machines which cut off the horizontal edge to more easily extract the contents. Likewise, where a bank has a large volume of outgoing mail, practical use is made of automatic sealers and postage meter machines to reduce labor.

In efficiently handling outgoing mail, clerks generally sort envelopes by weight so that letters requiring the same amount of postage are put through at the same time to avoid making changes in the meter. Personal mail is, of course, sealed by the sender, and it is the general and accepted regulation in every bank, that postage for personal mail must be provided by the sender.

In connection with the handling of mail, economies in operation and reduction in expense can be brought about, in many instances, by the redesigning or developing of forms which can be used in a window envelope, thus eliminating the addressing of a separate envelope.

Further economies can be effected too, by the use of lighter weight paper for foreign mail and multiple remittance and collection forms.

The Work of the Messenger. It is the function and the responsibility of bank messengers to present checks, bills of exchange, drafts, securities, coupons, in fact all sorts of valuable papers or documents payable on sight, to the drawer; and upon delivery to receive payment either in cash, certified check or a draft on a bank.

Messengers also present items discounted by the bank, or held as collateral, which mature from day to day and which must be presented in person for collection and payment.

The items presented by messengers are known as "city collections" and consist of the above items drawn on payees located in the town or area served by the bank as distinguished from "country collections" which are items sent by the bank to a bank in another town who use their messengers to present the item for collection and payment.

The responsibility of messenger in a bank is either a part time job or full time position.

In a smaller bank, messenger functions are generally a part time responsibility of the mail clerk, a clerk in the bookkeeping department, a teller, or even the janitor. In small towns, where there are one or two banks, it is generally the practice for one of the tellers or the proof clerk to act as messenger and present checks for exchange with the other bank in the morning, and to make the exchange and return items and final settlement in the afternoon. In such towns items for collection, unless circumstances are unusual, are very seldom "presented." Because everyone is known, it is the general practice of the bank which has a collection item drawn on a customer, to call him on the phone, telling him that the item has come in for collection, and make arrangements for its pickup and payment.

In a large bank the position of messenger usually is one held either by career men who enjoy meeting people, and spending a great deal of their time out of doors; by employees who do not have the ability or qualifications to advance to administrative positions within the bank and who, because of age and a desire on their part to remain active in the banking business, are delegated this responsibility; or by trainees in the process of applying what they learned from their lessons about banking to the actual business of banking. It is understood that a trainee, working as a messenger, is expected to possess all the qualities required to hold other advanced positions in the bank.

In making collections the messenger will come into contact with men in all walks of life, all types of businesses, and receive all sorts of treatment, which, if properly assimilated, will provide him with the background for getting along with people and adjusting himself. These qualities will serve him well in his future career as a banker.

Before assuming the responsibilities of the position of messenger, it is presumed that the trainee, through study and proper indoctrination, has become familiar with negotiable instruments; the various services of the bank; names of the officers and directors; and can intelligently answer questions about the bank which others are likely to ask of him.

Whether the messenger is a career man or a trainee, the position plays an important part in banking operation. The duties are simple yet responsibilities important, and his every act is surrounded by precedence or governed by banking law.

Unless he is an experienced and a career messenger, the messenger should not assume responsibilities and should only be sent out with explicit instructions as to what to do, what not to do, how to release items, and what to accept in payment of items. Generally he should not take anything but certified checks or cash in payment.

When business is being operated in a period of economic stability, it generally makes little difference whether payment of a collection item be made in cash, certified check or draft. However, it is well to remember that in the event of failure of the bank making the collection; or the bank on which the instrument received in payment is drawn, certain questions of law arise which can place responsibility on the presenting bank because of improper presentation. It is well for all messengers to be thoroughly acquainted with the responsibility which prudent bank management will place upon them, based upon the advice of their legal counsel.

Messengers should also thoroughly understand the value of the paper entrusted to their care. In the course of a normal day's business, a messenger may have entrusted to his care checks, bills of exchange, coupons, securities and other documents valued at thousands of dollars for which he must account and for which the bank is responsible in case of loss. Messengers, therefore, are usually provided with a stout wallet or case with a padlock which is generally attached to the messenger's wrist, which device is to prevent robbery or holdup.

In order to maintain control over items to be handled by the messengers, the messenger, or the section, usually give the section from which they received the item for presentation a receipt. Such items in return, which are to be handled by a messenger, are indexed on a register by date, name of section from which received, name of payer, name of payee, a brief description of the document, and the amount involved. The original of the register goes with the messenger, the duplicate remaining as the receipt and record for the bank. Such register usually has a space for the section or person who requested the messenger to present the item for collection to receipt for proceeds or item, if payment is refused when it is returned to them.

While every bank employee is adequately protected against holdup or robbery by insurance carried by the bank, which protects the employee and the bank in case of holdup or robbery while the employee is engaged in business of the bank, it is the usual practice to have messengers who are carrying large amounts of cash or valuables accompanied by another messenger or a guard.

As time is the essence to any collection item, a qualified messenger must become acquainted with the city and know the quickest way to get to any part of the city. Further, to avoid backtracking, he should be able to schedule stops to be made so as to cover the route in the quickest possible time. In a large city, where much territory has to be covered, regular routes will be laid out which the messenger will follow in presenting collections for payment, and in handling other business for the bank such as the pickup of clearings, return of checks which are dishonored, and delivery of mail to other banks.

Generally two collection runs a day are made by the messengers, one in the morning for items which have been received by the presenting bank late the previous day, or which have been held by the bank and are due to be presented and paid on that particular day; and the afternoon run consisting of items which were received for presentation and collection from other banks in the morning mail.

The position of messenger is a very important one for a trainee, as it is the first position in the bank which has responsibilities attached to it. It is well for every trainee to remember that is it from the position of messenger that many of today's bank presidents have come.

The accepted and standard procedure for personnel of the mail and messenger section to follow in performing their work and in discharging their responsibilities are generally covered by operating instructions. Such operating instructions, issued by the officer in charge of operations, are usually in connection with the following:

1. Schedule for delivery of incoming mail.
2. Schedule for pick up and processing of outgoing mail.
3. Assignment of locations for inter-bank pickup stations.
4. Procedure for handling Registered Mail.

CHAPTER XXVIII

THE PROOF, CLEARING AND TRANSIT SECTION

IT IS IMPORTANT THAT EVERY PERSON WHO aspires to be a successful banker should acquire knowledge and familiarity with the processes or mechanics through which wealth—represented by mediums of exchange in the form of promises to pay given in exchange for something of equal value—is transferred from one person to another.

Such promises to pay, written on pieces of paper known as checks, are handled for presentation, collection, and payment through the clearings and transit operations of banks. Clearings generally refers to the presentation and collection of checks drawn on other local banks, while transit refers to the collection and payment of checks drawn on banks located in towns other than that in which the bank is located.

In discussing checks and their collection it is well to remember that a check is nothing more than an order on a bank to pay MONEY, and it is subject to all the laws of negotiable instruments. It is well to remember, too, that before a check is of real value to the holder, it must be presented for encashment, in which case the presenter receives currency; or it must be deposited in a bank and collected so that the proceeds can be converted into cash upon demand by the depositor. Checks are only promises to pay dollars. They are not promises to pay anything else, and can only be converted into currency when actually presented on the bank on which drawn and a demand is made for currency.

In spite of the widespread use and the many advantages of using checks as a circulating medium, the fact that they are only promises, and must be redeemed in money (currency-silver) upon presentation and demand, does not make them a circulating medium.

One of the serious problems of the American banking system,

prior to the creating of the Federal Reserve System, was the fact that banks had no way to turn their assets into circulating medium to redeem the checks of depositors when cash on hand and cash on deposit with other banks was inadequate to cover the demand for exchange of checks into currency. When this occurred, a bank had no other alternative except to sell their notes, mortgages, and investment securities at whatever the market would bring for currency, which in time of depression or panic were subject to wide fluctuation and depreciation and resulted in the bank assuming such losses that often its capital was impaired and it was forced to suspend operations.

With the creation of the Federal Reserve Banking System, whose provisions have been modified over the years, notably in 1933, 1934 and 1935, it can be generally said that today practically any asset of a bank can be rediscounted or pledged with the Federal Reserve Bank as a loan in exchange for currency with which to honor checks presented for payment.

The collection of checks deposited or cashed by customers, or arising from business and banking transactions, is one of the most important services banks provide.

Checks which banks process in the usual course of business originate from many sources (customers, sections of the bank in payment of services, interest, fees, etc.)

Such checks, however, for the purpose of presentation and collection are classified to one of four sources of payment:

A. Checks drawn on the same bank in which they were deposited, cashed, or originated.

B. Checks drawn on other banks located in the same city, which will be paid through the clearing house.

C. Checks drawn on other banks located in the same city which do not belong to the clearing house, which must be presented either directly, in exchange for a draft drawn on a major reserve city bank, or handled through a correspondent bank.

D. Checks drawn on banks located in cities, other than the one in which the receiving bank is located, which must be presented for payment either through the Federal Reserve Bank or a correspondent bank.

The collection of local checks is handled through the clearing section of the bank, while the collection of items drawn on banks located in other cities is handled through the transit section.

THE PROOF SECTION

The mechanics through which clearings and transit items are presented for payment, which incidentally is a function performed ONLY by banks, begins simultaneously, or as a by-product of the process in connection with the accepting and proving of deposits.

When we refer to proving a deposit, we refer solely to the mechanics in connection with verifying the fact that the total as represented by the individual checks deposited to the credit of a customer's account agrees with the total as listed on the deposit ticket.

The procedure, used by banks in proving deposits and handling of cash items, is generally predicated on the volume of deposits handled and the type of business serviced. For example, in a small country bank or a bank located in a residential community, deposits will consist generally of one or two items with only an occasional deposit, usually from merchants or those engaged in industry, containing ten or more items. In a larger bank, of course, or those located in an industrial area, more of the deposits will consist of or contain a large number of checks. One of the peculiar aspects of the deposit transaction is that, in general, the errors in proving the deposits occur where more than one, but less than ten checks are deposited. This is due to carelessness, and also to the fact that deposits containing a large number of checks are usually prepared by an experienced bookkeeper who proves them on the adding machine or lists them on the deposit ticket by adding machine.

In some banks, the receiving teller proves the deposits and lists the items on his cage blotter sheet which he uses at the end of the day to record the balance of his cage.

In many small banks where they have a low volume of deposit activity, the teller, to make certain there is no error in the deposit ticket, will run the items on the adding machine while the customer waits.

In banks where there are more customers and more depositors and the tellers do not have the time to prove the deposits at the window, they merely extract the cash, substitute a cash ticket, and turn over the deposits, together with the cash ticket, to the proof clerk who handles the transactions from the individual tellers separately. This procedure effectively proves out the balancing of a teller with the proof section at the end of the day.

Activity, types of deposits, and the number of banks to which items are sent for collection, determines which system and equipment used in proving deposits is most adaptable to the bank. This will vary from the ordinary adding machine to the complex sorting and calculating equipment which has been used by larger banks for many years, and also to the new equipment utilizing electronics which by means of magnetic tape or a punch card system automatically does the sorting, calculating and listing.

There are several recognized methods commonly used by banks in proving deposits or in verifying the total of the aggregate checks deposited with the total on the deposit ticket.

A. Individual deposit proof.

B. Group deposit proof, or the batch system.

C. Central proof.

Individual Deposit Proof. Under the individual deposit proof system the teller, or some clerk, checks the addition on the deposit ticket after which the items are sorted into checks on us, checks drawn on other local banks, items drawn on banks outside of the city and miscellaneous items. After such proof and segregations have been made, the items are run on a teller's blotter sheet. Then they are sent to the clearing or transit section or to the clerks who handle these functions for relisting on a collection sheet, according to the bank on which the items are drawn, for later presentation for payment.

Group Deposit Proof or Batch System. Under a group deposit or batch system, the proof clerk works on the theory and premise that if each deposit is correctly totaled, the sum of the checks, after sorting to banks on which drawn and re-run, will equal the total of the deposit tickets. In operation of this system, the proof clerk takes a number of deposits and first runs a total. Next he takes all of the checks, sorts them out according to whether they are clearing checks, transit checks, on us checks, or cash tickets, and runs them by groups. If the total of all the deposit tickets, as determined by the proof operator, is exactly the same as the total of all items after being sorted and run, it is considered that the batch is in proof. If, however, there is an error, it is necessary to recheck the items back against the individual deposit tickets to discover the error.

Central Proof. The central proof system is strictly a machine operation, under which the teller is responsible only for the cash he receipts for in a deposit taken in at the window—or for cash paid out in cashing a check. In processing a deposit, the teller counts the cash and verifies that the actual cash agrees with the amount of cash as listed on the deposit ticket, entering it on a cash-in ticket which he substitutes for the cash which he places in his cash drawer.

After receipting for the full amount of the deposit in the customer's pass book, or issuing a teller's machine receipt, the teller sends the deposit ticket, together with the cash-in ticket and checks to the proof section for processing.

When a teller pays out cash he either records the amount on a cash-out ticket, or segregates such checks and periodically records the amount on his teller's sheet before turning over the checks he has cashed to the proof section for processing.

When the deposit slip, together with the checks and/or cash-in ticket is received in the proof section, the clerk or machine operator, who may be the same, depending on the size of the bank and volume handled, enters the amount of the deposit in the proof machine by punching out the amount, depressing the bar which records the amount, and adds it to the total of previously recorded deposits. The operator then enters the amount of each check in the proof machine by punching out the amount of the check and selecting a key for sorting, which directs the check to the slot in the name of the bank on which drawn, or through which it will be collected. All checks are listed by amounts and added to the totals on a master tape, while each individual check is added to the accumulated total of items sorted to respective banks. After all checks and cash-in tickets have been run and listed, the operator totals the items. Should the total equal the amount of the deposit, the machine automatically clears. If however, the total of the individual groups of checks does not balance with the deposit, the machine locks or indicates to the operator that an error has occurred. Periodically, or at the end of the day the checks are taken out of each compartment to which they have been sorted and the tapes attached. The tapes are used as clearing or transit letters for presentation of respective items to the banks on which drawn, for payment.

The proof clerks, in some banks, may also review each check before it is processed and mark on the deposit ticket, opposite the amount of the check, the number of days it will take to collect the item, or convert it into cash, so the bookkeeper can make a proper note on the ledgers and refer all checks drawn against uncollected funds to an officer for approval before paying.

Today, many banks are re-analyzing their situation in line with using special proof equipment. While there can be distinct advantages in using special proof machines, final decision should only be made after study and analysis of the contributions such equipment can make to economical operating efficiency.

There are several manufacturers of proof machines, each of whom produce models to fit any number of types of operation. It is not wise to assume that any one machine or any one system is better than another until proven. Each machine has its distinct advantages and, because of the changes which are constantly taking place, it is suggested before deciding on new equipment that up-to-date information be obtained on the operation of each of the respective machines, especially since many of these machines are being adjusted or adapted today to future use of automation and electronic equipment.

The proof section generally operates on a continuous schedule. The first thing in the morning they generally assist the clearings section in processing in-clearings. When this phase is completed, they begin their periodical picking up, proving, and processing of deposits and tickets from the tellers, and other sections of the bank.

TELLER BALANCING UNDER VARIOUS TYPES OF PROOF SYSTEMS

The teller's participation in the proof system comes at the end of the day when he balances.

When a teller proves his own deposits, he merely picks up the totals of the checks and deposits from his teller's blotter sheet, crediting the totals of deposits to the bookkeeping section; debiting the total of the checks on the bank which he has cashed or accepted for deposit to the bookkeeping section; the totals of the checks drawn on other local banks, which he has received in deposit or cashed to the clearings section; and the totals of the checks which he has cashed, or received in deposit drawn on banks in other cities, to the transit section. He thereafter effects his balancing through the counting of cash.

Where a batch system is used it is the customary practice for the tellers, at the end of the day, to include in their sheet a total for each group or class of checks cashed which have gone through their cages and report such figures to a general clerk or summary clerk, who consolidates the figures from the other departments to effect the balancing of the bank.

Under a batch or central proof system, the paying and receiving tellers merely balance to cash, that is, using cash on hand at the beginning of the day plus cash received in deposits, which is accounted for by cash-in tickets; balancing this against cash paid out through the encashments of checks, accounted for by cash-out tickets, plus the cash remaining on hand at the end of the day.

Under this system it is up to the proof operator to reconcile and balance the checks received in deposits using the cash tickets to balance with the teller and the items taken from the teller which they have cashed against the total cash-out tickets. Such a system simplifies the whole operation of paying and receiving and permits quicker balancing at the close of business.

While the proof work can be undertaken by a teller or a clerk as a part time job, most banks find it helpful to organize a separate proof section, or allocate work so that the proving of deposits becomes one person's principal responsibility, often with the additional responsibility of preparing local checks for presentation and payment and for the sending of transit items through correspondent banks or Federal Reserve Banks, for presentation and payment.

ERRORS IN DEPOSITS

No matter how careful depositors are, errors and mistakes are bound to occur in deposit transactions. Some errors and mistakes are those of judgment, other errors are in listing, while others are errors in addition. In any event, a qualified and experienced proof clerk or operator should be familiar with such errors and the procedures to follow in correcting them, should they occur.

In order to avoid adjustments it is the accepted practice in many banks to review all checks received in deposits for date, endorsement and irregularity, before being processed. Other banks leave the discovery of errors either to the proof operator or to the banks on which the item is drawn.

An experienced proof clerk or operator, however, in proving and processing deposits should be certain:

A. Checks are signed.

B. The date on the check is prior to presentation.

C. There has been no change or alteration in name or amount.

D. That by endorsement, the depositor has proper title to the check.

E. All items listed on the deposit slip are accounted for, and balance with the grand total of all items as entered on the deposit slip.

If the check is not signed but carries a printed name, bears a current date or is undated, and is of nominal amount but otherwise in order, many banks, assuming carelessness, follow the practice of processing the check and leave final decision as to honoring the item to the paying bank.

If the check discloses an apparent alteration or change in the name, date or amount, the item is generally referred to an officer for decision. Usually such items are deducted from the deposit and the customer is immediately notified to pick up the check so as to take proper steps as are warranted under the circumstances.

Where checks payable to the person who made the deposit are unendorsed, many banks follow the practice of stamping the check with an endorsement stamp which reads "Credited to the account of the within named Payee."

If the check is endorsed by the payee, but does not bear the endorsement of the depositor, such items are generally either deducted from the deposit and the item returned to the depositor—

or the deposit is held out and the depositor notified to come to the bank and supply the proper endorsement.

Where there are errors in addition, listing, or checks are missing, the deposit is generally first referred to an officer, after which the entire deposit is processed, with the necessary debit or credit to adjust the error, with an advice by mail or telephone, or both, to the depositor describing the error.

Most banks have established policy as to the procedure to follow in case there are errors in a deposit. Generally these policies are in the form of operating instructions, or standard procedures. Should there be any doubt as to the procedure to follow, the matter should be referred to an officer for official decision.

ERRORS IN PROVING DEPOSITS

Errors caused by failure of the items listed in a deposit to balance with the total amount as entered on the deposit ticket are often the result of transpositions or mistakes in the listing of items For example, the total of the amount as listed on the deposit ticket is $9.00 more than the totals of the individual checks. This could be the result of listing a check for $1.00 as 10.00. In like manner, the total as listed on the deposit tickt is $18.00 less than the totals of the individual checks which could be the result of listing a check of $20.00 as $2.00. The operator can also make such mistakes in running the items on the machine.

There are hundreds of similar transpositions and mistakes many of which experienced operators pride themselves in recalling—in solving and adjusting differences. Some of these, as an example are:

	REASON FOR THE DIFFERENCE	
If the difference in cents or dollars is:	if LESS than the total is in listing or in the running of,	if MORE than the total is in listing or in the running of,
2	3 instead of 5 or 7 instead of 9	5 instead of 3 or 9 instead of 7
3	5 instead of 8	8 instead of 5
5	3 instead of 8	8 instead of 3
6	1 instead of 7	7 instead of 1

9	1 instead of 10	10 instead of 1
18	2 instead of 20	20 instead of 2
27	3 instead of 30	30 instead of 3
36	4 instead of 40	40 instead of 4
45	5 instead of 50	50 instead of 5
54	6 instead of 60	60 instead of 6
63	7 instead of 70	70 instead of 7
72	8 instead of 80	80 instead of 8
81	9 instead of 90	90 instead of 9
90	10 instead of 100	100 instead of 10
99	1 instead of 100	100 instead of 1
180	20 instead of 200	200 instead of 20
198	2 instead of 200	200 instead of 2
270	30 instead of 300	300 instead of 30
297	3 instead of 300	300 instead of 3
360	40 instead of 400	400 instead of 40
396	4 instead of 400	400 instead of 4
450	50 instead of 500	500 instead of 50
495	5 instead of 500	500 instead of 5
540	60 instead of 600	600 instead of 60
594	6 instead of 600	600 instead of 6
630	70 instead of 700	700 instead of 70
693	7 instead of 700	700 instead of 7
720	80 instead of 800	800 instead of 80
792	8 instead of 800	800 instead of 8
810	90 instead of 900	900 instead of 90
891	9 instead of 900	900 instead of 9
900	100 instead of 1000	1000 instead of 100
990	10 instead of 1000	1000 instead of 10

PROOF SECTION OPERATING CHECK LIST

In order to operate in an efficient manner, many proof sections follow a daily procedure similar to that outlined on the following check list:

A. Before beginning the day's work, the operator should be certain that

1. All totalizers on the machine register zero.

2. All checks have been removed from the slots or bins.
3. The endorsement dater is set for the current day.
4. There is sufficient tape on tabulators to provide for the listing of the day's work.

B. Assist with the running and proving of in-clearings.
1. Run and prove items against list and sort to processing points.
2. When run is complete, remove checks from slots or bins, attach tapes, and
3. Enter totals on summary or re-cap sheet.
4. Deliver checks and tapes to other sections for processing.
5. Check to be certain machine is cleared, and totalizers register zero.

C. Begin with proof of deposit work.
1. Record amount of deposit in machine.
2. Scan check for signature and correctness of date. Enter amount in keyboard. Depress key, selecting bank to which item will be sent for collection.
3. Turn item over, in manner prescribed under standard procedure, and check for endorsement.
4. If in order, depress recording bar.
5. Process next deposit.
6. When run is complete, or it is cut-off time, close off individual tapes, remove checks from bins or slots, affix tapes to batches, deliver to proper section for processing. (In proofing deposits, considerable time can be saved if deposits containing one item are held aside and run in batches. That is, all such deposits are run at once and totaled, with the items sorted and totaled as if they they were part of a single deposit.)

D. When day's work is complete.
1. Close off individual tapes.
2. Remove checks from slots or bins. Bind with respective tapes.
3. Record totals of each section on blotter sheet and deliver to general bookkeeper or settlement clerk for use in effecting balance of the bank.

4. Deliver checks and tapes to respective sections for final processing of items.

The sources of items and routing for final processing are illustrated in Exhibit 88.

In connection with processing checks for collection, it should be remembered that the bank has either advanced cash, in the case of checks which have been cashed; or has credited the account of the presenter with the proceeds, sometimes permitting him to draw and use such funds; before the checks are actually converted into cash. As in both instances the bank is actually loaning the funds to the customer without the payment of interest, it is important that such items be collected as speedily as possible. It is the customary procedure, therefore, regardless of whether the teller, proof clerk, or central proof section prove the deposits, to have the transit clerk or section send all items drawn on out of town banks to the Federal Reserve Bank or their city correspondent as soon as possible after the close of business, so that the items can be presented to respective banks on which drawn, for collection and payment early the following morning.

It is also customary, where a city bank handles a large volume of mail deposit items or has a large volume of correspondent bank business, to employ a night crew to process such items so that they can be presented for payment through the clearings the following morning.

In connection with checks drawn on local banks, it is the customary practice to have all such checks prepared for presentation to other banks through the clearing house, or to other banks for exchange and payment the first thing the following morning. In some instances banks even exchange clearings with other local banks late in the afternoon, so that the work will be ready for processing by their bookkeeping staff early the following morning. It is also common practice, particularly among the larger city banks, where checks of substantial amounts are deposited, to present such checks to the bank on which drawn within a few hours after being deposited, in order that the funds may be converted into legal reserve with the Federal Reserve Bank the same day.

As items drawn on other banks, once they have been processed by the proof section, are passed on to other sections for further processing, our next study will be in connection with the collection

Exhibit 88

SOURCE AND ROUTING OF ITEMS PROCESSED BY PROOF SECTION

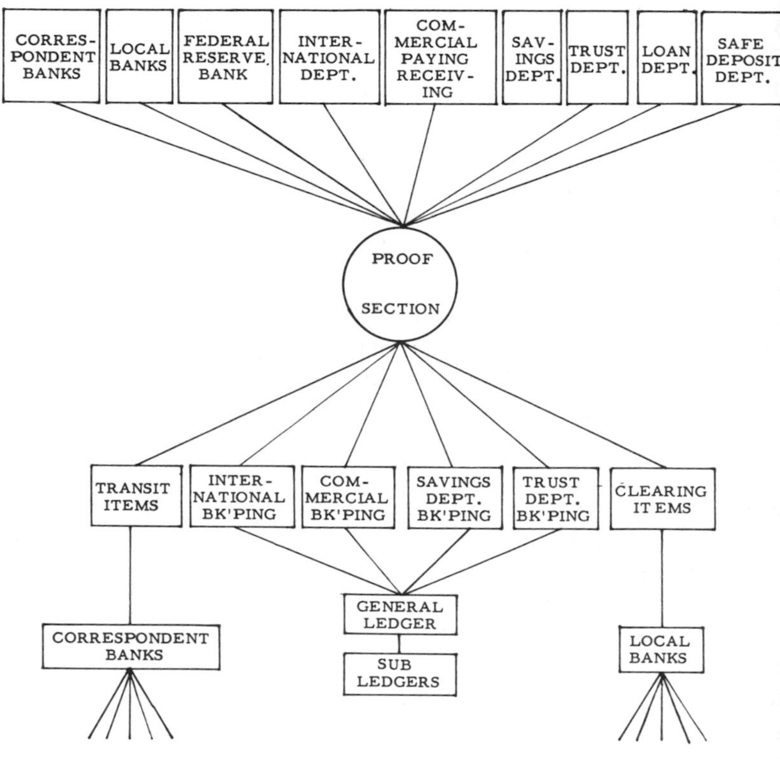

of checks drawn on other banks and functions of the clearings section and transit section.

THE CLEARINGS SECTION

The clearings section of a bank has two principal functions:

A. In-clearings function, or the acceptance, proving and processing all items drawn on themselves, presented for payment by other banks located in the same town; received from correspondent banks or the Federal Reserve Bank.

B. Out-clearings functions, or the presentation of items for collection drawn on other local banks, which the presenting bank received in deposits or in the settling of obligations.

In-Clearings. In the handling and exchange of items between other local banks, settlement is either made through the clearing house, if there is more than one bank in the town or area, or by direct exchange of items between banks.

In cases where a clearing house operates, all member banks take their checks drawn on other banks to a central point, at a mutually convenient time each day—usually the first thing in the morning. By means of debiting or crediting on a settlement sheet, they make one check to the clearing house settlement bank for the difference, or in turn receive a check from the clearing house settlement bank, should the checks charged against them and belonging to them be less than the checks which they have presented through the clearing house, drawn on and payable by other banks.

Should the clearing arrangement merely be for the exchange of checks, then each bank makes an individual settlement with the other banks tendering their draft, if the checks the other bank presents exceed those which the presenting bank has for them, or receiving in return, the draft of the other bank, should the presenting bank's checks exceed the checks the other bank is tendering them for collection and payment.

As soon as exchanges have been made, the respective bundles of checks are brought back to the individual banks where they are proven. Sometimes, particularly if automatic equipment is used, the checks are proven and sorted in one operation.

If the checks are merely to be proven, it is the customary practice to rerun the items on an adding machine, being sure the total of such items received from a certain bank equals the total shown by the check or tape attached to the checks. Under this procedure when all batches have been proven, the items are then sorted to several bookkeeping and other sections for final processing. If, however, the checks are processed on proof machines, they are proved and sorted in the same operation.

Whether a proof machine is used or not, checks after being proven, or during the time they are proven, are sorted to various bookkeeping, general bank or general ledger sections. Depending on the volume of checks, the number of accounts and activity, checks are generally sorted to the bookkeeping section breakdown which in the simplest form is the A to K section, and the L to Z section.

A secondary breakdown in a medium sized bank might be from A to E; F to K; L to R; and S to Z. In a larger bank, again depending on the breakdown of the proof machine used, would take any one of a number of combinations. In addition, in proving, sorts are also made, where proof machines are used, to cashier's checks, money orders, expense checks, trust checks and consumer credit loan checks.

It is even possible, where a bank is favored with an account which draws an exceptionally large number of checks, to provide a slot on the proof machine for immediate proving and sorting of such items, which can then be posted to a commercial account in total.

Once in-clearings are proven and found to be in balance, they are then turned over to the bookkeeping section for fine sorting and preparation for posting to the respective accounts, a process covered in the next chapter.

In reviewing checks presented by other banks through the clearings for payment, it is necessary that the bank check over and review all items presented to see that they are in proper and acceptable order before they are paid, posted to respective accounts and cancelled.

In order to discharge this responsibility, it is necessary that the bank assures itself that:

1. The signature is genuine and authorized.

2. The check does not bear a prior date.
3. The amount or name of payee has not been altered.
4. The item has been properly endorsed by the payee.
5. The maker has not stopped payment on the check.

While this responsibility is discharged in every bank, the procedure followed in carrying out these functions will vary between banks, depending on the size of the bank, volume, and methods and procedures used.

In some banks the checking of dates, endorsements and amounts is the function of the in-clearings section. In other banks this responsibility is the function of the bookkeeping clerks, or bookkeepers at the time they are fine sorting the items preparatory to posting them to the ledger sheets of respective accounts on which drawn. At this time they also pay signatures, and check for stop payment orders.

In other banks the proving and sorting of items to the bookkeeping section is the sole function of the in-clearings clerk. The paying of signatures, date and endorsement is the responsibility of the paying and receiving tellers, after the items have been posted to respective accounts on which drawn, prior to cancellation and filing. The procedure will vary with banks depending on operating methods, procedures used and other factors.

Out-Clearings. Out-clearings refers to the preparation of checks cashed or deposited by customers of the bank, and processed by the proof section or proof clerk, which are to be presented to the local bank on which drawn for payment.

If the sorting of checks to respective local banks on which drawn is not a function of the proof section or a by-product of the proving of deposits, it is then the function of a designated clerk, after the items have been proven, to sort them out according to the local banks on which drawn and to see they are properly endorsed and prepared for presentation.

In a small town, served by more than one, but less than five or six banks, the so-called clearings, when received from the proof section, if not automatically sorted at time of proving are sorted down to the respective banks. They are then balanced and packaged, together with the tape showing the amount of the collective checks, and presented the following morning directly or through the clearing house association, to the bank on which drawn, for payment.

In banks located in larger cities, however, several methods of collecting out-clearings are followed, again depending on the size of the bank and the number of banks in the area. Should the bank be a small bank deposit-wise; or be located where they have a small volume of items drawn on other banks, whether or not they use mechanized sorting equipment; it is generally the policy to only sort items to respective banks when there is a sufficient number of items daily to justify the sorting. In such cases banks generally will segregate and sort items out to the most important banks, bunching or collectively handling miscellaneous items drawn on the remainder banks, and depositing them to their account with one of their larger banks which acts as their correspondent.

If, however, they happen to be one of the larger banks, they will sort the individual items to respective banks and either make a direct presentation, receiving in return their checks or collectively handle the items through the clearing house association in the daily settlement.

Once the exchange of checks has been made between banks, the items received in exchange become in-clearings and are processed as previously described.

The clearing house section of a bank also performs another function, that is, the handling of items returned for insufficient funds, signature, date, endorsement or any reason which according to the law of negotiable instruments does not place the check in good delivery order. Generally, when these items have been refused by the bank, a slip is attached to the individual check describing the reason why payment has been refused on the check. Such items usually are placed in a special envelope and presented, together with the clearings, to the bank from which received as though it were a check drawn on them.

Once such returned items are received by the bank which originally presented them, adjustment is made by charging the account which deposited the check, or charging it back to a teller, in case the check was cashed, for collection of the item from the payee or last endorser.

TRANSIT SECTION

The work of a transit section, like the work of a clearings section is exacting and frequently performed under pressure.

Before considering the various channels through which checks drawn on banks located in other towns are collected, it is well to recall again that checks are only promises to pay money, which is only available for use of the holder when the check has been converted into cash. It is, therefore, the important responsibility of the transit section, or of a clerk who functions as a transit clerk, to see that all items are promptly presented to the bank on which drawn by the most rapid means, (messenger, regular or air mail, special delivery) so that such checks can be rapidly converted into cash and/or earning assets.

In order to properly discharge this responsibility, the transit section, like the mail section, maintains railroad and air line transportation schedules so that sending of checks for collection to respective points can be made at the earliest opportunity.

Checks drawn on out of town banks are of two classes, and are referred to as "par" and "non-par" items. Par items are those which are remitted for at face value by the bank on which drawn. Non-par items are those against which the bank on which the checks are drawn deducts a fee, referred to as "exchange" (which we shall cover later in this section) from the amount of the check, in making the remittance.

In connection with par and non-par checks or items, there are three principal ways in which checks drawn on out of town banks can be collected — directly, through a correspondent bank, or through the facilities of the Federal Reserve Banks.

The direct collection of items generally refers to the procedure banks follow in sending items drawn on out of town banks to another bank in the same town, as a regular collection item, requesting them to present the checks to the other bank for payment and to remit the proceeds, either by means of a draft on a Federal Reserve Bank or a major city bank. Obviously this process is not only expensive but slow, and is only used by banks when a check requires special handling.

The regular collection of checks through a correspondent bank, referred to as the "direct sending of items," is a service provided by major banks for their correspondent bank cutomers, in connection with the presentation and collection of checks drawn on banks located in other sections of the country, especially those which do not remit at par.

This service is also of particular value to banks which are not members of the Federal Reserve System, and to country banks that use the facilities of their correspondent banks located in the major cities in order to collect checks drawn on banks located in the city where the correspondent is located, and in other cities where the correspondent maintains a comparable relationship.

The collection of checks through the Federal Reserve Banks is a service provided to banks which are members of the Federal Reserve System. Only checks drawn on banks which remit at par, however, can be collected through their regular clearing facilities.

Checks received in deposits or cashed, as we previously learned are sent from the tellers and other sections of the bank to the proof section where they are processed. If they are checks drawn on local banks, they are then sent to the clearings section for presentation to the bank on which drawn, either through the clearing house association or directly by the clearings clerk.

If the checks are drawn on out of town banks, they are sent by the proof section to the transit section for processing and sending to banks located in various sections of the country for presentation and payment.

In preparing items on out of town banks for collection, if a batch system is used, the items are generally sorted to collecting points by hand, after which they are listed on a transit letter which shows the amount of the check, the number of the bank on which drawn, and the name and/or number of the endorser.

A copy of this transit letter is kept by the bank while the original accompanies the checks which are sent to the Federal Reserve Bank or a correspondent bank for presentation and collection.

However, where a bank makes use of a proof machine, through which deposits are proven and items sorted in the same operation, pockets or slots are generally allocated to banks at a certain sending point. Under such a setup, at the end of the day, the checks are merely extracted from the pockets; the original of the tape is affixed to them; the package is stamped with the name of the bank to which they are sent; and the envelope placed in the mail; with the duplicate or master remaining as the bank's record.

As protection to the bank in the event a transit letter is lost in the mail, stolen or destroyed, many banks follow the practice of photographing all checks so that in the event of such loss, copies of the check can be reproduced for presentation and payment; or charged back to the endorser in order to obtain a duplicate check from the maker.

The routing systems banks follow in presenting items drawn on out of town banks for collection and payment varies, depending on the size and location of the bank, and class of business handled.

Banks, whether they are members of the Federal Reserve System or not, may send both par and non-par items direct to the bank on which drawn for collection, or make full use of the facilities of their principal correspondent bank.

Other banks which are members of the Federal Reserve System may send checks drawn on non-par banks direct, or to one of their correspondent banks for presentation and payment, while collecting all par items through the Federal Reserve Bank.

Still other banks, which are members of the Federal Reserve System, may either send all or part of their par items for collection to their correspondent bank, or Federal Reserve Bank of their district, while sending items drawn on banks in the city in which the Federal Reserve Bank is located to their correspondent located in the same city, for presentation and payment through the clearing house.

In addition, if banks which are members of the Federal Reserve System have a large volume of par items drawn on banks located in other Federal Reserve Districts, they may send the items direct to the Federal Reserve Bank of that district with instructions to credit the proceeds to their account with the Federal Reserve Bank of the district in which they are located.

To facilitate the collection of checks between Federal Reserve Banks, a complete wire system connects all Federal Reserve Banks with other Federal Reserve Banks and their branches. Member banks are also permitted use of this facility for the purpose of transferring funds from one member bank to another member bank.

Larger banks, on the other hand, which use the facilities of their correspondent banks instead of, or in connection with, the facilities provided by Federal Reserve Banks generally, depending on the source of items for collection, volume, and location of banks on which the items are drawn, may either send all their items, drawn on out of town banks, to their city correspondent, or to the Federal Reserve Bank, or they may maintain one or more correspondent accounts with banks located in the East, Mid-West, South, South-West, and West, through which they will send both par and non-par items for presentation and collection.

However, when the facilities of the Federal Reserve Banks are used, because of the need to maintain reserve requirements, which, depending on class of bank, represent a percentage of time and demand deposit member banks must keep on deposit with the Federal Reserve Bank; and because funds from items drawn on out of town banks are not considered reserve until collected; member banks are required to sort their items according to availability.

Under this requirement, member banks must sort items to those:

A. Drawn on nearby banks, collectible the same day as received, which are available for immediate credit.

B. Drawn on banks located in the immediate area which are to be presented for payment and collected the following day, which are on a one-day credit basis.

C. Drawn on banks some distance away (regardless of where drawn) which are considered to be presented for payment and collected in two or more days, which are on a two day credit basis.

Both the one and two-day deferred credit items must be set up in a deferred account and daily transfers made to the reserve account.

Before determining the geographical places checks drawn on out of town banks should be sent to for presentation and collection, banks should undertake careful study and analysis, over a reasonable and representative period of time, of all items processed through the proof section. This study should show the location of banks on which such out of town items are drawn and enable the bank to set up routing sorts to effect rapid and efficient collection of items.

Such analysis will generally disclose that out of town items should be sorted manually or through the operation of the proof machine to several or all of the following or similar groupings:

Slot	*Sorting*	*Representing items for or*
1.	Federal Reserve Bank	(Immediate credit)
2.	Federal Reserve Bank	(1 day deferred credit)
3.	Federal Reserve Bank	(2 day deferred credit)
4.	Federal Reserve Bank	(Miscellaneous)
5.	Correspondent Bank	(Non-par items)
6.	Correspondent Bank-East	(New York City)
7.	Correspondent Bank-East	(Drawn on banks located in eastern states/cities)
8.	Correspondent Bank-Mid W.	(Chicago)
9.	Correspondent Bank-Mid W.	(Drawn on banks located in mid-western states/cities)
10.	Correspondent Bank-South	(Atlanta-Jacksonville)
11.	Correspondent Bank-South	(Drawn on banks located in southern states/cities)
12.	Correspondent Bank-S. W.	(New Orleans, Dallas)
13.	Correspondent Bank-S. W.	(Drawn on banks located in south-west states/cities)
14.	Correspondent Bank-West	(Los Angeles, San Francisco, Seattle)
15.	Correspondent Bank-West	(Drawn on banks located in western states/cities)

In order to facilitate the rapid collection of checks through proper routing, the American Bankers Association, on May 2, 1911, established a system of numbering banks so that the location of the bank could be quickly recognized by looking at a number, rather than trying to read the name of the bank and determine its location.

Under this system each check shows the number of the bank on which the check is drawn; the state in which the bank is located; the city in which the Federal Reserve Bank to which the item should be sent for collection is located; and information as to whether the item is subject to immediate or deferred credit to the bank which presents the item. Explanation of these numbers is shown in Exhibit 89.

Under this numerical arrangement the numbers on all checks 1 to 49 are assigned to principal cities, while the numbers 50 to 99 are assigned to states. The prefix numbers of respective cities and states under the plan are shown in Exhibit 90.

Under authority of the American Bankers Association, Rand McNally & Company of Chicago, who publish the Rand McNally "Bankers Directory," commonly referred to as the "Blue Book," and the "Key to Numerical System of the American Bankers Association" assign numbers to new banks as they are organized.

EXCHANGE

Any discussion or review of the mechanics involved in the collection of checks would be incomplete without reference to the matter of exchange charges.

In the early days of this country, with the expansion of trade and commerce, banks mushroomed wherever large settlements were located. Although the use of drafts as a transfer of wealth or in settlement of debt were widely used, such items were still considered "orders to pay" and funds were only made available to the payee (unless discounted, or accepted in exchange of something of value) after the draft had been presented to the bank on which drawn and converted into money.

In those days, the only way this could be accomplished was by having someone travel to the town where the bank on which the draft was drawn was located; present the draft; and transport "back home" the gold or silver tendered in payment of the draft. It is well to recall here, and refer to the Suffolk Bank; also to remember there was no Federal Reserve Bank at that time and facilities and methods of operation of correspondent banks had not developed to where they could make provision for the collection and exchange of drafts—except in relatively few instances.

Later country banks opened accounts with banks located in the major cities and deposited with them gold and silver, against which they drew drafts. Today, of course, banks do not transfer currency or coin to other banks in payment of drafts they draw against them. They "settle the account" by tendering a draft drawn against a deposit account which they maintain in another bank, or against their balance in a Federal Reserve Bank, or the proceeds of checks drawn on other banks which they deposit to their account with the bank on which they draw drafts. In other words they have a balance on deposit convertible into cash on demand.

Prior to 1914, banks all over the country consistently made a practice of what was known as an exchange charge. This charge, which was proper and legitimate at that time, arose out of two circumstances.

1. The cost of transporting currency and coin from the bank on which the draft was drawn to the bank which presented the check which they received for collection from their customer.

2. The cost of transporting gold, silver and currency from the bank on which drafts were drawn to a bank in a major city so that checks could be paid at the point of presentation instead of being sent back to the source or bank on which drawn.

With the advent of the Federal Reserve System process of settling balances and making transfers of funds between banks by

Exhibit 89

EXPLANATION OF A.B.A. ROUTING NUMBERS

STATE-------------------	70-1669	-------NUMBER OF BANK
(Illinois)	711	(Wilmette State Bank) (Wilmette, Illinois)

FEDERAL RESERVE BANK AND CITY IN WHICH LOCATED, TO WHICH ITEM SHOULD BE SENT, AND WHETHER ITEM IS FOR IMMEDIATE OR DEFERRED CREDIT.

(Collectable through Federal Reserve)
(Bank of Chicago on second day.)

Exhibit 90

AMERICAN BANKERS ASSOCIATION
CHECK PREFIX NUMBERS OF CITIES AND STATES

CITIES

1 New York, N. Y.
2 Chicago, Ill.
3 Philadelphia, Pa.
4 St. Louis, Mo.
5 Boston, Mass.
6 Cleveland, Ohio
7 Baltimore, Md.
8 Pittsburgh, Pa.
9 Detroit, Mich.
10 Buffalo, N. Y.
11 San Francisco, Calif.
12 Milwaukee, Wis.
13 Cincinnati, Ohio
14 New Orleans, La.
15 Washington, D. C.
16 Los Angeles, Calif.
17 Minneapolis, Minn.
18 Kansas City, Mo.
19 Seattle, Wash.
20 Indianapolis, Ind.
21 Louisville, Ky.
22 St. Paul, Minn.
23 Denver, Colo.
24 Portland, Ore.
25 Columbus, Ohio
26 Memphis, Tenn.
27 Omaha, Neb.
28 Spokane, Wash.
29 Albany, N. Y.
30 San Antonio, Tex.
31 Salt Lake City, Utah
32 Dallas, Texas
33 Des Moines, Iowa
34 Tacoma, Wash.
35 Houston, Tex.
36 St. Joseph, Mo.
37 Ft. Worth, Tex.
38 Savannah, Ga.
39 Oklahoma City, Okla.
40 Wichita, Kans.
41 Sioux City, Iowa
42 Pueblo, Colo.
43 Lincoln, Neb.
44 Topeka, Kan.
45 Dubuque, Iowa
46 Galveston, Tex.
47 Cedar Rapids, Iowa
48 Waco, Tex.
49 Muskogee, Okla.

STATES

EASTERN

50 New York
51 Connecticut
52 Maine
53 Massachusetts
54 N. Hampshire
55 New Jersey
56 Ohio
57 Rhode Island
58 Vermont
59 Hawaii

SOUTHEASTERN

60 Pennsylvania
61 Alabama
62 Delaware
63 Florida
64 Georgia
65 Maryland
66 N. Carolina
67 S. Carolina
68 Virginia
69 West Virginia

CENTRAL

70 Illinois
71 Indiana
72 Iowa
73 Kentucky
74 Michigan
75 Minnesota
76 Nebraska
77 North Dakota
78 South Dakota
79 Wisconsin

SOUTHWESTERN

80 Missouri
81 Arkansas
82 Colorado
83 Kansas
84 Louisiana
85 Mississippi
86 Oklahoma
87 Tennessee
88 Texas
89 Alaska

WESTERN

90 California
91 Arizona
92 Idaho
93 Montana
94 Nevada
95 New Mexico
96 Oregon
97 Utah
98 Washington
99 Wyoming

TERRITORIES

101 Puerto Rico

means of drafts drawn on Federal Reserve Banks, there was no longer a valid reason for banks to make a charge for expense incidental to converting checks and drafts into gold or silver.

It was common practice, however, for banks sometimes to advance funds to the presenter of a draft (by cashing) or by permitting them to draw checks against the balance represented by the draft they deposited, before it was collected or converted into gold or silver. (Today, if a person draws a check against a balance created by the deposit of checks which have not been collected or converted into money, without arrangements with the bank to do so, such checks are returned as being drawn against "uncollected funds.") Where such privilege was granted, it was customary for the banker to make a charge known as a "float charge" which consisted of interest for use of the funds for as many days as it took to collect the item. This was in addition to the so-called exchange charge.

With the organization of the Federal Reserve System, many banks who were not members continued to levy both charges, while the member banks, although eliminating the so-called charge for converting checks into gold or silver, continued to levy the charge for funds in the process of collection, whether used or not, which they continued erroneously to refer to as an "exchange charge." It was not until about 1930 when banks in many of the larger cities realizing that such charges drove deposits away, through action of their clearing house association, voted to do away with the so called "exchange" charge.

Even today, however, an ever declining number of small country state banks in the northwest and south, which are not members of the Federal Reserve System, continue to charge exchange which, under banking conditions of the last quarter century, can only be considered as legalized larceny.

Many of these banks fail to realize that the assessing of exchange charges, which are levied against the payee of a check and not the maker, implies that the funds customers maintain on deposit subject to check with banks which charge exchange (non-par banks) are at a discount, or worth less by comparison than funds customers maintain on deposit subject to check with par banks, or those banks which do not charge exchange.

Unfortunately, in many cases, exchange charges penalize only those customers who maintain substantial balances and bring business to the community. Unfortunately, too, many banks which charge exchange do so to produce income in lieu of assessing charges for rendering services, which, if properly and equitably applied, would result in having the customer who receives the service pay for the service.

In connection with the efficient operation of a proof, clearings and transit section, certain functions will probably be covered by standard procedures or operating instructions similar to the following:

1. Routing of items for collection drawn on out of town banks.
2. Schedule for closing off proof operations for processing of transit items.
3. Schedule for presenting checks for collection drawn on local banks.
4. Procedure for handling undated checks.
5. Procedure for handling unendorsed checks or checks improperly endorsed.
6. Procedure for handling checks where there is a discrepancy between the printed figure and the written figure.
7. Procedure for handling checks which have been altered.
8. Procedure for returning checks for stale date.

CHAPTER XXIX

THE COMMERCIAL BOOKKEEPING SECTION

IN THE PREVIOUS CHAPTER WE LEARNED that checks cashed, deposited by customers to the credit of their account, or received by departments and other sections of the bank in connection with banking transactions known as out-clearings, after being processed by the proof section, are distributed to the clearings, transit and bookkeeping sections for routing, presentation and payment.

We also learned how checks drawn on our bank, known as in-clearings are presented by other banks for processing and payment.

We will now take up the functions of the bookkeeping section which has the responsibility of seeing that checks, drawn on the bank by customers who maintain checking accounts, are in order and correctly charged against (deducted from) the balance the customer maintains in the account; and funds, in the form of checks, or cash, are correctly credited to (added to) the balance which the customer maintains in the checking account.

Before describing the functions of the commercial bookkeeping section and the methods and procedures followed by the personnel in carrying out their respective duties and responsibilities, it is well to remember that banks have the responsibility to maintain accurate records of all of the transactions in connection with a customer's account.

Not only does a depositor expect the bank to be accurate and to keep all of its transactions strictly confidential, but that the bank be in a position to provide him with information regarding the transactions of his account at any time, at his request.

The depositor also has a responsibility to the bank. The bank, and rightfully so, expects the depositor to keep a careful record of his own regarding his transactions.

The bank expects the depositor to list on the deposit ticket carefully and in detail the check which the bank is to collect and credit the proceeds to the account. The bank also expects the depositor to keep an accurate record of all the checks he writes, and to maintain a current balance so that it is not necessary for the bank to return checks for insufficient funds. This is always a source of embarrassment not only to the depositor, but to the bank as well.

In reviewing bookkeeping operations, it might be of interest to mention, for the information of the new generation of bankers, that the so-called mechanization of bookkeeping operations is of recent origin. Bookkeeping machines came into general use during the 1920/25 period. Prior to that period it was the single function of bookkeepers in banks to maintain huge bound books, known as Boston Ledgers which contained a permanent hand posted pen and ink record of all transactions of a customer's checking account.

Each day, in using this record, the bookkeeper would painstakingly by hand, enter opposite the name of the depositor, any deposits made and all checks presented and paid. The bookkeeper then would add the deposits to the previous balance, deduct the checks, and bring forward the new balance. Because of bulk and detail involved, it was not practical to provide the customer with a statement of his account. Instead, reconcilement was made by having the customer bring his pass book to the bank periodically, at which time the bookkeeper or an officer of the bank would add all the customer's deposits in the pass book, subtract from the total the aggregate of all checks which had been presented and paid since the last balancing, and bring forward the new balance for information of the customer. Later on, with the advent of machine posting, all transactions were posted both on a ledger and a statement, the latter of which was furnished to the customer. At this stage the pass book merely became a receipt book.

It is also interesting to point out that it has only been in recent years that pencils and erasers were permitted in banks, and when first used for figuring and preparing tickets were indelible and without erasers.

One of the first internal control and audit principles was in connection with erasures. It was the generally accepted practice, once a figure had been entered and had to be corrected, to draw a line through the original figure and list the corrected figure above or to the side. While later some use was made of ink eradicator in correcting mistakes, which too was frowned on, the common instrument for "erasing" was the "scratcher knife" which consisted of a small curved blade on a wooden handle.

While the principal function of the bookkeeping section, depending on the size of the bank, is in connection with the posting of deposits and checks to customers' accounts, it also has the following additional duties and responsibilities in connection with, or in relation to its principal functions, some of which are equally important:

1. The alphabetical or numerical sorting of all checks received from the proof and clearings section to respective bookkeeping sections and controls; and to respective accounts. within such control sections.

2. The reviewing and examining of all checks as to proper date; endorsement; agreement of amount as printed with amount written; and determining if the signature is authentic and authorized.

3. The reviewing of all checks received to be certain there are no stop payment orders or holds against the account.

4. The posting of checks and deposits to respective accounts.

5. The referring of all accounts overdrawn, or accounts against which the volume of checks presented exceeds the balance, to an officer for decision.

6. The handling of checks returned by the bank because of insufficient funds.

7. The sending out of proper notification to accounts on which checks have been honored creating an overdraft.

8. The proving and balancing of the ledgers after the day's posting is completed.

9. The photographing of checks.

10. The canceling of checks.

11. The filing of paid and cancelled checks by account.

12. The recording and maintaining of records in connection with the activity of accounts.

13. The periodical preparation and delivery of statements of the account to depositors together with paid and cancelled checks.

14. The maintaining of balance records for the use and information of the officers.

Duties and responsibilities will vary, between banks, depending on the size, the number and type of accounts handled, and other factors. In a large bank, one or several employees may be assigned responsibilities in connection with a single factor; while in a small bank handling several hundred accounts, all such duties and responsibilities might be handled by one person.

In order to more throughly understand these functions, they are herewith described in detail.

1. THE ALPHABETICAL OR NUMERICAL SORTING OF ALL CHECKS RECEIVED FROM THE PROOF AND CLEARING SECTIONS TO RESPECTIVE BOOKKEEPING SECTIONS AND CONTROLS, AND TO RESPECTIVE ACCOUNTS WITHIN SUCH SECTIONS. Sorting of checks to the various sections within the bookkeeping section does not present a difficult problem, but fine sorting, that is alphabetical sorting, is not such a simple matter.

Bank depositors, for some unknown reason, probably to disguise their signature to prevent forgery, have a tendency to write their name rapidly when signing checks. Unless one is very familiar with the signature, it is sometimes almost impossible to read.

In order to help bookkeepers to become familiar with the signatures on checks, it is sometimes the practice of banks to have a customer sign an additional signature card which is attached to the ledger sheet as assistance to the bookkeeper in recognizing the signature.

Another problem in connection with deciphering signatures and in sorting, however, arises from the use of joint accounts. When joint accounts are maintained in the name of husband and wife, even if it is a common name, it does not present too much of a problem because generally the account is never more than four or five names out of line. If the account, however, is maintained in the names of two or more individuals of no name relationship, for example a joint account in the name of John Jones and Raymond Peters, unless the sorters are familiar with the account, the checks will sometimes be sorted to the "J" and "Jo" section, while other times the checks will be sorted to the "P" and "Pe" section, resulting in errors, mis-sorts, and other problems. To overcome this problem, as well as the problem of deciphering signatures, it is becoming increasingly popular with banks to supply all of their customers with either personalized checks on which their name is printed, or to provide checks with an alpha/numerical identification number.

2. THE REVIEWING AND EXAMINING OF ALL CHECKS AS TO PROPER DATE, ENDORSEMENT, AGREEMENT OF AMOUNT AS PRINTED WITH AMOUNT AS WRITTEN, AND DETERMINING IF SIGNATURE IS AUTHENTIC AND AUTHORIZED. Work in connection with examination of checks may be done by the signature clerk, posting clerk or tellers; or it might be divided up among all three. An important fact to remember in examining checks is that the date, endorsement, and signature on checks reviewed are in proper order.

As to date—a check to be in proper date order must neither be postdated nor bear a stale date, even though an instrument is not invalid only for the reason that it is antedated or postdated. provided it is not done for illegal or fraudulant purposes. While the law holds that a person to whom an instrument so dated is delivered acquires the title thereto as of the date of delivery, a check dated in the future, however, is not an effective order on the bank until that date arrives.

Whenever a bookkeeper pays a check bearing a future date, the bank is exposed to possible loss unless the depositor confirms the action or accepts the check when it is returned to him together with his statement. Banks are very careful about accepting checks which bear a future date for it is presumed that the depositor can refuse to permit the item to be charged against the account until the date shown on the check—also up to that time the depositor has a perfect right to stop payment on the check.

Banks, as a matter of policy, discourage the practice of customers issuing postdated checks, and if they persist in the practice usually request them to transfer their account to another bank.

In cases where a check is presented for payment which bears a date 30 or 60 days prior to presentation, it is said to have a stale date. While holders of checks are legally responsible to present checks for payment within a reasonable time, banks can be held liable for honoring such checks unless they exercise ordinary precautions.

Generally bank policy determines if a check bearing a stale date should be cashed or accepted for deposit. As most banks try to conform to the wishes of their depositors in such matters, many banks follow the practice, when a check bearing a stale date is presented, to contact the customer before refusing payment.

As to endorsement—before a check is posted or charged against the balance of a customer's account it should be ascertained that the check was properly endorsed by the person to whom the check was made payable, and by subsequent endorsers.

Unless the checking of endorsements is done by someone other than the bookkeeper, most bookkeepers, when making a fine-sort, follow the practice of turning the checks over and looking at the endorsement as they put them in to the sorting compartments.

The reason banks require all checks to be endorsed is that, according to law, an instrument is only negotiated when it is transferred from one person to another in such a manner as to make the transferee the holder thereof. Unless the check is properly endorsed, it is not legally transferred.

Checks payable to bearer, of course, may be transferred by delivery. While not required by law, most banks require the person to whom they pay the money or from whom they accept the check for deposit, to endorse the check.

Checks made payable to the order of a named person or firm must first be endorsed by that person or firm before they can be transferred by delivery to another person.

When a person endorses a check he warrants that on due presentation the check will be accepted and paid; and if it is dishonored, and the necessary proceedings of dishonor are taken, he will pay the amount thereof to the holder or to any subsequent endorser who may be compelled to pay it.

The law is very specific on this point, and where a person places his endorsement on an instrument negotiable by delivery, he incurs all of the liabilities of an endorser. Endorsers are liable always in the order in which they endorse. Joint payees, or joint endorsers, are deemed to endorse jointly and severally.

In endorsing a check to a bank honoring the check, it is apparent that even after a person has received the money at a bank, other than the one on which it is drawn, that the person who negotiated the check could be required to return the money to the bank. This could come about through dishonesty of the drawer, who might have closed the account; because the balance was impounded; or because of a stop payment order. In any event, the negotiating bank would have recourse against the person to whom they turned over the proceeds of the check.

Obviously, in connection with checks payable to individuals or corporations who are not known to the bank, the bank has no way of definitely knowing that the funds were paid to, or exchanged for, value received by any of the parties who endorsed the item. Because a person who places his endorsement on an instrument, negotiated by delivery, incurs all the liability of an endorser, banks to protect themselves when cashing checks or accepting checks for deposit, require the check to be endorsed by the person who presents the check and has received the proceeds.

Once the proceeds have been paid to the presenter who has endorsed the check, the bank then becomes the holder in due course. However, in order for the bank to collect the funds which they have advanced to the customer, it is necessary for them also to endorse the check, which they do by placing a stamp on the back of the check which usually contains a special endorsement—the name of the bank, the A. B. A. number and the phrase "prior endorsements guaranteed," similar to the following:

Pay to the order of any Bank
or Banker
Prior Endorsements Guaranteed
January 18, 1961
First National Bank
2-1 of Chicago 2-1

Generally bookkeepers, members of the bookkeeping department, or others charged with the responsibility of paying endorsements, because it is universal practice for all checks coming through banks to bear the bank endorsement stamp, only check endorsements on checks in amounts of $500 and over, relying on the bank endorsement for recourse should prior endorsement be missing, or should questions arise as to the negotiability of the check. Whenever a question arises, in connection with the endorsement or negotiability of a check, it is up to the customer against whose account the check was drawn and paid, to file claim with his own bank for recovery of the funds so paid out. His bank, in turn, files claim against the prior endorser, who after reimbursing the claimant bank for the check, in turn files a claim for reimbursement against the previous endorser for whom it cashed the check, or accepted it for collection and credit. If the check was negotiated for a depositor, the general practice is to charge the customer's account with the amount of the item and return it to him for action against the party from whom he received the item, and so forth, until the item is back to the original endorser who is the payee of the check.

Most banks, in order to protect themselves against unauthorized signatures and forgeries, refer all checks to those who, by experience, are qualified to recognize and pay signatures on checks when presented to the bookkeeping section.

Sometimes it is the bookkeeper or a clerk in the bookkeeping section. Other times it is the responsibility of the tellers who, because of their seniority and experience, generally come to know signatures much better than the bookkeepers.

As to amount—checks should be very clear as to the amount it was the intention of the customer to have deducted from the balance of his account. Both the printed amount, and the amount written on the line where the amount is expressed in writing should be the same. The Negotiable Instruments Law states that where the sum payable is expressed in words and also in figures and there is a discrepancy between the two, the sum denoted by the word is presumed to be the amount authorized to be paid. Therefore, if the written amount is clear, it is considered sufficient evidence of intent to charge that amount against the account.

Where there is a discrepancy, on the other hand, some banks on the advice of counsel follow the practice of paying the lower amount. Other banks, particularly if the amounts involved are substantial, refer the check to the maker before being paid. Because of the difference in state laws, it is sound policy, whenever checks are presented which show a discrepancy between the printed and the written amount, to refer such items to a superior officer for decision as to payment.

As to signature—in order for a check to be in good order, it is necessary that the signature be genuine and authorized. A genuine signature is purported to be the signature written on the signature card, which authorizes the bank to pay out funds upon presentation of a check signed by that person in whose name the account is carried.

Signatures, however, must also be authorized. That is, the bank must have written authority to honor checks when signed by a genuine signature of an authorized person. While an unauthorized signature does not involve forgery, it does involve other serious considerations. For example: A person affixes the signature of his own name to a check of a corporation, association, partnership etc. on which he does not have any authority to sign. The check is presented to the bank for payment. The bank refuses to honor the check—not because the signature is not genuine—which it is—but because the bank has not been ordered to honor the genuine signature, as one authorized to order the bank to pay out funds on deposit in the account.

3. THE REVIEWING OF ALL CHECKS RECEIVED, TO BE CERTAIN THERE ARE NO STOP PAYMENT ORDERS OR HOLDS AGAINST THE ACCOUNT. Another factor to be considered in the processing of checks, is that there is no order to the bank, signed by the depositor, stopping payment on the check; or there have been no orders issued by the court, or under due processes of law, ordering the bank to hold the balance intact.

All banks are bound by the written instructions of their customers regarding the handling of their accounts. Since a check is nothing more than a written order to pay funds to another person, it follows that the depositor may rescind or revoke such an order in writing. This written instruction ordering the bank to stop payment on a check is known as "Stop Payment Order," similar to that shown in Exhibits 91 and 92.

Where there is a stop payment order against a check the customer generally signs a Stop Payment Order, covering the date, number of the check, name of payee, amount of check, and reason for stopping payment on the check. When received by the bank, tellers and bookkeepers are immediately notified to be on the lookout for such checks and, if presented for cashing, to refuse payment for the reason that "payment has been stopped"; and if

Exhibit 91

STOP PAYMENT ORDER

Please **STOP PAYMENT** on the following check:

Number__________ Date____________________ Amount__________

Payable to____

Reason____

The above check has not been charged against the account of the undersigned by you in any previous statement. The undersigned hereby agrees to hold you harmless and reimburse you for any and all loss, damages, costs, disbursements, expenses or liabilities (including attorney's fees) which you may incur or sustain either directly or indirectly because of your refusing payment of said check, and agrees further not to hold you liable on account of payment contrary to this request if same occurs through inadvertence or mistake.

NAME OF ACCOUNT ______________________________

Authorized Signature

Exhibit 92

STOP PAYMENT NOTICE

REMARKS

Date Stopped		Date of Check	Check Number
Maker	**Payee**		**Amount**

REMARKS

Date Stopped		Date of Check	Check Number
Maker	**Payee**		**Amount**

28—Kalco—Chicago

received from another bank, to return them, together with a prepared notice, with the reason for return.

Generally stop payment orders, are considered to be in effect for a period of 30 or 60 days unless renewed. This regulation, which is a good practice, is followed to prevent an accumulation of stop payment orders, most of which are issued in connection with checks to utility companies or stores of reputation, which cannot be negotiated because of the endorsement required, which have been lost, misplaced or stolen.

Accounts are also subject to what are known as hold orders. Hold orders are orders to the bank restricting them from paying out funds in an account under writ of attachment, garnishment, or some other type of court order.

Hold orders are also placed against the balance of an account by tellers to secure or hold all or part of the balance for a specific reason. For example: when a teller pays a check of a large amount or pays checks late in the afternoon, he may, to protect himself, notify the bookkeeper that he has negotiated a check for cash or exchange for a cashier's check or draft; and to place a hold on the account for the amount of the item. Holds incidentally are placed on every account, as a matter of record, whenever a check is certified.

Holds may also be placed against an account in the case of the death of a depositor, which in the case of an account in the name of an individual, immediately revokes all outstanding checks; or in the case of a person who is declared incompetent, bankrupt, or under other circumstances which render the depositor incapable of handling his own affairs. In such cases, however, the restriction is placed against an account as the result of a court order.

Regardless of the reason, when a hold order is received, proper notations are made on the ledger sheet of the account in such a way that no checks will be charged against the account as long as the hold order is in effect.

4. THE POSTING OF CHECKS AND DEPOSITS TO RESPECTIVE ACCOUNTS. The work of posting refers to the process or procedure in recording all deposits and checks to respective checking accounts. While it is not the purpose of this section of the chapter to detail the technical aspects of posting functions in

relation to methods, procedure and tools available, it will, however, be helpful in our overall study to summarize and review various methods, procedures, and some of the principal bookkeeping posting systems generally used by banks today. Such systems, exclusive of electronic processing, which we shall cover later, are of four principal types.

1. Dual posting.
2. Single posting, with a carbonized copy as a statement.
3. Single posting, with a photograph of the ledger as a statement.
4. Post to check process.

DUAL POSTING. Under a properly devised dual posting system, one bookkeeper will post checks and deposits to one section of individual records known as ledgers, while another bookkeeper is posting another batch of checks and deposits to another section of individual ledgers. Upon completion of posting the items to the ledgers, they exchange checks and deposits and post the same items to a duplicate set of individual records known as statements. After the posting is completed, the bookkeepers run and balance the ledgers with the statements and compare balances of individual accounts on the ledger with balances of the same account on the statement, to be certain items have been correctly posted to both sets of accounts. The theory of dual posting is that two persons would not make the same mistake, and by running and proving the balances, any errors would be detected.

The other advantage of a dual system is that the ledger becomes the bank's permanent record while the statement, at the end of the month, or periodically, is sent to the customer together with the cancelled checks. This system, as can clearly be seen, involves the duplication of posting all entries.

SINGLE POSTING. Many banks use a single posting system to eliminate the double posting and separate statement. Under a single posting system either a duplicate record of the account is made by the insertion of a carbon sheet between two records, making an original and duplicate, which at the end of the month is delivered to the depositor together with paid and cancelled checks; or, at the end of the month, the ledger sheet is photographed after which it is delivered to the depositor together with the paid and cancelled checks as a statement. The photo copy then becomes the permanent bank record.

Under the single posting system, however, it is usually necessary to verify periodically the correctness of the entries. This is done several times during the month by counting the checks and scanning from the lower right hand corner so as to check the signature, and then counting the number of checks posted on the statement to be certain the number of checks as counted corresponds with the number of checks posted. In addition, under a single posting system, it is generally the practice at the close of business each day to sight post the deposits, that is, to check the posting of the deposits to be sure the entries have been made on the proper account.

Another method of checking used with the single posting system is to sight post or sight verify checks after they have been posted. This, however, is quite tedious and unnecessary as long as periodical verification as to number of checks is made.

POST TO CHECK PROCESS. The post to check process, which is a system of recent origin eliminates the daily posting of checks and deposits to either a statement or a ledger. Under this system the balance is carried forward on the back of each check or deposit as the item is posted, after which, checks and deposit tickets are filed in a cellophane envelope with the most recently recorded item in the front. In obtaining a balance, instead of referring to a ledger record, the bookkeeper immediately refers to the envelope, finds the old balance on the last item posted and records the new transaction.

Under such a system, periodically, but at least once a month, either all of the items are posted to a ledger sheet which is then photographed and sent to the customer, or all checks are photographed and sent to the customer together with a statement which shows the balance.

Regardless of which system is used, or which new systems are recommended for adoption, public relation minded management should remember that while economical and efficient methods and procedures are essential to the profitable operations of a bookkeeping section, no changes should be made which can adversely affect the depositor-bank relationship.

While all of the described bookkeeping operations differ as to practices and procedures, they can be operated under several posting systems generally referred to as a current posting system, or as a delayed posting system.

A system referred to as a current posting system means that all checks received from correspondent banks or from local banks through the clearings; all checks cashed or received by the bank in payment of services; and deposits made by customers at the tellers window or by mail, are processed, charged against, or credited to the account the same day as received.

Deferred or delayed posting, on the other hand, is just what the word describes—the posting of checks and deposits to commercial accounts the day following, or the day after the transaction takes place. In other words, checks received from correspondent banks or the clearings and checks and deposits received over the counter are sorted, combined, and posted to the individual accounts on the following day. This is only practical and permissible, however, where the law and arrangements between banks provide for a day's delay in notifying the presenting bank of the dishonor or non-payment of items.

The use of a delayed posting system has been a boon in many banks as it enables them to schedule their operations in such a manner that straight posting can be accomplished and delays avoided in stopping posting routines to return checks. In addition, deferred posting enables a bank to eliminate either the morning or afternoon posting and to post both deposits and checks to an account at the same time.

Some banks follow a modification of the delayed posting system through which they post the counter work of the previous day, or all work which originates through the bank the day before, with the checks received in the mail the current day from correspondent banks, or from local banks through the clearings. Other banks, as a further modification, follow the procedure of only posting the deposits to accounts the same day as received, and deferring the posting of checks until the following day. Each system embraces its own merits and advantages depending on size of bank and type of business handled.

5. THE REFERRING OF ALL ACCOUNTS OVERDRAWN, OR ACCOUNTS AGAINST WHICH THE VOLUME OF CHECKS PRESENTED EXCEEDS THE BALANCE, TO AN OFFICER FOR DECISION. Most depositors are careful not to draw a check for more money than they have on deposit in their checking account. It sometimes happens, however, that the depositor has made a mistake in addition or subtraction, or has neglected to deduct the amount of a service charge from the balance of the account as shown in the check book, with the result that when a check is presented and deducted from the balance, a minus balance shows up on the ledger sheet. This minus balance known as an overdraft usually is printed automatically in red ink.

Overdrafts, which are considered unsecured loans without evidence of a note, are contrary to good banking practice in the United States even though the extending of credit by means of an overdraft is a recognized banking practice in England and other foreign countries. In addition, not only are overdrafts frowned upon by the supervisory authorities, but the person who authorizes an overdraft is considered to be personally liable for its repayment.

Generally when checks are posted which overdraw the account, the customary procedure, after posting, is for the bookkeepers to first check for a deposit or to attach the check to the ledger sheet and refer it to the officer who is authorized by the board of directors to approve overdrafts.

While it is a customary practice in many banks for the bookkeeper to check for a deposit before referring the overdrawn account to an officer, this practice in modern times, especially where a delayed posting system is followed, is an unnecessary waste of time. The circumstances of delay in posting is evidence that the customer did not have sufficient funds on deposit in the account at the time the check was issued. Therefore he either issued the check with full knowledge that the balance was insufficient, or issued the check in anticipation of being able to deposit funds in the account before the check was presented for payment. Under either circumstance the bank, as a routine matter, is justified in returning the check without checking for a deposit unless, of course, the officer to whom the matter is referred is of the opinion, because of the character of the depositor, that such a search should be undertaken.

The payment of checks which result in an account being overdrawn are generally predicated on several factors—the status of the customer and manner in which the account has been conducted—the amount of the overdraft—and the time of the month in which the overdraft occurs. If the depositor is considered to be a "good" customer; the amount is nominal and occurs about the approximate time it is customary for the customer to make a deposit; or if it appears the difference is the result of an honest mistake; the overdraft is favorably considered.

If the officer approves the overdraft, the items are sorted with the other posted checks and handled in a routine manner. If, however, the officer declines to approve the overdraft, the entries are cancelled on the ledger sheet; the control balance is credited with the amount, and the items turned over to the person who has the responsibility for handling the return of dishonored checks.

6. THE HANDLING OF CHECKS RETURNED BY THE BANK BECAUSE OF INSUFFICIENT FUNDS. When checks to be returned for insufficient funds are received from the bookkeeper, the person who is responsible for handling such checks enters the items individually on a register. The original is sent to the depositor as advice of the check returned and notification of the charge for returning check, the duplicate is the debit to the account covering the charge for returning the check, and the triplicate is the bank's record of the transaction.

If the check was received from another bank, the clerk makes out a debit for the amount of the check which accompanies it when it is returned to the bank from which received through the clearing house or correspondent bank.

If the check was cashed or deposited by a customer, a debit is made up in triplicate. The original accompanies the check when it is returned to the customer advising that payment on the check has been refused for insufficient funds and the item is being charged back to the account, the duplicate is the charge to the account, and the triplicate is the bank's record of the transaction.

If the check was received from another section or department of the bank or cashed by a teller for a non-depositor, the item is charged back to the section or department from which received, where it is held as "cash" until such time as the amount of the check can be recovered from the person for whom it was negotiated.

7. THE SENDING OUT OF PROPER NOTIFICATION TO ACCOUNTS ON WHICH CHECKS HAVE BEEN HONORED CREATING OVERDRAFTS. On accounts where the payment of checks has been approved creating an overdraft, a list of the overdrawn accounts is generally turned over to a clerk in the bookkeeping department at the end of the day. He prepares a notice which is mailed to the depositor, notifying him of the overdraft, and requesting him to deposit sufficient funds to cover. Banks generally make a charge for permitting the overdraft, which charge is prepared on a triplicate form of which the original is the advice to the depositor, the duplicate the charge to the account, and the triplicate the register copy.

8. THE PROVING AND BALANCING OF THE LEDGERS AFTER THE DAYS POSTING IS COMPLETED. After all checks and deposits have been posted to the ledgers (and statements) the accuracy of the work of the individual bookkeeper and the section as a whole must be proven.

It is generally the practice to balance the individual ledgers after the close of business so that the bookkeepers can check out and balance their totals with respective control accounts and with the general books.

In the general books, the liability account "Commercial Deposits" or "Individual Deposits" shows the total amount due to commercial customers or those maintaining checking accounts. During the day checks have been received from the tellers and other sections or departments of the bank and from other banks through the clearings and from correspondent banks, while deposits have been received from the tellers and from the mail. Respective checks and deposits and the sums represented by them have been used by individual tellers and departments to effect the balancing of their work. In order to effectively balance the bank, these totals must be reflected in the total debits and credits of the bookkeeping department, adding and subtracting the amounts from the "Individual Deposit" totals or "Commercial Ledgers."

In addition to balancing with the control accounts on the general ledger, it is necessary to prove that the individual ledgers balance with the statements, and that all items have been correctly posted so that the records of the customer will be accurate.

Where banks follow a dual system of posting, that is, posting items to both ledger and statement, a comparison of the balances after posting discloses any errors, or the fact that items have been posted to the wrong account. In a single posting system, however, there are no balances to compare with, except that of the previous day, which means a sight posting job, often time consuming and inaccurate. In order to prove work under a single posting system, the journal sheet can be effectively used for making a comparison with the old pickup balance and the current balance by calling back of the checks and the sight posting of deposits after the work has been completed.

9. THE PHOTOGRAPHING OF CHECKS. Regardless of protective steps which are taken, unfortunately from time to time, statements with cancelled checks are lost or destroyed; or transit letters enclosing checks sent to another bank for collection are lost, stolen or misplaced. Infrequently too, differences occur between banks and their customers where a customer issues a check and forgets to enter it in his check book and the check is lost or mysteriously disappears after it has been charged against the account, and was not returned to the apparent drawer with his monthly statements and other cancelled checks.

In order, therefore, to provide protection against loss occurring from such circumstances, many banks, in recent years, have resorted to the practice of photographing all checks after they have been charged to an account, before being filed away and later delivered to the customer. This provides a permanent record in case a question should ever arise either as to the authenticity of the signature, endorsement, or to establish the fact that such a check existed.

10. THE CANCELING OF CHECKS. In order to prevent checks being presented the second time, and to establish the date as to the payment of checks, it is the customary practice of

ll banks to cancel checks before filing and returning them to the ustomer.

Cancelling is done in three different ways—the automatic ancelling by stamping the word CANCELLED on the face of he check when is is microfilmed; the hand stamping of the word CANCELLED or PAID across the signature line which is very ime consuming; or the cancelling of checks by putting them hrough a machine which perforates the check with the word PAID and the date.

11. THE FILING OF PAID AND CANCELLED CHECKS BY ACCOUNT. After checks have been photographed and cancelled, the next step is to see that they are properly filed for periodical return to the depositor.

It is a general practice to set up check files with a guide card n alphabetical order by customer, behind which checks which have been paid and cancelled are filed. In addition to making ure that the checks are filed in the right compartment, it is also mportant to file checks in order of payment, which is the order n which they appear in the customer's statement. It is important and of value to the customer, when he receives his statement, to find the checks are in the order in which they appear on the tatement so he can check them off or reconcile the account much nore easily in case there is a difference between the balance as hown on the statement and the check book stub.

Before statements are mailed or delivered to the customer, cancelled checks should always be counted and checked against he number of checks shown in the statement, in order that the bookkeeper may have the opportunity to detect any posting or filing errors and the depositor only receive the checks which belong o him.

12. THE RECORDING AND MAINTAINING OF RECORDS N CONNECTION WITH THE ACTIVITY OF ACCOUNTS. In nearly every bank checking accounts are subject to either a form of service charge or an account analysis charge. Such charges are et up for the purpose of compensating the bank for the expense ncurred in handling checks, deposits, or performing other services where the income from the balance maintained is insufficient to cover the cost of performing such services.

In order to properly compute such charges, it is the function o either the bookkeeper by machine; a clerk in the bookkeeping sec tion, or a clerk in the analysis section to daily or periodically recor on an analysis sheet the number of items handled or services per formed, such as the number of deposits made; the number of loca or out of town items in each deposit; the amount of currency an silver deposited; the number and volume of checks cashed; th number of checks posted against the account, or other services. Th cost of all these operations should be covered by the incom earned from investing the balance maintained in the account.

At the end of the month, it is generally the practice to for ward the analysis sheet, or stub of the statements if the informatio is recorded by the bookkeeper by machine, to the analysis cler who computes the income from the minimum or average balanc maintained, deducts the cost of providing the services and deter mines the profit or loss of the account.

If the computation results in the account showing a loss, service charge debit is prepared and posted against the account In some banks the use of the debit has been eliminated bein recorded on the statement by the letters SC. In other banks where all analysis information is computed on the statement stub the stub is used as the debit after the information has been re corded on the analysis record.

Details in connection with the determining of item costs an charges, together with the basis for computing such charges ar covered more fully in Chapter XXXX Cost Analysis.

13. THE PERIODICAL PREPARATION AND DELIVER OF STATEMENTS OF THE ACCOUNT TO DEPOSITORS TO GETHER WITH PAID AND CANCELLED CHECKS. In orde to currently inform depositors of the balance of their account, pro vide them with receipts covering funds which they have paid ou and exchanged for goods and services, and to directly confirm th balances, banks periodically return cancelled checks with a pre pared statement of the account to all checking account customers

Generally, it is the practice to render statements and retur cancelled checks monthly to customers who maintain regular per sonal or business accounts, usually on the first business day o the month; while it is the practice to return cancelled checks an tatements on special checking accounts, such as "No Minimum Balance" or "Pay as You Go," accounts, usually when the ledger heet is filled up, or quarterly.

While many banks still adhere to the practice of rendering tatements on accounts for a current monthly period and deliver uch statements shortly after the first day of the month, many anks, in recent years, in order to eliminate the unavoidable overime work, are tending to adopt a cycling system of rendering tatements.

Under such a cycling system, while statements are made up nd mailed to depositors together with cancelled checks every 30 lays, depositors receive the statements on the 5th, 6th, 7th, 10th r 20th day of the month depending on the date the alphabetical r numerical section in which their account is carried, is scheduled or the makeup of the statements. In other words, under a cycling ystem, statements and cancelled checks covering approximately /20 of the number of accounts are made up and mailed each lay. This system eliminates peak periods and the payment of vertime, not to mention the general inconvenience under a five lay week when the end of a month comes on a Thursday or Friday r in a week which also contains a holiday.

14. MAINTAINING BALANCE RECORDS FOR THE INORMATION AND USE OF OFFICERS. In connection with nswering credit inquiries; providing information in connection vith credit analysis; and determining the value to the bank of a ustomer's relationship reasonable and accurate knowledge of he balances maintained are of great importance.

In order that such information may be available for use by the redit department and loaning officers, balance records are mainained on each individual customer. Information to post to these ecords, as we reviewed in a previous chapter, originates in the ookkeeping section and is either posted to such records by lerks in the bookkeeping section or by tellers, from the statement tubs, or from periodical review of the ledger balance.

Before concluding this section, and reviewing electronic deelopments it is well to point out that there are several nationally nown and highly regarded firms manufacturing machinery and quipment used in connection with bookkeeping operations. While each piece of equipment under certain conditions and circumstances can be preferred over another, depending on the type of business served, activity, volume, and over-all operations, it is well for an alert manager of a bookkeeping section, or officer who has the responsibility for supervising bookkeeping operations to maintain a file on the various bookkeeping systems and types of equipment so as to be currently informed, and be in a position to recommend the most efficient and practical equipment when circumstances and conditions warrant.

In connection with the operations of the bookkeeping section, some or all of the following operating instructions will apply:

1. Schedule for posting in-clearings to checking accounts.
2. Schedule for posting counter work to checking accounts.
3. Schedule for referring overdrafts to officers for approval.
4. Authorization for returning checks for insufficient funds.
5. Authorization for approving overdrafts.
6. Procedure for returning dishonored checks to correspondent banks or clearing house member banks.
7. Policy in respect to handling stale and post dated checks.
8. The acceptance and processing of stop payment orders.
9. Schedule for the preparation and mailing of commercial account statements.
10. Schedule for the preparation and mailing of "special" account statements.
11. Schedule of current service charges.

ELECTRONIC DATA PROCESSING AND BOOKKEEPING OPERATIONS

According to conservative estimates, banks within the next few years will spend over a billion dollars in electronic data processing equipment for the purpose of expediting the handling of checks and for solving problems in connection with processing the ever-growing volume of checks and financial paper work.

Before referring to uses of electronic data processing equipment in connection with the processing of checks and bank operations, let us remember the primary function and responsibility of a bookkeeping section is in connection with the recording of the payment of funds to designated persons or order—upon presentation of a check or order to pay—properly dated—signed by a person authorized to withdraw funds—and endorsed for by the recipient of the funds—and the maintaining of the records of such transaction.

Let us also remember that as long as banks provide checking account facilities, these functions and responsibilities will remain. What will change will be the method and procedures through which these functions and responsibilities are carried out.

Billions of checks are being written in this country every year and the volume is constantly increasing. It is a problem of every bank to find ways and means to process these items automatically and economically.

One of the solutions to the vast problem is through the use of of electronic data processing equipment which has:

1. The capacity to handle an increased volume of work in a shorter period of time and with greater accuracy.

2. The potential to reduce the number of tedious, routine accounting jobs.

3. The promise of reducing over-all operating costs.

Use of electronic data processing equipment can provide the answer to many banking problems in connection with processing and proving checks, providing the system adapted to the needs of the individual bank is used to its maximum potential.

Electronic data processing equipment because of its varied nature is perplexing unless a banker has a graduate degree in engineering, and even then there are misgivings, and he may have little understanding of how it works and why it works. All he knows is that by use of a highly developed electronic automated process he can expect certain results for spending a certain number of dollars.

Unfortunately, but it is best to realize the fact, we all have fear of the unknown. It is human nature to avoid that which we do not understand; yet lack of understanding encourages inactivity and a do-nothing attitude.

Before getting to the subject of automation and describing some of the equipment available for bank use, the stating of a few facts, definitions and principles might be of assistance in dispelling some of the mystery surrounding electronic data processing, commonly known as EDP.

Let us remember that while electronic data processing is apparently new, certain forms of automation have been used in banks for a number of years, such as addressograph equipment, punch card equipment, postage meter machines, letter folders and sealers, and in recent years, the microfilming equipment for use in photographing checks. In order to attempt to understand something about EDP, let us first define terms.

> *Automatic.* A machine or piece of equipment which has the power of self-acting or self-regulating. This definition is simple to understand. We are familiar with it in our ball point pens, automatic transmissions and the mechanics of our radios and television sets.
>
> *Electronics.* Electronics is the branch of physics which treats of the behavior and effect of electrons (which are particles associated with the elementary charge of negative electricity and constitute part of an atom) in vacuum tubes or photostatic cells.
>
> *Photostatic Cells.* Photostatic cells are vacuum tubes whose electrical properties and resistance are modified when exposed to light of certain wave lengths.
>
> *Automation.* Automation is nothing more than the technique of making a process or system automatic by electronic devices.

Let us remember too, in considering the field of electronics, that electric data processing equipment was developed by human beings from the knowledge, harnessing, and use of the elements of the universe which were created by Almighty God.

Let us also remember that electronic data processing equipment cannot think; it cannot interpret; it cannot analyze results nor can it make decisions. It can only provide an answer to a problem which a human being gives it to solve.

One of the major developments in the use of electronic data processing equipment for banks was through the development of the common machine language in connection with high speed paper check sorting known as MICR, or Magnetic Ink Character Recognition, which has been adopted by most check manufacturers who imprint the coding on all checks for use with electronic equipment.

To find the answers to problems in connection with the processing of checks, a great deal of research will be necessary. Let us realize here that research is not scientific but a process of trial and error. The only scientific part is in connection with knowing what to try and how to interpret our findings. All else is repetitious experimentation. As long as any variables exist, we will never get away from trial, error and repetitious experimentation. Review and analysis of the scientific developments which have taken place in connection with automation leads one to the conclusion that the problems of research have largely been covered. What remains in the future is the application of knowledge, which has been discovered through research, to the everyday problems in connection with banking.

In making this application and discovering the answer, it is going to be necessary for astute bankers to refer constantly to many of the searching questions used in connection with work simplification programs, such as:

Why do we do this?
Why do we do it this way?
Can it be done any other way?
Is there a faster, easier way of doing it?
Is this form necessary?
Can this form be combined with other forms?
Can we rearrange machinery and equipment to eliminate unnecessary steps?
Can we change our procedure or routine to provide a smoother work flow?

Regardless of whether or not a bank decides to install electronic equipment, many benefits should accrue to every bank considering its use, through exhaustive study of existing systems and practices, which should disclose many opportunities to make present methods and procedures more efficient, and result in reducing operating expenses. The savings could be passed on to customers in the form of better service and to personnel in the form of increased compensation.

Another confusing factor in connection with discussing electronic data processing is the terminology used to describe the various types and functions of electronic computers and other equipment, unfamiliar to many bankers and laymen alike.

In order to dispel some of this confusion and at the same time describe, in simple and understandable language, the use and functions of electronic computers and equipment, particularly as it applies to bank operations, I quote from an excellent article on the subject "Computers Can be Described in Simple English" authored by Mr. E. R. McClay, Administrator, Industry Applications Electronic Data Processing Division, Radio Corporation of America, which appeared in the December 8, 1960 issue of the *American Banker*.

"The word 'computer' often provokes mental images of science fiction marvels that out-think humans. Actually, the exploration of space, the use of atomic energy, and the defenses of the U. S. are heavily reliant upon computers. These devices can digest vast amounts of information and come up with the answers at speeds not much slower than lightning.

"How can such devices be used in the routine operations of a bank? The use of the word 'routine' is the key to the answer of how and where electronic data processing is useful in banking. Any banking function that is routine, that is repetitive, that is practically free of the requirement for human judgment, can be considered as a ripe field for a data processor.

"Notice that the words 'data processor' were used in place of computer. Actually, 'computer' is too limiting a term for today's flexible electronic data processing systems. By and large, a computer may be considered as a special purpose machine, designed and constructed to perform high-speed computation and a series of related operations at electronic speeds. Typical of such devices are fire control computers, scientific computers in use at Cape Canaveral, and other military and scientific machines. A data processor, on the other hand, is a general purpose machine, capable of performing a wide variety of routine operations over and over—including computation . . . .

"A business data processor consists essentially of four basic elements, input, storage, processing, and output.

"Input—Before data can be used by a system it must be put into a form acceptable to the data processor.

"Any method of data manipulation carries with it the basic requirement to get data into the system. Such items as checks and deposits, correspondent letters, new accounts are considered as being part of the necessary input to the demand-deposit system for a commercial bank.

"Input may utilize many media and many data processors have the facility to deal with any or all of them. Data input can be handled through punched cards, punched paper tape (prepared manually by communications equipment), mark sense EAM cards, magnetic ink character readers, and optical scanning equipment, capable of optically reading a printed document and recording its data on magnetic tape.

"Storage—Once the data has entered the system, provision must be made to store it until needed . . . .

"In magnetic recording, the tape disc has the facility to accept and hold indefinitely a magnetic charge. A series of these charges makes up the alpha-numeric characters and are stored. Magnetic bulk storage permits data to be recorded and read electronically, providing fast storage and data access . . . .

"Two other storage media in wide use at present are punched card or punched paper tape. Both are much slower and the punched card is a more cumbersome method of storing data, but if low volumes are anticipated, they will fit well into the data processing techniques.

"Processing—Some means of working on this data is needed—some place where totals may be balanced, where statements may be prepared, where checks and deposits may be credited or debited. This part of a data processor is called memory or high speed storage.

"Advanced electronic data processing systems use magnetic core memories as their processing medium. Magnetic cores use a very simple code represented by a magnetized or non-magnetized state—to provide the work area where information may be read in, worked on, rearranged, added to, merged, substituted, deleted, and otherwise manipulated.

"It is in the memory of the EDP System that a series of instructions are kept. These instructions, called a program, are written in such a way that every contingency is covered and the processor is able to handle all the situations it is intended to handle.

"A processor, of course, possesses no ability of its own. It must be told in complete and painstaking detail what to do in each situation. The series of detailed instructions are written and tested by personnel called 'programmers' and the written instructions must be stored in the memory while they are being executed.

"Output—The function of an electronic data processing system is work—the production of reports, the preparation of daily trial balances, the preparation of cycle statements, and hundreds of other types of processed information. Therefore, a data processor has as one of its major components a means of producing printed copy or some other output medum . . . .

"Input, storage, processing, and output devices working together make a complete electronic data processing system."

Now that basic principles have been stated, and terminology defined, a brief outline of some of the more important functions, uses and adaptations of electronic data processing equipment will be covered. Such an outline, however, will be brief and only cover the principal functions and uses, because of the continuous refinements and improvements being made through the application of EDP equipment to specific functions in both large and small banks, and the fact that each installation contributes to the solution of present and future bank operating problems.

In view of the fact that we are still in the field of research, no one person can be considered sufficiently qualified, both in the field of electronic data processing and bank operation, to accurately decide which type of equipment will provide the solution to each bank's particular problem. Each bank, therefore, must decide for itself if the electronic equipment presently available, through a number of manufacturers, provides the solution or answer to their particular problem.

Under these circumstances, therefore, we believe it is our responsibility, in covering the subject, to merely set forth certain factors which will acquaint bankers and students of banking with present electronic data processing functions and provide them with information which will assist them in their contacts with the manufacturers of equipment who are experts in their respective fields.

To those who wish current information on all aspects of electronic data processing equipment, and how such equipment can be economically utilized in solving the particular problems of the individual bank, it is recommended they contact any or all of the following companies who have made pioneering and distinct contributions to the development and use of such equipment now available for use in the field of financial accounting:

Burroughs Adding Machine Company
General Electric Company
International Business Machine Company
National Cash Register Company
Radio Corporation of America
Remington Rand Corporation

While electronic data processing equipment in a single or multiple unit can be used in performing a number of operations, every system, to properly function from a bank accounting standpoint, should conform to one or more of the following requirements.

A. Coding
B. Sorting
C. Recording-proving
D. Reporting

The key requirement in every system is in *coding*. This is the process of recording by means of slots or holes which are punched on cards, tapes, or the item itself; or by magnetic ink character reading figures which are either imprinted on checks before they are given to the customers, or added to the checks at the time of processing; the name of the account, amount of the check and the bank on which the item is drawn.

The recordings of the amount of the check and the bank on which the check is drawn are numerical and can be readily identified by slots or holes, or the printed numbers themselves. The coding of the name of the account, on the other hand, generally takes one of three forms.

1. Straight numerical, which consists of only arabic numbers.

This is the system, commonly known as MICR or Magnetic Ink Character Recognition, which was developed about 1959 by the Technical Committee on Mechanization of Check Handling, established by the ABA Bank Management Commission. In 1956 as a result of their research, together with the wholehearted assistance of the machine manufacturers, Type Font E-13B was adopted as the most efficient type of MICR.

In 1957, the lower ⅝″ of each check was designated as a clear band, free of magnetic ink printing other than the approved characters for the purpose of encoding in specific locations, the transit number, account number, and the amount, in Type E-13B magnetic ink characters.

The committee also recommended that certain standards be set up for all checks, among which was that the maximum dimensions of checks would not exceed 8 3/4″ by 3 2/3″ and the minimum would not be less than 6 by 2 3/4″.

2. Alpha Numeric, which is a system using both alphabetical and numerical numbers, with the alphabet or component parts prefacing the numbers which are assigned to accounts within alphabetical breakdowns.

3. Alpha Digit or electronic signature identification, refers to identification of the account through a setup whereby certain letters of each customer's name are electronically fused into magnetic strips on the back of each statement-ledger form (the last letter of the first name, the middle initial and the last letter of the proper name). In coding, the operator uses a comparator keyboard to set up the initials from each check on a card for selecting the correct ledger sheets.

The second requirement, *sorting*, is in using equipment which will interpret or read figures, names, etc. on the items which have been encoded, and sort them; or sort and prove them to a previously determined alphabetical or numerical classification.

The third requirement, *recording-proving*, is in using equipment which, after items are sorted, will record such debits and credits against the balance as shown on the ledger sheet or record, which also are electronically selected from the drawer, binder or tray by the coding on the check.

The fourth requirement, *reporting*, is in using equipment which will make a report, and furnish or provide records of accounting transactions resulting from the posting of such debits or credits to ledger sheets or other records.

In considering the use of electronic data processing equipment, it is well to realize that the machinery and equipment used in performing the various accounting functions is generally compatible, that is, a system can be set up using equipment manufactured by several different companies, and that once a system is initially established, it does not necessarily follow that a bank must purchase additional equipment from the same manufacturer from whom they purchased the original pieces of equipment.

Because of the great expense incurred by manufacturers in developing electronic data processing equipment, the cost of purchasing or renting such equipment, at the present time, is generally prohibitive for banks with resources under 50 million dollars, regardless of results to be obtained. Banks which are unable to take advantage of the economies which can be brought about through the use of electronic equipment, will have to continue to pass their increasing operating costs (which it is apparent will increase rather than decrease in the years ahead) on to their customers in the form of higher service charges and higher interest rates.

There could, however, be opportunities for aggressive management of smaller banks to take advantage of electronic data processing equipment, by means of cooperative effort.

This could be similar in operation to the following described programs, each of which have advantages and disadvantages depending again on the size of the cooperative banks, the area served by individual banks, and the respective fields of operation.

A. Service Bureau. Under the service bureau plan the servicing center is owned and operated by a manufacturer of electronic data processing equipment. Banks wishing to take advantage of the machinery and equipment rent or purchase time on the system.

B. Data Center. Under a data center arrangement the manufacturer of electronic data processing equipment provides the space and the equipment, but requires the banks to provide their own trained operators to operate the equipment while the work is being processed.

C. Cooperative Service Center. Under this plan, one or two

of the larger banks in the area set up the system and share the equipment with the smaller banks on a rental or lease basis with cost determined by the time and type of equipment used.

D. Processing Service Center. A processing service center is a separate corporation formed by a group of banks for the pu-pose of providing electronic data processing equipment and facilities for the members. Under such an arrangement, the staff is provided by the corporation with expenses prorated among the members based on services rendered.

E. Clearing House Processing Center. This type of an organization is where electronic data processing equipment is owned and operated by the clearing house, for the use of its member banks to the extent warranted under the circumstances, for the electronic processing of checks. This could even extend to where the bookkeeping records of a number of banks would be centrally located—where all checks would be processed, statements prepared and mailed, with a closed circuit TV used for reference purposes between the center and the tellers of representative banks.

The cost of electronic data processing equipment presently available, is prohibitive in cost for the small bank to consider. Many of these banks cannot even afford or justify the purchase or use of a proof machine or postronic bookkeeping machine, let alone magnetic ink sorter/readers, encoders or computers. However, they are not justified in ignoring the possible uses or future potential advantages.

The very fact that such bankers, in undertaking an investigation, check into their own processes, methods and procedures, with an open mind, is a guarantee they will discover ways and means to simplify, or effect economies in present operating methods and procedures.

One of the most interesting aspects in connection with the use of the electronic data processing equipment is in making future projection. Bankers and others should not lose sight of the fact that such equipment is not reserved for banks alone. Electronic data processing equipment has the ability to process anything in which numbers or amounts are recorded, processed, or used in financial computations. It should also be remembered that machinery merely counts, controls, and records numerical figures at the direction of a human being known as a programmer.

Future projections of the application of electronic data processing equipment to over all business, could open up a new field of opportunity for the small bank. For example: disregarding the factor of scheduling, which is of minor importance, such equipment owned and operated by a bank could be used for the recording and billing of accounts receivable for customers; for maintaining inventory control over finished goods and materials for manufacturers, lumber dealers, grocery stores; or in connection with any other business records where numbers, or dollars are used in computations. Another field could be in working closely with local municipal authorities and utility companies in connection with recording, billing and accounting functions.

In connection with this study, we must remember that electronic data processing equipment presently used by banks was developed in the process of developing computers in connection with requirements of our defense program in the so-called atomic age.

It is the opinion of this writer that within a few years, backtracking and application of known and existing facilities will make it possible for the majority of banks to economically process their work electronically. This could be through the development of three types of small, reasonably priced machines: A coding machine which, as part of the proof operation, would encode on each check the amount, bank on which drawn, and the account against which drawn. These checks when received by correspondent and Federal Reserve Banks would be run through a reading machine which would read and prove the checks as to amount, and sort and summarize totals to the bank on which drawn.

Once such checks were received by the bank on which drawn, they would go through another reading machine which in turn would prove, and sort to respective bookkeeping sections. From there on a check would be automatically handled by a bookkeeping machine which would not only select the correct ledger, based on the coding, but post and, in recording, incorporate many of the other features required in bank operations. Such facilities as mentioned are already available, but not in this form. Further research, it is believed, will develop such equipment so that in time the advantages of electronic data processing on an economical basis will be available to all banks regardless of size.

CHAPTER XXX

THE SAVINGS SECTION

A SAVINGS ACCOUNT IS JUST WHAT THE NAME implies—an account for the purpose of enabling individuals and others to set aside certain sums of money for a special purpose.

While special purposes can be for any one of a number of reasons, the principal reasons why people have savings accounts, in order of economic importance are to:

1. Provide funds to tide them over in case of temporary unemployment.
2. Create a nest egg to fall back on in case of illness.
3. Have a safe place to put aside funds to provide for the education of their children.
4. Have a place to put funds accumulated for the down payment on a home, automobile, household appliance.
5. Have a place to set aside small sums, accumulated from time to time for a trip or vacation.
6. Have a safe place where they can accumulate funds at interest for their retirement years, or to provide for their old age.

Before covering the subject of savings operations in commercial banks, it might be well to briefly review certain factors in connection with the saving of money, and the institutions which provide the facilities through which people save money.

The most common institutions which provide facilities for people to save money are those provided by:

A. Mutual Savings Banks.
B. Savings and Loan Associations.
C. Commercial Banks.

Mutual Savings Banks, as we learned, are cooperative institutions conducted without profit to the managers, for the purpose of receiving deposits and for safekeeping sums as may be offered; for the purpose of investing such funds for the account of the depositors jointly, in such manner as prescribed by law, and the paying to the depositor, as interest, all the earnings of the institution except the amount required for expenses and whatever part may be set aside and held in reserve to provide for losses.

Savings and Loan Associations, likewise, are mutual organizations, generally formed for the purpose of assisting people to own their own homes. Customers deposit funds in share accounts which the association loans out at interest, against first mortgage real estate security. A depositor in a Savings and Loan Association is known as a shareholder while the return he gets from the investment of his funds is known as a dividend.

In both Mutual Savings Banks and Savings and Loan Associations every depositor is, in a sense, a joint owner with equal rights as far as dividends are concerned, and a participant in net assets in the event of liquidation.

A savings account in a commercial bank, on the other hand, is a special deposit account on which the bank pays interest for the use of the funds in view of the depositor's promise to give the bank if required, at its discretion, 30 days prior notice of intent to withdraw funds. Because such funds usually will remain with a bank for a long period of time, it can safely invest such funds, as we previously studied in Chapters XX and XXI, in bonds, commercial loans, and mortgage loans at prime rates of interest, which justifies the payment of interest on the balances maintained. Interest, however, is only paid semi-annually to savings depositors for use of the funds deposited in an account and then only on that portion of the funds which have been on deposit for the entire six months or other predetermined period.

When a savings account is opened, the depositor signs a signature card similar to that shown in Exhibit 58 authorizing the bank to pay funds only to the depositor upon presentation of an order properly signed when accompanied by the passbook. The depositor, in opening an account, is given a passbook in which the initial deposit is recorded and in which succeeding deposits and withdrawals will be recorded. In addition, depositors sometimes affix their signature to the ledger card to assist the teller and bookkeeper in verifying signatures on withdrawals when they are presented for encashment.

One of the particular provisions in connection with a savings account is that funds on deposit are only payable to the person in whose name the account is carried, and then only upon presentation of a withdrawal slip properly signed, when accompanied by the passbook. In other words, the person in whose name the savings account is carried is the only one who can legally withdraw the funds and to whom the bank may legally pay the funds, which is different from using a check, which is an order on a bank to pay funds to cash, bearer, or a specified person.

While it is generally the policy, in handling savings transactions, to require the depositor to have the savings passbook with him, there are exceptions. For example, when a depositor wishes to make a deposit to the account, or to the account of another, and does not have the passbook. Under such circumstances, it is common courtesy for the teller to issue a duplicate deposit ticket, and request the depositor to return the ticket with the passbook the next time the depositor comes to the bank, so that the entries can be made in proper order. Generally in such cases the depositor does not remember the number of the account, so it is necessary for the clerk to refer to the signature card, which is usually filed alphabetically, in order to get the number of the account, and then refer to the ledger card.

It is also the general and accepted practice not to allow withdrawals without presentation of the passbook. Whenever a withdrawal is permitted without the presentation of the passbook, most banks generally require the approval of an officer, and take steps to follow up to be certain the passbook is presented so that the withdrawal can be recorded. This is most essential because a savings passbook, as far as the depositor is concerned, is a record of the account, and when time lapses between the time a withdrawal has been made without the passbook, and another withdrawal or presentation of the passbook, very often the depositor has forgotten the withdrawal. This makes it necessary to extract the withdrawal, evidencing receipt of the money from the vault, so as to assure the customer that he was the one who received the funds.

There is little difference between the mechanics involved in handling a deposit at the window for a savings account depositor, and handling a deposit for a checking account depositor; or in posting the ledger sheet of a savings account against the posting of a ledger sheet of a checking account. The only real difference between a checking and a savings operation, aside from the fact that generally a deposit to a savings account consists of only one item, (check or currency) where a deposit to a checking account may consist of many items, is in the withdrawing of funds. In connection with a savings account there is generally only one withdrawal to post and charge against the balance; while in connection with a checking account, there may be one or a number of checks presented at the same time, to be charged against the balance of the account.

Because there is usually only one item to post, either a deposit or withdrawal, banks generally follow one of three systems in handling savings transactions.

A. Delayed ledger posting.
B. Window posting.
C. Ticketless posting.

Delayed Ledger Posting. Under the delayed posting system the savings depositor fills out the deposit or withdrawal slip, which he presents to the teller at the window together with the passbook. Generally, unless volume and operating setup provide for separate windows for deposits and withdrawals, both types of transactions are handled by the same teller.

When a deposit is made, the teller merely enters the amount by hand in the passbook, being certain that the name and number on the deposit slip correspond to the name and number as shown in the passbook.

In connection with withdrawals, the teller verifies the balance on the ledger card and the signature while the customer is at the window, before he enters the amount of the withdrawal in the passbook.

Under a delayed ledger posting system, unless a central proof system is used, the teller either periodically during the day, or at the end of the day, lists all "on us," local and out of town checks received in deposits on the blotter sheet, and passes them on to the proof, clearings or transit clerk for processing.

In balancing, at the end of the day, the teller lists and totals the deposits on the blotter sheet, which he adds to the figure of cash on hand at the beginning of business. This is offset by the totals of the checks or withdrawals cashed and received in deposits which have been listed and totaled on the blotter sheet, which the teller adds to the cash on hand at the end of the day.

Some banks which enjoy a large volume of savings funds, with considerable activity, process the work through a central proof section setup. Under this procedure, cash received in a deposit is extracted by the teller and substituted for by a cash ticket, which is appended to the deposit slip which goes to the proof clerk together with the deposit slips and other checks which were deposited, for proving, distribution and balancing. At the end of the day a cash out ticket is sent to the proof clerk covering all withdrawals cashed. By use of cash tickets, the teller effects a balance at the end of the day merely by using these tickets together with the actual figures of cash on hand.

Regardless of whether the teller balances as a unit or through the proof section, after balancing has been effected, the deposits and withdrawals go to a bookkeeper who, generally the first thing the following day, posts the deposits and withdrawals to respective ledger sheets after which the withdrawals are cancelled and filed in numerical order.

Window Posting. Under the window posting system ledger cards are kept in or adjacent to the teller's window. When a customer comes to the window to make a deposit or withdrawal, after filling out the deposit or withdrawal slip, the ledger card is removed from the file and both ledger card and the passbook placed in a window posting machine.

After the old balance is recorded, the deposit or withdrawal is entered on the machine and the adding or substracting key punched, which not only makes the correct computation on the ledger sheet and the passbook at the same time, but accumulates the deposit and withdrawal totals for later balancing.

In smaller banks, or in banks which have a nominal amount of activity, it is generally the custom for the teller to extract the ledger card and also make the machine posting. In larger banks, where there is considerable volume, it is sometimes the practice for window work to be handled by one teller while a bookkeeper close by processes the transactions on the machine.

Under the window posting operation at the end of the day, regardless of whether or not a central proof setup is used, balancing and proof of work can be undertaken automatically, in that the window posting machine accumulates the totals of the old balances, current deposits and withdrawals, and the new balance.

Ticketless Posting. Under the ticketless posting system no deposit or withdrawal slips, as such, are used. In connection with handling a deposit, the customer hands to the teller the currency or checks which he wishes to deposit to his account. The teller enters the amount on the machine, and after placing both the ledger card and passbook in the window posting machine, punches the key recording the transaction on both the passbook and the ledger sheet at the same time.

In connection with withdrawals, the customer tells the teller the amount of money he wishes to withdraw from his account. The teller then obtains the ledger card from the file, and after being certain that there are sufficient funds to honor the withdrawal, places the ledger card in the window posting machine together with the passbook and punches the key recording the transaction at the same time on both the ledger card and the passbook. After the posting is completed the teller hands the ledger card to the depositor who affixes his signature as a receipt on the line where the amount of funds withdrawn has been recorded. If the signature compares with the signature on the card, the money is turned over to the depositor.

While the ledger card on a ticketless system carries a number of signatures, it has advantages in that the teller has an identification each time a withdrawal is made because the signatures for prior transactions are immediately above it.

As is done under the window posting system, the accounts are balanced at the end of the day by the figures which the machine automatically totals and accumulates as each transaction is processed.

Regardless of which system is used, identification is most important. In connection with a savings account, of course, the teller has the advantage of a passbook number under which many of the banks file their ledger cards for simplification in selecting and filing. Generally, too, by using a number for reference purposes, comparison can be made of signatures on the withdrawal slip with the authorized signature on the account, as most banks follow the practice of having the depositor affix his signature to the ledger card at the time the account is opened.

Due to the fact that periodic statements of the account are not rendered to savings depositors, which would give them an opportunity to reconcile their account in the same manner as a commercial account customer, special attention is required in handling savings transactions to periodically reconcile the balance as shown in the customer's passbook with the balance as shown on the ledger card. This is essential, not only to reconcile differences which might have come about due to the fact the customer was permitted to make a deposit or withdrawal without having the passbook, but often depositors forget to bring in their books to have interest which has been earned and credited to the account entered in the passbook record.

In the operation of a savings section some of the functions and procedures will generally be covered by operating instructions similar to, and covering the following:

1. Method to be used for computing interest on savings accounts.

2. Procedure to follow in accepting deposits or honoring withdrawals without presentation of the passbook.

3. Resolutions, letters or documents required in opening a savings account in the name of a minor, or for a person acting in fiduciary capacity.

4. Schedule of charges for excess withdrawals within interest periods.

5. Regulations in connection with waiving of charges for drafts and cashiers checks issued at the request of savings depositors.

CHAPTER XXXI

THE COMMERCIAL RECEIVING SECTION

ONE OF THE PRINCIPAL FUNCTIONS OF BANK management, we learned previously, is to obtain deposits. It is the investing of such deposits, and the funds belonging to stockholders, in loans, and bonds at interest, which provides income to cover the expenses of servicing such accounts, and pays a return to the stockholders for the risk involved in using their funds.

The competition among banks for deposits is extremely keen. Most banks, particularly the large ones, have a special department known as Public Relations or New Business departments, whose responsibility is to maintain pleasant and satisfactory relationships with present customers, and to solicit the business of prospects to make them customers of the bank. The success of banks in attracting and keeping customers depends on the services they provide, and the courteous manner in which they handle the affairs of their customers.

Some banks it can regrettably be said, buy deposits; that is, agree to provide arrangements and services not available to regular customers as an inducement to the person or company to open an account. Among such inducements are offering of a favorable rate of interest on funds borrowed; offering to provide special services at no cost; agreeing to permit the depositor to use uncollected funds; and last, but not least, and probably the most flagrant violation, the inducement of a preferential rate of interest on funds deposited in a special time or certificate of deposit account.

Such inducements, while often temporary, are not only unethical and unsound in that the relationship is not built on a solid foundation of courtesy and service, but provide funds for investment which must be considered unstable and vulnerable. This is so because customers who are influenced by the promise of certain inducements to transfer their account from another bank, can also be prevailed upon or induced by yet another bank to transfer their account on the same basis.

The greatest competition for deposits between banks, however, is in connection with the obtaining of the accounts of other banks. Here inducements are made to a country bank to maintain a correspondent relationship with a city bank through the opening of an account because of services the city can render the country bank. Such services are usually in connection with the collection of out of town checks, both par and non-par; the obtaining of credit information; the purchase or sale of commercial paper and securities for the banks own account; the safekeeping of securities; the participation in excess loans, and by the assistance the city bank can render the country bank and its customers in many other ways. Name it, and there is a correspondent bank which will provide it.

Fortunately, to the credit of both correspondent bankers and the country bankers who have seen the evils of relationships based on promises, not only are all services provided by correspondent banks practically uniform, but there is little switching of accounts between banks as long as a satisfactory and pleasant relationship is maintained.

New correspondent bank business, therefore, is generally obtained only when a new bank is organized, or when the nature of the business done by a customer of a country bank requires the facilities of a city bank not otherwise provided.

Well managed banks, which have soundly formulated policies in connectiion with new business, generally have a gentlemen's agreement with other banks serving the area in connection with the solicitation of commercial accounts and other business. This arrangement has come about because it has been learned, over the years, that out and out solicitation of the business of customers of another bank, without reason, often brings retaliatory measures with the result that banks end up swapping customers, and in many cases exchanging good risks for bad. Obviously, therefore, the source of new business is either new companies being organized; companies relocating in the areas served by the bank together with the personnel of such company; or normal changes occasioned by discourtesy and lack of service on the part of one bank, and the realization that other banks, because of their activities and advertising, provide the same, better or additional services which the customer needs.

This does not, however, preclude the following of the good neighbor policy of being friendly and courteous to non-customers as well as customers, both from a business and social standpoint, especially with the directors and officers of companies which enjoy a good credit standing and where the opening of an account might lead to a borrowing relationship, which, after all, is the most profitable relationship a bank can have with a commercial customer.

In connection with the organizing of a new business in the area served by the bank; or a business being re-located in the area served by the bank, a satisfactory correspondent bank relationship can be of real help. As a matter of practice and policy, city correspondent banks will generally only maintain an active relationship with one bank in a town. (This depends of course on the size of the town.) When a business is re-locating, therefore, and the correspondent has a relationship both with the bank in the town from which the company is moving, and the bank in the town to which the company is relocating, very often, even if the company is not a customer of the bank, the correspondent bank, through its relationship, can act as intermediary and assist the company in establishing banking connections in their new location.

The most important factor in establishing a relationship with a bank is in being properly introduced or in being satisfactorily identified. Unless a prospective depositor for the bank is properly introduced by another customer, or known to one of the officers of the bank, so that identification can be positively established, the bank will undertake an investigation and require references before permitting the relationship to be established. In this connection many banks even follow the practice of using identification cards which are sent to banks with whom the prospect maintains, or formerly maintained an account or other relationship, for verification of the signature.

New accounts are sometimes investigated by the credit investigator in the credit section to be certain that the customer is morally acceptable. Most important, however, is that positive identification be established so that the bank is certain that the person who has the authority to withdraw funds from the account is one and the same person to whom checks which will be deposited in the account are made payable.

THE RECEIVING TELLER. One of the most interesting positions in a bank, and the first one outside of a messenger where the young banker has the opportunity to come in contact with business concerns or individuals engaged in business, although he has had some contact with the public and other customers through discharging responsibility as a savings teller, is that of a commercial receiving teller. While most of the checks drawn by depositors are paid through the clearings or received from other banks through the mail, deposits, generally speaking, are all accepted by the bank at the receiving teller's window. The exception to this, of course, is deposits which are made by mail.

Being a receiving teller is an important step in the career of every young banker. While the officers are acquainted with certain accounts and meet the principals from time to time in connection with services or credit, the receiving teller comes in contact frequently with customers of the bank who maintain checking accounts and because of this can do much, from a public relations standpoint, to make the depositor feel at home. By being courteous and considerate a receiving teller can build a strong solid relationship between the depositor and the bank.

To each person who comes to his window to make a deposit, the receiving teller *is* the bank. It is his ability to be pleasant and get along with people that contributes most to the future of the bank, since the bank can only grow—through people.

Generally a person who makes banking a career, and has reached the position of receiving teller, has spent time in the bank learning the duties, responsibilities and functions of the messenger, proof clerk, bookkeeper, and has had experience in operating the various types of machinery and equipment.

In addition, before being delegated responsibilities in connection with being a receiving teller, he has studied and been made familiar with the laws of negotiable instruments so as to be able to determine the negotiability of a check. He has also studied and learned about the various denominations and types of currency, so as to be able to detect counterfeit bills if received in a deposit.

Before going into the functions, duties and responsibilities of a receiving teller, it might be well to reaffirm the relationship which exists between a bank and a depositor as soon as an account has been opened.

It is a generally accepted principle of law that the relationship between a depositor and the bank is that of creditor and debtor, and that a bank, by accepting an account which includes money and negotiable instruments which will be deposited from time to time, becomes the legal owner of same, agreeing to repay the amount upon presentation of a check or written order to pay, properly signed.

It is erroneous to speak of "having so much money in the bank," when actually all a depositor has are receipts evidencing the fact that certain sums have been deposited in an account with the bank or that on the books of the bank he has a credit, which the bank by practice and law agrees to pay to him or to other parties, in the amounts, and as ordered by the depositor. It is also well to remember that as a depositor has the right to issue an order to disburse the funds—he also has the right to recall the orders, at any time prior to payment, by issuing a stop payment order.

It is the principal function of the receiving teller to accept, in behalf of the bank, currency and coin for immediate credit to the account of the depositor, and checks, coupons for credit to the account, for use of the depositor after being collected.

While both currency and checks are entered on the same deposit ticket, banks make it clearly and distinctly understood that checks and coupons are accepted by the bank only for collection, and such funds only become available for use of the depositor when converted into cash.

In order to protect themselves in their relationship with the depositor, most banks state in the passbook, on the receipt form, or on the reverse side of the deposit ticket—or on all three forms, rules and agreements between the bank and the depositor governing the collection and manner of collecting such items.

Generally such agreements, similar to that as shown in Exhibit 57 A, contain provisions to the effect that—in receiving checks for collection the bank merely acts as agent—does not assume responsibility beyond due diligence—reserves the right to use any legitimate means to collect the checks—selects such agents as in their judgment they believe reliable—is not liable for neglect or failure of channels or parties to, or through, which items are sent for collection—and reserve the right, at any time, to charge the item back to the depositor in event of default.

The work of a receiving teller is in connection with discharging certain responsibilities concerning:

A. The acceptance, proving and receipting for currency and checks (cash items) deposited by a customer to an account.

B. The sorting, segregation, and packaging of currency received in a deposit as to denomination and quality.

C. The sorting and routing of checks (cash items) to the proof, clearings, transit, or other sections of the bank for processing.

RECEIVING SYSTEMS. The act of the depositor in making a deposit at the bank is generally performed under one of the following systems:

1. The segregated system.
2. The unit system.
3. The special system.
4. The universal system.

Under the segregated system, the bank provides separate cages for the acceptance of deposits and the cashing of checks, while under the unit system the same teller handles both functions.

Under the special system, especially if the bank is favored with a large number of business accounts, they will use the unit system for ordinary normal bank transactions, but have a special window for the exclusive cashing of payroll checks. Sometimes they will also have special windows for the exclusive handling of deposits of business concerns which contain large amounts of currency which have to be verified, or checks which have to be checked for endorsement, while the depositor waits.

Both the segregated and unit systems are sometimes modified, in the larger banks, under what is known as an alphabetical arrangement.

Under the alphabetical arrangement, tellers only handle work for customers whose names are within a certain alphabetical breakdown, such as A to E, F to M, etc., which means that all customers whose last names begin with an A, B, C, D, E, take their transactions to that particular window for processing, while those whose last name began with the letter F, G, H, I, J, K, L, M, take their transactions to window F to M for processing, etc.

Under the universal system, the first teller system used in banks, and still used in smaller banks throughout the country, the teller not only accepts commercial deposits and cashes checks; but handles savings deposits and withdrawals, loan payments, collections and issues drafts, cashier's checks and money orders.

It is worthy of comment, in covering the receiving tellers section, to point out that regardless of efficiency or controls which can be built in for protection, the universal system, which is being brought back into general use by some of the larger banks, by eliminating the annoying practice of having a customer go to several windows and often standing in line to transact several classes of business, not only provides flexibility and better use of tellers and resultant economy in operating expenses, but more closely conforms than any other system to the number one principal of any system—rendering the best and most courteous service to customers.

SPECIAL RECEIVING TELLERS. In addition to the several systems through which deposits are made at regular teller windows, deposits can also be accepted by special tellers located at openings on the exterior of the bank building known as Drive In, Drive Up, or Walk Up Tellers.

Drive Up windows are just what the name implies. They are windows located on the outside of the building, with access off a street or alley, so a person can drive up to the window and, without leaving his car, transact his business.

Walk Up and Drive In windows are similar in use except that such windows are maintained usually in connection with parking facilities where customers may drive in and park their cars in the parking space provided by the bank, get out of their car, walk up to the window located on the outside of the building, and transact their affairs.

In addition, many banks limited by lobby space and hampered by lack of proper parking facilities provide Walk Up Teller facilities accessible from the sidewalk.

Such tellers generally only accept deposits. In some cases, however, depending on the bank, they perform one or more other services such as cashing checks; handling savings withdrawals of nominal amounts when accompanied by the passbook, and the presenter is properly identified; providing currency and silver for change and payroll purposes; issuing money orders, cashier's checks and drafts; and accepting and receipting for payments on installment loans.

The decentralization of industry, the development of urban areas, the crowded condition of streets, and limited parking facilities are more and more bringing about the widespread use of Drive In, Drive Up, Walk Up Teller facilities.

In addition to deposits which are personally made by the customer or his agent at the teller's window, deposits for credit to a customer's account are also made by, or through:

1. Other departments and sections of the bank.
2. Lobby depositories.
3. Mail.
4. Night depositories.
5. Wire transfers.

DEPOSITS ORIGINATING IN OTHER DEPARTMENTS OR SECTIONS. Whenever a customer, who is a depositor, obtains a loan from the bank; has the bank present an item for collection such as an interest coupon or bond; collects the proceeds from the sale of stocks or bonds; or is the recipient of trust funds, he can either receive the proceeds in cash; through a draft or cashier's check, which he later can negotiate for cash or credit to an account; or deposit the proceeds directly to an account he maintains or opens, for the purpose of using it to disburse the funds.

When such proceeds are made available to a depositor by credit to an account, the originating documents consisting of a check, draft, or debit to the account of a corresponding bank, (collection) debit to bills receivable (loan) debit to trust deposits, (disbursement of trust funds) and the deposit ticket, are prepared within the department or section where the transaction originates. Such documents, once prepared, are either delivered to one of the receiving tellers or included in other transactions to the proof section, which accumulates the credits for various departments, and at the end of the day forwards them to the bookkeeping section for recording on the ledger of the customer.

LOBBY DEPOSITORIES. Many banks provide a chute or receptacle in the lobby of the bank which customers may use during busy periods for the depositing of checks and currency. The procedure followed in using this facility is that the customer fills out a deposit slip in the regular way and encloses the deposit slip and passbook, or, in the event he is not using a passbook, a duplicate deposit slip, together with the currency or checks, in an envelope which he drops in the chute. Later in the day such envelopes are extracted from the depository, opened and processed by one of the tellers. In the interest of good banking practice, such depositories are usually under the dual control of two or more tellers and all such envelopes while being processed are opened and proven by two or more tellers.

MAIL DEPOSITS. In order to avoid a trip to the bank, especially for the depositing of salary, income, and dividend checks, there is a growing use by depositors, of the post office department of the United States Government as a messenger. This service can be utilized by depositors entering the check on a deposit ticket, in original or duplicate; or original accompanied by the passbook; and mailing both check and deposit slip to the bank in an ordinary envelope.

When received by the bank, such envelopes are opened and delivered to a receiving teller or special teller for processing. This consists of extracting the items, checking for endorsement and to determine they are in proper order, and delivering the items to the proof section for further processing. The teller either stamps the duplicate with his teller's stamp or prepares a special form which is mailed to the depositor acknowledging receipt of the checks for collection and credit.

Banks also provide mail deposit envelopes for the convenience of their depositors. Such envelopes, self-addressed to the bank, contain a receipt form for use with a window envelope, which the depositor prepares in making up the deposit, and which is used in returning the receipt, together with a new envelope to the depositor. Because of the locations of mail boxes and conveniences of depositing by mail, it is truly said that a bank is as close as the mail box.

NIGHT DEPOSITORY SERVICE. Another service provided by banks is in connection with providing facilities for customers to make deposits and transact certain other types of business after regular banking hours. Such facilities, referred to as After Hours, or Night Depository Service, provide for deposits to be deposited in an opening in the lobby wall, or outside wall of a building to a specially constructed vault or safe. Such facilities are of two types, special and regular. The special type is where depositors using the service are provided with a key which when inserted in a lock, permits them to operate a rotating cylinder with a space for inserting the pouch containing the deposit. When the cylinder is turned back it dumps the pouch into the safe and automatically locks.

The regular type operates similarly to a mailbox, and does not require the use of a key. This service is used, not only by depositors who have special arrangements for night depository service, but other customers of the bank who wish to make a deposit to their account, pay a note, collection, or transact similar business, after regular banking hours.

Businessmen who do not wish to hold checks or cash in their place of business overnight and use these facilities, are provided with canvas or leather bags or pouches with locks, into which they place checks and cash for depositing in the night depository safe. Such facilities, for businessmen, are generally used under one of two arrangements, both of which are covered by an agreement covering the bank's rules for the handling of such deposits. One arrangement provides for the bank to extract the pouch from the safe, after which, as they also have a key to the lock, they open the pouch, extract the currency and checks which have been entered for deposit, and process them in the usual manner, entering them in the passbook which is returned to the customer together with the night depository bag when he comes to the bank later in the day.

The other arrangement provides for the bank to remove the pouch from the safe but hold it intact until such time as the depositor comes in when he is handed the bag on receipt, opens it and processes it in his own way. Many merchants use this arrangement for safekeeping their "till" cash, depositing it in the bag at night and picking up the bag the following morning, before their store opens. They make a deposit to their account later in the day, in the usual course of business.

In handling deposits made through a night depository, the safe is generally under dual control, that is, it requires two or more authorized employees to work the combination and open the vault, after which each bag or envelope is indexed on a register sheet which is signed and attested to by those who opened the vault. Such bags are then delivered to the receiving tellers or a special receiving teller, who signs for the envelopes and bags, and depending of course on the system used, opens them or not, as the case might be, and processes them in the usual course of business.

WIRE TRANSFERS. Customers wishing to transfer funds from their account in one bank to an account in another bank do so by instructing their bank to transfer funds by wire. In providing this service, for which the bank charges and receives a fee, the bank directly, or through a series of instructions and transfers, to, through, and from correspondent banks or Federal Reserve Banks, debits and credits respective accounts until the transfer has been effected.

PREPARING ITEMS FOR DEPOSIT. All items which are to be deposited after being endorsed, are entered by the depositor on a deposit ticket similar to that shown in Exhibit 57, which is a detailed record of items which are to be deposited to the account.

Such items are receipted for by the teller on behalf of the bank, by entering the total amount of the transaction in a passbook by hand, or by machine, according to date, amount, and appending his initials, as evidence he is the person who handled the transaction.

The reason banks require customers to make out their own deposit slips is because it is a document of original entry, in the handwriting of the depositor. It is an invaluable record, should a depositor claim to have deposited currency or checks other than that shown in the bank's record or as entered in the passbook.

In preparing a deposit ticket, the customer should list all checks individually according to type, that is checks on us, checks drawn on other local banks, checks drawn on out of town banks, in the space provided, and enter the total in the summary space together with the amount of currency or silver deposited.

In depositing currency, the depositor should use care to see that all bills are separated as to denominations and placed right side up. Silver should be wrapped in standard packages with the depositor's name or initial written on each package, for ready reference in case there happens to be a discrepancy.

It is the receiving tellers' function to sort the currency. Not all currency passed out by the paying tellers in cashing checks is new currency. Generally, however, a bank which is public relations conscious, will endeavor to use clean currency. It is one of the functions of the receiving teller to see that such currency is properly prepared. This is done in spare time by going through respective denominations of currency and sorting it out as to good, usable and unusable. The good currency which is reasonably new, is packaged and used by the paying tellers in cashing checks for individuals. The usable currency which is old but reasonably clean, is given out to storekeepers for change purposes or to business concerns together with new or good money for payroll purposes. The non-usable consists of old, dirty or mutilated currency which is sent back to the Federal Reserve Bank or correspondent bank for either cleaning and re-issue as good or usable currency, or cancelled and destroyed.

In packaging currency for use of both customers for payroll and change purposes, and the tellers, it is the customary practice in most banks to package one dollar bills in packages containing $50 or $100; five dollar bills in packages containing $250 or $500; and ten and twenty dollar bills in packages of $500.

DISTINGUISHING GENUINE CURRENCY FROM COUNTERFEIT CURRENCY. Because of the great responsibility tellers have in handling currency, not only should they become familiar with the identification marks which distinguish the various denominations, but such markings and points to check in distinguishing genuine bills from counterfeit bills.

Astute receiving tellers can generally avoid accepting counterfeit bills if they will but remember the following checkpoints taken from the bulletins issued by the United States Secret Service.

The United States Government only prints three types of currency for circulation:

1. Federal Reserve Notes which bear green serial numbers and a green seal.
2. United States notes which bear red numbers and a red seal.
3. Silver certificates which bear blue numbers and a blue seal.

Counterfeit bills can usually be distinguished from genuine bills through differences in the

1. Portrait
2. Seal
3. Serial numbers
4. Paper

Portrait. The portrait on a genuine bill, especially the eyes, is lifelike. It is oval and stands out from the background, which is a screen of fine regular lines. The portrait on a counterfeit, on the other hand, is usually dull and smudgy.

The following portraits identify denominations of bills printed for general circulation:

Washington	on all	$1.00	bills
Jefferson	on all	$2.00	bills
Lincoln	on all	$5.00	bills
Hamilton	on all	$10.00	bills
Jackson	on all	$20.00	bills
Grant	on all	$50.00	bills
Franklin	on all	$100.00	bills
McKinley	on all	$500.00	bills
Cleveland	on all	$1,000.00	bills
Madison	on all	$5,000.00	bills
Chase	on all	$10,000.00	bills

Seal. On a genuine bill, the saw-tooth points around the rim of the seal are identical and very sharp, while on a counterfeit, such points are usually uneven with some of the points broken off.

Serial Numbers. Serial numbers in genuine bills are of a distinctive style. They are sharply and evenly printed in the same color as the seal. Numbers on counterfeit bills, on the other hand, are usually of a different style, poorly printed, and uneven in appearance.

Paper. Genuine bills are printed on distinctive paper manufactured under a special formula containing very small red or blue silk thread. Counterfeit bills, on the other hand, may have such thread, but generally the color is made by the use of colored ink.

In connection with counterfeit currency, it is well to remember that not all strangers are counterfeiters, but all counterfeiters are likely to be strangers.

Should a customer include in his deposit a bill which appears to be a counterfeit, the accepted practice in banks is to explain the suspicion to the depositor, withdraw the bill from the deposit and give the depositor a receipt for the bill. The bill, however, under no circumstances should be returned to the depositor but sent to the Federal Reserve Bank for study and further action.

Should a stranger attempt to exchange a bill which appears to be a counterfeit, an alert teller will:

1. Delay the presenter under some pretext and call the floor guard, bank policeman or officer to apprehend him, meanwhile jotting down a description of the passer, particularly any distinctive physical identification features such as color of eyes, hair, height, weight and scars.

2. As generally such a passer, unless innocent, will flee once there is a delay in making change or undertaking the service, the teller, if at all possible, should endeavor to obtain the make, color and license number of the automobile used, if one is involved.

The counterfeiting of coin is seldom practiced, due to the fact that they are easily detected and the "profit" is not worth the work and effort involved in making molds and casting the metal. Periodically, however, people will attempt to counterfeit coins for use in meters and vending machines. Fortunately, with the increased use of such machines, mechanisms have been devised which will reject coins which are counterfeit.

Counterfeit coin generally can be distinguished from genuine coin by sound, feel and appearance.

1. Genuine coin has a bell-like ring when dropped on a hard surface, while counterfeit coin has a dull thuddy sound.

2. Counterfeit coin has a greasy feeling.

3. The corrugated outer ridge of a genuine coin is regular, even if aged and worn, while the edge of a counterfeit is uneven, bent and often crooked.

4. The edge of a coin suspected of being counterfeit can be easily cut or chipped by a sharp knife.

ITEMS ACCEPTABLE FOR DEPOSIT. Customers and non-customers of the bank use the facilities of the bank to effect collection of items representing wealth owned by them in the form of orders to pay and promises to pay which, from a bank collecting standpoint, fall into three principal categories, cash items, collection items and cash collection items. Only cash items which include coin, currency, checks and coupons, presented by a customer can be collected through the regular facilities of a checking account while collection items and cash collection items presented to a bank for service, either by a customer or a non-customer, must be handled and processed by the collection section. In general the following factors distinguish a cash item from a collection or cash collection item.

A. They are orders to pay, or promises to pay on demand, not at some future date.

B. There are no conditions attached to payment and have no documents attached to them.

C. The means and instructions for collecting such items, through presentation to the person or agency under whom drawn, are simple and uniform.

Collection items are those which have documents attached and can only be converted into cash after presentation to the person on whom they are drawn, and proceeds and payment have been actually collected. Such items are notes or drafts payable at a future or fixed date or with certain conditions which must be complied with before they will be paid.

Cash collection items are collection items with documents attached, against which the bank may advance the funds by either crediting the proceeds to the account or advance the cash. Such items require special handling and are usually processed by the collection section or a special section of the bank which has facilities for handling such items. Often an instrument in the form of a check, which looks like a check, is included in a deposit to an account. The instrument is not a check, however, but a draft drawn on the treasurer of corporation payable through a bank on presentation. Such items, unless in nominal amounts, and drawn an a well known and responsible corporation, should only be accepted for collection.

Alterations of the dates of checks are generally not serious, particularly around the first of the year where from force of habit the previous year's date is used. Checks, however, where the day and the month bear alteration, should be accepted with extreme caution and only accepted with approval of an officer. Post dated checks which are given generally in anticipation of funds being available, should not be accepted for deposit to an account.

Checks which show a difference between the printed amount and the written amount are accepted for deposit only at the figure represented by the written amount or the lesser amount. In either case, the amount for which the check is passed should be approved by an officer, and the amount stated by the bank on the check by means of a special stamp.

Checks received in a deposit bearing a forged signature are difficult to detect. Suspicion, however, is often called to a forged signature by the fact that the signature appears to be drawn or traced and not freely written. Should a receiving teller detect such an item in a deposit, it is prudent to call it to the attention of an officer, and if it is in a rather substantial amount, to place a hold on the account until the check has been cleared and any suspicion allayed.

In connection with the alteration of the name of the payee, checks in which the name has been changed in any way cannot be accepted and, where detected at the window, should be returned to the depositor or referred to an officer for approval before accepting.

Even though in a previous chapter the various types of endorsements were reviewed, it would seem in order to again briefly review endorsements in connection with the depositing of items for credit to an account.

In connection with checks, there are six types of endorsements.

Blank, which only bears the signature of the payee, which is transferred by delivery.

Special, in which the endorsement names the person to whom title is transferred.

Restrictive, where title is restricted such as the endorsement of a check to a bank "For deposit only."

Qualified, where the item bears the endorsement "without recourse" and places the holder on notice that the prior endorser assumes no responsibility for the honoring of the check.

Conditional, where payment of the check is conditional upon some act being performed.

Combination, which consists of a special endorsement and restrictive endorsement such as "Pay to the order of the First National Bank for deposit only."

Generally, any checks bearing any endorsement other than qualified and conditional can be accepted for deposit to an account.

Checks which bear qualified endorsements should not be accepted for collection, unless the depositor is reliable and well known.

When a bank accepts checks of an individual, partnership or corporation, drawn on another bank for deposit or encashment, unless such checks are certified, it is impossible for the bank to know if the signature is authorized and authentic; that there are sufficient funds on deposit of the drawee to provide for payment of the check upon presentation; or if the check is subject to a stop payment order, in which case the item will not be honored.

In order to speed up the collection of checks and to place responsibility for endorsements, every bank in presenting checks to the bank on which drawn or to another bank for collection endorses such checks with their endorsement guaranteed stamp. In other words, the presenting bank stands ready to redeem such a check from the bank through which it has been presented for collection, in the event it is dishonored by the drawer's bank.

Receiving tellers should be particularly attentive to deposits of corporations to be certain that all checks deposited bear, as the last endorsement, the endorsement of such corporation or business; also that the original payee of the check is not a business or corporation, other than the business or corporation which presents the check for deposit.

UNCOLLECTED FUNDS. One source of loss of income for a bank is the often undisclosed drain on funds available for investment, through permitting customers to use funds they have deposited before such funds have been collected and converted into cash.

When a bank honors checks drawn by a depositor against uncollected funds, it is making an unsecured loan to the depositor without interest.

So that a bank will not unknowingly permit a customer to use funds before collected, or draw against checks which might be dishonored, it is generally the responsibility of the teller or the clerk in the proof section in reviewing the deposit, to put the ABA number of the bank opposite the amount of checks, indicating the number of days required to collect such checks, which the bookkeeper notes on the ledger sheet. Should checks thereafter be presented which are drawn on a balance made up of checks still uncollected, they are referred to an officer for decision.

PROCESSING THE DEPOSIT. Mistakes in accepting deposits can generally be avoided if the teller will follow the same routine in processing each deposit. The recommended routine is for the teller to:

A. Verify the total of cash as shown on the deposit slip with the amount of currency and coin handed in. This is done by actual count at which time the teller scrutinizes the currency and coin to be certain they are genuine and not counterfeit.

If the cash count is correct, the teller either places the cash in his drawer, sometimes in a special section for further sorting, or if the bank operates under a central proof system, makes out a cash-in ticket which is attached to the deposit ticket.

B. Review all checks to be certain they are cash items, and in good delivery order—that is readily convertible into cash upon presentation to the bank on which drawn, and properly endorsed.

As assistance in determining good delivery order of items, tellers in reviewing items tendered for deposit, (this also applies to paying tellers in encashments of checks) may find the following check list of help.

1. Is the item a check and is it drawn on a bank?
2. Is the check recently dated?
3. Is the amount represented by numbers the same as the amount written?
4. Does the signature appear to be authentic, or has it been forged?
5. Has the name of the payee been altered in any way?
6. Does the first endorsement conform to the name of the payee?
7. Is the last endorsement the same name as that which appears on the deposit slip carrying the title of the account?

In checking endorsements, either the teller or a clerk assigned the responsibility, or the proof clerk, in proving the items, should check to see that the first endorsement on the back of the check is exactly the same as that of the payee, and that the last endorser is exactly the same as the name on the deposit slip.

Where there are two or more endorsements, the important factor is to be certain that the last endorser is the name in which the account is carried by the person who deposited the item.

Where a teller handles a large volume of deposits, there is no time generally to verify endorsements. A teller can, however, carefully scrutinize the last endorsement to see that it agrees with the name on the deposit slip.

Third party endorsements can be a source of annoyance and trouble and whenever possible should be noted by a teller. A third party endorsement is one made by a person who is not a party to the check. In other words, a check which is payable to one party, endorsed by them, and then negotiated for deposit or encashment by another person. Unless the last endorser is well known to the bank and reliable, a hold should be placed against the account if the item is substantial because, should the original or second endorsement be a forgery, the bank will look to the last endorser for recovery of the proceeds.

In connection with forgery and alteration, such checks are generally cashed or first negotiated with a local merchant rather than at a bank. Unless such forged checks or raised items are immediately detected, it sometimes is as long as a month before the forgery or alteration is detected by the party against whose account the item has been charged.

C. Run the checks and verify that the total amount of the checks as listed, agrees with the amount as set forth on the deposit slip; or prepare the deposit slip for verification by others. In such cases, where a bank operates under a central proof, the tellers merely verify the amount of the currency and coin, the amount of which they enter on a cash ticket which is attached to the deposit slip with the checks for later proving and sorting to banks on which drawn, by the proof department.

D. Issue a receipt for the deposit, either by making the entry in the customer's passbook, stamping a duplicate deposit ticket, or issuing a machine produced receipt.

E. Set aside the deposit slip to which the cash-in ticket and checks have been attached, for delivery to or pick up by the proof section for processing. If the bank does not have a proof section or special clerk handling proof operations, the teller will sort the checks as to checks which are drawn on his bank; checks drawn on other local banks; and checks drawn on out of town banks. He will list them on his blotter sheet periodically during the day, after which he will charge them to the clearings, transit or bookkeeping sections for final processing.

In proving deposits, should an error be discovered in the deposit, it should be called to the attention of an officer for immediate attention.

Errors, while generally explainable, sometimes are not all they seem. Very often a depositor will have meant to deposit certain checks and entered them on the deposit ticket, and then through an oversight forgot to include them. In like manner, depositors will sometimes include a check, with other checks, for deposit without entering it on the deposit slip. When such errors occur, alert banks which are public relations conscious, immediately call the discrepancy to the attention of the depositor and see that the corrected entries are made in one of the several ways previously described in covering the operations of the proof department.

The receiving teller is generally accountable for all items and cash from the time they are received by him until they are delivered to other sections for processing. Cash which a teller takes in is sorted as to condition, packaged in standard packages, and daily turned over to the head paying teller or some other officer who has charge of the bank's surplus cash.

In connection with the operations of the receiving teller, some or all of the following operating instructions will be probably used as a guide:

1. Procedures for tellers to follow in connection with handling altered checks tendered for deposit.
2. Schedule for pickup of checks for processing.
3. Handling of coupons tendered for deposit.
4. Regulations in connection with the use of night depositories.
5. Procedure for handling mail deposits.

CHAPTER XXXII

THE COMMERCIAL PAYING TELLERS SECTION

IT HAS BEEN ESTIMATED THAT OVER 90% of all business transactions are settled by check. Each year in excess of 9 billion individual checks are written and processed through the banking system, and the number is increasing daily as more and more people are coming to find the use of a checking account convenient as a medium of exchange for the purchase of goods and payment of bills.

The 9 billion checks become 63 billion items handled by banks and others, however, when we consider the channels through which a check travels from the time it is issued as an order to a bank to pay money to a particular party or order, until it is finally returned to the bank on which drawn and charged to the drawer's account.

The channels through which a check travels in its sometimes short life, may cover a distance only from the paying teller's window to the bookkeeping department, or may travel half way around the world during which time it is handled principally by:

1. The payee when the check is issued.
2. The teller when the item is deposited or cashed.
3. The proof or transit section of the receiving bank in routing it to the bank on which drawn for collection.
4. The correspondent, or Federal Reserve Bank to which the item is sent for presentation and payment to the bank on which drawn.
5. The proof section of the bank on which drawn in proving the items as received from the correspondent bank.
6. The bookkeeping section of the bank on which drawn when it is posted to the account of the drawee.
7. The file clerk of the bank on which the check is drawn when the check is filed after being posted and cancelled.
8. The drawer when he receives his statement at the end of

the month and files the check as a receipt for future reference purposes.

While there are a number of reasons why checks are in such widespread use, the following are the most important:

A. It is a convenient way to pay for merchandise and goods purchased or to pay bills in that it results in a vast saving of time and effort which would be entailed if it were necessary to pay bills by the actual exchange of mediums of exchange.

B. It represents safety because it makes it unnecessary for a person to carry large sums of money.

C. A receipt for payment of the bill or merchandise is automatically effected by endorsement of the check.

In previous chapters we learned about negotiable instruments. We studied the legal requirements covering the relationship of a depositor with a bank, and the requirements for opening a checking account. We also not only became familiar with the various types of accounts, the resolutions and signature cards required by banks as authorizations to honor such checks when presented but the various operating procedures through which a check passes from the time it is issued and tendered in payment of debt or exchanged for something of value, until it is paid by the bank on which drawn by deducting the amount from the balance in the account maintained by the person who issued the check.

We will now cover one of the most important steps in the handling of such checks—the function of the paying teller in discharging his responsibilities in connection with the paying or cashing of checks.

In this connection it might be well to again be reminded that a check, as referred to in banking, is a negotiable instrument generally defined as an unconditional order in writing, signed by one party, ordering a third party to pay a certain sum in money on demand or presentation of the order by a second party or bearer. Another definition is that a check is a streamlined letter of instruction to a bank covering the disbursal of funds which the maker has on deposit.

A check is a written order which a bank is obliged to honor upon demand. In doing so it must determine the genuineness of the order by an examination and approval of the depositor's signature. The bank also has the responsibility for seeing that the money is paid to the person named in the check as payee, or to another person or persons to whom the check has been properly negotiated by endorsement.

In connection with endorsements, it is well to remember that a check payable to bearer, cash, currency or to a fictitious payee, is payable to the presenter and may be cashed by a bank without identification or endorsement. While such checks are negotiable by delivery, as a matter of precaution all such checks should be endorsed, and use of checks made payable to bearer should not be encouraged. Many banks as a matter of practice and policy decline to cash such checks unless endorsed by the presenter, or they are given a receipt covering the funds paid out in exchange for the check.

ON PAYING OR CASHING CHECKS. Because of the legal technicalities involved, it might be well to explain here the difference between "paying" a check and "cashing" a check. Although the terms are widely and quite loosely used, it should nevertheless be understood that the term "paying" a check refers to the bank exchanging cash or its equivalent for a check drawn on itself; while the term "cashing" a check refers to advancing cash or money on a check drawn on another bank and which must be presented for payment.

When a bank is presented with a check drawn on itself, it is under legal obligation to pay the item providing the signature is genuine; it is properly dated; the person to whom the check is payable or order presents the item for payment; and the drawer has sufficient funds in the account to provide for the payment. Banks, on the other hand, only cash checks when they can recover the amount from the payee, if the check is not good, or payment is refused by the bank on which it is drawn.

The importance of tellers both from a public relations and operating standpoint cannot be overestimated. Tellers see and wait on more customers than all the rest of the bank combined. In fact, it is estimated that over 90% of the personal contact of customers with the bank is made through tellers. This being the case, obviously, they must be carefully chosen.

The receiving teller does business only with the bank's customers, as we learned in the previous chapter. The paying teller, on the other hand, does business with the public in addition to customers of the bank. There is more responsibility on a paying teller than any other teller in the bank, however, not only from a public relations standpoint, but because of the financial responsibility he assumes in performing the functions of his position.

A receiving teller's only real concern in handling transactions is in seeing that checks bear the endorsement of the one depositing them, and that cash in the deposit is accounted for, which he can verify at the window or later. The paying teller, on the other hand, if he has paid out more money than called for on the check, cannot detect the error until closing time and then may only know that an error has been made.

Paying tellers at times also work under pressure. On busy days they have long lines in front of their windows and because of the necessity to wait many customers become impatient. To avoid errors, a good paying teller must be calm in the paying out of money, keep a cool head, be courteous to all who come to his window, and not permit any customer to hurry him or speed up his work so that an error will occur.

It must be remembered that a paying teller has many opportunities or avenues to make mistakes. He may pay a forged check or a raised check. He may fail to compare the written amount with the printed amount and possibly overpay the item. He may pay the wrong party or pay a check that has not been properly endorsed. He may pay a post dated check or a stale check. He may certify a check against an insufficient balance; pay a check for more than the amount of the deposit balance creating an overdraft; or pay out funds on a check on which a stop payment order has been issued.

A paying teller is constantly taking risks, and it is therefore essential that a paying teller must be a person of unquestionable honesty and integrity, and have the ability to cultivate a memory for faces and names, so as to recognize the signature on checks. In addition, as he represents the bank in its relationship with the public, he should be dignified yet friendly, neat in appearance and pleasant in his contacts with the customers and the public.

Originally the cashier was the custodian of all of the bank's cash and generally was surrounded by a glass cage, bars and protective devices, in addition to the vault and safe in which surplus cash and currency was maintained. It is believed that the word "cashier" came originally from the Spanish word "cajero" which means cash keeper.

Later, as banks developed, the functions of money keeping by the cashier were turned over to the teller who became the assistant to the cashier. As banks continued to grow, with the services of many tellers required, the control and providing of cash to handle normal daily transactions became the responsibility of a head teller, while responsibility for surplus, reserve or cash in excess of that required to handle daily transactions was placed under the control of one or several officers. Today, because of convenience and the rapidity with which currency can be provided for requirements from correspondent or Federal Reserve Banks and to keep uninvested cash at a minimum, it is established policy in most banks for tellers to maintain only sufficient cash in their possession for their current needs. Each day, or as circumstances warrant, these tellers turn over excess cash to the head teller as reserve, or shipment to their correspondent or Federal Reserve Bank for conversion into deposits which can be drawn upon for investment in bonds or for loans.

FUNCTIONS OF A PAYING TELLER. While duties and responsibilities of a paying teller may vary as between banks, their principal functions are to:

1. Pay checks drawn on the bank presented over the counter by depositors for pocket cash or for payroll and other purposes.

2. Pay checks drawn on the bank presented over the counter by persons who are not customers of the bank, upon proper identification.

3. Certify checks payable to individuals when presented, providing there is no stop payment against the check and there are sufficient funds on deposit in the account to cover it.

4. Maintain control over the signature cards of the bank's depositors.

5. Maintain a record of all current stop payment orders.

In addition, in some banks, it is the responsibility of the paying tellers to examine the signatures and endorsements of checks drawn on the bank, presented through the clearings, correspondent bank, or Federal Reserve Bank and approve before they are posted by the bookkeepers to respective accounts.

RECORDS MAINTAINED BY PAYING TELLERS. The records maintained by a paying teller are relatively simple inasmuch as he begins with cash; exchanges such cash for checks during the day, which are forwarded to the proof, transit or bookkeeping department for ultimate collection; and ends with cash.

Generally, a paying teller maintains a cash book or blotter in which he records the amount of cash on hand at the beginning of the day and the totals of checks proven and processed by the proof clerk drawn on (a) his own bank, (b) other local banks known as clearing house items, and (c) checks drawn on banks outside of the local area known as transit items which he has cashed. When balancing at the end of the day, cash on hand plus the totals of checks drawn on other banks which he has cashed should equal the amount of cash he began with in the morning.

In most banks, at the end of the day after balancing, the total amount of cash is entered on the teller's daily cash sheet which discloses to the head teller the total amount of cash on hand. If the amount is in excess of the bank's normal requirements, the excess is shipped to the correspondent bank or Federal Reserve Bank for credit to the bank's account, while if the cash balance on hand is less than that normally required to handle daily transactions, the correspondent bank or Federal Reserve Bank is notified to charge the bank's account for the amount of currency required and ship it to them so that it will be available for transacting business the following day.

The other principal records maintained by a paying teller, in addition to the cash book or daily blotter sheet, are the files containing the signature cards of customers and those authorized to sign on behalf of partnerships, corporations and others who maintain accounts with the bank. Generally such signature cards are maintained in a file in the teller's cage, a duplicate of which is maintained in the bookkeeping department.

As protection to the bank in paying checks, and to maintain a proper relationship with the depositor, signature cards should be maintained on every account carried in the name of:

1. Individuals.

2. Several individuals under a joint account arrangement where the bank is authorized to pay out funds on the signature of one of several people individually, or on the signature of two or more people jointly.

3. Partnerships, where several people have an interest in the account, and where the bank is authorized to pay out funds on the signature of one of several people individually, or on the signatures of two or more people together.

4. Corporations, where the bank is authorized to pay out funds on deposit in the name of the corporation on presentation of checks signed by persons whom the corporation, by proper resolution of its board of directors, has authorized to sign checks in behalf of the corporation.

5. Clubs or associations, some of whose members are elected or appointed to transact financial affairs in behalf of the rest of the members.

6. Individuals acting in fiduciary capacity such as administrator, executor or trustee, where proper authorization, usually by court order, is filed in the resolution file.

In addition, such accounts may have attached a power of attorney or authorization by the person in whose name the account stands to permit checks to be honored and business transacted by one whom they designate their attorney to act in their behalf.

With reference to powers of attorney, it must be remembered that what a man may do himself, he may also do by his agent; and the acts of the agent when within the scope of the authority, are the acts of the principal. Sometimes depositors, therefore, for certain reasons and convenience, give the right to draw checks on the bank to others by delegating their authority through a properly executed power of attorney. Such powers of attorney may be limited or unlimited, and include, as a rule, the right to endorse checks on behalf of the principal. While the right to endorse only may be given, it should be remembered that such right to endorse does not include the right to draw checks. In connection with a power of attorney, it must be in writing and be explicit not only so that the bank will know the powers and rights of the agent or attorney, but the extent of their responsibility in dealing with the one acting in behalf of the principal.

Paying tellers or other tellers to whom are delegated the responsibility for certifying checks, also maintain the registers in which all checks certified are recorded by number, date, name of drawer or maker, and name of payee.

In negotiating a check for currency, a paying teller has greater responsibility when he pays a check drawn on his own bank, than when he is called upon to cash a check drawn on another bank. Where the item presented for encashment has been drawn by a depositor, there is no question as far as the signature of the maker is concerned; and bank records disclose information as to balance, any stop payment orders which may have been issued.

Where a check drawn on another bank is presented and cashed, however, the teller is not passing on the goodness of the check or fact that the maker has an account in the bank on which drawn, approving the genuineness of the signature on the check, determining there is sufficient funds in the account to pay the check when presented, or whether an order has been issued by the maker to stop payment on the check. Only the bank on which the check is drawn possesses this information.

The responsibility of a teller in cashing a check drawn on another bank, therefore, extends only to having assurance and reasonable knowledge that the person for whom the check was negotiated is able and willing to reimburse the bank for the funds advanced, if for any reason payment on the check is refused by the bank on which drawn.

In paying a check drawn on his own bank, a paying teller generally applies different tests to the transaction to determine if he is justified, on behalf of the depositor and the bank, to honor the order of the drawer to disburse the funds as directed, and to exchange cash for the check.

These seven tests, which well trained and competent tellers through experience undertake almost subconsciously, are all in connection with establishing the fact that:

1. The signature is authorized and genuine.

2. The date on the check is current. Generally this means it should not be dated ahead or bear a date more than 30 or 60 days prior to the date of presentation.

3. The check is not altered or changed in any way.

4. There is no stop payment order in effect against the check.

5. The drawer of the check has a collected balance sufficient to cover the check.

6. There is no hold on the account because of a bankruptcy, death, garnishment or order which has impounded the funds.

7. The check has been properly endorsed by the person to whom the check is made payable and by the person presenting the check for encashment.

AUTHORIZED AND GENUINE SIGNATURES. In a bank where procedures are well supervised, the paying tellers are provided with a well kept signature card file which carries the genuine signatures of those authorized to withdraw funds from specific accounts. Through practice, experience and process in paying checks drawn against the accounts which are posted by the bookkeeper, tellers soon learn to distinguish an authorized and genuine signature from an unauthorized or forged signature.

Where an individual draws a check on his account, there is no problem as the signature is genuine and he is the only one authorized to withdraw funds from the account.

In connection with a corporation, on the other hand, it is the bank's responsibility to not only see that the signatures on checks presented for credit or encashment are the genuine signatures of those who are permitted to sign checks, but that the signatures are those of persons who have been authorized by proper resolution to sign checks.

The danger to a teller in handling checks is that he might be confronted with a forged signature. Through practice and experience, however, an astute teller learns to watch for the peculiarities of the signature, such as little curlicues, the lines, the bearing down on the initials and other different marks which become part of the signature of the person authorized to withdraw funds. Such practice day after day enables an experienced teller, with surprising accuracy, to detect forgeries or at least question the authenticity of the signature and establish positive identification.

DETERMINING IF CHECK IS CURRENTLY DATED. A check which bears a date in the future is said to be post dated and is not an effective order on the bank to pay the check until that date arrives. Where a bank honors a check that is post dated, it is presumed that the depositor can refuse to permit the item to be charged to his account and has the right to issue a stop payment order against the check at any time prior to the date appearing on the check.

A check which bears a date in the past, on the other hand, is said to be stale dated. According to the general interpretation of the law, the holder of a check is obligated to present it to the bank on which drawn for payment within a reasonable time. This is generally assumed to be no later than 60 days from the date of the check. Checks outstanding for a longer period of time are generally referred back to the maker before being honored. The time lapse between the date on the check and the time when it is considered stale through non-presentation varies, of course, between states. Here again tellers should be governed by the laws of the state as applied to their bank and the recommendation of their legal counsel, as payment of a post dated or stale check by a paying teller can possibly result in loss or embarrassment to the bank. Particular attention, therefore, should be paid at all times by an alert paying teller that the item presented for encashment is currently dated.

ALTERATIONS OR CHANGES IN A CHECK. Every bank is obliged to accept a check for encashment or credit in strict acdance with terms established by the drawer at the time the check was issued; therefore, for a check to be in good delivery order and to be wholly acceptable by the bank, it must not be altered or changed in any way.

Although a bank is responsible for detecting alterations and for paying such checks, many depositors often are careless and negligent in the issuance of checks such as scratching out a date, writing over the amount of the check, or filling out checks in such a manner that it encourages alterations by unreliable holders.

One of the most common forms of alteration is in the raising of the amounts on checks. For example, where a check is made out for $1.00, $2.00, $3.00 etc. and the written amount is garbled, missing or can be erased, it can be raised to $100.00, $200.00, $300.00 accordingly. In like manner a check in the amount of $3.00, $30.00, $300.00, can be raised to $800.00. While obviously it takes the work of a clever penman to alter checks, it is occasionally done. When it happens and is detected, the bank has no authority to honor such a check and charge it to the depositor's account. Too much cannot be said for the use of good quality safety paper for check stock.

The date of a check may also be altered with the intention to defraud. This is done in cases where a customer will give a post dated check with the intent that when the check is due to be presented on the date as set forth in the check, he will have sufficient funds on deposit to cover the check. The payee, in the hopes of effecting a collection, will alter the date and attempt to negotiate it. Such alterations are generally difficult to detect and checks are usually returned for insufficient funds. If the balance is sufficient, however, to provide for payment of the check and the check is paid, the depositor accepts the situation, even though other checks might be returned, due to the fact that he had no right to issue the check in the first place knowing there were not sufficient funds on deposit to provide for payment of the check if presented.

THE BALANCE IN THE ACCOUNT MUST BE COLLECTED AND SUFFICIENT TO COVER THE CHECK. Unless the account has sufficient funds to cover the amount of the check and the check is paid, it results in an overdraft which is in effect an unauthorized loan.

Banks do not intentionally permit a customer to overdraw the account and only do so with the approval of an officer. Should the bank decline to honor the check, it is then marked "Insufficient Funds" and returned to the presenter. Overdrafts are not favorably regarded by banks and customers who constantly draw against insufficient funds, or issue checks when they do not have sufficient funds in the bank to cover same when presented, are usually requested to close the account.

Frequently, especially in connection with businesses which have a considerable volume of accounts receivable, the balance in the account, while usually sufficient to take care of any checks presented, is composed of funds which are in the process of being collected from, or through, other banks. As such funds are not considered cash or available for payout until checks which comprise the balance are collected, any checks drawn against such a balance are referred to an officer or person in authority for decision as to payment. Should the account warrant the accommodation, the bank will occasionally honor such checks. On the other hand, should the bank decline to honor such checks, they are marked "Drawn Against Uncollected Funds" and returned through the usual channels to the presenter.

THE BALANCE MUST BE FREE OF ATTACHMENT. Notice of bankruptcy, garnishment, attachment and death are circumstances under which a bank is generally and temporarily prevented from honoring checks drawn against the balance of the account of the person affected.

To avoid confusion and properly handle such matters, it is a general practice in most banks, to have writs of attachment and garnishments served on one officer of the bank, who then places the hold on the account for the reason specified, impounding such funds until the funds are released by a court order.

In cases where a bank learns or is notified of the death of a person in whose name an individual account is maintained, the usual practice is to refuse to honor any checks presented which have been drawn against the account until the funds are released by proper action of the state and federal government inheritance tax offices.

If a bank learns or is notified of the death of a person who has signing authority on a partnership or association account, or an account established under order of a court, it is the usual practice to hold up the honoring of checks presented which have been drawn against the balance of the account until ownership of the funds or new authority has been properly established. Because the laws in the various states differ, the practice and procedure of paying checks drawn against an account where the principal or one with signing authority is deceased, is usually covered by instructions adopted by the bank in accordance with the advice of its legal counsel.

Holds are also placed on an account by paying tellers or various sections of the bank, in the form of a notice to the bookeepers that they have cashed a check or paid out funds, and for the bookkeeper to hold back such amounts to cover the honoring of the debit or the check when it is received by the bookkeeping section.

CHECKS MUST BE PROPERLY ENDORSED BY THE

PAYEE AND THE PERSON FOR WHOM THE CHECK IS NEGOTIATED. The matter of proper endorsement and identification of the endorser or presenter is of great importance to a bank in cashing a check.

In order to negotiate a check for cash, for credit to an account, for exchange for something of value, or in settlement of debt, the right title and interest of the payee or holder in such check must be transferred to the person who accepts the check for cash, credit to an account, exchange for something of value or settlement of debt. Such right, title and interest can only be transferred by endorsement, and to be binding the endorsement must be that of the payee or holder who is positively identified and known to be the person to whom the check was made payable by the maker or owner of the rights, title, and interest in the check, or by endorsement of such payee and/or previous holders.

In connection with checks drawn on the bank, once identification of the holder or presenter has been established, it is the responsibility of the teller to determine that the check has been properly endorsed which means that:

A. The check, if presented for encashment by the person named as the payee, bears a blank endorsement and that the name, as signed on the back of the check, is the same as the name written or spelled in the payee space on the face of the check.

B. The check, if presented by a person other than the one named as payee on the face of the check, not only bears this name as the first endorsement, but that any or all additional endorsements are blank endorsements, that is only carry the signature of a person; and that the last signature is that of the person who is negotiating the check.

Checks payable to a corporation or to a person acting in a fiduciary capacity should always be deposited for credit to an account and not be cashed unless proper authorization is on file with the bank.

The matter of identification can be a problem, especially in cashing checks for strangers. The common and acceptable means of identifying a person with a name, aside from finger printing, is by knowledge gained from personal association with a person having certain physical characteristics, who answers to a certain name and is known by others through physical characteristics as a person who is known by a certain name.

Most persons presenting a check for encashment at a teller's window are customers of the bank and are well known to the teller, so no question arises as to identity. Sometimes such a customer will present a check of substantial amount drawn on another bank. Here, too, caution must be exercised and if there is any question as to the goodness of the check it is sometimes policy to have the customer deposit the check to his account and then draw a check for the amount he wishes to have, as evidence of the transaction. Banks also sometimes have a rule that all checks over a certain fixed amount presented for encashment by a depositor, if drawn on another bank, must be approved by an officer before being exchanged for cash or accepted for deposit for immediate use.

Where a check drawn on the bank is presented by a stranger, it is generally the policy of the bank to have both the amount of the check and the name of the payee or endorser approved by an officer, who will use means for determining identification as are warranted under the circumstances.

In connection with checks drawn on other banks, presented by non-customers or strangers, it is the customary practice of banks to refer such transactions to an officer, who, if he decides to accommodate the person, and after he has satisfied himself as to identification, may telephone the bank on which the check is drawn to ascertain that an account is maintained in the name of the drawer representative of the amount of the check. It is well to remember, as it has so often been said, that while all strangers are not forgers or check manipulators, all check manipulators and forgers are strangers.

If a person is not personally known, but has an account at the bank, identification is readily obtainable because the signature of the individual appears on a card somewhere in the bank, and it is presumed that proper investigation was made at the time the account was opened or the relationship established.

In connection with identification, it is generally the policy of banks to require proper and positive identification under the following circumstances.

A. When a person opens a new account. The identification

must be thorough and complete, even to the extent of requiring the customer to sign his name and send it to the bank where he previously maintained an account for confirmation of signature.

B. When a stranger wishes to cash a check. This is necessary, not only to establish the proper identification of the payee or the endorser, but for possible recourse in case payment on the check is refused.

C. When a person wishes to deposit part of a check and take the remainder in cash. Unless the individual is known to be the person in whose account part of the funds are to be deposited, the transaction should be scrutinized. Very often such a transaction is set up as means to negotiate a forged or raised check.

D. When a person who is not known presents a savings passbook and withdrawal slip properly signed and wishes to withdraw funds. Extreme caution is exercised by banks in handling this type of transaction because the withdrawal, while apparently conforming to the rules of the bank, might have been obtained under duress.

E. When a person tenders rolled coin and wishes to exchange it for currency or a check. Such precaution is necessary because often such rolls can contain leaded coin, pieces of pipe, or are short in the number of items supposed to be in the package.

While it is generally accepted practice in most banks to refer all checks presented by a non-customer to an officer for approval, it is helpful to know the ways in which identification can be established. As mentioned, if a person has an account with the bank or maintains a relationship, identification is generally easy to establish. Should the person not have an account or maintain a relationship, he usually tenders credit cards, social security card, or a driver's license or something which shows his signature.

Obviously, such credentials which bear the signature of the person are helpful, for then it is possible to make a comparison with the signature on the identification and the signature on the endorsement of the check. These documents for identification purposes, in order of importance are:

1. Automobile operator's license showing picture of the person.
2. Employee identification card.
3. A factory badge showing a picture of the individual and a signature.

4. Driver's license.
5. Passport.
6. Selective Service card.
7. Social Security card.
8. A travel credit card.
9. Voter's registration card.
10. A lodge card.
11. A library card.
12. A firearms permit.

There is no way for the person who examines such identification, however, to positively ascertain that such items tendered for identification purposes are those identifying the person who is presenting them as it is entirely possible that they could have been stolen or forged. At best, such documents act as a supporting guide to judgment acquired through experience over the years.

TELLER OPERATIONS. Depending on the size of the bank and volume of check cashing activity, several recognized systems are followed by banks in handling the encashment of checks. These are:

A. The segregated system where the sole function of the teller is to cash checks.

B. The unit system where the teller not only cashes checks but accepts deposits.

C. The special system where regular tellers cash checks and accept deposits, and special tellers are set up to cash payroll checks exclusively.

Both the segregated and unit systems are sometimes modified under an alphabetical arrangement. Under this system checks are cashed by tellers, each of whom handles a certain section. For example: A check issued by a person whose last name begins with the letter B. Such checks would be presented at window A to F for encashment, etc.

Regardless of which system is used, if the paying teller has a separate function from that of receiving, he should plan at the beginning of the day to have sufficient bills and coin to take care of the demands placed upon him by customers. This, of course, will vary from day to day and at different times of the month, depending upon whether it is a weekend or a payday, and the local requirements of merchants. It goes without saying that, in order to provide excellent service, the paying teller should have in his cage at all times sufficient currency to preclude the necessity, except on rare occasions, of having to leave the cage to go to get additional currency and coin to supply the needs of the customer. The amounts required from time to time generally can be ascertained by recording the daily volume of transactions. The most convenient manner in which to handle currency is as it is packaged by the paying tellers after they have sorted it out.

In many banks in recent years, because of the minimum risk involved and in order to facilitate handling of coin, especially with the use of women tellers, paying tellers are provided with small cage safes which contain an ample reserve supply of silver. Where such safes are provided, it eliminates the need for tellers to take their silver into the vault at night.

Where banks, however, follow the unit system, the amount of currency required daily for the encashment of checks can often be gauged by the teller from records maintained recording the amount of cash received in deposits on certain days of the week and certain hours of the day. By checking such figures, an astute teller or head teller can very often come approximately close to the minimum and maximum amounts of currency and coin each teller should have in his cage at the beginning of each day's business. Obviously, if this procedure is followed, excess currency is turned over to the head teller periodically for adding to the reserve, or, if that account is sufficient, for transfer to the correspondent or Federal Reserve bank so such funds can be invested to produce income for the bank.

FORGERIES AND CHECK ALTERATIONS. While it is a rule of law that the bank pays forgeries at its peril and is responsible for paying a forged signature or raised amount, many checks are issued by depositors who do not take due precautions and exercise diligence in preparing the check.

Even though depositors obviously cannot avoid giving checks to strangers or others in payment of goods and merchandise, they can, however, write them in such a manner that they will not be a positive invitation to the holder to raise or alter them for his own benefit.

Although the copying of a signature by a clever forger is easy, and amounts on a check can be raised by a clever penman with little effort, such manipulations could be made more difficult, if not impossible, if banks would suggest to their customers that they follow these rules of guidance in preparing and delivering a check.

1. Checks should be written on forms provided by the bank or printed on good safety paper.

2. Checks should be written out in ink and not in pencil.

3. Signatures should be complete so positive identification is possible.

4. The figures should be well written up against the dollar sign with a heavy hand, in a way that leaves no further room for the addition of other ciphers.

5. The written amount should be placed beginning well to the left and filling in the remaining open space with a wavy line.

6. Whenever possible a protective device should be used for cutting in the amount on the face of the check.

7. Checks should never be exchanged with another person or "sold" to another person for cash.

8. As soon as the statement and cancelled checks are received at the end of the current month, they should be reconciled with the check register or book and endorsements checked to be certain payment has been transferred in accordance with the original intent.

In connection with forgeries it is well to remember that forgers "draw" signatures, that is, they are not made free-hand.

When a signature is drawn, generally the forger, using the original signature as a model, reveals his dishonesty by what are known as hesitation strokes. These are lines drawn part way but not completed and are caused by the forger referring to the signature while in the process of completing it. Sometimes he will trace a signature through a carbon paper and then go over it in ink. In so doing he is quite likely to carelessly leave a slight mark which is made by the tracing and which has not been covered by the ink, due to hesitancy in the line of the pen. When this is noted, a forgery is suspected and can, of course, be determined by comparison with the authentic signature on the signature card.

Many times an alert teller can spot a person who is trying to pass a forged or altered check. He is nervous and his facial expression discloses anxiety. In such cases, unless the teller is absolutely certain of the worthiness of the check and the presenter is well known, the extra time taken to check out the item often pays off and prevents the teller from honoring the check.

Persons who try to cash checks which have a forged endorsement, forged signature, or where the amounts have been raised, generally try to negotiate such checks with a merchant, tendering the check in payment of goods. If presented to a bank, it is usually done so during a rush period with the hope that the teller will be so busy that he will be negligent in passing on the authenticity of the check. Experienced tellers, however, are unusually careful during rush periods and take their time in handling transactions, particularly if there is the slightest question of doubt regarding the legitimacy or authenticity of the check.

In cases where a teller is of the opinion that the person presenting the check is not the lawful holder or is party to a forgery, the proper procedure to follow is to refer the check and the item to an officer. If, however, the teller is certain that the item is a forgery and the bank is of sufficient size to have a floor guard, he should contact him, or act in accordance with the procedure to be followed under such circumstances as outlined in the operating instructions. In any event, an alert teller should carefully note the description of the person, that is the persons approximate height and weight, color of hair and eyes, and any distinguishing physical marks such as a mole on the chin, scar on the cheek etc.

PAYING OUT CURRENCY. In cashing checks, some customers will request the teller for payment of the proceeds in currency of a certain denomination. In the case of a depositor picking up currency and silver for payroll and change purposes, he may provide the teller in advance with a list of currency denominations and rolls of silver he wants. In such cases, the teller should make sure that the list totals the same as the total of checks offered, and that the checks tendered in payment total exactly the amount of currency and coin passed through.

The denominations and makeup of currency requested will vary between customers, depending upon the type of business. The change and currency needed by a proprietor of a gas station is quite different from the denominations required by the proprietor of a clothing store. Likewise, the currency and silver required by a person operating a variety store or drug store, will be entirely different from the requirements of a person operating a grocery store, where purchases are generally for higher amounts and where larger bills are generally tendered.

In connection with cashing checks, particularly payroll checks, an experienced teller will not only keep in mind the different combinations which may be tendered for different even amounts, but will make combinations generally found to be acceptable in cashing payroll checks. In no case, unless it is specifically requested, should a paying teller hand over the proceeds of a check in the largest bill, as for example, one $5.00 bill in exchange for a five dollar check; or a $50.00 bill in exchange for a fifty dollar check; or a $20.00 bill in exchange for a twenty dollar check.

Generally, and this sometimes varies between sections of the country, unless otherwise requested, the acceptable denominations for cashing checks of fixed amounts are as follows:

AMOUNT OF CHECK*	PAYABLE IN DENOMINATIONS*
$ 5.00	Five $1's
10.00	One $5; Five $1's
15.00	Two $5's; Five $1's
20.00	One $10; One $5; Five 1's
25.00	One $10; Two $5's; Five $1's
30.00	Two $10; Two $5's
35.00	Two $10; Three $5's
40.00	Three $10's; Two $5's
45.00	Three $10's; Three $5's
50.00	One $20; Two $10's; Two $5's
55.00	One $20; Three $10's; One $5
60.00	One $20; Three $10's; Two $5's
65.00	Two $20's; Two $10's; One $5
70.00	Two $20's; Two $10's; Two $5's
75.00	Two $20's; Three $10's; One $5
80.00	Two $20's; Three $10's; Two $5's
85.00	Three $20's; Two $10's; One $5

90.00	Three $20's; Two $10's; Two $5's
95.00	Three $20's; Three $10's; One $5
100.00	Three $20's; Three $10's; Two $5's
125.00	Five $20's; Two $10's; One $5
150.00	Five $20's; Three $10's; Four $5's

* Silver change paid out per changer or in easy denominations.

STOP PAYMENT ORDERS.

Banks are always bound by the written instructions of their customers. Should a check be lost, stolen, or used in a transaction in which the party presenting the check did not receive value; or become lost, misplaced or stolen while in the hands of the payee, it is customary practice for the drawer of the checks to notify the bank of the fact and instruct them to stop payment on the item.

Before accepting a stop payment order, the bank employee who has the responsibility for handling such orders first checks with the bookkeeping section to be certain the check has not already been presented and paid. If the item has been paid, the check is immediately scrutinized for possible evidences of fraud and steps taken to recover the funds or undertake whatever action is warranted under the circumstances.

If the check has not been paid, the depositor is asked to fill out and sign a stop payment order similar to that shown in Exhibit 90, after which notices similar to that shown in Exhibit 91 are prepared and given to the tellers and bookeepers for their information and guidance.

CERTIFYING OF CHECKS.

Another function of the paying teller is in connection with certifying checks, which is a warranty by the bank that the funds represented by the check are available and will be paid to the payee or order on presentation. Once a check is certified, it becomes the obligation of the bank rather than the bank's customer and for that reason the amount is deducted from the customer's account at once. A request for certification may be made by the owner of the account on which the check is drawn, or made by the payee. There are times when people receive checks and want to be sure, for some reason or another, that the check is good; and likewise, for some reason or another, do not wish to cash the check immediately.

Banks, of course, are not required by law to certify customers' checks either for a customer or for a payee. Certification, therefore, s an accommodation and a courtesy.

Obviously a check cannot be certified if the drawer's account does not have a sufficient balance to cover it.

In certifying a check, the paying teller first establishes the fact that the balance in the account is sufficient and that there are no stop payments or holds against the account. If it is in order, he teller then notifies the bookkeeper to put a hold on the account and enters the check by number, name, amount, date and payee on a triplicate form of which the original is a debit, deducting the amount from the account of the maker; the duplicate is a general ledger credit to certified checks; while the triplicate is the register copy. To complete the transaction the teller stamps the word CERTIFIED on the face of the check, together with the date and igns it. Thereafter it becomes the obligation of the bank rather than the customer.

In a well managed bank, many of the functions and responibilities of a paying teller are covered by operating instructions generally in connection with the following:

1. Procedure to follow in connection with forged signatures or altered checks.
2. Approvals of checks for encashment.
3. Guarantees of endorsement.
4. Procedure to follow in certifying a check.
5. Teller's cash control schedule.
6. Requirements in connection with cashing payroll checks.
7. Procedure to follow in accepting stop payment orders.

CHAPTER XXXIII

THE SPECIAL SERVICE SECTION

EVERY BANK, IN ADDITION TO PROVIDING loan and credit facilities and facilities in connection with deposit accounts, provides many special services to assist customers and the public in handling their financial affairs.

Some of these services which are in connection with facilities provided by the Trust Department, International Department and Safe Deposit Department we shall cover in later chapters. Other special services, including collections which are covered in the following chapter, are in connection with:

A. Issuing official checks such as:

1. Bank drafts on domestic banks.
2. Bank drafts on foreign banks.
3. Bank drafts on Federal Reserve banks.
4. Bank money orders.
5. Bank registered checks.
6. Cashier's checks.

B. Handling orders of customers and others for the purchase or sale of securities for their own account.

C. Providing temporary safekeeping services.

D. Arranging for the telegraphic transfer of funds.

In a small bank, providing for all or part of such services can be the responsibility of an officer, or in some cases one of the functions of the note or the collection teller. In a large bank, depending on volume, the responsibility for rendering respective services might be delegated to several individual sections or combined in a single service section. Regardless of deposit size or location of the bank, however, such services, which are important means of conducting trade and commerce, are provided by every bank.

ISSUING OF OFFICIAL CHECKS.

Bank drafts, either domestic or foreign, which are described in Chapter XVI and shown in Exhibit 34, are instruments drawn and payable against funds which the issuing bank maintains on deposit with the bank on which drawn. They are generally used by individuals, corporations and banks when it is desirable to have funds in other cities which can be immediately available for use in completing a transaction.

On the surface this would not seem to be possible or practical, for to accomplish this purpose would require each bank to maintain an account with every other bank. From a practical standpoint this is generally accomplished by banks maintaining accounts with banks to which they send their out of town items for collection and credit.

Actually, however, it is very nearly possible to transfer funds from one person to another person, and from one bank to any other bank in any part of the world, and have such funds immediately available through drafts and wire transfer facilities of the Federal Reserve Banks, and facilities provided by major city banks who have extensive correspondent banking relationships.

Bank money orders, registered checks, cashier's checks, which are also described in Chapter XVI and shown in Exhibits 35, 36 and 37, are instruments provided by all banks for those who believe they cannot afford to have the convenience of a checking account, or have not been properly sold by the bank on the many advantages of having a checking account, and wish an instrument other than cash, to use in transacting their financial affairs.

Cashier's checks, money orders, and registered checks are not drawn against or on any existing balance except that created by the funds which the purchaser of the check has tendered in exchange for the check; and against which the check will be charged when presented and paid. Such checks are considered drawn on the bank by itself.

Official checks, instead of personal checks, are also a great convenience to customers in completing financial transactions in other sections of the country where they are not known and in local areas where goodness of funds tendered in completing a transaction must be assured and rapid conversion into cash effected. In addition, cashier's checks (together with certified checks) are widely used in commerce, as when municipal or other agencies accept bids on construction work or on contracts, bids must invariably be accompanied by a bidder's check which must be in the form of a cashier's check or certified check.

Cashier's checks and drafts are also widely used to facilitate remittances for items sent to the collection department for presentation and payment, and by banks in making adjustments through the clearing house for the redemption of returned checks.

The special service or other sections in some banks may also issue travellers checks, letters of credit, and engage in foreign exchange transactions in connection with issuing drafts which, when presented to a bank in a foreign country, can be exchanged for the coin or currency of that country; and the exchanging of checks and redemption into United States coin, of checks and drafts drawn on banks in foreign countries. As these services, however, are customarily provided by other sections, they are covered in detail in Chapter XXXVIII, The International Department.

The functions of the personnel of the special services section in connection with the issuing of drafts, cashier's checks, and other official checks; the handling of items for safekeeping; and services in connection with handling the purchase and sale for customers, are mechanical operations governed, of course, by the law of negotiable instruments which has been covered in previous chapters and rules and regulations of the bank.

Customers or the public who wish to purchase a draft or certain type of official check generally fill out a requisition similar to Exhibit 93 on which they indicate the type of check they wish, to whom it should be made payable, the amount and their name as purchaser. The form also provides a space for the teller to mark down for control purposes the amount of the fee collected.

Once the requisition together with the funds to be used in payment of the check are tendered to the teller, he follows the same procedure as he would in handling a check for deposit or for encashment.

If cash is tendered in payment of the check, there is no problem. If a savings withdrawal slip is tendered, it either must have been approved by the savings teller and deducted from the passbook, or it is necessary for the special service teller to either refer the customer back to the savings section for approval, or to take the withdrawal slip together with the passbook and check it against the savings records to be certain the signature is authorized and is the signature of the person in whose name the account is maintained; the balance in the account is sufficient to honor the withdrawal; the person presenting the withdrawal slip and passbook, if someone other than the person in whose name the account is carried, has the right and authority to withdraw the funds in exchange for an official check.

If the funds tendered in payment of the official check are represented by a check on the bank signed by the person who wishes to exchange the funds for an official check, and the identification of the person is known, there is no problem.

If the check tendered in payment of the official check is drawn on another bank but presented by a customer to whom the check is payable or by whom endorsed, and the customer is known, the teller must satisfy himself as to the ability of the person pre-

EXHIBIT 93

REQUISITION FOR OFFICIAL CHECK

Requisition for

☐ Money Order ☐ Cashier's Check ☐ Chicago Draft ☐ New York Draft

PURCHASER ....
DATE

ADDRESS .... CO1—6

PAYABLE TO (PLEASE PRINT)	AMOUNT	
SERVICE CHARGE		
AUTOMOBILE LOANS — PERSONAL LOANS TOTAL		

FIRST NATIONAL BANK AND TRUST COMPANY OF EVANSTON
Low Rates **EVANSTON, ILLINOIS** *Friendly Service*

senting the check to make the check good in case payment is refused; or the check, when presented to the bank on which drawn, is returned for insufficient funds, or because a stop payment order has been entered. In any case, where doubt exists, it is good banking practice to refer such checks to an officer for official approval.

If a check tendered in payment of an official check, in addition to being drawn on another bank, is tendered by a person who is not known, or is not a customer, extreme caution should be exercised, not only because the bank has no control over the genuineness of the check nor assurance it will be paid when presented, but because it does not know the endorser. Generally, unless a person who is well known to the bank will endorse the check, thereby guaranteeing repayment in case of a dishonorment, banks will not, as a matter of policy, accept such checks in exchange for a draft or official check.

In order to assist personnel of the special service department in determining if checks tendered in payment of official checks are in order, use of the following check list will be found helpful.

A. Is the date on the check current?

B. Is the written amount the same as the printed amount?

C. Is the check signed?

D. If the check is drawn on this bank, is it free from a stop payment order?

E. If the check is drawn on this bank are there sufficient funds on deposit to provide for payment of the check?

F. Is the check properly endorsed?

G. Is the endorser known?

H. If the check is drawn on another bank, is the endorser and presenter known and, if so, sufficiently responsible to reimburse the bank for the amount of the check, in case it is not paid when presented to the bank on which drawn?

Most tellers satisfy themselves as to the goodness of the funds tendered in payment of an official check before writing up the check on the bank records. Records usually consist of a triplicate form of which the original is the check, the duplicate a receipt for the customer, and the triplicate the register copy which, at the end of the day, goes to the general bookkeeping section or the auditing section for future payoff.

After the check has been suitably prepared, it is run through a protectograph apparatus which records the amount of the check, sometimes by embossing or by scoring, but in such a manner that it is difficult, in fact almost impossible, to alter.

Next, depending upon the procedure followed in the bank, the check is either signed by the teller or referred to an officer for signature. In recent years considerable use has been made of a mechanical check signing machine which affixes the official signature on all checks or drafts merely by embossing or scoring in a manner which is practically impossible to duplicate. The machine has a locking device for the auditor to check at the end of the day to confirm the number of signatures with the number of checks on which the machine has been used.

In connection with the signing of official checks, not only is it costly and an interruption of administrative work to require all official checks to be signed by an officer, but an inconvenience to customers once they have purchased an official check, to wait in line, chase around the bank, or otherwise be delayed in finding an officer to place his official signature on the check, thus negotiating it. On the other hand, from an audit and control standpoint, it is considered to be somewhat risky to permit tellers wide latitude in disbursing the funds of the bank by the issuance of official checks.

It is therefore prudent policy, and again based on custom and practice in the locality in which the bank is located and the general use which is made of official checks, to permit tellers to sign cashier's checks, money orders, and registered checks, which in the final analysis are paid by the bank; and where several opportunities exist for checking of irregularities if they should occur, to permit the tellers to sign such checks in amounts not to exceed $500.00. Checks in excess of such amount are referred, as a matter of precaution, to an officer for signature.

A similar precaution can also be exercised by printing on the face of the money order or registered check the words "Not Good for More Than $———" and, as a matter of policy, only using checks for amounts less than the stated amount which the teller can sign; and using cashier's checks for amounts in excess of the maximum amount stated on the money order or registered check and requiring such checks to be signed by an officer.

In connection with drafts, banks generally discourage the use of drafts for small amounts and permit the teller some latitude as far as signing authority is concerned. One of the customary practices is for tellers to be able to sign drafts up to $1,000.00 providing they come within certain restrictions, such as being payable to a bank for a collection item, or are issued in connection with normal business transactions. Under this practice checks over $1,000.00, of course, require the signature of an officer.

Some banks, for additional protection, require all drafts to be signed by two persons, in which case the regulations usually provide for one of the signatures to be provided by the teller and the other by an officer or other authorized person.

Charges for the issuing of drafts and official checks will vary among banks. The most common practice is to use a minimum charge for the various types of official checks, graduating the charge upward, depending on the amount, similar to that disclosed in Exhibit 94.

In setting a charge schedule for providing official checks, it should be remembered, from a public relations standpoint, that the charges should be equitable, that is, they should closely conform to fees charged by the post office and commercial agencies for issuing money orders. In addition, charges should be made applicable to everyone alike and no favoritism should be shown. The providing of official checks is merely an accommodation available to anyone. Should a customer object to paying a charge or a fee for the special service which is provided because of the balance they maintain in their checking account, the protest should not be allowed for the following reason. Under normal circumstances the customer would have used a check drawn on his own account in connection with the transaction. The fact that his own check was not acceptable and required another form of payment justifies the charge for the service. Using the balance maintained in a savings account as a reason for free service is also unjustified due to the fact that compensation for the balance maintained in a savings account is paid in the form of interest—not service.

HANDLING ORDERS FOR THE PURCHASE OR SALE OF SECURITIES.

In connection with handling the purchase and sale of securities for customers and others, the bank merely acts as agent and assumes no responsibility beyond ordinary care and diligence. So that the relationship between the bank and the party for whom the transaction is handled is clearly understood, banks, except in the case of the purchase or sale of U. S. Government obligations, which have a form of their own, generally require customers to sign a written buy or sell order such as shown in Exhibits 95 and 96.

Such forms, in addition to recording the details in connection with the transaction, including the price at which the security is to be purchased or sold and instructions as to delivery of the security or disposition of proceeds, carry a disclaimer clause, similar to that shown in the form, which holds the bank harmless from loss incurred by the customer aside from failure to exercise ordinary care and diligence.

In buying securities, it is the responsibility of the teller, before

EXHIBIT 94

SCHEDULE OF CHARGES FOR ISSUING DRAFTS AND OFFICIAL CHECKS

AMOUNT	OFFICIAL CHECK	CHICAGO DRAFT	NEW YORK DRAFT
Under $ 25.00	$ .15	None issued	None issued
$ 26.00 to 99.00	.20	None issued	None issued
100.00 to 299.00	.25	$ .30	$ .35
300.00 to 499.00	.35	.40	.45
500.00 to 799.00	.50	.50	.60
800.00 to 999.00	.50	.60	.75
1000.00 and over	1.00	1/10 of 1%	1/10 of 1%

placing the order, to ascertain the identification of the purchaser; and that satisfactory and proper arrangements have been made between the customer and the bank, through an officer, for payment of the securities when purchased. In other words the customer must be known. If a check is tendered in payment of the approximate cost of the securities or a percentage of the cost, such check must be properly dated, signed, not altered and payable to the bank; or, if to the purchaser, properly endorsed. If the check is drawn on the bank which is handling the transaction, unless otherwise warranted under the circumstances, it is proper to place a hold on the account for the amount of the check. It is also customary practice to place a hold on the account for the amount of the purchase should no check be tendered at the time the order is placed.

Should the check tendered by an individual be drawn on another bank, it should be certified and properly endorsed before the order is placed.

Should the order be placed by a non-customer or person who is not known to the bank, not only should positive identification be established, but funds accepted in payment of the securities ordered to be purchased be readily converted into cash before the order is placed.

Once the order is signed, the bank places the order by telephone with a broker of its choice, confirming such order later by letter or by sending a copy of the order form which is made up in quadruplicate.

After the order has been executed the broker notifies the bank by sending a confirmation of the execution of the order which states the price, commission, and total amount due. The bank either requests the broker to send the securities to it with a draft attached for payment; present the securities with a draft to its correspondent bank; or instructs its correspondent bank to charge its account and remit a draft (or payment) to the broker, and forward the securities to it.

In selling securities, the teller must not only be certain of the identity of the person presenting the securities for sale, but that the person has the right to sell and convert the securities into cash. This does not present a problem when the securities are presented by a customer. In the case of a non-customer, however, positive

EXHIBIT 95

ORDER FOR THE PURCHASE OF SECURITIES FOR CUSTOMERS

BANK OF CHICAGO

No.

19

Gentlemen:

Without liability to yourselves you are hereby authorized to BUY for my account.

Quantity	Description	Price

It is understood that the above transaction is made at my request and for my accommodation; that the bank acts only as my agent and assumes no responsibility beyond ordinary care and diligence in the selection of a broker for the actual execution of the transaction subject to all the rules and customs of the Exchange (and of clearing house, if any) where executed; that the bank assumes no responsibility for the neglect, default or failure of any agent so selected or for the loss of items in transit. The bank has not solicited this transaction and has not made any statements or observations regarding the securities involved in it. It is understood that all open orders remain in force until executed or cancelled.

Sig. of Customer

Order Cancelled

Date

Sig. of Customer

B
R
O
K
E
R

ORDER

Order Placed

By

With

Time

Proceeds		
Int.		
Tax		
Brokers Com.		
Remit to Broker		
Service Charge		
Net Charge		

Payment

Disposition

BANK OF CHICAGO

By

Received Above Described Securities

Date

Sig. of Customer

20—Kelco—Chicago

EXHIBIT 96

ORDER FOR THE SALE OF SECURITIES FOR CUSTOMERS

BANK OF CHICAGO

No.

Gentlemen:

Without liability to yourselves you are hereby authorized to SELL for my account.

19

Quantity	Description	Price

Order Placed		
By		
With		
Time		
Proceeds		
Int.		
Tax		
Brokers Com.		
Recd. from Broker		
Service Charge		
Net Proceeds		

It is understood that the above transaction is made at my request and for my accommodation; that the bank acts only as my agent and assumes no responsibility beyond ordinary care and diligence in the selection of a broker for the actual execution of the transaction subject to all the rules and customs of the Exchange (and of clearing house, if any) where executed; that the bank assumes no responsibility for the neglect, default or failure of any agent so selected or for the loss of items in transit. The bank has not solicited this transaction and has not made any statements or observations regarding the securities involved in it. It is understood that all open orders remain in force until executed or cancelled.

Disposition

Sig. of Customer

BANK OF CHICAGO

Order cancelled and securities received

Date____________

Sig. of Customer

By____________

B
R
O
K
E
R

ORDER

19—Kalco—Chicago

identification should be established, even in the case of bearer bonds which might have been counterfeited, lost or stolen.

All registered bonds and stocks, in order to be negotiable for sale, must be in good delivery order, that is, properly endorsed and the signature guaranteed. This is usually done by the bank where the person is known.

When securities are sold, upon receipt of the confirmation, the bank either sends the securities by registered mail directly to the broker or to a correspondent bank with instructions to deliver the securities to the broker upon payment of the proceeds. Payment may be made by a regular check, certified check, cashier's check or draft at the direction of the delivering bank, unless otherwise instructed.

It is well to remember, in every banking transaction, that reliance must be placed on the laws of negotiable instruments, and laws governing the relationship of a bank with its depositors both as to form, terms and provisions; and to endorsements of instruments tendered in payment, as outlined in Chapters XV and XVI.

In connection with the purchase of United States Government securities, however, the procedure varies, depending on the type or class of bond purchased. Before covering this operation, because of the changes which have taken place, it might be well to point out that the government first started to issue special registered bonds in various denominations for sale to the public in 1935, beginning with series "A." Through the years such series progressed through B, C, D, E, F, G, H, J, and K, each for a special purpose. Some were sold on a discount basis, that is the purchase price was less than the maturity value, the difference representing accrued interest. Others were sold at a stated par maturity value with interest mailed by check semi-annually to the owners. At present however (1961) only Series "E" bonds (sold on a discount basis) handled by banks, and Series "H" (sold at maturity value) by Federal Reserve Banks, are available for purchase.

At the present time, in purchasing Series "E" bonds, the purchaser fills out an application which together with the check in payment is delivered to the special service section. After approving of the funds tendered in payment, the bank either issues a Series "E" bond which is delivered to the customer or sends the order for other Series, together with the proceeds, to the Federal Reserve Bank, which in turn issues other bonds and registers them in the name of the purchaser. They are then returned to the bank for delivery to the purchaser.

The purchase of United States Treasury Bills, Certificates of Indebtedness, and Treasury Notes, on the other hand, is handled in the same manner as the purchase of other securities except that the purchase order is placed through a bank, registered dealer, or Federal Reserve Bank.

In selling Savings Bonds, banks are only permitted to convert Series "E" bonds to immediate cash or credit to an account and then only, in accordance with the terms, upon satisfactory identification. Such bonds can only be negotiated by the person in whose name the bonds are registered. After the proceeds have been passed on to the payee, the bank sends the bonds to the Treasury Department (Federal Reserve Bank) for credit of the proceeds to the bank's account. Series "H" bonds (and other such series bonds outstanding) can only be accepted by banks for conversion into cash or credit to an account upon proper identification, for presentation for payment and collection through a Federal Reserve Bank.

Transactions in connection with the sale of other types and classes of United States securities, for the account of customers, are processed in the same manner as a sale of other securities, except that the order is placed through a bank, registered dealer or Federal Reserve Bank.

TEMPORARY SAFEKEEPING SERVICES.

Another service rendered by the special service section of a bank is in connection with the temporary safekeeping of securities or documents for customers and others.

Before considering safekeeping in connection with the special service section, it is well to remember that the term safekeeping in banking indiscriminately refers to three separate services or functions: (A) the regular safekeeping or custodianship of securities which is a service of the trust department for which it receives a fee; (B) safekeeping where property is placed in a safe deposit box rented to a customer to which the renter rather than the bank has access, for which the bank receives a fee (both of which we shall cover later), and (C) temporary safekeeping which is nothing more than service through which the bank, as a risky and unprofitable convenience, holds securities, mortgage papers and other valuable documents, on receipt without charge, until it is convenient for the owner to pick them up and either place them in a safe deposit box or take personal possession.

In connection with temporary safekeeping, such documents usually originate or consist of: (1) securities which a bank has purchased for the account of a customer upon his order; (2) documents which have been delivered to the bank with a draft attached and where payment has been effected by charging the amount of the draft to the customer's account, and where the documents are held pending pick up; or (3) securities originally pledged as collateral for a loan which were placed in temporary safekeeping upon payment of the loan.

In all such cases, it is the customary practice for the bank, in placing items in safekeeping, to enter them in a combination receipt and register form, the original acting as a receipt which is sent to the owner of the securities, while the duplicate is attached to the securities, and the triplicate remains as the registered copy. Upon presentation of the receipt and endorsement of the register, the securities or documents are delivered to the owner.

The holding of securities in temporary safekeeping is frowned upon by the supervisory and other authorities as being contrary to good banking practice inasmuch as other facilities are available, under proper control and protection, for the safekeeping of securities and other valuable documents.

TELEGRAPHIC TRANSFERS OF FUNDS.

Another service rendered by the special service section is in connection with the telegraphic wire transfer of funds, (also covered in Chapter XXXI) which are orders transmitted by telegraph or cable to pay money to a designated person. Sometimes such orders, when communicated by telephone, are also referred to as telegraphic transfers.

In connection with telegraphic wire transfers, the usual procedure is for the bank to act only on a written request and authorization by the depositor. When such authorization is received, the bank either through its correspondent bank, Federal Reserve System, telegraph or cable company, authorizes the agent to pay the funds in accordance with instructions.

In paying for such transfers the funds are either made available by the customer, tendering a check drawn on his account for the amount, or the bank charges the account of the depositor. The proceeds are then credited to the account of the Federal Reserve Bank or correspondent bank which, on receipt of the telegraphic order and upon proper identification of the payee, will pay such funds, generally by check, so it will have a record of the transaction and endorsement, which has been paid for by charging the account of the bank from which it received the order.

In the case, however, of telegraphic transfers of funds through a telegraph or cable company, the customary procedure is for the bank to deliver the actual cash to the telegraph or cable company together with instructions. Upon receipt of the funds at the point designated, the agent of the company, upon identification and receipt, then pays out cash to the designated payee.

In connection with the functions of the special service section, certain phases of operation most probably will be covered by operating instructions in connection with the following.

1. Schedule of fees to be charged for the issuance of official checks and drafts.

2. Schedule of fees to be charged for the transfer of funds by wire.

3. Schedule of fees to be charged for placing and executing orders for the purchase or sale of securities for customers.

4. Procedure to be followed in accepting stocks, bonds, deeds and other documents for temporary safekeeping.

CHAPTER XXXIV

THE COLLECTION SECTION

BEFORE DESCRIBING THE FUNCTIONS of the collection section and the duties of those who have the responsibility for presenting items representing wealth and value for conversion into currency or credit, it might be advisable to define the terms "collect" and "collection."

The general meaning of the term "collect" is to demand and receive payment of a debt. Ordinary payment of debt is made by cash, checks, and orders or promises to pay which are handled by and converted into cash or credit through facilities provided by banks.

If the item given in payment of the debt can be immediately converted into cash or credit and proceeds paid to the presenter of the item or owner, it is known as a cash item. If, on the other hand, the item is one which can only be converted into cash or credit:

A. Upon presentation to the debtor,

B. Upon the fulfillment of conditions or compliance with terms,

C. On, or after a certain date,

it is known as a collection item.

Most items handled by banks are cash items or checks which are simple to handle. Such items are either drawn on the bank at which they are originally presented, in which case they are known as "us" items; drawn on other banks located in the same town, in which case they are known as "clearing items"; or drawn on banks located in other sections of the country, where they are known as "transit items." Such items, if in order, are payable immediately and unconditionally upon presentation to the bank on which drawn unless, of course, there is a stop payment. No other documents are attached and instructions for converting them into cash or credit are uniform. From an operating standpoint they can be processed readily in volume at low cost.

Collection items, on the other hand, in contrast to cash items, because of the conditions surrounding payment, must be handled individually and generally under specific and individual instructions. Collection items generally consist of notes, drafts, bills of exchange, and coupons which have stated maturities and are not considered as being paid until the proceeds are actually converted into cash.

From an accounting standpoint, there is also considerable difference between a cash item and a collection item. In connection with a cash item, once the check has been deposited or cashed, it becomes either a part of the bank's assets if the item is converted into cash or used to reduce a loan, and a liability if it decreases a deposit account. Collection items, on the other hand, do not become either a part of a customer's account or an asset or liability of the bank until such time as the items are actually paid and proceeds converted into cash or credit.

Methods and procedures used to handle cash items are standardized. Generally such items originate from a teller or another section of the bank in the normal course of business and ultimately arrive at the proof section, where either as "on us" items, "clearing" items or "transit" items, they are presented to the bank on which drawn for payment.

Collection items, because they are payable on a certain date, upon fulfillment of conditions, or on compliance with terms, and are accompanied by documents, require special handling.

The services of a collection section of a bank are a convenience and widely used by individuals in the transferring of balances of savings accounts, for the collection of bonds, coupons, notes, mortgages and rent payments. Such services are more widely used by those engaged in business in collecting amounts due for merchandise or produce shipped where delivery of such merchandise or produce, from the carrier, can only be effected upon presentation of documents released by a bank upon payment of a draft drawn on the purchaser. These services are also used to effect collection of obligations in connection with any other type of financial or business transaction requiring an agent or reliable and trustworthy collection facilities.

In brief, the collection section collects items that cannot be collected through the clearing house or the transit department, or items which cannot be credited to an account or converted into cash until payment is actually received.

In addition to conditions and terms of payment, the element of time of payment is involved and will vary depending on the type of collection and the terms. Generally collection items are payable:

A. Upon presentation or on demand.
B. A designated number of days after presentation.
C. Upon arrival of merchandise.
D. On specific dates or at determinable intervals.

Items generally handled by, or through the collection agency most of which were covered in detail in Chapter XVI, consist of:

1. Acceptances.
2. Bonds.
3. Bond coupons.
4. Dishonored checks.
5. Drafts with documents attached.
6. Drafts without documents attached.
7. Promissory notes.
8. Purchase or sales contracts.
9. Real estate contracts.
10. Savings accounts for collection.
11. Miscellaneous items.

ACCEPTANCES. Acceptances are time drafts which by being *ACCEPTED* (acknowledged) are converted into promissory notes. See Chapter XVI and Exhibits 31 and 32 for details.

BONDS. Bonds are time promissory notes, either payable to bearer or registered in the name of the owner, against which property has been pledged as collateral security. Interest is generally payable semi-annually and evidenced by coupons which are attached. When bonds are due to be payable (at maturity—or when and if called for payment) they are presented to the paying agent for conversion into cash.

BOND COUPON COLLECTIONS. Coupons, which have been defined as "little promises to pay" as distinguished from the parent bond which is referred to as "a big promise to pay," are payable to bearer upon presentation at the office of the company or fiscal agency of the company.

Coupons (or bonds) of the United States Government, local municipalities, and others which the bank knows will be paid promptly upon presentation, are usually accepted as cash items and credited to the customer's account when deposited. Other coupons are customarily accepted by a bank only for collection.

In accepting coupons for collection, banks generally require the customer to insert the coupons in envelopes which show on the outside the name of the depositor, name of the issuing company, when due and where payable, the number of coupons enclosed and the amount.

If due, they are accepted for deposit or cash; if not, they are handled as a collection item.

Under the Federal Income Tax Law owners of coupons are required to include with the coupons a certificate of ownership and statement as to whether or not tax exemption is claimed. It is not the function of the bank to vouch for the statement made by the owner nor pass upon any point in connection with the tax. They merely act as agent and their only function is to see that the certificate is properly signed, filled out and accompanies the coupon.

DISHONORED CHECKS. Dishonored checks are generally those which have been deposited by customers and returned by the bank on which drawn because of insufficient funds; or checks drawn on the handling bank which have been returned to customers of other banks for the same reason. Such items may also include checks which have been returned for signature, guaranty of endorsement, payee, date or amount.

DRAFTS WITH DOCUMENTS ATTACHED. Drafts with documents attached, (see exhibits 39-40 Chapter XVI), are sight drafts payable on presentation and time drafts payable at a certain time after date, or on a future designated date, or upon delivery of goods. Generally time drafts are presented as soon as received, as by accepting (see Exhibit 31) which acknowledges the debt, the draft is converted into a promissory note which can be discounted by the drawer for immediate credit or cash. Documents attached to such drafts generally consist of:

A. Bills of lading to be surrendered only upon payment of the draft.

B. Bills of lading to be surrendered upon acceptance of the draft.

C. Warehouse receipts to be surrendered only upon payment of the draft.

D. Warehouse receipts to be surrendered upon acceptance of the draft.

When drafts with bills of lading attached are not paid on presentation, unless instructions are specific for the procedure to follow in case of non-payment, the presenting bank immediately notifies the customer or the company by mail or telegraph as to disposition of the item, that is, whether to hold it and present it later or to return it.

In handling a collection of a draft with a bill of lading attached, an astute collection clerk will apply the following check list:

A. Is the draft to be paid on presentation or held for the arrival of the goods?

B. Can the draft be accepted, and upon acceptance can the bill of lading be delivered to the payer, and the acceptance held for payment at maturity?

C. Does the bill of lading allow the payer the privilege of inspecting the goods before making payment?

D. Is the draft to be protested if not paid?

E. What are the instructions in the event of non-payment?

DRAFTS WITHOUT DOCUMENTS ATTACHED. In addition to drafts drawn against a purchaser arising out of such a transaction, it is the custom for many merchants to draw on their debtors if a bill is not paid according to terms; and for retail merchants to draw on their customers for delinquent current accounts. Such drafts (see Exhibit 41 Chapter XVI) are sent out by merchants and mercantile establishments to banks for presentation and for payment. A great many of these items are frequently what is termed "dun items" and the notice is returned with a notation "will send check." Some banks refuse to handle such items unless a modest presentation fee accompanies the draft.

PROMISSORY NOTES. Promissory notes are unconditional promises to pay money either on demand or on a specified date and must be presented to the maker for payment. (Refer to Chapter XVI and Exhibits 42 and 43 for details and further information.)

PURCHASE OR SALE AND REAL ESTATE CONTRACTS. In addition to cash items collected through the clearing or transit section and regular collection items handled by the collection section, the handling of special items which call for collections to be made at stated intervals, generally monthly, for a period of time in connection with real estate notes or sales contracts, and equipment sales, generally known as installment collections, are also handled by the collection section.

SAVINGS ACCOUNTS FOR COLLECTION. Persons moving from one town to another, as soon as they are located, generally transfer the balance of their savings account to a new bank of their choice. This is accomplished by presenting the passbook, together with a draft properly signed which is presented by the collection section to the bank in which the account is maintained for cancellation and return of the book together with a check for the balance.

Through rules and regulations of savings departments which require withdrawals to be made only upon presentation of a withdrawal slip and the passbook, it frequently happens that a person who maintains a savings account at a bank some distance from where he is located wishes to effect the transfer of funds to his present bank for his own particular use. Such transfers may be accomplished either by the depositor writing a note or letter to the bank with whom he maintains an account and sending it together with the passbook requesting the bank to charge his account for the amount so requested and to mail him a check; or by taking his passbook to a bank and signing a draft for the amount so required, which the collecting bank will send to the bank in which he maintains the account for presentation and remittance by draft or cashier's check.

Particular attention should be paid to handling collection items where a passbook is involved due to the fact that custom varies between banks. Sometimes, upon closing out an account, the bank will return the passbook to the depositor; other times the passbook remains in possession of the bank. Frequently, where a passbook is handled through several different sources, it is misplaced or lost, requiring considerable work in having the originating bank prepare a duplicate. Some banks are unwilling to do this unless the request is accompanied by an indemnity bond.

MISCELLANEOUS ITEMS. Frequently a person is interested in examining, with intent to purchase, a gem, a piece of jewelry, heirloom, manuscript, document or other article of value, but because of the distance from the owner (or buyer) finds travel for examination too expensive or inconvenient. Under these circumstances, it is often the practice for the owner (or buyer) to arrange for such articles to be sent for examination to a bank in the town where the tentative purchaser is located and, if acceptable, to arrange for delivery on payment and remittance. Miscellaneous items also include the delivery, upon payment, of securities which have been sold, and payment for securities which have been purchased, on delivery.

The various functions of the collection section in banks generally depend on the volume. In some banks the work in connection with handling collections is performed by a teller in addition to his regular duties. Sometimes collection items are sent direct, other times they are sent through the correspondent bank or through the non-cash collection division of the Federal Reserve Bank.

In banks where the volume warrants, the services of a full time teller for handling collections may be employed. This teller, again depending upon the size of the bank and volume, may also issue certificates of deposit, official checks and perform other miscellaneous functions.

In larger banks, however, because of the volume of special services required, collection work may be divided into subsections to handle various classes of collections, such as monthly payments on real estate contracts, grain and commodity drafts, coupons, or types of collections particular to the locale in which the bank is located or to the particular type of business engaged in by the depositors.

In connection with our study however, we are covering a bank which has one collection section handling all types of collection items for all classes of customers. The person in such a bank to whom is delegated the responsibility for supervising the operations and functions of the collection section should have a thorough working knowledge of the laws of negotiable instruments covered in Chapter XVI, which should be referred to again in studying this chapter.

In addition to possessing knowledge of negotiable instruments, the person in charge of the collection section should be currently informed on case study law regarding presentation and collection of items, for what happens in one bank may happen in another. Case law is simply the report of results of error which an astute collection teller can possibly avoid by knowing the details and circumstances of cases in which the decisions have been made. Such knowledge not only protects the bank from loss and assists the teller to acquire additional knowledge, but develops judgment which is essential if he is to progress with the bank.

Collections are governed by laws so strict that careful attention must consistently be given to presentation, protest, notice of protest, and funds accepted in payment, as we shall cover later in this chapter.

From an operating standpoint confusion sometimes exists because of the terminology used in connection with describing collections. Some banks classify collection items, regardless of their origin, by source of payment, that is, by location of the person or company which will pay the item. For example some banks will classify as:

A. Local or city items those which are payable by individuals and companies located in the area served by the bank.

B. Domestic or out of town or country items those which are payable by individuals or companies located in other cities or states, and which are sent to other banks for presentation and payment.

C. Foreign items those which are payable by individuals or companies located in countries outside of the continental United States.

Other banks classify collection items by sources or from whom received. In other words, if an item is received from a customer to be sent out by the bank for presentation and payment, regardless of whether or not the item is payable locally, out of state, or in a foreign country, it is referred to as an outgoing collection item; while a collection received from another bank for presentation and attempt to effect collection and payment, is referred to as an incoming collection item. As the use of the terms incoming collection and outgoing collection more aptly describe the operations referring to the collection of items, we will use such terminology in describing the functions of the collection section in this chapter.

OUTGOING COLLECTIONS. Outgoing collections are items such as notes, drafts, etc. which customers of the bank and people residing in the area bring to the bank for collection. Such items are either directly presented by the bank to the person on whom the collection is drawn for payment, sent to a bank in the area where the payer is located or a correspondent bank for presentation, or sent to the Federal Reserve Bank for handling through their non-cash collection system.

In handling a collection item it is necessary that complete instructions be obtained regarding such matters as identification, delivery of documents, negotiability, etc. In connection with accepting items for collection, the use of the following check list will be found helpful.

1. Is the presenter of the item for collection a customer of the bank or known to the bank?
2. If presenter is not a customer or known to the bank, has the endorsement been approved by an officer?
3. Is the item properly endorsed so it can be negotiated?
4. Are documents attached in proper delivery order?
5. Are orders for the handling of the item in case of nonpayment clear and understood?
6. Are instructions for disposition of proceeds clear and understood; that is, will proceeds be made available to presenter by cash, check or credit to an account?

After examining the documents and if found to be in good order, the collection teller or clerk in the collection section indexes the item on a form similar to that shown in Exhibit 97, after which a receipt is given to the presenter. Sometimes, depending upon the procedure followed, outgoing collection items will be receipted for upon presentation, followed up later by the formal receipt which is made up as part of the collection record.

The form used in connection with an outgoing collection will either consist of a single or multiple fanfold form for use with a window envelope and include a

1. Register,
2. Transmittal letter,

3. Receipt to the presenter,
4. Audit copy,
5. Advice of disposition of payment to the presenter,
6. Duplicate deposit slip.

The first or register copy is the bank's permanent file record. This copy shows the number of the collection, the date received, the person from whom received, the person or company under whom drawn, bank to which the item is sent, description of the item, date due, amount, interest, instructions as to protest, instructions as to proceeds.

The second copy is the transmittal letter which accompanies the item to the bank to which it is sent for collection.

The third copy is the receipt containing all the information which is given to the presenter or endorser as evidence that the bank has received the item for collection.

The fourth copy is an audit copy which is sent to the auditing department and used in auditing the collection section and accounting for the disposition of the proceeds.

The fifth copy is the advice of disposition to the presenter accompanying check or advice of credit to an account.

The sixth copy is a duplicate deposit slip used in the event the proceeds are credited to an account.

After being indexed on the collection register, the item, together with the transmittal letter is either sent to the collecting bank by registered mail or by regular mail, whichever is warranted under the circumstances, or delivered to the messenger section for local presentation.

Outgoing collections are filed under the name of the presenter or alphabetically under due date which, in case of a collection payable on presentation or at sight, is usually five to ten days after date of receipt.

In connection with endorsement of negotiable paper for collection, it is a set principle of law that in the absence of an indication to the contrary, the form of the endorsement controls the title of ownership. On the other hand, the title to or ownership of an item left with the bank for collection remains with the customer and the bank's relationship simply is that of an agent. Therefore, the endorsement "for collection only" is notice of ownership to

EXHIBIT 97

OUTGOING COLLECTION FORM

FIRST NATIONAL BANK
ILLINOIS

OUT No.

DISPOSITION OF COLLECTION ITEM DESCRIBED BELOW. **RECEIVED**

Payee or Maker	Payer	Description	Due	Amount
				$
				Exch.

TO
RF
TO
RF
TO
RF

We cr. your a/c $
We attach CC #
We return item for reason

DATE
BY

REGISTER

FIRST NATIONAL BANK
ILLINOIS

OUT No.

WE ENCLOSE FOR COLLECTION THE ITEM DESCRIBED BELOW. **DATE**

Payee or Maker	Payer	Description	Due	Amount
				$

TO
RF
TO
RF
TO
RF

Deliver only on Payment.
Do not protest unless instructed.
Do not hold unless instructed.

NOTICE

all parties through whose hands it passes, and the collecting bank, or its agents, acquires no title or interest therein.

THE ROUTING OF COLLECTION ITEMS. In the handling of outgoing collections it is very important that the person in charge of the collection section uses extreme care and good judgment in the routing of items to banks for presentation and collection. Particular attention should be paid so that the items will not be routed through several banks, and wherever possible, in keeping with prudent practice, should direct all drafts with bills of lading attached to the corresponding bank closest to the person or company on which the item is drawn to avoid any excess charges accruing because of delays in the mail. Where a bank has no regular correspondent it should send the items to the nearest town where it has connections or where there is a bank.

FEDERAL RESERVE NON-CASH COLLECTION SERVICE. Member banks and non-member participating banks, or banks which remit for items drawn on themselves at par, are eligible to use the facilities of the Federal Reserve Non-Cash Collection System.

This system, which operates much in the same manner as the collection department of a large bank, presents, collects and remits proceeds from non-cash items, as described when payable in any Federal Reserve District, Puerto Rico, dependency possession, or part of the United States outside the continental United States as the Board of Governors may designate.

Non-cash items according to the definition of the Federal Reserve System refer to:

A. Maturing notes; acceptances; certificates of deposit; bills of exchange and drafts with or without securities, bills of lading or other documents attached.

B. Drafts, and orders on savings deposits with passbooks attached.

C. Checks, drafts and other cash items which have previously been dishonored or on which special advice of payment or dishonor is required.

D. Maturing bonds and coupons and other obligations of the United States and its agencies, which are collectible through and payable at said Reserve Banks as fiscal agents.

E. State or municipal warrants, including orders to pay, addressed to officers of state and political subdivisions thereof, and any special or general obligations of state or political subdivisions thereof.

F. Other evidences of indebtedness, orders to pay, except checks and drafts handled under the provisions of regulation J or drawn on or payable by a non-member bank which cannot be collected at par in funds acceptable to the Federal Reserve Bank of the district in which the non-member is located.

Non-cash collection service is invaluable to member banks and non-member banks in facilitating the presentation and collection of items where doubt exists as to other facilities for collection.

In handling outgoing collections, banks should exercise due care as to sending items to other banks for presentation and payment. It is a general rule of law that the originating bank is liable for damage that has been sustained by the negligence of a subagent or collecting bank. Banks seeking to protect themselves are covered either by express agreements with presenters or by printed notices on their deposit tickets or passbooks, to the effect that the bank assumes no responsibility for the collection of any item beyond due care and diligence in the selection of collecting agents, and such items are taken for collection at the sole risk of the customer. Further, that the bank is not responsible for any loss through failure or default of the bank's agent.

Upon receipt of payment, the collection section marks the register and either mails the presenter a check, or credits his account with the proceeds with advice of credit. Should the item not be honored upon presentation, the record is marked to reflect action taken and the item returned to the presenter with advice of dishonorment.

INCOMING COLLECTIONS. Incoming collections are notes, drafts, etc. received by mail from other banks or business houses located outside of the service area of the bank, drawn on customers of the bank or people residing in or engaged in business in the service area served by the bank. Incoming collections should be accompanied by a letter of transmittal and full instructions as to protest and dispositions of proceeds, that is, whether to remit by cashier's check, draft, or credit to an account of a correspondent bank or the Federal Reserve System. Some banks follow a practice of acknowledging receipt of collection items particularly if received from another bank, with the request that the sending bank refer to the collecting bank's own number if further reference to the item is required.

In order to be certain all incoming collections are in proper order for acceptance and processing, the collection teller checks the transmittal letter to be certain it contains:

1. Instructions for delivery of documents,
2. Provisions for collecting interest in case payment is delayed,
3. Method to use in advising of payment or dishonorment,
4. Instructions as to disposition of proceeds (whether the funds are to be credited to an account or a check is to be mailed in payment).

Instructions are important because, although rules and regulations applying to all types of items are the same, conditions and terms under which payment will be made vary so widely that definite instructions should be provided with each item sent for collection in order that the bank can provide the utmost in service, and take actions which are in accordance with principles of good public relations.

If the item is in good form and order, it is indexed on the collection form similar to that shown in Exhibit 98.

While collection forms used and procedures followed will vary among banks, depending on the volume and class of collection items handled, forms for recording or registering incoming collections, whether in a single or multiple form, will include the following:

1. Register,
2. Notice to drawee,
3. Acknowledgement,
4. Audit copy,
5. Second notice or tracer,
6. Advice of payment.

The first copy or register is the bank's permanent record. This copy shows the number of the incoming collection, the date received, the name, date and number of the collection item of the sending bank, description of item, name of maker, name of payee, the amount, and instructions as to protest and disposition of proceeds.

Certain information, however, through use of blackout space will only appear on the succeeding copies where it is applicable or where it is required.

The second copy is a notice to the payer and usually made up for use with a window envelope. Information from this copy also may be recorded on the messenger's record.

The third copy is an acknowledgement form which some banks use to send to the bank from which they have received the item, acknowledging receipt and advising that the item is in the process of collection.

The fourth copy is an audit copy used for verification purposes and reconciling of disposition of proceeds of collection items.

The fifth copy is used as a second notice or tracer when the first notice has been mailed and no response has been received.

The sixth copy is the advice of disposition or of payment which goes to the sending bank, together with a check if the item is paid or with the collection item if payment has been refused.

After being entered on the register and reviewed to be certain it has been correctly recorded, the method of presentation is determined.

While all outgoing collection items are handled or processed in the same manner, incoming collections may be divided into two groups, those which are and can be presented for collection by a messenger; and those to whom notice of collection item received are mailed or who are called on the telephone and expected to come to the bank to make payment and pick up the item.

Incoming collections, after being indexed, are usually filed alphabetically under the due date. Items payable on sight, demand, or presentation, are currently filed under the date received, which indicates that all items in date order, prior to current date, are past due and no attention has been paid to the notices which require review and attention. If the item is to be presented by the messenger, the fifth and sixth copies are filed in place of the item in the file.

With regard to presentation, the law states that a note must be presented at the place where it is made payable if such a place

EXHIBIT 98

INCOMING COLLECTION FORM

FIRST NATIONAL BANK
ILLINOIS IN No.

Disposition of item received for collection described below. Date Received

Payee or Maker	Payer	Description	Due	Amount	Exch.	Total
				$	$	$

TO
RF
TO
RF
TO
RF

Your Ref. No.________
We cr. your a/c $________
We attach CC #________
We return item. Reason________

Date________
By________

REGISTER

FIRST NATIONAL BANK
ILLINOIS IN No.

We have received for collection the item described below. Date

Payee or Maker	Payer	Description	Due	Amount	Exch.	Total
				$	$	$

Please advise promptly disposition of same.

TO
RF
TO
RF
TO
RF

Your Ref. No.________

Checks on other banks tendered in payment of this item must be certified.

NOTICE

s named. If such a place is not named in the note, it is presumed o be payable at the maker's place of business, at his residence, or vherever he might be found on the day of maturity. General bankng customs make the hours at a bank from 9:00 to 2:00 and at a place of business from 9:00 to 5:00.

When a messenger takes an item from the collection section or presentation to the drawer, he is generally charged with the tems taken out and gives a receipt to the collection section. This unction was covered in the chapter on duties and responsibilities of the mail and messenger department which could be referred to at this point for reference as far as responsibilities of the messenger are concerned. Let it suffice to state again that a messenger's princ ipal duties consist of doing as he is told. He should not assume esponsibilities. He should be sent out with explicit and specific nstructions as to what to do, what not to do, and be held to them. A messenger, unless specifically instructed, should never permit any document to leave his possession or permit any modification of nstructions without receiving authority. He should not take paynent of items in anything but cash or by certified checks.

PAYMENT OF COLLECTION ITEMS. Under normal business conditions it may make little difference whether payment of a collection item is made by cash, cashier's check, draft, or personal check. In times of economic distress, however, in the event of a ailure of the bank making the collection or failure of the bank on which the instrument received in payment is drawn, the question of law arises which the collecting bank is bound to know.

When a cash item or check is cashed or credited to a customer's account, as stated in the rules and regulations to which the customer agrees when he opens an account, credit or payment is subject to final acceptance or payment by the bank on which the item is drawn. As to a collection item, however, once the remittance has been credited to an account or check paid, it is understood the item has been paid and the customer is entitled to regard the payment as final. Therefore, the collection section, as a rule, must be certain it does not report an item as paid or give credit for a collection item, until actual payment has been received and whatever is tendered in payment has been cleared and cashed. It is, therefore, a good rule for a collection department to only accept certified checks, cashier's checks, drafts or cash in the payment of collection items.

Upon return of the messenger with the proceeds of the collection, the register is marked, the check or draft in remittance to the presenter is prepared, and together with advice of disposition sent to the bank or person from whom the item was received.

PROTEST. If, however, the item has been presented by the messenger and payment has been refused, another problem arises with which every astute collection teller should be familiar.

In order to hold the endorsers of a note liable, it is absolutely necessary, if payment has been refused, that the item be presented to a Notary Public of record on the day the item falls due, and that notices of protest be sent to all parties concerned no later than the first thing the following morning. It is considered good business practice to protest notes and negotiable instruments presented for collection if payment is refused, not because it absolves the maker but because it is a sworn statement beyond dispute in case of a suit that the note was presented and payment refused at the place specified, on the date due.

By the terms of the negotiable instrument law, protests are necessary only on foreign bills of exchange, checks, notes and bills drawn in one state, payable in another; whereas common banking practice is to protest all instruments which are not paid on date, if the amount involved is substantial. In recent years it has been general practice, in connection with checks, not to protest items for less than $500 received by a bank for collection, and customary practice for the originating bank to indicate its wishes in regard to protests. The purpose, of course, in protesting an item is to legally hold the endorser responsible, for unless the protest is properly made, the endorsers under the law are discharged from their responsibilities. Further, when an item is protested, the document needs no other evidence in court as to having been properly presented for payment.

MONTHLY INSTALLMENT COLLECTIONS. In handling installment collection items where payment is received monthly once the item has been accepted, the collection section sets up the item in a separate file by date of payment, or alphabetically in the name of the person making the payment, in which case a cross reference card is prepared showing the date of payment.

In some cases a ledger sheet is also prepared covering the contract and recording the detail of the payments for the bank's records. Payments are also indexed on the contract or note itself.

Generally, records are maintained which provide easy reference, for example, if the contract is filed by name of the owner, the ledger sheet may be filed by name of the payer; while a tickler card will be prepared under due date. If the ledger card is filed by name of the owner, then the crossfile card is filed alphabetically by the name of the payer together with a tickler card showing date payment is due.

Where banks provide full collection system, a notice is prepared and sent to the payer about a week or ten days before payment is due, showing the amount to be paid, broken down as to principal, interest, taxes, insurance, or whatever else is called for by the terms of the contract.

When payment is received, a receipt is given to the payer or the payment is stamped in a receipt or coupon book after which the bank credits the account of the owner or mails him a check for proceeds in accordance with the provisions of the arrangement. Banks charge a fee for this service which is either collected on a per annum basis or deducted from each payment as received so that the owner receives credit for the net amount.

Because of the variations in laws between states, the methods and procedures within banks in handling collection items, and the application of the Negotiable Instruments Law and state laws to particular transactions, prudent bankers will review the laws which apply to their own situations with their own legal counsel, and provide rules of guidance for the person who has the responsibility for supervising the collection section.

In connection with the operations of an active collection section in a large bank, some or all of the following operating instructions will be in effect:

1. Schedule of fees for handling collection items.
2. Schedule of messenger runs.
3. Routing of items for collection.

4. Mail schedule for outgoing collections.
5. Protesting of dishonored items.

CHAPTER XXXV

THE LOAN TELLERS SECTION

AS WE LEARNED IN PREVIOUS CHAPTERS, millions and millions of checks representing millions and millions of dollars in the bank, and millions and millions of dollars of currency withdrawn from banks, are used every day by people in settlement of, or payment on a debt—for the exchange for objects of wealth—and for the purchase of the necessities of life.

While a considerable amount of currency remains in constant circulation, a substantial amount, together with checks, finds its way back into the banking system through being redeposited in a bank in an account.

A bank account in addition contains primarily the wherewithal the owner needs to meet his current checks, requirements for the operation of his business, funds awaiting investment and reserves for contingencies.

The check which reduces the bank balance of one person, that is the maker, when deposited, increases the balance of the endorser. Bank deposits, while subject to daily fluctuations in ownership, collectively remain sufficiently constant to form the greatest single source of funds available for investment which we studied in Chapter XX.

Through the medium of highly trained credit and investment personnel, as we have learned in previous chapters, the aggregate unused funds, less legal reserves, are put to productive use by banks through investment and conversion into earning assets. Such funds which are not invested in bonds are invested in the various types of loans we studied in Chapters XXII and XXIII.

LEGAL LOAN LIMITS. Banks, by state and federal law, are limited to the amount they can lend to any one borrower. This is referred to as the legal limit and varies among states and type of security and whether or not it is a national or a state bank.

The general limitation, subject to certain exceptions as outlined, for a national bank is to loan 10% of the paid-in capital and unimpaired surplus. In the case of state banks, the limitation is generally 15% of the paid-in capital and unimpaired surplus.

Banks, on a dividend basis, are generally required by law to transfer a minimum percentage, generally 10% of their undivided profits, periodically to surplus until the surplus account equals the paid-in capital. Every time a bank increases the surplus, it automatically increases its legal loan limit.

Frequently, in order to be able to undertake large commitments to important customers, banks will periodically transfer funds from undivided profits to surplus; or increase capital by paying out earnings in the form of stock dividends or increasing capital by public subscriptions. While it is generally the law that a bank is prohibited from loaning more than 10% of its capital and unimpaired surplus to any one person, if it is a national bank, and 15% if it is a state bank, regardless if the loan is endorsed or collaterized by stocks, bonds, real estate, or agricultural products, there are certain exceptions under provisions of the Federal Reserve Act. For example, there is no limit on the amount a bank can loan on:

A. Drafts or bills of exchange drawn in good faith against actual existing values. Such are self-liquidating transactions where the source of repayment within a short time is usually evidenced from an examination of the draft and attachments. It is also two name paper, where, if the drawee does not pay, the drawer is liable. In substance it is a secured obligation, for the customer as drawer is in a position similar to an endorser on a collateral note and his liability, therefore, is contingent rather than direct.

B. Rediscounted commercial paper which the bank may handle for the company or person negotiating it as long as it is an obligation arising directly from a business transaction such as the purchase of goods, and is the property of the negotiator/endorser.

C. Commodity obligations drawn in good faith against actually existing values secured by goods or commodities in process of shipment. The obligation can be drawn against actually existing values and yet not be secured by the values, such as drafts drawn to collect money due for merchandise shipped direct to the purchaser, or to which a "straight" as against a "shippers order" bill of lading is attached. A "straight" bill of lading is non-negotiable and, therefore, not classified as security. Also, goods are said to be in the process of shipment where a buyer is committed to purchase, but for his own convenience does not want them shipped until some later date.

D. Bankers' Acceptances consisting of drafts drawn on and accepted by a bank to run not more than 6 months, and growing out of the importation or exportation of goods or the domestic shipment of goods. Such acceptances must be secured at the time of the acceptance by warehouse receipts or similar documents conveying and securing title to readily marketable staples which are defined as articles of commerce, agriculture or industry; or by such uses as to make it the subject of constant dealings in ready markets with frequent quotations of price making the price easily and definitely ascertainable, and the staple itself easy to realize upon by sale at any time. The draft payable from the sale of the underlying merchandise is directly tied in with a self-liquidating transaction and is payable from the sale of the merchandise. There is no limit placed on the purchase of bankers' acceptances on other banks as long as such acceptances conform to section 13 of the Federal Reserve Act. Regulation C of the Federal Reserve Board.

Banks, however, cannot accept for any one name an aggregate amount exceeding the legal limitations unless the acceptances are secured by bills of lading, warehouse receipts or other actual securities growing out of the same transaction as the acceptance.

Including both secured and unsecured acceptances of all names, the aggregate amount which one bank can accept cannot exceed 50% of its capital plus surplus except that with prior approval and under conditions imposed by the Federal Reserve Board, and provided that the bank concerned has a surplus of at least 20% of its capital, it may carry acceptances up to 100% of combined capital and surplus.

Loans made by banks basically fall into two classifications—secured and unsecured. Both classes are further divided by types into commercial loans, which by their terms are fully repayable in a single payment on demand or at a fixed date; installment or consumer credit loans, which by their terms are repayable in monthly intallments; and mortgage loans, which are long term loans secured by real estate equities generally repayable in monthly installments.

The majority of commercial loans granted by banks are unsecured loans or loans extended on the general credit standing of the borrower, after careful investigation and analysis of his financial standing and other factors as described in Chapters XXII and XXVI. The evidence of such a loan is by use of an unsecured promissory note similar to that shown in Exhibit 42, in which the borrower has not pledged any specific asset to secure payment.

The secured loan, on the other hand, is one in which specific property belonging to the individual or to the company is pledged to secure payment. The evidence of such a loan is by use of a secured promissory note similar to that shown in Exhibit 43 which gives the lender authorization to sell the property pledged as security, and to apply the proceeds to the balance if the loan is not paid at maturity, or if the borrower fails to maintain a proper margin, in which case the lender has the right to sell whatever is pledged as security at public or private sale, with or without notice to the borrower. Margins, which we shall cover later in this chapter, refer to the difference between the price someone is willing to pay for the evidences of value pledged as security and the amount which the lender has advanced on the security.

In connection with secured loans it might be well to point out that there is not necessarily any difference between a secured and an unsecured loan as to use of the proceeds. There is, however, sometimes a relationship between the security pledged and application of proceeds of the loan. A case in point is in connection with an individual's purchase of listed stocks, who borrows from the bank to finance part of the transaction.

Under Regulation U, the Federal Reserve Board is empowered to set the margin which banks must require their borrowers to maintain in connection with loans for the purchase of securities traded on a national exchange. This margin varies from time to time depending on economic conditions. Where, however, the proceeds of such a loan secured by marketable stocks is not being used for the purchase of additional securities, banks are permitted to loan whatever seems advisable and prudent under the circumstances. It is up to the collateral teller, however, to know the purpose of such loans secured by marketable stocks so that proper margin, because of bank policy and Regulation U of the Federal Reserve Board, can be maintained and enforced at all times.

The instruments, documents or papers, evidencing or representing wealth or value, as described in Chapter XXIII, generally pledged as security for a loan, consist of:

1. Accounts receivable.
2. Bills of lading.
3. Cash surrender value of life insurance.
4. Chattel mortgages.
5. Listed and unlisted stocks, bonds of industrial and utility corporations, and bonds and notes of the United States Government.
6. Oil, land, and mining leaseholds.
7. Real estate mortgages.
8. Savings accounts.
9. Trust receipts.
10. Warehouse receipts.

In connection with accepting a pledge of property to secure payment of a loan, the following check list should be applied by the loan or collateral teller to each class of respective property delivered to be certain it is in good acceptance (delivery) order.

ACCOUNTS RECEIVABLE. In pledging accounts receivable as security for a loan, either the respective accounts on the books of the borrower are actually marked "assigned to ——Bank," and debtors of the company notified to make payment of their accounts directly to the bank, which function is either undertaken by the officer who made the loan or by an experienced clerk in the loan section; or the loan is made with the promise and assurance of the borrower that all payments received by the company will be turned over to the bank in the form received and the proceeds applied to the loan.

When accounts receivable are pledged, such evidence usually consists of a list of such accounts by name, date of the credit and the amount. Should the balance owed by the customer consist of more than one charge, or be subject to special terms such as being repayable over several months, the terms are noted on the list.

BILLS OF LADING. Bills of lading, which are defined as receipts for goods in transit, to be satisfactory security for a loan must be negotiable, that is, provide for delivery of the goods to the person named in the bill or to his order, and only on proper endorsement and surrender of the bill of lading to the carrier. In addition, the bill should show the name of the shipper, the carrier or vehicle by which the goods are to be transported, and a description of the goods together with the date shipped. Particular attention should be paid to the date of the bill of lading and its relation to the date the bill is accepted as security for the loan. Goods may have been sidetracked, spoiled, damaged, destroyed, which, if accepted as security, involves the bank in considerable inconvenience and possible loss. Should there be more than normal difference between the date of the bill and the time it is pledged as security for the loan, the teller should call the discrepancy to the attention of the officer and accept it only on formal approval of the officer.

CASH SURRENDER VALUE OF LIFE INSURANCE. The cash surrender value of a life insurance policy is the amount which the insurance company will surrender to the insured should he decide to give up the policy. Generally the approximate amount of cash can be readily computed from the tables appearing in the body of the policy.

In order to guide against the danger from failure of the insured to pay the premiums, banks generally only loan between 75 and 90% of the cash value and only make such loans after a proper agreement has been executed by the holder and accepted by the insurance company.

In connection with loans on the cash surrender value of life insurance, it should also be remembered that unless the beneficiary is the estate of the insured there could be complications should a loan be foreclosed without the knowledge and consent of the beneficiary. It is therefore prudent practice for banks to have the beneficiary join in the assignment to the bank, which puts the insurance company on notice that all parties of interest have consented to the assignment. It is always prudent to determine that the policy is assignable, that is, it is not involved in the existence of a trust, interests of minors, prior assignment, or agreement in case a person other than the insured pays the premiums. Life insurance policies whose cash surrender value is pledged as security should be accompanied therefore by a properly executed assignment of interest and consent of beneficiary.

CHATTEL MORTGAGES. Chattel mortgages are used to cover the pledge of property which is movable or can be removed, such as automobiles, machinery, equipment, cattle, crops and vest title to such in the lender.

Such mortgages, to be acceptable as security, must be dated, properly signed, conveyed to the lender, and carry a full and sufficient description of the property pledged to enable such property to be positively identified. Generally such chattel mortgage notes are recorded in the county in which the property is located as evidence of a lien against the property.

LISTED AND UNLISTED STOCKS. Listed and unlisted stocks and registered bonds should be in the name of the borrower and either endorsed or accompanied by a power of attorney bearing the signature of the person in whose name the certificate was made out, and properly guaranteed by a bank.

In connection with bonds, interest coupons for the current and subsequent periods should be attached.

OIL, LAND, AND MINING LEASEHOLDS. Leaseholds or production loans are loans made to finance the mining of minerals; production of oil; cost of seed; planting, cultivating and harvesting of a crop.

For security the bank generally takes a trust deed on the property and an assignment of the proceeds of the produce. It is agreed that as proceeds are obtained from sale of the product, such proceeds are percentaged and deposited toward reduction of the loan, the balance going to the account of the borrower.

Ordinarily a bank does not go more than 6 months on a crop loan, or more than 2 to 3 years on a mineral and oil production loan. Such property when properly assigned is considered good security for a loan, especially since geological methods in estimating oil, gas and mineral reserves are quite reliable and provide a basis for astute credit analysts and loan officers to estimate the extent of such reserves, their value, and arrange payment terms in line with production schedules.

In handling such leases as security for a loan, it is the responsibility of the loan or collateral teller only to be certain that the agreement or lease is properly signed and has been initialed and approved by the officer who made the loan; or has the approval of the discount or executive committee.

REAL ESTATE MORTGAGES. A real estate mortgage, if pledged as collateral, should be accompanied by a trust deed carrying a full description of the property which has been recorded in the county in which the property is located, mortgage policy or abstract, and, if encumbered with buildings, with fire and other required insurance policies or evidence that the property is covered by insurance.

SAVINGS ACCOUNTS. In connection with a loan against the balance of a savings account, not only should the savings withdrawal slip be properly signed, signature approved by the savings section and be accompanied by the passbook, but by an acknowledgement from the savings section that a hold has been placed against the account for the amount as shown on the withdrawal slip.

TRUST RECEIPTS. In addition to loans secured by chattel mortgages on automobiles and other property, bills of lading and warehouse receipts on commodities, similar security is provided through the use of trust receipts and floor planning agreements in connection with automobiles and appliances.

A number of dealers handling automobiles and appliances are not of sufficient financial strength to carry on their operations without bank credit. Usually their sales run into large figures, but because of their operation they are not entitled to a line of open credit without security.

Unless a financing plan is provided, the sale from the manufacturer to the dealer is cash on delivery, while the sale from the dealer to the retail purchaser is largely on credit. Automobiles and appliances are generally shipped to the dealer sight draft and bill of lading attached and before he can take possession of the merchandise, he must pay the draft.

In order to have possession of the automobiles or appliances for sale, he is in need of temporary financing. This is provided by banks, which generally are willing to make a loan to a reputable wholesaler or dealer under a floor planning arrangement. Under such an arrangement, a collateral note is signed and accompanied by a list showing each automobile or appliance by make, model, number and cost. However, instead of the article being covered by a chattel mortgage, a document known as a trust receipt is used. This document acknowledges receipt of the funds which are to be applied on the purchase of the automobile or appliance and vests title to the property in the bank. Under terms of such an arrangement, the dealer is allowed possession of the automobile or appliance but cannot sell it without the release from the bank. While the bank does not have a recorded lien on the merchandise, it is presumed to have actual ownership in that the person who signs the trust receipt promises to deliver such article as described in the receipt to the bank upon demand.

While the possession of the automobile or appliance by the dealer is in violation of a fundamental principle of loaning on security—that security back of the loan should at all times be under control of the lender – the nature of the business is such that there is no alternative, as obviously if the merchandise is stored in a warehouse it cannot be shown for display purposes or used to create a desire on the part of prospective purchasers for possession.

Under such arrangement, when the automobile or appliance is sold, the dealer pays the bank and obtains the release from the receipt. Generally, however, since most of the sales are on time, the dealer either has the purchaser sign an installment note payable to a finance company or to the bank secured by a chattel mortgage which upon receipt of the proceeds is turned over to the bank; or has the purchaser sign a note and execute a chattel mortgage on the bank's own form, which the bank accepts on a recourse or non-recourse basis from the dealer, crediting the proceeds of such new loan against the balance of the loan against which the property was pledged as security.

The loan teller, in accepting such property on trust receipt as collateral security for a loan, must be certain that such receipt is dated; signed by the owner; and that each receipt bears the model, number, make of the car or appliance and any other identifying description required to positively identify the property.

WAREHOUSE RECEIPTS. Loans are frequently made against the pledge of raw or finished goods such as wood, metals;

manufactured merchandise such as furniture, household appliances; commodities such as cotton, grain, canned fruit and vegetables; perishables such as meat, eggs, cheese, etc. stored in a warehouse.

Where such goods are pledged as security for a loan, they are generally placed in storage or in the custody of a licensed and bonded warehouse by the owner, and the receipt issued by the warehouse used as security for the loan.

When such commodities are seasonal; that is, processed at one time of the year, such as fruit in season, and are sold during the year, it is up to the loan officer to schedule payment so that the loan is paid off by the time the next season comes around. In addition, it is sometimes the responsibility of the loan or collateral teller to set up a tickler file to cover such repayments.

Warehouse receipts to be acceptable must show the location and name of the warehouse where the property is kept, the name of the owner, and provide for full or partial delivery of the goods to the person named in the receipt, or to his order, on proper endorsement and payment of storage charges due. In addition, depending on the property pledged, evidence should be provided showing such property is covered by insurance as is warranted under the circumstances.

The test of property acceptable as collateral security for bank loans is its ready salability under adverse conditions; or convertibility into cash. Obviously, if business conditions are good, the value of the property usually remains stable or increases; while if business conditions are bad, the price at which the property pledged can be sold or converted into cash is less. It is the responsibility of the loan teller or function of the loan and collateral section not only to see that all property pledged as security for a loan is in proper delivery order and, in the case of stock certificates, endorsed or accompanied by a power of attorney and property recorded in the collateral register, but to see that a sufficient difference, known as a margin, exists at all times between the price someone is willing to pay for the property pledged as security and the amount the borrower owes the bank.

In addition to property pledged as security for a loan, endorsements or guarantees, while not considered collateral in the true sense of the word, certainly can be considered security for payment of a loan.

Sometimes property or documents tendered as security for a loan are not delivered or not in proper order. Property which is not in good negotiable order should not be accepted by the teller unless such acceptance is approved by the officer who made the loan, in which case arrangements should be made for a followup to determine the completeness of the collateral at the earliest possible time.

FUNCTIONS OF THE LOAN TELLER

It is the function of the loan teller to set up, handle, and service the various classes and types of loans once they have been approved by the loaning officer.

In protecting and safeguarding the rights and interests of the bank, the personnel of the loan section are charged with principal duties and responsibilities for:

A. The acceptance of notes. In connection with this particular function it is the responsibility of the teller to (1) review the note and ascertain that it is properly signed, endorsed, and in good legal order, (2) obtain a proper receipt for the proceeds of the loan, (3) be certain that documents, papers, instruments, or evidences of wealth, pledged as security, are negotiable and in good delivery order.

B. Maintaining accurate loan records, safeguarding the notes as evidences of the loan, and giving proper notice or making presentation of the note at maturity.

C. Safekeeping and custodianship of instruments, documents or papers evidencing wealth pledged as security to the loan.

D. Calculating and collecting interest and other charges in connection with the loan.

E. Handling and processing loan payments.

The functions in connection with processing the various classes and types of loans and the duties and reponsibilities of personnel to whom are delegated operating functions are the same in every bank. In small banks, however, such functions perhaps might be performed by one single individual, distributed amongst several individuals, or performed individually by any one of a number of individuals. In a large bank, depending on volume, functions in connection with commercial, installment and mortgage loans can be performed within individual sections or set up under various combinations depending, of course, upon the volume and procedures used. In order to cover operations performed in handling the various types and classes of loans, however, in this study we will presume all of the operations in connection with handling commercial, installment and mortgage loans are performed within the same section, the personnel of which handle operations in connection with multiple duties and responsibilities.

ACCEPTANCE OF NOTES. When the note is delivered to the loan teller it is for the purpose of exchanging the note or promise to pay at a future date, or on demand, for cash in the form of currency, which is only given on receipt, a cashier's check which by endorsement is evidence of receipt of the funds, or by credit to an account where evidence of receipt of the funds is the credit to the account and disbursement of the funds by means of checks drawn by the borrower.

Before disbursing funds, however, the teller examines the note to be certain:

A. It is properly signed, and if discounted for a customer, properly endorsed.

B. It is dated.

C. It bears a maturity date or terms as to when payment will be made (30-60-90 days or in equal monthly installments, etc.)

D. It provides for payment of interest either at maturity or for discount (deducted from the proceeds).

E. The amount in figures is the same as the amount in writing.

F. If it is a secured note, that the property delivered as security is in good delivery order.

MAINTAINING ACCURATE LOAN RECORDS. Once the teller has ascertained the note is in proper order, he begins to prepare the loan records. The records of the loan section which are quite extensive, are characterized by their completeness. In a small bank where the loan volume is limited, the minimum of records are necessary, but since the bank may have to produce proof of the transactions, all records are set up on a permanent basis.

These records which provide a daily record of transactions

processed within the loan section and record the outstanding direct and indirect liabilities of each and every borrower are:

1. The teller's blotter, or the forms for recording the debits or credits to Notes Receivable on the general ledger.
2. The discount register.
3. The liability ledger.
4. The maturity ledger.
5. The notification record.

TELLER'S BLOTTER SHEET OR INDIVIDUAL DEBITS OR CREDITS TO BILLS OR NOTES RECEIVABLE. The payment of the proceeds of a loan is made either by a check which is cashed or used in connection with other financial transactions; cash for which a receipt is (or should be) given; or by credit to an account.

In order to obtain such funds for distribution of proceeds, the general ledger account, Bills Receivable, must be debited so that the offsetting credit can be made to either the general ledger control accounts, cashiers checks, or a commercial or savings account.

This transaction is either recorded on a form known as a teller's blotter sheet, or teller's discount sheet similar to that shown in Exhibit 99, or entered on an individual set of tickets, debits to Bills Receivable as shown in Exhibit 100.

The blotter sheet, it should be noted, provides for both disbursement of funds in connection with new loans and receipt and distribution of payments on loans. Such a form is found to be quite practical in banks which handle less than 50 transactions a day. Through its use, all essential detail in connection with a new loan; renewal or payment, such as name, amount, class or type, interest paid, or discount received, net amount and disposition of proceeds or source of payment are recorded in one place. In using this form, all new notes, renewals and payments are recorded as handled or as funds are disbursed. At the end of the day each column is totaled and respective debit and credit tickets are made up and totaled for each general ledger account which is affected and sent, together with other items originating in the section, to the proof section.

The blotter sheets, together with the notes, go to the clerk at the end of the day for posting the information to the liability ledger and for the filing of notes.

The bills receivable debit form, made up for use with a window envelope is found to be very efficient and convenient in a bank which has numerous daily commercial loan transactions. This form, which can be filled out in either pencil or ball point pen at the time the transaction is processed, consists of five parts. The original which is the general ledger debit to loans and discounts of respective class and type; a duplicate for use if the proceeds are credited to an account; a triplicate which is the advice of credit or used as a memo if a check is issued; a quadruplicate copy which is the credit to unearned discounts if the interest is deducted in advance from the proceeds; and a quintuplicate copy which is the memorandum to the clerk for use in posting the liability ledger.

After the note is entered on the blotter or bills receivable form and proceeds are disbursed, the teller's window operation is complete except that if the loan is secured, the documents are receipted for and set aside for later registration in the collateral register.

At the end of the day, if the bills receivable tickets are used, the teller either summarizes the respective tickets on his teller sheet or sends the tickets, together with checks received in payment of or on loans; general ledger tickets covering issuance of drafts or cashier's checks in payment of proceeds; general ledger credits to interest received or discount unearned accounts; credit tickets representing proceeds of loans credited to the account of the borrower; and record of cash; to the proof section for balancing and processing.

After the loans have been entered on the blotter, or recorded—either currently—at the end of the day—or the following day, the individual transactions are recorded or posted to the discount register or journal and to the liability ledger.

In connection with processing consumer credit or installment loans, the forms usually are prenumbered and prepared at the time the customer is notified the application is approved and consist of a note; a ledger card, with or without payments pre-scheduled; and an information card containing the number of the loan, name, address, security if any, date, amount of payment, dates of

EXHIBIT 99

LOAN TELLERS BLOTTER SHEET FRONT

THE WILMETTE STATE BANK
WILMETTE, ILLINOIS
DISCOUNT TELLERS SHEET

DATE________________

	DEBITS												CREDITS						
	LOANS AND DISCOUNTS				MISC. DEBITS	CASH RECEIVED	CHECKS		NAME	INT. RATE	PREVIOUS NOTE NO.	RENEWAL PERIOD	CASH PAID	MISC. CREDITS	INTEREST AND DISCOUNT	LOANS AND DISCOUNTS			
	DEMAND		TIME													TIME		DEMAND	
	UNSECURED	COLLATERAL	UNSECURED	COLLATERAL			BANK NO.	AMOUNT								COLLATERAL	UNSECURED	COLLATERAL	UNSECURED

EXHIBIT 99 A

LOAN TELLERS BLOTTER SHEET REAR

RECAPITULATION	DR.	CR.	GENERAL BOOKS			PAYMENTS		DEPOSITS		TICKETS		CASH		CHECKS			
			DEBITS	CREDITS		PER INST.	AUTOMOBILE	CHECKING	SAVINGS	DEBITS	CREDITS	ITEMS	ACTUAL	ON US	OUTSIDE	SAVINGS	
F. H. A.																	
F. H. A.																	
Demand—Unsecured																	
Collateral																	
Time—Unsecured																	
Collateral																	
Interest and Discount																	
Miscellaneous																	
General Books																	
Checking Deposits																	
Savings Deposits																	
Tickets																	
Cash																	
Checks																	
Cash Items																	
Paying Teller No.																	
Savings																	
Real Estate																	

payment for cross reference purposes, which is either filed by name or date of payment depending on the system. After signing, the note together with other papers are given to the teller who enters the note on a journal or blotter similar to that used in connection with commercial loans. This journal, in addition, generally provides space for other information such as the recording of the name of a discounter which is a matter of practice where notes on bank forms are taken by retailers in payment for purchases, after which they are discounted or sold to the bank.

After determining that the note is signed and the papers are in proper order and carry the approval of the loaning officer, the loan is entered in the journal and a check prepared for the distribution of the proceeds. At the end of the day the teller totals the respective columns in the journal and prepares respective general ledger tickets for the total of each column. These are sent to the proof section or the general bookkeeper for balancing after which the note, the liability card and supporting papers are filed by a clerk.

EXHIBIT 100

LOAN TELLERS GENERAL LEDGER DEBIT TICKETS TO BILLS RECEIVABLE

FIRST NATIONAL BANK
ILLINOIS

DEBIT—Bills Receivable CLASS [ ] DATE

REMARKS	DATED	TENOR	DUE	RATE	INT.	DISC.	AMOUNT	NET PROCEEDS
								XXXXXX XXXXXX

Loaning Officer ______

Prepared By ______

Approved By ______

Renewal ☐ Increase ☐ New ☐

GENERAL LEDGER DEBIT

Form 1-A Copyright 1944, Marshall Corns Co., Chicago

When the loan is entered in the journal it is usually indexed by number, date, name of mortgagor, location, and description of the property.

Most of the processing of mortgage loans is handled over a period of time with various details of respective financial transactions being computed and recorded as the loan is being processed.

In some cases an accounts receivable account is established in the name of the borrower. Where this is done, after the note has been signed, all funds advanced by the bank in connection with the pickup of the old mortgage, tax payments, title charges, and insurance, are charged to this account. When the loan is completed and put through the full amount of the loan is charged to "Bills Receivable-Mortgage Loans," the account receivable account is credited with the amount owing, and the borrower is given a check for the net proceeds.

Where the bank follows the practice of charging "Bills Receivable – Mortgage Loans" when the loan has been approved and the note signed the proceeds are credited to an accounts payable account in the name of the borrower to which all funds expended by the bank in connection with the picking up of the old mortgage, such as interest, taxes, insurance, abstract fees, etc., and other items of similar nature are charged. Under this procedure, when the processing of the loan has been completed the bank gives the borrower a check or credits his account for the net proceeds remaining in the account.

These computations are usually made by a mortgage closing officer who prepares a detailed statement for the mortgagor showing the amount of the loan, funds which have been disbursed by the bank, and the net proceeds. Once the closing arrangements have been made, the loan officer delivers the mortgage papers consisting of the note, trust deed and guaranty policy or abstract, to the loan teller together with a statement showing the amount of the proceeds to be payable to the mortgagor.

Upon receipt of such settlement statement, the teller prepares the necessary tickets to bills receivable, accounts receivable, or accounts payable together with a credit to cashiers' checks, in the event the proceeds are to be distributed by check; or to an account, if the proceeds are to be credited to the account of the borrower.

The loan is then entered in a register and maturity tickets prepared by month and date. Mortgage papers are filed in a document envelope for filing in the vault, while the note, together with the insurance, is filed by name or by number in the mortgage loan file. If the mortgage loans are filed by number, a cross reference file is maintained by number, depending on whether such loans are installment loans with payments due monthly or payments are due to be made quarterly or semi-annually.

THE DISCOUNT REGISTER. After a commercial loan has been processed by the teller the note is "registered"—that is indexed, either by hand or by machine in a permanent record, in chronological order by number, date, name, amount, rate of interest, and maturity.

Under some operating procedures this record is referred to as a journal, and becomes a book of original entry similar to a blotter where all details in connection with loan transactions are entered. Where thus used, the totals of new loans made, renewed and paid; interest collected in advance known as discount; and interest paid are computed at the end of the day and used to effect the balancing of the loan section. These figures are also used for reconciling and maintaining control figures on the current position of the various classes and types of loans with the balances of the same classes and types of loans as of the close of business of the preceding day on the general ledger.

In connection with installment or consumer credit loans such a register merely records the loans in chronological order by number, name, date, class, security, and if discounted, from whom received.

The mortgage loan register is used for the same purpose, that is, for recording in chronological order all mortgages made by number, name, date, amount, rate of interest, terms, maturity, and address or description of the property.

LIABILITY LEDGER. The liability ledger is a permanent record consisting of a separate ledger sheet similar to that shown in Exhibit 101 for every borrower on which is detailed each loan transaction, the extent of the borrower's indebtedness to the bank, and whether on a secured or unsecured basis, and if such loans are endorsed or guaranteed by another party.

When a loan is made, it is recorded in the debit column on the ledger sheet of the maker. As payments or renewal notes are received, the fact is recorded on the ledger sheet by posting the amount of the old note in the credit column and the amount of the new note in the debit column, reference being made to the notes and the history of each note by the recording of the date and number. This information, of course, is posted either by hand or by machine from the blotter, the discount register, or the memo section from the bills receivable debit form.

The liability ledger while it shows the total amount owing the bank by any one borrower, whether it is secured or unsecured, or whether it is guaranteed or endorsed, only discloses the total commercial loan liability of the individual borrower. It does not show if the borrower has endorsed or guaranteed notes for others, or if notes given in trade to other business concerns or individuals, have in turn been discounted with the bank.

In order to determine at any time not only the direct liability of a borrower, but his indirect liability on loans which have been discounted and loans on which he has assumed responsibility for payment through endorsement or guarantee, separate memo ledger sheets similar to that shown in Exhibit 102 and 103 are sometimes set up in the name of the borrower, on which the liability on loans discounted and liability as guarantor or endorser are recorded. These memo sheets are usually made up in colors to distinguish them from the ledger sheet on which the direct liability is recorded, and filed together with the direct liability sheet.

Such information can, at times, be of great importance in placing the bank on notice when an individual, company, or principal of a company, obligates himself through endorsing loans for others, thus spreading or depleting his credit; or a company is financing its business operations by giving notes in payment of invoices.

Because of the volume of transactions involved in handling the various types and classes of loans, most of which are secured, only so-called commercial loans are listed on the liability ledger sheet of the borrower. Sometimes, though infrequently, a notation will be made to the effect that the borrower is also liable to the bank under a real estate mortgage loan or on an installment loan. Generally this information can only be obtained from either a central file of information, if the bank has a central file, or by review and analysis of the loan borrowings of the real estate mortgage section and the installment loan or consumer credit loan section.

In the installment or consumer credit loan section, the ledger card, which is filed either numerically, by maturity (date payments are due), or alphabetically under payment date, to simplify the recording of payments, is also the liability ledger, except that it only shows the detail in connection with that particular loan.

Knowledge of the total amount owing the bank by one person through other consumer credit or installment loans is not too important inasmuch as such loans are for nominal amounts, amply secured, and generally are not made to individuals who have commercial loan facilities available to them. Should information be required, however, as to other borrowings of the individual in the consumer credit or installment loan section, such data can be easily obtained by referring either to the cross reference file or credit folder.

In connection with real estate mortgage loans, the ledger sheet is the liability record. This record, in addition to showing the number, name, original amount and present balance of the loan, together with description of the property, carries a record of the insurance coverage by company, number of policy and expiration date. In addition, the ledger sheet carries a record of payments showing distribution of proceeds as to principal, interest, reserve for taxes and insurance.

MATURITY LEDGER. According to law, in order to enforce collectability, a note must be presented to the maker for payment during business hours at the place specified in the note. If this place of payment is the bank, there is no problem. If, on the other hand, the note was discounted for a customer and must be presented to the signer or borrower at a place other than the bank, proper records must be maintained.

As it is the responsibility of the loan section to present all notes when they are due at the place where they are payable, it maintains what is known as a maturity tickler file or maturity ledger.

It is from this maturity ledger that the loan teller selects loans which have been discounted and are/or payable at places other

EXHIBIT 101

LIABILITY LEDGER SHEET

P-43

LIABILITY LEDG

DISCOUNT

PICK UP OF CLASSIFICATION BALANCES				NAME OF CUSTOMER	DATE	MAKER OR ENDORSER
SECURED	UNSECURED	INDIRECT	TOTAL LIABILITY			

KEY TO SYMBOLS—FOLLOWING NOTE NUMBER:

PRECEDING NOTE NUMBER:

ER JOURNAL

DIVISION

O. K.	NUMBER	RATE	DATE DUE	DEBIT	✓	CREDIT	BALANCES BY CLASSIFICATION			TOTAL OF BALANCES
							SECURED	UNSECURED	INDIRECT	

C—SECURED
U—UNSECURED
CR—SECURED REDISCOUNT
R—UNSECURED REDISCOUNT
UX—COLLATERAL PLEDGE
U—SUBJECT TO REGULATION "U"
PA—PREMIUM ADVANCE LOAN
CP—COMMERCIAL PAPER

LEDGER POSTED BY____________

BALANCES CARRIED TO MARGIN CARDS BY____________

EXHIBIT 102

LIABILITY LEDGER SHEET FOR LOANS DISCOUNTED

BANCO POPULAR

NAME

ADDRESS

INDIRECT LIABIL

DISCOUNTED FOR	DATE	LOAN NUMBER	TENOR

DE PUERTO RICO

____, PUERTO RICO

ITY DISCOUNTS

MATURITY	INTEREST OR COMMISSION	M E M O	DEBITS OR CREDITS	BALANCE

EXHIBIT 103

LIABILITY LEDGER SHEET INDIRECT AS ENDORSER OR GUARANTOR

BANCO POPULAR

NAME

ADDRESS

LIABILITY AS GUARA

GUARANTEED OR ENDORSED FOR	DATE	LOAN NUMBER	TENOR

DE PUERTO RICO

, PUERTO RICO

NTOR OR ENDORSER

MATURITY		M E M O	DEBIT OR CREDIT	BALANCE

EXHIBIT 104

MULTIPLE LIABILITY LEDGER FORM

LIABILITY LEDGE

DISCOUNT D

P-43

PICK UP OF CLASSIFICATION BALANCES				NAME OF CUSTOMER	DATE	MAKER OR ENDORSER
SECURED	UNSECURED	INDIRECT	TOTAL LIABILITY			
100.00	200.00	300.00	600.00	JOHN DOE	APR 1 APR 1	JOE DOADS J. BRAWL

THESE FIGURES WERE TYPED IN IN ORDER TO GIVE A BETTER PICTURE OF THE OPERATION
FIRST THE PREVIOUS BALANCES ARE ENTERED AT THE RIGHT SIDE OF THE JOURNAL. THEN
THE THREE PART TICKET AND CUSTOMER LEDGER ARE PUT INTO THE MACHINE. ALL NECESSARY INFORMATION
IS THEN ENTERED, SIMULTANEOUSLY PRINTING ON THE TICKET, THE LEDGER AND THE JOURNAL.

P-16

DATE	NAME OR ENDORSER
APR 1	JOE DOADS J. BRAWL

NOTICE

CITY NATIONAL BA
AND TRUST COMPANY of Chi
208 SOUTH LA SALLE STREET, CHICAGO 90,

YOUR NOTE DESCRIBED HEREON WILL BE DUE AND PAYABLE AT

MAIL TO	DATE DISCOUNTED	OTHER PARTIES
JOHN DOE		JOE DOADS

P-50

CHECKS ON OTHER BANKS MUST BE

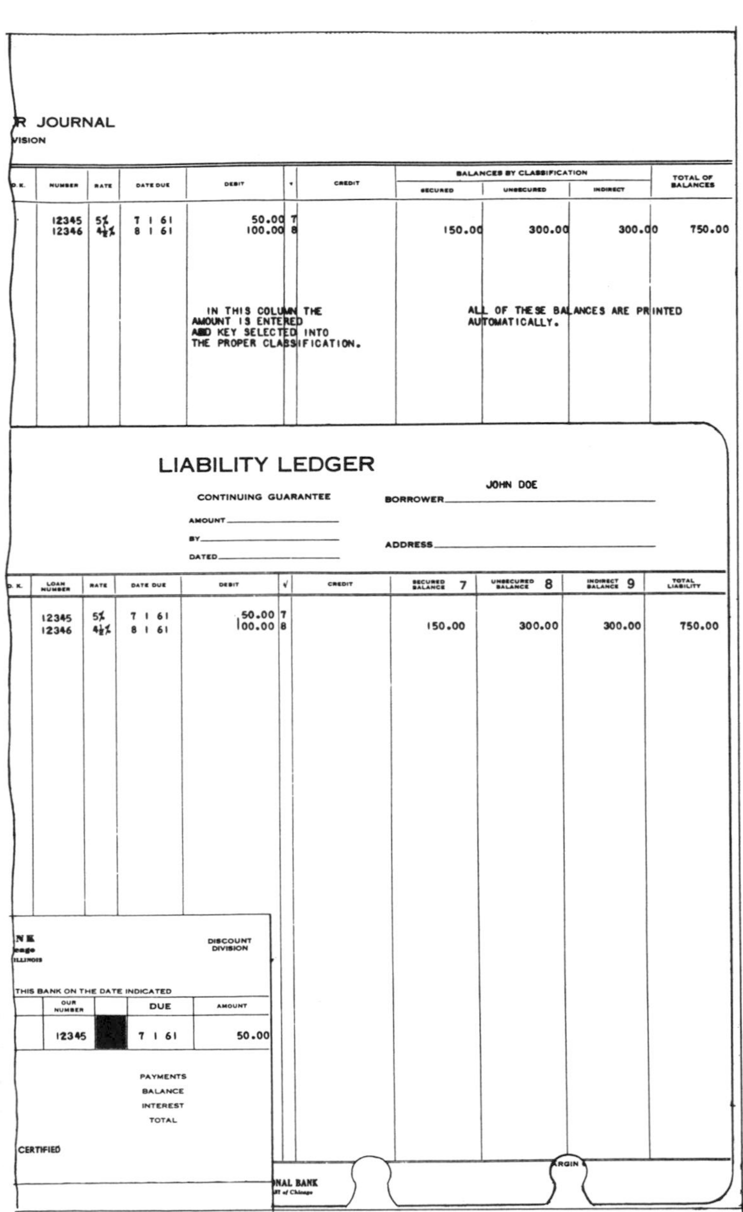
R JOURNAL
VISION

D. K.	NUMBER	RATE	DATE DUE	DEBIT	✓	CREDIT	SECURED	UNSECURED	INDIRECT	TOTAL OF BALANCES
	12345	5%	7 1 61	50.00	7					
	12346	4½%	8 1 61	100.00	8		150.00	300.00	300.00	750.00

(BALANCES BY CLASSIFICATION: SECURED, UNSECURED, INDIRECT)

IN THIS COLUMN THE AMOUNT IS ENTERED AND KEY SELECTED INTO THE PROPER CLASSIFICATION.

ALL OF THESE BALANCES ARE PRINTED AUTOMATICALLY.

LIABILITY LEDGER

CONTINUING GUARANTEE
AMOUNT
BY
DATED

BORROWER JOHN DOE
ADDRESS

D. K.	LOAN NUMBER	RATE	DATE DUE	DEBIT	√	CREDIT	SECURED BALANCE 7	UNSECURED BALANCE 8	INDIRECT BALANCE 9	TOTAL LIABILITY
	12345	5%	7 1 61	50.00	7					
	12346	4½%	8 1 61	100.00	8		150.00	300.00	300.00	750.00

NK
cago
ILLINOIS

DISCOUNT DIVISION

THIS BANK ON THE DATE INDICATED

	OUR NUMBER		DUE	AMOUNT
	12345		7 1 61	50.00

PAYMENTS
BALANCE
INTEREST
TOTAL

CERTIFIED

NAL BANK
of Chicago

RGIN

than the bank, for delivery to the messenger section for presentation; or for delivery to the collection section, if the note is payable in another town, or place where it cannot be presented by the messenger.

In certain instances, all loans are entered in a separate maturity ledger, not only for discounted items to have attention when due, but to show what loans will be coming due on certain dates, or within a certain period, for the information and guidance of the person charged with the responsibility of converting funds into investments.

In connection with installment or consumer credit loans where payments are made by coupon or passbook, no maturity ledger is maintained. The ledger card which is filed by month under the date of payment, sometimes alphabetically under due date, acts as the maturity record.

The maturity record in connection with mortgage loans repayable in monthly installments, generally is the ledger sheet, otherwise a separate maturity card is made up which is filed monthly by date. This card is used by the loan teller in sending notices of payment due on mortgages.

THE NOTIFICATION RECORD. The notification record consists of the notice to the borrower of the amount of principal and interest due on a certain date or at maturity. Sometimes a memorandum or tickler record is prepared from information provided from the note, blotter, or teller's receivable debit memo. Such records can be prepared under a system through which the liability ledger, discount ledger or journal, and notice and tickler are prepared by machine in one operation similar to that shown in Exhibit 104.

In certain banks where the liability ledger is posted directly from the blotter or bills receivable ticket, and items are not entered in a register, or the makeup of the notice and tickler is not a by-product of the posting of the liability ledger, a multiple copy form similar to that shown in Exhibit 105, made up from the note, blotter, or teller's receivable debit memo, is sometimes used. In connection with this form the original is the notice, the duplicate the maturity tickler, the triplicate is the accrual slip on which the interest earned but uncollected or discount paid but unearned is igured, while the quadruplicate copy is the register.

In using the accrual form which is filed numerically for figur-ng accruals, the interest earned or discount paid is spread over the eriod of the loan by months. Each month the amounts accrued uring the particular month are run on an adding machine from he form, and respective total amounts either debited to "interest arned but not collected" (accounts receivable asset account) or o "discount paid but unearned" (accounts payable liability ac-ount), and the total proceeds credited to the income account "in-erest earned on loans."

In other banks where the notice and tickler is not prepared as by-product of posting the liability ledger or journal, the notice s made up manually in original and duplicate, of which the original s the notice of payment due which is sent to the borrower and iled alphabetically, and the duplicate or tickler which is filed by ue date. Sometimes it is a practice to file both the original and uplicate together under due date. In either event, usually ten ays before maturity, the notice is sent to the borrower while the uplicate is referred to the loan committee for decision, depending n circumstances as to renewal, reduction or payment.

EXHIBIT 105

MULTIPLE NOTICE AND REGISTER FORM

FIRST NATIONAL BANK
ILLINOIS

No.

Your note as described will be due as indicated.

Dated	Tenor	Due	Amount	Rate %	Int.	Discount	Total Amount Due
			$				$
Endorser or Collateral							

Checks on other banks must be certified.

Please bring this notice with you.

NOTICE

SAFEKEEPING AND CUSTODIANSHIP OF DOCUMENTS PLEDGED AS SECURITY TO A LOAN. In connection with handling securities or documents pledged as collateral to a loan the person who is referred to as being "in charge of collateral" (whether such person is the loan teller, collateral teller, or referred to as property custodian teller of the loan section) depending on the size of the bank, has the responsibility for:

1. Checking the securities and documents tendered to be certain they are complete and in negotiable order.

2. Issuing a receipt to the borrower for the securities or documents pledged.

3. Seeing that securities or documents pledged are properly indexed in the collateral register.

4. Depositing such securities or documents in the vault under proper control.

5. Seeing that securities pledged are currently priced and that sufficient margin is maintained.

6. Approving the release and delivery of securities or documents upon payment of the loan, on proper receipt.

Documents evidencing wealth such as stocks, bonds, notes, chattel mortgages, warehouse receipts, accounts receivable, life insurance policies, guarantees, etc., pledged as security for a loan, after being tendered and examined as to order and delivery, are indexed in what is commonly referred to as a collateral register.

The registering and receipting for collateral is handled by banks in several different ways. With some banks the issuing of a receipt covering the depositing of securities or documents as collateral is standard procedure, while in other banks such receipts, as a matter of policy and to avoid possible hypothecation, are not given unless required by the customer, and then under approved circumstances.

In order to prevent hypothecation and possible fraudulent misuse, receipts should be numbered, clearly state that the securities as described are pledged as collateral security for a loan, and be marked "non-negotiable."

In connection with registration, it is the practice in some banks to use one register sheet for each borrower, wherein all securities pledged are listed. Under this practice, when securities or documents are pledged as collateral, the teller makes out a receipt form in triplicate of which the original is the receipt for the customer, the duplicate the auditor's copy, and the triplicate, which accompanies the collateral, the medium from which the register is posted. Under this system when securities or documents are withdrawn, the customer, in addition to returning the receipt, acknowledges receipt by inscribing his name in the register in the space provided.

In other banks it is the practice to issue an individual receipt or maintain a separate register sheet for each respective item deposited. Such receipts generally consist of a four part form of which the original is the register, the duplicate the receipt to the customer, the triplicate the auditor's copy and the quadruplicate the file copy.

While each system has its respective merits, proper consideration should be given at all times, whether a receipt is given or not, to provide some record for the person delegated audit and control responsibilities to use in maintaining control, and in periodically confirming and verifying securities or documents pledged as collateral.

While the combination form accomplishes all the objectives of collateral handling, it does have the drawback where several items of securities are pledged in connection with withdrawals or substitution. Further, it does not present a record from a historical point of view for the bank's information. The best procedure to follow, therefore, including a copy of the receipt for the auditor, is to maintain a collateral register with a sheet in the name of the borrower on which are entered securities and documents pledged as collateral and which provides a space for receipt by the borrower when such securities or documents are withdrawn.

After securities and documents deposited as collateral are checked and found in order and indexed in the collateral register, they are placed in a strong manila envelope or folder and filed for safekeeping in alphabetical order either in a teller's truck or special compartment in the bank vault.

To safeguard and maintain control over such property and prevent misuse, collateral is usually placed in the vault under dual control, that is under the joint control of the collateral clerk and a person in some other section of the bank. Under this procedure, when collateral is either placed in the vault for safekeeping or removed from the vault to be returned to the borrower, representatives from two sections are present to confirm the deposit, or its removal from the vault compartment.

MARGINS. Generally, when reference is made to sufficient or adequate collateral, it refers to margin, which is the difference between the current price at which securities or documents evidencing wealth or value of commodities pledged to secure a loan could be exchanged for currency, and the unpaid balance of the loan.

The price at which stocks, bonds and commodities are bought or sold are constantly changing, depending on the law of supply and demand and general business or political conditions. In order to provide proper and sufficient protection to the bank, every experienced credit or loaning officer takes the matter of margin into consideration at the time the loan is made, to protect the bank against any possible loss due to necessity for forced liquidation or sale of collateral under adverse market conditions.

For example, as a matter of policy, a bank may decide to only loan a fixed percentage, say 65% of market price, on a pledge of a certain stock or bond, feeling such security was overpriced in the market and the price is not justified by the earnings record or future sales projection.

A similar situation might also exist in regard to commodities. For example: A dealer in eggs purchases a carload of eggs at 50c a dozen. As he requires financing from the bank, he puts them in a warehouse and tenders a warehouse receipt to the bank covering the eggs. Because of general economic conditions and the law of supply and demand, the loaning officer feels that although the present market price of the eggs is 55c a dozen wholesale, it is quite possible for the market price to substantially decline due to the fact that the market is glutted with eggs. Therefore, in order to have ample margin, and to protect the bank against any loss, he will only loan the dealer 40c a dozen, using the differential as a "margin" of protection to the bank in event of possible forced sale on liquidation.

The pricing of securities is a relatively simple matter in a small bank. In other banks, however, when the volume is large and a great variety of collateral is handled, the records must be complete and quite detailed. Probably the most commonly used record, in addition to the collateral register, is the loan card which shows the amount of the loan, carries a complete description of the securities pledged to secure payment of the loan, and has space for periodically recording the date, per share value and total value of each type of security. By use of this record, the collateral clerk or loan officer can readily evaluate the market value of securities pledged to secure such loans.

Where a bank has a large volume of loans secured by listed or unlisted stocks or bonds it is also customary practice, in order to provide protection against being over-extended in any one class, issue, or type of security, to maintain a cross index reference under the name of the security. This is a very excellent practice to follow, particularly in a period of market activity or wide speculation, in order to prevent over-extension of credit against one issue or certain classes of stocks or bonds.

From the moment a loan is granted, it becomes one of the responsibilities of the collateral clerk or collateral section to make certain that such margin is continuously maintained. They, therefore, periodically check the current market value of all securities or property pledged as collateral against the unpaid balance of the loan, and whenever they find the current value of the securities or property is not sufficient to cover the loan plus desired margin, immediately refer the matter to the officer who approved the loan for corrective action.

Where, after investigation, the officer feels the loan is not properly secured, that is, there is not sufficient difference between the current price at which the collateral could be sold, and the unpaid balance of the loan to provide proper protection, he either calls on the borrower for more security or for a payment on the loan, either of which will restore proper margin.

Frequently the same borrower may have two or more loans, made at different times, against the same security. In such cases, for practical purposes, the collateral is treated as a single unit securing the total debt.

After a loan is paid, the property pledged as security is returned to the owner upon presentation of the receipt and acknowledgement of the return of the property on the register copy, or in case the bank does not follow the practice of issuing receipts, then by directly signing for such property, together with the date of release, on the collateral register.

In order to obtain such property from the vault, however, it is first necessary for the teller to obtain release of the collateral from those who have it under custody.

Following release of the collateral, the customer's receipt or copy of vault record is forwarded to the auditor for checking and verifying.

CALCULATING AND COLLECTING OF INTEREST ON LOANS. Another function of the loan teller or clerk in the loan section is the computation and collecting of interest owed by the borrower for the use of the funds.

In computing interest, several systems or methods of computing interest can be followed, depending on the policy and practice of the bank.

Notes payable 30-60-90 days after date are generally considered to become due on whatever date occurs after the designated period. Interest in such cases is computed on a 360 day basis. Where a note is payable one month, two months, or three months after date or on a specific date, interest is computed from the date of the instrument until the date for payment on a 365 day basis. Most banks endeavor to have notes on the term basis as interest computations on a 360 day basis produce more interest income than if computed on a 365 day basis.

Under the laws of negotiable instruments dealing with presentation, notes falling due on Sunday or a holiday, or if banks are closed Saturday, are considered to be due and payable on the first business day following, in which case additional interest is computed on the original basis.

Some banks, in order to avoid having notes come due on Saturday or Sunday, purposely set the maturity date as close to the term period as possible, but while dating maturity for a Friday or Monday, will compute interest on the 360 day basis for the actual number of days.

Interest on commercial or one payment loans, after being computed, may either be payable at maturity, in which case the face amount of the loan is paid over to the borrower; or the loan may be discounted, in which case the interest is deducted from the face amount of the loan and credited to an interest income account and only the net amount is paid over to the borrower.

Should the bank be on a cash basis, the interest when collected at maturity, or discount collected at the time the loan is made, is credited immediately to the income account, "interest earned on loans."

Where the bank is on an accrual basis, however, and the interest is paid at maturity, the amount of interest accrued each month is charged to "interest earned but not collected" and credited to "interest earned on loans." In case the bank is on an accrual basis and the interest is discounted, then the whole amount is credited to "interest paid but unearned," a liability account, and each month the account is charged for the amount of interest which has been accrued during the month and credited to "interest earned on loans."

Obviously, if the bank is on an accrual basis, payment of interest at maturity which is credited to "interest earned but not collected," cancels out the asset account, while if the loan is discounted, the multiple monthly withdrawals from "interest paid but unearned" in time will deplete the liability account. Regardless of which basis is used, however, it is the responsibility of the loan clerk or accrual clerk to make such interest computations which should be periodically verified by the auditor or person charged with audit and control responsibility.

In connection with installment loans and mortgage loans repayable in monthly installments, the interest is figured at the time the loan is made and included as part of each equal installment. With such loans, however, the total amount of interest, if the bank is on a cash basis at the time the loan is made, is credited immediately to "interest earned on loans" or, if the bank is on an accrual basis, the interest is credited to a liability account, "interest paid but unearned" and a proportionate amount deducted each month and credited to the "interest earned on loans" account.

Whenever a loan is paid before maturity, it is also the function of the loan teller or clerk in the loan section to recompute the interest charges and, after making a satisfactory adjustment to respective interest income accounts, to refund the over-payment of interest to the borrower by means of a cashier's check. Such refunds are only made, however, with the approval of an officer and are later checked and verified, both as to figuring and disposition of funds, by the auditor or the persons charged with the responsibility of control and auditing functions.

THE HANDLING AND PROCESSING OF LOAN PAYMENTS. Another important function of the loan section is the handling and processing of funds tendered by the borrower either in full payment of the loan or as payment on account.

In connection with the payment of commercial loans, the customer may come in any time after receiving the notice, up to and including the date the note is due. He can either make payment in full, partial payment and renew the balance, or renew the entire note, depending upon the judgment and decision of the officers or committee. Generally, in the absence of arrangements to the contrary, all unsecured loans are expected to be paid at maturity.

If the loan was made on an unsecured basis for a non-customer of the bank; discounted for a customer of the bank; or a loan made to a non-customer secured by acceptable collateral; the teller should only accept cash, a cashier's check on another bank, or a certified check of the borrower in payment before cancelling the note or releasing the collateral.

Should a personal check be tendered in payment, the note should not be cancelled or collateral released, until such check has been presented to, and paid by, the bank on which drawn.

If the loan is made on either a secured or unsecured basis, the bank generally will accept a check on the borrower's account in payment. Neither the note should be cancelled nor the collateral released, however, without the teller determining that the balance in the account is sufficient to cover the check, and placing a hold against the balance of the account for the amount of the check.

Payments on account, in connection with commercial loans, if made before maturity, are endorsed on the note itself by the teller, and indexed on the blotter sheet or bills receivable credit ticket.

In connection with payments made on loans secured by accounts receivable, warehouse receipts (when a partial release has been effected upon payment) or trust receipt (where payment has been made for an article or piece of merchandise) the amount of payment covering the account or article is endorsed on the note, while proper notation is made on the list or receipt form, after which it is entered on the blotter, or bills receivable credit ticket for later posting to the liability ledger. Checks are sent to the proof section for processing while cash is placed in a teller's cash drawer.

Payments in full or on account, when received by the teller are either indexed on a blotter, a general ledger credit ticket to respective class of bills receivable; or on a special bills receivable multiple form, similar to that shown in Exhibit 106, a four part form of which the original is the general ledger credit to "bills receivable" for the particular class of loan; the duplicate to "interest earned on loans" or "interest earned uncollected" in case interest is paid at maturity; the triplicate a debit to the account of the borrower, in case either the principal, a payment, or the interest is to be charged to the account; and a quadruplicate memo copy

EXHIBIT 106

LOAN TELLERS GENERAL LEDGER CREDIT TO BILLS RECEIVABLE

FIRST NATIONAL BANK
ILLINOIS

CREDIT—Bills Receivable CLASS DATE

REMARKS	NUMBER	DUE	RATE	INT.	AMOUNT	TOTAL CHARGE
						X X X X X X X X X X X X

Part Payment ☐
Full Payment ☐
Renewal ☐
Check Drawn on
Charged to Customers A/C ☐
Prepared By
Approved By

GENERAL LEDGER CREDIT

Form 1-B Copyright 1944, Marshall Corns Co., Chicago

for use of the teller or bookkeeper in posting the payment to the liability ledger.

Whenever a commercial time loan is renewed, the entire transaction is handled in the same manner as though a new loan was processed for one customer and payment in full of a loan was made for another customer. In other words, they are handled as two separate transactions with, of course, the interest received or discount being credited to the respective income accounts.

Consumer credit or installment loan payments, which are made monthly, generally are set up using a coupon book or passbook for payments. If the coupon style procedure is followed, the customer either tenders the coupon book at the loan window (or in some cases any paying and receiving teller of the bank) who extracts the coupon and upon receipt of payment, marks the coupon and the receipt with his paid stamp. Such coupons are either charged over to the installment loan section or to the loan teller, or go directly to the proof section with other work of the teller who has received the payment, for processing, balancing and return the following day to the bookkeeper who handles payments on installment loan accounts.

Payments on installment or consumer credit loans where coupons are used are either stamped off the ledger card by the bookkeeper from the coupon, if payments are pre-scheduled or machine posted to the ledger card the following day.

When the passbook system is used, the borrower goes to the loan teller, who extracts the ledger card from the file and enters it into a window posting machine which posts the passbook and ledger card simultaneously. At the end of the day proof of posting is made by the teller, after which the general ledger tickets are prepared which adjust the balances of respective bills receivable control accounts.

In connection with mortgage loans which are repayable in monthly installments, the payment acceptance procedure similar to that used in handling payments on installments or consumer credit loans is followed. When payments are posted to the ledger sheet by the bookkeeper, however, such payments are distributed by machine to payments due on principal, interest, and amounts reserved for payment of taxes and insurance.

DELINQUENCIES. In handling loan delinquencies several procedures are followed. In connection with commerical loans, whether secured or unsecured, it is the general practice to have the teller prepare a past due notice if the loan is unpaid at the close of business of the day on which the note is due. This is generally followed up within 5 days by a telephone call from a loan officer or by a registered letter. Should the loan be unsecured, prompt action is taken to contact the borrower and effect arrangement for payment of the loan.

If the loan is secured and there is ample margin, steps are taken by the loan officer to have the loan either reinstated on a current basis or paid, and failing in this, after proper notification has been given, to sell the collateral and apply the proceeds to the loan.

Where delinquencies on consumer credit and installment loans occur, it is generally the practice to send a notice 5 days after the payment date. This is followed up 15 days after payment date with a second notice, and the sending of a third notice 25 days after payment date.

Generally on the anniversary or when payment has been missed for the second consecutive month, a registered letter is sent to the borrower or the loan is turned over to a collector for proper handling by telephone or special letters. After a certain determinable period of time, such loans are turned over to the attorney for collection and attempts made to repossess the automobile or appliance which has been pledged as collateral security, and to sell it and apply the proceeds to the balance of the loan.

In connection with real estate mortgage loans and delinquencies, because of the security involved, the general procedure is to send a notice that payment has not been received for payment due on due date, following it up in about 10 days with a letter or telephone call for payment. Failing to obtain payment, generally the procedure is to send a letter by registered mail and after a considerable period of time, depending upon the circumstances, to file suit for foreclosure, to take title to the property, dispose of it, and apply the proceeds to the loan. Should, of course, the loan be made under the Federal Housing Administration Act, the procedure according to due process of law as covered by the Act is followed.

The matter of collecting interest on past due loans, or interest from date of maturity until date of payment, is generally of little concern where a commercial loan is involved, inasmuch as each loan is a transaction complete in itself and such interest owed becomes part of the unpaid principal.

The situation, however, is different with consumer credit or loans repayable in monthly installments. Here the amount of the payment not only includes repayment of principal, but interest for the use of the funds which has been prorated in equal installments over the term of the loan.

Where such payments are delinquent, some banks either compute the amount of the additional interest and collect it at the time the payment is made, or add it on to the last payment before releasing the security, or follow the practice of making a "late charge" which is the penalty charge for being past due or delinquent in payments. Depending on the bank, such late charges are usually collected 5 days after due date and either consist of a per diem payment such as 50c for each day past due, or a charge predicated on a percentage of the amount of the payment.

In the operation of the loan teller section, the functions will be covered by some or all of the following operating instructions:

1. The legal loan limits covering the various classes and types of loans.
2. Approvals required for various types and classes of loans.
3. Margin requirements for the various classes and types of loans.
4. Approvals required for withdrawals of property pledged as security to a loan.
5. Procedure for sending notices in connection with delinquent installment loan payments.
6. Schedule of charges in connection with delinquent installment loan payments.
7. Approval of interest rebates on loans.

CHAPTER XXXVI

THE SAFE DEPOSIT DEPARTMENT

THE FORERUNNER OF THE SAFE DEPOSIT function, presently performed by banks and independently organized safe deposit companies, was the service originally provided by goldsmiths and money changers, who accepted gold or silver coin, and/or bullion, from customers for safekeeping, on receipt.

Later, and in modern times, as the business of banking developed, bankers built stone and concrete vaults reinforced by boulders, steel bars, or pieces of iron, to which were attached a grille, and both an inside and outside door. Generally the inner door was equipped with a key, while the outside door was equipped with tumblers and several locks. In modern times the outside door consists of several thicknesses of armor plate, combination locks with electrical control mechanism, and is protected by alarm systems, poison gas, and other devices to make the vault burglar proof. In addition, combination locks to both doors are maintained under dual control and the whole operation subject to extensive internal control and audit procedures.

Originally, as an accommodation to their customers, banks rented the unused space to individuals or corporations for the purpose of letting them keep their own safe or strong box in the bank vault for safe keeping.

Later, banks purchased drawers or chests in a case or tiers, each equipped with an individual lock, which they rented out to individuals and corporations for the safekeeping and protection of valuables.

In addition to banks, the right to provide a "safe place" to keep valuables and wealth was granted to separate companies especially organized to rent out strongboxes or safes of various sizes within a vault which individuals and corporations could lease for storage and protection of their valuables. The first such independent safe deposit company, or corporation organized or chartered to engage in the business of providing a safe and secure place for the storage and safekeeping of valuables was The Safe Deposit Company of New York, chartered by the State of New York to Francis H. Jenks on April 15, 1861.

Because modern safe deposit boxes, constructed as they are of heat resistant steel and lodged in reinforced concrete and steel vaults, provide maximum protection for valuables or articles of wealth against fire, theft, flood and other disasters, they are widely used by:

A. Individuals alone.
B. Individuals with power of attorney to another party.
C. Individuals in joint tenancy with right of survivorship.
D. Individuals acting in fiduciary capacity.
E. Partnerships.
F. Corporations.

for the safekeeping and protection of valuable papers, documents, articles of wealth or value or evidences of such, as:

Agreements
Baptismal certificates
Bonds
Cancelled checks as evidences of debts paid
Cash
Coin collections
Contracts
Deeds to real estate
Gems
Heirlooms
Insurance policies
Jewelry
Keepsakes
Letters of importance
Marriage license
Miscellaneous valuable papers and letters
Mortgages
Notes
Property tax receipts
Receipts

Stock certificates
Titles to automobiles
Wills

The principal functions and attendant responsibilities of the Safe Deposit department are in connection with:

1. The leasing of safe deposit boxes, which consists of the identification of the renter, execution of the contract, and selection of the safe deposit box.

2. The servicing of renters of safe deposit boxes which consists of handling accesses and supervising activities of customers when they wish to place, remove, or refer to something contained in their box.

3. The terminating or cancelling of leasehold agreements.

IDENTIFICATION. Banks have the right to select customers with whom they intend to do business. Not everyone who wishes to rent a safe deposit box may be acceptable to the bank. Banks normally will not rent a safe deposit box or enter into any other type of business relationship with a known criminal, public enemy, or person who is of disreputable reputation, as such relationships may cause embarrassment to the bank and be of concern to other customers. It is important, therefore, that banks know with whom they are dealing.

If the applicant has a bank account, it is possible that the bank has already satisfied itself concerning the individual, that is, made the necessary references as to the person's background and found that they are acceptable. If, however, a prospect does not have an account, they should be properly identified, references verified and background investigated. Customers should not be permitted to give their address as "care of a bank" but use their legal mailing address, as any other practice complicates the matter of notice and contact for matters in connection with possible legal procedure.

TYPES OF SAFE DEPOSIT BOX LEASES. In connection with the leasing of safe deposit boxes, because of the legal relationship which exists between the bank and the renter of the box, a standard contract or agreement containing the rules and regulations of the lease arrangement, conforming to respective state laws, are signed by the renters or lessees. In addition, because of certain legal questions which are involved between the bank and the renter in connection with rights of parties at interest, separate documents or agreements are also executed in connection with the following relationships, to the extent warranted.

The Individual Alone. Where an individual alone rents a safe deposit box, a signed standard contract form similar to Exhibit 107 is sufficient to provide for the identification of the person entitled to have access to the box.

Individuals with Power of Attorney to Another Party. Under this type of arrangement, the individual either appoints someone to act as his deputy or under power of attorney. When the renter appoints a deputy or power of attorney and a special form is signed, both parties, the renter and the deputy or person to whom the power of attorney runs, should be present in order that the customer may properly identify and witness the signature of the person they have authorized to have access to the box in their behalf. Where a power of attorney form is used, as it is obviously for the express purpose of placing documents in or withdrawing documents from the safe deposit box, the power of attorney should specify that the right only covers having access to the box and has no bearing on the exercise of other powers.

Individuals in Joint Tenancy with Right of Survivorship. Where such an arrangement is entered into by a bank, the general contract is signed by both parties. In addition a separate agreement signed by the parties of interest is executed and filed with the bank. Because of the legal technicalities involved, some banks use the word co-lessee instead of joint tenants to avoid the implication that the property contained in a safe deposit box, regardless of the name in which it is carried, belongs to the survivor.

In connection with joint tenancy or co-lessee contracts, an agreement similar to the one as shown in Exhibit 108 is signed by the parties at interest.

In certain forms of agreement, if one lessee dies the survivor has the right of access provided there is compliance with any local tax or inheritance restrictions.

In other cases, access is only permitted to the survivor if accompanied by an accredited representative of the estate and in compliance with inheritance tax laws.

EXHIBIT 107

STANDARD SAFE DEPOSIT BOX RENTAL CONTRACT

BANK OF CHICAGO
Safe Deposit Regulations

The lessor shall have the exclusive right to fix the hours for opening and closing the vaults, and said hours may be changed by the lessor from time to time without notice.

The vaults may be closed upon any national, state or city holidays or upon any other days when the lessor shall deem such closing prudent and proper.

The use of the safe is in every instance granted by the lessor and accepted by the renter upon the express understanding and agreement that the lessor may terminate such use and require the vacation and surrender of the safe and of the keys or combination thereto at any time upon sixty (60) days' notice in writing mailed to the renter at the last known address of the renter appearing on the lessor's records and upon repayment or tender of repayment for the unexpired time, if any, of a prorata portion of the amount paid for the use of the safe.

Except as expressly otherwise herein provided, access to the safe shall be granted only to the renter and the duly authorized and designated agent of the renter or either of them, and in case of the death or insolvency of the renter to the duly appointed and authorized legal representative of the renter's estate. The lessor may require that the authorization of any agent or deputy shall be set forth on a form provided by the company.

If a safe is rented by two or more persons as joint tenants, it is understood that each of said persons, or his duly authorized representative, shall have all the authority regarding the contents of the safe, the power to surrender or to exchange the safe or to modify the terms of this lease or to appoint an attorney or deputy to have access thereto, and may cancel any such appointment made by either joint tenant. It is further understood that such rights or powers shall in no way be restricted or terminated by the death or incapacity of any one or more of such persons.

Deputies or attorneys may also be appointed by corporate, individual or partnership renters to have access to or surrender the safe. Such appointments must be in form satisfactory to the lessor, and in the case of corporations must be made by resolution of the board of directors, and in the case of individuals, partnerships and joint tenants must be in writing, blanks for which may be had on application.

An authorization restricted as to the purpose of access, such as specifying what is to be placed in or removed from the safe will not be recognized.

Until the receipt by the lessor at its office of written notice of revocation of any power of attorney or deputy appointment or of conclusive notice of the death or legal incapacity of the renter or of one of the joint renters, any action of the lessor in reliance upon such power of attorney or deputy appointment or in permitting the other joint renter to have access to the safe for any purpose shall be fully binding upon the renter or renters of the safe and their respective heirs, executors, administrators, personal representatives, committee, successors and assigns, and to that extent such power of attorney or deputy appointment and such authorization to each joint tenant shall not be deemed to have been revoked by the death or legal incapacity of the grantor of the power of attorney or deputy appointment or of such joint renter, and the respective renters will indemnify the lessor against any unauthorized act of the attorney, deputy or joint renter.

Fiduciaries are required to file papers evidencing their authority as such.

The contents of a safe should not be examined in the vault, but in the rooms provided for that purpose.

Rentals for the use of safes are due and payable annually in advance.

If a key is lost, the lessor should be notified without delay, and the remaining key brought to the office of the lessor in order that the lock may be changed. Lost keys must be paid for by the renter. When both keys to a safe are lost, the safe must be broken open and the lock changed in the presence of the renter, the cost of which must be paid for by the renter.

The lessor reserves the right, from time to time to make such further rules and regulations for the conduct of its business, and such changes in the rules and regulations, as it may, in its judgment, deem necessary or desirable. Notice of such other or additional rules and regulations should be given renter by mailing a copy thereof, postage prepaid, addressed to renter at the last known address appearing on the records of the lessor, and by posting a copy in one or more conspicuous places in or near said vault.

"If possession of any safe is withheld by the renter upon termination of the lease (or its renewal), and the rent thereof remains unpaid thirty (30) days thereafter, the lessor is authorized and empowered by the renter, without notice to the renter, to open the safe at the expense of the renter, in the presence of at least one of the officers of the lessor and one other witness, and remove the contents therefrom. Money or securities found therein may be deposited in any bank or repository in the City of Chicago to the credit of the renter, or held by the renter for the renter without, however, any liability on the part of the lessor. The remainder of contents may be sealed and stored at the expense of the renter in any storage room in said city of Chicago and the lessor shall thereafter incur no further liability with respect thereto."

The liability of the lessor to the renter is expressly limited to loss proved to have been caused by the neglect of the lessor to exercise ordinary care and diligence to prevent other than the renter or the duly authorized representative of the renter, and is assumed upon the express agreement that such unauthorized opening shall not be inferable or presumed from proof of loss of any of the contents of the safe.

Lessor shall not be liable for any damage caused by any act or neglect of any person or persons not in the employ of the lessor, nor for failure of any of the vault doors or locks to operate.

If, by any act, writ, decree, or proceeds against the renter or other person having authorized access to the safe, the lessor is forbidden to permit the safe to be opened by such person, access thereto may be suspended or denied by the lessor without incurring any liability therefor until such act, writ, decree, or process be annulled. The lessor shall be justified and excused from any liability in relying on advice of counsel as to its rights or obligations arising out of notice or service of any such act, writ, decree, or process.

If the renter has left no address with the lessor, then the lessor shall be relieved from giving notice as hereinbefore provided, and shall be entitled to take any action or excerise any right hereinabove given predicated on such prior notice, without notice to the renter.

DATE ____________________

ACCEPTED ____________________

____

____

Individuals Acting in Fiduciary Capacity. Wherever a contract is signed by a person acting in a fiduciary capacity, such as a trustee, executor, administrator, or guardian, it should be accompanied by proper documents or a court order certifying as to appointment. It is a matter of general policy that a safe deposit agreement with a person acting in fiduciary capacity should only be accepted by a bank after review and approval of the bank's legal counsel.

Partnerships. The contract for boxes rented to partnerships should be signed by all partners. In addition, a partnership arrangement should be placed on file clearly indicating the relationship of the partners; whether they are general or special, and their respective rights, if any, to the contents of the box; or the rights, if any, to have access to the box.

Corporations. Where corporations enter into a leasehold arrangement for the rent of a safe deposit box, the contract is signed by those to whom access has been granted by the corporation. This is always accompanied by a corporate resolution, properly

EXHIBIT 108

SAFE DEPOSIT BOX JOINT TENANCY OR CO-LESSEE AGREEMENT

Joint Tenancy Agreement

It is hereby agreed that all articles and property at any time now or hereafter placed or contained in the safe rented by the foregoing lease, now do and shall, so long as they are contained therein, continue to belong to the undersigned renters as joint tenants with right of survivorship therein, and may be withdrawn therefrom, in whole or in part, by all or any one or more of the renters; and upon the death of any one or more of the renters, the title of all articles and property then contained therein shall, upon such death, vest and be in the survivor or survivors jointly with right of survivorship therein, and such survivor or survivors, or any one or more of them, shall have the right to remove and withdraw from said safe all or any part of the articles or property now or at any time hereafter therein contained.

DATE

____________________ ____________________

____

31—Kelco—Chicago

attested to by the secretary, covering the rental of a safe deposit box and authorizing the bank to honor or to grant access privileges to those who are designated in the resolution as having the authority to have access to the box.

IDENTIFICATION. In addition to the signed contract or agreement, the records of the bank generally disclose the full name of the renter, the address and identification. Some banks, as a means of positive identification, show a physical description of the individual and information for coding purposes, such as the name of the renter's parents or another code name which is not likely to be known by a person presenting a key and attempting to forge the signature.

SELECTING A BOX. Safe deposit departments generally have samples of the various size boxes, together with the annual rental, on display to enable prospective renters to make a choice of a box in the price range they can afford to pay and to select a box of sufficient size to contain their valuables and documents.

After selecting the box, the safe deposit clerk, whenever possible and practical, generally takes the renter into the vault and points out the unrented boxes of similar size so customers can make a choice of location.

After the box is selected and the contract signed, the renter is given a sealed envelope containing two keys for which he receipts on the contract form similar to that shown in Exhibit 109, which also provides a space for the recording of the rentals, and for the release, upon removal of the contents and the surrender of the keys. Unless such information is printed on the envelope, the attendant should explain the procedure in respect to the interchange of locks when keys are lost or the lease to the box is terminated.

SERVICING. Servicing, in connection with safe deposit customers, refers to the functions of approving accesses, and providing facilities where renters can examine or refer to the contents of their boxes.

In permitting accesses to safe deposit boxes, a procedure similar to the following, and which should be reviewed and approved by the bank's legal counsel, should be used:

EXHIBIT 109

SAFE DEPOSIT BOX KEY ACKNOWLEDGEMENT RECORD

I, WE, the undersigned, having rented Safe No. __________ at $__________ a year in the vault of BANK OF CHICAGO, hereafter called lessor, acknowledge receipt of TWO keys to said safe, and agree to the Rules and Regulations of the lessor in force at this date and such additional Rules and Regulations as may be hereafter adopted.

Date______________________ ______________________

Witness ______________________

______________________ ______________________

Keys issued by

______________________ ______________________

The contents of Safe No.__________ in the vault of BANK OF CHICAGO having been removed, the said safe with ______ keys is surrendered by (me) (us) and said lessor is hereby released from all liability by the undersigned.

Date______________________ ______________________

Witness ______________________

______________________ ______________________

Keys surrendered to

______________________ ______________________

PAYMENT RECORD

Date Billed	Amount	Date Paid	Date Billed	Amount	Date Paid

Weight	Height	Eyes	Birth Date	Mother's Maiden Name	SIGNATURE

BILLING ADDRESS	Special Instructions

Number Signatures Required	Type of Account	Individual	Joint A/C	Ptnsp.	Corp.	Ass'n.

Safe No.	Name	RENTAL DATE											
		Jan.	Feb.	Mar.	Apr.	May	June	July	Aug.	Sep.	Oct.	Nov.	Dec.

1. The renter should be asked to show the attendant his key. This is to identify the key as belonging to the bank.

2. The renter should be asked to sign the access slip and to list the number of the box. Sometimes the record of box renters is made by the number and others by name. Having both the name and number on the access slip sometimes eliminates the need for referring to the cross reference file.

If the person is not known personally, the renter should be requested to enter the number and sign the access slip after which it is compared with the contract or signature card on file. Particular attention should be made to the way a stranger signs an access slip. If the signature is made rapidly, you have the first assurance that the individual signing the slip is the person he claims to be. If, however, the person wishing access signs his name very slowly or seems to be drawing it, you have a right to be suspicious. The suspect could be a forger, as generally forgers do not write their names freely but are said to draw signatures. In cases of this kind, identification marks such as the color of eyes, identifying birthmarks, peculiarities of teeth, dress, etc., may be of help in corroborating identification of the person wishing access. Where banks follow a practice of using an access card for use with a time stamp device, they should guard against having the cards in an open bin accessible to anyone who enters the vault. Such cards should be maintained under close scrutiny of the clerk and only made available to the renter upon positive identification.

The signature on every access slip should be checked with the contract or access records to be certain that the signatures are authorized.

In the case of corporations, the authorization comes from the board of directors who pass a resolution, a copy of which is filed with the bank. Such resolution authorizes the bank to permit access to the box to certain individuals and is a binding order until it is rescinded. To be certain that no changes have been authorized it is necessary to check the signature on every access slip with the record.

In the case of a joint account, signatures which can be verified should be on file. The card should be scrutinized to be certain that the formal contract has not been changed and that the person presenting the key and wishing access has the right to present access.

In connection with an agent or a person operating under power of attorney, as such authorizations may be rescinded without notice to the deputy or to the person holding the power of attorney, current authorization should be determined by referring to the contract.

Safe deposit departments which are operated properly require the renter to sign an access slip regardless of how well he is known to the vault clerk. Also, to avoid omissions of carelessness, the signature on every access slip should be checked by the clerk against the safe deposit box contract record to avoid claim of negligence, or the charge of carelessness which can be brought about through familiarity with the renter. It is only through continuous observance of this rule that the clerk can ascertain that the renter has the right of access to a particular box. Whenever a clerk, in checking the signature on the access slip, is in doubt either as to the signature or person applying for access, or documents presented to authorize access, the matter should immediately be referred to an officer or person of authority.

Banks, through services rendered by their safe deposit departments, assume great responsibility as to accesses, so much so that it is a cardinal rule that no one, not even a relative, must be admitted to a safe deposit box unless he has the proper legal authority or has his signature registered with the bank on the contract.

3. The clerk or attendant should also note on the access slip the number of persons, if any, who accompany the renter. This could be important. Also, if the renter is accompanied by others and seems nervous; or it appears that access is being requested under duress, the attendant should excuse himself and notify an officer or person of authority of his apprehension.

4. Once identification has been established and the access slip approved by the attendant by initialing and the time of the access marked on the card, the customer is taken to the vault to obtain his box. Once inside the vault and the box is located, the attendant should request the renter to place his own key into the box door, after which the vault attendant places the guard key in the lock and opens the door of the box. In a large bank, the work

of the access clerk differs from that of the vault attendant, in which case the renter will present the access slip to the vault attendant who will handle the access and will place his initials on the slip as evidence that he was the one who permitted the box to be removed.

5. After the compartment door is opened, the vault clerk or attendant should ask the renter to handle his own box. Sometimes this is very inconvenient due to the location of the box. However, once the box is removed, it should be immediately placed in the hands of the renter and the renter escorted to the coupon room.

Should it be necessary, because of circumstances, for the attendant to carry the box to the coupon room for the renter, which sometimes happens in the case of elderly persons, the attendant should be certain, or endeavor to see, that the box is kept at all times in full sight of the renter. The best way this is done is for the attendant to walk close by the side of the renter with the box held so that it can be seen at all times.

6. After the box is removed from the compartment, the clerk or attendant should close the door, remove the guard key, return the key to the renter and lead the renter to the coupon room where he can examine or have access to the contents of his box without being disturbed.

7. After the renter has been taken to the coupon room, the clerk or attendant should index the number of the room on the access slip as a record that the renter in question used a particular room, at a certain time, on a certain day.

8. When the renter returns from using his box in the coupon room, the clerk or attendant should ask the renter to insert his key in the compartment lock, after which the clerk or attendant inserts the guard key. When the door is opened, the renter is requested to replace the box in the compartment, close and lock the compartment door and remove his key, after which the clerk or attendant removes the guard key.

9. After the access is completed, the clerk or attendant should initial the access ticket in the space provided as evidence he was in attendance when the box was replaced in the compartment, and mark the time at which the compartment door was locked.

10. The coupon room used by the renter should then be ex-

amined and the initials of the clerk or attendant who examined the room affixed to the access ticket in the space provided or on a special record designed for that purpose.

The purpose of this procedure is not only to make sure that the booth is clean before someone else uses it, but also make certain that the last customer did not overlook any item which might have been removed from the box and left it on the counter; and to check the waste basket to see that nothing of value has been thrown away, misplaced or fallen into the waste basket by accident. In examining the booth, which usually contains a desk or a counter, the clerk should lift up the blotter, if there is one, move around the inkwell and make certain there is nothing under it. The clerk should also carefully scrutinize the floor, examine any cracks or holes in which small articles such as a jewel or ring might be lodged. Should the booth not be equipped with good lighting, it is a good practice for the attendant examining the booth to make use of a flashlight.

Safe deposit procedure usually provides for waste baskets to be emptied in one place after a coupon room has been used. In doing so, one piece of paper at a time should be removed, examined and only be disposed of permanently when the attendant is certain that the paper is worthless and of no value. If there is any possibility at all that the paper might be valuable, it should be placed in an envelope on which is indexed the number of the coupon booth, name of the last renter together with the box number and should be referred to an officer, who may or may not contact the customer depending upon the value of the article. The wise policy, of course, is to refer the matter to an officer who will call the customer if the article appears to be of value. By handling the item in such a manner, very often the matter can be disposed of immediately, sometimes before the renter discovers something is lost or missing.

If the article found is of value, it should be indexed in a register by description, date, time, number of coupon room where found, name and box number of renter who last used the room, and placed under proper control to be delivered only to the owner on proper receipt.

As a precautionary measure, and to prevent the use of the coupon booth without being examined after being used by a customer, safe deposit booths are usually equipped with special locks, the doors of which can only be opened from the outside with a key, so that once a customer is inside the booth no one else may have access. Under such an arrangement, once a customer leaves the coupon booth, the door automatically locks and is not placed in "ready order" until the attendant has had the opportunity to examine the booth. As a means of determining whether or not a booth is still occupied and in use, the doors to most safe deposit booths are composed of a glass panel through which a reflection may be seen from the outside or have a space underneath the door where it is possible for the attendant to see the feet of the person occupying the booth.

In addition to contracts, cross reference files, and access records, most banks also maintain a vault record for use of the auditor or control officer, which lists by days, the time the vault containing the safe deposit boxes is opened; by whom it is opened; the time the timer is set; the persons who set the timer; the time the vault is closed; and the persons who effected the closing of the vault.

RESTRICTIONS ON ACCESSES UPON DEATH OF LESSEE. The death of a renter of a safe deposit box, in most cases, alters the relationship.

When the box is maintained in the name of an individual, death precludes access by anyone else except on a court order or by the accredited representative of the estate. Certain states, however, permit the opening of a box by next of kin to search for a will, cemetery deed, or any other document essential to closing the estate. Upon the death of an individual, any power of attorney becomes null and void.

In some states, under certain conditions which should be clearly set forth by the bank's legal counsel for the guidance of those who have responsibility for handling safe deposit operation, a safe deposit box can only be opened on court order and in the presence of representatives of the state or federal taxing body, at which time an inventory is made of the contents of the safe deposit box.

In cases where the box is rented to individuals in joint tenancy with right of survivorship or as co-lessee, if one of the parties dies, sometimes it is necessary for the survivor to be present before access is permitted to any accredited representative of the estate of the decedent. In other states the death of a person other than an individual or co-lessee does not serve to interfere with access by those authorized to have access. Each case, depending on the state, must be covered by rules and regulations approved by the bank's legal counsel.

The death of an individual acting in a fiduciary capacity, usually precludes any access to the box except through a successor appointed by the court; or receiving appointment from the same source as the original appointment was made.

The death of one of the signers in the case of a partnership, unless the contract provided for right of survivorship, automatically stops access to the box unless authorization is shown.

To provide protection for the bank and to parties of interest, whenever notice of a death or incompetency of an individual to act is called to the attention of a bank, records should be marked and access refused unless approved by terms of the contract or under provisions of the law.

TERMINATION OF LEASEHOLD, OR SURRENDER OF A SAFE DEPOSIT BOX. In connection with the surrender of a safe deposit box, banks follow certain procedures, for the protection of the bank and the safeguarding of the articles which have been kept in a safe deposit box.

Generally, when a box is to be given up and the lease terminated, the customer either brings his keys to the bank and announces he wishes to terminate the lease on the safe deposit box; mails the keys to the bank upon receiving notice of the rental due; or makes a customary access to the safe deposit box, after which he stops by the attendant's desk and turns in the keys.

When the customer either brings in his keys before making an access or turns in the keys after making an access, it is sound procedure for the attendant to ask the renter to accompany him to the safe deposit box so they can jointly examine the box to be sure that nothing has been left in the box; and then to have the renter sign the termination acknowledgement on the contract.

If keys are mailed in, it is the customary procedure for the vault attendant to examine the box in company with some other employee; and to jointly sign the termination agreement on the contract attaching thereto the letter received from the renter.

Whenever a box is given up; surrendered, or the lease terminated; in order to be certain there is no possibility of the former renter having duplicate keys made to effect access at a later date, the keys are stapled together with a tag showing the box which has been used and set aside. Periodically, a representative of a safe and lock company or the locksmith, following established procedure, takes these keys; removes the lock from the safe deposit box; mixes up the locks; places them on different safe deposit boxes; and places the keys in a sealed envelope for use by the next box renter. This provides absolute assurance that such keys to a lock of a safe deposit box rented to a new customer are especially for him and that no one else can have access to the box.

PROCEDURE FOR COLLECTION OF RENTALS FOR SAFE DEPOSIT BOXES. Generally the procedure for collecting rentals for safe deposit boxes follows one of two systems. In some banks the rents on all safe deposit boxes become due and payable on the same day each year. Under such circumstances each time a box is rented, the rental and the tax is adjusted for the unexpired term.

Under the other and most frequently used system which is by far the most simple from an accounting standpoint, the safe deposit boxes are rented for one year in advance of the date of the rental which, of course, eliminates adjustment both from a tax standpoint and rental adjustment standpoint. In collecting rents for renewals of box leaseholds, the customary practice is to send a notice 10 days in advance. Such notice, similar to that in Exhibit 110, consists of an original which is the notice; a duplicate which is the second notice; a triplicate which is the receipt for payment; a quadruplicate which is the credit to the general ledger income account "safe deposit box rents received," while the quintuplicate is the register.

If the renter of a safe deposit box is a customer of the bank, very often it is the practice to charge the account of the customer for the amount of the rent and taxes due. Where this is not the practice, checks on other banks, given in payment of box rent should be noted on the register by number and name of bank; and if the account is different from the name in which the box is rented, this also should be noted.

LOST KEYS. In connection with lost keys, safe deposit departments usually follow the following procedure.

If one key is lost, the customer is required to return the duplicate in exchange for two keys to a new lock which is inserted in the present safe deposit box.

If both keys are lost, the services of a locksmith are required to drill the lock on the box to effect entry, after which the customer is given two new keys to a new lock which is inserted in the box. The records, of course, are changed accordingly. In case it is necessary to replace a lock due to loss of one or both keys, it is the general practice for safe deposit departments to require the renter to pay for the cost of drilling the box and for the installation of the new lock.

In addition to providing safe deposit box facilities, banks also provide what is known as storage facilities.

In providing storage service, which is separate and distinct

EXHIBIT 110

SAFE DEPOSIT BOX NOTICE FORM

FIRST NATIONAL BANK
ILLINOIS

The annual rental on your Safe Deposit Box is due as indicated.

Box No. Due

Annual Rental $________

Tax $________

Total Amount Due $________

By________

FIRST NOTICE

Form No. 10 Copyright 1944, Marshall Corns & Co., Chicago

from safe deposit service, the bank acts as a warehouse; and provides, for a fee, space for storage of unidentified, undescribed items contained in a locked trunk; sealed packages or sealed crates usually used for the storage of rugs, paintings, family heirlooms, silverware, manuscripts, valuable books and papers. Such items as are left for storage are covered by the customer's own insurance. The bank assumes no liability beyond ordinary diligence and care unless otherwise formally provided in writing.

Banks which provide safe deposit facilities, in addition to providing physical protection and safeguards, should see to it, in order to efficiently and safely operate, that from an overall functional responsibility standpoint:

A. Contracts and agreements for handling the relationship between the box renter and the bank are reduced to formalized instructions approved by the banks legal counsel.

B. Personnel, to whom are delegated responsibility for performing functions in connection with safe deposit work, understand the rules and operating procedures established for conducting the affairs of the department.

C. Personnel are sufficiently familiar with other departments, divisions and sections of the bank, and are informed on the various services provided to intelligently answer questions which may be asked of them.

As it is assumed personnel have been made familiar with the bank and services provided through study of a handbook; and contracts and agreements have been approved by the bank's legal counsel; our principal concern is in connection with carrying out the operations of the safe deposit department and observing the following standard rules adopted by most banks, in this or similar form, for their own protection and the protection of box renters.

1. All renters of safe deposit boxes must be positively identified.

2. Contracts should be properly signed and, wherever required, accompanied by agreements warranted under the circumstances.

3. Records should show the addresses of all renters, together with suitable identification.

4. Keys, as a matter of additional protection, should not bear the name of the bank.

5. The bank, as a matter of policy protection, should not hold keys for customers, as by doing so it has full control of the access.

6. Access to a safe deposit box should only be permitted to authorized persons.

7. No access to a box will be permitted unless the access slip is signed and approved by authorized personnel of the safe deposit department.

8. Keys shall not be left in the safe deposit box door after the customer removes the box and takes it to a coupon room. The box should be locked shut and keys maintained in possession of the renter at all times to preclude claim that someone made an impression (wax mold) from which a duplicate was made.

9. Booths must be carefully searched for misplaced items after each use.

10. When a box is given up or lease terminated, both keys must be returned, the lock interchanged, and new keys sealed in an envelope maintained under dual control until released to a new renter.

11. If a safe deposit key is lost or stolen, the customer should immediately report such loss to the safe deposit departments, and upon release of the remaining key obtain a new box and a new lock.

12. Should both keys be lost or stolen, the services of a locksmith must be obtained since the lock must be drilled, at the expense of the customer, so as to replace it with a new lock and key.

13. If a safe deposit key is found on the premises, it should be immediately placed in the proper custody and if when claimed, upon proper identification, should be turned over to the safe deposit department with the other key and the box exchanged for a new box with a new lock.

In the operation of a safe deposit department, the following are a few of the operating instructions which would be in use:

1. Schedule of safe deposit box rentals.
2. Identification of renters or lessees of safe deposit boxes.
3. Policy of the bank in connection with lost safe deposit keys.
4. Recording of the time of entrance to a safe deposit box.

CHAPTER XXXVII

THE TRUST DEPARTMENT

BANKS WHICH HAVE BEEN GRANTED TRUST powers provide many important, technical, and highly specialized services. Some of these services, as we shall learn, originated many centuries ago. Others have been originated in recent years by the trust departments of banks to assist individuals and businesses in conducting their financial affairs. All developed, however, from the ever increasing need for some vehicle to provide fiduciary services or to act in fiduciary capacity.

In studying the early relationships between goldsmiths and persons of wealth we learned that people often left gold, silver and other objects of value with the goldsmith for safekeeping. The reason the goldsmith was selected was because people had confidence in him—they believed he was honest—and they trusted him. They also recognized the desirability, under certain conditions, of having someone stand in their place and act in their behalf to safeguard their property and protect their families in the event of their death.

From this need there grew a relationship under which a man gave or willed his property to another to be used or managed in accordance with his wishes. Originally this was for the purpose of safeguarding and managing his property and providing income for his wife and children until his oldest son became of age and became head of the family. The person to whom he delegated this responsibility became known as a trustee. By the terms of a written document, he directed this person to take, administer, and manage the property which he owned for a specified time when the estate should be distributed or turned over to the son as oldest heir for further management.

It wasn't long, however, before it became a matter of common knowledge that private individuals did not make the best executors or trustees. Often they lacked the experience and inclination to perform the work efficiently and economically. Frequently private trustees made mistakes of omission or commission and unfortunately, in many cases, did not possess the financial responsibility to make good these mistakes.

In addition, individuals acting as trustees often got sick, took vacations, moved away or became incompetent to act. Sometimes, too, they died in the midst of handling the trust which caused confusion, delay and expense in appointing a successor. There also were many cases, unfortunately, where the property of the trust was comingled or mixed up with the property of someone else.

It gradually became quite apparent that there was need for a trustee in whom would be combined the qualities of ability, availability, honesty and financial responsibility; and for laws to protect beneficiaries of such trusts against dishonest acts of trustees. It was evident, however, that no law or statute acts against death or the constant availability of the trustee. As time went on it became obvious that only a corporation, because of the continuity of its existence, could supply these factors which are vital and essential to a sound and competent trusteeship. For these reasons, the use of qualified institutions as executors, trustees and agents became a matter of common adoption and necessity.

Originally corporations were licensed only to conduct trust business, that is, acting in fiduciary capacity. Later, because of circumstances peculiar to the area in which they served, they accepted time deposits. Many institutions today, as evidence of that situation, have the name Trust Company or Trust & Savings Bank in their name. Later, with the development and expansion of the country, such institutions were given the right to accept commercial deposits.

Trust services, in one form or another, touch upon practically every phase of our personal and business life. It is of great importance, therefore, that all employees of a bank are made familiar with the services their bank has to offer through the facilities of their trust department so they can at all times recognize how and when such services and facilities can be used profitably by customers and friends.

The services provided by trust departments of banks in America have developed along well defined and distinctive lines. First of all, a trust institution is a corporation engaged under authority of law in the business of settling estates, administering trusts, and performing agency services for individuals, partnerships, associations, business corporations; and for public, social, educational, recreational and charitable institutions, and even for units of government. Secondly, such a corporation continues to have full power, authority, and responsibility even though it is engaged in other kinds of business. Today, however, there are only a few corporations engaged exclusively in trust business. The great majority of trust institutions or corporations which are permitted by law to provide trust services are also engaged in banking, with the results that there are trust companies with banking departments and banks with trust departments.

According to Mr. Gilbert T. Stephenson, author of *The American System of Trust Business* and widely known authority to whom this author is indebted for much of the early history of trust business and other material, the first corporation in the United States to receive expressed powers to engage in the trust business was the Farmers Fire Insurance and Loan Company (later the City Bank Farmers Trust Company of New York and now, in 1961, part of the First National City Bank of New York). It received its charter from the State of New York on February 28, 1822 to engage in the loan and insurance business. In April of that year the charter was amended, following which the company was granted trust powers.

During the next few years other corporations began to exercise trust powers. The New York Life Insurance and Trust Company (now the Bank of New York) assumed a guardianship in 1831. A living trusteeship was accepted in 1835 by the Pennsylvania Company for Insurance on Lives and Granting Annuities. In 1839, the Girard Life Insurance Annuity & Trust Company (now, 1961, the Girard Trust Corn Exchange Bank, Philadelphia) accepted both an administratorship and executorship.

Prior to 1850, even though a number of banks had trust powers, they did not provide trust services in the modern sense of the term. Most of their activity was in the nature of savings banking, such as the issuance of interest bearing certificates of deposit and the investing of funds of individual customers.

The development of trust services to corporations came later.

In 1836 the Pennsylvania Company for Insurance on Lives and Granting Annuities and the Girard Life Insurance Annuity and Trust Company received express authorization, under their charter, to execute corporate trusts. In 1839 the Girard Life Insurance Annuity & Trust Company served as trustee under a bond issue. It is said that the first instance in which a corporation chartered to execute trusts served as a registrar and transfer agent for a corporation in connection with an issue of stock was in 1864. As late as 1865 no corporation was serving as a trustee under any one of the 17 railroad bond issues then outstanding, and it was not until 1890 that the practice of naming individuals as trustees, under corporate bond issues, practically ceased.

The providing of full trust functions through the development of American trust institutions has only taken place since 1890. At that time there were only 63 trust companies in the United States all of which were chartered by respective states. Within the next 10 years, however, events occurred which rapidly developed trust business, foremost of which was the organization of a Trust Company Section of the American Bankers Association in 1896; and the holding of the first meeting in Detroit in 1897. This meeting not only served to form a common bond between corporations providing trust facilities, but to focus the attention of the American people upon the valuable services being offered by such trust institutions.

The authority of a corporation to engage in trust business and provide trust facilities, according to Mr. Stephenson, is a granted and not inherent or implied right. The corporation does not acquire authority to engage in trust business merely by obtaining a charter. Such right must be obtained either from the federal government, in the case of national institutions, or from the state government in the case of other institutions. In order for a corporation to obtain authority it first must satisfy the requirements of the supervisory agencies of the charter granting department of the federal or state government and comply with all the rules and regulations. Even after a corporation has obtained the charter powers to engage in trust business, it must, in most states, also secure a license to begin to engage in the trust business.

Each state has the right to prescribe the conditions upon

which a corporation may do trust business within its borders, and all corporations, whether local or out of state, either federally or state chartered, must meet the individual requirements.

Prior to 1913 the right to engage in the business of serving trusts was confined to banks and corporations licensed by the state in which they intended to engage in business. In 1913, however, national banks were granted trust powers under regulations of the Federal Reserve Act.

It is well to know, however, regardless of whether the charter is granted by the federal government or the state, the power to engage in trust business in one state does not carry with it the power to engage in trust business in another state.

In obtaining a license to engage in trust business, a corporation, whether a state chartered bank or trust company, national bank or other corporation, must apply to the authority of the state which grants licenses to engage in trust business, usually the state banking department, which then investigates the needs of the community, the fitness of the applicant to engage in trust business and either issues or refuses the license.

A national bank, in addition, must apply to and receive its license from the Board of Governors of the Federal Reserve System. The license is granted only after investigation as to the need of the community for a trust institution and the fitness of the applicant to render trust services.

Before engaging in trust business or exercising trust powers, banks and other corporations must comply with certain legal requirements of the state in which they are licensed to do business, among which are:

1. The capital or capital and surplus must be of a certain amount.
2. The corporation must deposit with the designated state authority a required amount of securities for the special protection of trust property.
3. Operations of the trust department must be subject to periodical examination by the supervisory authority of the state in which the bank or trust corporation is doing business.

Should these periodical examinations indicate that the corporation is not properly equipped to engage in trust business or properly exercising its authority and responsibility, the license to engage in trust business may be revoked by the same agency which granted the license in the first place.

Regulation "F" of the Board of Governors of the Federal Reserve System, under which all national banks exercise trust powers, provides that before they are licensed to act in a fiduciary capacity a national bank must provide space for a trust department which must be separate and apart from every other department of the bank. This same provision is required by the laws of several states and is a sound provision inasmuch as it is essential that the property of the bank be kept separately from the property entrusted to it in fiduciary capacity; and that property entrusted to the bank by one customer be kept separate and distinct from the property entrusted to it by another customer.

BASIC PRINCIPLES OF TRUST BUSINESS

All trust institutions in conducting their business are governed and guided by the cardinal principles common to those acting in a fiduciary capacity; that is, fidelity, integrity and respect for the confidential relationship which should never be revealed except when required by law.

It should be remembered that trust institutions or corporations exercise their rights and privileges under authority of law, and although operating as a private institution, in relationship to customers, must be ready at all times to give full information of their own financial responsibility, their staff, equipment and safeguards thrown around trust business.

The underlying principles under which trust institutions operate have been formulated, approved and adopted by the Trust Division of the American Bankers Association and approved by the executive council of the American Bankers Association, as well as by corporate fiduciary associations and other associations composed of institutions engaged in trust business. In complying with these principles, certain of which should be of interest to all students of banking, any trust institution should:

1. Limit its functions to settling estates, administering trusts, performing agency services in all appropriate cases for individuals,

partnerships, associations, business corporations, public, educational, social, recreational, and charitable institutions and units of government.

2. Carry out the wishes of the creator of the trust as expressed in the trust instrument.

3. Administer a trust solely in the interest of a beneficiary without permitting the intrusion of interests of the trustees or a third party that may in any way conflict with the interest of the trust.

4. Keep accurate accounts with respect to the administration of the trust.

5. Keep the beneficiaries acquainted with all material facts in connection with the trust.

6. Exercise the care a prudent man familiar with such matters would exercise as trustee of the property of others, adhering to the rule that a trustee is primarily a conserver in administering the trust.

7. Keep the properties of each trust separate from those of all other trusts; and also from the property of the trust institution.

8. Devote all the care and skill it can reasonably acquire to its trust investments.

9. Only buy, retain, or sell securities in a trust account upon the authority of the investment committee composed of capable and experienced officers or directors of the institution.

10. Promptly seek the guidance of the court in verifying or interpreting the terms of a trust instrument, should it become unlawful, impossible, or against public policy to literally follow the terms of the trust instrument.

11. Not buy from or sell to estates or trusts any securities or other property in which the trust institution has any personal or financial interest.

While banks employ many men with law degrees or former practicing attorneys to act in administrative capacity on behalf of the bank in administering trust accounts, it is a well understood and ethical principal of conduct that such men will not draft wills, or will such trust institutions engage in the practice of law.

It is, however, a common practice and policy of most banks providing trust services to employ the attorney of the testator, or creator of a trust, for such legal services as may be necessary.

Banks, however, reserve the right to employ other counsel if in their opinion the best interests of the estate or the beneficiary require it. Further, banks generally comply with any wishes expressed in writing by the creator of the trust regarding the employment of certain brokers, life insurance counsellors, accountants, realtors or other professional representatives, although reserving the right to employ their own advisor if in their opinion it becomes necessary to efficiently and properly carry out the terms of the trust.

Before discussing some of the specific services which banks are prepared to render, a statement concerning bank trusteeships in general may be helpful. Unfortunately the business of trusteeship has often been regarded, even by bank people themselves, as too complex and technical for the average person to understand. Not only is bank trusteeship simple to comprehend but likewise challenging in its possibilities for constructive service to others.

The essence of trust service is simply taking care of other people's property, its management for the living and its conservation for the dependents of those who have died. In the main a trustee is simply in the business of property management.

Depending on the circumstances, the trustee, to a limited or large extent, handles the finances and performs all the administrative details of the estate, including the investment and reinvestment of the property for the benefit of the persons named in the will or trust agreement. In some cases women must be helped in the management of their incomes, homes, and living conditions, and with the education of their children. Frequently the trustee must assume the management of a business. Sometimes such properties comprise the principal assets of the trust and the good or ill-fortune of the whole estate may depend upon proper handling by the trustee. Nevertheless, whether in small or large degree, this is simply a matter of caring for other people's property.

It is also well to remember that every estate, that is real and personal property that a person has possession of or owns at the time of his death, must be settled and administered by someone unless it is so small that it is considered to be a no administration matter.

If a person dies without a will, his estate is settled by an administrator. If he dies leaving a will, his estate is settled by an executor.

In the former case, the administrator is appointed by the court on the petition of the heirs or of creditors. Although members of the family, if they are willing and competent to act, are entitled to preference, it is possible in some cases that an utter stranger may become the administrator. If they so desire, the members of the family may relinquish their right to the administration by nominating a disinterested person or a trust institution to serve as the administrator.

In the case of a will, a property owner has the right to select his own administrator by expressly naming him in his will. In that case the court will respect his choice provided the person named in the will is still living, is not dishonest and is not incompetent.

The contribution a trust institution makes to a community is measured in terms of its influence on the economic wealth of the community and upon the welfare of beneficiaries.

It is not, nor was it ever the intention that a trust department or trust institution be designed for the production of wealth but for the purpose of conserving wealth. Through the course of years a trust institution properly managed conserves and protects the property and funds placed in its care. Without this careful handling much of the property left, if placed in inexperienced or incapable hands, would be lost or dissipated.

Wherever there is a trust institution there are several different classes of people to whom trust services are particularly designed. These are the immature, those inexperienced in property management and those incapacitated. Sound trust administration requires that the property be conserved and invested on behalf of these individuals so as to produce a regular income consistent with safety and geared to the protection of the principal.

Recognizing the need for such services, the question logically arises as to whether a trust institution or individual can more uniformly render the most satisfactory service. While it is agreed that an individual could possess all of the qualifications necessary to competently act in fiduciary capacity, there are, however, certain recognized and admitted advantages in having a trust institution act over an individual in rendering services such as:

1. CONTINUED EXISTENCE. A trust institution is not subject to illness, incapacity, absence or death to which every indivdual is subject.

2. EXPERIENCE AND SPECIALIZATION. Bank administration brings to every trust account the combined skill and experience of trained individuals, people who have made banking, investments and property management a profession in all of its legal, technical and confidential aspects.

3. DECISIONS BASED ON GROUP JUDGEMENT. National banks by regulation, and many state banks under the law of respective states, are required to have the acceptance and administration of all trust accounts approved by a trust investment committee of at least three members who must be capable and experienced officers or directors.

4. ACCESS TO CREDIT, INVESTMENT AND FINANCIAL INFORMATION. Being licensed to administer trusts, such institutions undertake extensive research and maintain extensive records which are used in the investment of funds and the conducting of trust business.

5. FINANCIAL RESPONSIBILITY. Unless a qualified trust institution is appointed, any individual appointed administrator, executor, trustee or guardian is generally required, under the law, to post bond with the county or state for the faithful performance of his duty, regardless of whether or not the will exempts the individual from giving such bond. The expense of these surety bonds is usually substantial and is paid by the estate, with the result that the annual renewal continues as expense during the life of the estate.

The state laws under which most trust institutions act exempt them from giving such bonds because the institutions must deposit securities with the state treasurer for the special and continuous protection of trust assets and trust funds against mistakes or wrongdoings of the institution. In addition, the entire resources of every trust institution stand behind all trust obligations.

6. GOVERNMENT SUPERVISION. While it is true that the

courts have the same jurisdiction over individuals, executors, administrators, trustees and others acting in fiduciary capacity as they have over trust institutions, trust institutions are subject to periodic and unexpected examinations by officials of the state banking authority, Federal Reserve System, Comptroller of the Currency, and the Federal Deposit Insurance Corporation.

Individual fiduciaries, on the other hand, are not subject to governmental supervision, therefore, such trust accounts do not receive the benefit of constructive suggestions or corrective regulations which may be suggested.

7. AUDITING, VAULT AND INSURANCE SAFEGUARDS. In addition to financial responsibility and government supervision, the trust departments of most banks are subject to continuous audit and control, and not only are proper vaults provided where securities are to be maintained with safety, but proper insurance is carried as additional protection for the assets of the trust.

8. LEGAL PROTECTION. In addition, bankers through long practice and experience are better qualified than an individual to determine if the provisions of a will are unworkable or against public policy, thus providing further assurance of the careful administration of such trusts in conformance with the express wishes of the testator, by referring such matters to the court for decision.

Before describing the various trust functions of banks or institutions chartered to exercise trust functions, it might be well to again define some of the principal terms used in describing the function of a trust department, trust instruments, and action taken in administering trusts.

1. *Administrator.* One appointed by the court in the absence of a will to settle an estate.

2. *Agent.* One who acts for, and in behalf, and with the authority of, another.

3. *Beneficiary.* The person who derives the benefits from property held in trust.

4. *Codicil.* An amendment to a will. An instrument which adds to, takes from, or changes the terms of a will.

5. *Corpus.* The amount represented by all types of assets which comprise an estate.

6. *Executor.* The one named in a will to settle an estate.

7. *Holographic Will.* One that is written wholly and completely in the handwriting of the testator, and which contains the name of the testator.

8. *Intestate.* A person who dies without leaving a will.

9. *Letters of Administration.* An instrument in writing issued by a court having jurisdiction over the settling of an estate of persons leaving no will, authorizing the person appointed as administrator to settle the estate.

10. *Letters Testamentary.* An instrument in writing issued by a court having jurisdiction over the probate of wills empowering the executor named in the will to dispose of the estate in accordance with its terms.

11. *Nuncupative Will.* A will made by word of mouth and generally applying only to personal property and in amount depending on the laws of respective states. It is generally used by soldiers or sailors in active service, or by persons on their deathbeds, in stating how they wish their personal property to be distributed. Such wills, depending again on the state, are only valid when the person who made such a will dies within a specified number of days or is unable to make an ordinary will and where the witness reduce the statements to writing.

12. *Principal.* A fund which is invested for the purpose of yielding income – also the donor or person who creates a trust relationship or grants authority to another to act in his behalf.

13. *Probate.* The term given to a document and action which constitutes the legal proof of a will.

14. *Settlor.* One who creates a trust by agreement or declaration.

15. *Testate.* A person who dies leaving a valid will.

16. *Testator.* One who makes a will.

17. *Trust.* A situation where one person holds legal title to property and another person is entitled to the benefit derived from such property.

18. *Trustee.* A person holding legal title to a property for the benefit of another person or persons entitled to the benefit derived from such property.

19. *Will.* An instrument by which a person may direct to whom, and upon what terms, his estate shall go at his death; or a legal declaration of a person's desires concerning the disposition of his property to take effect after his death.

A trust may be created by will, by agreement, declaration, or order or court; or it may be the outgrowth of a relationship between certain parties; or might arise by operation of a law because of a relationship between parties.

Perhaps the best known of all trust services rendered by banks is that of settling estates of deceased persons by acting as executor, or trustee. When a person dies, the property of the estate must be administered according to law; that is, the assets must be inventoried; debts, death taxes, state taxes, if any, paid; and the remaining assets distributed to the heirs at law.

Every individual in the United States, subject to certain exceptions, who is 21 years of age or over, and of sound mind, may make a will disposing of his or her property. There are exceptions to this general rule, however. In some states the legal age for making a will is different for a man than for a woman, while in other states a married person may make a valid will even though under 21 years of age.

If a person who dies leaves a will, he is said to die testate and the one named to settle the estate is referred to as the executor. While the court generally makes the appointment of an executor, it usually appoints the executor named in the will, unless, of course, there are compelling reasons why they should not do so. Where more than one person is appointed, they are known as co-executors.

If a person dies intestate; that is, without making a will, or the executor named in a will is unable or refuses to serve, the court must appoint some other individual to settle the estate in accordance with the terms of the will. Individuals, or a bank so appointed, who settle an estate in the absence of a will, are known as the administrator with the will annexed. Where the court appoints two or more administrators, they are known as co-administrators.

Strange as it may seem, many persons who pride themselves on being reasonably good business executives fail to make wills.

Not to make a will is probably one of the most slip-shod things a person can do in respect to his property and family.

If one dies without a will, the property is divided in accordance with state law known as the statute of descents which directs the court to allot the estate to the heirs and next of kin in certain amounts and in the order of priority fixed by that law. This law is inflexible and under it persons in the immediate family sometimes do not inherit as much of the estate as the head of the family intended them to receive.

The only way to be sure that one's property will be divided exactly as intended is to make a will in which is expressed exactly who shall receive the estate, in what amounts, and how it shall be managed.

If properly drawn and executed, the courts and the world will uphold and respect such a will. It is a business-like act and may save many heartaches, misunderstandings, dissentions, spurious and far-fetched claims of distant kin. It takes but a short time to make a will and lawyers are usually very modest in their charges for drafting it.

If a person intends to appoint a bank as executor or trustee, it is always a good practice to consult with the bank before actually completing or executing the will in order to inform the bank of the duties and responsibilities it is expected to discharge, so that objections, if any, can be reconciled and advantage taken of the many good recommendations and suggestions a bank can make by virtue of its wide experience in such matters.

Trust services of banks fall into two principal classifications; those performed for, or in behalf of individuals, known as personal trust services; and those performed for, or in behalf of corporations, known as corporate trust services.

PERSONAL TRUST SERVICES

Personal trust services, in order of importance, are those where the bank acts for individuals in the capacity of:

Executor
Administrator
Guardian
Trustee
Agent

or has available facilities to provide services in connection with:

Estate planning
Investment counselling

Executor. The procedure followed by an executor in settling or winding up an estate, may be grouped under five principal headings.

1. Obtaining proper authority from the court to settle the estate.
2. Assembling the assets of the estate.
3. Safeguarding the assets of the estate.
4. Paying the debts and other charges of the deceased or estate.
5. Distributing the net estate to the beneficiaries.

Obtaining Authority from the Court to Settle the Estate. The first step in the settling of an estate is to obtain the authority from the court to settle the estate. Where a deceased person leaves a will, it is usually presented to the court a few days after death, whereupon the court, variously called a probate court, surrogate court, orphans court, or ordinary court, examines the witnesses to the effect that the deceased person signed or acknowledged his or her signature to the will and that, in their opinion, the testator was of sound mind when he or she did so.

When the court is satisfied the individual or trust institution named as executor is the proper one to settle the estate, it issues letters testamentary which constitute the authority of the executor to proceed with the settling of the estate.

Assembling the Assets of the Estate. Once the executor receives letters testamentary his responsibility is to assemble the assets and bring them under his control. This includes the transferring of bank or brokerage accounts of the deceased to the name of the executor; taking possession of all securities and contents of safe deposit boxes; collecting life insurance payable to the estate; taking charge of the business of the deceased and either managing it, arranging to close it out or for it to be carried on, collecting any open accounts and securing any claims due the estate.

Safeguarding the Assets of the Estate. As the assets are assembled, the executor takes steps to safeguard them, which includes the proper inventory and appraisal as required by law. If the decedent was engaged in business at the time of his death, the business must either be liquidated or reorganized as in the absence of court order or express authority in the will an executor is not permitted to carry on the business and take the additional risk.

In this connection it might be necessary for the executor (or trustee) to compromise and adjust claims owed by, or due to the estate by virtue of the business enterprise; dispose of perishable goods; take over the protection of certain valuables and personal property such as works of art, heirlooms, and other items; and oftentimes even arrange for the borrowing of money or use of cash to pay up debts of the estate.

Paying the Debts and Other Charges of the Deceased of Estate. It is the function of the executor to raise the funds (insofar as the estate is solvent) with which to pay all expenses of administration, general expenses, taxes and debts. Generally where an executor has discretionary powers, odd lot parcels of stock and securities will be sold or disposed of and the proceeds used as part of the estate.

It is also up to the executor to file notice with the Collector of Internal Revenue and the State Inheritance Tax Office of the death of the testator, prepare all tax reports and returns in connection with local, state and federal income, inheritance, estate or gift taxes, and pay such taxes when due.

The executor must also see that all debts are paid in the order provided by the statues and if the estate is not solvent, that the amount paid on debts is prorated proportionately. If an executor is unable to pay off a debt and fails to notify creditors, or pays the debt out of the statutory order, any creditor of an estate, who is prejudiced by payment of the claims of others, may be able to collect his claim or pro rata share from the individual property of the executors. During all these steps decisions must be made and action taken to divide and distribute the property in the manner directed by the will.

Distributing the Estate. Once all assets of the estate have been collected and debts have been paid, it is the final step of the executor to distribute the net estate, that is, what remains of the estate after payment of debts, administration and taxes to the beneficiary according to the terms as provided by the will under such forms of distribution as are approved by the court when the final accounting is presented to the court for approval.

Administrator. The procedure followed by an administrator in settling an estate, that is, where a bank or individual is appointed administrator by a court where the deceased died without leaving a will, is exactly the same; that is, obtaining authority from the court to settle the estate; assembling the assets of the estate; safeguarding the assets of the estate, paying the debts and distributing the net estate. The only difference of consequence is that instead of the administrator distributing the net proceeds of the estate in accordance with the wishes of the testator as outlined under the will, the distribution is made to kin in accordance with the statutes of the state of which the decedent was a resident. In order to become familiar with the laws of descent as it applies to your state, it is well to consult legal counsel of the bank on this important phase.

Guardian. Banks also serve as guardians of the property of minors and incompetents, by appointment of the court.

It is generally recognized that a minor is a person under 21 years of age, while an incompetent is a person of any age who is regarded by the law as being incapable of taking care of his or her property. Incompetents not only include persons who are mentally defective, but in some states also those persons who are unable to manage their own property. Although a guardian may be recommended by the family, the appointment is made by the court. In some states the bank or individual appointed by the court to act as guardian of the property of an incompetent is also known as a conservator.

When a bank is appointed guardian or conservator, it takes possession and control of the assets of the minor or incompetent, generally referred to as a ward. It is its responsibility, once it has taken possession and control of the assets, to prepare and file an inventory and appraisement with the court, to invest cash not needed for the immediate needs of the ward in accordance with orders of the court, and to periodically distribute funds for support, maintenance and education of the ward, or the incompetent as the court shall direct. In the case of minors, the corpus of the estate is generally distributed to the ward or turned over to the ward upon his attaining 21 years of age; or to the incompetent upon regaining sound mind; or to a legal representative upon death.

There are two main types of guardians, one of the property or possessions of the minor or incompetent; and the other of the person. Generally it is the responsibility of the guardian of the property to take care of and manage the property of the ward while the guardian of the person, who takes the place of the parent as far as upbringing and protection is concerned, looks after his housing, food, clothing, schooling, and the like. Banks seldom are appointed nor will they accept guardianship of the person, but generally manage the estate, turning over to the person appointed as guardian of the person such funds as are required for the maintenance of the individual.

In addition to guardianships under court appointment, there are guardianships known as veterans guardianships, that is, guardianship of funds paid by the government through the Veterans Administration to, or for the use of incompetent veterans, minors, or incompetent dependents or beneficiaries of veterans. Such veteran guardianships, in addition to being governed by the general state law applicable to the guardianships, are governed by special laws adopted by the state at the recommendation of the Veterans Administration which are applicable only to the estates of wards of the Veterans Administration.

The usual duties of a bank guardian are similar to those of a trustee, that is, to receive, hold and manage property for the benefit of the beneficiary, which, in the case of a guardianship, is for the benefit of the ward if a minor and the incompetent if unable to manage his own property. While wide latitude is permitted a trustee, the duties and responsibilities of a bank guardian in administering the estate are, for the most part, defined and limited by the law of the respective states.

Trustee. A trustee is one holding legal right to property. As such, a trustee has all the basic rights of any other legal owner of the property, such as the right to hold the property against the world, to sue and be sued, and to prosecute and defend actions at law or in equity with respect to the trust property. It may be said in general that a trustee can do anything to or with trust property that the outright owner can do, except use the trust property for his own benefit.

A bank named trustee acts either in capacity as trustee under a will, or trustee under agreement. As trustee under a will, the bank acts as trustee under appointment of the last will and testament of a person to administer the person's estate. A trustee under will is named when an individual wishes his estate to be properly managed over a period of years in a competent and conservative manner after his death in order to provide income for his wife, children, heirs, and others he wishes to share in his estate.

Trusts under agreement are established either for a general or fixed period of time during the lifetime of the donor either with provision for distribution, termination or administration in the event of death; or for continued administration of the service, in a manner prescribed under provisions of the trust indenture after his death.

A bank is appointed trustee under agreement when an individual deems it advisable to have someone manage all or part of his estate during his lifetime, for a fixed or indefinite period of time, or for a particular reason or purpose.

Trusts under agreement are principally of two types; revocable and irrevocable. A revocable trust, sometimes called a voluntary trust, can be revoked or changed at any time by the donor. An irrevocable trust, on the other hand, is one which, once it has been set up, must be administered until terminated or extinguished by fulfillment of the terms of the trust indenture or instrument.

In setting up a trust under agreement, some donors retain certain authority, principally in connection with the right to decide on matters of investment of principal, while others vest full authority in the trustee through provisions of the trust agreement.

In acting as trustee, the bank receives title and possession of all the assets comprising the trust. After appraising and analyzing them, it determines those suitable for retention, disposes of those not suitable, and reinvests the proceeds of such sales in proper trust investments, except in cases where the donor has retained some right as to the reinvestment of funds.

Once a trust is set up, the bank then pays the income to those entitled to receive it under terms of the trust; and distributes the principal to the beneficiary or beneficiaries under the terms of the trust agreement.

All provisions under which a trust is operative are set forth in the trust indenture for the guidance of the trustees and information of the beneficiaries. All investments, the disposing of assets, and the decision as to action to be taken, is made by the trust committee of the bank composed of capable, experienced and qualified officers and directors.

A person need not wait until death to provide gifts in trust to members of the family, or to charities or institutions. If during his lifetime a person desires to establish a separate income for his wife, for the education of his children or to give them a financial start in life, he can establish a living trust and observe while he is still living, the results of his benefactions.

Such a trust is of considerable advantage to a property owner because by breaking down his total income through gifts of property to several persons, his annual income tax can be softened through the lowering of his former tax brackets. A living trust may also substantially soften federal estate taxes. The gift, even though made in trust, automatically reduces his general estate and, at his death, no federal estate tax will apply against the amount previously put into the trust unless the gift has been made in actual contemplation of death.

The creation of living trusts, however, is a highly technical matter and it is important that the property owner contemplating such a trust consult not only the bank but his tax advisor and lawyer before doing so.

Another important service which banks render as trustee is in connection with life insurance trusts.

In setting up such a trust, the donor has his life insurance policies made payable to the bank as trustee, directing the bank to pay the income on the principal after his death to beneficiaries, which he may designate, and to distribute the principal upon the terms set up in the trust instrument.

If the donor continues to pay the premiums on the insurance policies, the trust is referred to as an unfunded insurance trust. If, however, the donor places additional property in the trust so that the rents, dividends or interest from securities is sufficient to pay the insurance premium and used for that purpose, then the trust is known as a funded insurance trust.

Making all or part of one's life insurance payable to the bank as trustee has a number of special advantages. It protects the owner's general estate by providing his executor with cash for the payment of expenses, debts, estate taxes, and legacies, thereby avoiding a sacrifice sale of a business or other assets of the estate to raise the necessary cash. It also provides immediate cash for the family's living expenses while the estate is being settled.

A life insurance trust for business purposes also can be created to enable surviving associates to buy the interest of a deceased associate without straining the resources of the business. This type of trust is frequently used between partners of a business or the stockholders of a corporation whose stock is held among a small group.

By creating a trust either by will, called a testamentary trust, or by agreement or voluntary trust, and appointing a bank as trustee, a person can secure to his loved ones, the benefits of his properties and estate without the burdens of management. Often in the case of testamentary trusts, it is possible not only to avoid the second set of transfer taxes, but effect important savings in reducing income, inheritance and state taxes, and in expenses of administration.

The basic duties of a trustee are found in the fundamental laws of trusteeship. Included in these laws are the responsibilities and duties to:

1. Safeguard and protect the trust property.
2. Make the trust productive of income insofar as possible through the proper investment of funds.
3. Be faithful alike to the creator of the trust and to the beneficiaries under the trust.
4. Maintain accurate and strict records of trust administration.
5. Carry out any special duties such as are described in the trust instrument or in the court order creating the trust.

The fact that trusts are created for a special purpose brings up the question as to the length of time property may be trusteed. It is a general rule in many states, subject to modification of course, that a trust under will may continue during the life or lives in being at the time of the testator's death and 21 years thereafter; whereas a trust under agreement ordinarily may continue during a life or lives in being at the time a trust is created and 21 years thereafter. This is called the rule against perpetuities.

Where the general rule applies, it is generally assumed a person may create a trust under will to continue during the lifetime of the last survivor of his own children and until his grandchildren are 21 years of age; or, may create a living trust or trust under agreement to continue during the lifetime of the last survivor of his children who are in being at the time of the creation of the trust and until the children of those children are 21 years of age. Provisions of the law are to prevent a person creating a trust to continue indefinitely, except for a charitable purpose.

The question as to how long a trust should continue brings into being another set of principles. Generally a trust for a minor continues until he is of legal age, while a trust for an incompetent continues until he has either recovered his mental competency or dies. The general opinion is that a trust should continue only as long as it is needed and that the donor of a trust should not project the program to where it could interfere with unforeseen future personal and social developments.

Where certain beneficiaries are minor children or have not manifested ability to suitably engage in business, the trust should continue as long as there is need for protecting the child from his own unwise or extravagant management. Some of these provisions provide for such a person to receive his share upon reaching the age of 21. Others provide that such funds shall be distributed over a period of years after reaching 21, while other provisions in a trust indenture give the trustee discretionary powers as to distribution, when and if in its opinion, such beneficiaries are capable of managing their share of the estate.

AGENT. Every trust institution performs many and varied kinds of agencies for individuals. In creating an agency a person commonly known as the principal authorizes another known as the agent to act for, in behalf of, and subject to, the control of the principal. In this capacity the bank assists customers in many ways in administering their affairs and matters of their estates, under one or more of the following agency arrangements:

Escrow Agency. When a bank acts as an escrow agent it is acting in behalf of one or more individuals in a transaction involving one or more other individuals.

Escrow accounts are established for the purpose of setting

forth terms and provisions of an agreement between two or more parties wherein, when certain terms and conditions as set forth in the agreement are fulfilled or complied with, other terms and provisions of such agreement will be complied with or executed. The escrow agent determines that the provisions and conditions under the agreement are complied with.

Escrow accounts are usually established in connection with the purchase or sale of real estate and other property, where the owner deposits title or deed to the property or real estate with the escrow agent under provisions of a written agreement through which the escrow agent is to deliver the title or deed to the other party or parties when other provisions of the agreement, or terms of payment have been complied with.

Escrow arrangements are widely used by lawyers and businessmen in closing deals where actual deliveries cannot be made at the time the parties sign the agreement, or are contingent upon some conditions being fulfilled. By using a responsible stakeholder while waiting for the event to take place, all parties are protected. If and when the contemplated event takes place, then the escrow agent delivers the cash, documents or property as provided in the contract, receiving in return for delivery to the other party, cash or documents as called for under the agreement. If, however, the event fails to take place, the escrow agent then reinstates the parties to their former positions by redelivering the items in the form and amount originally deposited.

Safekeeping Agency. Under a safekeeping arrangement banks, as agents, provide service for custody of stocks, bonds, mortgages and notes. Safeguarding arrangements do not provide for service in connection with collection or investment of securities, but merely for the holding and delivery of the securities upon the order of the principal.

Custodian Agency. As custodian, the bank as agent not only receives, holds and delivers property held for safekeeping, but performs certain active duties with respect to the property committed to its custody, such as collecting interest and maturing principal on bonds, notes and mortgages, dividends on stocks, and handling the proceeds in accordance with provisions of the trust agreement.

Management Agency. In a management relationship, the bank acts as managing agent of both real and personal property.

In connection with personal property, the bank performs all the usual duties of the safekeeping agent and the custodian agent. In addition, to the extent specified in the agreement, it engages in the active managing of the securities such as analyzing and reviewing the securities, advising on or recommending changes in investments, handling the investing and reinvesting of cash, maturing principal and interest, all in accordance with the trust agreement.

As managing agent of the real property, such as land and buildings, the bank may rent, lease, or in some cases, operate the property for the principal, handling all matters in connection with leases, collection of rents, payment of taxes, supervision of repairs and improvements, attending to the insurance and general management of the property for the benefit of the owner.

ESTATE PLANNING. The trust departments of most progressive banks provide without cost the service known as estate planning. This confidential service consists of counselling and assisting customers of the bank and others in the planning of the distribution of their estates and counselling on the impact of income, gift and death taxes on the estate.

Family situations frequently make it undesirable to leave an estate as an outright and unprotected gift to certain members of the family. The creation of trusts may not only be a sound protection against dissipation, but soften income and death taxes.

Banks which are to be appointed executor or trustee find these conferences very desirable and helpful, because they are given the opportunity in advance, to become familiar with the problems and the character of the estate which they will ultimately be called upon to handle.

In providing this service banks do not provide legal advice or accounting service, but merely point out such tested objectives for the consideration of the customer. Where such recommendations are found acceptable, it is up to the customer to take the matter up with his or her legal counsel for placing the recommendations in legal form.

INVESTMENT COUNSELLING SERVICE. Another service

provided by trust departments of progressive banks is in connection with advising customers and others on investments.

Under this service, qualified and competent men advise people of means how they may go about building or rebuilding their estate, not only for the purpose of rearranging their holdings as to better serve the purpose for which the estate was designed, known as estate planning, but for the conversion and investment of funds. In providing this service it is generally the practice to only provide factual information and investment advice along general lines, and to instill in the customer's mind a sound viewpoint to enable him to make his own decision.

Customers and investors make wide and practiced use of this service for the reasons that the bank has no securities for sale and therefore provides unbiased information. This service is not only of assistance to the customer in managing his affairs but to the bank, as it often provides an opportunity to discuss trust services with the investor such as executorships, trusteeships, safekeeping or custodian accounts, which can relieve the customer of some of the detail in connection with managing his own estate. In addition, it provides the opportunity for banks to sell the investor on the idea of appointing the bank as the executor or trustee to handle his affairs after his death.

CORPORATE TRUST SERVICES

Trust institutions exist not only to assist individuals in managing their wealth and estates during their lifetime and dispose of their estate upon their death, in accordance with their wishes, but to serve all types of businesses, institutions and organizations where, in the course of their respective operation, they require the services of a reliable and competent trustee or agent to carry out a plan, program or instructions.

To accomplish this purpose, banks and trust institutions provide trust services to corporations acting in the capacity of:

1. Trustee under trust deed
2. Trustee under a pension plan
3. Trustee under a profit sharing plan
4. Trustee under an insurance trust
5. Trustee under land trust

6. Trustee as liquidator of a business enterprise
7. Transfer agent
8. Registrar
9. Dividend paying agent
10. Paying agent for bonds and coupons under a trust indenture.
11. Depositary

TRUSTEE UNDER TRUST DEED. A business or corporation desiring to raise capital through the sale of its bonds and notes transfers property to a trust institution by a deed of trust through which a lien on certain property is vested in the trustee for the benefit of those who have or will invest money in the corporation through the purchase of bonds, notes, debentures, or trust certificates.

Under such an arrangement, a trust indenture issued by the corporation, propertly recorded, shows what it is purported to be; that is, a first mortgage on real estate, etc., mortgage on equipment, etc., or any type of property which can be pledged as collateral for the bonds, notes, debentures, trust certificates which are to be issued.

The type of security called for under the trust indenture is property identified by the trustee with the trust indenture and certified by the trustee that such bonds, notes, debentures or certificates covered by the trust indenture are of the issue mentioned in the deed of trust. After certification, bonds, notes, debentures or certificates are delivered to the corporation, to the purchasers, or to the underwriter for sale and distribution.

It is the duty and responsibility of the trustee to maintain proper custody over the deed to the property, insurance and other supporting documents, and if collateral is pledged as underlying security for the bonds, notes or debentures issued under the trust indenture, to see that such property is properly covered by chattel mortgages or whatever other documents are required under the circumstances.

A further duty of a trustee is in connection with maturing bonds which are called for redemption and to see to it that when they are presented they are properly cancelled and released from the trust indenture.

In the event of failure of a corporation to meet its obligations or retire the bonds, debentures, or trust certificates covered by the trust indenture in the manner prescribed, or on the dates they mature, it is the obligation of the trustee through foreclosure under order of court, to sell or dispose of the property for the benefit of the bond holders, note holders, debenture holders, and apply the proceeds to the satisfaction of the obligation, paying over whatever remains after satisfaction has been made for the indebtedness, to the corporation or to its order.

TRUSTEE UNDER A PENSION PLAN. This type of trust has been used widely by corporations in recent years as a stabilizer of employee relations and an inducement to secure high grade personnel. In addition, pension plans have been favorably regarded by corporations in that the contributions to a pension fund under certain and approved conditions are deductible expense, at the present time, under the Internal Revenue Code.

Generally, under the terms of a pension trust, the employer and the employees, if it is a contributory trust, contribute a predetermined amount at stated times to a fund which is held in trust by a trust institution for the purpose of (a) either purchasing annuity contracts for the participants, effective at retirement age, (b) investing of funds from which proceeds a payment will either be made directly to such participating employee upon reaching retirement age in a lump sum or for certain amounts to be paid them monthly as long as they shall live. In certain of these trust arrangements the bank merely purchases annuity contracts with an insurance company for each of the employees and acts only as a recording or safekeeping agent. In other instances the bank actively manages the employees' pension trust by reinvesting the funds and distributing the proceeds to the beneficiaries when they reach retirement in accordance with the terms and provisions set forth in the trust instrument.

TRUSTEE UNDER A PROFIT SHARING PLAN. Profit sharing plans are used by corporations as another means of stabilizing employee relations. Such plans receive their great impetus from the fact that they permit employees to share in the profits of the company in some relation to their contribution.

Under the terms of a profit sharing plan the employer contributes a percentage of the annual profit, arrived at by the application of a certain formula, to a fund which is either distributed to all participants annually or periodically, based on salary, length of service, production results, or a combination of all three; or trusteed with a bank for the purpose of having them invest and reinvest the principal amounts and the income for the benefit of the various employees who have participated in the trust, for distribution to them upon reaching retirement age or upon termination of the plan.

Generally most profit sharing trusts provide that the amounts due the participant, which have accrued to him during his employment with the company can either be paid to him in a lump sum or, upon reaching retirement age, depending on his wishes and terms of the trust indenture, be payable to him over a period of time in the form of an annuity.

TRUSTEE UNDER AN INSURANCE TRUST. Under various, yet particular circumstances, it becomes practical and advantageous, sometimes, for a group of stockholders of a corporation to insure one anothers lives, or the life of their chief executive, to compensate for their loss in event of death. In like manner, partners will often insure each other's lives for the benefit of the business and to compensate for the loss of income in the event of the death of one of the partners.

Whenever such a plan merits adoption, the insurance policies are generally payable to a trust institution as trustee, for the benefit of beneficiaries as set forth in the trust instrument. The purpose of such an arrangement is to assure prompt distribution of the proceeds of the insurance in accordance with the predetermined wishes of the stockholders or the partners, without running the risk of the proceeds becoming a part of the general assets of the business. One of the principal reasons for such an arrangement is to provide cash to the corporation or partnership to retire the stock or interest in the partnership owned by the deceased, so that the remaining stockholders or partners do not have their interest jeopardized by the sale of stock to an outsider; or the partnership finds it necessary to liquidate assets in order to turn over to the deceased partners estate his share of the partnership interest.

TRUSTEE UNDER A LAND TRUST. In a number of states it is the practice of owners of real estate to transfer title to trustees under trust agreements commonly known as Land Trusts. Frequently title is transferred to such a trustee to conceal the identity of the real owners who are the beneficiaries named in the trust agreement.

Under trusts of this character, while the title to the real estate is recorded in the name of the bank as trustee, the management of the property, the collection of rents or proceeds of sale are generally vested, by the terms of the trust agreement, in the beneficiaries. Such an arrangement has the advantage of preventing judgments obtained against the owner from being attached as liens to the real estate and thus cloud the title.

Another advantage of this type of trust arrangement is that the owner of a beneficial interest in the trust may assign his interest through a simple assignment of the beneficial interest on the books of the trustee, without actual transfer of the title to the real estate itself.

This type of land trust sometimes has considerable appeal because the trustees' powers can be expanded to include management of the property and actual sale of the real estate.

TRUSTEE AS LIQUIDATOR OF A BUSINESS ENTERPRISE. Trust institutions are also authorized to serve as an assignee for the benefit of creditors under a voluntary assignment, or creditor's agreement. Under such authority the bank takes over the assets of an embarrassed corporation, attends the orderly sale of assets and preserves the resources for the protection of both the creditors and the corporation. The liquidation of a business is similar in some repects to the settlement of the estate of a deceased individual.

A trust institution may also accept an appointment as receiver under court order and operate a business until such time as the creditors are paid off; or until it becomes evident that complete liquidation or bankruptcy cannot be averted. In such case, the trust institution may accept the trusteeship in bankruptcy, liquidate the assets and distribute the proceeds to the creditors. This, however, is a specialized field and unless the commercial department of a bank is involved with extensions of credit, a bank will not generally accept this type of an appointment.

TRANSFER AGENT. Any corporation may issue or transfer

its own stock in its own office or may make any arrangements it wishes for that purpose. Because a transfer of stock in a corporation having numerous stockholders entails an enormous amount of detail it has become the accepted practice of larger corporations, particularly those whose stock is listed on one or more of the registered stock exchanges, to appoint a trust institution as its transfer agent.

In acting as transfer agent, the trust institution is the agent of the corporation. Thus the corporation is liable for the omissions and acts of the transfer agent in transferring stock in the same manner as it would be if the acts were performed by its own employees.

In acting as transfer agent, the trust institution issues certificates for the number of shares the corporation is authorized to issue, either by its charter, by-laws, or proper authorization of the stockholders, but only to those stockholders of record is it authorized or directed to issue stock.

In issuing stock the transfer agent issues such certificates in respective numbers of shares each in accordance with the wish of the respective stockholder.

It is the responsibility of the transfer agent, with respect to the transfer of stock, to see that the present holder of the certificate has the right to transfer the certificate to another, that all requirements of the transfer are met, the certificate is properly endorsed, and the endorsement is guaranteed. Such transfers, particularly those which arise in connection with transfers by and to partnerships, executors, administrators, guardians, trustees and others holding stock in fiduciary capacities, which arise as a matter of course in a days work, require a great deal of technical knowledge on the part of the agent. Such duties and responsibilities, procedures to follow, methods to be used in handling such transfers are, however, simplified by the issuance of operating instructions and standard procedures for the guidance of personnel.

In addition to acting as transfer agent for stock, trust institutions are also called upon to act as transfer agents for registered bonds, receivers' certificates, voting trust certificates, certificates of deposit, warrants and rights to subscribe to shares of stock. Regardless of the capacity in which the trust institution acts, responsibilities and liabilities are substantially the same.

REGISTRAR. It is the function of the trust institution acting as registrar to prevent an overissue of stock, voting trust certificates, certificates of deposit, receivership certificates, debentures or whatever type of instrument for which they are appointed as registrar.

With respect to new issues, it is the responsibility of the registrar to check the issuance of new certificates to see that only certificates covering the authorized number of shares are issued. In connection with transfers, the registrar checks both the old and new certificates to see that the number of new shares equals the number cancelled, which shares are registered in a general stockholders ledger or in other records suitable for the purpose intended.

As the main purpose of a registrar is to keep a check on the corporation or its transfer agent to prevent an overissue, the registrar is responsible both to the corporation and to the stockholders to see that only stock which is authorized is issued.

In operation, when certificates of stock are sent in for transfer, they are cancelled by the transfer agent except for the signature of the registrar, and then sent together with the new certificates to the registrar. After the registrar has checked both the old certificate and new certificate and has satisfied himself that the proposed transfer does not involve an overissue of stock, he cancels the signature on the old certificate and affixes the signature to the new one, then returns both the old and the new certificate to the transfer agent who retains the old certificate and delivers the new certificate, in accordance with the instructions received.

Because of the wide distribution of stock, and the requirements of stock exchanges, every corporation whose stock is listed on such exchange must have a transfer agent and registrar in the city in which the exchange is located.

Corporations in recent years have adopted the practice of having co-transfer agents and co-registrars wherever they desire to have stock transferred and registered for purposes of convenience or service to their stockholders. Where such an arrangement exists, the co-registrars and co-transfer agents must keep in constant touch with each other so that the records coincide and are in agreement at all times.

DIVIDEND PAYING AGENT. Because the clerical work

involved in the payment of dividends by large corporations is so heavy and exacting, many corporations have come to employ trust institutions to serve as paying agents. Frequently, because the trust institution, which is acting as transfer agent already, has an up to date list of the stockholders, the corporation appoints the same institution to serve as paying agent for dividends.

In operation, when a corporation declares a dividend, the corporation notifies the dividend paying agent to prepare checks for each stockholder for the amount of the dividend declared on each share, in accordance with the resolution of the Board of Directors. Generally the declaration of a dividend is made to be payable at a future date to stockholders of record as of a prior date, which gives the paying agent ample time in which to prepare the individual checks. Formerly this entailed a considerable amount of work on the part of the dividend paying agent for each check had to be personally typed up with the name of the stockholder, amount of the dividend and signed. In recent years, however, with the use of special equipment, many thousands of such checks can be processed automatically each hour. Before the checks are mailed out, however, the corporation has made financial arrangements for the dividends, and has deposited, usually in a special dividend account, sufficient funds against which the bank will charge the dividend checks when returned to the bank and presented for payment.

Corporations sometimes pay dividends in a form of stock. In such a case, the paying agent must prepare and send to each stockholder of record, in accordance with the terms of the resolution as passed by the board of directors of the corporation, a stock certificate or rights to purchase stock which are traded in and handled in the same manner as a stock certificate.

Where rights are given in lieu of a cash dividend, the stockholder either must sell the rights, obtaining cash; or purchase additional rights to enable him to obtain full shares of stock, in which case the rights are sent to the transfer agent and registrar to be processed in connection with issuing a new stock certificate.

PAYING AGENT FOR BONDS AND COUPONS UNDER A TRUST INDENTURE. Trust institutions are also called upon to act as paying agents for matured bonds, and for the interest due and payable on bonds. In acting as paying agent for interest on bonds, the trust institution must not only handle the actual pay out, receiving and paying of funds as the coupons are presented, but comply with the requirements of the federal government with respect to income tax returns. Where a trust institution acts as paying agent for unregistered bonds, the coupons usually are presented through another bank or through the collection department. Before the remittance is made by the paying agent the coupons are checked to determine that the coupons are bona fide and have been clipped from bonds authorized under the trust indenture.

In case, however, bonds are registered and there are no coupons attached, it is up to the paying agent to send out interest checks payable to the person in whose name the bonds are registered on the books of the transfer agent or registrar.

Because of the convenience, it is a general practice to have the same trust institution which acts as trustee under the bond issue serve as paying agent for called or maturing bonds or the payment of interest.

In operation, funds are deposited with the paying agent prior to date of the maturing bonds or interest date of the coupons in sufficient amount to retire bonds which mature as of the particular date, and to pay the interest on all bonds outstanding as of that date. Once the coupons have been presented and paid according with instructions, the trust institution makes a complete accounting to the corporation, making a satisfactory arrangement for the future payment of interest coupons which have not been presented, or bonds which have not been presented for payment as of the date. Generally, the bank will hold such funds in escrow in a separate account to provide for future payments.

DEPOSITARY. Trust institutions also provide another form of agency service known as a depositaryship. Under such an arrangement, the trust institution receives stocks, bonds and other securities in connection with corporate readjustments, reorganizations, subscriptions to new issues and other securities deposited with it, holds them in accordance with the trust indenture, and eventually accounts for the funds or securities or other property so deposited.

In addition to services provided for individuals and corporations, trust institutions also provide services to charitable, educational, religious and other institutions and organizations designed for the benefit of groups of people. Such trust institutions generally provide services in connection with escrows, safekeeping, management, investment counselling and acting as custodian.

In recent times trust institutions, to an increasing extent, provide safekeeping, management, and investment counselling services in connection with endowment funds of colleges and universities. They also provide services in connection with acting as agent for the treasurers of churches, schools, and hospitals, in which capacity the bank provides books, maintains records, furnishes bookkeeping services, and generally serves as financial secretary.

Many civic clubs, religious bodies and professional associations have also established foundations for the express purpose of promoting a special objective in which they are interested. They too, in order to take advantage of many services offered by a trust institution, appoint them as trustee for the property with specific instructions contained in the trust indenture.

It is well to point out, however, that a public institution cannot trustee its endowment no matter how greatly it needs or desires the services of a trust institution, unless it is the outright owner of the property. It is of particular importance where a public institution receives property or funds for a specified purpose, such as for endowment of wards or beds in a hospital, scholarships in a college, or for the maintenance of a church. Having received the property for a special purpose the institution cannot pass it on to a trustee and divest itself of the title. It can, however, appoint a trust institution as its agent to receive, safeguard and manage the property or the funds. Such arrangements are known as institutional agencies which enable trust institutions to do for some public institutions what they do for others through a trusteeship.

Trust institutions also can undertake some of the record keeping, custodianship, and safekeeping duties of an individual fiduciary. While a trust institution cannot assume the discretionary duties of an individual fiduciary, the individual may relieve himself of many of the burdensome features of this undertaking, with the assurance that such duties will be properly taken care of, by naming a bank or trust institution as his agent.

ACCEPTANCE AND SUPERVISION OF TRUST BUSINESS. Trust institutions like banks, while semi-public corporations, have both a moral and financial responsibility to operate profitably and conduct their affairs in such a manner as to reflect favorably on the stockholders, customers and people of the communities they serve.

This being the situation, it is a well recognized and accepted fact that banks and trust institutions are under no obligation either moral or legal to accept all business offered to them.

In considering the acceptance of personal trust business in which the relationship is private and confidential and the trust institution is responsible only to those who have or may have a financial interest in the account, the two determining factors are:

A. Is the trust service needed?

B. Can the service be properly rendered?

In connection with acceptance of corporate business, which can be either public or private, the determining factors are:

A. Is the company which the bank has been asked to serve in fiduciary capacity in good standing?

B. Is the purpose of the relationship legal and acceptable by bank policy?

C. Can the service for which the bank has been asked to act in fiduciary capacity be rendered properly?

Because of the relationship involved, national banks by regulation are required to have all new trust accounts approved and accepted by the board of directors, or by a committee of capable and experienced officers and directors of the bank known as the trust committee. Such committee, in addition, is required to exercise supervision and approve the purchase, retention or sale of the assets of each trust account. The various states, to varying degrees, have similar requirements. In addition to the regulations provided by national banks, all national banks must also conform to the regulations in connection with the acceptance and supervision of trust accounts as provided by the laws of the respective states, inasmuch as the acceptance of trusts and acting in fiduciary capacity is covered by laws of the state in which the bank or trust institution operates.

OPERATIONS AND MANAGEMENT OF A TRUST DEPARTMENT. Trust functions are carried on under several different forms:

A. By a trust institution alone. These are relatively few, as such institutions in recent years are qualified to accept savings business, commercial business or both.

B. As a trust department of an originally organized savings bank or commercial bank.

C. As a department of a bank originally organized to handle commercial and savings business and to provide such services.

Under each of these forms the functions, operations and regulatory requirements are basically the same and provide that:

a. Trust activities must be carried on in a section or department physically separate, if possible, from any other activities.

b. Supervision of the trust activities and approval of conversions of funds in a trust account must be made by a committee of the directors or committee appointed by them.

c. Active management of the trust operation shall be under an executive officer, or officer qualified and competent to administer trusts.

d. Books and records reflecting trust operations must be maintained separate and distinct from books and records in connection with other operations.

e. The safekeeping and control of trust property shall be maintained separate and distinct from other property owned by the bank or belonging to other trust accounts.

The difference among the three forms of institutions handling trust functions is in the organization, management, and delegation of responsibilities—which depends on volume.

In an institution organized only to conduct trust business, or act solely in fiduciary capacity, as provided for by the law of the state under which it is organized, it has its own stockholders, capital, board of directors, officers, committees and employees. In keeping with a traditional precedent, the title of officers in a strictly trust institution, outside of the president and secretary, which do not necessarily reflect authority or responsibility, are trust officers instead of vice presidents; assistant trust officers, and assistant secretaries instead of assistant vice presidents; a treasurer instead of a cashier; and assistant treasurers instead of assistant cashiers.

Where a bank was originally organized as a savings or commercial bank, and later qualified and was granted trust powers; or was organized as a commercial bank with trust powers; the trust functions, depending on the size of the bank, are conducted as a separate department of the bank with officers holding title as trust officers or assistant trust officers, sometimes together with the additional title of vice president or assistant vice president.

Frequently, when a bank operates an active commercial department and active trust department, it is facetiously referred to as a bank with two institutions operating under the same roof. Unfortunately, too often this is true because of the invisible wall which not only separates the activities of the commercial department from the trust department, but divides personnel as to their loyalties, reflecting in poor esprit de corps and lack of cooperation from a new business development standpoint.

In a small bank, depending on volume, where the officers have the title of trust officer or assistant trust officer, designating their qualifications to act competently in behalf of the bank in fiduciary capacity, it is usually another title, such as president, vice president, assistant vice president or cashier which denotes that they also handle commercial banking business.

In all such institutions it is well to point out that the type and volume of trust business depends upon the location of the institution, and the services required by people residing in the area served by the bank.

In larger cities all types of personal and corporate trust business are handled. In smaller towns, banks will generally confine their trust activities to acting as executor, administrator or trustee in connection with estates of individuals. Regardless of size or volume, however, each bank must have a trust committee or have the board of directors pass on the acceptance and management of all trust accounts.

The responsibilities of a trust officer acting in fiduciary capacity are varied and require knowledge and a high degree of skill and experience, in order to safely and competently discharge the duties of the relationship. These duties in general are to:

1. Carry out the terms of the trust indenture exactly as stated.
2. Analyze and periodically review the trust.
3. Keep the principal safely invested.
4. Maintain uninvested principal and undistributed income at a minimum consistent with the provisions of the trust indenture.
5. Promptly collect income and maturing principal on all investments.

6. Control, pay out and distribute funds only as authorized by the trust instrument.

7. Study and be acquainted with the needs of the beneficiaries at all times.

8. Promptly remit payment in acceptable form for coupons and bonds presented for payment or redemption.

9. Expeditiously prepare and mail checks representing dividends declared.

10. Competently manage or supervise the management of any real estate holdings, farms, etc. as required in the discharge of the trust relationship.

11. Operate in a competent manner any business or liquidate same if directed by the will.

12. Advise and consult with donors and beneficiaries of a trust on their business and personal problems.

13. Promptly prepare and handle income tax matters.

14. Make prompt reports and accountings to donors or beneficiaries of a trust as required.

The principal activities of the personnel of the trust institution or trust department of a commercial bank can be further summarized into three phases:

A. The acquiring of business.

B. The administration of business.

C. The servicing of business or operations.

ACQUIRING OF BUSINESS. The acquiring or solicitation of personal or corporate trust business by a trust institution, or trust department of a bank is highly specialized, technical and confidential.

Personal trust business, where the bank acts as executor, trustee, or in an agency capacity, develops principally because the donor or person creating the trust is either a customer of the bank, who has been told about the services of the bank by one of the officers who knows the person has means and is a prospect for fiduciary services or by attorneys who are familiar with the bank, have confidence in its administration of trust accounts and recommend the services to their client. It is for this reason that banks which are not permitted to practice law, assiduously cultivate the friendship of lawyers and work with them closely so as to be named by them as executor or trustee under the wills they draw up for their clients.

Lawyers, in drawing a will, may appoint a bank to act in fiduciary capacity, yet in order to be properly compensated for their work, continue to serve the client during his life and after his death, by being named as attorney for the estate, in which capacity they receive a fee for handling the decedent's estate matters. This in no way creates an additional expense for the estate, but literally means that the bank performs the technical bookkeeping work in connection with the estate and receives a proportionate fee based on the work performed.

Directors, officers and even stockholders of banks can develop trust business by recommending the trust facilities of the bank to their friends and acquaintances who have means. Well informed bank officials should be able to discuss the facilities offered by the bank in connection with the particular estate problem of their friends, and provide an introduction to an officer of the trust department who can explain currently and in detail the many advantages of a trust relationship in line with the particular problems or setup of the person interested in making a trust. When such a relationship develops to the point where the person wishes to name the bank as executor or trustee under his will, then, of course, the matter is handled by the prospective client's attorney, who draws up the necessary papers, sees that the will is properly executed and contains the various legal provisions which will assist the bank in the distribution and management of the estate in accordance with his client's wishes.

Therefore, it behooves the personnel of every trust department to acquire as much information as they can regarding the wealth or means of their important bank customers, and to place such names on the mailing list to receive certain releases which a trust department will send out from time to time to its most prominent prospects. They will also cultivate, in a most discreet and courteous manner, members of the legal profession and keep them advised and acquainted with the facilities offered by the bank so they too will be in a position to recommend the bank's services to their clients.

Solicitation of trust business is made by general announcements as to trust services in the form of statement insertion pluggers and direct mail advertising; also by personal calls by trust department representatives, after interest in the bank's services has been indicated by a prospective customer, or when the bank has been invited to discuss matters of a confidential and trust relationship with the prospective customer.

A substantial amount of trust business, in which the bank acts as executor or trustee, arises when people become convinced that they should make a will and name the bank executor or trustee under their will. Generally a copy of such will is sent to the bank and placed on file at the insistence of the attorney. At other times, the bank only has knowledge of its appointment as executor or trustee after the donor or maker of the will has died, and the will is found in the safe deposit box. This procedure, however, should be avoided as in many cases the will is not all inclusive and fails to provide for contingencies brought about by economic circumstances, modifications of tax provisions, and changes in the family due to death, divorce, etc. It is for this reason that most progressive banks, where they know they are named as executor or trustee and the wills are on file, periodically advise the maker to review and bring the will up to date, and make any necessary revisions so that when the time comes to execute or administer the will, in accordance with the wishes of the donor, it can be done effectively and comply as closely as possible with the wishes of the deceased.

In addition to using pluggers and direct mail advertising of trust service, many progressive banks periodically keep members of the legal and accounting professions advised on other bank services and consult with them on ways and means through which the bank can cooperate more closely with them in developing business for their mutual interests, and in providing services which are required or could be of assistance and use to their clients in conducting their financial and personal affairs.

Activities in connection with acquiring new business are either part of the assigned duties and responsibilities of the officers of the trust department or, if the bank is of sufficient size to warrant the expenditure, the responsibility of an officer in charge of the development of new business for the trust department.

ADMINISTRATION OF BUSINESS. This phase of trust organization covers the activities of respective trust committees, officers and administrative personnel, to whom have been delegated responsibilities for: (a) establishing policy in connection with the acceptance and administration of trust services, (b) the supervision over the execution of instructions in connection with administering trusts, (c) consultation and counselling with donors and beneficiaries of trusts, and (d) the supervision of activities of clerical personnel assigned operating functions and responsibilities in connection with the maintenance of records, safekeeping of securities, collections, and distribution of trust funds.

SERVICING OF BUSINESS. This phase of trust organization is in connection with the actual performance of operating functions, routines and procedures followed in administering trust accounts. Many of the routines and procedures, with slight modifications, are identical with those followed in commerical banking operations. For example: each trust relationship is carried as an account. Instead of it being a personal account, joint account, corporation account, however, it is an executor account, trustee account, agency account.

Checks received in payment of rent, interest, dividends on securities held in trust accounts, are collected through the facilities of the proof and clearing house section of the bank similar to checks on other banks deposited and cashed for customers who maintain a checking or savings account.

Checks for making disbursements of trust funds are charged against the balance of the account on which drawn. However, instead of beng honored on the signature of the person in whose name the trust account is carried, checks are honored on the signature of the trust officer and disbursements made in accordance with the terms of the trust indenture.

Statements showing the balance and details of respective trust accounts are periodically rendered to those who have an interest in the trust account similar to statements rendered on commercial checking accounts.

The functions of the trust department can best be described by reviewing an organization plan of a trust department for a medium sized commercial bank with trust powers, which has a board of directors, and president; and where delegation of responsibility of the directors for the trust administration is delegated to committees responsible to the board of directors.

In reviewing this chart as shown in Exhibit 111 and describing the respective functions, it is well to remember again that each bank providing trust services performs similar functions as described, the difference being in the size of the bank. In a large bank respective duties, responsibilities, and functions may be assigned to one particular person; where in a small bank, depending on volume, many functions may be assumed by several individuals or all by the same person.

The same delegation of responsibility applies to operations. In a large bank, depending upon the size, certain clerical personnel will be held responsible for performing one phase of trust operations; where in a smaller bank the same clerk might perform a number of distinct and separate operations, or might even be assigned other duties in connection with commercial or savings functions.

Under the Plan of Organization of the trust department of the bank we are using as an example, the board of directors determines the general policies of the bank, delegating to the trust administration committee and/or trust investment committee, specific responsibilities in connection wth the functions of the trust department somewhat along the following lines:

TRUST COMMITTEE

Membership: The Chairman of the Board as Chairman, the President, the officer in charge of the trust department, and two non-officer directors.

Principal functions are to:

1. Review the terms and conditions of all accounts presented to the bank in which the bank is to act in fiduciary capacity.
2. Accept or reject such accounts.
3. Review and approve the termination or closing of all trust accounts.
4. Advise and consult with the officer in charge of the Personal Trust Section and Corporate Trust Section in

EXHIBIT 111

ORGANIZATION PLAN OF THE TRUST DEPARTMENT

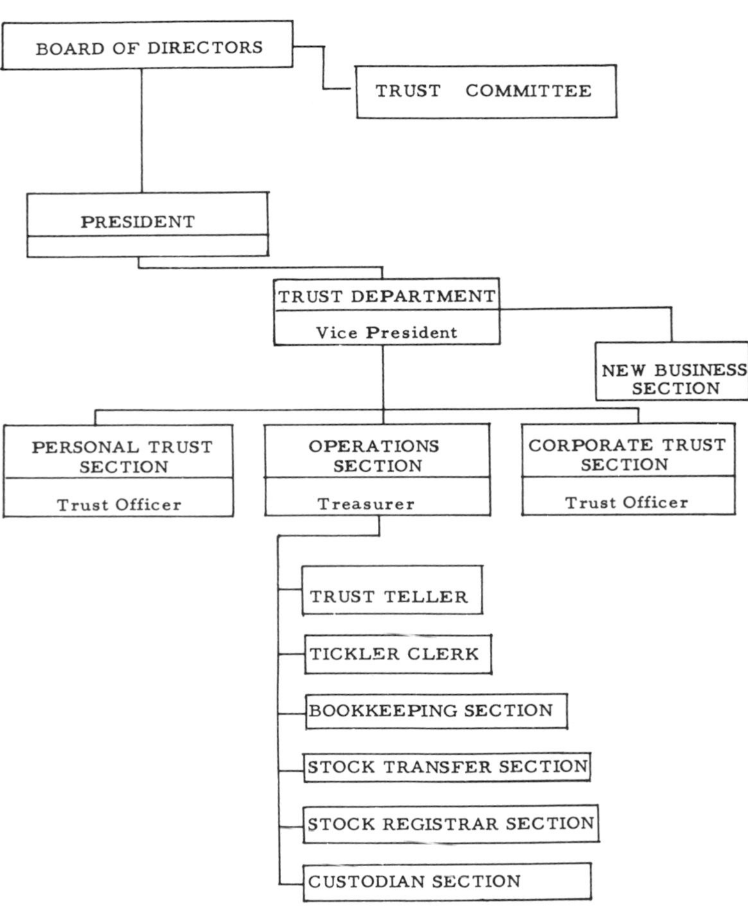

respect to administration and policy to be followed in conducting the operations of the trust department.

5. Review all trust accounts at least once a year for the purpose of determining compliance with the terms of the trust instrument; and to formulate policy and make specific recommendations in respect to management of the particular trust.
6. Review all assets held in each trust at least once a year to determine value, and the advisability of retaining or disposing of such assets. (Should the trust committee decide upon a change in the securities of one account, the decision immediately brings the security under review and leads to the independent consideration of that security in every other trust account, in which such security is held.)

   In order to enable the trust committee to take proper action, it shall be the duty of the officer in charge of the trust department or the secretary of the committee to make reports of the committee's review of each trust account. As assistance to interested parties, it is well to make such minutes with respect to the review of each trust account in triplicate, of which the original will be the minutes; the duplicate for the board of directors as a report of the committee; with the triplicate filed in the trust file for the information and guidance of the trust officer.
7. Authorize and approve the purchase of securities for all trust accounts.
8. Authorize and approve the sale of securities from all trust accounts.
9. Determine whether trust funds awaiting investment or disposition are in excess of the cash required to properly conduct the trust in accordance with the terms of the instrument and, if so, to see that such funds are invested or disbursed.

In connection with the functions of the trust committee, it is the duty of the trust officer or the secretary of the committee to prepare and maintain minutes of the actions of the committee. Here, too, it is well to maintain such records in triplicate for use of the board of directors, and memo to the trust file of the account.

Prior to reviewing a trust account, it is generally the responsibility of the trust officer or officer in charge of the respective administration division to prepare from the master or control register of the trust account a summarization of the matter on which the trust administrative committee, or trust investment committee, is required to take action. In order to expedite the review, it is advisable to have copies of this summary prepared in advance for distribution to each member of the committee following a current meeting so they will have an opportunity study it before the next meeting.

Recommendations and approvals of the investment of trust funds, or for the sale of securities held in trust accounts, are generally made only after carefully reviewing the information on the various securities, thorough study and research, and the selecting of trust securities which in their judgment are safe, dependable, and will provide suitable income for the needs of the beneficiaries of each particular trust.

To accomplish this and other objectives the trust committee either independently, through the investment officer of the bank, or through other sources, takes the widest and most complete advantage of the investment information supplied by brokers, investment counselling services, and correspondent banks. It is the aim and objective of trust departments to provide a sound balance or stability of principal, as well as to assure income on which the beneficiaries must depend for their security and financial protection.

Oftentimes the trust instrument, whether it is a will, trust agreement, or order of court, is ambiguous on the subject of trust investments. In the absence of instructions to the contrary, it is incumbent upon the trustee to follow the law of the state under which the trust is administered. Should the state provide a list or class of securities in which the trustee must invest, in the absence of direction or discretion granted by the trust instrument, securities for investment must be selected from that list. Should no list be available, then the trustee must make investments for the trust in accordance with certain standards or classes approved by the state.

In the final analysis it is incumbent upon the trustee to make investments in line with the letter and spirit of the trust instrument.

In reviewing the various responsibilities of the committee as outlined, it is well to point out that, depending on the size of the bank and type of trust services, such functions as here outlined as being performed by one committee, could be performed by two or more committees. By the same token, all such functions could be performed by a trust officer, or officer appointed with trust responsibility, reporting periodically to the full board of directors of the bank.

Responsibility for the general administration of the trust department is vested in the officer to whom the directors have delegated responsibility for trust administration. In some banks, depending on the volume and type of service provided, he may handle both personal and corporate trust relations and new business. In other banks he may only exercise supervision; delegating, with the approval of the directors, responsibility for the administration of personal trust accounts, corporate trust accounts, new business and trust operations, to several assistants responsible to himself. Whether performed by one or twenty one individuals, the functions of administrative personnel are to an extended or limited degree in connection with the following responsibilities, leaving to the operating division the operating methods and procedures used in executing the decisions of administrative personnel:

1. General supervision and responsibility for execution of policy in connection with respective trust accounts assigned to them.
2. Solicitation, negotiation and opening of new accounts.
3. Authorizing action to be taken on each trust account in accordance with the trust indenture.
4. Validating documents, and certifications on behalf of the bank.
5. Approval of all tickets effecting changes in the trust account.
6. Executing sales or purchases of investments.
7. Handling all correspondence in regard to trust matters.

Operating functions of a trust department generally begin when: (a) the bank is notified of the death of a person who has named it executor or trustee under will and it has received letters testamentary from the court; (b) the court has appointed it administrator and it has received letters of administration; (c) it is notified by the court of its appointment as guardian; (d) assets or documents for which it is to act in fiduciary capacity are deposited.

Following notification, or after preliminary arrangements have been completed, either the trust officer or a clerk in the trust department:

1. Prepares a folder containing a work sheet which details the various steps and necessary procedures which must be undertaken to establish the account, and which has space for the person undertaking the work to initial as proof of completion. In addition, step sheets will be prepared carrying various essential data and outlining steps to be taken in the administration of the trust. The folder will also include a schedule of claims, register of the heirs at law or beneficiaries, plus an abstract of the will or trust agreement.

2. Indexes the account in the register by date accepted, name of account, description of duties, account number assigned according to type of account, and the code.

Generally accounts maintained in the bookkeeping section and documents and correspondence are filed alphabetically, while for accounting and control purposes they are filed by code and number, similar to the following:

ADM.	Administrator
AGT.	Agent
CU.	Custodian
D. P.	Dividend paying agent
ESC.	Escrow
EXEC.	Executor
GDN.	Guardian
IN.	Investment duties in addition to safekeeping
L. T.	Land trust
P A.	Paying agent under bond issue
P. M.	Property management
REG.	Registrar of stocks or bonds
SK.	Safekeeping
T. A.	Trustee under agreement
T. B.	Trustee under bond issue

T. D.	Trustee under trust deed
T. I.	Trustee under life insurance trust
T. L.	Trustee, liquidation of business enterprise
T. W.	Trustee under will
TRAN.	Transfer agent

For cross reference purposes the bookkeeping and file sections usually maintain a file showing all numbers in chronological order opposite which the name of the account is indexed. However, systems will vary as between banks, depending on volume and other factors.

3. Prepares the inventory. Whenever a new account is opened, particularly in the case of executors, administrators, trustees, or guardians, the inventory sheet carrying a detailed description of each asset received must be prepared with sufficient copies for the trust teller, document file and bookkeeper.

In preparing such an inventory, the par value of stocks, bonds and mortgages is shown, together with their appraised value and, if possible, the cost. In addition, all items should be grouped separately, totalled and summarized; that is, all the various types of bonds grouped together and summarized, totalled; stocks summarized and totalled; and all other items handled in similar manner so that the corresponding classifications will correspond to the bookkeeping ledger sheet. Such items as jewelry, documents, heirlooms of undeterminable value are generally carried at one dollar each, as are stocks of no par value which are carried at one dollar per share.

Upon completion of the work sheet, all securities and documents, together with copy of the inventory are delivered to the trust teller or the trust cage for processing.

It is well to observe that all orders and instructions covering the deposit or withdrawal of documents, no matter where initially originated, generally are placed in the respective types of operating routines called for by the type of trust, in the trust cage which acts as a clearing house and distribution center for all types of trust operations. Sometimes, of course, depending upon the volume and circumstances particular to the individual trust department, the trust cage may be bypassed in connection with registrarships, trusteeships, and trust services of similar nature.

TRUST TELLER

After checking out securities and documents received and recorded in the inventory, the trust teller receipts for same. He then sends a copy of the work sheet and inventory to the tickler clerk for processing; the document and securities to the custodian for safekeeping or to other sections for processing, obtaining their receipt which is included in the folder and sent to the file.

In addition to being the originating agency for all trust operations, the trust teller has other principal duties, among which are to:

1. Process "in" and "out" tickets affecting trust accounts which will go to the bookkeeper, vault and the general books.

2. Accept securities and documents for deposit to trust accounts and issue the bank's receipt.

3. Release, upon proper authorization, securities and documents from trust accounts.

4. Handle any direct transactions with customers.

5. Accept cash and checks received in payment of trust collection items and effect their collection through the proof department of the bank.

6. Forward and collect all maturing items for payment.

7. Prepare credit tickets to respective trust accounts for the proceeds of collections.

8. Clip coupons from bonds held in trust accounts and make collection of the proceeds and remittance to the trust accounts.

9. Prepare and deliver checks to beneficiaries in payment of trust income, or disburse trust principal under terms of the trust indenture on proper authorization.

As the trust tellers initiate all operating procedures, once authority has been given, to effectively operate they usually prepare and maintain the following separate reference files:

1. Card file arranged in alphabetical order by name of trust.

2. Card file arranged in numerical order of the trust.

3. Cross reference card file where there are several names appearing in the title of the trust.

4. An "interested party" file which consists of cards alphabetically arranged in the names of all persons interested in any particular trust such as beneficiaries, attorneys, creditors, or all those who possibly have an interest in the trust. In addition to the names

of the interested individuals arranged in alphabetical order, the card also contains the number classification and the name in which the account is carried.

TICKLER CLERK

In carrying out the terms of a trust agreement, there are many duties and operations which must be done at fixed intervals. For example, income from each earning asset and principal on bonds, mortgages, accounts receivable and rents must be collected when due. Remittances must be sent to beneficiaries on time. Statements must be prepared periodically for beneficiaries. Reports must be prepared for the court and other interested parties. Insurance premiums must be paid when due. Tax returns must be prepared and filed at specified times.

To avoid mistakes of omission and commission, any of which could be costly and for which the bank would be held liable, separate controls and reminders known as tickler cards are maintained to assure the processing of work in conformance with the terms of the trust instrument.

It is the principal responsibility of the clerks in the tickler section to prepare, according to the original work sheet or by special direction of the officer who handles the account, such reminder cards as may be necessary to bring up the duties for attention on the proper date. In addition to maintaining the tickler record, the clerk maintains a cross reference card on each kind or issue of bonds, stock, or other readily marketable security belonging to a trust which shows the par value, number of shares and the book value of each issue, together with the name and number of the trust account in which the security is carried.

Such cards are essential for quick reference, because changing market conditions on securities may make it necessary or imperative for the trust officers to take action with regard to a particular security. Use of this file enables the trust officers to know immediately, should any reference be required, whether a certain security is held, the quantity in which it is held, and the account in which it is held.

Once the tickler cards have been set up they are filed under due date. In using the cards the entire file for the next succeeding month is pulled well in advance of the first day of the month and referred to the administrative officer or trust teller for execution; that is, to clip a coupon, mail a check, present a security for collection or redemption, collect a rent, or whatever the circumstance happens to be for which the tickler was made up. Once the collection has been effected or the work taken care of, the tickler is returned to the file and advanced to the next period for action indicated on the card.

Tickler cards are made up in duplicate. Generally, the first card is the master card which is never pulled, while the duplicate is used as a work sheet.

Tickler cards are also prepared and set up for the collection of trust charges or fees so the account may be referred to the trust officer and bills prepared for services rendered. The responsibility for preparing the cards and pulling the cards when due for reference to the proper party is vested in the tickler clerk, who also has the responsibility to follow up these file tickler cards and see to it that the matters referred to on the card are promptly handled. The use of tickler cards will vary between institutions depending on the volume.

BOOKKEEPING SECTION

The bookkeeping section of the trust department has many responsibilities among which are to:

1. Maintain all trust department financial and inventory records.

2. Post all tickets to respective trust accounts and control accounts as they come from the teller section.

3. Prepare financial statements and reports for each trust as required.

4. Provide income and expense figures to be used in preparing required tax returns.

Bookkeeping section records generally consist of two sets of records:

A. Individual books consisting of separate ledgers containing ledger sheets for assets and liabilities of each trust account.

B. General books consisting of control accounts reflecting the summarized totals of all types of assets and liabilities which make up the individual trust accounts.

Maintaining All Trust Department Financial and Inventory Records. The records for each trust account are prepared by the bookkeeping section from the work sheet or inventory, generally at the time the account is opened, and are posted and maintained as transactions occur. These records consist of, where applicable to the particular type of trust, a ledger sheet for each of the following items (plus a control sheet reflecting a total of financial data on all items in each particular classification):

1. Abstract—information in the trust account as to the donor, purpose, powers and beneficiaries.
2. Corpus—master control sheet showing the total value of all assets.
3. Principal cash—cash awaiting investments or re-investments.
4. Income cash—cash for distribution to beneficiaries or investment in principal.
5. Real estate
6. Mortgages
7. Stocks
8. Bonds
9. Notes
10. Sundry

Such respective ledger sheets which show the number, name of the trust and code are usually distinctively colored; that is, they are either blue, buff, pink or some other pastel shade, or have a colored line across the top or bottom indicating the particular asset classification.

Individual records of each trust account are maintained not only because the law requires all books, records and property of each trust to be kept separate from every other trust; but from the standpoint of internal control, and to facilitate the prompt rendering of statements for the information and use of donors, beneficiaries, trust officers, trust committee and the courts.

Posting of All Tickets to Respective Trust Accounts and Respective Control Accounts. All detail affecting increases or decreases in trust accounts must be recorded in considerable detail so that at statement time, when a run off is made, it will disclose sufficient information to fully advise the beneficiaries and any interested parties as to the transactions which have taken place in the account.

Particular attention must also be paid between principal and income. Cash in the principal account usually is to be reinvested and ultimately distributed at the time and in the manner directed under the trust instrument, while income from the investment of principal is usually distributable periodically to beneficiaries. It is necessary to keep such funds separate for proper accounting to be made of them in preparation of income taxe statements.

Preparation of Financial Statements and Reports for Each Trust as Required. Financial statements and reports must be prepared periodically for each trust account as an accounting of the stewardship of the bank to the beneficiaries or the courts, and as a report to the members of the trust committee as to the bank's compliance with the trust indenture. These statements, depending upon the type of the account, generally consist of:

A. A condensed statement of assets and liabilities.

B. A detailed statement showing the inventory of the asset and liability accounts.

C. A statement of the invested assets.

D. A statement of the income received.

E. A statement of any expenses.

F. A statement of the principal for the period showing the receipts, disbursements and balance on hand.

Such statements, again depending upon the type of trust and use, may show the assets by description, price at which they were acquired by the trust, and market value, in order to enable the trust committee and those who have a beneficial interest in the trust to make proper decision as to realization of profit from sale of such securities which have increased in price.

Providing Income and Expense Figures for Use in Preparing Required Tax Returns. This information is taken off respective records usually following a guide or schedule set up on a tickler as part of the statement preparation as outlined above. Such information is taken off respective records, when requested by the tickler section, and delivered to the tax attorney for his information in filing the proper tax returns.

GENERAL BOOKS. The general books of the trust department, posted from the daily tickets which effect each individual account, consist of the totals of the various transactions effecting the control accounts and reflect summarized figures of assets and liabilities of each respective trust account.

A balance sheet of a trust department of a small bank would reflect financial figures somewhat as follows:

ASSETS		LIABILITIES	
Cash	$ 7,000	Administrator	$ 420,000
Due from banks	213,000	Escrow	200,000
Bonds	847,000	Executor under will	840,000
Stocks	554,000	Trustee under agreement	691,000
Mortgages	417,000	Trustee under will	310,000
Real Estate	305,000		
Sundries	118,000		
TOTAL	$2,461,000	TOTAL	$2,461,000

The statement of an individual account would be similar as to detail of assets except that under the liabilities there would be a single heading noting the type of account.

The controls of respective accounts on the general ledger always balance against the totals of respective individual asset and liability accounts. All assets except cash are kept in safekeeping. Actual cash is maintained under control of the teller, while funds in trust accounts awaiting investment or disbursement are maintained in an account with the banking department either as a demand deposit, against which all checks and disbursement of trust funds are drawn, or in a special time account which is interest bearing.

STOCK TRANSFER SECTION

It is the function of the stock transfer section or stock transfer agent, whether it be the officer or clerk of the corporation or trust institution, to see that title, as evidence of ownership of shares of stock originally authorized by a proper resolution of the board of directors of the corporation, sold to, or purchased from others, is recorded on the capital stock books of the corporation in the name of the new legal owner. This is most important in case of a purchase, however, as according to law, a new purchaser is not recognized as being the legal stockholder of record until the transfer has been effected on the books of the corporation or transfer agent.

When the trust department of a bank is appointed to act as transfer agent for stocks or registered bonds of a corporation, it only assumes responsibility as agent after a proper resolution of the board of directors of the corporation has been passed, with a certified copy being delivered to the bank authorizing it to act as their agent. Once this authorization has been granted, then a trust agreement outlining the duties of the bank as the agent for the corporation, duly signed by an authorized officer of the corporation and the bank, is executed.

Stock certificates are personal property and ownership is passed from one person to another by assignment. To be effective as far as voting rights and dividends are concerned, such transfers must be recorded on the books of the corporation.

When shares of stock are sold it is necessary that the seller, in whose name the stock certificate was issued and whose name appears on the face of the certificate, assign the certificate to the purchaser (or leaving the assignment space blank if the stock is sold through a broker and the purchaser is unknown to the seller) by signing (endorsing) the certificate and having such signature witnessed and guaranteed. This must be done before the certificate is presented to the transfer agent for cancellation of the old certificate, and issuance of the new certificate to the new owner.

In making a transfer, it is necessary to determine first if the stock transfer books are still open. It is a general practice to close transfer books for short periods, whenever dividends are declared, in order to make up the list of the current stockholders entitled to have the right to receive the dividends.

Where there is wide and extensive trading in certain stocks, they are traded in street name, that is, in the name of the broker, which circulates from person to person until such time as the holder wishes to have the stock registered in his own name.

A form of assignment which usually appears on the stock certificate is shown at the top of the following page.

The signature of the assignee must correspond with the name as written on the face of the certificate in every particular, without alteration, enlargement or any change whatsoever.

Transfers of stock from one individual to another individual or to a bank or a corporation are accomplished with little trouble. The transfer, however, of securities registered in the name of a person who is deceased or who is acting in fiduciary capacity requires additional steps.

For value received (I) (We) (Name) ____________
hereby sell, assign and transfer unto (Name) ____________
________ shares of the capital stock represented by the within certificate, do hereby irrevocably constitute and appoint (Name) ____________ attorney to transfer the said stock on the books of the within named company with full power of substitution in the premises.

Signature (Name of Holder) ____________
Date ____________
Signed in the presence of: (Witnesses) ____________
Signature Guaranteed (Date) ____________
By: ____________

If the stock is registered in the name of a deceased person, it may be assigned by the executor or administrator of the estate. If the decedent died testate, to effect transfer it is usually necessary to provide a certified copy of the will, and a certificate of appointment as executor dated within 6 months of the presentation.

If the decedent died intestate, it is usually necessary to have a certified copy of the court appointment as administrator before such stock can be transferred.

It is usually a good policy, in connection with stock certificates registered in the name of a deceased person, for the administrator or executor to check with the transfer agent as to what papers are required or necessary to effect a transfer.

Where stock in the name of a trustee or guardian is transferred out or sold, it is usually necessary to furnish the transfer agent with a properly authenticated copy of the court order showing the appointment of the individual as trustee or guardian.

Where title to stock registered in name of a corporation is to be transferred, it is necessary that transfer of certificates be authorized and certificates signed (or endorsed) by a duly authorized officer of the corporation. Such authorization usually consists of a resolution of the board of directors authorizing certain officers of the corporation to assign a certificate in behalf of the corporation. A copy of the resolution, affixed with the corporate seal, is usually required by the transfer agent in making a transfer of the certificates.

Because conditions and circumstances vary under which a transfer agent is called upon to transfer ownership of stock on the books of the corporation, he must use proper precaution in protecting the interest of his principal and also the old and new stockholders; the former by seeing that the stock is transferred only upon a properly executed assignment; and to protect the new stockholder, by seeing that the wording of the new certificate correctly describes the ownership.

In operation, stock certificates when received from individuals, brokers, stock exchange houses, and banks and are properly assigned to the new owner and endorsed by the person in whose name the certificate is registered, are entered in the stock transfer journal by date, number of the certificate, name of the owner, number of the new certificate, and name of the new owner.

After being entered in the journal, the transaction is recorded in the stock register which contains a page or ledger sheet in the name of each stockholder showing the date acquired, number of shares acquired, certificate number and the balance.

After the transaction is recorded in the stock transfer journal, the new certificate is issued in the name of the new owner in the stock certificate book, and signed. The old certificate is then cancelled and affixed to its respective stub in the stock certificate book after which the certificate is mailed to the stock registrar for certification and delivery to the new owner. Sometimes, after being registered, the stock will be returned to the transfer agent for return to the party from whom originally received.

STOCK REGISTRAR SECTION

It is the function of the registrar to compare the number of shares represented by the certificates with the number of shares authorized and if there are no irregularities, to register the certificates on his own records and sign his name to each stock certificate.

Banks and trust companies authorized to act in fiduciary capacity are appointed by a corporation for the purpose of giving certification that all of the shares issued and in circulation do not exceed the number of shares authorized by proper resolution of the board of directors.

The relationship between a corporation and its registrar is a matter of contract. In the case of a new corporation, it is the duty of the registrar to see that only certificates representing the amount of shares authorized are authenticated. In the case of transfers of outstanding shares, it is the responsibility and duty of the registrar to make certain that each new certificate issued by the transfer agent, which in some cases is the corporation itself, is accompanied by a genuine certificate representing the same number of shares to be cancelled. It is the registrar's responsibility, too, to see that there is a cancellation for each issuance, and to validate new certificates, which have been presented to him, by affixing the authorized signature.

In operation, stocks or registered bonds are presented to the registrar either from the bank which acts as a stock transfer agent, or from the corporation itself. Generally, after registering the stock, it is returned to the corporation or the transfer agent for delivery to the new owner.

CUSTODIANSHIP OF TRUST ASSETS

As custodian of trust assets, the bank assumes not only a great responsibility which it zealously protects through physical safeguards, insurance safeguards, management safeguards, and custodian safeguards, but it assumes the responsibility for the clipping of coupons on bonds when due, presenting bonds in their custody for collection and payment when called or maturing, and seeing that all other assets receive maximum protection.

Well managed banks generally follow the principle of providing protection for the property of others as if it were their own.

Physical Safeguards. Physical safeguards of real property consist of devices for the protection of such property against fire, theft, burglary or damage.

Physical safeguards for personal property such as silverware, glassware, furniture, works of art, heirlooms, consist of providing the type of storage, whether in vaults or warehouses, that a prudent person would require or provide to safeguard and protect such property.

Physical protection of other personal property such as certificates of stock, bonds, notes, mortgages, valuable papers or documents, consists of providing space in a vault adequately protected against fire, theft and burglary.

Insurance Safeguards. Insurance safeguards consist of the bank maintaining a sufficient capital which is regulated by law; maintaining fidelity insurance under a blanket bond policy which provides protection to assets of the bank and assets belonging to others against loss by fire, theft, robbery, holdup, and acts of embezzlement or defalcation on the part of bank employees; and covering respective assets with other types of insurance warranted under the circumstances.

Intangible assets, and stocks, bonds and securities, are generally covered by the bank's blanket bond; while real and other property, in addition to physical safeguards, is covered by insurance protection such as public liability, fire, property damage, earthquake, wind storm, tornado, or whatever type and coverage is warranted under the circumstances.

In the conduct of its regular business the bank carries registered mail, special safe deposit, burglary and robbery, misplacement and theft insurance, all of which cover assets under the direct custodianship or management of the bank where it is acting in fiduciary capacity.

Management Safeguards. Management safeguards of real property not only consist of insurance, but the providing of management. This often involves the actual management of real estate properties including the rental services, upkeep and maintenance. If the trust department is not equipped or qualified to undertake such property management, it hires qualified people to engage in such activities, or places the property with a recognized and acceptable firm for management purposes.

Custodian Safeguards. It is the responsibility of the trust clerk to handle the securities. This begins when the securities are delivered on receipt by the trust teller and are checked against the work sheet. After all securities have been checked in, the custodian sees to it that title to all stocks, bonds, real estate, trust receipts, and legal title to all other types of investments and other property have been endorsed or assigned to the bank as trustee. Such securities are then sent out on receipt to the transfer agent to be transferred into the name of the bank or its nominee. A nominee is usually a fictitious company or person whose name is registered with other banks, stock exchanges and transfer agents, to facilitate the handling of trust securities.

Securities belonging to each trust account must be kept separately in an envelope under the name of the trust in a separate section of the vault. In the case of larger banks, the trust department will have its own individual vault where securities are properly stored and serviced.

The key to trust operations is the tickler system. In operation, sometime during the current month, tickler cards covering the coupons, bonds, interest on mortgages, notes, etc. due in the coming month are sent to the custodian. Prior to due date, and usually during the same month, the custodian of the trust assets, together with a representative of the auditing department, will remove the coupons from the bonds and process them. In processing, coupons are sorted as to issue, amount and maturity date. Coupons from each issue are placed in a special envelope on which is inscribed the name of the issuing agent, where the coupons are payable, the due date and the name and address of the trust account, certificates of ownership, the number of coupons, and the dollar amount. On due dates, respective deposits are made to respective accounts for the amount of the interest collected, and the coupons are sent to the paying agent or to the collection department for presentation and payment.

When new securities are delivered to the custodian of the safekeeping section, they are checked in and receipted for. A numbered safekeeping receipt, generally in quadruplicate, is then issued by the custodian which shows the name and number of the trust, amount, description of security or asset deposited, and other pertinent information.

The original of the receipt is used for the permanent record; the duplicate usually is filed in the trust file; the triplicate goes to the auditing department; and the quadruplicate goes to the tickler clerk for checking against the work sheet and preparation of the tickler cards.

On securities withdrawn from the vault, the trust officer prepares a withdrawal memorandum giving the amount and description of securities being taken out, which is presented to the custodian, who delivers the securities as requested, obtaining a receipt on the original receipt form. Receipts for securities deposited with a custodian are generally filed in the trust envelope.

It is the responsibility of the file clerk to file all receipts, copies of correspondence and schedules in the trust file; and to maintain such files in good order so that the information is readily available to the officer whenever the tickler calls attention to the fact a report should be rendered or a matter reviewed.

INTERNAL CONTROL SYSTEMS AND AUDITING PROCEDURES

Additional protection for donors and beneficiaries is provided through examinations, internal control systems and audit programs provided by the supervisory authorities and the bank's own personnel.

Supervisory authorities examine the trust departments of banks from time to time as provided by law. Such examinations are undertaken by experienced trust examiners in order to see that all legal regulations are being complied with, and that the operations of the trust department are being conducted in a manner consistent with good business practices.

Provisions of the Federal Reserve Act applying to national banks require that a committee of directors, exclusive of any active officers of the bank, shall at least during each 12-month period make suitable examinations or audits of the trust department or cause such examinations or audits to be made by auditors responsible to the board.

This annual examination or audit, which must be made in addition to any examination made by the state or federal bank examiners, must be undertaken by the board of directors, the trust auditing committee or someone appointed by them. Such an examination or audit should include not only an examination and review of the different documents in the trust accounts, verification of the securities with the inventory, review of the correspondence and the trust instruments to see that the terms of the agreement are being followed but that every asset, as disclosed by the work sheet and receipts, is properly recorded.

In undertaking such an examination or audit each asset, if income bearing, should be checked to determine that all the income has been received and credited to the proper account, and that the income as recorded on the ledger account reconciles with receipts shown on the income cash account. This is readily discernible from review and analysis of bonds, notes, mortgages. However, it is sometimes difficult to ascertain income in connection with stocks. For this purpose the auditor should maintain records or check with financial services to determine the amount of dividends paid during the period and the date such dividends were declared.

Where real estate is involved, the leases or tenant contracts should be checked and income traced to the proper income account.

Expenditures in connection with trusts should be traced from the trust account to the check disbursing same, and endorsement of the parties receiving the proceeds verified.

Once the annual examination or audit has been completed, the committee or auditor should make a full deport to the trust auditing committee which in turn presents it to the board of directors for acceptance, together with recommendations and suggestions for correcting any omissions or meeting criticisms set forth in the report.

In a well managed bank, most of the routine custodianship controls should be set up under a daily control system which provides for the use of receipts and written orders for the deposit and withdrawal of securities and other assets, with a copy to the audit section for later verification.

From an internal control standpoint, depending upon the volume, the internal auditor, daily or periodically as the case might be, checks out from the work sheet all items which comprise the corpus of a trust. He follows through with the collection department or with the safekeeping department on certificates sent out for transfer in the name of the bank's nominee for compliance. On the matter of coupons and bonds sent for collection and rents or other income received, he sees that proceeds are properly credited to the proper trust account.

INCOME TAX RETURNS

In connection with certain types of trust accounts, it is the responsibility of the trust department to prepare and file income tax returns, or to prepare and forward such information to the beneficiaries for their use in preparing their own returns. In order to provide this information, security ledger sheets generally show in their headings the tax status of each income producing asset, so that at the end of the period, in taking off the report, it is easy to determine income which is taxable and income which is not taxable.

As all tax returns are prepared in accordance with the generally accepted practice on a fiscal year or calendar year basis, each account is set up on tax tickler cards. To simplify the work of the trust department, it is the customary practice of some banks to adopt the fiscal year basis for preparation of tax returns so that the work can be spread over the period of a year's time instead of having all returns prepared for filing at the same time.

COMPENSATION

Trust services are rendered by separate trust institutions or trust departments of commercial and savings banks licensed to act in fiduciary capacity. Being a business enterprise with capital either provided solely for the risk involved in rendering trust services, or where capital provided for undertaking the banking business is used to assume the risk involved in acting in fiduciary capacity, the stockholders who own the enterprise are supposed to make a profit and should not be expected to render free service or accept unprofitable business. In order to render such trust services while being properly compensated for the risk involved, the value of such services should be determined.

The value of trust services can be gauged two ways:

1. The monetary cost of providing the service.
2. The responsibility assumed.

The monetary cost of safekeeping a large volume of securities, considering the insurance and providing other protection, may be negligible but the responsibility assumed in having the custody of such securities could be burdensome.

A statement of principles of trust institutions by the Executive Committee of the Trust Division of the American Bankers Association clearly states that trust institutions are entitled to reasonable compensation for services. Further, that the minimum compensation for services in any community should be uniform, and applied uniformly and impartially to all customers alike. It is not meant, however, that compensation cannot be graduated according to the size and nature of the trust account, far from it. It does, however, mean that regardless of the basis of compensation, fees should be applied uniformly and impartially to all customers, and the same schedule of fees charged by all banks serving a particular area.

To accomplish this objective, and in order to be assured of obtaining proper and equitable compensation for services rendered, trust departments of banks in any given area are generally guided by and follow a schedule of fees for regular services, set up somewhat similar to the following:

ADMINISTRATOR OR EXECUTOR	
Gross value	Approximate rate
Under $25,000	5%
On the next $25,000	4%
On the next $50,000	3½%
On all over $100,000	3%

INSURANCE TRUST	
Acceptance fee	$50
Distribution fee at the time of death	
On the first $100,000	1%
On all additional amounts	½ of 1%

MANAGEMENT SERVICE	Annual charge
Improved income property	6% of the gross income

REGISTRAR	Annual charge
Minimum charge covering registration of 100 certificates	$100
For each additional certificate	$.25

SAFEKEEPING	Annual fee*
Bonds, notes, mortgages	
On first $100,000	$2.00 per $1,000 par value
On next $100,000	$1.50 per $1,000 par value
On all over $200,000	$1.00 per $1,000 par value
Stocks	.06 per share
*Minimum $75.00	

TRANSFER AGENCY	Annual charge
Minimum charge for issuance of 100 certificates, and maintenance of 100 accounts	$100
Each additional account and each additional share issued	.40

TRUST UNDER AGREEMENT	Annual fee
On the first $50,000	½ of 1%
On the next $50,000	¼ of 1%
On amounts over $100,000	1/5 of 1%

TRUSTEE UNDER CORPORATE INDENTURE	
First $100,000 or fraction of principal	$200
All over $100,000 of principal	1/10 of 1%

TRUSTEE UNDER WILL	
Acceptance fee	$100
	Annual charge*
On the first $100,000	½ of 1%
On next $100,000	¼ of 1%
On all over $200,000	1/10 of 1%
*Minimum charge $500	

Cost of special records where required, such as ledger cards, binders, checks, transfer registration reports, and expense in connection with postage, insurance, etc. are to be added to the regular charges for services.

Due to the increased development of trust facilities of banks, not only are more and more people seeking trust services in providing assistance in managing their financial affairs and protecting and safeguarding their estate, but are making wide use of the counselling services which most banks have available to assist their customers in their financial planning.

To acquaint customers not only with the services available, but with the ethics followed by a bank in administering trusts, many banks have found it advisable to make public the principles under which they conduct relationships in fiduciary capacity. One of the most complete is the declaration of trust principles of the First National Bank of Leesburg, Florida, promulgated for the information of customers and the public alike. It can serve as a guide for banks in making their principles known to the public they serve.

FIDELITY

FIDELITY is and forever shall be the cardinal principle governing the administration of estates and trusts by this bank.

SECRECY

INFORMATION ACQUIRED by a director, officer or employee of this bank relating to any estate or trust in its care, of the beneficiaries thereof, MUST NOT BE REVEALED except when required by law.

COMPLIANCE

THE FIRST DUTY of this bank shall be to promptly and faithfully carry out the wishes of the creator of every trust as expressed in the will or trust agreement.

IMPARTIALITY

EVERY TRUST shall be administered in the interest of the beneficiaries thereof, without the intrusion of any personal interest of the bank itself or that of outside parties.

GRATUITIES

NO DIRECTOR, OFFICER or EMPLOYEE of this bank shall accept or receive, either directly or indirectly, any personal gratuity whatsoever from or through any trust administered by the bank unless he shall be a named beneficiary thereof evidenced by the appointing document or a court order relating thereto.

INDIVIDUAL SERVICE

THE PROPERTY, securities and records of every trust shall be kept separate and apart from those of every other trust and from the property and assets of the bank itself.

SECURITY

FUNDS received or held by this bank in a trust capacity shall not be used by the bank in the conduct of its business unless fully secured by the deposit of bonds of the United States or other securities approved by the Board of Governors of the Federal Reserve System.

INVESTMENTS

TRUST INVESTMENTS held or made by this bank shall be governed at all times by consideration of SAFETY OF PRINCIPLE and DEPENDABILITY OF INCOME and shall not be influenced in any wise by the hope of unusual gain for the trust through risk or speculation.

NON-PARTICIPATION

THIS BANK shall not have or acquire any personal interest in the trust investments of any of its estates.

NO DIRECTOR, OFFICER or EMPLOYEE shall purchase from or sell to any estate committed to the care of this bank, any property or securities of any kind whatsoever.

THIS BANK shall not at any time buy or sell to any such estate, any property or securities in which the bank itself or any of its directors or officers has any personal financial interest.

COMPENSATION

THE COMPENSATION of this bank for trust services shall be based on the reasonable cost of such service, and the responsibilities involved, and shall be applied impartially to all customers alike.

Depending on the size of the bank, trust services provided, and volume of business some or all of the operating instructions issued in connection with the operations of the commercial and other departments and sections of the bank will apply. In addition, some or all of the following instructions will be operative:

1. Schedule of trust fees.
2. Regulations in regard to opening and closing trust vaults.
3. Procedure for investing of trust funds.
4. Authorization for withdrawals of trust securities.
5. Classification of trust accounts.
6. Approval of debit tickets covering disbursement of cash from trust accounts.

CHAPTER XXXVIII

THE INTERNATIONAL DEPARTMENT

WHILE THE TERM INTERNATIONAL DEPARTMENT is of recent origin, many of the functions performed in such departments today in connection with providing servces for customers, originated in ancient times with the money changers and goldsmiths, when they accepted and used receipts of other money changers as mediums of exchange.

Such receipts, when carried by a local merchant traveling in a foreign city, enabled him to obtain funds with which to make purchases simply by signing over such right title and interest in such receipts as he had, to the foreign money changer in exchange for "local money" he required for his business dealings.

These receipts passed as "currency" between towns until they were finally presented to the goldsmith or money changer who had originally issued them; and exchanged them for the actual metal called for in the receipt.

The development of commerce and business required the money changers and goldsmiths to provide other services. Then when the business of the money changers and goldsmiths developed into the business we now call banking, the services in connection with the importation and exportation of goods began to be provided by specially organized departments or sections of commercial banks.

Originally such departments were developed by seaboard banks, that is banks located in cities which provided harbor and dock facilities for the shipping, receiving and storage of foreign goods and commodities, such as those located in Boston, Providence, New York, Mobile and New Orleans.

Later, with the development of commerce and trade between foreign countries and the westward expansion of the United States, banks in other cities located on waterways, such as Savannah, Jacksonville, Tampa, Galveston, Houston, San Francisco, Portland and

Seattle, provided this service. In recent years the opening of the Great Lakes Waterway has made the servicing of foreign trade an important function of banks located in the Great Lakes cities such as Buffalo, Detroit, Cleveland, Chicago and Milwaukee.

Almost all of the foreign business engaged in by United States companies, where banking or financial assistance is required, is handled by less than 100 banks, several of which maintain many branches throughout Central and South America, Europe, Asia and Africa, and have in turn correspondent banking relationships with banks located in countries on those continents.

Inland banks, that is banks not located directly on waterways, while making foreign services available to their customers, generally handle and complete transactions involving foreign trade through the facilities of seaboard banks which are their correspondents.

The fact that most foreign banking business is concentrated in relatively few banks is due to the fact that it is a highly specialized field. It is therefore most advantageous for a domestic company conducting business with a company located in a foreign country, to have the financial end handled by a bank which has connections with a bank located in that country so as to be able to obtain up-to-date financial reports and be provided with reports on current economic and political conditions.

It is also most important that a domestic company, when engaged in foreign business, not only establish a relationship with a bank which can provide it with proper service, but one which has a thorough knowledge of the various methods used in financing foreign trade so that the particular needs of the business can be handled.

It is also advisable that the bank with which a domestic concern does foreign business be familiar with the language and customs of such country and have reliable sources which can be depended upon for providing current credit information regarding the important business concerns doing business in respecitve countries.

Another reason for the concentration of foreign department business among a few banks is because foreign department operation can only become profitable if, in addition to developing a relationship with domestic customers, the bank also develops a deposit and credit relationship with customers located in foreign countries and with foreign banks, through which acceptance business and advances can be developed.

In order to properly operate, domestic banks recognized as leaders in the field of foreign business maintain either directly or through correspondent arrangements, accounts with leading banks located in the principal cities of the world such as Lima, Rio de Janeiro, Buenos Aires, Alexandria, Cape Town, London, Venice, Hamburg, Barcelona, Istanbul, Stockholm, Bombay, Calcutta, Hong Kong, Shanghai, Yokohama, Manila, Sydney, Melbourne and others.

In order for a domestic bank to enter the foreign trade field it is first necessary for it to establish its own credit standing abroad in order that its letters of credit and travelers checks may be easily negotiated. It is a generally accepted fact that the operations of a foreign department in connection with selling foreign drafts, letters of credit, handling the ordinary routine collections and accommodations, are a service generally provided by a bank to customers of the bank at a loss. For this reason, even some of the largest banks prefer to process their foreign business through one of the top major banks of the country.

Where it is advisable for an American business concern to maintain bank accounts in foreign countries to facilitate trade, it is considered more efficient to maintain such accounts in an American bank which has a branch in the country or city where the domestic concern is doing business, not only because of the ease with which his funds may be transferred, but from the standpoint of providing credit information and other facilities.

Concurrent with development of the country came our present generation of Americans from the great influx of foreign born. Attracted by the money making possibilities in this land of opportunity, they located wherever commerce and industry beckoned their talents—the coal mines of Virginia; the steel mills of Pennsylvania and Indiana; the tillable land of the Middle West; the ranges and mining of the great Northwest; the fishing and commercial opportunities of the Atlantic and Pacific coasts.

Once settled, many of these foreigners sent money home for passage for their families to come to join them in America. During this time many banks, located in areas where these people settled, opened foreign departments which were just what the name implies. Originally a foreign department was set up to serve those whose tongue was different than ours—a place for foreigners, unfamiliar with the American system of banking, to exchange their dollars into foreign money to remit home; or to place such funds in a savings account to build a nest egg for a home or a farm and lay the foundation for financial security. That they were successful is evident today by those with foreign sounding names who occupy positions of prominence in business, commerce, finance and government. During this period millions and millions of dollars earned here in the United States were sent "home" to Greece, Italy, Germany, Poland, China, Japan, Sweden, Scotland, and Ireland, which not only enabled other people of these countries to come to the United States, but most important, provided funds which contributed to the economy of those nations.

Many of the restrictions which have curtailed the flow of such money in recent years have also contributed to the need for the Federal Government, through Lend-Lease, the Marshall Plan etc., to make loans and grants to such countries to bolster their economy.

About the turn of the century, and with the development of travel, many banks in major cities all over the country, in addition to making American Express Company travelers checks, and travelers letters of credit drawn on their New York correspondent banks available for use and convenience of their customers traveling in foreign countries, began to provide additional travel service in the form of arranging for hotel reservations and obtaining railroad and steamship tickets.

As a result of these developments, the international departments of most of the leading banks today not only handle commercial transactions between their domestic customers and those residing and doing business in foreign countres, but provide practically every type of facility for their customers in conducting trade and traveling ouside the continental United States.

Before going into the operations and functions of the international department of banks, lest its absence be questioned, it may be well to comment briefly on the matter of gold. This should be covered from the standpoint of use as a medium of exchange in the settlement of debt between countries arising out of the export and import trade, so as to not confuse the flow of gold with normal transactions handled by international departments of banks.

For thousands of years gold, as we have learned, has been recognized as the prime medium of exchange and the use, sacredness and respect for gold in the beginning of the 19th century became the base for what has been known as the gold standard. This gold standard, developed primarily by the Bank of England, came about by giving British pounds a constant value in terms of a specific quantity of gold, thus the English pound became the universally accepted substitute for gold. It wasn't long before other countries, and in time practically the entire world, adjusted their medium of exchange to gold because of its convertibility. The basing of currencies of nations on gold was effective until the first World War, not only in settling international accounts, but as a basis for currency and credit. Freely flowing as it did, it had an almost immediate effect on credit and interest rates. First of all, a physical outflow of gold reduced the credit base which could only be countered by raising the discount rate which curtailed credit. If gold came into the country in vast amounts, it brought about the re-reduction in the discount rate making it cheaper to borrow thus absorbing the gold.

Prior to World War I gold movements to a great extent were determined by interest (discount) rates. It was the main function ot central banks to maintain the international stability of their currency through the raising or lowering of the discount rate.

In recent years the increased role of government in influencing business activity has upset the functions of central banks as to controlling the gold supply.

The increased role of government in managing the economy of a country and the importance of gold as a basis for currency and credit has also declined. Formerly, under the gold standard principles, the currency of central banks was generally supported by a stipulated or fixed percentage of gold. Such percentages are virtually non-existent in a managed economy with the result that the principal function of gold in recent years has been to settle trade balances between nations.

The beginning of our present problems occurred toward the end of World War I after the Communists succeeded to power in

Russia and forbade the exporting of gold. Both Germany and Italy went off the gold standard as soon as the socialists and fascists came to power, and in 1931, prior to the world-wide depression of the 30's, Britain placed an embargo on gold and ceased redeeming the pound in gold.

In the dark days of 1933 and 1934, with the backing of Congress, the United States seized all the gold in the Federal Reserve Banks, compelled individuals to surrender gold, repudiated the gold redemption clause in government obligations and internationally devalued the dollar. The unrest in Europe in the late 30's; the fear of Naziism, Fascism and Communism; the confiscation and expropriation of wealth in Russia, Italy, Germany and their satellite countries resulted in a liquidation by nationals of their foreign assets, conversion to gold and the depositing of gold in the United States.

The beginning of World War II found the United States in the untenable position of being the prime supplier of merchandise, goods, and supplies of war, for which payments had to be made in gold. It was not long before foreign countries ran out of gold because they were buying from us more than they could sell to us and due to the fact their productive capacity was involved in war goods. When the gold supply was depleted we had two choices. We could loan them the money; or provide them with funds with which to purchase commodities and supplies, by means of lend-lease or gifts. This latter solution was decided upon by the realization that if assistance was in the form of loans the allies would be saddled with such a great mountain of debt at the end of the war they would not have the wherewithal to resume normal trade relations with us. In this hodge-podge of finance the United States taxpayer was called upon to carry the load which took the form first of Lend-Lease, the Marshall Plan, International Cooperation Program, and other plans through which the resources of this country have been dissipated, depleted and used to assist other nations to compete with us in the commercial areas of the world.

The phenomenal recovery of England, France, Germany and Japan following the cessation of hostilities was truly remarkable; but due almost entirely to our financial assistance, debt forgiveness and long term credits.

Because of this widespread assistance, our national debt has constantly increased, depleting our resources. This ever-increasing government debt is vicious, especially when the Treasury Department, by the very acts of Congress in appropriating vast sums of money in excess of what is provided through taxes, is compelled to meet current obligations by selling bonds directly to the banking system. Because of this complex procedure, government bonds when purchased by the Federal Reserve System or by individuals add to the reserves, as gold used to do, and can be multiplied through liberalized reserve rules by a process of private bank loans, thus creating new money. As a result there has been a tragic decline in the dollar's purchasing power, the value of wages, salaries and retirement funds, even in the Social Security funds for millions of Americans.

What people do not realize, in this matter of gold, is that for the last ten years the United States has been sending abroad more dollars in payment for imports, foreign and military aid, tourist travel and private investments, than have returned to the United States in payment of exports, return on investments and repayment of foreign loans.

Since 1950 military expenditures have aggregated in excess of 27 billion dollars. At the present time we are spending about 3 billion dollars a year for maintenance of our armed services abroad which funds, used for the purchase of food, commodities, housing and services, bolster the economy of the country in which the money is spent.

Since 1950 we have made grants, loans and outright gifts to foreign countries which have aggregated another 27 billion dollars, and now continues at the rate of about 2½ billion a year.

In the same period we have invested some 12 billion dollars in direct investments in foreign enterprises, and have spent or left another 10 billion dollars in foreign countries as a result of our travels, all of which has gone to assist their economy.

Because of our gratuitous attitude; failure to impose certain restrictive embargos; inability to compete in foreign markets; we have only been able to realize approximately 5 billion dollars a year from our export trade and other payments. As a result the deficit of about 3½ billion dollars a year has been settled in the last 10 years through an outflow of gold or earmarking of gold for foreign countries in settlement of trade.

The reason for this deficit and the problems we are experiencing today in respect to gold is due to the fact that in the United States, as used in settlement of international trade, there are two kinds and types of dollars. One type of dollar, with which we are very familiar, is the one which consists of a piece of green paper known as currency or a piece of ordinary paper used as a medium of exchange when properly scrawled with a signature known as a check. The other kind is the same dollar except that we give it to foreigners. Under the present management of our monetary system, however, all dollars used in foreign countries, through devious ways and means, can be used in settlement of trade balances through the International Monetary Fund through which process the presenting nation converts such dollars into credit on the books of the International Monetary Fund which credit can be converted into actual gold and delivered on demand.

The principles of foreign exchange in operation at the present time are nothing more than the continuation of the principles of barter and exchange in effect from the beginning of time. Trade is nothing more than an exchange of commodity for commodity. One section manufactures or raises one type of commodity which it trades or sells to another section, receiving in return something of like value or a medium of exchange.

The same principles apply in the credit between nations. One country sells cotton; another jewels; another farm machinery; still another country sells steel and various manufactured goods. Each nation takes in return or in exchange, wheat, cotton, raw material, or manufactured goods of the other country. However, inasmuch as the amounts traded do not always balance because one country buys more than it sells, there is a difference in the balance of trade payments which must be settled in money. This is accomplished by the transfer or settlement of debt through the major bank of one country and a bank of another country in the International Monetary Fund. This is done in final form by allowing debits and credits for trade to accumulate between merchants in certain countries; and periodically settling with merchants in another foreign country for the difference through an exchange on the books of respective banks. Settlement of debt is exactly the same as the practice followed by commercial banks. They provide funds for the customer by drawing on an account they maintain in another city, except that in relationships between the United States and foreign countries, differences are settled by a transfer of gold through the International Monetary Fund.

Credit or money which foreign countries can convert into gold arise from the following sources:

1. Funds to pay for goods imported by merchants and dealers for sale in this country.

2. Payments for securities representing domestic investments in foreign companies.

3. Tourist expenditures.

4. Payment of principal, interest and dividends from stocks and bonds in domestic corporations held by nationals of a foreign country.

5. Remittances for insurance and freight charges due foreign countries.

Credit, or the money owed us or owed domestic corporations by foreign customers or customers located in foreign countries, arises out of the following transactions:

1. Goods manufactured in the United States and sold abroad against which drafts are drawn.

2. Securities, stocks and bonds of foreign corporations which have been sold and for which proceeds must be remitted.

3. Remittances for freight and insurance due American companies.

4. Funds spent by nationals of foreign countries visiting and touring the United States.

Ultimately or periodically, whenever one country accumulates more funds of another country than it disburses, there must be a settlement to balance trade which can only be accomplished by a transfer of gold. At the present time this is accomplished by the transfer of gold on the books of the International Monetary Fund. The basis of all exchange dealing is always the price at which the monetary unit of one country is expressed in gold, in relation to the monetary unit of the other country expressed in gold.

Interim settlements and payments, or the settlement of amounts due and owed between individuals, which arise out of normal business transactions, however, are made by commercial credits developed from the importation and exportation of goods.

The International Departments of banks maintain the facilities through which such commercial credits are handled, and provide other services which assist customers in developing foreign trade and handling commercial transactions. Before we cover the various services provided by the International Department it is well to point out that there are varied and significant differences between handling domestic and foreign operations and between concerns engaged in domestic and foreign business.

In a domestic trade, goods are generally passed directly from a manufacturer or seller to the buyer or consumer with few, if any documents required. Financing is done between the buyer and his bank or between the manufacturer and the bank by discounting the paper, use of an open line of credit, or through various facilities available for financing the manufacture and sale of goods.

In connection with foreign business, operations are concerned primarily with the movement of goods between the United States and a foreign country, and use of the various documents required covering the shipping, delivery and payment of the goods. Fundamentally, principles of foreign trade are exactly the same as used here in the United States in domestic trade where commercial transactions take place between principals located in different states except that we have no boundaries, no trade barriers, no exchange charges between states. There is no ultimate settlement of net balances owed through the transfer of gold.

The principal services provided by the International Departments (or Foreign Departments) of banks, either through their own facilities or through the facilities of their correspondent banks, are in connection with:

1. Issuing commercial letters of credit to finance the importation of foreign goods and commodities.

2. Issuing travelers letters of credit to provide those traveling in foreign countries with funds.

3. Selling foreign exchange necessary to pay for imported goods purchased in foreign currency.

4. Financing importers to enable them to carry goods between the time of payment and arrival in the United States.

5. Making advances to importers against warehouse receipts covering foreign goods and commodities.

6. Collecting drafts drawn by domestic exporters on foreign importers.

7. Paying drafts drawn by domestic exporters under letters of credit issued by foreign and domestic banks.

8. Making advances on drafts presented for collection drawn against letters of credit.

9. Selling foreign money.

10. Selling travelers checks.

11. Purchasing and selling cable transfers and checks in foreign currency.

In addition, the International Departments of banks:

A. Render reports on the credit standing of suppliers of goods and commodities located in foreign countries.

B. Provide letters of introduction to bankers and third parties abroad.

C. Obtain hotel accommodations, direct or through travel agencies and correspondent banks, for customers and for customers of correspondent banks.

D. Make railroad, steamship, and airline reservations direct, through travel agencies and correspondent banks, for customers and for customers of correspondent banks.

In connection with financing foreign trade and in providing the services as above described the following instruments and documents (as previously outlined in Chapter XXIII) are used by customers and the International Department, in handling foreign trade transactions:

1. Acceptance credits.
2. Bank drafts and bills of exchange.
3. Bills of lading.
4. Cable transfers.
5. Commercial letters of credit, both import and export.
6. Travelers checks.
7. Travelers letters of credit.
8. Trust receipts.

9. Warehouse receipts.

Acceptance Credits. By use of acceptance credits banks finance importation and exportation of readily marketable goods and commodities.

To finance the purchase of goods, once they have been ordered and shipped, the bank's customers draw a draft on the bank at 60 to 90 days sight which, when presented, the bank accepts to mature in 60 to 90 days. In addition, the customer executes an agreement with the bank to reimburse it at maturity for the amount of the acceptance.

Such acceptance may either be discounted for the customer by the bank at the regular buying rate, or returned to the customer in order to enable him to dispose of it on the market through one of the discount houses. The proceeds received are used by the customer of the bank to pay for the merchandise. After the transaction is completed, the proceeds are deposited with the bank to pay off the acceptance when it is presented for payment at maturity; or if the bank has discounted the acceptance itself, to retire it.

Many companies which manufacture and sell goods not only in domestic but foreign markets, finance their foreign sales by use of time or sight drafts drawn in dollars on the purchaser. However, instead of waiting to get the proceeds of sale from the foreign buyer as remitted generally in New York exchange, the manufacturer finances the export by a bank acceptance.

After the goods have been shipped the customer sends the draft and shipping documents to the bank for collection. At the same time he draws a time draft on the bank for approximately the amount of the purchase or sale to mature at approximately the time the proceeds from the collection will arrive in the states in the form of New York exchange. The bank accepts the draft and discounts it, using the draft drawn on the foreign purchaser with the documents attached as collateral security. The bank then sends the draft and documents abroad to its correspondent bank for presentation and payment. The proceeds when received are applied against the acceptance at maturity.

Acceptance credits for financing an import or export can also be established so as to be repayable in a foreign currency.

Under such an arrangement where the customer is obligated to provide foreign exchange to pay the foreign acceptance at maturity, and to protect himself from loss due to the exchange rate fluctuation, he buys the required exchange from the bank for future delivery at a fixed rate. The bank obtains reimbursement by sending abroad for acceptance, the time drafts they have purchased which after acceptance are sold in the foreign discount market with the proceeds deposited in the foreign branch or an account with a correspondent bank.

When the transaction has been completed, the customer takes up the future contract by paying for the foreign exchange at the fixed rate in dollars, after which the bank remits foreign currency to the foreign financial center or by a check on its own bank or that of its correspondent to provide for the maturiting acceptance. Under such an arrangement the customer received American dollars by selling the bank the foreign exchange time draft and pays his obligation with a fixed amount of dollars. The advantage of this type of transaction is that at the time the goods are shipped or negotiations entered into, the buyer also knows the cost of financing which can be figured in the retail sales price of the goods.

This procedure is only used for protection when there is wide fluctuation in exchange rates or if the borrowing and discount rates abroad are lower than they are in the domestic market.

The reverse is also true; that is, when the borrowing or discount rates are lower in the United States than in foreign countries it may be more profitable to finance the transaction in the New York market.

In studying foreign exchange transactions it must be again remembered that money is a commodity and can be bought, sold, traded and exchanged just like any other commodity. Borrowing, therefore, in connection with foreign transactions, or borrowing by domestic companies in foreign markets can be profitable or advantageous, depending upon the exchange rates and the availability of funds for investment.

Bank Drafts and Bills of Exchange. A bank draft or bill of exchange, as we learned, is a written order drawn by one bank ordering another bank with whom the first bank maintains an account, to pay a certain sum of money to a third party on sight or on a specified time after date.

In foreign exchange transactions, because of the delay and inconvenience incurred when documents are lost or destroyed and because bills of lading, insurance certificates, instructions are usually prepared in multiple form, drafts and bills of exchange are also usually prepared in duplicate or triplicate and attached to copies of the documents.

Such drafts and bills of exchange bear on their face either one of two phrases, depending of course upon whether or not the original document has been paid or lost. These phrases are "Pay against this Check (Duplicate being unpaid) to the order of" or "Pay against this check (Original being unpaid) to the order of————."

When a draft is drawn it is the customary practice for the issuing bank to advise the drawee bank that it has drawn a draft on its account with them so that the bank will be in a position to pay the draft upon presentation, subject of course to local laws governing exchange restrictions, identification and endorsement.

Some foreign buyers prefer to negotiate and pay for goods manufactured in other countries in the currency of their own country. In such cases it becomes necessary for the exporter to figure the cost in his own currency and then convert the selling price into the currency of the foreign country. After the sale and terms are completed, the seller then, in order to protect himself from loss due to fluctuating exchange value, contracts at a fixed rate of exchange to sell the documentary draft to a bank for currency and draws a draft on the bank. After the goods have been shipped, he draws a draft on the buyer abroad, attaches the shipping documents and presents to his own bank for negotiation against the future exchange contract, whereupon the domestic bank pays the seller the equivalent in dollars. The purchasing bank then forwards the draft and documents abroad for collection and credit, generally with its correspondent bank in the country in which the purchaser is located, for conversion into the foreign currency called for.

When there is a wide fluctuation in exchange, manipulation of discount rates, or inflationary factors working, often foreign sellers of goods to American importers insist on taking payment in dollars. Instead of taking payment for the goods in dollars in this country or establishing a credit balance in dollars in an American bank which could be used for the purchase of American goods, they prefer to receive payment in actual United States dollars in their country. Such an arrangement enables the seller or holder of the draft to retain the value of the goods sold in dollars, whereupon it can be converted into dollars or converted into money of their own country. While such drafts can be issued in dollars, when they are presented to foreign banks there is no warranty that the bank on which the draft is drawn has dollars available or will pay out actual United States currency. In such cases the holders are only entitled to receive in exchange currency of the respective country in which the draft is presented, at the current buying rate, however, for dollars as of the date of presentation. To provide this service for their customers, however, many foreign banks accumulate U. S. dollars so as to be able to pay the holders of dollar drafts in actual United States dollars.

In prior years, however, because of the stabilization of currencies of various foreign countries, there was very little demand for dollar drafts. Foreign trade to a great extent was negotiated with the use of drafts payable in the currency of the foreign country. In the last ten years, however, because of the relationship of the dollar to other currencies, and the very fact, as was explained earlier in this chapter, that actual dollars when held in foreign countries can be presented by the governments of those countries for actual exchange into gold, there has been a recurrence of the payment of goods in dollar drafts.

Bills of Lading. A bill of lading, as we studied in Chapter XXIII, is an instrument issued by a common carrier acknowledging receipt of merchandise for transportation to point of destination, and guaranty of delivery of such goods to the person named in the document or his order.

Foreign exchange order bills issued by steamship companies, known as ocean bills of lading, are used in the majority of foreign exchange transactions where acceptances, bills of exchange and letters of credit require some document to be included or attached to the accompanying draft. Once such goods are delivered by the carrier, upon presentation of the bills of lading, such goods can be removed and either placed in a warehouse and covered by a warehouse receipt, in which case the goods become collateral to a warehouse loan, or they can be stored on the premises or property of the borrower, in which case the goods can be pledged as collateral to an inventory loan.

Generally, in connection with the importation or exportation of goods, the shipper is required to provide marine insurance covering reimbursement for loss in case the merchandise is lost or destroyed in transit. Such documents, usually in the form of a separate insurance policy or a rider, cover the specific shipment and warrant that the merchandise as described is insured for a specified number of dollars from a certain time until another time in the future or until delivery.

Cable Transfers. A cable transfer is simply an order drawn by a domestic bank on one of its foreign branches or correspondents for immediate delivery of a specified amount of money either in dollars or in the exchange of the country where the bank called upon to make payment is located. Cable transfers are used when it is desired to settle obligations immediately and avoid delays incidental to sending remittances by mail. A cable transfer is the same as a draft except that it calls for immediate payment. Authorization to the bank to which the cable is sent to pay out funds is usually accomplished by use of codes for the purpose of authenticating cables. Through the use of code books, banks arrange among themselves private test keys, although most of the standard codes are widely used by banks which maintain relationship with foreign banks.

In settling claims by a cable transfer, it is necessary for the customer to make arrangements with his bank to transfer such funds. In doing so they sign an agreement protecting the bank from any delay beyond its control, and protection for the exchange rate by which the cable amounts are transferred into the exchange of the country in whose currency the cable transfer is payable.

Commercial Letters of Credit. In the importing and exporting of goods and commodities, dealers very often must obtain such goods or commodities when and where available. In transacting their business, merchants and manufacturers very often must enter into contracts and commitments which are much larger than normally would be considered justifiable in relation to their working capital. As a result a purchaser may require a larger credit than the seller is willing to extend, or in excess of the loan the buyer's bank is willing to extend to finance the business. Further, if the buyer has to pay cash for the order, or is in possession of funds and deliveries are delayed by bottlenecks in transportation, he may have a large portion of his working capital tied up for long periods, depleting his bank balance and over-extending himself as far as bank credit is concerned.

The seller, on the other hand, may be in a position of needing cash to discount bills, pay for other purchases and use the funds for the general operation of his business. In addition goods which he has sold may be pledged as collateral security for a loan under warehouse or trust receipts. In any event, some means is needed to facilitate the transaction without the layout of immediate cash.

To provide means by which such imports or exports can be properly handled, the wide use of commercial letters of credit has come to be recognized as one of the prime mediums for financing foreign trade.

Under the usual recognized terms, commercial letters of credit constitute an agreement through which the bank of the buyer commits itself, under certain stipulated conditions, to pay the seller's draft drawn on its customer when presented and accompanied by an invoice and other documents. Ordinarily the credit takes the form of a letter from the bank to the seller stating the terms under which the drafts must be drawn, and the latest date on which the draft may be presented for payment or acceptance. In addition. the letter provides for payment of the drafts immediately upon presentation, or for acceptance which in effect is the bank's guarantee to pay such drafts on a specified later date.

Such an arrangement protects the importer because he is provided with a means of purchasing goods from a foreign country on a cash basis without being required to put up the actual cash. On the other hand, the exporter, once he has possession of the letter of credit and has surrendered documents evidencing the shipment of the goods ordered, can go to his bank and obtain the funds.

In arranging for a letter of credit the buyer, after completing negotiations as to price and date of shipment, makes application to his bank for a letter of credit. If the buyer has completed the necessary arrangements and is in good credit standing, the bank will issue a letter of credit providing for drafts payable at sight or after 30, 60 or 90 days.

Once the seller has been notified by mail, cable advice, or advice through the foreign correspondent bank of the domestic bank that the credit has been established, the seller prepares the goods for shipment and delivers them to a steamship company, in exchange for a set of bills of lading. Once the seller has these bills of lading, together with consular invoice, commercial invoice, certificate of insurance, and presents them to the bank, they are attached to a draft on the bank which issued the credit and presented to the seller's local bank. If the documents are in good order, the bank will pay over the proceeds of the draft to the seller.

The draft then may be sent to the bank on which drawn for collection and payment; or the negotiating bank may forward the draft and the documents to its bank correspondent in the city which issued the letter of credit in the first place where the issuing bank, after carefully examining the documents, will stamp its "acceptance" on the face of the draft. After the draft, together with the documents, has been presented and accepted, the bank then advises the customer of the receipt of the documents and the date of maturity of the accepted draft.

Upon receipt of a notification that the vehicle carrying the goods or commodities has arrived, the customer applies to the bank for the documents and obtains them either by paying cash, or if his credit standing warrants it, by signing what is known as a trust receipt; or he will avail himself of an open line of credit or have them warehoused. Generally, in the ordinary course of events, the merchandise is sold on or before arrival or shortly thereafter, and the proceeds of the sale are turned over to the bank and the obligation generally liquidated before maturity; otherwise the usual commercial credit provisions apply and the merchandise is disposed of in the usual course of business.

The commercial letter of credit offers great advantages to both the buyer and the seller. The buyer gains the advantage of cash buying, better price, and better delivery, without having to pay for the goods until the documents are presented. The seller, on the other hand, does not have to make an extensive investigation of the buyer's financial responsibility, and his payment is assured through the letter of credit. Most of all it is the only form of financing in which a secured accommodation can be made available by a bank to its customers before the actual collateral is at its disposal. The reason for this is that the bank is not required to make any payment until the documents and title are in its hand, while the advantage to the seller is that the draft on the letter of credit provides the same assurance as if cash accompanied the order.

Travelers' Checks. Travelers' checks usually issued in denominations of 10, 20, 50, 100 and 500 dollars, and payable in United States dollars, are a specialized form of negotiable instrument sold by banks and others. It is essentially the same as a cashier's check. When these checks are purchased the holder signs the checks generally in the upper left hand corner. At the time of encashment, the holder again signs his name, this time in the lower left hand corner in the presence of the person from whom he will receive the funds, thus providing immediate self-identification.

Travelers' checks are the safest form of a medium of exchange to use when traveling, not only because they are a bank's guarantee of payment, but because they are not restricted to cashing at banks at any certain hour, but are acceptable for cashing at hotels, railroads, steamship and airline offices. These checks are negotiable at the current rate of exchange for checks, generally in New York; and the holders, when cashing, receive the value in the equivalent of the money of the country where they are staying, at the current rate of exchange.

Traveler's Letter of Credit. Traveler's letter of credit, also known as circular letters of credit, are considered to be the best means for providing for financial requirements when traveling. Such letters, when issued by an internationally known bank, are readily negotiable in practically all parts of the world and especially at banks with which arrangements have previously been made for this service.

Owing to the instability of many foreign monetary forms in the past, and because, in recent years, of the wide demand for dollars, most traveler's letters of credit are payable in dollars. On the other hand, if a person is traveling in one country and wishes to have unlimited funds for the purchase of goods, a traveler's letter of credit can be issued in the money of that country; that is, either in francs, guilders, pounds, yen, etc.

In obtaining a traveler's letter of credit, the customer applies to the bank for a letter of credit for a fixed amount which he either pays for by a special deposit of funds; or arranges for through a loan. The issuing bank then provides him with a letter of credit which sets forth the amount of funds which he has available, together with a formal letter of introduction to the paying bank. Such letter also contains a guaranty of the signature which appears in the letter of identification.

A customer holding a traveler's letter of credit, when he wishes to obtain funds, presents the letter to the bank and upon proper approval of identification, signs a draft, which is negotiated. The amounts advanced or withdrawn under the credit are entered on the reverse side of the letter, thus reducing the open balance. This not only provides the traveler with a running record of the amount he has withdrawn, but also shows the remaining balance available for payout by the bank.

Trust Receipts. Trust receipts are also used by banks in handling and financing the import of goods and commodities. When a customer pledges goods or commodities, either accompanied by a bill of lading or represented by a warehouse receipt, providing the credit standing of the importer is well rated, the bank will release the documents so that the customer may obtain custody of the goods for sale so as to apply the proceeds to the loan.

Under a trust receipt arrangement, the bank retains title to the goods or commodities as long as requirements are met or the agreement is complied with. Such receipts which are pledged provide for the return of the commodities specified or their equivalent, and generally are used where the bank has established a credit for the importer using the goods imported as collateral security.

Warehouse Receipts. In assisting an importer of goods or commodities, banks frequently establish an open line of credit, or loan against the goods or commodities when received and placed in storage, using the warehouse receipt as collateral security for the loan. A warehouse receipt, as we learned in Chapter XXVIII, is nothing more than a bill of lading covering goods stored in a permanent place in custody of the warehouse. When a bank makes a loan using the warehouse receipt as collateral, it permits the owner to take delivery either by releasing the warehouse receipt on trust receipt, or by authorizing the warehouse to deliver specified articles.

In connection with the financing and storage of raw materials and commodities, banks generally find it easier to operate with a non-negotiable receipt. For example, partial deliveries can be made by means of a delivery order, signed by the person in whose name the warehouse receipt is issued.

AMERICAN AND FOREIGN TRADE DEFINITIONS. In connection with the exporting and shipping of merchandise, confusion sometimes occurs between the buyer and the seller resulting in dispute, litigation and financial loss. A bank can become involved because of the misuse and erroneous interpretation of common shipping terms used in exporting goods and commodities, and differences in interpretation of weights and quantities. For example; acceptances and bills of lading frequently bear the initials of abbreviated terms and general conditions of shipment as follows:

F.O.B.——————Free On Board (name of carrier or place). Under this term the price quoted applies only at an inland shipping point, and the seller arranges for loading of the goods on, or in, railway cars, trucks, lighters, barges, aircraft, or other conveyances furnished for transportation.

F.A.S.——————Free Along Side (name of vessel). Under this term the seller quotes a price including delivery of the goods along side an overseas vessel and within reach of the loading tackle.

C.& F.——————Cost and Freight (named point of destination). Under this term the seller quotes a price including the cost of transportation to the named point of destination.

C.I.F.——————Cost, Insurance, Freight (named point of destination). Under this term the seller quotes a price including the cost of the marine insurance and all transportation charges to the named point of destination.

Many of these terms were originally used in foreign trade to refer to the handling of goods and commodities; and the responsibility of the exporters and importers from the place of origination, or from where the goods and commodities were manufactured or stored or from where such goods and commodities were delivered;

to a wharf or alongside the vessel which was to transport the goods to a point of destination. Later such terms were used in domestic transactions and applied to inland shipments. Some of these terms are still being used today.

As each term has many variations and interpretations and designates certain other particular responsibilities between buyer and seller, importer and exporter, it is recommended that those who are actively engaged in handling foreign trade operations become familiar with the responsibilites under each principal form. This can be accomplished by studying the revised American Foreign Trade Regulations, adopted July 1941 by a joint committee representing the National Foreign Trade Council Inc., United States Chamber of Commerce, and National Council of American Importers Inc.

In connection with weights and measures it is also recommended that particular attention be given in making weight quotations. Between countries, even between sections of a country, there is often a difference in what is meant by a net ton, gross ton and a metric ton; and wherever a price per ton is quoted, the pounds in that ton should be used.

It is also important to note that in the United States a carload lot means the quantity of a particular commodity in question necessary to obtain the carload freight rate. As some commodities are heavier and bulkier than others, it naturally results in a difference of space and weight. It is recommended, therefore, that the weight in addition to the quantity be quoted.

Another point of difference arises in connection with insurance protection. Ordinary marine insurance gives no protection against deterioration or damage to the merchandise itself while in transit caused by recognized hazards. Banks should see to it, especially when financing shipment by steamer, that insurance coverage is obtained giving full protection from the primary shipping point to the designated seaport delivery and/or foreign point delivery, to avoid possible losses.

OPERATING METHODS AND PROCEDURES OF THE INTERNATIONAL DEPARTMENT. As documents and instruments used in connection with International Department transactions are either in the form of "notes or drafts," operating methods and procedures used are those followed by the loan and collection sections in processing work.

Operating instructions used in connection with operations of the International Department will vary, depending on size of the bank and volume, but will generally include the following:

1. Schedule of fees and commissions charged in connection with letters of credit, travelers' checks, cable transfers.

2. Routing for collection of drafts drawn on foreign banks.

3. Current government regulations in connection with foreign exchange transactions.

CHAPTER XXXIX

BUDGETING

IN EVERY BANK FROM THE SMALLEST to the largest, one or several members of the staff have the responsibility for seeing that:

1. Accounting is performed and proper financial records of the bank maintained.
2. Financial statements of condition are periodically prepared as required by law.
3. Directors are currently informed on income, expenditures and the results of operation.

The person who performs such functions may be a clerk, a general bookkeeper, have a title of assistant cashier, cashier, or even president, depending on the size of the bank. As a bank gets larger and duties and responsibilities are charted, defined, and delegated to administrative personnel, the responsibilities in connection with accounting and control functions are usually vested in a comptroller or the comptroller's division.

One of the most important functions of the comptroller's division, as we learned in Chapters XI and XII, is in connection with establishing budgets of income and expense.

The term "budget" has several definitions and several interpretations. According to the dictionary, a budget is the annual estimate of financial needs for the year to come. To the layman, a budget is a distribution of fóreseeable income to expenditures essential to provide the necessities, conveniences and pleasures of life.

In developing a budget, the gross income is first determined. From this figure fixed expenses such as rent, light, utilities, time payments plus insurance and savings are deducted. The remainder (after deducting fixed expenses from gross income) is then prorated to such items as food, clothing, charity, medical expenses and sums to be set aside for some special project.

Generally such budgets require considerable manipulation and revision in order to balance outgo with income with the result that amounts, generally set aside for future purchases and for saving, are currently used for the immediate purchase of automobiles, utilities, household appliances, which can be paid for over a period of time through installment financing.

The purpose of budgeting in banking, however, is to project items of income and expense to enable management to determine operating profits or losses. It is from such projections that the directors approve all operating expenditures and authorize the setting aside or disbursement of funds for dividends, reserves, advertising, and public relations activities, justifiable salary increases, bonuses, and for the purchase of new machinery and equipment.

Budgeting in banking, in addition to controlling the expenses, has another at least equally important function—the projection and controlling of income.

The purpose of an income budget is not only to disclose the sources of earnings, but by analytical projections in connection with the investment program, to act as a sales quota, or an incentive to the officers who have the responsibilities for the various types of loans and investment to maintain quotas in accordance with the policies established by the board of directors.

A properly devised and operated expense budget not only limits or controls overall expenditures, but acts as a lever on divisional and section heads to encourage them to reduce expenses through the introduction of more efficient and economical operating methods and procedures.

Income from a control and policy standpoint is vested in the directors and administrative personnel. It is the responsibility of the directors, from a policy standpoint, to approve the conversion of funds program based on the vulnerability of funds available for investment, which funds consist of capital funds supplied by or belonging to the stockholders, and funds belonging to the depositors carried in time and demand accounts. In other words the percentage of respective funds which shall be invested in the various types of loans, United States Government and municipal bonds. It is also their responsibility to determine the amount of such earning assets which shall be rendered sterile by investment in fixed assets, machinery and equipment.

Control of income from an administration standpoint is vested in active management—in the various officers to whom are delegated the responsibility for investing funds available for investment in the various types of loans and United States Government and municipal bonds.

Expenses, on the other hand, are controlled by three groups: supervisory management, administrative management and executive management.

SUPERVISORY MANAGEMENT

Supervisory management consists of those to whom is delegated the responsibility in connection with the direct supervision of operating functions of departments, divisions, and sections. Supervisory management is held responsible only for controllable expenses; that is, expenses over which they have some control, such as:

Compensation and salaries.
Employe welfare.
Maintenance, machinery and equipment.
Overtime.
Postage.
Repairs, machinery and equipment.
Stationery and supplies.
Subscriptions.
Telephone.
Water and towel service.

ADMINISTRATIVE MANAGEMENT

Administrative management consists of administrative personnel who are in charge of the principal departments and divisions of the bank. Such administrative personnel are responsible for the execution and administration of policy and control of items of expenses such as:

Attorney fees.
Donations.
Dues.
Entertainment of customers.
Heating.
Interest paid on borrowed money.

Maintenance of the building.
Rent of premises.
Rent of machinery and equipment.
Repairs to the building.
Supplies for the building.
Travel on bank business.
Travel on new business.
Travel to conventions and meetings.

EXECUTIVE MANAGEMENT

Executive management refers to the directors and the control exercised by them in approving expenditures in connection with:

Advertising.
Depreciation.
Directors' fees.
Donations.
Examinations.
Insurance.
New business activities.
Professional services.
Rates of interest on time accounts.
Taxes.

While the setting up and developing of bank and department budgets is under the direction of administrative personnel working in close cooperation with department managers or those held responsible for the operating functions of respective sections, it is up to the directors to approve such budgets and to see that provisions of the budget are carried out by those in charge of departments, divisions and sections of the bank.

The first step in developing a budget is to determine in detail, as required for control purposes, the respective items or sources of income and expense.

Once this is done, each item of income is listed by sources in a manner and form similar to that shown in Exhibit 112. After this has been completed, and rate of return determined, the interest income from bonds and various types of loans should be analyzed in connection with the conversion of funds program as covered in Chapter XX.

Exhibit 112

SOURCES OF INCOME

Source	Average Daily Outstanding	Average Yield	Total Income	Income Each Class	% of Income
INTEREST					
1 U.S. Govt. Bonds					
2 Municipal Bonds					
3 Other Bonds					
4 Div. FRB Stock					
(A) TOTAL INT. ON INV.					
5 Comm'l. Loans Sec.					
6 Comm'l. Loans Unsec.					
7 Installment Loans					
8 Mortgage Loans					
(B) TOTAL INT. LOANS					
FEES - CHARGES, ETC.					
9 Collection Fees, etc.					
10 Charges Drafts - M.O.					
11 Rents Received					
12 Rents - S. D. Boxes					
13 Tr. Dept. Fees					
14 Miscellaneous					
(C) TOT. OTHER INCOME					
15 Ser. Chg. Ck. Accts.					
16 Other Chg. Ck. Accts.					
(D) TOT.CHG.CK. ACCTS.					
(E) TOTAL OPERATING INCOME					

In undertaking this analysis, questions similar to the following are applicable to each class and type of loan and investment:

1. Is the total volume outstanding in line with the conversion of funds policy?

2. Would changes in type of bonds in respective classes result in increasing the yield?

3. Would changes in the types of loans in respective classes result in increasing the yield?

4. Would there be a favorable difference from a net profit standpoint, if policy was changed to permit a greater investment in tax exempt bonds?

5. Has stability of deposits changed, and if so, would review of percentages in connection with conversion of funds program be advisable?

6. What is the anticipated trend in commercial deposits in the coming year?

7. What is the anticipated trend in savings deposits in the coming year?

8. What is the anticipated trend in loan demand in the coming year?

9. Will demand for mortgage loans exceed available funds?

10. If it appears there will be a great demand for funds, should attempts be made to sell mortgage loans, retaining a servicing arrangement?

With reference to analysis of fees and other income, the following questions should be asked, particularly in connection with the profit and loss statement of respective divisions and sections where fees are collected for respective services rendered:

1. Are charges being properly applied to all customers who use or benefit from the service?

2. Does analysis disclose present charges of fees are sufficient to cover the cost plus a profit?

3. Should charges or fee schedules be increased or modified, based on cost, so as to produce greater income?

When the answers to such questions have been determined, respective figures should be adjusted and the information entered on a budget spread sheet similar to that shown in Exhibit 113, for monthly and periodical indexing of budget information.

Before indexing amounts in the expense budget, it should be first ascertained or determined that the respective expense accounts accurately reflect expenditures as charged to them. For example—that all charges to advertising are legitimate advertising expenses, and that the account does not include items which more properly should be charged to dues, donations, entertainment, etc. Once it has been established that all accounts correctly reflect expenditures attributable to the respective classifications, then the officer in charge of budgets should consult with the department, division and section managers, and the directors, on each type of expense controllable by them.

In undertaking this analysis, in addition to making a searching inquiry on each of the expense items as to: (a) the necessity for the expenditure, (b) possible use of a substitute which would be cheaper; the following questions should be applied to respective items, from an exploratory and analytical standpoint, if control and possible reductions in expense are to be effected:

ADVERTISING

A. What is the objective hoped to be attained from use of respective radio, television and newspaper advertising mediums?

B. Is the objective being attained in each case? If not, is the reason identifiable?

C. Is the amount expended for radio, television and newspaper advertising sufficient to produce results?

D. Should present forms of direct mail advertising be changed?

E. Should greater effort be made or used in direct mail advertising? If so, for what services?

F. Is the advertising budget, as such, set up to show the various mediums used and the amounts to be expended on a month by month basis?

ATTORNEY FEES

A. Does analysis indicate attorneys are being frequently consulted for opinions which could be set up under standard procedures or operating instructions?

B. Would a more equitable arrangement in connection with legal expense be to have the bank's counsel operate under an annual retainer?

C. Are items charged to "attorney fees" which should be recoverable from the customer, actually recovered?

D. Are attorney fees in connection with foreclosures, loans and collections unrecoverable?

E. Should fees in connection with foreclosures or the collection of loans be more properly charged to "other losses" than to "attorney fees"?

COMPENSATION

A. Has the salary schedule of officers and employees adjusted within the last 12 months been predicated on performance, review of assumption of duties and responsibilities?

B. Should such review be made?

C. Have departments, divisions and sections provided management with estimates of increases in salaries for the ensuing year?

D. What are the prospects, if any, for the reduction of personnel in various departments due to economies in operation or the use of more efficient methods and procedures?

DEPRECIATION

A. Is the depreciation schedule covering furniture, fixtures, machinery, equipment and building sufficient to amortize the cost over the estimated life of the article?

B. Would it be advisable, where depreciation has already written off any article, to continue to charge such amounts setting them up in a special reserve account for the purchase of new equipment?

C. Are charges to depreciation accounts and credits to reserve accounts sufficient to provide for replacement of the article at present cost?

D. Is the present depreciation schedule equitable and in line with Internal Revenue Department rulings on accelerated depreciation and, if so, would there be a tax savings by accelerating the depreciation?

DIRECTORS FEES

A. Are directors paid fees whether or not they attend the meetings?

B. Are fees paid directors sufficient to warrant their attendance

Exhibit 113

BUDGET ANALYSIS SPREAD SHEET

	DESCRIPTION	ANNUAL BUDGET	JANUARY	FEBRUAR
	INCOME			
A	Interest on Investments			
B	Interest on Loans			
C	Fees and Commissions			
D	Service Charges Checking Accts.			
E	TOTAL INCOME			
	EXPENSES			
1	Advertising			
2	Attorney Fees			
3	Compensation-Officers-Employees			
4	Depreciation			
5	Directors Fees			
6	Donations-Dues			
7	Employee Welfare			
8	Entertainment			
9	Examinations			
10	Heating			
11	Insurance			
12	Int. Paid on Borrowed Money			
13	Light and Power			
14	Maintenance			
15	Overtime			
16	Postage			
17	Professional Services			
18	Rent of Premises			
19	Rent of Machinery and Equipment			
20	Repairs to Building			
21	Repairs to Machinery-Equipment			
22	Stationery and Supplies			
23	Supplies-Building			
24	Subscriptions			
25	Taxes-Real Estate-Personal Prop.			
26	Telephone-Telegraph			
27	Travel			
28	Water and Towel Service			
29	F.D.I.C. Insurance			
30	Interest Paid			
31	Federal Income Tax-Reserve			
32	Intangible Tax			
F	TOTAL OPERATING EXPENSES			
G	NET OPERATING PROFIT (E less F)			
33	Less Reserve for Dividends			
34	Less Additions to Reserve Accts.			
35	Plus Profits Securities-Recoveries			
36	Less Losses Securities-Chg.-offs			
H	NET UNDISTRIBUTED PROFIT			

	MARCH	RESULTS 1st QUART	BUDGET 1st QUART	DIFF.	APRIL	MAY

This sheet should be extended in the same manner to cover the other three quarters of the year with a column at the extreme right for Total for Year; Budget for Year; Difference; and Reasons.

and the contribution of their knowledge and experience to affairs of the bank?

C. Would it be to the advantage of the bank to place members of the executive committee on an annual retainer or monthly salary basis to relieve officers of certain responsibilities and enable them to have more time for business development and assumption of other responsibilities?

DONATIONS

A. Are items being charged to "donations" which more properly should be charged to "advertising"?

B. Has a schedule been presented covering the donations made in the name of the bank for the coming year?

C. Does such schedule adequately cover various charities to which the bank, as a matter of public relations, should make donations?

D. Are donations being made out of proportion to the good will engendered on behalf of the bank; or because of favoritism of one of the officers or directors with the respective projects?

E. Is the bank making donations to certain projects which more properly should be paid in behalf of, and in the name of an officer or director, or in connection with pleasing a good customer? If so, could these be reduced or eliminated?

DUES

A. Has a list been prepared covering dues and membership fees for clubs and associations to which members of the staff belong?

B. Do benefits from such membership accrue directly to the bank?

C. Is use being made of each club or association for which dues are paid?

D. Could some of the dues for clubs and associations be eliminated; or could better use be made of such memberships?

EMPLOYEES WELFARE

A. Are proper benefits obtained from whatever contributions are being made and charged to "employees welfare"?

B. Are expenditures being charged to "employees welfare"

which more properly should be charged to other classifications or paid for by the employees themselves?

C. Are sufficient funds being set aside for the "employees welfare" to accomplish the objectives as set forth by the directors and management?

D. Should budget provisions be made for expenditures for greater and increased benefits for employees?

ENTERTAINMENT OF CUSTOMERS

A. Does review of entertainment expense indicate such expenditures are justified?

B. Are expenditures for entertainment in all cases for the benefit of the bank from a public relations standpoint; or for the benefit of individual officers in the discharge of their own personal social obligations?

EXAMINATIONS

A. Does examination expense include fees for the employment of outside accountants and, if so, does the bank pay for certain phases of the examination or audit which more properly should be undertaken by the bank's own auditors?

B. If outside auditors or accountants are employed, does the routine followed justify the expenditure; and do results obtained compare with results of a similar program if set up under the direction of the bank's own auditor, if properly held responsible for performance, by the board of directors?

HEATING

A. Is proper thermostatic control maintained over all areas of the building?

B. Can such control be maintained so that one section is not overly warm, which results in personnel raising windows, with the corresponding overuse of heating facilties in other sections?

C. Would conversion from the present type of fuel to another type effect reduction in operating expenses?

INSURANCE

A. Has the entire insurance program of the bank been analyzed and reviewed recently by an independent outside insurance counsellor?

B. Are there any duplications in coverage?

C. Do provisions for insurance adequately cover the exposure of the bank from the standpoint of theft, holdup, public liability, etc?

D. Could some items for which insurance is carried, be carried by the bank under a self-insurance program?

INTEREST PAID ON BORROWED MONEY

A. Is the amount expended for such interest out of line with a loss of income which could be brought about through a modification in the conversion of funds program which would permit larger balances to be maintained with correspondent or Federal Reserve Banks?

B. Does this account include deficiency charges by the Federal Reserve Banks in connection with reserve requirements?

C. Would concentration of funds with fewer correspondent banks provide more funds for investment and eliminate the necessity for periodical borrowing?

LIGHT AND POWER

A. Is proper control exercised over the use of lights?

B. Are separate switch controls maintained so that minimum lighting can be effected for different areas?

C. Is machinery turned off when not in use?

D. Are thermostatic arrangements properly set for both heating and air conditioning units to provide minimum use at hours when the bank is not open for business?

MAINTENANCE

A. Is the cost of maintenance of machinery and equipment high in comparison with other banks using similar equipment?

B. Would service contracts be more economical than individual calls for maintenance and repair?

OVERTIME

A. Is overtime in all cases justified?

B. Do personnel records show "time" on entering the bank

quarters in the morning and when personnel leave at night regardless of the time; or when they take up their positions in the department to which they are assigned and begin their work?

C. Is departmental overtime sufficient to warrant a re-adjustment or reassignment of work or an indication of need of additional personnel?

D. Can a rearrangement of work, or rescheduling of work in departments subject to overtime charges, be arranged to eliminate overtime?

POSTAGE

A. Is proper control maintained over postage?

B. Do employees pay for postage when sending out their own personal mail?

C. Is review periodically made of the mail sendings to be certain that "Airmail" and "Special Delivery" are not used where ordinary postage would suffice?

D. Are statements of accounts weighed in bulk before postage is affixed; or by estimating the weight and postage required?

E. Would it be economical to deliver local statements by messenger instead of mailing them first class postage?

PROFESSIONAL SERVICES

A. Are any charges made to this category which more properly should be made to "examinations"?

B. If certain professional services are required over an extendend period, would it be more economical to employ such a person on a permanent basis as a member of the bank's staff?

C. Are professional services necessary?

RENT OF PREMISES

A. Would it be cheaper to build and own than to rent?

B. Would a savings in taxes be incurred, and greater net profit accrue to the bank, if they were to build a building or have one built for them and lease it back on a long-term basis with option to purchase?

RENT OF MACHINERY AND EQUIPMENT

A. Is it more economical to rent such machinery and equipment than to own it?

B. Does the rental contract provide for servicing?

C. From a tax standpoint, would it be cheaper to purchase the equipment than to rent, charging the depreciation and service contracts to expense, considering possible accelerated depreciation schedules?

REPAIRS TO BUILDING

A. Are there items charged to "repairs" which should more properly be capitalized?

B. Would it be more economical to have a service contract cover repairs and maintenance than it would be to pay for the repairs as required?

REPAIRS TO MACHINERY AND EQUIPMENT

A. Are any items charged to "repairs" which should capitalized?

B. Are charges made against machinery and equipment which should be replaced?

C. Would it be more economical to pay for repairs as required or should such machinery and equipment be covered by a service contract?

STATIONERY AND SUPPLIES

A. Are there any items charged to "stationery and supplies" which should be charged to "advertising"?

B. Are certain items of stationery and supplies purchased in quantity charged to "stationery and supplies" as received, whereas from a proper accounting standpoint they should be capitalized and only charged to "stationery and supplies as used"? (This refers particularly to letterheads, envelopes, and checks.)

C. Can forms be combined to effect savings in printing costs?

D. Can forms be revised to be used with a standard-size window envelope?

E. Are the various sizes of envelopes presently stocked necessary?

F. Are quantities of stationery and supplies purchased in keeping with normal use; and do such orders take advantage of quantity discounts without running the risk of spoilage?

SUPPLIES – BUILDING

A. Are supplies used in the maintenance of the building properly priced and of the quality to do a good job?

B. Would use of other products result in a saving of expense, time, or more efficient operation?

SUBSCRIPTIONS

A. Are magazines, periodicals, trade journals to which the bank subscribes, read and used?

B. Are any subscriptions in duplicate?

C. Could the objective be accomplished by one subscription and having it routed to interested persons?

TAXES – REAL ESTATE, PERSONAL PROPERTY

A. Have schedules in connection with real estate and personal property taxes been reviewed and prepared by qualified personnel who are familiar with allowable exemptions and deductions?

TELEPHONE AND TELEGRAPH

A. Is proper provision made for telephone and telegraph expenses in connection with customer service, to be recovered by being charged to the customer's account?

B. Are employees required to reimburse the bank for telephone expense incurred in connection with personal business?

C. Are officers, or those who have occasion to make long distance calls, conscious of time or provided with three minute hour glasses?

D. Has the telephone equipment and need been recently surveyed from the standpoint of providing more economical service through use of a different type of equipment based on current development and need?

E. Are telegram and telephone charges, in connection with the collection of checks, paid for by the endorser?

TRAVEL

A. Are reimbursements for expenses incurred by officers and others in traveling approved by a senior officer?

B. Is the automobile allowance expense to bank personnel sufficient to cover operating costs?

C. Is the automobile allowance in excess of that charged by automobile rental agencies?

D. Could economy be effected by use of public transportation as against use of individual cars?

E. If bank transportation and travel is by means of bank-owned automobiles, would economy be effected through leasing cars from others?

WATER AND TOWEL SERVICE

A. Is special water and towel service necessary?

B. Would use of paper towels against linen towels be more economical?

C. Are drinking fountain outlets in proper mechanical working order to avoid waste of water?

FDIC INSURANCE

A. Are computations of FDIC insurance rechecked by someone other than the person who prepared the report?

B. Are reserves set up from current operations to provide for FDIC insurance assessments?

INTEREST PAID

A. Are interest computations checked by the auditor?

B. Is the proper interest table being used in the computation of interest on "certificates of deposit" and savings accounts?

C. Are any interest payments paid through exceptions to the terms of the contract?

FEDERAL INCOME TAX

A. Is the federal income tax return made by a person familiar with the law?

B. Is such federal income tax return checked before payment is made?

C. Are ample reserves set up monthly, by charges to expense, for the estimated tax owed?

Other searching and exploratory questions, similar in character to the above, can be added to provide answers to budgetary control problems.

Upon completion of such analysis and investigation, the respective adjusted figures should be entered in the budget spread sheet Exhibit 113. Where both income and expense figures have been prepared, it is generally the accepted practice to submit the complete schedule to the directors, or to a committee appointed by them, for final approval after which each person who has responsibilities for some particular expenditure is advised in writing, or provided with a schedule of the figures as a guide in complying with the approved budget.

Where a bank is of sufficient size to be departmentalized or sectionalized, the same careful analysis is made of each section such as the bookkeeping, proof, mail and messenger, with the combined totals of individual items of expense from respective sections being submitted to the board of directors or committee appointed by them for the final approval.

By referring to the chart, it is seen that such a setup provides management with current information on both income and expenditures. In connection with income from bonds and loans, unless the bank is on an accrual basis, it is recommended that estimates be used in computing the monthly figures so as to show a rather constant trend in income received.

Maintenance of the budget chart, once it is set up, is completed each month from the information provided the directors, with quarterly comparison of actual expenditures with budget estimates; thus enabling management, wherever warranted, to make necessary adjustments so that the net profit at the end of the year is in line with the forecast.

CHAPTER XL

COST ANALYSIS *

ONE OF THE MOST IMPORTANT TOOLS used by an ever increasing number of progressive bankers in managing the affairs of their bank is a cost system.

Under such a system, if properly devised, all income and direct and indirect expenses of a bank, by means of logical and scientifically developed formulas, can be allocated to departments, divisions and sections of the bank so that not only can the profit or loss of each department, division and section be determined; but functions performed, or services rendered by each department, division or section properly costed. Without this knowledge it becomes impossible for management either to accurately price services so that they will provide a profit, or purchase funds for conversion into loans and investments at a price which will provide a profit.

In connection with a cost system, every bank has three principal sources of income:

1. Income from converting funds belonging to stockholders and depositors into loans and investments.
2. Income from fees and commissions.
3. Income from the sale of services.

While individual bankers have little control over the wholesale price of money which is governed by general economic conditions, they have the control over the retail price of money, the cost of investing funds, and the retail price charged for providing services or performing functions for others. Unfortunately, the retail prices of bank services in recent years have not correspondingly increased, with the result that such services today, almost without exception,

* Principles of cost accounting described in this chapter are condensed from the book "PRACTICAL COST ACCOUNTING FOR BANKS" by the author, published by Bankers Publishing Company. Procedures to be followed in setting up a cost system and determining item costs and departmental profit or loss will be found in this book.

are priced below cost. In addition, because of the competitive factor, and in some instances because of the false approach of bankers as to what constitutes good public relations, many bankers today are using service charge schedules and account analysis systems which were adopted from another bank, which were adopted from another bank in the first place. As a consequence in many banks today there is little, if any, relationship between the charges presently being made for services rendered and the cost of providing such services.

The banking business as we previously learned consists of three distinct phases of activity:

1. The acquiring of deposits.
2. The converting of such deposits into earning assets.
3, The servicing of such deposits.

From a management and scope of service standpoint, these separate phases are classified into major departments, generally referred to as:

A. The Commercial Department, whose activities are in connection with the servicing of customers who maintain funds on deposit subject to withdrawal on demand by check; and the providing of general banking services.

B. The Savings Department, whose activities are in connection with the servicing of customers who maintain funds on deposit at interest, subject to withdrawal upon notice.

C. The Safe Deposit Department, whose activities are in connection with providing, for a rental fee, a safe and convenient place for people to keep their securities, jewelry and valuable papers.

D. The Trust Department, whose activities are in connection with the servicing, investing, and managing funds and property of others in fiduciary capacity.

E. The International Department whose activities are in connection with financial services required by customers and others in the exporting or importing of goods; or in conducting trade and commerce with those residing or engaged in business in foreign countries.

F. The Capital Department, whose activities are in connection with the providing of capital, the acquiring of deposits, and with the general direction and management of the bank.

From an operating and cost determination standpoint all divisions and sections within departments, depending on their particular function or on the service they render, are further classified as:

A. *Operating sections,* whose personnel perform work or provide services directly for customers such as those provided by the:

1. Collection tellers
2. Commercial bookkeeping section
3. Draft and money order tellers
4. Paying tellers
5. Proof section
6. Receiving tellers
7. Safe deposit section
8. Savings bond teller
9. Savings bookkeepers
10. Savings tellers
11. Transit section
12. Trust clerks
13. Trust tellers

B. *Non-Operating sections* whose personnel perform work similar to that of the personnel in operating sections but whose functions are generally in connection with the converting of funds into loans and investments such as the:

1. Collateral teller
2. Commercial loan bookkeeper
3. Commercial loan teller
4. Credit analyst
5. Credit clerk
6. Credit correspondent
7. Credit investigator
8. Installment loan bookkeeper
9. Installment loan teller
10. Investment analyst
11. Investment clerk
12. Mortgage loan bookkeeper
13. Mortgage loan teller

C. Capital sections representing ownership whose personnel performs work in connection with:

1. New business
2. Public relations
3. Stockholder activities

D. Administrative sections whose personnel and functions are in connection with the direction or management of the bank such as:

1. Auditor or assistant auditor
2. Cashier or assistant cashier
3. Comptroller or assistant comptroller
4. Directors
5. General bookkeeper
6. President
7. Secretaries to the officers
8. Vice presidents or assistant vice presidents

E. Service sections whose personnel perform functions principally in connection with serving the other divisions of the bank; that is, performing work or providing services which they use such as:

1. Addressograph
2. Mail and messenger
3. Maintenance
4. Occupancy
5. Personnel
6. Stenographic
7. Telephone-switchboard

In smaller banks it is customary to combine some operating sections such as commercial paying with commercial receiving or commercial paying and receiving with savings deposit and withdrawal functions. Likewise, in larger banks, it is sometimes customary to separate loan teller functions according to the type of loan handled.

DISTRIBUTION OF DIRECT EXPENSES

In setting up a cost analysis system, in order to determine the total cost of operating respective divisions and sections and the respective amounts of direct, indirect and administrative expenses of each section, it is first necessary to distribute all direct expenses to all of the operating, non-operating, capital, administrative and service sections on a special spread sheet similar to that shown in Exhibit 114. In making such distribution we will follow the formula for each item of expense as hereafter outlined.

Before beginning the distribution of expenses, it might be well to point out that the secret of scientific and simplified expense distribution is distribution by absorption. This means to distribute expenses to sections in such order or sequence so that the sections whose expenses are first distributed, have little or none of the expenses from the remaining sections as part of their direct, indirect, or operating expense.

In making distribution of expenses the closest dollar amount wherever practical should be used.

ADVERTISING

All funds which are expended for advertising come from the stockholders' profits which they are willing to spend in the hope of attracting additional business from which they will benefit.

Funds expended for billboards and newspaper advertising of bank services, are distributed to the public relations and new business section, while funds expended for publication of the bank's statement of condition, and season's greetings in the newspapers are charged to the stockholders section.

ATTORNEY FEES

Attorney fees consist of fees and expenses paid to lawyers for performing services in connection with a specific matter, or as a retainer to act in an advisory capacity on any of the technical and legal matters which arise in connection with loans, resolutions, returning checks, garnishments, estate matters, etc. Fees, if paid for a specific service, are charged to the section for which the service is provided, unless it is in connection with general bank matters when it is charged to the stockholders section. If the attorney fee incurred is in connection with recovery of a loss the amount should be charged to respective reserves. If the attorney fee is in connection with a trust or estate matter, it should be charged to the respective trust.

COMPENSATION

Compensation expense consists of salary and other compensation paid each officer and employee during the period including bonus and contributions to a pension plan.

If an officer is engaged in administrative work, his total compensation is charged to his title. If an officer is engaged in clerical work, such as a teller, his total compensation is charged to the section in which he performs his work.

Compensation of employees is charged to the sections in which they perform their work.

DEPRECIATION – FURNITURE AND FIXTURES

Depreciation of furniture and fixtures represents the percentage of the purchase price charged off annually to expense over the lifetime of use of the item. Such respective amounts are charged to sections based on the value of the furniture and fixtures used.

DEPRECIATION – MACHINERY AND EQUIPMENT

Depreciation of machinery and equipment represents the percentage of the purchase price charged off annually to expense, and is applicable to respective sections based on the value of the machinery and equipment used.

DEPRECIATION – BUILDING

Depreciation of building represents the annual depreciation on fixed assets taken in accordance with current tax provisions. The total amount is charged to the occupancy section when it is distributed to other sections of the bank based on space occupied.

DIRECTORS' FEES

Directors' fees cover the amounts paid the directors, as representatives of the stockholders, for counselling and advising management of the bank on general management and policy matters. Directors' fees are charged to the directors section and included

Exhibit 114

EXPENSE DISTRIBUTION SHEET

EXPENSES			OPERATING SECTION				NON-OPER SECTION			
NO	DESCRIPTION	AMOUNT								
1	ADVERTISING	$								
2	ATTORNEY FEES									
3	COMPENSATION									
4	DEPRECIATION F & F									
5	DEPRECIATION M & EQPT.									
6	DEPRECIATION-BUILDING									
7	DIRECTORS FEES									
8	DONATIONS									
9	DUES AND MEMBERSHIPS									
10	EMPLOYEES WELFARE									
11	ENTERTAINMENT-CUST.									
12	ENTERTAINMENT-OTHERS									
13	EXAMINATIONS									
14	HEATING									
15	INSURANCE									
16	INT. PAID-BORROWED MONEY									
17	LIGHT & POWER									
18	MAINTENANCE-BUILDING									
19	MAINTENANCE-MACH-EQPT									
20	OVERTIME									
21	POSTAGE									
22	PROFESSIONAL SERVICES									
23	RENT-PREMISES									
24	RENT-MACH. & EQPT									
25	REPAIRS-BUILDING									
26	REPAIRS-MACH & EQPT									
27	WATER-TOWELS-MSCL									
28	STATIONERY-SUPPLIES									
29	SUPPLIES-BUILDING									
30	SUBSCRIPTIONS									
31	TAXES-R. E & PERS PROP.									
32	TELEPHONE-TELEGRAPH									
33	TRAVEL-BANK BUSINESS									
34	TRACEL-NEW BUSINESS									
35	TRAVEL-CONVENTIONS									
(A)	DIRECT DIV. OPER. EXPENSE									
	SERVICE DIVISION EXPENSE									
	OCCUPANCY									
	PERSONNEL									
	TELEPHONE									
	MAIL-MESSENGER									
	ADDRESSOGRAPH									
	STENOGRAPHIC									
(B)	TOTAL SERVICE EXPENSE									
	ADMINISTRATIVE EXPENSE									
	SECY-PRESIDENT									
	ASST. CASHIER									
	ASST. CASHIER									
	CASHIER									
	VICE PRESIDENT									
	VICE PRESIDENT									
	PRESIDENT									
	AUDITING									
	GENERAL BOOKS									
	DIRECTORS									
(C)	TOTAL ADMINISTRATIVE EXP (of Opr-Non-Opr-Cap. Divisions									
	TOTAL OPERATING DIV. EXP (A plus B plus C)									

Columns are to be added for respective sections required as listed on pages 856-857

CAPITAL SECTION			ADMINISTRATIVE SECTION					SERVICE SECTION			

with other expenses for later distribution to the other sections of the bank, based on services performed.

DONATIONS

Donations consist of amounts contributed by the bank to the various civic, church and charitable organizations. Generally such donations made on behalf of the American Red Cross, Community Fund, hospitals, etc., are charged to the stockholders sections, while any donations made to local churches, schools and civic organizations are charged to the public relations section.

DUES

Dues and membership expense covers the expenditure of the bank for memberships in national, state and local banking associations; and for memberships and dues in civic and local service clubs and associations. Banking association dues are charged to the stockholders section; dues in local service clubs are charged to new business and public relations section; while dues in connection with the local Clearing House Association are charged to the proof section.

EMPLOYEES WELFARE

Employess welfare consists of the expenditures the bank makes in connection with parties, gifts, the providing of coffee, cokes, lunches, etc. All such items are charged to the personnel section.

ENTERTAINMENT – CUSTOMERS

Entertainment of customers covers expenses of the bank in the entertainment of present customers or prospects for new business; such as lunches, dinners, club affairs, and are all charged to public relations section.

ENTERTAINMENT OF OTHERS

Entertainment of others covers expenses of the bank in the entertaining of stockholders, expenses of the annual meeting, and expenses incurred by officers at conventions. All such expenses are charged to the stockholders section except dinners and luncheons for directors which are charged to the directors section.

EXAMINATIONS

Examination expense consists of fees paid the federal or state supervisory authorities for conducting their periodical examination; and fees paid outside accountants for conducting audits in behalf of the directors.

Such expense is allocated to the sections based on the time spent in examining the affairs of the respective divisions.

HEATING

Heating covers the expense incurred by the bank in heating the bank building. It also includes air conditioning. This direct expense is charged to the occupancy section for later distribution to other sections of the bank based on the amount of floor space occupied.

INSURANCE

Insurance covers the expenditure of the bank for protection of assets against fire, theft, robbery or damage; against dishonest acts of personnel and customers; and against claims for damages due to accidents and negligence.

Such expenses in connection with liability, blanket bond, health and accident insurance are charged to the personnel section, while all expense in connection with insurance on premises is charged to occupancy section.

INTEREST PAID ON BORROWED MONEY

Interest paid on borrowed money is the price paid for additional working capital and is charged to the stockholders section.

LIGHT AND POWER

Light and power covers the expenses of the bank for lighting, illumination of the outside signs, and is charged to sections of the bank based on the number of outlets used or estimates of power supplied.

MAINTENANCE OF THE BUILDING

Maintenance of the building covers any expenses in connection with painting, decorating, window washing performed by those not on the bank's payroll and are charged to the occupancy section for later distribution to other sections of the bank based on space occupied.

MAINTENANCE – MACHINERY AND EQUIPMENT

Expenses in connection with maintenance of machinery and equipment represent service in connection with maintaining machinery in good working order. Generally this work is performed under a service contract. In any event, the expense is charged to respective sections based on the location and use of the machinery for which the maintenance charges are levied.

OVERTIME

Overtime covers the expense of the bank in paying employees who work more than the hours permitted by the wage and hour law. Such expense is charged to respective sections where the employees incurring the overtime are assigned; or to the other sections where the work is actually performed.

POSTAGE

Postage covers the expenditure of the bank for mailing letters, statements, notices, and is charged to respective sections incurring the expense. Expense in connection with postage for monthly statements, which is a sizeable item, should be segregated as part of the general account overhead.

PROFESSIONAL SERVICES

The amounts expended for professional services cover the expenditures of the bank for employing outside counsel or advice. Generally these expenses are in connection with taxes, investments, management consulting fees, pre-employment medical examinations, and aptitude testing of personnel. Where such expenses directly affect personnel, they are charged to the personnel section otherwise to the stockholders sections or the investment section depending on the purpose for which such counsel was employed.

RENT

Rent covers the expenditure of the bank for the cost of space required for its operations. If the bank rents its space from others, then the annual rent is the rent expense. If the bank owns the building and does not consider rent as part of its operating expense, then for cost analysis purposes, an estimate of the rent the bank would have to pay if it did not own its building should be used as rent expense. Because sections of a bank are generally interchangeable as to location, and are related to each other in many of their operations, it is not practical to attempt to charge separate rates, depending on location. Rent expense, covering the total rent paid, or estimated rent the bank would have to pay if it did not own its building, is charged to the occupancy section.

RENT – MACHINERY AND EQUIPMENT

Rent for machinery and equipment covers the use of specialized equipment and is charged to the respective sections using such equipment.

REPAIRS – BUILDING

Repairs to the building covers the expenditures of the bank for minor repairs such as the repairing of windows, doors, floors, etc. If such items are charged off to expense and not capitalized, they are charged to the occupancy section.

REPAIRS – MACHINERY AND EQUIPMENT

Repairs for machinery and equipment cover the expenditures of the bank for the actual repair of machinery and equipment such as the elevators, heating and air conditioning sytems, etc. Such items of repair expense are charged to the section using the machinery and equipment being repaired.

STATIONERY AND SUPPLIES

Stationery and supplies cover the expenditures of the rest for stationery, forms, and supplies, used by each section of the bank. Generally a bank charges all such items of expense to the stationery and supplies account when paid for, regardless of the period of time the items will last. Under a properly devised cost system, however, sections should only be charged with major items of stationery and supplies as taken from inventory for current use.

SUBSCRIPTIONS

Subscriptions covers the expenditures of the bank for newspapers, magazines, and services such as Moody, Poors, Commerce Clearing House, etc. All such expense is distributed to sections based on benefit received.

SUPPLIES – BUILDING

Supplies for the building or such items as maintenance supplies, mops, polishing and cleaning products, lavatory supplies, etc. are generally charged directly to the occupancy section for later distribution to other sections of the bank based on space occupied.

TAXES – REAL ESTATE, PERSONAL PROPERTY

Taxes both on real estate and personal property are allocated to the occupancy section.

TELEPHONE – TELEGRAPH

Telephone and telegraph expense covers rental of equipment plus toll and unit calls. Such expense is distributed to sections based on number of phones and service.

TRAVEL – BANK BUSINESS

This expenditure only covers transportation and living expenses of personnel of the bank when engaged in bank business. Such expenses, when incurred in connection with visits to the supervisory authorities are charged to the stockholders section; when incurred in connection with visits regarding the investment portfolio, are charged to the investment section; when incurred in connection with credit or loan matters are charged to the respective loan sections; when incurred in connection with new business or public relations are charged to the new business and public relations sections.

TRAVEL – CONVENTIONS

Travel-conventions covers the expenses of bank personnel when attending banking conventions, meetings or schools. Such expenses, when incurred in connection with attending conventions or group meetings, are charged to the stockholders section; when incurred in connection with attendance at credit or mortgage conferences, are charged to the respective section; and when incurred in connection with attendance of personnel at schools to the personnel section.

WATER, TOWELS & MISCELLANEOUS

The expense for water, towels and miscellaneous covers expenditures of the bank for drinking water, general use of towels, etc. which should be charged to occupancy section for later distribution to other sections of the bank based on space occupied.

DISTRIBUTION OF EXPENSES OF SERVICE SECTIONS

After distributing the direct expenses of the bank to the Operating, Non-Operating, Capital, Administrative and Service sections, the next step in developing the cost system is to distribute the total expenses of the respective service sections to the Operating, Non-Operating, Capital and Administrative sections according to the following formulas. In applying these formulas let us again be mindful of the fact that the secret of cost distribution is distribution by absorption; that is, distributing expenses of respective sections in such order or sequence that the expenses of respective sections, once distributed, are not appreciably affected by distribution of the expenses from other sections.

OCCUPANCY SECTION

The total expenses of the Occupancy section consists of rent and other direct expenses which are most equitably distributed to the other sections based on the number of square feet of floor space occupied.

PERSONNEL SECTION

The total expenses of the Personnel section consisting of direct expenses, and expenses of occupancy, are most equitably distributed to other sections based on the number of personnel assigned to those respective sections.

TELEPHONE

Where expense of the telephone is not directly distributed to the other sections, and such expenses is charged to the Telephone and Switchboard section, the total expense including salary, rent, etc. is distributed to other sections of the bank based on service provided plus cost of calls and rental of the equipment.

MAIL AND MESSENGER SECTIONS

The total expense of the Mail and Messenger section is charged to the respective sections of the bank based on the services rendered by the Mail and Messenger section to the other sections of the bank.

ADDRESSOGRAPH

Total expense of the Addressograph section is distributed to the other sections of the bank based on the amount of time analysis discloses, the Addressograph section spends in serving the other sections such as making up lists, addressing envelopes, or performing other services of a similar nature.

STENOGRAPHERS

The expense of stenographers, which includes the proportionate cost of occupancy, personnel, mail, messenger, and addressograph services is first reduced to an hourly cost and then distributed to other sections of the bank based on the amount of time the stenographer spends in taking dictation, transcribing and typing letters, and doing other work.

It is at this point that we begin to apply the principles of cost distribution to services, and develop factors which can assist management in conducting more profitable operations.

In making a cost analysis very often an item is handled or a service performed by more than one person, or in more than one section. Therefore, to obtain the overall cost of handling an item or performing a service, the cost of handling such item in each section which has anything to do with the item, must be accumulated.

In determining costs, in addition to volume of activity and expenses applicable to the handling of the particular item or performing the service or function, two other factors must be taken into consideration—the percentage of time the employee spends in handling or processing the particular item, or performing the particular service—and where more than one item is handled or more than one service is performed by the same person—the relative "weight" of each respective item or service.

As to work hours in a year, it is generally considered that each employee is paid for working 40 hours a week for 50 weeks, or 2000 hours annually.

For example, analysis discloses that the stenographer spends about 10% of her time in opening new accounts, ordering check books, answering inquiries and 2% putting up statements at the end of the month. These functions have nothing to do with service or item costs. This 12% of her total expense is allocated directly to overhead.

It is further determined that she devotes about 12½% of her time to handling detail and writing letters for the cashier, about 18½% of her time to handling correspondence and detail for the executive vice president. The balance of the time, analysis discloses, is used in preparing coupon books in connection with installment loans and in issuing savings bonds.

By use of a stop watch, the time it actually takes the stenographer to prepare a coupon book and prepare a savings bond is determined, which provides the weight for handling respective transactions. Study further discloses it takes the stenographer 360 seconds to prepare a coupon book and ledger card in connection with an installment loan, and 66 seconds to issue a savings bond. Dividing the 360 by 66 indicates it takes 5.45 times longer to prepare a coupon book for an installment loan than it does to issue a savings bond. Therefore issuing a savings bond has a weight of 1 while preparing a coupon book has a weight of 5.45.

Next the weights involved in handling respective items are multiplied by the number of items handled to get the total units, after which the total expense applicable to handling respective items is divided by the total number of units to get the unit cost.

By multiplying the number of units in each item by the unit cost, the cost of handling any particular item is determined.

DISTRIBUTION OF EXPENSES OF ADMINISTRATIVE SECTIONS

After expenses of the Service sections have been distributed to the Operating, Non-Operating, Capital and Administrative sections, the expenses of the respective Administrative sections, which have functions and responsibilities in connection with supervision of operations, investment of funds, and new business activities, are totalled and distributed to the remaining Administrative, Operating, Non-Operating and Capital sections. This distribution is based on analysis of the functions and responsibilities of the personnel in respective administrative sections, and the percentage of their time to 100% that they devote to other sections or to other functions. This distribution is based on the percentage of their time and expenses that their services are engaged in:

1. Supervising operations of operating sections.
2. Accounting and auditing work.
3. Installment loan activities.
4. Commercial loan activities.
5. New business activities.
6. International department activities.
7. Trust department activities.
8. Safe deposit department activities.
9. Functions in behalf of the directors, stockholders.
10. Functions in connection with the investment of funds.

OFFICERS

The distribution of the total expenses of respective administrative personnel is made by applying respective percentages to the total expense and distributing the amounts so determined to the other divisions for whom they work or devote their time. This provides for the distribution of expenses of official personnel engaged in administrative work.

AUDITING

It is the function of the auditing department or the person

charged with the responsibility for maintaining the internal control system and the audit program to serve all of the various sections of the bank in accordance with the audit program approved by the directors. In distributing the expense of the auditor, all expenses for the routine control program are distributed to the various departments and sections of the bank based on the amount of time spent in executing the control program. In like manner, expenses in connection with executing the audit program are charged to respective sections of the bank based on the amount of time spent in undertaking phases of the audit program as approved and directed by the board of directors.

GENERAL BOOKS

The general bookkeeper has the responsibility of posting the general and subsidiary ledgers and for performing other functions in connection with the responsibilities of the position. The total expenses of the general bookkeeper are distributed to the other sections of the bank on the basis of time involved in posting or handling transactions for such sections.

DIRECTORS

It is the principal function of the directors to direct and not manage the affairs of the bank. It is also their responsibility to approve general policies in connection with loans, investments, new business and public relations; and to specifically approve each loan or investment made. If the bank has a trust department, it is also their responsibility to select and approve the acceptance of trust accounts, and supervise the management of trust accounts. The total expense of the directors after analysis is distributed to the Operating, Non-Operating, and Capital sections, based on the percentage of time the directors spend in directing, or time engaged in operations and functions of the respective sections.

After the expenses of the Service and Administrative sections have been distributed to the Operating, Non-Operating and Capital sections, the next step in cost analysis is to analyze the functions of each of the Operating and Non-Operating sections and determine the cost of performing each service or function or handling a particular item within each respective section.

Before doing this, however, it is well to briefly comment on the Capital section. Also, in case the study has not made it evident, it is well to point out that the total expenses in connection with Non-Operating sections are all incurred in connection with the investment of funds while all of the expenses of the Operating sections are incurred in connection with the providing of services.

The Capital section is composed of the Stockholders section and the Public Relations-New Business section, both of which represent the stockholders' interest and equity in the bank. To these sections all expenses in connection with services, functions or assistance rendered in their behalf, or in their interests are charged; and certain expenses incurred by management, which should not be assumed or borne by depositors or customers, are allocated.

Later, as we shall point out in the study, the net operating income from all operating sections will be adjusted to the Stockholders section. It is from the crediting of the net profits, or debiting of the net losses from these other sections, plus the income from the investment of their own funds, that the stockholders derive the profits from which are paid dividends, taxes, and their equity is increased by the crediting of undistributed earnings to the Reserve Surplus and Undivided Profits accounts.

Expenses of the Operating and Non-Operating sections are all incurred in connection with either rendering various services or performing various functions. The cost of rendering respective services or performing functions can best be arrived at by applying the following fixed formula to expenses of each operating section:

1. Outline the principal or main functions performed or services rendered within the section.

2. Deduct from the expenses of the section any expense items which are applicable to a particular service or function.

3. Determine the time it takes to perform each function or service to be costed, which establishes the individual weight.

4. Multiply the respective weight by the number of items handled to obtain the total weights.

5. Divide the remaining expense of the section by the total weights to get a unit cost.

6. Multiply the respective weights in each transaction by the unit weight which determines the cost.

7. Divide any expenses attributable to a particular function or service (item 2) by the number of transactions to obtain the special expense and add to the cost determined in item 6 to obtain the actual cost of performing a particular function or rendering a certain service.

The application of this formula gives the ACTUAL cost of performing a service or function.

The next and probably the most important step is to determine the POTENTIAL cost of handling respective functions or providing the certain services. This is done by taking the actual time it takes the teller or clerk to perform any respective service or function computed at the actual time cost of the person performing the service or function. This is generally arrived at by determining the per second cost of the clerk or teller, and by multiplying this cost by the seconds required to perform a certain function or service.

Such analysis, if accurately undertaken, will disclose that the POTENTIAL cost can be as low as 10% of the ACTUAL cost for performing the same service. The difference between the ACTUAL cost and the POTENTIAL cost indicates the degree to which management is failing to utilize the physical facilities, equipment, and available "time ready to work" of personnel. Proper delegation of responsibility, efficient scheduling of work, use of a floating staff, and conscientious use of work flow studies and studies of peak and valley periods will disclose many and sundry ways in which progressive management can obtain maximum production at minimum expense.

The same procedure is followed in costing the respective functions performed or services rendered in the Non-Operating sections in connection with handling the various and respective types of loans, loan payments or other services or functions performed.

It should also be remembered that any costs for performing a function or providing a service only applies to the cost of performing a function or providing a service *within a certain section.* Very often a particular function or service is handled in more than one section, therefore, in order to obtain the actual or total cost it is necessary to accumulate the respective costs for performing the function or providing the service or handling the item in the various sections through which it passes.

This can be best illustrated by referring to the following schedule of costs for performing certain functions or services undertaken in a typical bank:

Rental cost per square foot annually		$ 1.95	
Personnel cost annually		285.83	
Stenographic cost per hour		1.43	
Preparation cost, Installment Loan Coupon Book		.768	
Issuing U.S. Savings Bond		.14	
Cashier's time per hour		3.53	
Executive Vice President's time per hour		5.39	
Posting Liability Ledger, Commercial Loan debit or credit		.35	each
Posting Liability Ledger, Mortgage Loan		1.06	each
Commercial Deposit (credit only)			
Teller Cost	.053	.083	plus cost of items deposited
Proof Cost	.0059		
Bookkeeping	.024		
Savings Deposit (credit only)		.112	plus cost of items deposited
Teller	.082		
Proof	.0059		
Bookkeeping	.024		
Savings Withdrawal		.325	plus cost of currency paid out
Teller	.295		
Proof	.0059		
Bookkeeping	.024		
Cashing a check		.035	plus cost of currency paid out
Teller	.029		
Proof	.0059		
Currency deposited per $100		.088	
Currency paid out per $100		.103	
Overhead per month per account		.102	

Item	Component	Cost
Overdrafts		.96 each plus interest
Returning checks NSF, each		.984
Check deposited, each		.0059
Check "on us" paid		.024
Safe Deposit access		1.558 each
Cashier's Check or Draft (issuing cost only)		.323
Commercial Loan – 1 payment		6.54
Administration	4.79	
Teller	.747	
Bookkeeper	.35	
Teller, payments	.308	
Bookkeeper payment	.35	
Installment Loan – 12 payments		7.41
Administration	1.92	
Coupon Book	.768	
Teller, payments	4.72	
Mortgage Loan – 5 years – 60 payments		140.36
Administration	56.00	
Teller, payments	20.76	
Bookkeeping	63.60	
Loan Teller cost, handling payment on Commercial Loan		.308
Loan Teller cost, handling payment on Installment Loan		.393
Loan Teller cost, handling payment on Mortgage Loan		.346
Outgoing Collection		.554 plus postage
Incoming Collection		.785 plus cost of presentation remittance

THE PROFIT OR LOSS OF RESPECTIVE DEPARTMENTS AND SECTIONS OF THE BANK

The next step in cost analysis is determining the gross and net profit or loss from operations of respective departments or sections of the bank. This information is obtained by first determining the gross and net earnings of respective departments and deducting the expenses which leaves the net operating profit.

The principal source of bank earnings is the interest income obtained from the investment of funds:

A. Contributed by stockholders and augmented by undistributed profits

B. Maintained by depositors in checking accounts and payable on demand upon presentation of an order to pay (check)

C. Maintained by depositors in savings accounts at interest subject to payment upon notice and presentation of a receipt book

D. Deposited with the bank in an interest bearing Certificate of Deposit payable at a fixed maturity to the payee or to his order

E. Maintained by the Trust Department representing trust funds awaiting investment or held for distribution.

In order to produce income, such funds less a percentage required for providing cash for the needs of the depositors and for legal reserve requirements, are invested in commercial loans, installment loans, mortgage loans and in securities of the federal, state, and municipal governments.

All interest income, however, is not "net" to the bank, for against the gross income (considering amortization of premiums) the expense or cost of investing or converting such funds into loans and investments must be deducted.

The first step in this phase of cost analysis is to determine the net income from the investment of funds. This is done by deducting from the gross income received from the investment of funds in respective types of loans and investments, the expense incurred in investing such funds, such as the expenses of the loan teller incurred in connection with handling loan payments, and the administrative expenses of the officers in handling the various types of loans.

After the net income from the investment of funds in loans and investments has been computed, the next step is to apply the net income to the respective classes of funds for investment contributed by Commercial, Savings, Trust and Stockholders departments.

In order to obtain this information, cash and legal reserve requirements of respective classes of funds are deducted from gross funds to obtain the amount of net funds invested.

Next, the proper allocation of net income from the investment of funds in loans and investments is made to the net funds of the Commercial, Savings, Trust and Stockholders departments based on the conversion of funds program as covered in Chapter XX. However, where no investment program or conversion of funds program is followed, the net income from the investment of funds is pro-rated to the net funds of the respective departments available for investment.

After total operating income has been determined, the next step is to allocate the total expenses of the operating sections to respective departments of which they are a part which determines the gross operating profit.

From the gross operating profit the cost of providing FDIC insurance is deducted. This is done by taking the FDIC expense and pro-rating it to the Commercial and Savings departments funds based on the net funds. Next, interest paid on savings accounts is deducted from the Savings department profit which shows the gross department operating profit or loss.

The revenue each department receives from fees and commissions for specific services they render is then added which gives each department its gross departmental profit or loss. After this computation is made, the proportionate share of income tax is charged to each department on the basis of operating profit. The final result indicates the net income which the stockholders have realized from the operations of the bank. Such net income is available for distribution in the form of dividends, (after certain requirements have been met) added to the Undivided Profits account or appropriated for the development of business, capital expenditures, or for other purposes which are in the interests of the stockholders.

The logical question then arises. How can banks increase their net profits? There are a number of answers to this question among which are:

1. Converting investments to longer maturities to obtain a higher rate of income which, however, increases the risk of loss on forced liquidation.

2. Increasing the rate for borrowed money. This is unsound in that it penalizes one group of customers for the benefit of another group.

3. Increasing certain types of loans, which because of risk, demand a higher rate of interest. This practice is fraught with danger and places an additional contingency on reserve accounts and often capital.

4. Arbitrarily allocating the income from higher yield securities and loans to time deposits so as to justify the payment of a higher interest rate. This practice, followed by inexperienced management, is unsound in that it distorts the income picture as far as departmental earnings are concerned.

5. Reducing expenses. This is a sound approach, if it can be accomplished without penalizing warranted salary increases, advertising programs or public relations activities.

6. Increasing income through an increase in service charges and fees for services. Generally banks have been reluctant to approach this matter intelligently. Most banks are still giving their services away and using service charge schedules and account analysis methods which are moth-eaten. Banks, if they really knew their costs of operation and would properly apply such costs plus a reasonable profit to each transaction, could increase their service charge and fee income 50% to 100%—even higher. It is unwise, however, for banks to increase fees and service charges at the same time they increase interest rates on savings deposits—as customers are liable to react to the thought that the bank is penalizing one group of customers for the benefit of another. If money is so valuable, why service charges—or—why only a nominal earning allowance?

While banks may follow one or several of the above described methods for increasing departmental income, the most practical and equitable way is through adoption of an equitable and properly devised service charge schedule, applying account analysis formulas to services, and by becoming conscious of the profit formula, as used under our free enterprise system that *cost plus profit equals sales price.*

HISTORY OF SERVICE CHARGES

In connection with service charge schedules and account analysis methods, some of the background and history in connection with the development of service charges as we know them, should be of interest to students of banking.

Bank service charges developed out of economic conditions, the need and growth of banking services, increased use of such services by the public and realization by bankers of the need to develop a compensating plan or basis to cover the cost of supplying these services.

Cost analysis, the basis for soundly formulated service charges and account analysis was developed originally from the application of principals of cost accounting originated by the Scotch and English accountants in the latter part of the 19th century.

The first service charges, it is believed, were assessed about the turn of the century after several New York banks had undertaken a form of cost analysis and applied an "account charge" in an effort to have some of their customers either reimburse them for handling the account or to transfer their account to another bank. Even though banks had some idea of their costs, they were unwilling to pass these costs on to their customers preferring customers to maintain compensating balances. To bring this about, many banks of that period required customers to maintain a minimum balance of a certain amount, otherwise their business "was not welcome."

History of banking indicates it was a quite common custom of certain banks to only permit customers to maintain a checking account with them if their balance, at all times, was in excess of a certain figure which ranged from $1,000 to even $25,000.

In considering service charges, it is well to keep in mind that initially the underlying reason for banks making studies in connection with costs was to provide ways and means to provide services without assuming a loss; and *not to provide services at a profit.* Every basis of compensation in the handling of the small account up until about 1930 was in connection with increasing balances.

The failure to recognize the many advantages from adopting equitable service charge plans at the time, it would seem now, completely distorted the picture and precluded management from developing a solid base from which to use cost analysis as a means to reduce expenses through more improved and efficient methods and procedures, and devise more simplified routines in order to be able to render greater service—at a profit. Many banks, however, began to set up minimum average balance requirements. Depositors were required to maintain such a balance in order to carry a checking account. This minimum balance varied with banks. Some banks required a monthly minimum average balance of $100, while other banks required a minimum monthly average balance of $500 or even $1000. One of the major banks of the country at that time (1928) required a minimum monthly average balance of $25,000. Failure to maintain such a balance was met with a request to either increase such balance or move the account elsewhere.

In time, many banks established the policy of only permitting individuals or corporations to open a checking account if they agreed to maintain the bank's minimum average balance. Later they found, however, that while the minimum average balance requirements kept the small account from opening, they had no provision for controlling the account once opened, or control over accounts already on their books—except to request the depositor to either increase his balance or close the account. The latter course, obviously, was a drastic measure contrary to good public relations as we now view them.

Banks then devised a plan through which they endeavored to have depositors who maintained accounts below the minimum average balance requirements, reimburse them for the expense of handling the account by assessing a monthly service charge of $1.00, $2.00, or more. This charge was levied across the board against all accounts which failed to maintain the required minimum monthly average balance unless the depositor had connections or other business which, in the opinion of the officers of the bank, warranted the waiving of the charge. As a result of this policy many depositors went from one bank to another whose minimum average balance requirement they could maintain.

It should be understood, however, that this first form of service charge was a *penalty charge* and was in no way related to *services* or meant to be a source of income; rather it was a *charge to discourage people of small means from having a checking account.*

In respect to such a situation, however, it would seem evident, in the light of past history, that the fault lay with the bankers themselves for failing to "sell" the principal of service charges and profit to the public. However, at the turn of the century banks were in need of funds and made intensive efforts to have corporations, firms and individuals of means place large amounts with them on a demand basis on which they paid interest. These arrangements were usually made on the basis of the bank agreeing to pay interest on that portion of their balance over a certain amount. The customary arrangement at that time (1924-1930) was for the bank to pay 1%, 2% or more on that portion of the monthly average collected balance over $1000, $2000, $5000, $10,000, etc.

About the same time, some of the larger banks of the country began to apply the principles of cost accounting to their own operations.. As a result of such analysis they were appalled to discover that it cost them between .03 and .05 to process a check drawn against a depositor's account—.05 to .09 to handle each and every deposit at the paying and receiving window; .20 to .50 per thousand to process currency deposited; .01 to .04 to collect a check through the clearings and .02 to .04 to collect a check deposited by their customers drawn on another city. Even so, the larger banks which recognized the need for charges for services were undecided as to their course of action—charge for services and pay interest on the balances—or pay no interest on the balances and make no charge for services.

About 1925 bankers began to work toward a solution of the problem of the small account and the larger unprofitable account. John F. Tufts, writing in the American Banking Journal and quoted in Kniffin's "Practical Work of a Bank" said: "There are three principal causes making the question (of unprofitable and small accounts) of charging the unprofitable account of importance to commercial bankers.

"First—The tremendous increase in recent years in the number of people who have become acquainted with the convenience, security and other advantages afforded by a checking account.

Many of these people desiring to have checking accounts, have no idea of bank costs and their accounts are not self sustaining. They would willingly comply with a reasonable service charge plan or balance requirement if the need were explained to them." *(Author's note:* 30 years later many bankers are still reluctant to adopt proper charge plans and shy away from satisfactory explanations.)

"Second—The war period (World War I, 1914-1920) and the consequent rapid advance in cost of employees salaries, check books, pass books, stationery and other supplies has greatly increased bank expense. An average balance sufficient to pay for carrying a checking account ten years ago is entirely inadequate today." *(Author's note:* If this was true in 1925, how much more true is it today? In these comments note the emphasis is on a charge to cover the expense—nothing is said about profit!)

"Third — Unprofitable accounts as a class require proportionately more care and time, and involve greater risk than profitable accounts. Tellers windows have been congested and transit and bookkeeping departments are clogged to such an extent by the transactions of hundreds of unprofitable accounts that it is increasingly difficult to render the best type of service." *(Author's note:* In this period about which Mr. Tufts writes it should be remembered that nearly all of the banks of the country were still using the Boston Ledger system in their bookkeeping departments. Under this system, all checks and deposits were listed by hand on the ledger sheets in pen and ink and extended manually. It was not until the early 20's that banks began to use manually operated posting machines. Now, 1961, emphasis is on automation.)

Banks which decided to adopt some form of monthly "service charge" began by assessing the flat charge of $1.00, $2.00, or other amounts each month against all accounts which did not maintain the required minimum average balance. Banks which already used this flat charge basis but felt a change was in order, instead of scientifically approaching the unprofitable account from an analysis standpoint, attempted to correct the situation by either raising the minimum average balance requirement or increasing the flat penalty charge, or both.

In discussing this type of charge, it should be remembered that only the average balance was considered. For example, if the average balance requirement was $200.00 and one depositor maintained an average balance of $220.00 during the month and drew 45 checks and made 10 deposits containing 30 checks no charge was assessed. On the other hand, a depositor in the same bank who maintained an average balance of $180.00 and drew 5 checks and only made one deposit would be charged $2.00. Similarly a depositor maintaining an average monthly balance of $100.00 and drawing only 5 checks would pay the same charge as another depositor maintaining the same average balance but drawing 50 checks. Obviously the basis for the assessing of such charges was unfair.

The first notable change in setting up a service charge schedule which had some relationship to activity, and was only applicable to personal accounts, it is believed occurred in 1930 when the graduate form of service charge was devised and applied by the author as an equitable solution to comprising respective minimum average balance requirements of three banks brought together as a result of a consolidation.

In this type of service charge schedule various balances were subject to a fixed charge for which they were permitted a fixed number of checks, with an additional charge for each check issued and paid over the number permitted by the balance charge, similar to the following:

Average Balance	Charge	Free Checks Allowed
Under $300	$3.00	10
$301 to $400	2.00	10
$401 to $500	1.00	10

Additional checks over 10 at .05 each

It is believed that this was the first instance, at least by a major bank, to recognize the activity in the service charge. Even at that time the schedule was adopted not for the purpose of producing profit, but as *a subtle means for discouraging the small depositor from doing business with the bank.*

The larger banks, now that they were getting rid of the smaller and unprofitable checking account, were concentrating their efforts again to getting increased balances from the more important customers. Even though in this process they were going through the routine of some form of analysis, they were content to waive any charge in order to obtain an increase in balance or attract a new account regardless of activity just to have the funds. They needed deposits to supply the ever demanding need for funds to loan and became motivated by ideas of glamour—to be the biggest bank in the city—or the state. (It is interesting to observe that conditions in 1961 haven't changed much. Bankers everywhere are still harping on size and growth.)

As a result of this practice, active accounts which carried rather large balances moved from one bank to another which would either charge them less for the handling of their account or waive the charge entirely.

When the larger banks, finally becoming aware of the expense of handling the smaller accounts, began to get rid of them by assessing high service charges, the outlying city, neighborhood, and country banks, having little or no knowledge of costs, began to vie with each other for these small accounts which, in relationship to deposit totals, were insignificant. The advertising "Pay by check," "A checking account is a convenient way to pay your bills," became the gospel of many bankers.

The outlying city, neighborhood, and country banks, in going after the small account, merely followed the practice of the larger banks in previous years and were motivated by a desire to attract additional business. In this approach they, like their city cousins of a decade before, failed to realize the opportunity for profit in the smaller account through the assessing of equitable charges for service, based on cost—plus a profit.

When the large banks entered into the fierce competition for balances, (as they are again doing in 1961) the idea seems to have been conceived that the depositor was entitled to a share of the profits which his account earned—a reversal of the old axiom of need. Now the bank's need for deposits was greater that the depositor's need for a safe place in which to keep his funds. No one up to that time had given much thought to the depositor's share of the profit. Whatever profit the bank made from the use of the funds, outside of interest paid on the balance, it was entitled to keep because it was supplying the need of the depositor for a safe place in which he could keep his money.

The theory of paying a "profit" to the depositor came into existence through the idea of allowing an earning credit on the net average loanable balance. This was generally applied in a very unsound manner as only a few of the items of service rendered were considered as expense in arriving at the cost of handling an account. For many years there was strong opposition, which still exists, to include in any form of analysis the charges for making a deposit or for depositing checks and currency in a deposit. (Why penalize a customer for putting money in the bank?)

In analyzing accounts, it was the customary practice to first determine the average balance. This was done by adding together the daily ledger balance for each day and then dividing the total by the number of days in the month.

Banks also maintained float sheets on each depositor whose account was being analyzed. On this sheet they noted the numbers and amount of checks deposited by customer and the number of days it would take to collect such items. At the end of the month the total and the extension of such funds, were totaled and divided by the number of days in the month and was known as Average Uncollected Funds which was deducted from the average balance, leaving what was referred to as the Average Collected Balance. From this balance a percentage was deducted to provide for cash and legal reserve requirements. The remainder was known as the Net Loanable Balance on which an earning credit, commensurate with the return on funds loaned was allowed.

Because of the exchange charge, which had become unjustified, the amount of exchange collected was included as part of the income produced by the account. Later exchange charges, levied by the major banks in the big cities, were eliminated entirely for obviously if a customer was charged for the use of funds while they were in process of collection, he was entitled to the full earning credit allowed. Against the gross earnings of the account the banks charged the amount of interest paid on the balance, the costs of handling checks issued and paid, and for other services rendered which at their discretion they included in the analysis of accounts. A sample of the analysis sheet used at the time is shown in Exhibit 115.

The difference between the gross earnings and the total expense

EXHIBIT 115

ANALYSIS WORK SHEET

ACCOUNT MONTH OF

DATE	NO DEP.	CHECKS DEP. US	LOC	O.T.	CY DEP.	CPNS DEP.	OTH CHG.	SUMMARY
								AVERAGE BALANCE $.........
1								AVG. UNCOLL. FUNDS ....
2								AVG. COLL. BALANCE ....
3								CASH-LEGAL RES. ....
4								NET LOANABLE FDS. ....
5								EARNINGS CREDIT ....
6								EXCHANGE RECEIVED ....
7								GROSS EARNINGS .... $.........
8								
9								EXCHANGE PAID ....
10								INTEREST PAID ....
11								DEPOSITS @ .06 ....
12								US CHECKS @ .03 ....
13								LOCAL CKS @ .01 ....
14								OTHER CKS @ .02 ....
15								CY. DEP. @ .50 M ....
16								CPNS. DEP @ .08 ....
17								OTHER CHG ....
18								
19								TOTAL EXPENSE ....
20								PROFIT OR LOSS ....
21								DESIRED PROFIT ....
22								NET P or L ....
23								
24								
25								CHARGE ACCOUNT $
26								
27								APPROVED BY.
28								
29								
30								
31								

was either a profit or a loss, against which the banks sometimes charged an amount considered as desired profit, or the amount the bank thought they should earn on the account. Remember that in analyzing accounts, the items of service were charged only at cost and did not purport to return a profit. Most banks were closing their eyes to rendering services at a profit and only looking for reimbursement of expense—the profit came from the loaning of funds. (Unfortunately this is still the thinking of too many bankers.)

When an account showed a net loss, the first adjustment was to eliminate the payment of interest, increase the so-called free balance, or request the depositor to increase the collected balance. Only in rare instances was the charge levied. In many banks, it is said, the cost of operating the so-called Analysis Department was greater than the income from the service or analysis charges levied.

Enactment of Section Q of the *Federal Reserve Act in 1933* prohibited the payment of interest on demand deposits. Banks, however, continued to share their income through the subterfuge of allowing the earning credit in the analysis of accounts.

Beginning about 1935, as nearly as it can be determined, banks became conscious of the cost of "averaging balances" and work involved in determining float. There then began to come into use, the considering of the *minimum balance* as the balance subject to service or analysis charges. This was a step in the right direction in that it recognized the fact that it was only the minimum balance a depositor maintained which could be safely loaned out or invested.

As business began to return to normal after the depression in 1933 progressive bankers, awakening to the profit potentialities in time loans on automobiles, home improvements, and household appliances, organized Installment Loan and Consumer Credit Loan departments.

At the same time, banks again started to give considered thought to how they could serve the smaller depositor. They realized the inequalities of the flat service charge on the minimum balance, and the prohibitive cost of analyzing the small personal account.

The plan was then devised of permitting a depositor to maintain a checking account without requiring him to maintain a required minimum balance provided—the depositor paid for having an account by paying a charge for each check he issued. There were a number of such plans, the more prominent of which was known as the "NO MINIMUM BALANCE" plan. Under this plan the charge of .10 for each check was deducted from the balance at the time the check was posted against the balance of the account.

Later, recognizing the unnecessary operation and cost of deducting the fee at the time each check was paid, banks devised a plan of selling a book of checks, usually 20, for a $2.00 fee. There are a number of variations of this plan in effect today.

In connection with service charge schedules, account analysis methods, and other charges for services rendered by banks, it is well to remember money is a commodity just like a pair of shoes or a bushel of corn. It is bought through loaning and transferred in payment of obligations by means of checks which the owner has the privilege of drawing against his own account.

Every individual and corporation finds the use of a checking account a real convenience because it enables them to have a safe and convenient place to keep their money which is available to them at any time merely by drawing a check against their account.

A checking account also provides them with a means for converting checks they have received from others to cash and their own use.

Every bank, through extending the privileges of a checking account, also acts as a financial accountant to individuals and corporations through periodically providing them with a statement of the account which shows the funds received, the funds paid out, and the balance available for distribution.

Individuals, corporations and business concerns, in addition to benefiting from the use of a checking account, also have frequent use for other banking facilities such as the collection of drafts, notes, and interest coupons; the certifying of checks; the immediate transfer of funds from one section of the country to another; the providing of credit information which enables them to arrange satisfactory credit terms; the obtaining of credit information on a prospective customer which provides protection against possible loss from over extension of credit; and many other services.

Some of the services which a bank provides for the use of its customers cost more than others. The only way a bank can cover the expense in connection with providing checking account services is through the interest income it obtains from investing the net collected funds a customer has on deposit, less the amount it is required to keep on hand in cash and on deposit with the Federal Reserve Bank as reserve, in loans and investments.

The only way a bank can cover the expense of providing other bank services is by making a charge for each service. Such charge should not only be sufficient to cover the cost of rendering such service but provide a small profit to the bank for its work as well.

Because present day conditions call for a new and higher standard of bank management and the use of new and improved modern machinery and equipment to provide modern and up-to-date service, it is necessary for banks to adjust their schedule of charges to meet rising costs and current economic conditions.

Under these circumstances, and in order to carry out what should be the first objective of every bank, *to provide the best service in the most efficient manner possible*, many banks have adopted a schedule covering charges for all services provided and rendered by the bank, similar to the following, which schedule as a matter of policy, they make available to both customers and the public.

It is interesting to note that not only does such a schedule of charges disclose the basis or method of computing the charge for providing checking account facilities but by listing numerous services acquaints customers with other facilities and services the bank has available.

SCHEDULE OF SERVICES AND CHARGES
THE PROGRESSIVE BANK

Effective January 1 ______

CHECKING ACCOUNTS OF BUSINESSES AND CORPORATIONS

Accounts of corporation and accounts of individuals engaged in business under their own name shall be subject to monthly analysis on a uniform basis. (Accounts of churches, charitable organizations, and members of the clergy may be exempt from such charges at the discretion of the bank.)

Earnings

Under the system of analysis as adopted, an income rate predicated on the net return from investment of funds, as determined by the directors, shall be allowed on the minimum balance the depositor maintains during the month.

Expenses

Against the income allowance the bank shall charge the aggregate expense incurred in rendering the following direct services:

Maintenance (Providing of monthly statement)	$ .50
Deposits; each	.10
Checks paid, each	.06
Checks on this, and other local banks deposited, each	.03
Checks on out of town banks deposited, each	.05
Currency deposited, per thousand	1.00
Rolled silver furnished per roll	.04

The Charge if any

If the income allowance is greater than the aggregate expense of the services rendered no charge shall be assessed. If the aggregate expense of the services rendered exceeds the income allowance the difference shall be charged to the depositor's account in the following month.

CHECKING ACCOUNTS OF INDIVIDUALS

As checking accounts of individuals are maintained as a convenience in paying current and household bills and generally require little direct service, the bank simplifies the analysis of such accounts by handling them on a metered plan.

Under the following plan, the depositor pays a base charge, depending on the minimum balance maintained, for which he is allowed to draw a fixed number of checks. Should additional checks be drawn, a nominal charge is made for those exceeding the number of checks allowed.

Minimum Balance	Base Charge	Checks Allowed
Under 100.00	1.50	10
101 -200	1.00	10
201 -300	.50	10
301 and over	one check allowed for each $25.00 of minimum balance	

Excess checks over the number allowed at .10 each

COLLECTIONS

The bank provides facilities for handling the various types of collection items. Fees covering the presentation and the collection of respective items for customers and non-customers are as follows:

Bonds, others	$ .50 per $1000.00 plus postage Minimum charge .50
Bonds, U. S. Government	.50 per $1000.00 plus postage Minimum charge .25
Coupons, others	.15 per $100.00 plus postage Minimum charge .25
Coupons, U. S. Government	.10 per coupon
Incoming drafts, with or without documents attached	.15 per $100.00 Minimum charge .25
Lease/rental collections	.25 per payment Minimum charge .25
Outgoing drafts, with or without documents attached	.25 per $100.00 plus postage Minimum charge .25

As a convenience to customers the bank provides the following special financial services for which it either makes a direct charge, or in the case of business and corporation accounts, includes the charge in the analysis of accounts. Certain "public" services as shown are available to non-customers.

Balance requests	....	$ .25 each
Cashier's checks	Under $5.00	.15 each
	$5.01 to 24.99	.20 each
	25.00 to 99.00	.25 each
	100.00 and over	.25 each plus 1/10 of 1%
Cashing checks for customers		
Drawn on this bank		No charge

Drawn on another bank	.15 each plus 1/10 of 1%
Cashing checks for non-customers	
Drawn on this bank	No charge
Drawn on another bank	.15 each plus 1/10 of 1%
Certifying a check	.25 each
Credit report obtained for a customer	.50 plus cost
Credit inquiry on a customer	.50
Currency provided for a customer	.50 per $1000.00
Currency provided for a non-customer	.50 per $1000.00
Drafts-domestic and foreign	
Under $100.00	.25
$100.00 and over	.25 plus 1/10 of 1%
Endorsement stamps	Cost
Imprinting checks	Cost
Overdrafts	.50 per check
Night depository service	
1 bag per year	12.00
Each extra bag	2.50
Returning checks for insufficient or uncollected funds	.50 each
Rolled coin supplied customers	.05 per roll
Rolled coin supplied non-customers	.05 per roll
Special statements	1.00 each
Stop payment orders	.50 each
Travellers checks	At prices specified by company issuing
Wire transfers	
Under $100.00	.25 plus cost of wire
Over $100.00	.25 plus cost of wire and 1/10 of 1%

SAFEKEEPING

The bank, as a matter of policy, discourages the use of safe keeping services and suggests the use of a safe deposit box or trust department facilities.

As a convenience, however, the bank will hold items in temporary safe keeping no longer than 60 days, or until such items can be delivered to the owners for disposition, at the following charges:

Abstracts	.50 each
Deeds	.50 each
General issue bonds	1.00 each
Insurance policies	.50 each
Mortgage notes	.50 each
Stock Certificates	.50 each
U. S. Savings Bonds	.25 each

SAVINGS ACCOUNTS

The bank encourages the use of savings department facilities. Interest at a rate determined from time to time by the directors, depending on economic and investment conditions, will be paid January 1 and July 1 of each year in accordance with savings department regulations.

In computing the interest earned, the bank will deduct from the minimum balance maintained during the six month period all withdrawals; and allow interest on all deposits made before the 10th of the month in which the deposit was made until the end of the interest period.

Net interest earned in any one period will not be credited to the account unless the amount so earned amounts to $.25 or more.

As thrift is the purpose of a savings account, unusual activity will be charged for at the following rates:

Minimum balance for period under $100	1 withdrawal
Minimum balance for period $101 to $200	2 withdrawals
Balance $201 and over	1 withdrawal for each $100 minimum balance

Withdrawals in excess of the number allowed will be charged for at $.50 each at the end of the period.

Accounts which close out within 6 months of opening shall be subject to a charge of $.50.

SAFE DEPOSIT BOXES

The bank provides safe deposit boxes in its fire and burglar proof vault for the safe keeping of securities, valuable papers, heirlooms, and jewelry. Boxes, with two keys, when available, are rented on an annual basis, payable in advance. No boxes are rented for less than a year period.

The sizes and annual rental are:

Size	Annual Rental*
2 x 5	$ 4.00
5 x 5	7.00
4 x 10	10.00
7 x 10	12.00

* Plus Federal Tax

Should keys be lost or misplaced, a charge will be made for replacing them as follows:

Loss of one key	$ 2.00
Loss of both keys including cost of drilling	10.00

LOANS – COMMERCIAL

Loan applications from individuals, businesses, corporations based on financial responsibility or collateral security are solicited. Rates covering respective types of loans are determined from time by the directors based on economic conditions, class of security or financial responsibility.

A minimum interest charge of $5.00 shall be made on all commercial loans, with any amount in excess of the interest earned to be collected as a service charge.

LOANS – MORTGAGES

The bank welcomes applications for real estate mortgage loans from individuals, builders and contractors.

The percentage of appraised value the bank will loan against, the terms of repayment, and the interest rate, is determined from time to time by the directors based on economic conditions. No charges are made for submitting an application, except where the application is not accompanied by an acceptable appraisal. The bank reserves the right to have its own appraisal made for which a charge of $10.00 will be made.

LOANS – INSTALLMENT

The bank makes loans with co-signers, and secured by chattel mortgages on automobiles, household appliances and merchandise repayable in 6-12-18-24-30-36 monthly installments.

Rates and terms of repayment for respective classes of loans are determined from time to time by the directors based on economic conditions.

A minimum interest charge of $10.00 discount will be made on all installment loans, with the excess over the interest earned to be collected as a service charge.

Borrowers delinquent 3 days in making their payment shall be subject to a "late charge" of 5% of the payment due with a minimum charge of $.50.

Borrowers delinquent 30 days or more shall, in addition to the charge of 5% of the payment due, be subject to a charge of $1.00 for each letter, notice or call made plus costs of legal or collection services if required.

SECURITY TRANSACTIONS

To enable customers of the bank, and the public, to conveniently transact the purchase and sale of securities for their own account, the bank provides investment service, with fees as follows:

Exchange of U. S. Bond	$1.00 per issue plus postage
Guarantee of signature	.20 per certificate plus postage
Mailing of securities for transfer or delivery	1.00 per transaction plus postage
Purchase of general market bonds	1.00 per order or issue
Purchase of stock	1.00 per order or issue
Purchase of U. S. Bonds	2.50 per $1000.00 to $5000.00
	1.25 per $1000.00 over $5000.00
Registration of securities	1.00 per item plus postage

Sale of general market bonds	1.00 per order or issue plus postage
Sale of stock	1.00 per issue or order plus postage
Sale of U. S. Bonds	2.50 per $1000.00 to $5000.00 1.25 per $1000.00 over $5000.00

CHAPTER XLI

AUDIT AND CONTROL[1]

THE THEORY AND PRACTICE OF AUDITING PROCEDURE, as applied to the banking field, found its inception in the accounting practices of the Scotch and English firms of registered accountants about the turn of the century.

Since then many recommendations and suggestions have been made and programs and plans developed in connection with the establishing of audit controls, accounting procedures and protective routines which would prevent a person from embezzling or stealing from his or her employer.

One of the first practical and manualized approaches to an audit program applicable to banks was born in the United States in the late 20's as an answer to the common need for devising a set of standards and procedures which could be used not only in evaluating the assets and in recognizing the liabilities of a bank, but in providing effective control of such assets and liabilities.

Since, then, but particularly beginning about 1931, banks in a constantly increasing number have been setting up internal control procedures and audit programs. Unfortunately, in too many banks, such routines and controls have been established *after* a crime has been committed. In other banks procedures have become routine and stagnant instead of being alive, while in other banks the auditor has lost his alertness and curiosity as to opportunities for defalcation and embezzlement.

Strange as it seems, we generally catch crooks by blundering. We first become suspicious of the way in which a transaction is being handled, we think something is wrong, we analyze it and pin it down to a certain place or person. In the majority of cases

---

[1] Much of the condensed information in this chapter is taken from "HOW TO AUDIT A BANK" by this author, published by Bankers Publishing Company. It is suggested and recommended that readers interested in the subject refer to this book for complete information on audit programs and procedures.

the person who is being observed or investigated becomes jittery and makes a mistake, which, when followed up, exposes the embezzlement or defalcation.

There are hundreds of ways in which funds can be embezzled from a bank. It is unwise, we believe, to describe even some of the ways in which embezzlements or defalcation can take place. I have always refrained from discussing or writing about the details of such matters from the fear that in so doing I could be supplying a would-be embezzler with the very tools needed to pull a job or help continue the peculations.

Defalcations and embezzlements cannot be wholly prevented as long as we are dealing with people. Amounts of defalcations and embezzlements, however, can be held to a minimum and their frequency controlled through the establishing of routines and procedures known as internal controls.

Such internal controls, referred to as preventative accounting procedures, have for their objective the protection and shielding of:

1. Weak people from temptation.
2. Strong people from opportunity.
3. Innocent people from involvement.

It is the belief of the author that the objectives of preventive accounting can be attained if those charged with the management responsibility of banks, and the protection and welfare of bank personnel, establish and place into operation the internal controls, audit routines and procedures tailor made to fit the operating conditions and exposure of their own individual bank.

It is impossible to cover all the essential points in connection with bank auditing and control in a single chapter. It is the purpose and intent of the author, therefore, to cover the subject from the standpoint of general overall information only with the hope that the reader will undertake further studies of the subject and thus contribute to better auditing standards; and assist and guide those who have the responsibility for bank auditing and control, to more properly and conscientiously conduct thorough audits on behalf of the directors of banks.

The disclosure of an embezzlement or defalcation occurring in a bank is frightening and of concern to all conscientious bank directors, alert bank officers, trusted bank employees and dedicated auditors because no single circumstance retards the growth and development of a bank, engenders lack of confidence in management, results in financial loss to stockholders, creates fear and distrust on the part of the public and often brings economic stress and ruin to a community, more than an embezzlement or defalcation occurring in a local bank.

Before continuing, let us define the terms embezzlement and defalcation and briefly explain the functions performed in conducting an examination or undertaking an audit.

Embezzlement refers to the taking of funds belonging to depositors or customers.

Defalcation refers to the appropriation of funds belonging strictly to the stockholders such as interest income, fees and commissions, or through the use of fictitious notes, or fraudulent expense vouchers.

For purposes of reference we will use the collective term *peculation* when referring to any and all types of embezzlement, defalcation or misappropriation in this chapter.

Examination generally refers to the review and analysis of assets and liabilities of record, for the purpose of ascertaining that such assets and liabilities exist, are in order, and represent real value as shown by the dollar amounts.

Audit on the other hand not only refers to confirmation of the fact that assets and liabilities of record exists, but that the figures which represent such assets and liabilities represent the results from normal business transactions.

As studied in earlier chapters of this book, the ownership of over 14,000 banks in the United States through which commerce and industry are carried on, is vested in thousands of stockholders. The stockholders obviously, in many cases, find it impossible to participate actively in the management of the bank and therefore elect at annual periods from their membership a prescribed number of stockholders as directors to represent them in the management of the bank. Generally the caliber and reputation of directors does not depend on the bank. On the contrary, the reputation of the bank, to a great extent, is a reflection of the reputation and integrity of its directors who are supposed to represent the highest type of citizenry.

Directors, as the name implies, are supposed to direct and not manage. They are not expected to take an active part in the normal day by day routine operations of the bank, but to delegate this responsibility to competent officers selected by them.

The responsibility of directors to "direct" and their obligation to administer the affairs of the bank in an honest and diligent manner does not end with the selection of trustworthy and competent personnel, nor does it end in establishing policies and sound management principles for the officers to follow in accordance with, and conforming to, federal and state laws. It is also most important that they establish safeguards which diligently protect the assets of the bank and see to it that the funds entrusted to the bank by depositors for protection are safely handled and invested.

Unfortunately, many directors do not recognize the extent of their responsibility for the maintaining of adequate records, or for the establishing of adequate internal controls and other safeguards which should be devised for the protection of assets and the funds of depositors.

On the other hand, officers of many banks, while recognizing the need for protection, are reluctant to call the attention of the directors to such matters for fear it will reflect on their ability. In a well managed bank, however, it is up to the directors to see that proper internal controls are enforced and a proper audit system established to enable the directors to discharge their responsibility.

AUDIT AND CONTROL IS THE RESPONSIBILITY OF THE DIRECTORS

Regardless of the opinions expressed and harbored by many bank officers and directors, audit and control is the responsibility of the directors. The various state and federal laws may vary in their language, but without question state it is the responsibility of the directors (not the officers), to examine, or appoint a committee of stockholders, outside accountants, or others properly selected, to examine the affairs of the bank at least once a year. While from practical experience we know it is often difficult for directors to examine the bank because of lack of know-how, insufficient time, and other factors, it is not impossible or impractical for them to delegate this responsibility.

Unfortunately, too many bankers and bank directors take the attitude, in connection with the adoption or installations of sound audit routines or in employing the services of a full time auditor, that it can't happen to their bank because "they know everybody," or "they are thoroughly familiar with what goes on." Other boards of directors believe they are exercising their responsibility because the bank maintains adequate fidelity insurance.

It is a generally accepted fact that embezzlers and defaulters are made and not born. Usually embezzlers are basically honest people who find themselves in adverse circumstances and are tempted beyond their power to resist. Psychologically, it is realized, the conduct of most people is governed to a great extent by fear of consequences. Rules of conduct are followed because people are afraid of criticism or the consequences; or fail to do something wrong because the end to be obtained or objective to be accomplished does not justify the risk or trouble involved.

While the carrying of adequate surety coverage may discharge the directors and management of the bank from the financial obligations which they owe the stockholders, it does not, or will not, discharge the moral obligations which they owe the employees.

Failure to provide adequate internal controls to prevent or retard embezzlements sometimes is admitted because of the excuse that the bank is too small to have a full time auditor. This is a gross misconception of the facts. Auditing and control functions in a small bank, or in any bank for that matter, do not have to be performed by the same person to be effective. It is practical and possible, in developing an audit program, to allocate control and auditing functions and responsibilities to more than one person, providing the routine assigned is not in connection with, or directly related to, the operating work the person performs in connection with his regular and principal job.

Also, in every bank, no matter how small, there are always duties which should be performed in connection with cost analysis, operational research, new business, public relations, and conservation of business. Someone should be doing them—why not the person assigned audit and control responsibilities, if he does not have enough to do?

In developing an audit program and internal control system

we should cover all operations and all classes of personnel and be mindful of the fact that the position or title of the peculator has little to do with the peculation. It is the character of the individual, opportunity, and cause of temptation, which influences a person to peculate. It is for this reason that we should emphasize that the purpose of setting up internal control procedures and following an audit program is not to catch a peculator, but to set up vehicles to protect weak people from temptation, strong people from opportunity, and innocent people from involvement.

Now, just what are the principal causes of peculations in banks? While many reasons are given, it is generally agreed that they fall into the following categories:

Gambling – The "innocent" bets on horses – the "sociable" poker or crap game–the sure tip on the stock market. Then the inevitable loss of savings set aside as the down payment on a home or for the education of the children, followed by the attempted comeback–the "temporary borrowing," and, finally, the peculation.

Pride and envy – The gripe because of being passed over for promotion–the discouragement which comes from the realization that there is little hope for advancement or an increase in salary–lack of fortitude to quit–or seek another job.

Living beyond income – Keeping up with the neighbors, relatives, friends or associates–the lack of courage to face financial dilemma.

Unsound salary practices – The failure of bank directors and management to periodically review salaries of personnel and make proper adjustments predicated on the cost of living, domestic obligations, and money handling responsibilities, which frequently results in the person making his own adjustment.

Poor employee relations – The negligence of management to be even a little interested in their employees. Officers who look down on their subordinates and consider themselves to be in a class by themselves as far as "privileges" are concerned. The "policy" of some banks that the cost of employee participation in civic and banking association affairs be borne out of their own pockets.

The extra marital affair – The clandestine romance which is tinsel, costly, generally unsatisfactory—and a game in which everyone loses.

The best preventative against peculations being committed is through the establishment of an adequate internal control system. Now internal controls, contrary to some misconceptions, are not operating procedures but a check on operating procedures.

Internal controls are not a part of the audit functions—but the establishing of rules and regulations, proofs and balances covering transactions, which under an audit program are verified, and their authenticity established.

Every good and adequate internal control system is composed of two distinct parts – *Rules and Regulations*, and *Proofs and Balances.*

Rules and Regulations are procedures established for the purpose of preventing one person from handling an entire transaction without having his work checked or proven by another; guarding against one person having complete control over an entire department or section without someone else exercising rights of approval; or preventing one person from maintaining sole custody and control over any major subsidiary accounts, and generally cover or provide for:

1. The establishment of a dual control system over all vaults and compartments containing reserve cash, securities and unissued checks.

2. Separation of teller functions from bookkeeping and accounting functions.

3. An unsystematic but periodical program of rotating tellers, commercial and savings bookkeepers.

4. The periodical exchange and verification of cash between tellers under official supervision.

5. The official approval and control of all cash items.

6. The daily review and scrutiny of all general ledger tickets by a senior officer.

7. The segregation of all inactive or dormant accounts, and the placing of them under dual control.

8. The substitution of the regular signature card by one with a typewritten signature on all dormant or inactive accounts with the original card held under dual control.

9. The frequent test checking of signatures on checks pre-

sented and paid against signature cards and resolutions by someone other than the person who pays the checks.

10. The frequent test checking of savings withdrawals against the signature cards and other authorizations by someone other than the person who pays the items.

11. Compulsory annual vacation by all officers and employees, of which at least two weeks shall be continuous, during which time they shall not come to the bank.

12. An established procedure under which no work in connection with reconcilements, complaints, or confirmations, no matter how complicated, normally handled by such person on vacation, be held for their return.

13. The referring and handling of all customer complaints to a person not actively connected with the transaction.

14. The handling and checking of all mail returned for address by a designated person.

15. Annual review of salaries paid all personnel, together with review and appraisal of their responsibilities and obligations, by the directors.

16. Control and approval of all purchase orders for stationery, supplies, machinery, and equipment, and verification of merchandise received before payment by a senior officer or the auditor.

Proofs and Balances, under an internal control system are procedures and routines established for the purpose of determining that the work performed balances and is correct as far as the general ledger accounting operation is concerned.

These procedures and routines, among others, comprise:

I. The periodical trial balancing, at undetermined times, of the savings, checking, loan, investment, official checks, expense and other ledgers, with the general ledger control figures, by someone other than the person regularly handling.

II. The periodical reconcilement of Due From Bank accounts by someone other than the person who issues or handles drafts or posts the general ledger.

III. The periodical or daily checking, refiguring or verification of interest income received on loans and investments.

IV. The periodical mailing of all cancelled checks and statements to checking account depositors with direct verification of the balance as shown, either on a positive or negative reply basis.

V. The periodical direct verification with borrowers of amounts owed and collateral pledged.

VI. The prohibition for tellers to plug their cash, use a kitty, and compulsory reporting of each and every cash difference.

The setting up and developing of a properly devised internal control system and audit program in every bank depends not only on the size of the bank but on the four following factors, all of which, in the final analysis depend on and are the responsibility of the directors:

A. The directors themselves.
B. The physical exposure of the bank.
C. The personnel exposure of the bank.
D. The development and execution of the internal control system and audit program.

A. *The Directors.* It is their responsibility to:

1. See that they are periodically furnished with complete information on the condition and operations of the bank. This means that at the monthly director's meeting each director will be furnished with:

a. A comparative statement of condition showing the financial position of the bank for the current month, previous month, and corresponding month in previous year.

b. A comparative statement of income and expense, gross profit and net profit after reserves for taxes, charge-offs, etc. for the current month, and—for comparative purposes, the figures representing the cumulative figures for year to date, and previous year to date.

c. A report of all changes in the bank's investment portfolio since the last report. Securities bought or sold by issue, rate, par value, book value, cost or sales price, and the profit or loss where securities were sold.

d. A list of all loans made, paid or renewed since the last report.

e. A list as of the date of the report of all overdrafts and the officer approving.

f. A list of all accounts opened and closed since the last report, together with the reasons, if known.

2. Periodically, but at least annually, review and discuss a formal report prepared by the chief executive officer covering the duties, responsibilities, salary, and obligations of each employee, to be certain the bank is paying adequate salaries based on money handling responsibilities and sufficient for the employee to properly live in keeping with his or her position.

3. Independently confirm, by employing outside consultation, that the bank is adequately covered by fidelity and other forms of insurance.

4. See that all bank personnel is protected from emergency by provisions of group health, accident, life and hospitalization insurance.

5. Establish some form of pension or retirement plan effective at age 60/65 to provide income for those who have faithfully served the bank during their productive years.

6. Insist that each officer and employee take at least two weeks vacation each year on a continuous basis.

7. Be certain that duties and responsibilities of officers are defined and properly delegated so that too much power or authority isn't concentrated in one person. Avoid having a one man bank.

8. Set up, devise and approve a system of internal controls and an audit program to be followed by those in the bank to whom is delegated internal control and auditing functions; and see to it that such persons formally report to them periodically on the scope of their work.

9. Provide proper external protection for the assets of the bank and the lives of personnel.

10. Insist that all employees be rotated in their duties and functions.

11. Insist that cancelled checks and statements be mailed to all depositors monthly or periodically.

12. Insist that some system, subject to the approval of the directors, be devised for the periodical direct verification of deposit balances with depositors and loan balances and collateral with borrowers.

B. The physical exposure of the bank. Under this phase the directors should see to it that:

1. There is control over possession and use of keys to the premises.

2. Doors to the bank premises for public use are not opened before regular hours and that they are promptly closed or guarded after regular hours.

3. Some system is devised whereby designated employees will be the first to enter the bank in the morning, and that others will not enter unless they receive a pre-arranged signal that everything is normal.

4. All entrances to tellers' cages be protected by doors with self-closing locks which can only be opened from the inside.

5. The bank is protected by an alarm system which can be tripped by the tellers or officers, notifying the police, without alerting the robber that he has been discovered.

C. The personnel exposure of the bank. Under this phase the directors should see to it that the internal control program provides that:

1. All vaults or compartments containing bank surplus cash, securities and collateral are placed under dual control.

2. A system be provided for all personnel to sign in or out when entering or leaving the bank.

3. Each teller be provided with an individual compartment in the vault under combination lock for the protection and safeguarding of his cash—and that duplicate combinations for emergency purposes are sealed and placed under dual control of officers who do not have the combinations to the vault proper.

4. Where each teller has his own cage, that doors are provided with self-closing locks which can only be opened from the inside.

5. Where tellers share a common cage, that each teller, when leaving the cage, place his cash in a drawer provided with a lock.

D. The developing and execution of the internal control system and audit program. (These are covered in detail, later in this chapter.)

These are the tools the directors must provide. In a small bank any non-officer director, through periodical checking and investigating can determine if the physical and personnel exposure is covered. Where the bank is of sufficient size to employ the services of a competent auditor on a full time basis responsible to the board of directors, such responsibility can be delegated to him through the audit program or internal control system.

We have now reviewed all factors and determined that while it is the responsibility of the directors to safeguard and protect the assets of the bank, they can delegate this responsibility to one or several individuals, providing they exercise supervision. All that remains, therefore, is to set up an internal control system which is workable and practical; and develop the audit program, both of which should be tailor made to fit the particular needs and exposure of the bank.

THE INTERNAL CONTROL SYSTEM

An internal control system, regardless of the size of the bank, should be set up along the following lines and executed either by the auditor, members of the audit staff or, if the bank does not have an auditor, by the person or persons to whom are delegated internal control and auditing responsibility.

Functions or Detail of Work To Be Undertaken	**Frequency Work Should Be Undertaken**

TELLERS DIFFERENCES — OCCURRENCE

A. Whenever a teller, after taking a balance, is over or short more than $50.00 the auditor shall be notified and endeavor to locate difference. Should difference not be located, auditor shall make a written report of such difference to the cashier, attested to by the teller.

ACCOUNTS PAYABLE – OTHER LIABILITIES — DAILY

A. Review all entries (debits and credits) for proper authorization and order.

ACCOUNTS RECEIVABLE – OTHER RESOURCES — DAILY

A. Review all entries (debits and credits) for proper authorization and order.

DEMAND DEPOSITS DAILY

A. Observe situation and frequency of depositors calling about balance and advising "bank deposit is being made and not to return checks."

B. Review new accounts opened for presence of properly signed signature card and necessary supporting papers.

INCOME RECEIVED DAILY

A. Check charges received from returning checks for insufficient funds and overdrafts against number of checks returned and overdrafts approved. Report discrepancies.

B. Check all fees and commissions received against actual transactions to confirm or verify amounts received and credited to respective income accounts.

INTEREST PAID DAILY

A. Recompute and verify all disbursements of interest paid on certificates of deposit or special time accounts. Report discrepancies and variances by name and amount to cashier.

LOANS AND DISCOUNTS DAILY

A. Review all new loans and renewals as to proper computation of interest or discount.

B. Verify computation and trace disposition of all interest rebates.

C. Check new loans and renewals for proper approval and evidence of necessary or required supporting papers.

OFFICIAL CHECKS DAILY

A. Check duplicates or register against report of fees collected as shown by general ledger ticket to ascertain proper fees were collected.

PROPERTIES – STATIONERY AND SUPPLIES DAILY

A. Verify delivery and physical possession of all items of furniture, fixtures, equipment, stationery, and supplies for which invoices have been received and payment authorized. Indicate delivery and proper authorization by initialing general ledger ticket.

TIME DEPOSITS DAILY

A. Review new accounts opened for presence of properly signed signature cards and necessary supporting papers.

B. Review all withdrawals $300.00 and over for proper signature.

VAULT DAILY

A. Check report of opening and closing of vault for recording of time and signature of officer supervising.

OVERDRAFTS MONTHLY

A. Make report to cashier of all overdrafts, resulting from putting through of charges for returning checks or for overdrafts which have been on the books for 30 days or longer.

OVERDRAFTS WEEKLY

A. Review outstanding overdrafts for proper authorization. Report unauthorized overdrafts to cashier.

TELLERS CASH PERIODICALLY

A. Check to determine if currency is placed in drawer and drawer locked when tellers go to lunch.

B. Check to determine if tellers lock the door to their cages when away for a few minutes.

C. Check on workings of doors and locks through which ingress and egress is made to tellers' cages.

D. Check tellers' vault compartments to be certain tumblers are thrown if they contain currency.

All exceptions, in addition to being immediately referred to the person designated for attention, are to be recited in the monthly report to the directors.

THE AUDIT PROGRAM

Any audit program, to be effective, must not only be sufficiently broad and detailed so as to periodically cover all exposure points, but be formally approved and understood by the directors if they are to fully discharge their responsibility.

All phases of an audit program, whether applicable to a small bank which is not of sufficient size to have a full time auditor or to a bank which has a full time auditing staff, to be effective should be conducted at undeterminable times, that is, on a surprise basis. In addition, the frequency of such phases of the program should be periodically modified within reason by the person to whom is delegated the auditing control responsibility in order to avoid a "pattern." The person to whom is delegated audit responsibilities, unbeknown to anyone else, should also determine the respective months during which certain phases should be undertaken so that the entire program is covered within each 12-month period.

Where a bank is of sufficient size, or has an accounting system where there is more than one classification of an asset or a liability account, the auditor or person to whom is delegated audit control responsibility, at his discretion, may undertake the audit on a classification basis; that is, one subsidiary account at a time.

Regardless of the program used, whether it is adaptable to a small bank or a large bank, the auditor or person to whom is delegated audit control responsibility should report monthly to the directors the scope of the work performed, and what the audit disclosed, including a detailed list of exceptions or any variations of practice in accordance with established policy.

AN AUDIT PROGRAM FOR A SMALL BANK

In a small bank where every employee from the chief executive officer to the clerk receives commercial and savings deposits, handles loan payments, posts commercial and savings ledgers, pays checks and withdrawals, issues and signs drafts and cashier's checks, and even posts the general ledger, the greatest protection is in the flexibility. Under these circumstances the conducting of periodical checking where warranted, must be done by the directors themselves or by someone from the outside who is qualified to execute the program which study and analysis determines is required to afford maximum protection.

Where a bank, however, has one or two officers and a secretary who are not engaged in routine operations; two or three tellers; several proof and bookkeeping operators, who do not accept deposits or cash checks or withdrawals; and a general bookkeeper; internal control and audit responsibility can be divided in an efficient and satisfactory manner.

Such a program, including the periodical trial balancing of respective ledgers or registers, and balancing with the general ledger control accounts, where necessary, can be developed along the following lines:

Account or Function To Be Audited	Frequency Of Audit	Audit to Be Performed By
Charges on official checks	Daily	Secretary
Exchange charges	Daily	Secretary
Interest received	Daily	Secretary
Approval of bills	Monthly	Directors
Cash-cash items	Monthly	Junior officer
Due from banks	Monthly	Chief executive officer
Running-balancing of official checks	Monthly	Head bookkeeper
Safe deposit box rent	Monthly	Head bookkeeper
Service charge-fee income	Monthly	Secretary
Tellers difference	Monthly	Junior officer
Clearings	Quarterly	Junior officer
Collections	Quarterly	Head bookkeeper
Running and balancing of commercial ledgers	Quarterly	Savings bookkeeper Junior officer
Running and balancing of liability ledger and notes	Quarterly	Comml. bookkeeper Junior officer
Running and balancing of savings ledgers	Quarterly	Comml. bookkeeper Junior officer
Salaries	Quarterly	Chief exec. officer
Unissued official checks	Quarterly	Junior officer
Capital a/c-reserves	Semi-annually	Directors
Collateral	Semi-annually	Directors
Interest paid on deposits	Semi-annually	Officers
Investments	Semi-annually	Head Bookkeeper
Losses on securities	Semi-annually	Directors
Stationery and supplies	Semi-annually	Chief exec. officer
Sundry losses	Semi-annually	Directors
Direct verification of commercial and savings accounts; loans	Annually	Directors

Other divisions of audit responsibility can be made, depending on individual circumstances, and can be effective, providing daily operating routines and functions are divorced from control functions, and a system of checks and balances are established which can effectively check or discourage peculations. To maintain control, however, each person delegated respective responsibility should formally report the scope and results of his work to the directors when it has been accomplished. Further, the frequency and scheduling of such programs should be varied and uncertain as to time, so as to disguise any semblance of fixed routine or pattern.

AN AUDIT PROGRAM FOR A LARGER BANK

For a larger bank, which either has an auditor or someone charged with the responsibility of auditing functions, a program similar to the following should be adopted:

Description of Account To Be Audited	Recommended Frequency For the Audit
CASH ON HAND	MONTHLY

A. At the close of business, or first thing in the morning, seal all cash in vault and take possession of cash and cash items held by tellers. Balance with tellers journal and with respective control figure.

B. Instruct proof clerk to hold all cash letters containing checks drawn on other banks. List all checks $300.00 and over by bank on which drawn, date, endorser, maker and amount, and trace to source.

C. Review deposit slips for prior dating or date alteration. Directly confirm with depositor if date on deposit slip is prior to date deposit was credited to account.

D. Intercept all items $300.00 and over returned by correspondent banks for insufficient funds for six days following audit. Check against list "B," trace any such items, as are found, to source to determine validity.

NOTE: Tellers can be audited separately in which case the procedure suggested under "B" and "D" is not followed.

EXCHANGE FOR CLEARINGS SEMI-ANNUALLY

A. Take possession of all clearing letters containing checks drawn on other banks for collection after they are ready for presentation for payment.

B. Re-run, balance and prove totals with general ledger control figures.

C. Review all checks for correct presentation date and proper endorsements.

D. Prepare confirmation letter and send to all banks on which items are to be presented to have them directly confirm amount; and to send all items which they are returning unpaid to the auditor direct. All such items are to be traced to source.

DUE FROM BANKS PERIODICALLY

A. Monthly, check reconcilements of all "Due from Bank" accounts.

B. Annually, or oftener, request all banks with which the bank maintains an account to send a statement of the account as of the close of business, together with items in their possession. Upon receipt reconcile and confirm all outstanding items.

LOANS AND DISCOUNTS SEMI-ANNUALLY

A. Balance all notes in file and in process of collection in each classification with respective liability ledgers and with general ledger control figures.

B. Test check all new and renewal notes made within the ten days prior to date of examination to see if they were properly drawn and accompanied by required supporting documents.

C. Test all notes $1000.00 and over as to proper approvals within authorization of officer. List exceptions.

D. Check out business loans $5000.00 and over as to proper authorization and approval by the directors.

E. Check out collateral. List omissions or irregularities.

F. Review credit files on loans $5000.00 and over to be certain current financial statements are on file. Prepare list of all borrowing accounts, in such category where statements on file are over one year old, for attention of directors.

G. Prepare list of all loans 30 or more days past due as of date of examination.

H. Test check slow and renewal loans against overdraft list as to periodical "clean up" in liability ledger. Prepare list of all such items.

I. Directly confirm outstanding balances on a representative number of accounts with the borrower.

BONDS AND INVESTMENTS SEMI-ANNUALLY

A. Prepare list of securities in all classifications from the investment ledger. Run and balance with respective general ledger control accounts.

B. Examine all securities in the bank's possession. Check for matured coupons and bonds.

C. Verify by direct correspondence all securities in safe keeping with other banks, or out on trust receipt to secure deposits.

D. Check out all the purchases and sales of securities made for the bank's investment account since the last examination, with minutes of directors meetings for proper approval and authorization. Reconcile purchase price and premium, if any, with entries on the accounts.

E. Reconcile "Interest Due and Payable" and other computations with entries on respective income accounts.

PROPERTIES ANNUALLY

A. Review each class of property as to charges and credits since last examination. Verify correctness of entries. List exceptions or omissions.

B. Prepare a report covering each piece of real estate owned by the bank and indicate condition, need for rehabilitation, repairs, painting, decorating, etc.

C. Check out furniture and fixtures, machinery and equipment used by the bank with inventory control. Account for all exceptions and list.

D. Analyze sufficiency of depreciation schedule and make recommendations, if necessary, for required adjustments.

E. Review insurance coverage applicable to all classes of

property and exposure of the bank as to sufficiency. Report exceptions or exposure.

INCOME EARNED, UNCOLLECTED SEMI-ANNUALLY

A. Verify all debits to respective accounts for past 30 days by comparing periodical entries with summary as shown on detailed interest record. Test check and re-foot schedule.

B. Verify transfers from respective "Interest Receivable" account to respective interest income accounts.

C. Audit where practical, respective "Interest Receivable" accounts by listing on work sheets, all items against which interest is accruing. Recompute and adjust difference.

EXPENSES FROM OPERATIONS SEMI-ANNUALLY

A. Verify and recompute "Interest Paid on Borrowed Money" account.

B. Verify all debits to expense covering interest paid on deposits by comparing the amount of interest expense with corresponding credit to "Accrued Interest Payable" account.

C. Verify debits to expense for taxes paid with corresponding credit to "Accrued Taxes Payable" account.

D. Verify all debits to expense for depreciation by comparing charges to expense with offsetting credits to respective "Reserve for Depreciation" accounts.

E. Check and confirm salaries and overtime paid against payroll records. Confirm presence of all personnel listed on payroll records.

F. Review minutes of board of directors meetings for proper authorization of bonuses paid and salary increases to executive personnel.

G. Review all operating expense items. Test check for proper authorization and approval. List exceptions.

CHARGES OR LOSSES QUARTERLY

A. Prepare transcripts of respective accounts since last examination showing all debits and credits. Check for proper authorization and approval.

B. Review all charged off items and report on action being taken.

INCOME TAXES ANNUALLY

A. Verify all debits to expense for income tax by comparing charges to expense with offsetting credits to "Accrued Taxes Payable" account. Reconcile differences.

OTHER RESOURCES SEMI-ANNUALLY

A. Prepare schedule showing by date, amount, payee and purpose all open accounts receivable items. Include a report and comment on any items which appear irregular or slow.

B. Review tellers difference account. Scrutinize for date or amount irregularity.

C. Review and analyze prepaid expense account items for order, proper authorization and disposition.

D. Review and comment on any capital items temporarily being held in other resources accounts for proper authorization of the board of directors.

REG. - SPL. DEMAND DEPOSITS SEMI-ANNUALLY

A. Seal and place under control all ledgers containing subject accounts.

B. Make adding machine listing of respective ledgers and balance with control figures. Verify totals with general ledger control figures.

C. Test check signatures on checks drawn against a representative number of accounts for authorization. Check signatures on checks with signature cards and other authorizations.

D. Check out on a test basis cancelled checks for endorsement and date of payment.

E. Spot check deposit slips for date alteration. Make list of exceptions and check out to be certain they arise from normal business transactions.

F. Test check active accounts for use of uncollected funds.

G. Directly confirm balances on a representative number of accounts selected at random.

H. Test check corporation and partnership accounts for proper supporting resolutions or authorizations.

ESCROW OR FIDUCIARY ACCOUNTS SEMI-ANNUALLY

A. Make adding machine listing of all accounts in respective ledgers and balance with control figures.

B. Test check and review withdrawals for proper authorization and disposition.

OFFICIAL CHECKS SEMI-ANNUALLY

A. Make adding machine listing by class of outstanding checks. Balance with general ledger control account.

B. Take off for future reference a list of all official checks outstanding and unpaid for over two years, by date of issue, number, name of payee, purchaser and amount.

C. Check endorsements and trace to source all checks paid since last examination, which at the time of examination were outstanding and unpaid two years or more.

D. Check out and account for by number all unissued checks.

REG. - SPL. TIME DEPOSITS SEMI-ANNUALLY

A. Seal and place under control all ledgers containing respective classes of accounts.

B. Make adding machine listings of respective ledgers and balance with control figures.

C. Spot check a number of accounts at random to determine if signatures on withdrawals compare with signature cards or other authorization.

D. Spot check deposit slips for date alteration. List exceptions and check out to determine if they arise from normal business transactions.

E. Test check interest computations on a representative number of accounts. List discrepancies.

CAPITAL ACCOUNTS ANNUALLY

A. Prepare a schedule of the stockholders of each class of stock (or debentures) by name, numbers of certificates, and number of shares registered in each name.

B. Make an adding machine listing of the outstanding shares of the various types of stock from the stockholders ledger. Confirm the respective amounts of capital by multiplying the number of shares outstanding by the par value of the stock. Balance with the general ledger.

C. Make an adding machine listing of the stubs in the various stock certificate books and balance with the respective stockholders ledgers.

D. Check the respective stock certificate books to be sure that all certificates, both issued and unissued, are in numerical sequence and that unissued certificates are present and accounted for.

E. Review all classes of stock certificates cancelled or exchanged since the last audit to determine that all certificates were correctly endorsed, properly cancelled and filed in the respective stock certificate book.

F. Prepare a transcript of the surplus account showing all debits and credits made since last audit. Review all entries for proper authorization.

G. Prepare a transcript of the undivided profits account showing all debits and credits made since last audit. Review all entries for proper authorization. Trace all contra entries to the account from respective income and expense accounts. Determine proper authority for authorization for such transfers.

RESERVE ACCOUNTS ANNUALLY

A. Prepare a transcript of respective reserve accounts showing entries since last examination. Reconcile credits to respective reserve accounts with charges to expense.

B. Review all charged to respective reserve accounts for proper authority.

INCOME COLLECTED UNEARNED ANNUALLY

A. Verify all credits to unearned discount for past thirty days by comparing daily entries with totals as reported on tellers proof sheet.

B. Audit unearned discount account by listing notes by amount and number of days to maturity and compute interest. Balance or reconcile with control account. Adjust difference.

EXPENSES ACCRUED AND UNPAID QUARTERLY

A. Prepare transcript of respective accounts showing entries since last examination.

B. Verify all credits to respective accounts by comparing credits with the monthly charges to expense.

C. Verify and trace all debits to respective accounts with checks or credits tendered in payment.

CURRENT INCOME FROM OPERATIONS SEMI-ANNUALLY

A. Review each respective principal and subsidiary account.

B. Reconcile and verify accrued interest on investments and loans with debits to accrued interest receivable account.

C. Test check computation of non fixed fee income such as commissions.

D. Spot test and refigure income from charges and fees.

RECOVERIES AND PROFITS QUARTERLY

A. Prepare transcript of respective accounts showing all debits and credits since last examination.

B. Reconcile and trace to source funds tendered in payment of items carried under respective accounts.

OTHER LIABILITIES SEMI-ANNUALLY

A. Prepare a schedule showing all open accounts payable by date, amount, payee, and reason or purpose. Report any irregularities.

BOARD OF DIRECTORS SEMI-ANNUALLY

A. Prepare a list of the directors showing their attendance at meetings.

B. Prepare a list of directors, officers and employees and check against the liability ledger. Show all obligations to the bank either on a direct or indirect basis (endorser). Check all such borrowers against the minutes of the directors meetings for proper authorization. Report any omissions and details of borrowings.

C. Review minutes of the directors meetings for decisions regarding policy, management authorizations, etc. Check action taken by management and others to determine if action taken was in conformance with by-laws, federal and state banking laws, and order of the board of directors.

D. Review last report of examination made by the bank supervisory authorities. Check to see if criticisms have been eliminated or are in the process of being corrected. Comment and report on matters which require further attention.

COMMITTEES OF THE BANK — ANNUALLY

A. Review minutes of respective committees. Check action taken to determine compliance with decisions made.

ACCOUNTING DEPARTMENT — ANNUALLY

A. Review general ledger and subsidiary accounts for completeness. Check erasures or corrections with ticket of original entry.

B. Re-run and balance several days' statements of condition selected at random. Test check posting of tickets to proper accounts.

OPERATIONS DEPARTMENT — ANNUALLY

A. Review operating instructions against procedures followed to determine observance.

B. Based on audits of the various departments of the bank and branches, report on procedures and methods which should be covered by new operating instructions or revision of current operating instructions.

C. Check with officer in charge of operations as to contemplated changes in procedures or methods so as to set up proper controls and include coverage under the audit program.

PERSONNEL DEPARTMENT — ANNUALLY

A. Review the personnel record of each individual to determine that performance was reviewed by management and action taken during the year. Report on omissions.

B. Report on a department by department basis, all personnel who did not have a vacation during the year. Give reasons.

C. Prepare list of all personnel who resigned their position with the bank during the year. Give reason for leaving.

D. Review overtime payments. Prepare list of employees who habitually draw overtime payments and check as to reason. Report findings.

STATIONERY AND SUPPLIES ANNUALLY

A. Undertake physical inventory, either on a complete or test basis, of stationery and supplies. Compare with inventory control. Comment and adjust if necessary.

B. Determine if unissued official checks and receipts are under proper·control. Comment.

Sometimes there are objections to an audit program, or phases of an audit program, because it is felt that the procedures or routines might reflect upon the personnel of the bank or create adverse public opinion. Before seriously considering such objections let us remember that the function of checking someone else's work to determine that it has been properly performed is as old as civilization. In fact, it is a protective device which society itself imposed to insure honesty and freedom from error in all types of transactions.

For example: Our federal, state and municipal government constantly check on weights and measures to guard us against short weights and dishonest measures.

Our police force constantly patrols property to protect it from thieves.

Our fire department is constantly examining buildings to be certain that no fire hazard exists.

Our safety patrols periodically check the brakes and lights on automobiles to be sure that they provide safe driving.

The fact remains that some pattern, practice and procedure of checking and verifying is followed in handling every business transaction which takes place in our complicated world.

This being the case, why should depositors object to having some authorized person verify with them the amount of funds they have on deposit—or confirm the balance of their loan? The answer is that *they do not object when they are properly informed as to the purpose of the verification.*

It is the considered opinion of the author and of many persons recognized as authorities in the field of bank auditing that direct verification of account balances with the depositors and loan balances with borrowers is the most important phase of any audit program. This is true not only because direct verification frequently turns up defalcations, but reveals facts of importance to the bank and its customers. In addition, the fact that the bank has a verification program acts as a deterrent, in many cases, to employees from manipulating accounts.

While it is rather difficult to disguise the fact from the employees that a verification program is being followed, every bank can properly arrange the schedule so that the section or group of accounts being verified is not obvious to the employees.

It is also well to point out that where a verification program is adopted, especially in a small bank, the depositors be requested to mail the verification or confirmation to the bank or special post office box and not refer it to an officer for possible assistance in reconciling the balance as shown on the verification letter with the stub or record of his account.

As to the reaction of depositors and the public to direct verification of deposit and loan balances: customers of banks and the public are well aware of the harm and havoc resulting from peculations, and are apprehensive over the safety of their funds, especially if they personally maintain or are responsible for funds on deposit with the bank which exceed $10,000.

Most leading and conscientious citizens welcome evidence, as disclosed through a direct verification program, that directors of the banks in their community are on the job and alert to the proper discharge of their responsibilities; for in so doing they give assurance that they are zealously guarding the welfare of society and protecting community interests.

BIBLIOGRAPHY

Authoring a book of this kind not only entails considerable analysis and research, but study and review of material developed by others recognized as authorities and students of respective phases of the business we call banking.

As much of the material, the result of painstaking research on their part, has either been incorporated into this book, or has provided the basis for developing the text material for the book, the author not only acknowledges credit, but gratitude and appreciation to the following authors and their works.

ADAMS, James Truslo "History of the United States" New York, 1933

AMERICAN INSTITUTE OF BANKING Principles of Bank Operation" New York, 1956

ANDERSON, B. M. Jr. "The Value of Money" New York, 1917

ATKINS, Paul M. "Bank Secondary Reserves and Investment Policies" New York, 1930

BARNETT, George E. "State Banking in the United States since Passage of the National Banking Act" Baltimore, 1902

BEATY, John Y. "The Bank Employees Library" Cambridge, 1952

BLOCK, Maurice "Le Progres de la Science Economique" Paris, 1897

CONANT, Charles A. "History of Modern Banks of Issue" New York, 1896
"Principles of Money and Banking" New York, 1905

CORNS, Marshall C. "Better Bank Management" New York, 1937
"How to Audit a Bank" Cambridge, 1955
"Practical Cost Accounting for Banks" Boston, 1959

CRUCHON, Gustave "Les Banques dans l'Antiquité" Paris, 1879

DELOUME, Antonin "Les Manieure d'Argent à Rome Jusqu'à l'Empire" Paris

DEWEY, Davis Rich "Financial History of the United States" New York, 1903

FISHBACK, Benjamin L. "Risks of the Tellers Department" New York, 1932

GEORGE, Henry "The Science of Political Economy" New York, 1898

GUARANTY TRUST COMPANY OF NEW YORK "A Review of Export and Import Procedure" New York, 1957

HEPBURN, A. Barton "History of Coinage and Currency in the United States and Perennial Contest for Sound Money" New York, 1903

JEVONS, W. Stanley "The Theory of Political Economy" London, 1888

KABERNA, Joseph J. "Importance of Financial Statements in Bank Lending" Chicago, 1957 (Auditgram)

KANE, Thomas P. "The Romance and Tragedy of Banking" New York, 1922

KELLER, Albert E. "Embezzlement and Internal Controls" Washington, 1945

KNIFFIN, William H. "The Practical Work of a Bank" New York, 1928

MAC LEOD, Henry Dunning "The Theory and Practice of Banking" London, 1892

McCLAY, E. R. "Computers Can Be Described in Simple English" New York, 1960 (American Banker)

McCULLOCH, Hugh "Men and Measures of Half a Century" New York, 1889

MILL, John Stewart "Principles of Political Economy With Some of the Applications to Social Philosophy" New York, 1893

RICHARDSON, James D. "A Compilation of Messages and Papers of the Presidents 1879–1897"

ROGERS, James E. Thorold "First Nine Years of the Bank of England" New York, 1887

SCOTT, William A. "Money and Banking" New York, 1916

SMITH, Adam "An Inquiry Into the Nature and Causes of the Wealth of Nations" Oxford, 1880

STEPHENSON, Gilbert T. "The American System of Trust Business" New York, 1936

STRONCK, H. N. "Bank Administration" Chicago, 1929
"Bank Loan Management" Chicago, 1930
"Bank Management Controls" Chicago, 1941

USHER, Abbott Payson "Early History of Deposit Banking in Mediterranean Europe" Cambridge, 1943

WALKER, Francis A. "Money and Its Relation to Trade and Industry" New York, 1891

WELLS, H. G. "Outline of History" New York, 1930

WHITE, Horace "Money and Banking" New York, 1895

WOOLEY, E. S. "Bank Management Controls" Chicago, 1940

The author also expresses appreciation to the following banks, business establishments, and publications for their cooperation and permission to reproduce forms and adapt other material to the text.

BANCO POPULAR DE PUERTO RICO, San Juan, Puerto Rico

BANK OF CHICAGO, Chicago, Illinois

CITY NATIONAL BANK AND TRUST COMPANY OF CHICAGO, Chicago, Illinois

CONTINENTAL ILLINOIS NATIONAL BANK AND TRUST COMPANY OF CHICAGO, Chicago, Illinois

FIRST COMMERCIAL BANK OF CHICAGO, Chicago, Illinois

FIRST NATIONAL BANK AND TRUST COMPANY OF EVANSTON, Evanston, Illinois

FIRST NATIONAL BANK, Leesburg, Florida

LA SALLE STATE BANK, La Salle, Illinois

WILMETTE STATE BANK, Wilmette, Illinois

CADWALLADER AND JOHNSON, Chicago, Illinois

DUN & BRADSTREET, New York, New York

AMERICAN BANKER, New York, New York

AUDITGRAM, Chicago, Illinois

BANKERS MONTHLY, Chicago, Illinois

COMMERCIAL WEST, Minneapolis, Minnesota

FINANCE MAGAZINE, Chicago, Illinois

HOOSIER BANKER, Indianapolis, Indiana

MID-CONTINENT BANKER, St. Louis, Missouri

NORTHWESTERN BANKER, Des Moines, Iowa

PRUDDEN'S DIGEST, New York, New York

INDEX

— A —

— B —

– C –

— D —

– E –

– F –

– G –

– H –

—I—

– J –

– K –

– L –

—M—

— Mc —

– N –

– O –

– P –

– Q –

– R –

— S —

– T –